SYMBOLISM

SECOND EDITION

ALSO BY STEVEN OLDERR

The Pan American Games / Los Juegos Panamericanos:
A Statistical History, 1951–1999, bilingual edition /
Una Historia Estadística, 1951–1999, edición bilingüe
(McFarland, 2003; paperback 2009)

Reverse Symbolism Dictionary:
Symbols Listed by Subject
(McFarland, 1992; paperback 2005)

SYMBOLISM

A Comprehensive Dictionary

SECOND EDITION

Steven Olderr

McFarland & Company, Inc., Publishers
Jefferson, North Carolina, and London

LIBRARY OF CONGRESS CATALOGUING-IN-PUBLICATION DATA

Olderr, Steven.
Symbolism : a comprehensive dictionary /
Steven Olderr — 2nd ed.
p.   cm.
Includes bibliographical references.

ISBN 978-0-7864-6955-0
softcover : acid free paper ∞

1. Symbolism — Dictionaries.
I. Title.
CB475.O38 2012   302.2'22303 — dc23   2012004954

BRITISH LIBRARY CATALOGUING DATA ARE AVAILABLE

Front cover images © 2012 Shutterstock

Manufactured in the United States of America

*McFarland & Company, Inc., Publishers
Box 611, Jefferson, North Carolina 28640
www.mcfarlandpub.com*

Pour
Patricia Pingatore Olderr
toujours une rose sous un autre nom

Contents

Preface

If you are new to the use of symbolism, it is well to remember that it is an art, not a science. The meaning of a symbol is always affected by its context. Different people use symbols in different ways even within the same culture or genre. For the sake of convenience, however, symbols herein are usually listed under the culture or genre where they first appeared or have their greatest use. It doesn't mean the symbol hasn't migrated to other cultures. The information is offered primarily as a starting point for your analysis.

Symbols that are in general use or whose source is unknown are listed directly after the headword and before specific cultures or genres. For example:

> **azalea** transitoriness; the ephemeral; fire • **Chinese** great abilities; feminine grace; tragedy • **heraldic** temperance; passion • **Japanese** associated with April

The order of listings within a heading is largely random and should not be taken to mean an item has greater or lesser importance.

Please note that this is a historical work; regrettably, some symbols may be offensive.

A Few Subheading Conventions

- **Christian** includes the New Testament. Old Testament symbols are generally listed under the subheading **Jewish**, unless they have a specifically Christian application, such as Adam being considered a precursor of Jesus.
- **Greek and Roman** cultures intermingled greatly, and as such, these symbols are usually combined under the heading **Greco-Roman**.
- **Indic** is used for those symbols that cannot be pinned to a specific religion in India. Listings for the country of India are far more likely to be under the headings **Hindu** or **Islamic** as their meanings can be quite distinct.
- **Jewish** includes all Jewish culture, including the early Hebrews and the Old Testament

Further Information

The unique feature of this dictionary is its breadth. There are more than 15,000 entries—more than any other source. While space constraints preclude explanatory text, the liberal use of subheadings combined with context will generally be adequate to help the discerning reader understand meanings.

Those seeking greater depth and background can often find it in standard encyclopedias and common reference sources such as *The Reader's Encyclopedia* and *Butler's Lives of the Saints.* For still greater depth, the following books are just a few of those commonly available:

Bell, Robert E. *Dictionary of Classical Mythology, Symbols, Attributes and Associations.* Santa Barbara, California: ABC-Clio, 1982. A source of great breadth within its topic, with brief background of the legends.

Chevalier, Jean, and Alain Gheerbrant. *Penguin Dictionary of Symbols.* London, New York: Penguin, 1994. 1,700 terms. Probably the single best source for succinct additional information on a symbol.

Cirlot, J.E. *Dictionary of Symbols.* 2nd ed. New York: Philosophical Library, 1971. 800 terms. Lengthy discussions with a distinct Western bias. Still, there is probably more general background material here than anywhere else. Includes a 45-page introduction on the use of interpretation of symbols.

Cooper, J.C. *Illustrated Encyclopedia of Traditional Symbols.* London: Thames and Hudson, 1978. 3,000 entries. Less detailed than the Cirlot book, but has more entries and is broader in scope.

Ferguson, George. *Signs and Symbols in Christian Art.* London, New York: Oxford University Press, 1954. 400 terms. An excellent book dealing especially with Renaissance Christian art. Individual articles are not comprehensive, however, and the index must be used to gather complete information.

Hall, James. *Dictionary of Subjects and Symbols in Art.* Rev. ed. New York: Harper, 1979. 900 terms. Very good for art symbols.

Leach, Maria, ed. *Standard Dictionary of Folklore, Mythology and Legend.* New York: Funk and Wagnalls, 1950. A two-volume work with worldwide coverage. An excellent background source for symbols derived from folklore.

If one is careful, there is a wealth of useful background material on the World Wide Web. Be aware that anyone can put up anything on the Web and you really have to consider the source. It is best to use scholarly proprietary databases available through colleges or libraries, but materials published on sites with an ".edu" domain are generally trustworthy. There are also a large number of books from reliable publishers available in whole or in part that are available on the Web.

THE DICTIONARY

NUMBERS

-0- latency; potentiality; eternity; non-being; beginning; the feminine principle; the womb; Cosmic Egg; the primordial androgyne; vulva; nothingness; ultimate mystery; the incomprehensible; failure; an intensifier after a number; associated with the dwarf planet Pluto, the infinite, eternity, unity, ether, the archangel Lumiel • **Buddhist** the Void; non-being • **Islamic** divine essence • **Kabalistic** boundlessness; limitless light; the Ain • **Mesopotamian** the perfect number; associated with totality, the universe • **Pythagorean** the perfect form; the Monad • **Taoist** the Void; non-being • **tarot** the Fool

-1- reason; the cosmos; uniqueness; the universal; starting point; the transcendent; related to the Creator, mankind, moral purpose, existence, the active principle, spiritual revelation, unity, light, paradise, the infinite, mystic center, wholeness, individuality, indivisibility, the germinal, isolation, phallus, the masculine, the sun, intellectual power, will power, change, travel, domination, selfishness, ruthlessness, the archangel Raphael, orange (color); has the value of letters A, J, S • **Babylonian** unity • **Buddhist** an auspicious number; associated with the male, the heavenly • **Chinese** yang; the celestial; the auspicious; the Monad; associated with the element water • **Christian** associated with God the Father; the perfect unity of the Trinity • **Greek** basis of all numbers; associated with man, the sun • **Islamic** the self-sufficient; the unity of God; the Absolute • **Jewish** life force; power and will of the universe; hidden intelligence; God • **Kabalistic** associated with the archangel Metatron • **Pythagorean** spirit; essence; the Monad • **tarot** the Magician • **Yoruban** mediation between man and the orishas; power over sexual desire

-2- duality; positive and negative; diversity; conflict; dependence; day and night; echo; reflection; equilibrium; stability; nature; shadow; disintegration; an ominous sign; separation from unity; sin; polarity; diversity; conjunction of opposites; otherness; resistance; associated with opinion, the material, the feminine, intuition, emotion, cooperation, tact, diplomacy, timidity, deceit, secrecy, domesticity, helpfulness, instability, the moon, cycles, reproduction, pacification, inner peace, the archangel Gabriel, green, the left side • **two animals** a doubling of their traits • **alchemic** opposites such as sun/moon, king/queen, sulfur/Mercurius • **Babylonian** associated with the dichotomy of the universe • **Buddhist** the duality of samsara; the blind and lame united to see the way and walk it; associated with disaster, the male and female, theory and practice; the earthly • **Chinese** yin; the terrestrial; the inauspicious; associated with the element water • **Christian** Jesus Christ; the dual nature of Christ; angels at the tomb of Christ, thieves at the Crucifixion, etc. • **Greek** associated with evil, woman, the moon • **Hindu** duality; shakta-shakti • **Islamic** the Spirit • **Jewish** life-force; the parents of mankind; the tablets of the Ten Commandments • **Kabalistic** knowledge; wisdom; self-consciousness, associated with the archangel Uriel • **Platonic** a number without meaning • **Pythagorean** the Duad; the divided terrestrial being • **Taoist** the K'ua; the Two Determinants; yin-yang; a weak number • **tarot** the High Priestess

-3- generally a favorable, godly number; multiplicity; creative power; growth; forward movement; beginning/middle/end; past/present/future; related to the right side, moral and spiritual dynamism, intellectual and spiritual order, sufficiency, heaven, childbirth, conflict resolution, perfection, love, joyfulness, hope, destiny, children, achievement, carelessness, intrigue, marriage, good fortune, happiness, material success, the masculine principle, fame, activity, catalyst, concern for others, completion of a phase of growth, Mars (planet), the archangel Anael, red • **three days** the dark of the moon; days of death of the initiate or harvest god before rebirth • **African** Ashanti • **alchemic** sulfur, Mercurius, and salt representing spirit, soul, and body • **Arabian** Manant is threefold • **Babylonian** the three spheres of the universe • **Buddhist** the Three Precious Gifts; the Three Precious Jewels; the Buddhist triad of personality, church, and law; *Tibetan Buddhism:* the Three Poisons • **Carthaginian** *three pillars:* the Great Goddess • **Celtic** Bridget is threefold; the Three Blessed Ladies • **Chinese** sanctity; yang; an auspicious number; the perfect number; legs of the moon toad or bird; associated with the element wood • **Christian** the Trinity; crosses on Calvary, Theological Virtues, Marys, gifts of the Magi, denials by Peter, appearances of Christ after death, days in the tomb, temptations of Christ, days of Saul's blindness • **Druidic** degrees of priesthood • **Egyptian** the cosmos; *Memphis:* the godhead of Ptah, Sek-Het, Nefer-Tem; *Thebes:* the godhead of Amen-Ra, Maut, Khonsu; *Abydos:* the godhead of Osiris, Isis, Horus; Thoth the thrice great • **Greco-Roman** the Moirae/Fates, the Graces, the Erinyes/Furies, Gorgons, sirens, judges of hell; sacred to Aphrodite/Venus; associated with Zeus/Jupiter, reconciliation of opposites; *three-headed dog:* Cerberus; *three sickles of Megara:* lucky • **heraldic** *three legs joined at the thigh:* emblem of the Isle of Man; *three legs joined at the thigh with Medusa's head in the middle:* emblem of Sicily, Palermo • **Hermetic** the Supreme Power; Trismegistus • **Hindu** the godhead of Brahma, Vishnu, Shiva; wheels on Soma's chariot • **Jewish** limitless light; sanctifying intelligence; sons of Noah, days of Jonah in the fish's belly • **Kabalistic** energy; action; the three souls of man and the three worlds they inhabit; associated with the archangel Cassiel • **Japanese** the Three Treasures • **Maori** the Great Spirit; *three raised fingers:* mind, character, body • **Mayan** associated with women • **Norse** lucky; the three Norns; the godhead of Odin, Thor, and Frey; fate; new, full, and waning moon; *hare with three legs:* the moon hare; *three-headed deity:* Thor • **Persian** the three Yazatas who judge the dead; *three fires:* Anaid, Mihr, Berisov • **Pythagorean** completion • **Slavic** *three-headed deity:* the moon god • **Taoist** yang; Heaven-Man-Earth; multiplicity; an auspicious number; center point of equilibrium • **tarot** the Empress •

Teutonic Holda and her two daughters • **Yoruban** associated with iron, minerals, forests, keys, jails, tools • *see also* **triangle; trident; triskelion**

-4- usually a human number, but may be associated with divinity; the earth; the terrestrial order; material aspect of life; the feminine; balance of nature; the Elements; rational organization; tangible achievement; justice without mercy; hard work; stability; coldness; the seasons; order; reason; wholeness; the functional aspects of consciousness— thinking, feeling, sensation and intuition, concentration; double vision; the corners of the earth, phases of the moon, chambers of the heart, limbs of man, cardinal directions, winds; associated with the square, mind, teacher, taskmaster, reality, Saturn (planet), the archangel Samael, bright blue, Mercury (planet) • **four cherubs** the four corners of the earth, the elemental powers guarding the center of Paradise • **arm with the number four** force • **alchemic** synthesis • **Amerindian** perfection; the four winds, cardinal directions • **Babylonian** the four corners of the world, directions, winds, seasons, phases of the moon • **Buddhist** associated with the earth, the four boundless wishes of humanity, directions of the heart, streams of immortality, branches and roots of Damba, celestial guardians of the cardinal directions, deva kings, travels of Buddha • **Chinese** yin; the four streams of immortality; associated with the earth, the element metal • **Christian** divine equilibrium; the four Evangelists, Gospels, major prophets, rivers of Paradise, cardinal virtues, horsemen of the Apocalypse, winged beasts of the Apocalypse; *four cherubs:* the Evangelists • **Egyptian** the sacred number of time; the four pillars supporting the heavens, sons of Horus, cardinal directions, winds and/or gods of the winds, canopic jars placed around the dead • **Gnostic** Barbelo • **Greco-Roman** associated with matter; sacred to Hermes/Mercury, Uranus/Caelus • **Hermetic** God • **Hindu** totality; plenty; perfection; Brahma; the winning throw in dice; the square; the four tatvas, bodies of man, kingdoms of nature, yugas, castes, cardinal directions, seasons, pairs of opposites, petals of the Muladhara chakra (spine's base) • **Islamic** primordial matter; the four angelic beings, houses of death, fundamental duties, wives allowed a man, rivers of Paradise • **Japanese** associated with misfortune • **Jewish** measuring; beneficence; intelligence, the four living creatures of Ezekiel • **Kabalistic** memory; completion; the four directions of space, levels of the Torah; associated with the archangel Zadkiel • **Mayan** giants who support the vault of heaven • **Norse** rivers of milk in Asgard, dwarves who support the world • **Pythagorean** perfection; harmonious proportion; justice; the earth; the Pythagorean oath; double duality • **Sumero-Semitic** the four cardinal directions, astral gods • **Taoist** the four celestial guardians, Sacred Creatures • **tarot** the Emperor • **Yoruban** associated with Shango, war, power, masculinity, thunder and lightning

-5- associated with Jupiter (planet), Mercury (planet), God, indigo, change, new beginnings, the five senses, good judgment, sympathy, the universe, divine will, fertility, health and love, marriage, the powers of nature, change, travel, new experience, new friends, spring, growth, organic fullness of life, the erotic, man, man after The Fall, the human microcosm, freedom, hedonism, changeability • **five-pointed star** wholeness; the godhead; marriage; meditation; religion; versatility; the five senses (except in the East); spiritual aspiration • **five-pointed star pointing downward** witchcraft; black magic • **five-pointed leaves** the microcosm • **five-petaled flower** the microcosm • **alchemic** *five-petaled flower, or five-pointed star:* the quintessence • **Aztecan** the five eras; associated with the center of the world • **Buddhist** the heart; universality; the five Dhyani Buddhas, Bodhisattvas, disciples of a Buddha, commandments of Buddha • **Central American Indian** associated with the maize god • **Chinese** associated with the masculine, the cross, the center, the Five Elements, Atmospheres, Conditions, Planets, Sacred Mountains, Grains, Colors, Tastes, Poisons, Powerful Charms, Cardinal Virtues, Blessings, Eternal Ideas, Relations of Mankind • **Christian** the five wounds of Christ, yoke of oxen, talents, sparrows sold for a farthing, wise virgins, foolish virgins, lesser sacraments, points of the Cross, fish for the feeding of the 5,000, Patriarchates of the Greek Orthodox Church, associated with man after the Fall • **Egyptian** the five crocodiles of the Nile • **Greco-Roman** the five qualities of Apollo; associated with Aphrodite/Venus, Hermes/Mercury, marriage, sensuality, masculinity, sexuality, marriage of heaven and earth, light • **Hindu** conjunction of the male and female; the five faces of Shiva, elements of the subtle and coarse states, primary colors, senses, Powers of Brahma; the twice-five incarnations of Vishnu • **Islamic** a lucky number; the five pillars of religion, times of daily prayer, Divine Presences,

fundamental dogmas, actions, elements of the hajj, types of fasting • **Jewish** aspiration; hope; optimism; strength; severity; radical intelligence; the five books of Moses, stones David had to kill Goliath; associated with the archangel Anael; *five hearts:* Judah's five sons • **Kabalistic** fear; perfect man; associated with the archangels Michael, Samael • **Mayan** perfection; associated with the maize god • **Pueblo** associated with the center, manifestation • **Pythagorean** the marriage of heaven and earth; light; Apollo and his five qualities • **tarot** the Pope • *see also* **pentagon; pentagram**

-6- a perfect number; associated with divine power, majesty, justice, creation, perfection, balance, material comfort, education, marriage, institutions, harmony, responsibility, beauty, art, time, happiness, health, luck, evolution, family life, love, peace, life, good fortune, wisdom, mercy, spirituality, virginity, stabilizing influences, trial and effort, the soul, equilibrium, completion of a creative process, ambivalence, the duality of all things, feminine power, longevity, Venus (planet), the archangel Raphael, yellow, light blue, the letters F, 0, X • **Babylonian** the six ages of the world; the number of Hadad • **Buddhist** the six transcendent virtues; associated with the universe • **Chinese** the universe; heaven; the six senses; periods of day and night • **Christian** perfection; completion; the six hours of Christ on the cross, sins against the Holy Spirit, gifts of the Holy Spirit, attributes of the Creator, jars of water at Cana • **Greco-Roman** associated with Aphrodite/Venus, marriage, harmony, luck, happy coincidence • **Hindu** the six petals of the Swadhistana chakra (genitals) • **Islamic** the six days of Creation • **Jewish** creation; meditation; intelligence; the six days of Creation • **Kabalistic** experiment; creation; beauty • **Mayan** an unlucky number; associated with death • **Occidental** winning number in dice • **Pythagorean** chance; luck • **Sumerian** the six days of creation • **tarot** the Lovers • **Yoruban** associated with war, power, masculinity, thunder and lightning

-7- completeness; totality; perfect order; perfection; planetary order; exceptional value; transformation and unification of all hierarchical orders; reintegration; conflict; pain; the moon; the sun; charity; grace holiness; consecration; stability; security; safety; rest; creation; cosmos; the universe; the macrocosm; space; wisdom; an indefinite number; associated with the closing of a cycle, Saturn (planet), culture, coldness, virginity, the Great Mother, intellect, wealth, stubbornness, unexpected and willful action, fate, courage, heavy responsibilities, gray, the archangels Asariel, Gabriel, the personifications of Music, Health, Philosophy, Deceit; the letters G, P, Y; the seven liberal arts, days in the week, cosmic stages, circles of the universe, ages of man, divisions of the rainbow, days of the week, notes of the musical scale, wonders of the world • **alchemic** the seven metals involved in the Work • **Assyrian** *pine with seven branches and seven buds:* Tree of Life, completeness • **astrologic** the seven stars of the Great Bear, the Pleiades, major planets, rays of the sun • **Babylonian** the seven cosmic towers, stages, curls of Gilgamesh, branches of life, Pleiades.• **Buddhist** ascent; the seven steps of Buddha • **Chinese** the seven days of creation • **Christian** the Holy Spirit; the seven virtues, vices, deadly sins, major prophets, angels of the Presence, demons of Mary Magdalene, councils of the early Church, gifts of the Holy Spirit, joys of the Virgin Mary, sorrows of the Virgin Mary, sacraments of the Church, last words on the Cross, penitential psalms, heads of the Beast of the Apocalypse; *lamb with seven horns and seven eyes:* the seven gifts of the Holy Spirit; the Apocalypse • **Egyptian** sacred to Osiris; associated with eternal life, a complete cycle, dynamic perfection; the seven Hathors, daughters of Ra, hawks of Ra, underworld houses; *seven cows with a bull:* fertility • **Gnostic** *the seven Greek vowels arranged in a Kabalistic manner:* the Creator • **Greco-Roman** sacred to Apollo, Athena/Minerva, Ares/Mars, Pan/Faunus, Poseidon/Neptune; the seven strings in Apollo's lyre, pipes of Pan, Wise Men of Greece, minor planets; associated with birth, death, magic • **Hindu** the Seven Jewels of the Brahmans, gods before the flood, wise men saved from the flood, mansions of created spirits, chakras, sun rays • **Islamic** the first perfect number; the seven heavens, climates, earths, colors, seas, prophets, active powers, states of the heart, circuits around the Ka'aba, attributes of God, duties of the faith • **Japanese** the seven household gods • **Jewish** occult intelligence; the Ark rested on the seventh day; Noah sent out the dove after seven days; the seven trumpets of Jericho, circuits around Jericho, altars of Balaam, bonds of Samson, times Naaman bathed in the Jordan, sneezes of the child raised by Elisha, great holy days, menorah branches, pillars of wisdom, years to construct the Temple, Patriarchs • **Kabalistic** victory; associated with the archangel Anael • **Mithraic** the seven doors and altars of the cave of Mithras, grades of initiation; *ladder with seven rungs:* passage of the soul through the seven heavens • **Nigerian** *seven bracelets:* attribute of Oshun • **Norse** the seven oxen that pull the sun chariot • **Persian** the seven steps of progress toward heaven • **Pythagorean** the cosmic number; perfection; the god of the world • **Sumero-Semitic** the seventh day is dangerous for undertakings; the seven zones of the earth, branches of the Tree of Life, leaves on each branch of the Tree of Life, lunar divisions, days of the week, gates of hell, demons of Tiamat, colors, seals • **tarot** the Chariot • **West African** perfection; unity • **Yoruban** associated with Yewa, death • **Zoroastrian** the seven skies

-8- regeneration; entering into a new soul state; goal after passing through the seven stages of initiation; Paradise regained; resurrection; a twin or binary, symbol; perfect blending of the conscious/unconscious, knowledge/love, action/reaction; perfect rhythm; connection between heaven and earth; inspiration; ruthlessness; coldness; opposition; power; wealth; self-destruction; good deeds; justice with mercy; good health; endurance; discipline; discrimination; the letters H, Q, Z, the planets Mars and Uranus, violent passions, Scorpio, rose color, abnormal tendencies, material success, self-assertion; related to the gods, the eternal movement of the sea, solidity, rain and thunder, health, immortality, punishment; the eight winds, pairs of opposites, directions of the winds; associated with the archangel Anael • **Arabian** sacred to the sun • **Babylonian** sacred to the sun; associated with Ishtar • **Buddhist** completion; the Eight Things of Good Augury, eightfold path of Buddha • **Chinese** the whole; all possibilities in manifestation; totality of the universe; lucky; the Eight Delights of Human Existence • **Christian** regeneration; rebirth; baptism; the eight Beatitudes, sides on a baptismal font • **Egyptian** the eight disciples of Thoth; sacred to the sun; associated with balance and cosmic order • **folkloric** hours of sleep needed by merchants • **Greco-Roman** the eight gods of the winds, divisions of the sky; associated with the material world, justice, Cronos, Dionysus/Bacchus, Poseidon/Neptune • **Hermetic** magic number of Hermes; the eight minor gods • **Hindu** the eight regions of the world, suns, divisions of the day, chakras, sacred myths, great gods of the Vedas, modes of marriage, forms of Shiva, arms of Vishnu • **Islamic** the eight divisions of space, divisions of letters in Arabic, angels who support the throne of the world, animals that accompany believers to Paradise • **Japanese** the eight gods in the heavens; multiplicity • **Jewish** resurrection; atonement; eternity; endlessness; splendor; perfect intelligence; Yahweh; associated with circumcision; the eight days of the sanctification of the Temple, persons saved from the Flood • **Kabalistic** associated with the archangel Raphael, balance, silvery-blue • **Norse** the eight legs of Sleipnir • **Platonic** the eight spheres surrounding the pillar of the heavens • **Pythagorean** associated with love, friendship, prudence, solidarity, stability, thinking • **Sumero-Semitic** the magic number of Nebo • **Taoist** all the possibilities of manifestation; the eight immortals • **Tibetan** the eight guardian deities • **tarot** Justice, Strength • **Yoruban** associated with Obba, Obtala • **Zoroastrian** the eight categories of priests • *see also* **eight ball; octagon**

-9- a mystic number; truth; perfection; completion; attainment; the triple triad; synthesis of body/mind/spirit; truth and wisdom resulting from completion of a cycle; associated with the occult, philosophy, culture, fine arts, humaneness, spiritual or mental achievement, patience, meditation, harmony, Neptune (planet), hidden factors, the archangels Azrael, Lumiel, violet (color), the letters I, R, the moon, the Great Goddess, the underworld, hell, motherhood, fertility, the corporal, intellectual, spiritual worlds, months of human gestation • **Aztecan** the nine underground worlds, heavens, stages, souls, travels to reach eternal rest; associated with the nocturnal and terrestrial • **Amerindian** the nine underworlds • **Buddhist** supreme spiritual power; the nine celestial levels of the sky • **Celtic** the eight directions together with the center; the nine virgins attendant on Bridget, connected with the Beltrane Fire rites; *nine white stones:* attribute of Bridget • **Chinese** celestial power; associated with fertility; most auspicious of all numbers; the nine classes of officials, social classes, sky plains, prostrations before the emperor; the eight directions and the center • **Christian** the nine Gifts of the Holy Spirit, Fruits of the Spirit, circles of hell • **Egyptian** a sacred number; the nine great Osirian gods (the Ennead) • **Greco-Roman** the nine gods, muses; a sacred number; associated with Ares/Mars • **Hindu** associated with karma; Agni; fire; the nine avatars of Vishnu • **Islamic** channels of communication with the world; *walking down nine steps without falling:* tamed senses • **Jewish** pure intelligence; truth; the nine choirs of angels • **Kabalistic** achievement; foun-

dation; associated with the archangel Gabriel • **Masonic** the eternal number of human immortality; associated with the Mountain of the Sun • **Mayan** the nine underworlds; monogram of Bolon Tiku; a lucky number • **Mithraic** the nine celestial levels of the sky • **Mongolo-Turkic** the nine layers of heaven, servants of God • **Norse** the sacred number; the nine days and nights Odin hung in Yggdrasil to win the secrets of wisdom for mankind, months Skeldi lives by Niord's sea each year • **Pythagorean** the limit of numbers • **Siberian** the nine notches of the birch world axis • **Taoist** the nine nodes of bamboo; associated with fulfillment, yang • **tarot** the Hermit • **Tibetan** an auspicious number; longevity • **Yoruban** associated with Oya

-10- the perfect number; associated with the cosmos, return to unity, balance, completeness, kingship, infinite power, wonders of the world, beginning, originality, perfection, finality, androgyny, marriage, spiritual achievement, order, harmony in matter, involution and evolution, the archangel Lumiel; multiplication of the powers of one • **Buddhist** the ten moral duties of the code of Manou • **Babylonian** associated with Marduk • **Chinese** the Ten Celestial Stems, the souls each man possesses • **Christian** the ten talents, faithful disciples, wise and foolish virgins, their lamps, horns of the Beast of Revelation, the days between the Ascension and Pentecost • **Gnostic** the ten Aeons that become Sephiroth • **Hindu** the ten incarnations of Vishnu, rules of wisdom that Krishna received in his torment, petals of the Manipura chakra (solar plexus), the Pradjapati Brahma created • **Jewish** the ten Commandments, Levites that minister before the Ark, men needed for a minyan, Temple lavers, Temple tables, Temple candlesticks, wicked brothers of Joseph, Plagues of Egypt, servants of Joshua • **Kabalistic** the eternal word, wealth, resplendent intelligence; divine support; numerical value of Yod; number of the Sephiroth; the ten evil spirits; associated with the archangels Lumiel, Sandalphon • **Mayan** associated with the end of one cycle and the beginning of another, life and death • **Pythagorean** the godhead; perfection; infinite expansion; the recommencement of a series; the universe; the whole of human knowledge • **Roman** completion; the ten sibyls • **tarot** Wheel of Fortune

-11- associated with transition, excess, peril, sin, transgression, conflict, martyrdom, incontinence, balance, unity, a surfeit of completion and perfection, courage, power, the archangels

Azrael, Michael; sometimes has an infernal character; an intensification of the powers of ten; harbinger of conflict • **African** an especially holy number; associated with the mysteries of fruitfulness • **Babylonian** the 11 rays of Marduk, the 11-stringed harp of Telloh • **Buddhist** the 11 kinds of witnesses • **Chinese** associated with the union of sky and earth • **Christian** sin; transgression; intemperance; transition; the 11 disciples who did not betray Jesus • **folkloric** hours of sleep needed by wicked people • **Islamic** associated with the knowledge of God • **Jewish** the 11 Temple curtains, brothers of Joseph; generally considered a bad number • **tarot** Justice, Strength • **Yoruban** associated with power over sexual desire, mediation of messages between people and gods

-12- universal order; inner complexity of the universe; salvation; perfection; completeness; fulfillment; holiness; harmony; power; justice; temperance; beauty; grace; mildness; space and time; the 12 zodiac signs, sibyls; associated with the archangel Azrael • **Benedictine** the 12 steps of humility • **Buddhist** the 12 Nidanas, members of the Dalai Lama's council • **Celtic** the 12 paladins of Charlemagne, knights of the Round Table • **Chinese** the 12 animals of the zodiac • **Christian** the Church; the 12 Apostles of Christ, Epistles of Paul, gifts of the Holy Spirit, days of Christmas, pearl gates of the New Jerusalem • **Confucian** the 12 disciples of Confucius • **Egyptian** the 12 gates of hell; the 12 white pyramids and 12 black pyramids in the Egg of Osiris • **Greco-Roman** the 12 labors of Heracles/Hercules, gods and goddesses of Olympus, Titans, days and nights of Saturnalia, tables of Roman law • **Hermetic** the 12 months, torments, verses on the Emerald Table • **Hindu** the 12 petals of the Anahata chakra (heart); the 12 petals of the Sahasrara chakra (top of the head) • **Islamic** the 12 descendents of Ali, orders of dervishes, disciples of Mohammed • **Japanese** the 12 cushions of the Creator • **Jewish** the archangels Uriel and Gabriel together; the 12 tribes of Israel, sons of Jacob, legions of angels, gates of Jerusalem, foundation stones of Jerusalem, fruits of the Tree of Life, loaves of the Table of the Temple, stones on Aaron's breastplate; associated with completion of a perfect and harmonious unit • **Mithraic** the 12 disciples of Mithras • **Norse** the 12 companions of Odin, imposing rooms in Paradise • **Russian** the 12 "fevers" • **Sanskrit** the 12 names of the sun • **Sumero-Semitic** the 12-day duel between Chaos and Cosmos • **tarot** Hanged Man •

Yoruban associated with war, power, masculinity, thunder and lightning

-13- unlucky; the 13 lunations in a year, playing cards in each suit; associated with the archangel Raphael, betrayal, faithlessness, misfortune, death, birth, beginning anew, cleansing, purification, passage to a higher level of existence • **Aztecan** time; the days in a week; associated with divination, the skies, completion of a temporal series • **Christian** Judas Iscariot; the 13 Tenebrae, people at the Last Supper • **Druidic** the 13 segments in the sacred cord • **Egyptian** pieces of Osiris recovered by Isis • **Jehovah's Witnesses** the 13 fundamental doctrines • **Jewish** the 13 fundamental doctrines of Maimonides • **Kabalistic** the 13 evil spirits; associated with snakes, dragons, murderers, Satan • **Mayan** the 13 heavens; a sacred number • **Sumerian** the 13 constellations in their zodiac • **tarot** Death • **witchcraft** the 13 members of a coven • **Yoruban** associated with infections, diseases

-14- associated with fusion, organization, temperance, justice, good, charity, delusion, loss, sacrifice, Croesus, the archangel Zadkiel • **biblical** a holy number • **Buddhist** 14 Manous control the world in successive reigns during the great cycle of Mahakalpa • **Christian** associated with the Holy Spirit being spread in nature • **Egyptian** Osiris was cut into 14 pieces • **French** age of majority for kings • **Jewish** associated with King David • **tarot** Temperance

-15- associated with ascent; progression, the devil, the archangel Cassiel; generally an unlucky number; may have erotic connotations • **Christian** the 15 mysteries of the rosary, fruits of the spirit; associated with the plenitude of science • **Jewish** the 15 Temple steps, gradual Psalms • **tarot** the Devil

-16- associated with happiness, luxury, love, sensuality, fertility, increase, the archangel Samael, the achievement of material power, construction and destruction, Lucifer; the ideal age for a lover • **Buddhist** the 16 Arhats • **Hindu** the 16 petals of the Visuddha chakra (front of the throat) • **Jainism** the 16 goddesses • **tarot** House of God

-17- associated with the archangels Azrael, Uriel • **Christian** associated with the Holy Spirit • **Hindu** associated with the evolution of the cosmos and its tendency toward karmic liberation • **Islamic** the 17 liturgical gestures used in the five daily prayers, words in the call to prayer • **Italian** an unlucky number • **Roman** age of majority; an unlucky number • **tarot** Star

-18- life; associated with the archangels Asariel,

Zadkiel, Gabriel • **Christian** a sign of great reward • **Jewish** an evil number • **Kabalistic** associated with emotions, secrets, lies, selfishness, criminality, destruction, accidents, difficulties, sickness, danger • **tarot** Moon

-19- lucky; associated with the archangel Michael • **Japanese** misfortune • **tarot** Sun

-20- continuity; dynasty; an intensifier; the whole man; an indefinite number; shares in the symbolism of -10-; multiplication of the powers of -2-; associated with the archangel Lumiel • **Gallic** base of their number system • **Kabalistic** physical strength • **Mayan** associated with the sun god; days of a month in the religious calendar; the base of their number system; Primal Oneness • **tarot** Judgment • **Zoroastrian** volumes in the Zend-Avesta

-21- absolute truth; a lucky number; a sacred number; traditional age of majority; associated with the archangel Cassiel, excellence, harmony of creation • **Christian** union of the Trinity • **Italian** letters in the alphabet • **Jewish** perfection • **tarot** World

-22- generally an unfavorable number; associated with movement, infinity, manifestation of being in all its diversity • **Hindu** associated with a cycle's end, end of the obligatory reincarnations on earth

-24- usually a lucky number; the 24 cranial nerves that lead to the body's five senses; associated with the harmony of sky and earth • **Chinese** the 24 paragons • **Christian** the 24 elders of Revelation • **Hindu** the wheel of rebirth • **Jainism** the 24 tirthankaras

-25- • **Jainism** the 25 precepts of Mahavira

-26- letters in the Latin alphabet

-27- associated with the tendency of evolution to unify duality, divine light • **Christian** associated with the Holy Spirit • **Hindu** 27 women accompanied Soma

-28- an unlucky number • **Chinese** animals in the zodiac

-30- associated with sacrifice, perfect balance in cosmic organization; a multiplication of the powers of three • **Buddhism** the 30 transcendent virtues of Buddha • **Christian** traditional age at which Jesus began his public ministry; age at which John the Baptist began to preach; age of St. Paul at his conversion; the 30 pieces of silver Judas received to betray Jesus • **Jewish** age at which Ezekiel began to prophesy, David began to reign • **Kabalistic** sacrifice • **tarot** the Hanged Man

-32- • **Pythagorean** justice

-33- associated with mystery, perfection, culmi-

nation • **Christian** the traditional number of years in Christ's life; often the number of buttons on a cassock; the 33 Doctors of the Church • **Japanese** misfortune • **Masonic** the 33 degrees of the hierarchy • **telegraphic** fondest regards

-36- associated with initiation, the angelic world, the sky, heaven, cosmic solidarity • **Chinese** the 36 beneficial stars • **Christian** associated with Satan, evil • **Jewish** the renewal of life

-37- • **Chaldean** the Force, the Power, and the Capacity • **Christian** associated with Christ, the living word of God

-40- highest functioning of the intellect; multiplication of the powers of four; associated with wholeness, totality, probation, trial, initiation, preparation, penance, death, purification, expiation, maturity, castigation, punishment, death of the self and spiritual rebirth, perfection • **British** days it will rain if it rains on St. Swithin's Day • **Buddhist** Buddha's age when he began his ministry • **Christian** the church Militant; the days of Lent, days of Christ in the wilderness, days of the Resurrection, days of sanctuary in a church, days after Christ's birth until his presentation at the Temple • **Egyptian** days of fasting for the death and absence of Osiris • **Islamic** change; death; reconciliation; return; Mohammed's age at his call • **Japanese** the beginning of old age • **Jewish** the days of Moses on Mt. Sinai, Elijah in hiding, the Deluge, probation of Nineveh under Jonah; the years of the Jews wandering in the desert, David's reign, Solomon's reign, Eli as judge, under the yoke of the Philistines; age at which Moses was called by God • **Kabalistic** transformation

-42- weakness; being cut off halfway to perfection; creative generation; punishment; trial; expiation; correction

-49- • **Buddhism** days Buddha remained near the bo tree; *Tibetan Buddhism:* the ending of a journey; days needed for a soul to reach its new abode

-50- expansion to infinity; space; understanding and sympathy; a special rapport with the deity; by multiplication, shares in the powers of five; a jubilee year; a return to the beginning; the primordial state; a favorable number; associated with the total man, spiritual ascension, illumination • **Christian** remission of sins; the Holy Spirit; days from Easter to Pentecost • **Greek** lunations between the Olympic Games • **Jewish** days from Passover to Pentecost • **Kabalistic** initiative

-53- • **Japanese** stations on the highway between Kyoto and Tokyo; the noble path of empire

-60- a multiplication of the qualities of six; associated with time, happiness, harmony, destiny, the earth • **Buddhist** disciples Buddha sent out to evangelize • **Chinese** years for a complete cycle of the Chinese lunar calendar • **Christian** beads in a Roman Catholic rosary • **Egyptian** longevity • **Hindu** associated with the global karma of the universe • **kabalistic** destiny

-61- • **Islamic** Mohammed died at age 61 or 62

-62- • **Islamic** Mohammed died at age 61 or 62

-63- • **Jewish** books in the Mishna

-64- perfect actualized wholeness; plenitude; bliss; squares on a chessboard; earthly fulfillment; associated with paramount chaos • **Buddhist** Buddha's birth family had 64 kinds of virtues • **Chinese** pallbearers for emperors • **Christian** generations from Adam to Jesus (also said to be 77) • **Confucian** Confucius was the 64th generation from the founder of his line

-66- associated with loss of faith in the divine plan • **Jewish** days of purification for a woman who gave birth to a girl

-67- associated with the completion of Creation

-68- associated with the mercy of God

-69- a lucky number; associated with Cancer (the numbers are usually on their sides, one above the other); simultaneous oral-genital sex • **Hindu** the perfection reached by those who liquidate their karma

-70- a fortunate number; multiplies the qualities of seven; associated with finality, death. resurrection, the totality of evolution • **Buddhist** 70 virgins tended Buddha as a baby • **Egyptian** mummification took 70 days • **Islamic** 70 sails cover God's face • **Jewish** man's allotted lifespan; the number of elders; universality • **Kabalistic** catastrophe • **tarot** associated with the House of God, termination of a cycle, collapse, catastrophe

-72- a ritual number involving solar increase and lunar wisdom; associated with the earth, angels, mercy, but also evil and confusion; the average heart rate • **Chinese** number of malevolent stars • **Christian** the disciples sent out by Jesus • **Confucian** the disciples of Confucius • **Jewish** the races resulting from Noah; the languages at Babel • **Kabalistic** the 72 intelligences governing the 72 zodiacal terms; letters in the name of God • **Taoist** the Immortals of Taoism

-73- • **Benedictine** chapters in the Rule of Benedict • **ham and CB radio** end of a conversation; best regards

-74- associated with the absence of light

-76- Capricorn

-77- • **Christian** the generations from Adam to Christ (also said to be 64); associated with sinners who lived before the advent of Christ

-78- • **Hindu** individual karmic liberation reached through evolution • **tarot** cards in the deck

-80- enduring hope; multiplies the values of eight • **Buddhist** advisors of Buddha • **Christian** years of life given to man in the Psalms • **Hindu** associated with the karmic liberation • **Islamic** lashes given to those who falsely accuse free women • **tarot** associated with the Star

-81- truth [-9-] multiplied by itself; sometimes associated with the moon • **Buddhist** age at which Buddha died • **Chinese** a perfect number; age at which a man is considered completed • **Taoist** chapters in the Tao te Ching; the number of skies

-82- • **Hindu** associated with the creature liberated from karmic bonds enjoying the material world without transgressing the Law of the Cosmos; harmony in matter

-88- the double directions of the infinity of the universe; the infinitely small and the infinitely large

-89- • **Hindu** associated with those who have freed themselves from their karmic bonds

-90- divine discontent; striving toward perfection; reflection; the close of a cycle; multiplies the qualities of -9- • **Kabalistic** disappointment

-95- theses of Martin Luther

-96- • **Hindu** petals of the Ajna Chakra (between the eyebrows)

-99- a realized state of perfection • **Islamic** the names of Allah • **Jewish** age of Abraham when God appeared to him and made an alliance

-100- perfection; plenitude; an indefinite number; associated with perfection, plenitude, martyrdom • **Christian** associated with celestial beatitude • **Islamic** lashes for adulterers prescribed by the Koran; beads in a rosary • **Jewish** the prophets saved by Obadiah; Philistine foreskins Saul demanded as a bride price for Merab; age of Abraham when Isaac was born • **Kabalistic** perfection

-105- • **Jewish** Judith's age at death; age of Seth when he fathered Enosh

-106- associated with man's redemption by Christ

-108- a universal number; associated with man • **Buddhist** number of names of Buddha; solar years in a mahakalpa; beads in a rosary • **Hindu** the Upanishads, names of Vishnu, names of Shiva • **Japanese** bangs on the gong at main temples for the New Year • **Rosicrucian** cycles of the Rosicrucian brotherhood • **Taoist** the lords of Tao • **Tibetan** the names for Tara; the great and initiated masters in Shambala

-109- associated with achievement

-110- a canonical number; the perfect age to die; associated with a life of holiness and virtue glorifying the soul

-111- associated with plentitude, the sky, the Trinity (especially God the Father) • **Kabalistic** a solar number • **tarot** a solar number

-113- associated with the immolation of Christ on the Cross

-114- chapters of the Koran

-115- • **Christian** associated with the Immaculate Conception

-117- • **Druidic** number of atoms composing the earth

-118- associated with an unknown latent potential actively working to appear

-119- associated with high treason and the rejection of God

-120- a magical number • **Christian** associated with the power and glory of Christ the King • **Jewish** a large crowd; age of Moses when he died; the limit of man's age as fixed by God; the years that Noah had to build the Ark • **Mesopotamian** the Ark of Gilgamesh prescribed by Anu was a cube 120 cubits on each side

-123- associated with the Trinity

-126- satanic influence in man where is manifested as deceitful and deformed divine truths

-144- good omen • **Rosicrucian** the different kinds of atoms in the universe

-153- universality • **ancient times** the number of all the types of fishes in existence • **Christian** the catholicity of the Church; the Trinity; the number of fish taken by the apostles when Jesus directed them where to cast their nets

-175- • **German** associated with homosexuals

-200- • **Kabalistic** reincarnation • **tarot** corresponds to upheaval, antagonism

-222- associated with the Temple, the earth

-300- a large or infinite number; associated with the breath of God; a free and autonomous agent • **Buddhism** number of days Buddha was carried by his mother • **Christian** the victory of the faithful soul over; the victory of God over Satan; the popes and antipopes who will gather before the Second Coming of Christ • **Jewish** length of Noah's Ark in cubits; the invincible soldiers of Gideon; the foxes of Samson; number of angels in the Garden of Eden; the concubines of Solomon • **Kabalistic** compensation

-318- occasionally an abstract and universal number • **Gnostic** the number for Christ • **Jewish** men Abraham used to attack the captors of Lot

-333- associated with change, travel, transition, spiritual awakening, physical awakening

-360- degrees in a circle; symbols of the zodiac • **Chinese** human bones in traditional medicine • **Egyptian** number of pharaohs from the beginning to 1 CE; urns used by priests to honor Osiris • **Gnostic** number of eons • **Hindu** solar years in a divine year • **Islamic** number of idols Mohammed destroyed in Mecca • **Orphic** number of gods

-365- days in a year; a sacred number • **Egyptian** the tables of offerings around the tomb of Osiris • **Gnostic** the number of skies • **Jewish** Enoch's death age; angels involved in the creation of Adam's body

-400- associated with human fragility, life, sacrifice, the rotational cycles of nature in microcosmic creatures • **American** upper class society (especially in the East) • **Jewish** years the descendants of Abraham wandered; years of captivity in Egypt • **Kabalistic** reward • **Mayan** the innumerable; the inexpressible; days in the Mayan year

-444- the first divine woman • **Assyrian** the number of Lilith

-500- the cosmic germ; the physical life of the microcosmic creature • **Buddhist** at the birth of Buddha, 500 white elephants came to touch his father's feet • **Gaelic** infinity • **Jewish** age of Noah when he fathered Shem, Ham and Japheth

-515- the Holy Spirit

-540- • **Norse** number of gates or doors in Valhalla

-555- associated with discernment of spirits, lust, desire, swift attack, emotion

-600- perfection; conjunction and internal fruitfulness • **Far Eastern** years at which a crane eases to eat and only drinks • **Hindu** karma of the microcosmic • **Jewish** Philistines Shagmar challenged with an ox-goad; age of Noah when the flood began

-666- perfect imperfection; impiety without measure • **Christian** the Beast of the Apocalypse; the Antichrist; also applied to Martin Luther and other Protestants, Adolf Hitler • **Hindu** human karma in contact with cosmic karma and divine providential balance • **Jewish** the sons of Adonikam that returned to Jerusalem with Zerubbabel • **Kabalistic** the number of Sorath; a solar number

-700- • **Jewish** the wives of Solomon

-777- ascension of the soul through the physical body • **Jewish** age of Lamech (Noah's father) • **Tibetan** celestial man; the transmutation which takes place when a man becomes conscious of the necessity to follow the path of initiation and first perceives that the goal is in God

-800- • **Hindu** individual karmic liberation; general karmic liberation at the end of a big cosmic cycle • **Norse** warriors in each room at Valhalla

-888- sacred number of Jesus in the Hebrew alphabet; resurrection; baptism; redemption; a perfect number

-900- cosmic solidarity felt in the microcosm; deaths distinguished in the Kabala

-999- the infinitely large; justice; truth

-1,000- absolute perfection; eternity; a very long time; an indefinite number; a multitude; multiplications and additions to one thousand are intensifiers • **Christian** the totality of generations; the perfection of life; guardian angels of the Virgin Mary; years Satan would be bound in a pit at the Second Coming; the reign of God before the Last Judgment • **Gnostic** *1,000 days:* a cosmic day • **Hindu** *thousand-petaled lotus:* the Sahasrara chakra (above the crown of the head); *city with 1,000 gates:* Amaravati • **Jewish** imperishable doctrine; men killed by Samson with the jawbone of an ass; those who perished at Schechem; pieces of money Abimelech gave to Abraham; years Adam would have lived if he had not sinned; generations the alliance God made with Abraham would last

-1,008- persons who mocked Christ on the Cross • **Hindu** names for Shiva

-1,100- betrayal; caddish behavior

-2,000- • **Far Eastern** age at which a crane becomes all black

-6,666- the legions of Satan • **Gospel of Barnabas** demons in a person cured by Jesus

-7,000- • **Ethiopian** years in the ten cycles of Enoch • **Gnostic** years in a cosmic week

-10,000- plenty; fertility; abundance • **Chinese** the Ten Thousand Things; the whole of manifestation; the uncountable • **Zoroastrian** verses of each of the 20 books of Zoroaster

-12,000- associated with the force of the historical events, the impact of changes, the presence of the beings evolving through these changes, the passage of the external visitors of this dimension, such as Jesus, Buddha • **Christian** the seals of each of the tribes of Israel; the length, width, and height in stadia of the New Jerusalem • **Hindu** years in one cycle of a Mahayuga • **Zoroastrian** skins of cows Zoroaster used to write his 20 books; years the world would last

-18,000- • **Chinese** an indefinite period • **Jewish** worlds that could exist simultaneously in the universe

-25,920- average number of breaths per day; solar years of the Great Cosmic Year

-55,555- • **Taoist** the myriads of floors and offices in the Crimson Slenderness celestial palace; the myriads of celestial officials dressed in green feathers who work in the Crimson Slenderness celestial palace

-70,000- • **Islamic** in Mohammed's vision, he saw an angel with 70,000 heads each of which had 70,000 mouths

-99,999- • **Zoroastrian** the sicknesses launched by Ahriman

-100,000- • **Gospel of Barnabas** times the archangel Michael will strike Satan with his sword on the Day of Judgment

-144,000- the stones on the outside of the Great Pyramid • **Christian** the elect of the tribes of Israel • **Hindu** petals of the main chakra; the rays of light originated from all the seven chakras; the vibrations of the divine creation which travel in the cosmos and that are source of life • **Jehovah's Witnesses** the number who will be saved

-600,000- • **Jewish** the Israelites who left Egypt with Moses; interpretations possible with each verse of the Torah; Jewish souls that God created

-999,999- the infinitely great • **Persian** the fravashis in the sea of Kancu

-1,728,000- • **Hindu** solar years in a satayuga

-16,798,000- • **Buddhist** solar years in a regular kalpa

-306,720,000- • **Hindu** solar years in a manvantara

-320,000,000- • **Buddhist** solar years in a medium kalpa

-1,280,000,000- • **Buddhist** solar years in a great kalpa

-4,320,000,000- • **Hindu** solar years in a day of Brahma

-16,000,000,000- • **Buddhist** solar years in a small kalpa

-259,200,000,000- • **Hindu** solar years in a month of Brahma

A

A primal cause; the Trinity; initiative and leadership; beginning; equivalent to -1-; associated with happiness, creativity, the new year, spring, Aries, the sun • **medieval** alternate replacement for Roman numeral V • **tarot** the Minstrel

a'a bird • **Tahitian** manifestation of 'Oro

abacus the mysterious way of the Orient; sometimes an emblem of the Orient; attribute of

Arithmetic personified • **Far Eastern** prosperity; business acumen

abandonment death; guilt; loss of contact with God or nature; prelude to resurrection

abatina • **flower language** fickleness

abbey *see* **monastery**

abbot *see* **monks**

Abdera • **Greek** stupidity

abduction loss of control; primitive marriage; punishment for wickedness

abecedary • **flower language** volubility

Abel • **Jewish** the first man to die; the first murder victim; the first victim of jealousy

ablution *see* **washing**

abnormality indication of magical powers

abortion repression; denial of nature; may indicate a defect in the soul or spirit

Abraham • **Jewish** obedience to God; sacrifice to God; the father or seeker

absinthe (liquor, plant) grief

abstinence the soul refraining from temptation

abyss depth; profundity; inferiority; abasement; the Underworld; associated with the Great Mother and earth-god cults; female sexuality • **watery abyss** primordial source of the universe • **Gnostic** the Supreme Being

acacia fecundity; prosperity; purity; the soul; immortality; friendship; life; platonic love; dualities such as life/death, death/rebirth; associated with the archangels Michael, Samael, Azrael • **Chinese** smoke from acacia bark chases away demons and ghosts and puts the gods in a good mood • **Christian** immortality; moral life • **Egyptian** rebirth; immortality; initiation; innocence; residence of Osiris; associated with the sun; *acacia thorns:* emblem of Neith • **flower language** chaste love; friendship; *rose acacia:* friendship, platonic love, elegance; *pink acacia:* elegance; *white acacia:* elegance, platonic love; *yellow acacia:* secret love • **heraldic** *branch and leaves:* eternal and affectionate remembrance • **Hindu** smoke from acacia bark chases away demons and ghosts and puts the gods in a good mood • **Jewish** sexual abstinence; immortality; moral life; mourning; associated with funerals, the month of Purification, the golden bough; associated with the Ark of the Covenant • **Masonic** resurrection of the soul; immortality; purity • **Nepalese, Tibetan** smoke from acacia bark chases away demons and ghosts and puts the gods in a good mood

acalia • **flower language** temperance

acanthus heavenly gardens; heaven; immortality; felicity; art; the fine arts; love of art; artifice; solicitude about lowly things; stunting; regression; horns of the crescent moon; associated with Cancer • **Christian** awareness and pain of sin • **flower language** the fine arts; artifice; persistence; persistent genius • **heraldic** admiration of the arts

ace (playing cards) the best • **ace of clubs** associated with Summer, new beginnings, growth • **ace of diamonds** associated with Winter, material gain, wealth • **ace of hearts** associated with family ties, Spring, productivity, fresh starts • **ace of spades** associated with death, high rank, Fall, conquest, harvest, blackness • **pair of aces and pair of eights** the dead man's hand

ache mental or spiritual disorder

Acheron • **Christian** a white river or lake into which the repentant are cast by the archangel Michael before they can enter the City of God that sits within in it • **Greco-Roman** the river of pain in Hades • **Jewish** the river one must bathe in or cross before entering paradise

achillea millefolium lasting love; treatment for wounds; used in casting spells; a specific against witchcraft • **astrological** associated with the feminine, Venus (planet), water • **Chinese** used for I-Ching sticks

Achilles • **Greek** the hero who prefers glory to longevity; the vulnerable superhero

aconitum *see* **monkshood; wolfsbane**

acorn strength; virility; latent greatness or strength; independence; impenetrability; a germinal idea; untapped potential; protection against plague; attribute of the Golden Age personified • **Celtic** life; fecundity; immortality; aid to prophecy • **heraldic** antiquity; strength; *oak leaf and acorn wreath:* service saving a life or in homeland defense • **Norse** life; fecundity; immortality; sacred to Thor • *see also* **oak**

acrobat inversion; reversal

Adam • **Christian** prefiguration of Christ • **Jewish** wisdom; temptation; the weak, sinful side of man; the pristine equality of man; primitive agriculture; kingly power; spiritual consciousness made flesh; descent in consciousness

adamant (mythical stone) hardness; tranquility of the soul; sometimes associated with the underworld, hell

adder hidden evil; deadly malice • **Christian** evil; the sinner who closes his ears to the Word; one of the four aspects of the devil • **Jewish** *serpent with one ear to the ground and its tail stopping the other ear:* prudence

Aditi • **Hindu** the feminine principle in creation; infinity; boundless space

Adonis (mythology) • **Greek** youthful beauty; early death

Adonis (plant) • **flower language** sorrowful memories; painful recollections

adrenal glands corresponds to Mars (planet) • **Christian** associated with the Church of Pergamos • **Hindu** associated with self-preservation and physical energy

adultery forsaking a higher life for a lower one

aegis protection; productive power; magic power; preservation; the nutritive principle of nature • **Egyptian** attribute of Bast • **Greco-Roman** attribute of Zeus/Jupiter, Athena/Minerva, Achilles

aerolite *see* **meteorite**

Africa youth; primitiveness; the mysterious; the unknown; the subconscious

afterbirth the water and earth from which life springs; the external and separable soul • **Bagandan** the twin of a child • **Javanese** a crocodile

afternoon Autumn; fatigued or languorous state

agate strength; courage; birthstone for June; associated with Mercury (planet), 14th wedding anniversaries, the archangel Raphael; charm for strength, wisdom, calmness, eloquence, sanctity, safety at sea, and protection against snake bite, scorpion bite, contagious diseases, stomach diseases, the evil eye, poison • **black agate** charm for boldness, courage, vigor, prosperity • **moss agate** charm for success, especially in agriculture and gardening • **red agate** charm for wealth, longevity, peace, spiritual love, good health • **Arabian** charm for healthy blood • **Jewish** charm to prevent stumbling or falling

agave • **Aztecan** *agave milk:* used by Xolotl to nurse the first man and first woman • **Mexican Indian** the Cosmic Tree; attribute of Mayauel; *agave with falcon:* the power of the sun, the liberation of the new moon • **Nahuan** Tree of Life

Agni • **Hindu** the personification of fire

agnus castus • **flower language** coldness; indifference

agriculture fertility; cyclic existence; simple existence; cultivation and concern with the soul • *see also* **farmer**

agrimony associated with Jupiter (planet) • **flower language** gratitude

Ahriman • **Zoroastrian** the spirit of evil; the personification of evil

ailanthus virtue growing out of, but untainted by, sin

air the masculine principle; the mental plane; creation • **mountain air** purity; heroic and solitary thought; corresponds to Aquarius, Gemini, Libra • **night air** evil • **Masonic** corresponds to the mind, philosophy • **Mongolian** associated with East • **Tungun** associated with East

Airi • **Indic** the ghost of a man killed while hunting

airplane ambition; a spiritual vehicle • *see also* **flight; vehicle**

Ajax • **Greek** strength; courage; offense

alabaster purity • **alabaster box, vase, or dish** attribute of Mary Magdalene

Aladdin self-realization through a journey

Aladdin's Lamp male masturbation and its objectified emotional consequences

Alastor • **Greek** an evil spirit that haunts a family; man's inner evil driving him to sin

alb an undertunic in Greece and Rome, later a woman's chemise, and then adopted for wear by priests of a goddess • **Christian** chastity; purity; eternal joy; the innocence and the prophetic office of Christ; the white garment in which Christ was clothed by Herod; *with the sleeves, chest, and hem embroidered:* the five wounds of Christ

albatross lucky; beneficent nature; distant seas; long sea voyages; guilt • **Ainu** servant of the chief god of the sea; seeing one brings luck • **folkloric** omen of bad weather and/or high winds; killing one brings bad luck to your ship; one hovering over a ship brings continued bad weather; embodiment of a dead sailor's soul

Alburz • **Persian** dwelling of Mithras; mother of mountains; world center

Alcestis • **Greek** sacrifice

Alchemist (tarot) *see* **Temperance (tarot)**

alchemy salvation; illumination; foolish occultism

alcohol conjunction of opposites; mutually occurring opposites, such as male/female, active/passive, creation/destruction, good/evil • **alchemic** aqua vitae as both fire and water

alcove feminine symbol of containment; childbirth; doorway to another world

Alcyone (star) • **Greek** River of Heaven

Aldebaran • **astrologic** lucky; a harbinger of wealth for those born under it

alder tree solidity; firmness; associated with fire, evaporation, the smith's fire, Spring festivals, fire festivals, the archangel Cassiel • **alder bark** fire • **alder blossoms** water • **Anglo-Saxon** associated with Eostre • **Celtic** fairy tree; divination; resurrection; endurance; strength; passion; source of the first man; associated with rubies, Mars (planet), March, April • **Greco-Roman** associated with Pan/Faunus, Cronos/Saturn, Calypso • **Norse** source of the first woman • **Slavic** *alder stake:* used to kill a vampire

Alecto *see* Erinyes/Furies

Alectorian stone charm for strength, bravery, wealth, the prevention of thirst

alexandrite emblem of Russia; undying devotion; associated with June; stone for 15th and 55th wedding anniversaries

algae longevity

Alglaia *see* Three Graces

allerion • heraldic strength of will; authority of mind

all-heal *see* woundwort

alligator *see* caiman; crocodile

alloy marriage; the union of male and female, fire and water; impurity

allspice languishing • flower language compassion

almond awakening, wakefulness; revival; spring; hope; divine approval or favor; sweetness; delicacy; virginity; fruitfulness; prophecy; haste; giddiness; hope; death; yoni; vulva; conjugal happiness; the self-productive • almond tree stupidity; thoughtlessness; associated with the archangels Gabriel, Metatron, Raphael • Chinese divine favor and approval; virginity; feminine beauty; fortitude in sorrow; *almond blossom:* emblem of Spring • Christian attribute of the Virgin Mary; *almond blossom:* attribute of the Virgin Mary • European folklore a girl who falls asleep under an almond tree and dreams of her lover will wake up pregnant • flower language stupidity; indiscretion; thoughtlessness; the impetuousness of youth; *flowering almond:* hope, haste, watchfulness, discretion, thoughtlessness • Greek associated with Phyllis and Demophon; constancy; *almond milk:* seminal fluid • Hindu yoni; *eating an almond:* sexual intercourse • Islamic hope of heaven • Italian *double almond:* charm against the evil eye, witches, headache, and for luck • Jewish new life; attribute of Aaron; *almond blossom:* attribute of Aaron; *almond tree:* entrance to the underworld • Phrygian Spring; the father of all things; associated with the birth of Attis • Persian Tree of Life

alms *see* charity

alms bowl poverty; begging; charity; benevolence; aloofness from life; renunciation; surrender of the ego • Buddhist emblem of Buddhism; attribute of a Buddhist monk

almuce dignity

aloe sorrow; embalming; purification of the dead; contempt; bitterness; integrity; wisdom • Christian *myrrh and aloes:* the Passion of Christ • Egyptian charm for longevity, success• flower language affliction; grief; bitterness; religious superstition • Greco-Roman sacred to Zeus/Jupiter

alpha (Greek letter) beginning; the origin of all things • alpha and omega the beginning and the end; creation and destruction; Christ; totality; infinity • *see also* omega

Alsirat • Islamic the narrow bridge to paradise over the abyss of hell; the narrow path of salvation

altar intersection of heaven and earth; worship; mystic center; presence of God; thanksgiving; integration • tomb-shaped altar passage from death to life, and/or time to eternity • altar stairs ritual ascent • stone altar eternity of the deity • Christian death transformed into life; the Eucharist; the sacrifice of Christ; *table-shaped altar:* the Last Supper; *tomb-shaped altar:* the death of Christ; reminiscent of the early Church when the Eucharist was celebrated in the catacombs • Jewish *altar with flames:* altar of sacrifice; *two altars:* Cain and Abel; *bronze altar horns:* gave sanctuary to the person who grabbed them

althaea frutex • flower language persuasion

aluminum associated with the archangels Azrael, Raphael

alyssum exemplary modesty; attribute of Tranquility personified • flower language worth beyond beauty

AM *see* A.M.

A.M. • Christian stands for *auspice Maria*, Latin for "under the protection of Mary"; may also stand for *ave Maria*, Latin for "hail Mary"; attribute of the Virgin Mary; associated with Annunciation; *on a shield:* attribute of archangel Gabriel

amaranth a cockscomb; foppery; affection; crown of saints; love of God excluding all other affections; immortality; fidelity • globe amaranth faith; stability; cheerfulness; steadfast love; decorum; indifference • Chinese *red amaranth:* an offering to the lunar hare at the Moon Festival • flower language immortality; *globe amaranth:* unchangeableness • Greco-Roman sacred to Artemis/Diana • *see also* love-lies-bleeding

amaryllis pride; haughtiness; beauty; splendor; timidity

amazement part of the process of spiritual awakening

Amazon • Greek fearlessness; the higher emotions which oppose the desires

amazone friendship

amber (stone) beauty; strength; sorrow; joy after sorrow; the sun; immortality; fertility; electricity; magnetism; congealed light; protection against evil and disease; magic strength; aid to the dead; associated with Lithuania, the archangel Michael • **Chinese** courage; the soul of a tiger after death • **European** charm against croup, epilepsy, spinal paralysis • **Greco-Roman** tears of the Heliades; charm for the prevention of fever and throat infections; charm of gladiators for protection; attribute of Apollo, Helios/Sol, nobles • **Islamic** cure for jaundice, sore eyes, weak hearts • **Italian** charm against witchcraft • **Jewish** the tribe of Benjamin • **Norse** Freyja's tears for Svipdag • **Yoruban** *amber necklace:* sacred to Oshun

ambrosia (mythological food) truth; wisdom; love; the nourishment which these foregoing qualities provide in the soul

ambrosia (plant) • **flower language** love returned

Amemait *see* **Ammit**

American Indians the darker side of the personality; base forces; the instincts; natural men; natural spirituality; life in harmony with nature; emblem of the early Americas • **North American Indians** emblem of the American West

amethyst sympathy; sincerity; humility; resignation; chastity; piety; sobriety; abnegation; happiness; peace; peace of mind; wealth; courage; usually deep love, but sometimes dalliance; associated with Pisces, Aquarius, healing, 6th, 9th, 27th wedding anniversaries, the archangels Asariel, Zadkiel; birthstone of February; charm for overcoming alcoholism, healing, psychic power, peace, love, protection against thieves • **purple amethyst** penitence • **Christian** absolution; episcopacy; a foundation stone of the New Jerusalem; *amethyst ring with a carved Eros/Cupid:* attribute of St. Valentine • **English (Medieval)** sovereignty of kings and princes • **Gnostic** *sardonyx, jasper, and amethyst:* attribute of Abraxus • **Greco-Roman** charm against plague, hailstorms, evil spells, and for the preservation of a husband's affections; one drinking wine from an amethyst cup would not get drunk • **Jewish** charm for pleasant dreams; part of the High Priest's breastplate

A.M.G.P.D.T. • **Christian** stands for *Ave Maria, gratia plena, Dominus tecum,* the first words of the Hail Mary prayer in Latin; attribute of the Virgin Mary; associated with the Annunciation; *on a shield:* attribute of archangel Gabriel

AMGPDT *see* **A.M.G.P.D.T.**

amice • **Christian** the Helmet of Salvation; divine hope; purity of heart and soul

Ammit • **Egyptian** judgment of the dead; retribution; destruction of the soul

amphibian the parting of spirit and matter; evil

Amphion (son of Zeus and Antiope) • **Greek** beguiling charm

amphisbaena • **Greek** an ambivalent situation; the anguish caused by ambivalence

amphora *see* **jar**

ampulla • **Christian** consecration; attribute of a pilgrim to Canterbury

amputation castration; weakness or defect in the soul • **amputation of thumbs and great toes** incapacitation of a warrior • *see also* **maiming**

amulet the higher nature of the soul; the divine present in the worldly; resistance to evil

Anael, Archangel associated with -3-, -5-, -8-, copper, brass, emeralds, turquoise, rose quartz, lapis lazuli, Venus (planet), the 3rd heaven, Taurus, Libra, Friday, doves, rabbits, sparrows, love birds, elder trees, apple trees, eucalyptus trees, quince trees • **Kabalistic** associated with water, green, -7- • **tarot** associated with the Empress

analogion • **Eastern Orthodox** the word of God

anchor hope; steadfastness; salvation; stability; tranquility • **19th Century sailor's tattoo** service in the Atlantic • **anchor and dolphin** slowness and speed respectively; the middle way • **anchor with entwined serpent** union of the male and female • **Christian** Christ; salvation; disguised form of the Cross; hope; the true faith; attribute of SS Clement of Rome, Nicholas of Myra; *anchor and dolphin:* Christ on the Cross; *fish with an anchor:* hope in Christ • **heraldic** hope; religious steadfastness • **Mediterranean** *dream of an anchor:* ill omen for a voyage

androgyne integration of opposites; Oneness; primordial perfection; wholeness; totality; intellectual activity; self-creation; Adam before Eve was created out of him; the productive powers of nature; autonomy; the unconditioned state; two becoming one; union of heaven and earth, male and female; the all-father all-mother; fertility; loss of the sense of separation of the personality • **man's head on a woman's body** solid and profound judgment • **alchemic** the Great Work; silver and Mercurius after Conjunction • **Egyptian** Neper • **Hindu** Shiva

androsphinx emblem of Egypt • **Christian** the Beast of the Second Coming; the Flight into Egypt; the dual nature of Christ; the divine light of the world • **Druidic** *female androsphinx with many breasts:* fertility, mother • **Egyptian** abundance; wisdom; intelligence; riddle; truth; unity; intellect; power; enigma; spirit triumphant over matter; secrecy; silence; mystery; vigilance; strength; royal dignity; union of binary functions (spirit/matter, harmony/peace, creator/created, etc.); watchdog over the meaning of life, forever beyond man's reach; union of intellect and physical power; the elements of earth, wind, fire, and water; associated with Harmakhis, Horus, Ra; sometimes associated with lust, pleasures of the body, the libido; *female androsphinx:* the reigning queen, Isis; *pair of androsphinx with the Tree of Life:* fertility, conception • **Greek** arcane wisdom; protector of graves; wanton destruction; enemy of mankind; *female androsphinx:* pestilence, secrecy, the Terrible Mother • **Jewish** Israel in Egypt • **Persian** prophecy; magus • **Sumero-Semitic** lamassu; rulership; guardian of temples and palaces • *see also* **criosphinx; hieracosphinx**

anemone (flower) anticipation; frailty; early death; brief blossoming; sorrow; abandonment; associated with Adonis, Cancer • **Christian** sorrow; the Crucifixion of Christ; the Trinity; *the red spot:* the blood of Christ • **Greco-Roman** sorrow; death; attribute Aphrodite/Venus, Hermes/Mercury; sacred to Adonis • **flower language** sickness; expectation; *garden anemone:* forsaken; *meadow anemone:* sickness; *pasque flower anemone:* you have no claims, you are without pretension; *wood anemone:* forlornness • **North American Indian** (Great Plains) *pasque flower anemone:* courage; endurance; faithfulness until death

angel spiritual influences acting upon the earth; messenger of God; intermediary between man and God; saintliness; enlightenment; sweetness • **angel with book** a Cherub • **winged infant's head** a Cherub • **red or golden yellow angel** a Cherub • **angel with candle** a Seraph • **angel with crown** a Dominion • **angel with scepter** a Dominion; divine authority • **angel with red roses** a Virtue • **angel holding a lily** purity; a Virtue • **angel with crown held in the right hand** a Virtue • **angel with a throne** a Throne • **angel with armor** a Power or other lower order • **blue angel** a Seraph • **angel with three pairs of wings** a Seraph • **black angel** death • **cloud or circle of angels** spiritual ecstasy • **angel holding a sword upright** justice • **angel sheathing a sword** God's wrath turned aside • **angel kneeling** intercession • **angel holding a censer** heavenly adoration; prayer • **angel holding a branch with white flowers** mercy • **angel without sandals** on heavenly service only • **angel with garments belted** on active service • **angel with one hand extended** guardianship • **angel with two hands extended** invitation • **angel with trumpet** the voice of God • **angels with musical instruments** felicity in heaven • **alchemic** sublimation • **Christian** spiritual intelligence and wisdom; *angel bearing a sacramental wafer:* attribute of St. Bonaventure; *angel bearing an inkhorn:* attribute of St. Matthew; *angel holding a chalice:* the agony of Christ in Gethsemane; *angel holding a trumpet:* Resurrection Day; *angel placing crowns of roses on a man and a woman:* Valerius and St. Cecelia • **heraldic** belief; gaiety; striving for perfection; a good reputation; dignity; honor; glory; bearer of joyful news; inspiration; a purified existence; missionary service • **Islamic** *eight angels around a throne:* the throne of Allah; *angel with 70,000 heads each of which has 70,000 mouths:* Mohammed's vision; *angel with green wings:* Gabriel; *two angels hanging upside down in a Babylonian well:* Harut and Marut • **Jewish** *angel's feet emerging from cloud above mountain:* Nahum's vision; *angel holding a flaming sword:* judgment; expulsion from Eden • **Persian** *angel with golden balances:* Rashnu • *see also* **archangel; cherub; seraph** • **NOTE:** The attributes of angels have historically been used inconsistently.

angelica ecstasy; magic; inspiration • **flower language** inspiration • **heraldic** inspiration

angrecum • **flower language** royalty

Aniel, Archangel *see* **Anael, Archangel**

animals instinctual and emotional urges; fertility; passivity • **friendship and/or communication with animals** restoration or re-entry into the state of Paradise; oneness with nature • **slaying, sacrificing, or taming animals** bringing one's animal instincts under control • **wearing an animal mask or skin** access to animal wisdom; understanding or communication with animals • **Maori** ancestral people

ankh life; Tree of Life; key of knowledge; power; authority; covenant; the union of heaven and earth; immortality; health; truth; union of the sexes; reconciliation of opposites; hidden wisdom • **ankh held by a god or sovereign** command over life and death • **Egyptian** the union of Isis and Osiris; eternal life; attribute of Maat; *woman with the head of a lion, globe, ankh, and staff:* Tefnut

ankles associated with Uranus (planet)

annulet • **heraldic** a fifth son; rank; fidelity • *see also* **orle**

anointing (with oil) endowing the soul with divine love; consecration; prosperity; joy

anonymity loss of identity; absorption into the divine

anqa *see* **simurg**

ant industry; humility; foresight; modesty; wisdom; community spirit; an aphrodisiac; the fragility and impotence of existence • **in swarms** anger • **sudden increase in ants** omen of war • **Chinese** order; virtue; patriotism; subordination • **Greco-Roman** attribute of Demeter/Ceres • **heraldic** wisdom; providence in one's affairs; cleverness; artfulness; great labor • **Hindu** transitoriness; the fragility of life • *see also* **anthill**

anteater unlucky; associated with occult power

antelope struggle; presumption; associated with the Great Mother, the moon, fecundity • **African** sometimes a shape-shifted deity • **Egyptian** Osiris; Horus; sacrifice to Set • **heraldic** political cunning; peace; harmony • **Hindu** emblem of Shiva; steed of Pavana, Vayu; *chariot drawn by antelopes:* attribute of Soma, Chandra • **Malian** teacher of agriculture to humans • **Sumero-Semitic** associated with the subterranean ocean; creation

anthill fertility • **Alur** *burial in an anthill:* treatment for insanity • **Susun** residence of demons

anthurium the heart; emblem of Martin Luther

Antichrist • **Christian** adversary of the soul

Antigone • **Greek** faithfulness; nobility; incest; an independent woman; a woman in rebellion against the state

antimony a state close to perfection, but with the most difficult part remaining • **alchemic** the penultimate stage in the search for the philosopher's stone

antlers fertility; supernatural power; power over nature • **ten-point antlers** attribute of shamans • **Celtic** *deer antlers and/or skin:* ritual vestments • **Gallic** attribute of Cernunnos • **Greco-Roman** *golden antlers:* attribute of the Arcadian Hind captured by Heracles/Hercules • **heraldic** strength; fortitude • **Sumerian** attribute of Ea, Marduk • *see also* **horns (animal)**

Anubis • **Egyptian** life-giving, favorable, uplifting light

anvil the brain; the intellect; the force that created the universe; primal furnace; earth; matter; the feminine principle; attribute of warriors, Hephaestus/Vulcan, storm gods, thunder gods, blacksmiths, SS Adrian, Eloi • **with cross or swords** male and female; forge of the universe • **tied to the feet of a woman** Juno as Air personified • **hammer and anvil** the male and female forces of nature respectively, the male and female respectively, the active and passive respectively, the positive and negative respectively • **heraldic** honor

ape sin; malice; lust; cunning; fraud; vice; scoffing; uncleanness; the slothful soul of man; lev-

ity; Taste personified • **ape in chains** the devil; sin overcome • **Chinese** mischievousness; conceit; mimicry • **Christian** malice; lust; sin; luxury; Satan; idolatry; perversion of the Word; heresy; paganism; the devil • **Hindu** benevolence; gentleness; emblem of Hanuman • **Jewish** *with an apple in its mouth:* the Fall of Man • **Middle Ages** painting; sculpture • *see also* **baboon; monkey**

Apep • **Egyptian** the personification of evil

Aphrodite/Venus • **Greco-Roman** love in the physical or sexual sense; sexual perversion; casual or illicit sex; chastity; related to spring, April, dawn, fish, fertility, ritual prostitution, Cyprus

apocynum *see* **dogsbane**

Apollo • **Greco-Roman** balance; harmony; spiritualization; reason and intuition; self-control; acquired wisdom; *woman with cupped hands before Apollo:* the Cumean sibyl • *see also* **sun**

apparition *see* **ghost**

apple (fruit) earthly desires; indulgence in earthly desires; procreation; productiveness; discord; immortality; rejuvenation; death; beginning; Autumn; deceit; unity; temptation; sexual enjoyment; vulva; joy; fertility; divination; luxury; deceit; death; unity • **golden apple** discord; immortality; attribute of Vigilance personified and of the harpies that accompany Avarice personified • **offering an apple** declaration of love • **golden apple** discord; attribute of Discord personified • **apple cider** rural festivities • **Celtic** fertility; marriage; completeness; fruit of the Underworld; associated with magic and infernal powers • **Chinese** peace; concord • **Christian** attribute of Eve; *apple in the hand of the Christ child:* Christ as the new Adam, the fruit of salvation, alludes to Christ as the redeemer of man from Original Sin; *apple in the Virgin Mary's hand:* Mary as the new Eve; *three apples (often with three roses):* attribute of St. Dorothea • **Danish** the color fades when a lover is unfaithful • **Greco-Roman** liberality; attribute of Aphrodite/Venus, the Three Graces; *golden apple:* discord; attribute of Eris/Discordia, the Hesperides; *three golden apples:* attribute of Atalanta in her race with Hippomenes • **heraldic** love; rejuvenation; fullness of life; earthly kingdom; peace; perpetual concord; felicity; liberality • **Jewish** the Fall of Man; *ape with an apple in its mouth:* the Fall of Man; *apple in Adam's hand:* sin; *apple eaten with honey:* the hope for sweetness and joy in the future • **Norse** procreation; attribute of Freyja, Idunn; *golden apples:* attribute of Idunn • *see also* **crab apple**

apple tree man's happiness; health; immorality; associated with Taurus, the archangel Anael • **apple blossom** fertility • **Celtic** beauty; love; generosity; *apple tree branch:* has the power to erase sad memories with its magic music • **Chinese** *apple blossom:* peace, beauty • **flower language** temptation; *apple blossom:* preference, fame speaks one great and good • **Greco-Roman** sacred to Apollo; *branch:* attribute of Nemesis/Invidia, Artemis/Diana • **heraldic** love; rejuvenation; fullness of life; earthly kingdom; peace; perpetual concord; felicity; liberality • *see also* **crab apple; thorn apple**

apricot woman; self-fruitfulness; vulva; androgyny • **apricot flower** timid love • **Chinese** death; timidity

April beginning; youth; inconstancy; associated with rain

apron service; purity of life and conduct; fertility; slave nature; repression of sexuality; attribute of housewives • **woman's apron falling off** omen of bad luck or an unwanted child within a year • **putting an apron on backwards** lucky • **apron of bones** protection from the dead; invocation of aid from the dead • **leather apron** Ancient Craft; attribute of masons and other craftsmen, Freemasons • **Chinese** innocence; friendship; attribute of sacrificial rites; divides the body between the nobler and baser parts • **Egyptian** attribute of royalty

aquamarine (stone) youth; hope; health; treasure of mermaids; associated with Aries, Aquarius, Neptune (planet), 18th and 19th wedding anniversaries, the archangel Gabriel; birthstone for March, occasionally October; charm for safety at sea

Aquarius the waters of creation and its destruction; cyclic death and renewal; the masculine; associated with air, idealism, eccentricity, unpredictability, progressivism, the loosening of bonds, the immanence of liberation, the dissolution or decomposition of the world of phenomena, social cohesion, brotherhood, indifference to material things, Saturn (planet), Uranus (planet), the archangel Cassiel, buttercups, fennel, edderwort, amethysts, zircons, cold, rain, darkness, floods • **Egyptian** associated with Khnum • **Far Eastern** associated with the Rat • **Greco-Roman** associated with Zeus/Jupiter, Ganymede, Deucalion, Aristaeus

aqueduct channel of truth from a higher to a lower nature

Aquilo *see* **Boreas/Aquilo**

Ararat, Mount • **Jewish** the second cradle of humanity; World Navel

arbor vitae • **flower language** unchanging friendship; live for me; old age

arbutus associated with immortality • **Greco-Roman** food of man in the Golden Age; if snakes fed upon it they ceased to be poisonous; attribute of Cardea

arc growth; moving life • *see also* **circle**

Arcadia • **Greek** the Golden Age; associated with romantic love

arch the feminine principle; heaven; sanctuary; triumph; a secret place; associated with purification • **single arch** triumph; the heavens; associated with the sky • **multiple arches** hospitality • **Gothic arch** aspiration; spirituality • **Romanesque arch** dependability; authority • **broken arch** defeat • **passing through an arch** rebirth • **Christian** *trefoil or three-lobed arch:* the Trinity; *chancel arch:* passage from this world into eternal life, or from the Church Militant to the Church Triumphant • **Greek** Zeus • **Roman** Jupiter (god); *soldiers marching under a triumphal arch:* cleansing of bloodshed, imposing a barrier between the victors and the ghosts of the enemy

archangel primordial divine power on the highest level • **with sword** Michael • **with dragon underfoot** Michael • **with lily** Gabriel; the Annunciation • **with trumpet** Gabriel • **with staff and gourd** Raphael • **with scroll and book** Uriel • **with cord** Metatron • **with dagger** Zadkiel • **with sickle** Azrael • **covered in fire** Camael • **with chalice** Cassiel • **twin archangels** Metatron and Sandalphon • **holding flame** Uriel • **Islamic** four archangels inhabit the heavens beneath the throne of Allah; *archangel with green wings:* Gabriel • *see also* **angel;** and individual archangels such as **Gabriel; Michael; Raphael**

archer soldier of the lower classes; Sagittarius • **Christian** *archer threatening woman:* the woman is St. Ursula

Archpriest (tarot) *see* **High Priest (tarot)**

Archpriestess (tarot) *see* **High Priestess (tarot)**

Arcturus associated with storms • **astrologic** omen of wealth and fame for anyone born under it

Ares/Mars • **Greco-Roman** war; brute force; anger; aggressiveness; bungling; bullying; oafishness; loutishness; impetuousness

Arges • **Greco-Roman** the brightness of lightning • *see also* **Cyclops**

Aries associated with the creative impulse, courage, energy, selfishness, impatience, volatile temper, brute force, the masculine principle, dawn, Spring, the beginning of any cycle or process, renewal of solar energy, the head, the undifferentiated, Mars (planet), the archangel Samael, sage, water milfoil, bloodstones, diamonds

Aristotle Logic personified

ark salvation; regeneration; the womb; treasure chest; the heart; individual preservation and resurrection; place of transmutation; microcosm of the world; associated with the moon, the sea • **Noah's Ark** resurrection; the covenant God made with Noah and the Church; the Ark of the Covenant; baptism; the Church; the Deluge; the Virgin Mary as the bearer of Christ • **Egyptian** *Ark of Isis:* the womb • **Sudanese** attribute of Nommo

Ark of the Covenant peace; Old Testament worship • **Christian** Jesus Christ; the Virgin Mary • **Jewish** the presence of God; the Holy of Holies; associated with the Cherubim

Armageddon • Christian, Jewish the conflict of good and evil within the self

armillary the universe; astronomy; attribute of Astronomy personified

armor chivalry; self defense; security; resistance to evil; protection; chivalry; knighthood; the Christian faith as protection against evil • **Christian** the Christian faith as protection against evil; attribute of the archangel Michael, St. Liberalis (especially when shown leaning against a spear or holding a banner), St. Demetrius (usually with a shield and lance, or hand resting on a sword); attribute of any warrior saint; *armor with red cross:* attribute of St. George of Cappadocia; *soldier in armor with red cross on breastplate:* St. Maurice • **Japanese** attribute of Bishamon • **Mongolian** *blue steel armor:* attribute of Er Toshtuk, father of Genghis Khan • **Norse** *white armor:* attribute of Heimdall • **Tibetan** *gold chain mail:* attribute of Da

arms (body) action; activity; protection; strength; the position usually shows the activity — offering, worshipping, inviting, etc. • **one raised arm** taking an oath; bearing witness • **raised arms** invocation; self-defense; supplication; surrender • **a maiden's arms upraised, sprouting branches** Chastity personified • **arm with the number four** force • **arm behind the back** submission to God's will • **Celtic** *king with missing or artificial arm:* Nuada • **Greco-Roman** *maiden whose arms are sprouting myrrh branches, with nymphs standing nearby holding a baby:* birth of Adonis; *group of maidens, arms upraised, sprouting poplar branches:* the Heliades; *maiden's arms upraised, sprouting branches:* associated with Apollo • **Fulani** *god*

with twelve arms: Kaydara • **heraldic** *in armor:* leadership; *bare arm:* industry • **Hindu** *four-armed green man:* Yama; *four-armed man with elephant head:* Ganesha; *four-armed man with four faces:* Brahma; *four-armed man with fish bottom:* Matsya; *four-armed man with tortoise bottom:* Kurma; *four-armed man with boar's head:* Varaha; *four-armed man with noose:* Varuna; *four-armed man with four or five faces and three eyes:* Shiva; *dancing man with multiple arms:* Shiva; *woman with four arms:* Kali, Manasa, Sitala (may be red) • **Japanese** *woman with ten arms:* Benzaiten • **Jewish** *hairy arms:* Jacob's deception of Isaac • **Sri Lankan** *20 arms:* attribute of Ravana • *see also* **triskelion**

arms (military) *see* **weapons**

Arnold, Benedict • American traitor

arrow a spiritual weapon; fertility; the masculine principle; semen; penetration; virility; power; war rain; lightning; war; famine; disease, especially the plague; sun rays; the light of divine power; communication between heaven and earth; remorse; persecution; attribute of Sagittarius, warriors, hunters • **arrow pointed up** spiritual aspiration; message to heaven • **arrow pointed downward** power of the godhead; thunderbolt; sunshine; rain • **flight of arrows loosed** ascent to the celestial • **arrow piercing a heart** love, especially romantic love • **golden arrow** kindles love • **lead arrow** drives love away • **bundle of arrows** thunderbolt; attribute of Concord personified • **flint arrowhead** charm against evil; attribute of fairies • **Armenian** *triangular arrow:* attribute of Hayk • **Christian** martyrdom; the nails of the Cross; suffering; *arrow piercing a stag protected by a man:* St. Giles of Provence; *arrow piercing the hand:* St. Giles of Provence; *arrows piercing a nude man:* St. Sebastian; *arrows held by a rudely dressed woman:* St. Ursula; *two arrows piercing the breast or a heart:* St. Augustine of Hippo; *three arrows:* attribute of St. Edmund; *arrow held by maiden with a millstone:* of St. Christina • **Egyptian** *two crossed arrows:* emblem of Neith • **Greco-Roman** pain; disease; *Apollo's arrows:* sun rays in both the negative and positive sense, also pain and disease; *heart pierced by an arrow:* union; *arrow in woman with grieving hunter:* Cephalus and Procris respectively • **heraldic** readiness for battle; *arrow with cross:* affliction • **Hindu** swiftness; intuition; associated with -5-; attribute of Shiva, Rudra, Karttikeya, Indra; *man struck in the eye by an arrow:* the sensations aroused by the impact upon the senses of their object; *five arrows of Kama:* the senses • **Islamic**

destroyer of evil and ignorance; the wrath and punishment of Allah inflicted on his enemies • **Mithraic** emblem of Mithras • **North American Indian** sun ray; thunderbolt; protection; *crossed arrows:* friendship; *broken arrow:* peace; *arrowhead:* alertness • **Ural-Altaic** bird flight to heaven; transcendence of the earthly state • *see also* **archer; bow and arrows; bow (archery); bowstring; quiver (archery)**

arson regression, especially male

Artemis/Diana • **Greco-Roman** the woods; nature; fertility; virginity; jealousy; the Terrible Mother; moodiness; volatility; connected with childbirth, hunting, the moon

artemisia (plant) purgation • **Amerindian** the feminine, lunar, and nocturnal life principles • **Chinese** dignity; one of the Eight Precious Things • **Greek** sacred to Artemis

Artemisia (wife of Mausolus) • **Greek** a widow's devotion to her husband's memory

artery channel of truth from a higher nature to a lower one

Arthur, King • **Celtic** the soul's search for truth, enlightenment, self-realization; archetype of the journey of life

artist the externalization of inner emotions, thoughts, purposes

arum soul; ardor; androgyny • **flower language** ardor; *spotted arum:* warmth

Asariel, Archangel associated with Neptune (planet), emerald, amethyst, -7-, -18, water, ash, elm, pine, willow, fish, dolphin, stag • **tarot** associated with Temperance

asbestos associated with Mars (planet)

ascending an increase in intensity; a raise in value or worth; the human condition being transcended and a higher spiritual level being attained; transcendence; breaking through to a better plane of existence; going from darkness to light, from earth to heaven; reintegration; regaining Paradise • *see also* **descending**

Ascension Day • **Christian** victory; transcendence

asceticism voluntary abandonment of worldly activities in preparation for renewed life on a higher spiritual plane

ash tree adaptability; prudence; modesty; lamentation; grandeur; nobility; prudence; adaptability; flexibility; modesty; associated with Libra, the archangel Raphael • **Baltic** slow-wittedness • **Celtic** connection; surrender; wisdom; associated with coral, Neptune (planet), February, March, the archangel Asariel • **Chinese** *ash staff:* mourning for a father • **Greco-Roman** stability; charm against serpents; sacred to Zeus/Jupiter; associated with Meliae, the blood of the cas-

tration of Uranus/Caelus that gave birth to Erinyes/Furies; *ash leaves in wine:* antidote for poison • **heraldic** power; toughness; rebirth; intelligence; source of wisdom • **Norse** immortality; sovereignty; Yggdrasil; emblem of Odin; source of the first man • **Scottish** *ash sap:* protection against witches for children • *see also* **Yggdrasil**

asherah pole • **Sumero-Semitic** a symbolic tree associated with the feminine aspect of divinity; phallus; associated with Asherah, Astarte, Baal worship • *see also* **pole**

ashes death; mourning; defeat; mortality; the perishable human body; humility; penitence; failure; the lower mind; death of the body; an ending that is also a beginning; the shortness of life; worthlessness; purification • **eating ashes** utter misery • **ashes and dust** mourning; penitence; deep humiliation • **sackcloth and ashes** sorrow; abject humiliation; mourning, penitence, affliction • **ash heaps** wasteland • **Chinese** yang; *damp ashes:* death omen; *dry ashes:* the cessation of mental activity during meditation • **Hindu** renunciation of worldly vanities • **Mayan** the cyclic return of life

ashlar material to be worked to attain perfection through creative activity sorrow • **rough ashlar** unregenerate man • **finished ashlar** perfected man; spiritual accomplishment • *see also* **stone**

ash-leaved trumpet flower *see* **trumpet flower**

Asmodeus • **Jewish** lechery; revenge

asp suicide, especially Cleopatra's suicide • **Christian** evil; venom • **Egyptian** the solar; royalty; dominion; power; divine goodness and immortality; *white crown with asps, horns, and plumes:* attribute of Thoth • **Greek** protection; benevolence • *see also* **serpent, uraeus**

aspalathus the wisdom of the Lord

asparagus sexuality; aphrodisiac

aspen fear; uncertainty; excessive sensitivity; trembling; horror; fear; lament; pride; emblem of Judas; the wood of the Cross; associated with the archangel Raphael • **Celtic** transformation; victory; vision • **flower language** lamentation • **heraldic** *aspen leaves:* determination; overcoming fears and doubts

asperges • **Christian** expulsion of evil; purity; purification; holiness; *asperges with water pot:* attribute of St. Martha

aspergillum • **Christian** exorcism of evil spirits; attribute of SS Martha, Benedict, Anthony the Great, and other saints famed for their contests with the devil

asphodel death; loss of consciousness; humility; associated with Saturn (planet) • **Christian** attribute of the Virgin Mary • **flower language** my regrets follow you to the grave • **Greco-Roman** emblem of Persephone/Proserpine, Dionysus/Bacchus; associated with the Elysian Fields, paradise, the Islands of the Blessed; in later times associated with the dead, Hades, the afterlife, regret, cemeteries, ruins

aspiration the yearning of lower nature for the higher

Asrafil, Archangel • **Islamic** recording angel

ass (donkey) humility; patience; stubbornness; ignorance; honesty; courage; wisdom; cleverness; obstinate stupidity; greatness; steadiness; peace; salvation; lust; lewdness; sensuality; subservience; foolishness; sentimentality; inconstancy; pride; conceit; jealousy; a man between 80 and 90 years of age; messenger of death; associated with the poor, the sun; attribute of the personifications of Sloth, Inconstancy, Stupidity, Temperance • **she-ass** humility; peace; poverty; patience; courage • **ass and millstone** attributes of Obedience personified • **stumbling ass** an unbeliever • **chariot drawn by an ass** attribute of the personifications of Idleness, Peacemaking • **ass skin coat or cloak** humility • **ass in a lion's skin** a coward who hectors; a fool who apes a wise man • **head of an ass** fertility • **ass ears on a human** stupidity; a buffoon; folly; a lewd character; attribute of jesters • **Chinese** stupidity; *white ass ridden backwards:* steed of Chang Kuo • **Christian** the Flight into Egypt; Christ's entry into Jerusalem; emblem of St. Germanus; sometimes the Jews, the Synagogue; emblem of early Jewish Christians; *kneeling ass:* attribute of St. Anthony of Padua; *ox with an ass:* attribute of the Nativity • **Egyptian** evil; inert power; associated with Ra; emblem of Set as the god of evil; *red ass:* the most dangerous beast in the Underworld • **Greco-Roman** sloth; infatuation; sacred to Cronos/Saturn, Dionysus/Bacchus, Typhon, Priapus; *ass-eared man:* Midas; *chariot drawn by an ass:* attribute of Silenus; *she-ass:* wife of Ocnus; *ass eating a rope:* attribute of Ocnus • **heraldic** stamina; patience; contentment; humility • **Hindu** steed of Sitala • **Islamic** *speaking ass:* Balaam's ass • **Jewish** stubbornness; the Gentile nations; associated with Balaam; attribute of Zechariah; *white ass:* steed of kings, prophets, and judges; *jawbone of an ass:* attribute of Samson; *ass with two burdens:* associated with Issachar • **Hindu** steed of Nairittita, Kalaratri; drew the chariot of Ravana when he abducted Sita; manifestation of Dhenuka • **Persian** *three-legged ass:* the three phases of the moon;

purity; power against evil; *giant three-legged ass with six eyes:* Khara • **Spanish** *fat man on an ass:* Sancho Panza • *see also* **onager** with which the ass is frequently confused

Assyria • **Jewish** punishment from God

Astaroth • **Jewish** accusation; inquisition

aster • **Chinese** beauty; elegance; charm; humility • **flower language** *China aster:* afterthought; variety; *double aster:* I share your sentiments; *single aster:* I will think of it • **Greek** love; sacred to Aphrodite

athanor • **alchemic** place of physical, moral, or mystical transmutation

Athena/Minerva • **Greco-Roman** wisdom; Wisdom personified; fertility; man's higher nature; emblem of Athens; associated with spinning, weaving, and other women's crafts

Atlantis • **Greek** ancient mysteries, wisdom, enlightenment; the lost Paradise

Atlas • **Greek** strength

Aton • **Egyptian** the unique force from which all living things come

attic the head; the mind; the conscious; the soul; the superego; the past; the repressed

Audumla • **Germanic** fertility

aum the most sacred sound; affirmation; the reflection of absolute reality; the entire cosmos; the imperishable Word; the Absolute; the totality of all sounds; the Self • **Buddhist** *Indic:* the unity of all; *Tibetan:* pure spirit • **Hindu** Brahman; the manifestation of God in form; the primordial sound that was present at the creation of the universe; the original sound that contains all other sounds, words, languages, mantras; an emblem of Hinduism • **Jain** associated with the five paramesthis • **Sikh** pure spirit; one God

aureole *see* **nimbus**

auricula • **flower language** painting; *scarlet auricula:* avarice

aurora borealis a manifestation of the otherworld; omen of war, bloodshed, disaster, death of a king or leader • **Eskimo** spirits of the dead playing • **Finnish** souls of the dead • **Kwakiutl** deceased family members dancing for those living or about to die • **Makah** a small race of Indians cooking seal and walrus meat • **Mandan** medicine men and warriors boiling their enemies in huge pots • **Norse** light reflected from the shields of Valkyries • **Salteaux** spirits of the dead dancing • **Tlingit** spirits of the dead playing

automobile *see* **vehicle**

Autumn death; deterioration; middle to old age; harvest; incipient decay; the afternoon; associated with Libra, Scorpio, Sagittarius • **Greco-Roman** sacred to Dionysus/Bacchus

avalanche sudden loss of control; overwhelming forces

awl • **Roman** euphemism for penis

awl root associated with Dionysus/Bacchus

awning protection either granted or received • **square awning** earthly protection • **round awning** spiritual protection

axe thunder; lightning; the fecundity of rain; fertility; the power of light; the sun; the critical faculty; sacrifice; help; support; primitive warfare; war; fertility; execution; chastisement; attribute of divinities, carpenters, sky gods, lumberjacks • **axe and trident** fire and water, respectively • **double-headed axe** duality; the sun; the union of the sky god and earth goddess; thunder and lightning; attribute of royalty, St. Cyprian • **axe embedded in a stone, cube, pyramid, etc.** the revealing of secret or hidden knowledge; the final stage of initiation • **Buddhist** severs the cycle of birth and death; emblem of Buddhism • **Celtic** attribute of a deity, chief, warrior • **Chinese** justice; authority; judgment; punishment; *sacrificial axe:* death of sensual unenlightened man • **Christian** martyrdom; destruction; attribute of SS Matthew, Boniface, Thomas of Canterbury, Joseph (especially when shown with carpenter's tools), John the Baptist, Prolcus; *axe embedded in monk's head:* St. Peter Martyr; *axe with one or two oars:* attribute of St. Simon; *double-headed axe:* attribute of St. Cyprian; *double-headed axe with crown:* attribute of St. Olaf; *double-headed axe with a stone or open Bible:* attribute of St. Matthias • **Egyptian** the solar • **Greco-Roman** Intercidona; attribute of Zeus/Jupiter, Apollo, Athena/Minerva, Artemis/Diana • **Gallic** attribute of Esus • **heraldic** military service • **Hindu** attribute of Parashurama; *axe with wood and bellows:* attribute of Agni • **Jewish** *axe-head:* attribute of Elisha • **Mexican Indian** attribute of Tlaloc • **Nordic** attribute of a divine being, chief, warrior • **Sumero-Semitic** sovereignty; attribute of Tammuz, Teshub, Ramman • **Yoruba** *double-headed axe:* the magic power and thunderbolt of the storm god

axle phallus; axis of the universe; Tree of Life

axle tree axis of the universe; the sun azalea herald of spring; fragile and ephemeral beauty; fatal gifts; temperance; woman • **Chinese** woman • **flower language** temperance

azalea transitoriness; the ephemeral; fire • **Chinese** great abilities; feminine grace; tragedy • **heraldic** temperance; passion • **Japanese** associated with April

Azrael, Archangel angel of death; associated with the dwarf planet Pluto, -9-, -11-, -12-, -17-, rubies, garnets, topaz, bloodstones, Southwest, acacia, cedars, cypress, pines, foxes • **Kabalistic** associated with green, water

azurite charm for psychic power, healing, divination

B

B associated with the Savior, science, the moon, spirit, life force, emotion, cooperation, introspection; equivalent to -2- • **as a brand** punishment for blasphemy • **medieval** occasional Roman numeral for 300 • **tarot** High Priestess

Baal the tendency of civilizations to return to animal instincts • **Jewish** idolatry; devolution; paganism

Babel, Tower of • **Christian** confusion; sinful presumption • **Christian Science** false knowledge • **Jewish** an impractical dream; pride; confusion of speech; the lower self trying to rise above the higher self • *see also* **ziggurat**

baboon enlightenment; stupidity; lust; associated with Capricorn • **Egyptian** death; time; dawn; scribe of Ptah, Anubis; conductor of souls of the dead; associated with Babi, Thoth; *baboon with uplifted hands:* Hapi, wisdom saluting the rising sun; *god with a baboon head:* Hapi • *see also* **ape; monkey**

baby *see* **infant**

Babylon an impractical dream; the Terrible Mother; selfish ideals; self-gratification; earthly pleasures; associated with scarlet women • **Christian** the Anti-Christ • **Jewish** pride; confusion of speech; the lower self trying to rise above the higher self the antithesis of Paradise; luxury; vice; the material world; idolatry; worldliness; corrupt and fallen existence; desertion of matter by the spirit; turning away from spiritual values • **Islamic** *two angels hanging upside down in a Babylonian well:* Harut and Marut

baby's breath (plant) *see* **gypsophila**

Bacchantes *see* **Maenads/Bacchantes**

Bacchus *see* **Dionysus/Bacchus**

bachelor's buttons • **flower language** celibacy • **folkloric** if the flower stayed fresh in a man's pocket, he should marry his sweetheart; if it wilted he should find a new sweetheart

back (**body**) the unconscious; one's vulnerability; associated with Venus (planet)

backbone *see* **spine**

bacon wealth; life; money; material support; female sexual pleasure

badger vigilance; suspicion; savagery; ferocity; laziness; clumsiness; hostility; aggression; independence; the solitary life; forecaster of weather; steed of Avarice personified • **American** emblem of Wisconsin • **Chinese** mischief; playfulness; a lunar yin animal • **Celtic** associated with Moritasgus • **Japanese** deceit; mirage; false allurement; associated supernatural powers; emblem of prosperity, self-satisfaction • **North American Indian** *badger tracks:* lucky omen

bag secrecy; winds; feminine symbol of containment; hiding • **pig skin bag** attribute of a tinker • **Celtic** where Manannan kept all the treasures of the world • **Chinese** *leopard skin bag:* attribute of Vaisravenna • **Greco-Roman** where Aeolus kept the wind • **Mayan** *man with a scorpion tail carrying a bag:* Ekchuah • *see also* **money bag; purse**

Bagala-mukhi • **Hindu** sadistic and destructive instincts

bagpipe wind; melancholy; associated with shepherds, peasants, Scotland • **Celtic** associated with amusement, war • **folkloric** *17th century:* the devil's favorite instrument

baking love making; pregnancy

balances judgment; death; constancy; sobriety; economy; equality; equilibrium; androgyny; impartiality; justice; any binary function, good/evil, life/death, etc.; the equilibrium of opposites; harmony; emblem of Libra; associated with September; attribute of Justice personified, judicial courts • **balances on a razor's edge** attribute of Opportunity personified • **Chinese** justice; righteousness; attribute of a mandarin • **Christian** associated with the Last Judgment; attribute of Christ, the archangel Michael; *unbalanced:* the trial of Christ • **Egyptian** attribute of Osiris, Thoth • **Gallic** *sword thrown into a balance pan:* associated with Brennus • **Greco-Roman** attribute of Hermes/Mercury, Nemesis/Invidia, Themis, Cronus/Saturn • **heraldic** justice • **Hindu** associated with the Kshatriya caste • **Islamic** associated with the Last Judgment • **Jewish** attribute of Melchizedek, the archangel Michael • **Persian** *angel with golden balances:* Rashnu

balcony love; romance; spying; authority

Baldur • **Norse** the life principle; love; eloquence

baldness • **Christian** attribute of St. Paul • Da-

homean *bald-headed man with a vulture's body:* Suvinenge • **Japanese** *elongated bald head:* attribute of Fukurokuju

ball the earth; perfection; eternity; childhood play; sun; moon • **golden balls** associated with the harpies that accompany Avarice personified • **bouncing ball** chance; fate • **three balls** emblem of pawnbrokers • **tennis ball** youthfulness; fate-tossed man • **Christian** *three balls:* attribute of St. Nicholas of Myra • **Greek** fecklessness; chance; humility; attribute of Victory personified, Fate personified • **Roman** *golden ball:* charm against evil • *see also* **eight ball; globe; orb; sphere**

balm anointing; cure; relief; kingship • **balm tea** cure for melancholy • **flower language** sympathy; *balm of Gilead:* healing, cure, relief; *gentle balm:* pleasantry

balsam consolation; love; sympathy; the zealous benefactor; rejuvenation • **Christian** emblem of the Virgin Mary; *balsam with olive:* the dual nature of Christ • **flower language** impatience; ardent love; rashness; *red balsam:* touch-me-not; *yellow balsam:* impatience

bamboo longevity; constancy; gracefulness; resilience; growth; versatility; pliability; good breeding; enduring friendship; hardy old age; emblem of the Orient • **Chinese** modesty; filial piety; protection from defilement; open-mindedness; culture; refinement; longevity; emblem of Buddha, Winter; *bamboo and sparrow:* friendship; *bamboo and crane:* longevity and happiness; *seven-knotted bamboo:* the seven degrees of initiation and invocation; *bamboo, plum, and pine:* the Three Friends of Winter; *bamboo staff:* mourning for a father • **Formosan** Tree of Life • **Hindu** friendship; emblem of the sacred fire • **Hmong** Tree of Life • **Japanese** devotion; truthfulness; longevity; one of the Three Trees of Good Omen; associated with the moon • **Philippine** *bamboo cross:* aids the growth of crops • **Southeastern Asian** *flowering bamboo:* omen of famine • **Taoist** *rustling bamboo:* signal of enlightenment

banana the tropics; continuing life; wisdom; associated with the monkey and ape families; simian nature; phallus • **Tutsi** *banana beer:* drink of the warrior class

banana tree continuing life • **Buddhist** the weakness and instability of matter • **Solomon Island** sometimes the dwelling of the dead

bandages psychic wound; the winding sheet of the tomb; swaddling clothes • **burial bandages** the robe of resurrection • *see also* **wounds**

bandicoot *see* **rat**

banjo • **folkloric** a favorite instrument of the devil

bank (**river**) *see* **shore**

banner victory; triumph; conquest; protection; attribute of kings, princes, warrior saints • **red banner** revolution • **waving a banner** dispersal of evil spirits • **banners in superfluous numbers** aggressive militarism • **banner and cross** attribute of the Phrygian sibyl • **Christian** *banner and white horse:* attribute of St. *James the Great; white banner with red cross:* attribute of SS Ansanus, Ursula; *banner with cross or words "Ecce Agnus Dei:"* attribute of John the Baptist; *banner with a cross:* victory over sin, death, or persecution; attribute of SS George of Cappadocia, Reparata, Wenceslas; *banner with cross held by lamb:* Christ's victory over death, attribute of SS John the Baptist, Reparata; *Christ with a banner:* refers to his rising from the grave, the descent into hell, and appearances on earth after the Resurrection and before the Ascension • **Hindu** action against maleficent powers; *Ketu, the banner of India:* light ray, a shining forth, manifestation, victory over darkness; *banner stirring in the breeze:* attribute of Vayu • **Islamic** *black banner:* revolt • **Taoist** magical protection; summons to deities, spirits • *see also* **flag**

banquet *see* **feast**

banshee death; messenger of fatality

banyan tree the close union of the spiritual and physical in man; expanding knowledge • **Hindu** Vishnu's birthplace; Tree of Knowledge; invoked for vengeance; emblem of Siva; associated with sages, seers

baptism purification; rebirth; death and interment of the old, birth and resurrection of the new; initiation; regression into the undifferentiated; crossing the sea of life; passage of the soul from matter to spirit; emergence from the womb to the outer light • **fire baptism** purging of dross • **wind baptism** winnowing away of chaff • **Mayan** associated with burial • *see also* **font**

bar • **heraldic** *on a female symbol (circle, oval, etc.):* virginity; chastity

barbel • **Egyptian** an unclean fish; hatred; emblem of Typhon

barber gossip; primitive medicine

barberry • **flower language** sourness; sharpness; ill temper; tartness

bard *see* **poet**

barkeeper *see* **tapster**

barley love (especially red barley); poverty; jealousy; prophecy; divination; resurrection; fertility; renewal of life; associated with the White Goddess • **grains of barley** sperm • **Greco-Roman** fertility; associated with Demeter/Ceres, Kore, Janus

basement *see* **cellar**

basil poverty; associated with death and destruction, especially in the Middle East where it was planted in graveyards • **Congolese** projection of misfortune; evil; protection from evil spirits • **flower language** hatred; poverty; *sweet basil:* good wishes • **folkloric** cure for basilisk poison; associated with the devil • **Greco-Roman** emblem of hatred; had to be planted with cursing or it would not grow • **Hindu** sacred to Vishnu, Lakshmi; opens the gates of heaven; charm for bodily protection • **Italian** associated with lovers

basilisk evil; poverty; death; cruelty; mesmerism; the unconscious which is dangerous if not faced; the king of serpents; deadliness; possessed the look and breath of death; an insidious treacherous person bent on mischief; sovereign power that destroys when disrespected; the mortal dangers of life; an evil woman who can corrupt the innocent • **basilisk with two heads** an amphisbaena • **alchemic** the melding of man's higher and lower natures; the destructive fire that precedes transmutation • **Christian** the devil; the Antichrist; one of the four aspects of the devil • **folkloric** can only be killed with a mirror that will reflect the deadly glance back upon the creature • **heraldic** terror to all beholders • **Swiss** emblem of Basel, Switzerland • see also **amphisbaena; dragon; rooster**

basin (or basin and ewer together) cleanliness; innocence; purity; Pilate washing his hands; the humility of Christ's love; attribute of a barber

basket the maternal body; the feminine principle; fertility; sanctity; womb; vagina; scrotum; charity to the poor • **emerging from a basket** birth; escape from death • **basket with flowers or fruit** abundance; opportunity; reward; fruitfulness; victory; success; attribute of Hope personified • **spilled basket** end of the fruitful season • **basket of glassware** Alnaschar's dream (Arabian Nights) • **willow basket** protection • **basket of fruit or wool** fertility; women's quarters; women's housework • **Buddhist** *three baskets:* Buddha/the Law/the Community, Vinaya (discipline)/Dhamma or Suta (discourse)/Abhidamma (exposition) • **Chinese** *basket of flowers:* longevity; fruitful old age, attribute of Lan Ts'ai Hok, Han Xiang • **Christian** attribute of St. Philip; *man suspended in a basket by a rope:* St. Paul; *Christ with baskets of bread:* Feeding of the 5,000 • **Egyptian** attribute of Bast, Isis; *standing on a basket:* lordship, mastery, supremacy; *basket chalice:* wholeness; togetherness under heavenly rule; *basket in a ceremonial procession of Isis:* hiding place of religious secrets; *vulture on a basket:* conception within the womb • **Greco-Roman** *basket of fruit and a covered phallus:* powers of life and death, Dionysian/Bacchic fertility; *three maidens with baskets on their heads:* associated with Hermes/Mercury; *ivy-covered basket:* Dionysian/Bacchic mysteries, emblem of Demeter/Ceres • **Hindu** *winnowing basket:* attribute of Dhumavat • **Italian** *female warrior among shepherds and basket-makers:* Erminia • **Jewish** *infant in basket:* the birth of Moses

bat (animal) night; death; misfortune; envy; black magic; infernal power or being; desolation; stalled spiritual development; cunning; terror; madness; hidden fears; the dark side of the unconscious; blindness; revenge; idolatry; longevity; wisdom; a woman between 80 and 90 years of age; attribute of the devil, Dracula, witches, vampires, the personifications of Night, Pride • **chariot drawn by bats** attribute of Night personified • **African** perspicacity; darkness; obscurity; a dead soul; associated with rain • **alchemic** androgyny • **Apache** invoked to prevent horses from falling • **Australian aboriginal** the soul of a man • **Aztecan** attribute of Nahua • **Babylonian** ghosts • **biblical** idolatry • **Buddhist** darkened understanding • **Cakchiquel** Chamalkan • **Central American Indian** attribute of Mictlantecuhtli • **Chami** attribute of Aribada • **Chinese** a yin animal; happiness; contentment; peace; longevity; lucky; *two bats:* good wishes; emblem of Shou-hsing; *five bats:* the blessings of longevity, wealth, health, virtue and a natural death; *fungus with bat:* longevity, happiness • **Christian** duplicity; hypocrisy; melancholy; an incarnation of the devil; *bat wings:* attribute of the devil • **Egyptian** *bat's head:* charm to keep doves from leaving the dovecote • **Fulani** clear-sightedness; enemy of light; blindness to patent truths; filth; topsy-turvy world view • **Greco-Roman** vigilance; aphrodisiac; Minya's daughters; attribute of Artemis/Diana • **Guatemalan Indian** Camazotz • **heraldic** cunning; coolness in the time of danger; awareness of the powers of darkness and chaos • **Indic** *bat flying into a house:* death omen • **Irish** death • **Ivorian** souls of the deadl • **Japanese** chaos; unhappy restlessness; attribute of Fukurokuju • **Jewish** impurity; idolatry; fear; an unclean anima • **Kwakiutl** ghost; charm

for a child's cradle to make it sleep • **Macedonian** *bat's bone:* good luck charm • **Maori** evil omen • **Mayan** ruler of fire; destroyer of life; eater of light; associated with underworld gods; death • **Mexican Indian** death god; associated with North • **North American Indian** associated with rain; *Great Plains:* trickster • **Polish** lucky • **Renaissance** prolific motherhood • **Samoan** Sepi Malosi; Taisumale • **Taoist** a food of immortality • **Tongan** souls of the dead • **Tupi-Guarani** death god • **Tupinamba** a bat will swallow the sun at the end of the world • **Zuni** harbinger of rain

bat (fuller's) *see* **fuller's bat**

bath purification; initiation; regeneration; luxury; **warm bath** return to the womb, sensual pleasure, an assault on chastity • **cold bath** self-mortification • **bathing in sacred waters** promotion of fertility

baton *see* **wand**

battering ram destruction; fertilization; phallus

battle conflict with ideas, beliefs, a portion of oneself

battle axe *see* **axe**

Baubo • **Greek** mature feminine wantonness

bay (topography) vagina • *see also* **harbor**

bay laurel inspiration; triumph; victory, especially in a spiritual sense; renewal of life; immortality; achievement in poetry, song, and the arts in general; fecundity; glory; merit; reward; joy; peace; death; mourning; protection; truce; perfidy; Winter; chastity; eternity; immortality; associated with Leo, the archangels Gabriel, Michael • **wreath** distinction in literature or music; death; mourning • **British** resurrection • **Chinese** immortality • **Christian** crown of martyrs • **flower language** glory; reward of merit; the Arts; I change but in death; *common laurel:* perfidy; *ground laurel:* perseverance; *mountain laurel:* ambition, glory; *spurge laurel:* coquetry, desire to please; *red bay* love; memory; *rose bay (oleander):* danger; beware • **Greco-Roman** victory; truce; peace; inspiration; chastity; sacred to Daphne, Dionysus/Bacchus, Hera/Juno, Artemis/Diana, Silvanus, Hestia/Vesta, sometimes Apollo; associated with the Muses, poetry; *bay laurel sprouting from the arms of a maiden:* Daphne; *bay laurel grove:* Parnassus; *bay laurel wreath:* victory at the Pythian games, intellectual and military glory, attribute of Apollo, Clio; *withering bay tree:* death omen • **heraldic** peace; triumph; renown; success; victory; glory; poetry • **portraiture** implies the subject had literary or artistic merit

bayberry illusions; appearances • **bayberry candles** the New Year; lucky; prosperity

beach *see* **shore**

beacon safety; vigilance; watchfulness; religion; the Final Port; warning of danger; communication; guidance; man's remoteness and solitude; salvation; refuge • **beacon fire** communication between men • **Christian** Christ; the Bible; the Word of God • **heraldic** watchfulness; service giving an alarm

beads memory; rosary; the feminine principle • **blue beads** protection against the evil eye • **gold beads** protection against the evil eye, malevolent spirits, and throat diseases • **string of beads** children; continuity; perpetuity • **stringing beads** coition • *see also* **rosary**

beans false philosophy; immortality; transmogrification; worthlessness; energy; ghosts; resurrection; reincarnation; a humble food; sunshine in solid form; connected with witches, magic power; attribute of Gratitude personified • **beanstalk** usually a favorable symbol; the ladder to heaven; World Tree • **Egyptian** *bean fields:* place where the dead awaited reincarnation • **Greco-Roman** souls of the dead; communion with the dead; Spring gift of the dead to the living; *black bean:* a negative vote; *white bean:* a positive vote • **Hindu** *bean seedling:* love charm • **Japanese** *kidney beans (usually roasted):* exorcism; preservation; charm against demons, unlucky, lightning

bear bravery; strength; self-restraint; cruelty; evil; danger; a difficulty; obstacle; violence; clumsiness; solitariness; martyrdom; Satan; Gluttony personified; nobility; stubbornness; silliness; ugliness; triviality; melancholy; voluptuousness; the Terrible Mother; danger of the unconscious; crudity; emblem of Russia, the Kingdom of Persia; associated with moon goddesses, pessimism or declining prices on the stock market, the archangel Samael • **hibernating bear emerging from its den** resurrection • **bear emerging from its den with its newborn cub** new life; initiation • **bull and bear** two contending powers of the universe, such as positive/negative, male/female • **bear and lion** emblem of the devil • **Ainu** divine messenger; ancestor of the race; mountain god • **alchemic** instincts; primary phase of development; associated with black • **Algonquin** grandfather of the race • **American** *grizzly bear:* emblem of California, Montana • **Celtic** a lunar power; the warrior caste; temporal power; emblem of Berne; *boar and bear:* spiritual authority and temporal power respectively • **Chinese** strength;

bravery; herald of the birth of a boy • **Christian** the devil; evil; cruelty greed; carnal appetite; attribute of SS Blandina, Gall, Florentinus, Maximus, Euphemia; *David fighting with a bear:* the conflict between Christianity and the devil; *bear cubs:* the transforming power of Christianity • **Greco-Roman** Arcas, Kallisto/Callisto; companion of Artemis/Diana; attribute of Atalanta, Euphemia • **heraldic** power; strength; cunning; tenacity; ferocity in the protection of one's kindred • **Inuit** *polar bear:* a form of Tuurngasuk; *ten-legged bear:* Kokogiak • **Islamic** a wretched, disgusting creature • **Japanese** benevolence; wisdom; strength • **Jewish** the Kingdom of Persia • **Norse** sacred to Thor; the she-bear Atla was the feminine principle, and the he-bear Atli was the masculine principle; *bearskin:* attire of berserkers; *bear with human eyes:* a berserker • **North American Indian** supernatural power; strength; fortitude; *bear tracks:* good omen • **Pueblo** associated with powers of the underworld • **Russian** friend of mankind • **Samian** *bear-man:* Leib-olmai • **Siberian** omniscience; associated with the moon • **Siouan** guardian of the East • **Tibetan** *black bear:* attribute of Da • **Ural-Altaic** messenger of the forest spirits; ancestor of the race; omniscience

beard honor; strength; virility; manhood; sovereignty; age; wisdom; protection from one's emotions or environment • **bearded woman** a witch, androgyny • **blue beard** evil • **gold beard** the sun; attribute of a sun hero • **gray beard** old age • **white beard** attribute of a sage • **art** in early art, a beard indicated a person still living (the dead were shown clean shaven) • **Chinese** *white-faced long-bearded man with bow and arrows and small boy:* Chang Hsien • **Christian** *white beard:* attribute of SS Roulade, Paul the Hermit, Bernardino of Siena; *red beard:* attribute of the devil • **Egyptian** *bearded queen:* power equal to a king • **Far Eastern** old age • **Greco-Roman** *bird with a bearded woman's head:* a siren; *gray beard:* attribute of Chronos; red beard: attribute of Odysseus/Ulysses • **Japanese** *long white beard:* attribute of Jurojin • **Jewish** *cutting a beard:* infamy, shaming, penance, servility, punishment, mourning, sorrow; *unkempt beard:* a sign of madness; *kissing a beard:* sign of respect; *covering a beard:* mourning, sorrow • **Norse** *red beard:* attribute of Thor • **Sumero-Semitic** *cutting a beard:* infamy, shaming, penance, servility, punishment, mourning, sorrow; *unkempt beard:* a sign of madness; *kissing a beard:* sign of respect; *covering a beard:* mourning, sorrow

bearded crepis • flower language protection

beast selfishness; self-centeredness; the lower instincts • **Christian** *four beasts of the Apocalypse:* desires of the four lower chakras

beating punishment • **beating one's breast or thighs** anguish; grief; repentance • **beating one's forehead** grief; shame; wonder • *see also* **flagellation**

beauty nobility; charity; virtue; immortality; strength • **Celtic** *beautiful woman washing bloody clothes at a ford:* death omen; *beautiful woman weeping:* death omen

beaver industriousness; engineering; wisdom; self-mutilation; self-sacrifice; peace; vigilance; emblem of Canada, formerly an emblem of Germany • **American** euphemism for female pubic hair; emblem of Washington state • **Christian** chastity; asceticism; the Christian who makes sacrifices for the sake of his spiritual life • **heraldic** sacrifice; peacefulness; tolerance; vigilance; industry; perseverance; skill (especially in castle building) • **Siouan** guardian of the South

bed repose; marriage; procreation; coition; rest; illness; childbirth; secrecy; anguish; reflection; languishing; place of regeneration, procreation, birth, death; a phase of thought or opinion; dispensation of justice; luxury • **Christian** *man carrying bed:* Christ's healing of the paralytic

bee industry; creative activity; obedience; diligence; good order; bureaucracy; wealth; eloquence; poetry; a soul; sweetness; prophecy; death; immortality; virginity; chastity; fertility; rebirth; wisdom; flattery; temptation; madness; punishment; stars; messengers to the spirit world; messengers of oak and thunder gods; emblem of Beethoven, Napoleon, Assyria • **bees carved on a tomb** immortality • **Celtic** secret wisdom coming from the other world • **Chaldean** royalty • **Chinese** industry; thrift • **Christian** diligence; good order; courage; economy; chaste virgins; purity; cooperation; sweetness; religious eloquence; the ordered and pious community; the risen Christ; Mary's virginity; Christian vigilance; Christian zeal in acquiring virtue; *beehive with bees:* the Church and Christians respectively; *bee and honey:* the Virgin Mary and Christ respectively • **Egyptian** regal power; birth; death; resurrection; chastity; harmonious living; royalty; the soul leaving the body at death; emblem of the pharaoh of Lower Egypt; *worker bees:* the tears of Ra • **Essene** *"king" bees:* priestly officials • **folkloric** a woman who was not stung when thrown into bees was a virgin • **Greco-Roman** industry;

prosperity; immortality; purity; a lunar and virgin insect; bestowers of eloquence and song; harbinger of a stranger; emblem of Cybele, Demeter/Ceres, Eros/Cupid, Rhea, Artemis/Diana; *beekeepers:* Pan/Faunus, Priapus; *lion and bees:* Demeter/Ceres and her priestesses • **heraldic** industry; sovereignty; well-governed industry; the Carolingians • **Hindu** Soma; *bee on a lotus:* Vishnu; *blue bees on the forehead:* attribute of Krishna; *bee surmounting a triangle:* Shiva; *bowstring made of bees:* attribute of Kama • **Islamic** the faithful; intelligence; wisdom; harmlessness • **Jewish** government in good order • **Mithraic** the soul; androgyny • **Roman** breath of life; justice; sobriety; monarchy; *swarm of bees:* misfortune; *headless bee:* averts the evil eye • *see also* **beehive**

beech victory; honor; prosperity; divination; sacred to Zeus/Jupiter; associated with books, sexuality, the archangels Cassiel, Michael; emblem of Denmark • **flower language** prosperity • **heraldic** historical knowledge; tolerance

beehive cooperation; industry; thrift; abundance; well-being; activity; society thriving on rapacity; eloquence; earth soul; protective motherhood; workshop; maternal protection; attribute of Hope personified • **American** emblem of Utah • **Christian** the Church; the papacy; a monastic community; attribute of SS Bernard of Clairvaux, Ambrose (especially with two scourges), Chrysostom; *beehive with bees:* the Church and Christians respectively • **Gallic** *beehive on a pole:* attribute of Nantosuelta • **Greek** *beehive-shaped tomb:* immortality • **Roman** *staff topped with a beehive:* emblem of Mellonia • *see also* **bee**

Beelzebub • Christian, Jewish gluttony; worship of false gods

beer masculinity; drink of the common man; in very ancient times, the drink of the gods • **Celtic** drink of warriors and royalty • **Egyptian** drink of immortality • **Tutsi** *banana beer:* drink of the warrior class

beetle death; witchcraft; fairies; sundown; life reduced to smallness; a stupid person; the Self; blindness • **Egyptian** rebirth; prosperity; resurrection; abundance; lucky; *ram-headed beetle:* the West wind, Hutchaiui; *dung beetle:* Khepri • **folkloric** *beetle flying through the house:* unlucky • **heraldic** modesty; a reminder of worldly sorrows • **Irish** *dung beetle:* slander, sin, leprosy • *see also* **ladybug; scarab**

beggar indigence; poverty; independence • **female beggar holding a heavy stone** Poverty personified • **Chinese** *beggar taking the pill of immortality:* Han Chung-li • **Christian** St. Alexis; attribute of SS Elizabeth of Hungary, Martin of Tours, Lawrence, John Chrysostom; *beggar kneeling before a monk:* the monk is St. John of God • **Lithuanian** *old beggar:* Dievas Senelis

begging bowl *see* **alms bowl**

beheading separation of the body and spirit; an opinion, idea, or institution at the end of its cycle; loss of control; typical punishment of the upper classes • *see also* **head**

Behemoth the power of the land; monstrous size; oppressive power; brute force • **Jewish** will be served as food at the End Time

belfry call to prayer; religiosity undone by clerical weakness; the head

Belial • **Christian** the Antichrist • **Jewish** gambling as a vice; rebelliousness; lawlessness; worthlessness; the underworld; the personification of evil

bell virginity; alarm; death; fertility; consecration; health; the masculine and feminine principles together; the priest; the heavens; exorcism; purification; call to worship; freedom; motion of the elements; notice of change; attribute of Music personified, unmarried women • **hanging bell** connection between heaven and earth • **magic handbell** summon to the spirits of the dead, the underworld • **bells on one's person** protection from evil spirits • **Buddhist** the sound of perfect wisdom • **Burmese** *temple wind bells:* music of the gods • **Chinese** respect; veneration; obedience; honor for warriors; protection from the evil eye and evil spirits; faithful ministers; harmony between man and the divine; thunder; *evening temple bells:* prayers to the gods; *bell ringing:* call for rain • **Christian** Christ's joy; the bell is the mouth of the preacher, the clapper his tongue; *sanctus bell:* the coming of Christ in the Eucharist; *bell on a crutch:* attribute of St. Anthony the Great; *bell on a rope:* the feeding of St. Benedict in his hermitage • **European** church bells were once rung to break the power of thunderstorms, drive off witches, and cleanse pestilence • **German** church bells frightened away trolls, giants, and dwarves • **Greco-Roman** associated with Priapus, Dionysian/Bacchic rites; *bell clapper:* phallus • **heraldic** dispersion of evil spirits; *hawk's bells:* fearless of signaling approach; *bell tower:* integrity • **Hindu** rank; dignity; virginity; hearing; echo of primeval vibration; *handbell on a trident:* attribute of Shiva • **Islamic** Koranic revelation; the reverberation of the power of God in the world • **Japanese** *evening temple bells:* prayers to the

gods • **Jewish** thunder; lightning; virginity; attribute of King David; *golden bells on the hem of a garment:* attribute of Aaron, virgins • **Norse** church bells frightened away trolls, giants, and dwarves • **Teutonic** *hawk bell:* nobility • **Tibetan** *prayer bell:* call the attention of good spirits, drives off evil spirits; *handbell:* the world of senses, illusion • **Yoruban** drive away abiku

belladonna *see* **nightshade**

Bellerophon • **Greek** vanity; overweening ambition; military power attempting to seize civilian control • *see also* **Pegasus**

bellflower • **flower language** *white bellflower* gratitude; *pyramidal bellflower:* constancy

bellows breathing; flattery; temptation; attribute of Cinderella • **old man with a bellows at furnace** an alchemist • **Christian** *devil with a candle and a bellows:* the devil's attempt to extinguish spiritual life; attribute of St. Genevieve • **Hindu** *wood, bellows, and axe:* attributes of Agni • **Taoist** *cosmic bellows:* the space bounded by heaven and earth where life exists

belly physical man; antithesis of the brain or spirit; gluttony; destruction; matter; sensuality; compassion; intuition • **being in the belly of a monster or large sea creature** hell; Sheol; descent into the underworld; cosmic night; embryonic state of being • **emerging from the belly of a monster or large sea creature** rebirth; resurrection; salvation • **fat belly** gluttony; prosperity • **belly dance** *Asian:* mimics childbirth; *Greek:* promotes fertility, sexuality • **Hindu** *large belly:* occasional attribute of a rakshasa • **Oriental** seat of life • *see also* **stomach**

Belphegor • **Jewish** sloth

Belshazzar, King • **Christian** upholder of paganism; a type of Antichrist

belt virginity; power; strength; virtue; biding to power or office; dedication; fulfillment; victory; virtue; restraint • **twisted belt** a woman in love • **Norse** *belt of Thor:* doubling of strength • *see also* **cincture; girdle**

belvedere • **flower language** I declare against you

bend • **heraldic** knightly service

bend sinister • **heraldic** royal descent

Benjamin • **Jewish** the youngest son in a family

Bennu • **Egyptian** self-generation; associated with the rising of Nile, resurrection, the sun, the calendar, Ra, Osiris

Bermuda • **English** *Elizabethan:* enchantment, tempest, brothel district, underworld district

berry fruit of marriage; close relation; immortality; knowledge; rejuvenation • **berries on a branch** friendship; ephemeral beauty • **heraldic** liberality; felicity; peace

beryl love; married love; everlasting youth; inner happiness; goodness; associated with Scipio • **golden beryl** stone for a 7th wedding anniversary

betel • **Indic** aphrodisiac • **Vietnamese** love; conjugal fidelity; love potion

betony associated with Aries, Jupiter (planet) • **flower language** surprise

bezoar antidote for poison

Bible the Word of God; sanctity; holiness; spiritual guidance; truth; Protestantism in particular, Christianity in general • **opened to the Gospel of St. Matthew** attribute of SS Barnabas, Bartholomew • **opened to Romans 13** attribute of St. Augustine of Hippo • **New Testament** Christian worship • **Old Testament** Jewish worship; attribute of St. Stephen • *see also* **book**

bicycle humble transportation; free-spiritedness; self-control of the unconscious; balanced progress

bilberry • **flower language** treachery

billows overwhelming trials; loss of control

bindweed • **flower language** *great bindweed:* insinuation; *small bindweed:* humility

birch meekness; gracefulness; beginning; the new year; self-propagation; phallus; fertility; light; associated with love and death; charm against witches • **silver birch** associated with the archangel Raphael • **birch rod or switch for whipping** drives out evil spirits; school authority; corporal punishment; drives out insanity • **Celtic** beginning; renewal; youth • **Estonian** the personification of Estonia • **heraldic** new beginnings; vision quest • **Norse** the return of spring; the last battle in the world will be fought around a birch tree; attribute of Frigga, Thor • **Russian** associated with Spring • **Slavic** associated with Baba Yaga • **Teutonic** attribute of Donar • **Ural-Altaic** the Cosmic Tree

bird the soul; thought; imagination; spiritualization; transcendence; divine manifestation; the spirit; spirit of the dead; the ability to communicate with the gods and/or to enter a higher state of consciousness; link between heaven and earth; messenger; supernatural aid; air; wind; time; immortality; creation; the feminine principle; aspiration; prophecy; love; freedom; haste; betrayal; attribute of the personification of Touch, Hera/Juno personifying Air; associated with the archangel Raphael • **large birds** the solar; wind gods; thunder, especially if they have tongues of lightning • **night birds** associated with Saturn (planet) • **bird accompanying a hero** divine assistance • **solitary birds** the isolation of those who live on a superior mental plane • **talking and singing birds** amorous yearning • **bird on a pillar** union of spirit and matter; a sun god • **white bird** *ancient times:* eroticism • **dark bird and light bird together** dualism; the manifest and unmanifest; darkness/light, etc. • **red bird** *ancient times:* the supernatural • **black-colored bird** intelligence • **flock of birds** often have a negative connotation; magic powers; the supernatural • **flock of birds taking flight** orgasm • **brass-backed bird** fever • **metal bird** phoenix • **bird with a woman's head** a siren (mythology) • **bird fighting with serpent** the conflict of solar and underworld powers respectively • **bird freed from a cage** the soul freed from the body • **bird tapping at a window or flying into a house** death omen • **bird in a cage** hope of freedom or of salvation; a kept woman; the mind • **carnivorous bird** greed • **giant bird** creative deity; storm • **bird of prey flying from left to right before a battle** omen of defeat • **chariot pulled by birds of prey** attribute of Greed personified • **tree with ten or 12 birds** the solar cycle • **tree with three birds** the lunar phases • **African** strength; life; fertility; the soul; *battle between a bird and a serpent:* the battle between life and death respectively • **alchemic** *ascending bird:* volatilization, sublimation; *descending bird:* condensation, precipitation; *birds fighting or flying up and down:* the nous, the dual nature of Mercurius, distillation • **Aztecan** *feathers surmounted by a blue bird:* emblem of Huehueteotl • **Buddhist** auspiciousness; the Buddha • **Celtic** messenger of the gods; divinity; the happy otherworld; magic power; malevolence; *birds linked together with a golden chain:* omen of an important event • **Chinese** usually the solar yang principle, longevity, luck; *two birds with a shared wing:* fidelity, lovers, indissoluble unity; *blue bird:* an Immortal, fairy, messenger from heaven; *red bird:* West; *red and yellow bird with six feet and four wings:* chaos; *bird destroying its own nest:* harbinger of disorder and trouble in the empire; *bird hopping on one leg:* omen of rain • **Christian** souls; souls in Paradise; the imagination; *birds feeding on grapes:* the faithful gathering sustenance from Christ through the Eucharist; *birds in a vine:* souls abiding with Christ; *white bird:* divine messenger, purity, beneficence • **Egyptian** the soul; *bird with a human head:* a ba, a dead person's soul, deities visiting the earth; *purple firebird:* a dead person's soul • **Greek** *bird with a woman's head (sometimes bearded):* a siren; *woman with bird legs (and sometimes wings):* a siren • **heraldic** *bird* *claw:* the preyer who has been preyed upon • **Hindu** intelligence; the soul; vehicle of Vishnu; sometimes equated with the phoenix; friendship among the gods; manifestation of the gods; divine freedom • **Islamic** angel; souls of the faithful living on the Tree of Life; *birds of prey:* the souls of infidels • **Jewish** *birds with food:* attribute of Elijah; *green bird:* soul of a martyr flying to heaven; *speckled bird:* the Law, the Word of God • **Maori** strength; valor; *the Bird Man:* the divinity, the all-seeing, the all-wise • **Mayan** *bird demon:* Vucub Caquix • **Mesopotamian** a soul of the dead • **North American Indian** lightheartedness; *bird with its head surrounded by clouds:* rain; *bird with a broken circle around its head:* creation of life, opening of the gate of heaven • **Norse** the spirit freed from the body; wisdom; *dark red bird:* attribute of Hel • **Persian** *bird with a woman's or a dog's head:* a simurg; *talking bird:* Karshipta • **Russian** *woman with a bird body:* alkonost, gamayun, sirin • **Semang** *nocturnal bird:* a soul of the dead • **Shinto** the creative principle • **Sumero-Akkadian** *half-bird/half-man:* Zu • **Taoist** message from heaven; forewarning; manifestation of the Immortals; *willful, rapacious birds:* barbarians • **Tinguinian** *half-man/half-bird with toes and fingers reversed:* an alan • **Ural-Altaic** ascent to heaven; magical travel; *bird wings:* communication between this world and the spirit world; *small bird:* a child's soul • *see also* **Feng-huang; Ho-o; nest; phoenix; Roc; simurg; Ziz; Zu** and specific birds: **blackbird; bluebird; dove,** etc.

bird cage man's contrariness; imprisonment; deceit • **bird freed from a cage** the soul freed from the body • **single bird in a cage** hope of freedom or of salvation; a kept woman • **birds in a cage** the mind

bird nest *see* **nest**

bird of paradise (plant) • **heraldic** freedom

biretta • **Christian** *black:* attribute of a priest; *purple:* attribute of a bishop; *red:* attribute of a cardinal • *see also* **cardinal's hat**

birth new beginning; rebirth; second chance; new ideas • **folkloric** Sunday's child is full of grace / Monday's child is fair in the face (or, full in the face) / Tuesday's child is solemn and sad / Wednesday's child is merry and glad / Thursday's child is inclined to thieving / Friday's child is free and giving / Saturday's child works hard for a living -or- Born on a Monday, fair of face / Born on a Tuesday, full of (God's) grace / Born on a Wednesday, sour and sad (or, full of woe) / Born on a Thursday, merry and glad

(or, has far to go) / Born on a Friday, worthily given (or, is loving and giving) / Born on a Saturday, work hard for your living / Born on a Sunday, you'll never want (or, lucky and happy and good and gay) • **Jewish** *one twin born clutching the heel of another:* Jacob and Esau respectively • *see also* **virgin birth**

birthmark curse; karmic memory; destiny; personal mission

biscuit dryness • **Christian** the consecrated Host distributed without love

bishop • **Christian** the spiritual principle; spiritualized mental qualities; religious authority; *bearing a youth aloft:* St. Nicholas of Myra; *struck by a Jew:* the Jew is Rebellion personified; *foot on a fallen oak:* St. Boniface; *with a broken chalice:* St. Donatus; *with flames at his feet:* St. Januarius; *with robin:* St. Mungo; *with sword piercing his skull or hand:* St. Thomas Becket; *with sword piercing a book:* St. Boniface; *with three children in a tub:* St. Nicholas of Myra • *see also* **chess**

bison untamed nature; base forces; strength; intimidation; fortitude • **American** emblem of the American West, the state of Wyoming • **North American Indian** supernatural power; the whirlwind; prosperity; plenty • **Siouan** manifestation of the Great Spirit

bit and bridle (or just a bridle by itself) law; restraint; worldly interests and cares; control; endurance; forbearance; temperance; attribute of the personifications of Temperance, Fortune • **old man bridled, on all fours, ridden by a woman** Aristotle and Campaspe • **Egyptian** *turquoise on a bridle:* charm for sure-footedness • **Greco-Roman** attribute of Nemesis/Invidia; *golden bridle:* used by Bellerophon to capture Pegasus

bite seal of the spirit upon the flesh; love mark; mark of divine love; the dangerous action of the instincts upon the psyche

Biton *see* **Kleobis and Biton**

bitter herbs • **Jewish** servitude; slavery; affliction; misfortune

bittern grossness; rudeness; desolation

bitterness suffering undergone in purification of the soul

bittersweet (plant) truth

black associated with constancy, death, depression, destruction, error, evil, fertile land, germinal stage of a process, gravity, grief, humiliation, humility, ignorance, instinct, mineral life, mortality, mourning, nothingness, abyss, ocean depths, penitence, primordial chaos, primordial darkness, punishment, renunciation, sadness, shame, sin, sleep, superstition, the absolute, the non-manifest, time, wisdom, womb, Capricorn, the Terrible Mother, the earth, -8-, Saturn (planet), witchcraft, fertility goddesses, the North-South axis of the world; attribute of the personification of Death; the antithesis of white, color • **black and white** humility and purity of life respectively; clarity; the printed word; all opposites (light/dark, good/evil, etc.) • **red and black** life and death respectively • **red, white, and black** the three stages of initiation • **black flag** death; pirates; execution of criminals • **black hand or spot** impending death or murder • **black virgin** opposing aspects of the Great Mother —creator/destroyer, birth/death, etc. • **black garments** renunciation of worldly vanities; mourning for an irrevocable loss • **black sails** an ill-fated ship • **African** associated with night, ordeal, suffering, mystery; *North Africa:* earth, fertility • **alchemic** the absence of color; associated with the first stage of the Great Work, the arcane, matter, sin, penitence, dissolution, fermentation, the sinister, descent into hell • **Algonquin** associated with North • **Andaman** associated with the human spirit • **Aztecan** associated with North • **Buddhist** the darkness of bondage • **Chaldean** emblem of the moon • **Chinese** evil; North; yin; water; *black clouds:* portent of floods; *Black Tortoise:* primordial chaos; associated with Winter; *black face on stage:* a humble but honest person; *ritual face-blackening:* self-abasement; appeal for pardon • **Christian** associated with hell, death, mourning, sorrow, humiliation, humility, despair, spiritual darkness, corruption, witchcraft, penance; liturgical color for Maundy Thursday, Good Friday, masses for the dead; attribute of the devil; *black clerical garments:* humility, penitence, renunciation of worldly vanities; *black with dark red:* colors of Satan; *black nimbus:* occasional attribute of Judas Iscariot • **Egyptian** associated with rebirth, resurrection, earth, fertility, eternal life, destruction, Osiris, Anubis, Min; attribute of evil Genii; *black dove:* a woman who remained a widow until death • **English** (Elizabethan) *black blanket hung on a theater:* a tragedy being performed • **Greco-Roman** mortality; attribute of Castor, Cronus/Saturn; *black bull:* sacrifice to Poseidon/Neptune • **heraldic** prudence; wisdom; grief; penitence; constancy • **Hindu** time; the dark aspect of Kali, Durga; tamas; sensual and downward movement; antidote for envy, the evil eye; the color of Vishnu • **Islamic** divine essence; the color to which all colors lead; associated with destruction, rebellion, the Abbasids; *black banner:* revolt; *black dog:* brings death in a family; *black garments:* renunciation of worldly vanities; *black hen:* used in witchcraft; *black turban:* mission of vengeance • **Italian** emblem of the Guelphs • **Kabalistic** understanding; the Kingdom of God; associated with the archangel Cassiel • **Masonic** associated with Malkut, the Kingdom • **Mayan** associated with West, death, the mother, the hidden center, misfortune • **Mexican Indian** associated with North • **Norse** *half-white/half-black goddess:* Hel • **Persian** associated with mourning • **Pueblo** associated with the underworld

black moon the intangible; the unattainable; the overwhelming presence of absence and absence of presence; hyperlucidity; energy that must be mastered; karma that must be cleansed; the extremes of attraction and repulsion; the quest for the Absolute at all costs; annihilation; maleficent passions to be overcome; absolute void; associated with Lilith • *see also* **moon**

blackberry repentance; worthlessness • **Celtic** *British:* a taboo food; associated with death, fairies, the devil

blackbird an underworld deity; unlucky; evil; the darkness of sin; temptation; cunning; vigilance; resignation; inspiration • **black-colored bird** intelligence • **Christian** the devil; temptations of the flesh; the devil tempting St. Benedict; attribute of St. Kevin • **heraldic** a clear sounding family name

black-eyed Susan *see* **rudbeckia**

blacksmith the demiurge; mental qualities disciplined by the spirit; related to thought, creation, destruction, the diabolical, initiation, Creation • **Celtic** Gobniu • **Chinese** Ch'e Yu; Huang Ti • **Christian** Tubalcain; sometimes Cain; *blacksmith shoeing a horse, having first removed its leg:* St. Eloi • **Dogon** associated with soothsaying • **Egyptian** Ptah • **Greco-Roman** Hephaestus/Vulcan • **Hindu** Tvashtri • **Montagnard** Bung • **Norse** *dwarf blacksmith:* Regin • *see also* **forge**

blackthorn unlucky; difficulty; strife; associated with Scorpio • **British** attribute of Morgan le Fay, Gwynn ap Nudd; *blackthorn cane:* formerly an attribute of witches, in modern times an attribute of officers in the Irish Guards; *blackthorn pyre:* used to burn witches • **Christian** evil; associated with witches • **flower language** difficulty • **German** Tree of Life; divine guidance and succor • **Celtic** control; discipline; perspective • **Irish** traditional wood of the shillelagh; associated with war, blood, death; attribute of Morrigan, Dagda • **Scottish** associated with Winter, witches; attribute of Cailleach • **Welsh** attribute of Cerridwen • **witchcraft** the dark side of witchcraft; the waning moon

bladder grief; attribute of a fool

bladder nut the rosary • **flower language** amusement; frivolity

blaeberry • **flower language** ingenuous simplicity

blanket comfort; security; the night sky • **English** (Elizabethan) *black blanket hung on a theater:* a tragedy was playing

blindfold moral or spiritual blindness; sin; ignorance; deceit; carelessness; willful refusal to see or understand; contemplation; inner withdrawal; attribute of the personifications of Idolatry, Avarice, Fortune, Justice • **blindfold of Justice personified** impartiality • **blindfold of Fortune personified** randomness • **Christian** attribute of SS Paul, John the Baptist at their executions; *linen blindfold:* blindness to the vanities of the world; *woman with blindfold:* the Synagogue personified • **Greco Roman** attribute of Eros/Cupid; *blindfold of Nemesis/Invidia:* randomness; *blindfold of Eros/Cupid:* the blindness of secular love

blindman's bluff trying to solve a problem without sufficient knowledge

blindness darkness; ignorance; sin; bias; impartiality; dereliction of duty; the undiscerning; the irrational; error; prophecy; euphemism for castration; mentality immersed in the concerns of the lower life; the mind not awakened by the spirit; lack of spiritual perception; willful refusal to see or understand; punishment of deities; indication of heightened or supernatural powers; ability to see past the vanities of the world to deeper truths; attribute of sages, prophets, poets • **Buddhist** the blind old woman in the Round of Existence shows absence of knowledge, ignorance leading to death • **Greek** *blind man with bay laurel wreath and/or two tablets and/or stringed instrument:* Homer; *blind man with broken lyre sitting in Hades:* Thamyris

blister *on the tongue:* sign of a lie

blizzard overwhelming circumstances; the full force of nature • **Greek** *blizzard of gold:* fell on Athens at the birth of Athena

blood sacrifice; passion; war; life; the soul; strength; rejuvenating force; solar energy; guilt; covenant; fertility; martyrdom; fire; heat; powers of the sun • **menstrual blood** connected with magic, witchcraft • **drinking blood** enmity; absorbing the power of whatever or whoever bled • **stepping over blood** confers fertility; avoiding contamination • **blood on the moon** evil omen • **Christian** Christ's redemption of man; *blood and water at the Crucifixion:* the life of the body and the life of the spirit respectively; *blood flowing from a shroud pierced by a knife:* attribute of St. Gregory the Great • **Chinese** *blood and water:* yin and yang • **Hindu** *bowl of blood:* attribute of Shiva; *woman drinking blood from a skull:* Kali; *monster drinking blood from a skull or the palm of its hand:* a rakshasa; *woman in a boat in an ocean of blood:* Kali; *river of blood, hair, and filth:* Vaitarani • **Jewish** *blood on doorpost:* the Passover; *bloodstained tunic given to an old man:* the old man is Jacob, father of Joseph • **Tungun** associated with West • **Tibetan** *woman drinking blood from a skull:* Lha-mo

bloodroot healing; strength; growth

bloodstone courage; victory; longevity; wealth; strength; endurance; vitality; mourning; understanding; peace; devotion; faithfulness; granter of wishes; birthstone of March; charm for courage, presence of mind, stopping of bleeding, healing, legal success, business success, invisibility, agriculture; associated with Aries, Mars (planet), fourteenth wedding anniversaries, the archangels Azrael, Samael • **bloodstone placed in a glass of water during a drought** said to soak up sun rays and cause a storm • **Babylonian** divination; invulnerability; a sacred stone of the gods • **Christian** the red spots were said to be Christ's blood from the Crown of Thorns

blot death; the abnormal; defectiveness; weakness; sin; the transitory; associated with the passage of time

blowing female orgasm; passion; euphemism for fellatio • **blowing on a person** expelling evil spirits; conferring the Holy Spirit

blue sanctification; sincerity; piety; intuition; time and space; truth; intellect; revelation; eternity; devotion; loyalty; occasionally a royal color; harmony; candor; glory; spirituality; innocence; courage; fairness; love; justice untempered by love; coolness; coldness; Puritanism; calmness; philosophical serenity; contemplation; heavenly love; heaven; the unveiling of truth; modesty; prudence; hope; religion; faith; the subconscious; loss of love; despondency; half-mourning; non-erotic, tender love; passivity; the spirit of man; peace; tranquility; peace; expiation; humility; chastity; innocence; spotless reputation; sincerity; piety; mediation; purification of the mind; the least substantial of the colors; associated with water, the sky, the spirit, thought, surreality, royalists, right-wing politics, the sixth heaven, Sagittarius, Libra, Jupiter (planet), Mercury (planet) • **blue flower** spiritual happiness; magic or special powers • **blue ribbon** first prize • **blue-colored glasses** make one take a pessimistic view • **blue and red** love and authority; sometimes used for the color of God's clothes • **bluish green** associated with Scorpio • **violet-blue** associated with Capricorn • **pale blue** associated with Venus (planet) • **light blue** associated with Uranus (planet), the sky, daytime • **sky blue** associated with sky gods and sky powers, the Great Mother, the Queen of Heaven, etc.; the void; primordial simplicity; infinite empty space that can contain everything; the lunar • **dark blue** associated with Capricorn, a stormy sea, night sky; Mercury (planet) • **ice blue** associated with Cancer • **alchemic** associated with the sky • **American** associated with the Republican party • **Amerindian** the sky; peace • **Aztecan** *blue and yellow:* colors of Huitzilopochtli • **British** associated with the Whig party; *blue ribbon:* Order of the Garter • **Buddhist** the coolness of the heavens above and the waters below; the wisdom of the Dharma-Dhatu; associated with East, bearing holy witness; attribute of Akshobhya; *red, white, and blue:* Brahma, Vishnu and Shiva; intelligence, order, and unity • **Byzantine** *sky blue:* worn by emperors • **Celtic** associated with bards, poets • **Chaldean** emblem of Mercury (planet) • **Chinese** associated with the heavens, clouds, the Azure Dragon of the East, Spring, wood; *blue sedan chair:* attribute of a high government official; *blue man with wings, claws, drum, mallet and chisel:* Lei-kung • **Christian** heaven; heavenly truth; eternity; faith; fidelity; attribute of the Virgin Mary, the Trinity, sometimes Christ in his earthly ministry • **Druidic** associated with bards, poets • **Egyptian** associated with truth; *blue skin:* attribute of Amon • **European** *blue clothes:* attribute of servants, peasants, manual laborers, tradesmen • **folkloric** *blue flame:* a spirit passing; witches about • **Gnostic** baptism by water • **Greco-Roman** attribute of Zeus/Jupiter, Hera/Juno, Aphrodite/Venus • **heraldic** faithfulness; loyalty; steadiness; spotless reputation; humility; chastity; science; truth • **Hindu** antidote for envy, the evil eye; *blue rain cloak:* attribute of Indra; *god with blue skin:* Krishna; *blue mountain:* the southern face of Mount Meru; *blue neck usually with entwined serpents:* attribute of Shiva • **Iranian** *sky blue:* the national color • **Islamic** mourning; *dark blue:*

blessing; *azure blue:* intuitive conviction • **Jewish** *blue city:* Luz • **Kabalistic** mercy; associated with the archangel Zadkiel • **Kalmyk** South • **Masonic** haven; the Temple; the Starry Vault; beauty; foundation; the Crown; *blue scarf:* attribute of the French Rite; *blue scarf trimmed with red:* attribute of the Scottish Rite • **Mayan** defeat of an enemy • **Middle Ages** associated with worldly love, folly • **North American Indian** *prairie tribes:* North • **Pueblo** West • **Tibetan** potentiality; transcendent wisdom • **Tierra del Fuegan** associated with the sky, North • *see also* **indigo; turquoise**

bluebell sorrowful regret; constancy; kindness • **flower language** constancy; kindness • **folkloric** their bells called fairies to their midnight processions

bluebird happiness; the impossible; ideas; spiritual messenger; associated with Spring, Summer

bluebonnet • **heraldic** grace; forgiveness; mercy

bluebottle happiness; the modesty of the Virgin Mary; celibacy; single wretchedness; hope in love; emblem of Germany • **flower language** delicacy; felicity

bluejay *see* **jay**

bo tree • **Buddhist** heavenly light; contemplation; perfection; meditation; the tree under which the Buddha attained enlightenment; Sacred Center; the Great Awakening; the Great Wisdom Tree; the essence of Buddha

boar intrepidness; licentiousness; irrational urge toward suicide; courage; fertility; low animal nature; lust; anger; gluttony; attribute of Lust personified • **golden boar** the solar principle • **white boar** the lunar principle; associated with water • **boar underfoot** attribute of Chastity personified • **lion killing a boar** the sun overcoming Winter • **Celtic** the supernatural; magic; warfare; hospitality; the priestly caste; prophecy; a sacred animal; associated with trees, wheels, ravens, the human head; form of Cian in his escape; sacred to Lug; sacrifice to Derga; *boar's head:* health; preservation from danger; the life-force; abundance; lucky; *boar and bear:* spiritual authority and temporal power respectively • **Chinese** the wealth of the forest; *white boar:* associated with water and the lunar • **Christian** brutality; ferocity; anger; evil; sins of the flesh; cruel princes and rulers; divine anger; the Anti-Christ; the devil • **Druidic** spiritual power • **Egyptian** evil; attribute of Set • **Gallic** emblem of the priestly caste • **Greco-Roman** destruction; strife; Winter; sacred to Ares/Mars; attribute of Demeter/Ceres, Atalanta, Heracles; *boar surrounded by hunters:* Meleager; *crown of bay laurel held in the hand:* attribute of Calliope • **heraldic** hunting prowess; bravery; will fight to the death; *boar's head:* hospitality • **Hindu** associated with agriculture, fertility; *boar-headed, four-armed man:* Varaha • **Hyperborean** spiritual authority • **Japanese** courage; rashness; conquest; warrior qualities; last animal of the zodiac; Usa-hachiman; steed of war deities; attribute of Shinto Wakenokiyomaro shrines; *white boar:* the moon • **Jewish** the enemy of Israel • **Mediterranean** *dream of wild boars:* omen of violent storms at sea • **Mycenian** *boar's tusk helmet:* attribute of a warrior • **Norse** fertility; harvest; associated with storms, funerals; steed of Odin, Frey, Freyja; *boar mask or helmet:* put the wearer under the protection of Frey and Freyja; *boar with golden bristles:* Gulliburstin; the bristles represent sun rays; *boar's head:* emblem of Freyja; *monster boar:* Saerhrimnir • **Persian** associated with the sun; *wild boar:* incarnation of Verethaghna • **Siberian** courage; steadfastness; conquest; warrior qualities • **Sumero-Semitic** messenger of the gods; *winged boar:* slayer of Tammuz • *see also* **sow; swine**

boat the human body; the soul; the womb or cradle rediscovered; a venture; security; resurrection • **little boat** euphemism for vagina • **man in the boat** euphemism for clitoris • **Christian** attribute of St. Julian the Hospitator; *several monks in a small boat:* St. Brendan • **Egyptian** the throne of a god; vehicle to the afterlife; *boat with eight oars:* Tchetetfet • **Greco-Roman** *blue boat:* Charon's boat on the Styx; *woman pulling a boat upstream:* Claudia; *woman holding a boat in her hand:* Claudia personifying Confidence or Trust • **Hindu** occasional attribute of the Ashvins; *woman in a boat in an ocean of blood:* Kali • **Japanese** attribute of Prince Ninigi; *god with a boat-shaped nimbus:* Amida • *see also* **ark; ship**

boathook • **Christian** *with a fish:* attribute of St. Simon; *with a builder's square:* attribute of St. Jude; *with a saltire cross:* attribute of St. Andrew

boil (**disease**) a psychological affliction or spiritual shortcoming

boiling fury; an extreme state

Bologna, Italy • **Christian** *model of the city:* attribute of St. Petronius

bolt *see* **latch**

bomb • **heraldic** one subjected to bombing in battle

Bonaparte, Napoleon aggression; hostility; delusion of grandeur; emblem of France

bondage *see* **entanglement**

bones life; resurrection; death; the essential; mortality; the transitory; resoluteness; strength; virtue; the indestructible part of man • **destruction of bones** the preclusion of resurrection • **apron of bones** protection from the dead; invocation of aid from the dead • **Christian** *bonfire of bones:* attribute of John the Baptist • **heraldic** *crossed thighbones:* mortality • **Indic** *musical instrument of bone:* asceticism; access to immortality • **Jewish** *shank bone:* a reminder of burnt offerings and of the ancient glory of the Temple; *jawbone of an ass:* attribute of Samson; *valley of bones:* Ezekiel's vision • **Slavic** *hut surrounded by fence of bones:* dwelling of Baba Yaga • **Tibetan** *musical instrument of bone:* asceticism; access to immortality; *sash of human bones:* attribute of Nag-pa • **Tungun** associated with North • *see also* **skeleton; skull**

boneset fixing; mending; regeneration; strengthening

bonfire death; resurrection; fertility; warning; victory; strengthening the power of the sun, especially at solstices; encouraging the powers of light and good • **Christian** *bonfire of bones:* attribute of John the Baptist

bonnet one's attitudes, ideas; *green bonnet:* attribute of a bankrupt person • **Chinese** *goat's head bonnet:* attribute of Yang Ching • *see also* **hat**

bonsai tree • **Japanese** nature in its austerity and wisdom

book wisdom; secret or divine knowledge; magic; spiritual or mystical power; the Bible; the universe; the totality of God's decrees; related to the Creation, knowledge, teaching, 4th wedding anniversaries; attribute of the sibyls, authors, prophets • **closed book** secrecy; chastity; virginity • **open book** the Bible; perfect knowledge; honesty; dissemination of the truth; the book of life; learning; the spirit of wisdom; revelation • **Buddhism** akashic records • **Chinese** scholarship; *book pages:* the leaves of the Cosmic Tree, all beings in the universe, the Ten Thousand Things • **Christian** the Bible; attribute of the Apostles, the Doctors of the Church, the Virtues, SS Anne, Bernard of Clairvaux, Bonaventure, Thomas Aquinas, Augustine, Cyprian, and other saints famous for their learning; *sealed book in the lap of Christ:* the Apocalypse; *St. John eating a book:* the Apocalypse; *book with chalice:* attribute of St. Chrysostom; *book between two Doric columns:* attribute of St. Athanasius; *book with eagle:* attribute of St. John; *book with spear:* attribute of St. Thomas; *book with sword:* attribute of SS

Matthias, Paul (especially with legend "Spiritus Gladius"); *book with "alpha" and "omega" printed on it:* Christ; *sealed book:* the Virgin Mary; *closed book:* attribute of St. Jude; *closed book with seven seals and lamb:* Christ, John the Baptist; *book with halberd:* attribute of St. Matthias; *book with scroll or tall cross:* attribute of SS Philip, Andrew; *book with stone and whip:* attribute of St. Jerome; *book with writing table and pen:* attribute of St. Ambrose; *three books with pen:* attribute of St. Hilary of Poitiers; *book pierced by a sword:* attribute of SS Boniface, Anthony of Padua; *book with a fish:* attribute of St. Simon; *book with two vials:* attribute of St. Januarius; *book with flaying knife:* attribute of St. Bartholomew; *book with cross laying on it:* attribute of Faith personified; *monk with an open book:* often the rule of the order; *book inscribed "ad majorem Dei gloriam:"* attribute of St. Ignatius of Loyola • **Greco-Roman** attribute of Clio; *sealed book:* chastity; *book and sword offered to warrior sleeping under a tree:* the warrior is Scipio • **heraldic** *open book:* manifestation; *closed book:* counsel • **Islamic** truth; mercy; the Koran; *book with pen:* static being and the creative principle respectively • **Jewish** attribute of the archangel Uriel, Virtues • **Italian** *lovers sharing a book:* Paolo and Francesca • *see also* **Bible**

boomerang fate; karma; a situation that will not go away; emblem of Australia

borage bluntness; talent • **the whole plant** roughness of character • **flower language** bluntness; rudeness

border *see* **shore**

Boreas/Aquilo • **Greco-Roman** the personification of Winter; the North wind

boring (drilling) coition

bottle rain; refreshment; intemperance; consumption of alcoholic beverages; phallus; anything swollen; the womb; the containment principle; the enclosure principle; emblem of a tavern • **gold bottle** attribute of a banker • **with colored liquid** sign of pharmacists, later also of confectioners, grocers • **smashed bottle** rage; impending punishment • **Buddhist** the womb of Buddha nature • **Christian** salvation; attribute of St. James the Great • **Jewish** attribute of Jeremiah

bottle brush tree strength; resilience; associated with beauty, the archangel Raphael

bottomless pit or well insatiable desire

bouget *see* **water bouget**

bough hospitality; protection; offspring; phallus; flagellation; scourge; martyrdom, (especially a branch with thorns); Tree of Life; fertility; bridal festivities; occasional attribute of the personifications of Spring, Logic, Chastity • **bearing fruit or blooms** ephemeral beauty; friendship • **budding bough** agriculture • **bough with green leaves** friendship; protection; sign of a tavern; waved at heroes as a sign of their immortal glory • **green bough with flames** the endurance of a hopeless love • **olive bough** peace, reconciliation • **boughs of flowering broom** cover for corpses at funerals • **silver bough** the link between this world and the fairy world • **broken bough** death of a king • **Assyrian** *pine bough with seven branches and seven buds:* Tree of Life; completeness • **Celtic** renewal of youth; may take the place of a magic wand; *apple tree bough:* has the power to erase sad memories with its magic music • **Jewish** attribute of Isaiah; *tent of boughs:* the Feast of the Tabernacles • **Scandinavian** *boxwood boughs:* used in lieu of palms on Palm Sunday; grave decoration • *see also* **golden bough; tree**

boundary *see* **threshold**

bouquet sweet thoughts; tribute • **flower language** gallantry; *large group of gathered flowers:* we die together

bow (archery) war; power; death; hunting; exhausting strain; the will; the tension between physical and spiritual forces; the tension from which desires spring; worldly power; weapon of kings, hunters, common soldiers; fate; emblem of Sagittarius • **Christian** worldly power • **Egyptian** attribute of Anubis • **Greco-Roman** *silver bow:* attribute of Apollo; *silver bow of Artemis/Diana:* the crescent moon; *bow with quiver:* attribute of Orion, sometimes Heracles/Hercules • **heraldic** martial readiness • **Hindu** will power; warlike power; military superiority; emblem of kingship; attribute of Arjuna, Vishnu, Karttikeya, Rudra; *rainbow-like bow:* attribute of Shiva • **Islamic** divine power • **Islamic** the power of God; the grip of the bow is seen as uniting Allah and Mohammed • **Sumero-Semitic** spiritual authority; ultimate decision-making power; attribute of Ishtar, Inanna, sovereign high priests, those who held authority from deities • **Taoist** the Tao that brings down the high and raises the low, takes away excess, and supplies needs • **Yoruban** *miniature bow:* emblem of Ohossi • *see also* **archer; arrow; bow and arrows; bowstring; quiver (archery)**

bow and arrows penetrating inquisitiveness; fire and lightning; action as a means of effecting the will; attribute of America personified (both continents), putti • **arrow shot from a bow** action that cannot be taken back; ejaculation • **bow shooting arrow upward** the sublimation of desire • **centaur with bow and arrows** the fiery darts of the wicked • **Chinese** *white-faced long-bearded man with bow and arrows and small boy:* Chang Hsien • **Buddhist** will power; the bow is the mind that dispatches the arrows of the five senses; emblem of Buddhism • **Greco-Roman** attribute of Eros/Cupid, Aphrodite/Venus, Apollo, Selene/Luna; *silver bow and arrows:* attribute of Artemis/Diana • **heraldic** war power; marksmanship • **Hindu** *flower bow and arrows:* attribute of Kama • **Japanese** love • **Jewish** attribute of Esau • *see also* **archer; arrow; bow (archery); bowstring; quiver (archery)**

bowels *see* **intestines**

bower the feminine principle; shelter; protection • **Christian** the Virgin Mary

bowing honor; respect; humbleness

bowl limitation; family; poverty; begging; charity; gossip; attribute of Diogenes, the Cumean sibyl • **overturned bowl** the emptiness of worldly things • **filled bowl** riches; plenty; gluttony • **bowl of water** the feminine receptive principle; fertility • **Buddhist** *seven bowls at a shrine:* the seven offerings for an honored guest • **Christian** attribute of the Virgin Mary, St. Alexis • **Hindu** attribute of Ganesha; *bowl of blood:* attribute of Shiva; *ladle and bowl:* attribute of Kali • *see also* **alms bowl**

bowstring • **Hindu** *bowstring of stinging bees or flowers:* attribute of Kama • *see also* **arrow; bow (archery); quiver (archery)**

box the feminine principle; the maternal body; the unconscious; containment; treasure; secret keeper; container of tradition, the divine • **alms box** charity; benevolence • **closed box** secrecy • **opening a box** taking a risk • **putting something into a coffer** sanctification; safeguarding; tradition • **opening a box in good circumstances** divine revelation • **unsanctioned opening of a box** presumption; a dangerous act with unforeseen consequences • **Christian** *box of ointment:* attribute of SS Mary of Bethany, Mary of Egypt, Cosmas, Damian; *alabaster box:* attribute of Mary Magdalene • **Greek** *box of ointment:* attribute of Phaon • *see also* **Ark of the Covenant; Pandora's Box**

boxwood prosperity; grace; tenacity; resolve; perseverance; stoicism; incorruptibility; immortality; youth; vigor; vitality; perpetuity • **Christian** the abiding grace of the Church • **flower language** stoicism • **Gallic** eternity • **Greco-Roman** sacred to Aphrodite/Venus, Cybele;

Hades/Pluto; associated with burial, death, love, immortality, sterility, the life cycle • **Scandinavian** *boxwood boughs:* used in lieu of palms on Palm Sunday; grave decoration

boy immaturity; the future; neophyte • **Chinese** *white-faced long-bearded man with bow and arrows and small boy:* Chang Hsien • *see also* **child; man; putto**

Boyne River • **Irish** an aspect of the cosmic river from which all comes and all returns

bracelet continuity; wholeness; marriage; eternity; a cycle; learning; a gift to bind; attribute of royalty • **serpent bracelet** succession; dissolution and reintegration; the eternal cycling of the ages • **Nigerian** *seven bracelets:* attribute of Oshun

braces (dental) the need for restraint of ideas or emotions; immaturity; attribute of adolescents

bracken poor man's soap; associated Mercury (planet) • **Irish** fecundity • *see also* **fern**

Brahman caste *see* **caste**

braids *see* **hair**

brain fantasy; memory; reason; intellect • **Tibetan** *woman eating brains:* Lha-mo

bramble lowliness; envy; remorse; sin, sometimes major sin (especially when growing); death; entanglement • **Christian** Christ's crown of thorns; attribute of the Virgin Mary • **Jewish** divine love; dangerous pride • *see also* **briers; thorn**

branch *see* **bough**

branding membership in or separation from a group; subjugation; humiliation; punishment • **the letter B as a brand** blasphemer • **M branded on the thumb** a murderer • *see also* **tattooing**

brass boldness; shamelessness; baseness in comparison to gold or silver; obstinate resistance; mentality; firmness; strength; hardness; drought; eloquence; sometimes associated with the underworld, the devil, Venus (planet), the archangels Anael, Michael, Zadkiel, Samael • **Armenian** *demon with brass fingernails:* an al • **Christian** *brass feet:* understanding • **Greek** *brass tower:* prison of Danae • **Jewish** *laver of brass:* Old Testament worship • **Middle Ages** strength; durability; Christ's Divinity

brazier attribute of Constancy personified • **Jewish** *brazier with wood and knife:* associated with Abraham and Isaac • **Roman** *woman snatching coals from brazier:* Porcia Catonis; *soldier with hand in brazier:* Mucius Scaevola

bread fecundity; life; goodness; hospitality; the means of sustaining life and soul; nourishment; visible and manifest life; care and nurture; food of the poor • **breaking of bread** hospitality; killing, in a ritual sacrifice • **loaf of bread** charity to the poor; can have a sexual connotation according to shape • **shared bread** shared and united life • **bread and water** prisoner's food • **round loaf of bread** fertility; sacred food • **crust of bread** something valueless; poverty; deprivation • **white bread** once the food of the rich, now sometimes considered soulless, without taste • **brown bread** once the food of the poor, now considered hearty and healthful • **bread and wine** man and divinity respectively; the feminine and masculine respectively; androgyny; the visible manifestation of the spirit and divine ecstasy respectively; the combination of solid and liquid; food of funerals • **Christian** the body of Christ; the sustainer of life; God's providence; *bread and wine:* the body and blood of Christ respectively; the two natures of Christ; *Christ with baskets of bread:* Christ's Feeding of the Five Thousand; *loaf of bread with a serpent emerging from it:* attribute of St. Benedict; *loaf of bread carried by a raven:* God's providence, attribute of St. Paul the Hermit; *two loaves of bread:* attribute of St. Philip; *three loaves of bread:* attribute of St. Mary of Egypt; *Capuchin monk receiving bread from a child:* St. Felix of Cantalice • **Jewish** *loaf of bread:* attribute of Elijah; *bread with chalice:* associated with Melchizidek; *twelve loaves:* the 12 tribes of Israel, months of the year, zodiac signs; *communal eating of bread and salt:* friendship that cannot be broken • **Sumero-Semitic** communion; attribute of Anu; *breaking of bread:* providing food for the souls of the dead

breaking destruction; despoiling; the lunar cycle • **breaking a glass** the transitoriness of human life • **breaking a tablet** the contract or partnership or the rescinding of a debt • **breaking a funeral object** releases its soul so that the dead can take it to the next world • **breaking bread** hospitality; killing, in a ritual sacrifice • **Christian** *breaking the Host in the mass:* the death of Christ's body • **Sumero-Semitic** *breaking bread:* providing food for the souls of the dead • *see also* **dismemberment**

breastplate righteousness as a defense; courage; heroism; protection; preservation; judgment • **Christian** *soldier in armor with red cross on breastplate:* St. Maurice • **Greco-Roman** *mounted on a pole:* attribute of Athena/Minerva • **Jewish** attribute of Aaron, priests; *breastplate in the middle of the ephod:* the Cosmic Center • **Tibetan** *metal mirror breastplate:* attribute of Nagpa

breasts charity; plenty; innocence; devotion; motherhood; nourishment; protection; fertility; consolation; comfort; wisdom; prudence; happiness; hope; love • **left breast** the moon • **right breast** the sun • **woman with one breast exposed** attribute of a warrior, courtesan • **bare breasts** candidness; humility; grief; repentance; penitence • **woman squeezing her breasts** generosity • **woman with bare breasts and veiled face** Prudence personified • **toad hanging from a woman's breasts** attribute of Lust personified • **multiple breasts** fertility; abundance; fertility • **breasts thrust forward** courage; challenge; wantonness • **woman expressing milk from her breasts** Mercy, Benignity personified • **breast milk from a Muse falling on a book or musical instrument** inspiration • **beating one's breast** anguish; grief; repentance • **woman with many breasts** Diana of Ephesus; Mother Nature (especially when surrounded by flowers, fruits, and/or vegetables) • **Christian** *breasts in a plate:* attribute of St. Agatha of Sicily • **Druidic** *androsphinx with many breasts:* fertility, mother • **Finnish** *beautiful woman with enormous breasts she can throw over her shoulder:* a nakinneito • **Mexican Indian** *woman with 400 breasts:* Mayauel • *see also* **milk; nursing**

breath soul; spirit; purification; the divine element in man breathing assimilation of spiritual power; life; passion; life-giving power; power of the spirit; the spirit of God; the transient, insubstantial, elusive; spiritual insight • **breathing** the alternating rhythm of life and death, manifestation and reabsorption into the universe • **breathing or blowing on a person** expelling evil spirits; conferring the Holy Spirit • **Celtic** possessed magical powers

breeches *see* **trousers**

breeze the spirit energizing the mental plane; the clearing away of misconception; amorous yearning; fertility; the voice of the gods • *see also* **wind**

briars *see* **briers**

bricks dependability; substance; permanence; birth; a settled way of life; restraint • **Akkadian** Marduk created bricks immediately after earth, water, and life • **Babylonian** emblem of Mami • **English** lower class upstart • **Jewish** *bricks and whip:* Israel's Old Testament captivity and forced labor; *making bricks without straw:* punishment

bride the soul; fertility; freshness; innocence; inexperience; expectation • **Christian** the Church; *bride and groom together:* the Church and Christ respectively

bridegroom fertility; freshness; expectation • *see also* **bride**

bridge connection between worlds; connection between heaven and earth; transition from one state of being to another; link between the perceptible and the imperceptible; change; peace; man as mediator • **crossing a perilous bridge** return to the lost paradise; proof of spiritual worth; victory over death; the way to enlightenment • **narrow bridge, knife-edged bridge** the narrow separation between opposites; the spacelessness of the supernatural realm; things accessible only by mind and spirit • **river or gorge crossed by a bridge** the banks or sides represent different worlds life/death, mortality/immortality, body/spirit, etc. • **devil's bridge** a bridge so difficult to make that the devil's aid is enlisted for the cost of the first soul who uses it • **heraldic** patience; stability; justice; governor; magistrate • **Islamic** *bridge of seven arches:* the seven duties of the faith • **Italian** *naked man wrestling a knight on a bridge:* the rescue of Angelica • **Persian** *bridge guarded by two dogs:* the Cinvat Bridge

bridle *see* **bit and bridle**

briers sins, sometimes major sins (especially growing); death; grief; rejection; modesty; solitude; parasite • *see also* **bramble; sweet brier; thorn**

brimstone *see* **sulfur**

briony *see* **bryony**

broccoli tranquility

Brontes • **Greco-Roman** thunder • *see also* **Cyclops**

bronze mentality; firmness; endurance; purification; a sacred metal; incorruptibility; immortality; unswerving justice; associated with 8th, 19th wedding anniversaries, the archangels Zadkiel, Samael • **Christian** *bronze feet:* understanding • **Greco-Roman** *bronze hooves:* attribute of the Arcadian Hind • **Greek** *bronze gong:* struck at the death of a king, the eclipse of the moon; *bronze giant:* Talos • **Jewish** *bronze serpent:* healing, God's protection, attribute of Moses; *bronze altar horns:* gave sanctuary to the person who grabbed them • **Roman** *bronze palace:* attribute of Fama

brooch may indicate the wearer's trade • **as a gift** broken love or friendship • **in the shape of an animal** endows the wearer with the characteristics of the animal

brook deceit; spiritual guidance; morning; vulva

broom (plant) war; zeal; servitude; humbleness; rejected love; associated with North, kingship • **branches of flowering broom** used to cover

corpses at funerals • **flower language** neatness; humbleness • **heraldic** humility; ardor; House of Plantagenet • **Hindu** *bundle of broom in her right hand:* attribute of Sitala • **Jewish** associated with Elijah on Mt. Carmel

broom (sweeping) victory; dominance; insight; wisdom; sacred power; power to do away with worry and trouble; servility; witch's steed; emblem of housework; attribute of housewives, well-meaning fairies • **broom placed by a cottage door** the woman of the house is not at home • **Chinese** wisdom; insight; removal of worries and difficulties • **Japanese** used for ritual purification

brothers deep friendship; family devotion; duality; often contrasting pairs of opposites such as Romulus and Remus, Cain and Abel, and in Southeastern European folklore, God and Satan • **younger brother** the youthful part of oneself • **older brother** the wiser part of oneself; Christ • *see also* **monks; twins**

brown the earth; the material world; grief; barrenness; depression; spiritual death and degradation; renunciation of the world; modesty; melancholy; sorrow; calmness; trustworthiness; conservatism; practical knowledge; Victorian lack of emotion or spirituality; associated with Autumn, Virgo, Neptune (planet); drabness • **Chinese** the Sung dynasty • **Christian** spiritual death; renunciation; poverty; penitence; death to the world; degradation; *brown habit tied with a knotted rope:* attribute of Franciscans • **Hindu** associated with the Northern region • **Kabalistic** associated with the archangels Lumiel, Sandalphon

Brunhild • **Norse** the dormant earth brought to life by the sun; the unattainable object of inordinate passion; the renunciation of personal advantage for the sake of love; the dual knowledge of heaven and earth

brush *see* **broom (sweeping)**

Brussels sprouts light heartedness; gaiety

bryony associated with witchcraft • **flower language** *black bryony:* be my support • *see also* **mandrake**

bubble hollowness; emptiness of material existence or personality; a dream; fragile hope; joy; brevity of life; transience; lack of substance; gaiety; mindlessness; folly • **Buddhist** the transience of the world of illusion

Bucentaur • **Italian** the powers of instinct and procreation

Bucephalus • **Macedonian** the deathless devotion of a servant to a single master

buck *see* **stag**

buckbean • **flower language** calm, repose

bucket attribute of Fortune personified • **knocking over a bucket** death • **Christian** attribute of St. Florian; *bucket of milk:* the spiritual nourishment of Christ and the Church

buckeye *see* **horse chestnut (buckeye)**

buckle virginity; aristocracy; fidelity in authority • **buckling up** defense; protection • **unbuckling** freedom • **Egyptian** strength; power; the goodwill and protection of Isis • **heraldic** tenacity; steadfastness; readiness; fidelity; authority; victory

buckler divine defense

Buddha • **Buddhist** love; contemplation; realization of selfhood; divine wisdom; virtue • **Japanese** *fat laughing Buddha:* Hotei

buds future promise; virginity; patent or undeveloped power; youth; immaturity • **half-opened** vitality

buffalo untamed nature; base forces; strength; intimidation; fortitude • **riding a buffalo** mastery over man's animal nature • **Buddhist** Yama (also shown as a man with the head of a buffalo) • **heraldic** valor; bravery; generosity • **Hindu** steed of Yama; *demon buffalo:* Mahisha • **Taoist** steed of Lao Tzu (usually a green buffalo) • *see also* **bison; water buffalo**

buffoon *see* **jester**

bugle call to action; sign of a cuckold • **American** emblem of the US Cavalry • **Christian** the Horn of Salvation • *see also* **trumpet**

bugloss attribute of Lying personified; once used as a cosmetic • **flower language** falsehood • **heraldic** hope; joy

building *see* **construction**

bull the masculine; fertility; the father; the king; usually the masculine principle in nature and connected with the solar, but it also can symbolize the earth and be connected with the lunar; power; male sexual desire, impulsivity; virility; brute strength; tyranny; world-bearer; fertility; Taurus; peace; self-denial; patience; a man 20 to 30 years of age; hoax; rising prices or optimism on the stock market; linked with heaven, death, sacrifice; associated with sky gods, rain, storm, thunder, lightning • **black bull** death • **bull tied to a fig tree** lascivious fury appeased; a man subdued in marriage • **winged bull** guardian spirit • **chariot pulled by a bull** attribute of storm, sky, and solar gods • **man riding a bull** steed of storm, sky, and solar gods • **bull ridden by a woman** the taming of masculine and animal nature • **slaying a bull at the new year** death of Winter and the birth of the creative life force • **sacrifice of a bull** the tri-

umph of spiritual nature over animal nature; suppressing the influence of a dominant father figure • **bull-man** guardian; protection; wards off evil • **bull and bear** two contending powers of the universe, positive/negative, male/female, rising stock market/falling stock market, etc. • **bull's head** sacrifice; death • **bull and lion** death • **roaring of a bull** thunder; rain; fertility • **American** falsehood • **Anatolian** *bull head:* the god Men • **Assyrian** steed of Ashur • **Babylonian** Enlil • **Buddhist** the moral self; the ego; reincarnation; attribute of Yama (also shown as a man with a bull head) • **Celtic** divine power and strength; *brown bull:* Donn Cuailnge • **Chinese** one of the animals of the Twelve Terrestrial Branches • **Christian** brute force; associated with St. John; attribute of SS Sylvester, Ambrose; *brass bull:* attribute of St. Eustace; *bull with wings and nimbus:* emblem of St. Luke; *woman tied between two bulls:* St. Thecla • **Druidic** the sun • **Egyptian** temperance; passive power; Mnevis; Apis; sacred to Ra; associated with Bata, Nut; *thigh of a bull:* the phallic leg of Set, fertility, strength, the North Pole; *seven cows with a bull:* fertility; *black bull with white triangle on the forehead:* emblem of Ptah; *bull with a solar disk between its horns:* fertility, funeral god associated with Osiris • **Fulani** *rooster and/or bull in the streets:* a secret told to everyone • **Gnostic** emblem of Ormuzd • **Greco-Roman** the unleashing of violence; attribute of Zeus/Jupiter, Ares/Mars, Aphrodite/Venus, Europa, Dionysus/Bacchus; *black bull:* sacrifice to Poseidon/Neptune; *white bull:* Zeus; attribute of Dionysus/Bacchus; *white bull bearing a maiden to the sea:* Zeus raping Europa; *two fire-breathing bulls:* guards of the Golden Fleece; *man with the head of a bull:* Dionysus/Bacchus; the Minotaur; *bull ridden by a woman:* Europa • **heraldic** magnanimity; valor; power; servility; bravery; generosity; *bull horns:* strength; fortitude • **Hindu** strength; speed; fertility; reincarnation; the procreative power of nature; Agni; Dyaus; Rudra; Indra; attribute of Agni; *white bull:* Nandi • **Hittite** a form of Teshub • **Jewish** the might of God; associated with Ezekiel; *bull with censer:* Day of Atonement • **Mesopotamian** Gugalanna • **Minoan** the Great God; the reproductive force of nature; associated with earthquakes • **Mithraic** the solar god; victory over man's animal nature; life through death; *bull and lion:* death; *stag and bull:* the moment of death • **Norse** attribute of Thor; sacred to Freyja • **Persian** soul of the world; associated with the moon and the fertility of rain clouds; *bull with golden horns:* incarnation of Verethraghna • **Phoenician** *man with a bull's head:* Moloch; *bull roar:* Baal • **Sumero-Semitic** fertilizing power; Baal; El; steed of Ramman, Adad; a form of the lunar god Sin; the zodiacal year; *winged bull:* guardian spirit; *bull horns:* attribute of Astarte; *bull ridden by a woman:* the woman is Astarte; *bull roar:* Dumuzi • **zodiacal** Taurus; sun, the creative resurgence of Spring • **Zoroastrian** the first animal created and the germ of all later creation • *see also* **cattle; calf; cow; minotaur**

bulldog perseverance; tenacity; stolidity; generosity; courage; emblem of Great Britain; attribute of St. Margaret of Cortona

bullfight the struggle between one's higher and lower natures

bullfinch a scholar; imitation

bullroarer thunder; wind; invocation of a deity • **Amerindian** invocation of the Great Spirit; emblem of the All-Father • **Australian aboriginal** initiation; rainmaking • **Greco-Roman** attribute of Dionysian/Bacchic mystery rites

bulrush salvation; lack of stamina; attribute of Moses; the humble faithful who abide with Christ • **flower language** docility; indiscretion • **heraldic** peace; prosperity

bun with a cross originally the moon and its four quarters • **Anglicanism** eaten on Good Friday

bundle burden; problem • *see also* **fasces; sheaf**

burdock fever remedy • **flower language** persistence; don't touch me; rudeness; pertinacity

burglar *see* **thief**

burial honoring the dead; sorrow; consummation, in its various senses; return to the primal parent; initiation into manhood; being overwhelmed • **burial alive** common criminals were buried in the earth; monks, nuns, noblewomen, wives of knights, Vestal Virgins, etc. might be walled in to save them the shame of execution

burning passion; lust; indignation; shame; venereal disease • **burning animal bones** sends their souls to heaven so that they may be reborn

burning bush *see* **bush**

burr importunity; coherence; discomfort • **burr sticking to one's clothing** being in love

bush place for lurking, ambush, spying, illicit love; barrenness; usefulness • **Christian** *burning bush:* the Annunciation; the Virgin Mary; divine love; the Church being persecuted but not perishing • **France** *burning bush:* vulva • **Jewish** *burning bush:* the presence of God; the giving of the Law to Moses

buskin nobility; vagina; tragedy, especially in drama

bustard polygamy • **as a day bird** uncatchable prey • **as a night bird** the changeful world • **as a migratory bird** the questing human soul • **African** the union of souls and fertility; interpenetration of matter by the soul • **Berber** marriage of souls; fertility; the descent of souls to the material world

butler masculine subservience; order; helpfulness • *see also* **servant**

butter divine love and wisdom; luxury; food in general • **churning butter** coition; masturbation; creation • **buttered hay** deceit; cheating • **Hindu** associated with sacrifice; *put in a fire:* restores Agni to life

butterburr associated with Mars (planet)

buttercup • **flower language** cheerfulness; childishness; ingratitude; desire for riches • **Greco-Roman** mockery; spite; madness; emblem of Ares/Mars

butterfly the soul; freedom; unconscious attraction toward light, God; life; rebirth; joy; the psyche; inconstancy; love; liberty; frivolity; superficiality; transitoriness; rashness; wantonness; lightness; spring; resurrection; eternal life; the Great Goddess; intuition as opposed to logic • **red butterfly** a witch • **Australian aboriginal** a returning spirit of the dead • **Aztecan** the soul that escapes at death; spirit of a woman who died in childbirth; associated with -5-, Itzpapalotl; *butterfly among flowers:* dead warrior's soul; *pectoral butterfly ornament:* emblem of Huehueteotl • **Celtic** the soul; fire • **Chinese** immortality; joy; abundant leisure; high spirits; the pleasures of good living; *butterfly with chrysanthemum:* beauty in old age; *butterfly with plum:* longevity • **Christian** abundant life; Easter; occasional attribute of the Christ child • **Egyptian** *winged foot crushing a butterfly:* Hapi • **Greco-Roman** immortality; the soul; the psyche; Psyche; *winged foot crushing a butterfly:* Serapis; *butterfly wings:* attribute of Zephyr, the Horae • **heraldic** frailty; transitory life; psyche; soul • **Japanese** a vain woman; a geisha; a fickle lover; *pair of butterflies:* conjugal happiness; *white butterfly:* a spirit of the dead • **Maori** the soul; longevity; immortality • **Mexican Indian** the sun that passed through the Underworlds at night; associated with death, resurrection, sacrifice • **North American Indian** everlasting life • **Siouan** guardian of West • **Vietnamese** the wish for longevity • **Zairean** the soul

butterfly weed associated with rebirth, healing transformation • **flower language** let me go

buttons (clothing) unification; connection; associated with wealth • **Chinese** *large buttons on* *ceremonial robes:* sun and moon; *small buttons on a ceremonial robe:* stars

buzzard despicability; death; old age; the feminine; the maternal; harbinger of death, destruction

C

C the crescent moon; associated with intellectual qualities, optimism, happiness, success despite obstacles, -3-, Earth, Venus (planet) • **Roman** numeral for 100 • **tarot** the Empress

cabbage disentanglement; peasantry; sun emblem; the self-willed • **flower language** gain; profit

Cabeiri • **Mediterranean** unknown spiritual powers; the hidden aspect of the godhead; the mystery of divine energy

cabin rustic life; adversity; hermitage

cabinet heart

cable strength

cacalia • **flower language** adulation

cactus protection; the desert; a waste land; warmth; ardent love; grandeur; hidden treasure • **flower language** warmth; *serpentine cactus:* horror • **heraldic** bravery; endurance • **Mexican Indian** *peyote fluid:* dew of immortality • **North American Indian** *cactus flower:* courtship

caduceus moral equilibrium; self-control; health of body and spirit; union of the sexes; fertility; phallus; eloquence; reason; peace; protection; truce; commerce and industry; magic wand; human ambiguity; attribute of sacred persons, heralds, ambassadors, messengers, doctors, Peace personified • **caduceus in a woman's hand** felicity; peace; concord; security; fortune • **caduceus wings** transcendence; air • **caduceus wand** power • **caduceus snakes** dualism, such as healing/poison, male/female, good/evil; opposites eventually to be united • **alchemic** *caduceus snakes:* sulfur and Mercurius, sleeping and waking; the power of transformation, sythesis of opposites • **Egyptian** attribute of Anubis, Serapis, Thoth • **Greco-Roman** moral equilibrium; safe conduct; attribute of Hermes/Mercury, Heracles/Hercules, Aphrodite/Venus, Asclepius, Concordia • **heraldic** medicine; balance; union of opposing forces • **Jewish** attribute of the archangel Raphael • **Sumero-Semitic** attribute of Baal

Caelus *see* **Uranus/Caelus**

cage imprisonment; marriage; cruelty; slavery; bondage; entrapment • *see also* **bird cage; prison**

caiman attribute of America (both continents)

personified • **Aztecan** attribute of Cipactli • **Gurani** ferryman of the dead • *see also* **crocodile**

Cain • **Christian** the Jews who killed Christ • **Jewish** agriculture; jealousy; rage; vengeance; selfishness; human responsibility; murder; the first murderer; fratricide; the attempt to win salvation or God's love by works

cairngorm • **Scottish** patriotism; homesickness

cake feast; fertility; offering to a god; food of the rich • **sacrificial cakes with a cross** the moon and its four quarters

calabash *see* **gourd**

caladrius • **Christian** Christ • **Roman** *turning away from a sick person:* death; *turning toward a sick person:* recovery

caldron *see* **cauldron**

calendar • **Christian** *red dates:* holy days

calf *see* **leg**

calf (cattle) weakness; clumsiness; sacrifice; immaturity; innocence; endearment; childishness; folly; stupidity; a boy of up to 20 years of age; the young Dionysus/Bacchus • **chariot pulled by calves** attribute of Spring personified • **lion lying with calf** peace; Paradise regained; primordial unity; the Golden Age; the end of the temporal world • **Christian** associated with the prodigal son's return; a beast of the Throne of God; *unblemished calf:* Christ • **Hindu** the mind of Aditi • **Jewish** *golden calf:* wealth; materialism instead of spirituality, the recurring temptation to worship wealth, power, sensuality; associated with Aaron, Baal • *see also* **cattle; bull; cow**

Caliban spiritual decay

calla aethiopica • **flower language** magnificent beauty

Calliope • **Greek** muse associated with eloquence, heroic poetry, epic poetry

calliope (music) emblem of the circus

calumet *see* **pipe (smoking)**

calycanthus • **flower language** benevolence

camel asceticism; patience; long-suffering; endurance; resistance; temperance; obedience; submission; prudence; sobriety; slyness; greed; salaciousness; pride; awkwardness; clumsiness; emblem of the Middle East; attribute of the personifications of Asia, Fury, Discretion, Obedience; Middle East, Temperance • **camel's hair clothes** penitence; royalty • **kneeling camel** humility; docility; submission • **herd of camels** wealth; prosperity • **Arabian** a term of endearment • **Bedouin** wealth • **Christian** temperance; royalty; dignity; obedience; stamina; attribute of the Magi; *camel's hair clothes:* attribute of John the Baptist • **German** a large stupid person • **heraldic** stamina; contentment; docility; patience; perseverance; stubbornness • **Hindu** rarely, an emblem of malevolence • **Jewish** an unclean animal; *flock of camels:* wealth; *camel's hair clothes:* attribute of Elijah • **Persian** associated with the dragon-serpent; incarnation of Verethaghna • **Middle East** royalty; dignity • **Roman** the personification of Arabia on coins

camellia steadfastness; ephemeral, fragile beauty; exotic, seductive beauty; pure beauty; • **Chinese** beauty; health; physical and mental strength • **flower language** *red:* unpretending excellence; *white:* perfected loveliness • **Japanese** sudden death; *camellia japonica:* emblem of Japan

camomile *see* **chamomile**

camphor chastity; the senses; an anti-aphrodisiac; charm against evil spirits • **Christian** attribute of the Virgin Mary

canary idle chatter

canary grass • **flower language** perseverance

cancer (disease) spiritual decay; impending doom; a debilitating situation; war with oneself

Cancer (zodiac) the mediator between the formal and non-formal worlds; the threshold through which the soul enters upon its incarnation; associated with sensitivity, imagination, moodiness, self-pity, emotionalism, the Moon, the ocean, bodies of water, mother's milk, plant sap, the feminine principle, sheltering, preserving, the subconscious universal soul, subjectivity, memories, dreams • **Chaldean** gateway for souls coming from heaven to earth

candelabrum life; spiritual life; the spiritual light of salvation; the presence of God • **seven-branched** Menorah, the chakras • **Christian** *three-branched:* the Trinity; *two-branched:* the dual nature of Christ • *see also* **candle; candlestick; Menorah**

candle life, especially that of an individual; hope; learning; festivity; the external soul; charm against evil spirits; light; light in the darkness of life; the vitalizing power of the sun; evanescence; romance; attribute of Faith personified, the Libyan sibyl • **funeral candles** light in the world to come • **bayberry candles** the New Year; lucky; prosperity • **spark in a candle flame** a stranger or letter will come • **Christmas tree candles** souls; heavenly bodies • **Halloween candle** *going out between 11 and midnight:* evil omen; *staying lit between 11 and midnight:* one year free from witchcraft • **Christian** the divine light; spiritual joy; Christ as the light of the world; attribute of St. Gertrude; *candle held by a nun, blown out by a demon:* St. Genevieve; *two candles:* the dual nature of Christ; *three candles:* the Trinity; *five candles:* the five wounds of

Christ; *five candles lit, with five candles unlit:* the five wise virgins, and the five foolish virgins; *seven candles:* Jesus; *vigil candle:* the presence of the Host at the altar in Roman Catholic and Anglican churches, honor to an icon; *burial with an unlighted candle:* an excommunicated person; *crossed candles or candles with an iron comb:* attribute of St. Blaise; *Paschal candle:* the presence of Christ with the disciples for forty days after his Resurrection; the light of the risen Christ; the pillar of fire that guided the Israelites for forty years; *candles set around a wheel rim:* attribute of SS Blaise, Donatian • **Eastern Orthodox** *two candles joined:* the dual nature of Christ; *three candles joined:* the Trinity • **folkloric** *blue flame:* a spirit passing; the presence of witches • **heraldic** transitoriness; life; light; spirituality • **Kabalistic** *three candles:* wisdom, strength, and beauty • *see also* **flame; candelabrum; Menorah; candlestick**

candlestick the beauty of ripe age; spiritual illumination • **Christian** *seven golden candlesticks:* the seven early Christian churches of Asia Minor • **Kabalistic** *three candlesticks:* wisdom, strength, and beauty • *see also* **candelabrum; Menorah**

candy associated with sixth wedding anniversaries

candytuft indifference

cane (walking cane) old age; cripple; blindness • **gold-headed cane** attribute of doctors, gentlemen • **white cane** attribute of the blind • *see also* **crutch**

cannibalism absorbing the power of the person eaten • **Australian aboriginal** *cannibal giant:* Thardid-Jimbo

cannon war; destruction; fecundation • **Christian** attribute of St. Barbara • **heraldic** *cannon and/or cannon balls:* one who has endured artillery fire

canoe the crescent moon; a lunar barque; primitive transportation; vagina; associated with North American Indians, voyageurs • **Iroquoian** *miniature canoe model:* charm against drowning • **Maori** the Mother of the Race

Canopus • **Hindu** home of Agastya

canopy regal dignity; royalty; sovereign power; protection; paradise; the celestial realm • **round canopy** the sky, sun • **square canopy** the earth • **baldachin** spiritual and/or temporal authority • **Buddhist** the Sacred Tree of Enlightenment; one of the Eight Emblems of Good Augury; *white canopy:* the pure mind embracing the Dharma and protecting human beings • **Chinese** official rank; royalty; sovereign power; protection • **Hindu** spiritual and temporal power • **Indic** *square canopy:* attribute of a priest; *round canopy:* attribute of a king

Canterbury, England seat of Anglicanism; mystic center

Canterbury bell • **flower language** acknowledgment

cap nobility; used to hide the horns of a cuckold • **cap with colored feathers** unaccountable actions; fancy • **Egyptian** *bearded man wearing a cap with two tall plumes:* Amen-Ra • **Greco-Roman** *eggshell or conical caps of Castor and Pollux:* the two halves of Leda's egg from which they were born, also the two hemispheres; *cap of invisibility:* made by Cyclops for Hades, worn by Perseus and Hermes/Mercury • **Japanese** worn on the sixty-first birthday • **Jewish** *blue ritual cap:* the heavens, the sky • **Teutonic** nobility; power; *cape of invisibility (Tarnkappe):* owned by Alberich, worn by Siegfried • **Ural-Altaic** worn by a shaman as a sign of power • *see also* **hat; skullcap**

cape *see* **cloak**

capon dull fool; love letter; bribe for judges; eunuch • *see also;* **chicken; rooster**

Capricorn (zodiac) prosperity; the dual tendencies of life toward both the high and the low, the physical and the spiritual; the end of a cycle; associated with the winter solstice, earth, reliability, good humor, patience, rigidity, pessimism, miserliness, Saturn (planet), the archangel Cassiel • **Chaldean** Gate of the Gods through which souls passed into heaven

Capricornus (mythology) associated with the Winter solstice, Pan/Faunus • **Babylonian** a form of Ea-Oannes

capstan • **Christian** attribute of St. Erasmus • *see also* **windlass**

captive the spirit held latent • **captives** attribute of St. Vincent Ferrer

car *see* **vehicle**

carbuncle (stone) blood; war; bloodshed; anger (especially when related to the eyes); martyrdom; suffering; constancy; self confidence; energy; determination; assurance; success; strength; charity; love • **Christian** Christ's Passion and suffering; *five carbuncles:* the five wounds of Christ • **folkloric** *carbuncle losing its luster:* omen of disaster • **Islamic** illuminates the fourth heaven • **Jewish** attribute of the High Priest's breastplate

cardamine • **flower language** paternal error

cardinal flower • **flower language** distinction

cardinal's hat • **Christian** attribute of SS Vincent Ferrer, Jerome (although he was not a cardinal); *lying on the ground or hanging in a tree:* attribute of St. Bonaventure

cards *see* **playing cards; tarot**

Carmel, Mt. • **Baha'i** World Axis • **Christian** associated with the founding of the Carmelite order • **Jewish** associated with Elijah

carnation endurance; fidelity; the Virgin Mary; admiration; fascination; love; divine love; female love; caprice; associated with Scorpio, Jupiter (planet); emblem of Persia • **green carnation** emblem of St. Patrick's Day, homosexuality • **pink carnation** motherhood; a mother's undying love • **purple carnation** capriciousness • **light red carnation** admiration • **dark red carnation** betrothal; admiration; marriage; passionate love • **white carnation** pure love • **yellow carnation** rejection • **striped carnation** a love that cannot be shared • **American** *white carnation:* associated with Mother's Day • **Christian** *pink carnation:* the tears of the Virgin Mary • **flower language** fascination; woman's love; bonds of affection; health and energy; *red carnation:* admiration, my heart aches for you; *deep red carnation:* alas, my poor heart; *striped carnation:* refusal, Sorry I can't be with you, I wish I could be with you; *solid color carnation:* acceptance; *yellow carnation:* disdain, you have disappointed me, rejection; *pink carnation:* I'll never forget you; *purple carnation:* capriciousness; *white carnation:* sweet and lovely, innocence, pure love, a woman's good luck gift • **Chinese** marriage • **French** misfortune; *purple carnation:* funeral condolence • **heraldic** caprice; admiration; fascination; impulsiveness; joy; capriciousness; devotion • **Korean** *red and pink carnations:* filial affection

carnelian courage; distinction; self-confidence; friendship; associated with the archangel Michael; charm for reproduction, sexuality, peace, eloquence, health, protection from jealousy, anger, hatred, storms, black magic; stone for a 17th wedding anniversary; formerly the birthstone for August • **biblical** emblem of hope, patience • **Islamic** *carnelian ring:* attribute of Mohammed

carnival invocation of primordial chaos; the desperate quest for a way out of time; the desire to concentrate all the possibilities of existence in a given period of time

carp perseverance; fortitude; voracity; war; energy; courage; longevity; a talkative person; complaint; considered a masculine fish • **eaten as food** poverty • **Bambaran** vulva, clitoris • **Chinese** perseverance; literary eminence; courage; longevity; lucky omen; steed of the Immortals; *twin carp:* the union of lovers; *carp model on rooftop:* charm against fire • **Japanese** courage; dignity; resignation to fate; perseverance; ambition; lucky; success; love; longevity; virility; emblem of boys, young men, samurai • **Vietnamese** *Golden Carp:* an evil spirit

carpenter one who brings order out of chaos; the Creator • **Christian** Christ; St. Joseph; *carpenter visited by an angel:* St. Joseph • **Greek** Dedalus; *carpenter building a wooden cow:* Dedalus working for Pasiphae • **Jewish** *building an ark:* Noah

carpenter's square *see* **square (tool)**

carpet luxury; sovereignty • **unrolling carpet** unfolding of life • **red carpet** honor; special treatment

carriage elegance; upper class vehicle • **golden carriage** spiritual qualities allied with wisdom • **pumpkin carriage** attribute of Cinderella • **Lithuanian** *small twin horses pulling the carriage of the sun:* the Asvieniai • *see also* **vehicle**

carrion low life; the flesh; death; despair

cask famine; the maternal body; wealth; pleasure • **bottomless cask** useless labor; the apparent futility of earthly existence • *see also* **box**

casket death • **Christian** *three caskets:* Epiphany • **Hindu** the head; the inner void that surrounds and protects the Self; *golden casket:* dwelling place of the Self • *see also* **sarcophagus; chest**

Cassandra • **Greek** unheeded prophet

cassia • **Chinese** Tree of Life in Paradise; lucky; a rise to greatness; nobility; a staple food of the Immortals; immortality • *see also* **cinnamon**

Cassiel, Archangel associated with Saturn (planet), lead, North, onyx, sapphires, turquoise, salt, -15-, -21-, 7th heaven, Capricorn, Aquarius, Saturday, alders, beech, cypress, evergreens, oaks, yews, crows, ravens, crocodiles • **Kabalistic** associated with -3-, black • **tarot** associated with the World

cassock • **Christian** devotion to Christ and the Church; *white:* attribute of a pope; *red:* attribute of a cardinal; *violet or purple:* attribute of a bishop; *black:* attribute of a priest; *black cassock with square hat:* attribute of a Jesuit; *black cassock with red piping:* attribute of a monsignor, dean; *cassocks of other colors:* may indicate that the person depicted was originally a member of a religious order, and the cassock color is used for habits of that particular order

castanets little annoyances; associated with Spain, Spanish dancing • **Taoist** the two contending powers of the universe; emblem of Ts'ao Ko-Chu

caste the pattern of the universe; the four cardinal points • **Brahman caste** associated with the sacerdotal, the polar regions, Winter, North • **Kshatriya caste** associated with the royal, warriors, the rising sun, spring, East • **Sudra caste** associated with servants, darkness, obscurity, Autumn, West • **Vaishya caste** associated with trade, agriculture, the setting sun, Summer, South

castle safety; impregnability; heavenly wealth; that which is difficult to obtain; authority; sovereignty; defense; the transcendent soul; the psyche; inner refuge; cavern of the heart; an embattled spiritual power ever on watch • **black castle** evil; abode of Hades/Pluto, evil powers; an alchemist's den; another world; place of no return; utter failure; unsatisfied desire • **castle of darkness** the unconscious; unfocused desire; bewilderment • **white castle** achievement; treasure; spiritual perfection; salvation; abode of a heavenly power; a beneficent place • **castle of light** awareness; aroused desire • **assaulting a castle** spiritual testing • **capturing or breaking into a castle** gaining spiritual treasure • **crossing a castle moat or drawbridge** *see* **bridge** • **Christian** *turreted castle:* attribute of the Virgin Mary • **heraldic** grandeur; nobility; solidity; strategy; safety; protection; strength • **Jewish** *turreted castle:* attribute of David • *see also* **palace**

Castor and Pollux • **Greco-Roman** brotherly love; power in battle; safety at sea; the dual worldly and spiritual nature of all things

castration emasculation; death of a fertility god or hero; a life sacrifice; punishment for rape, adultery • **Frisian** punishment for temple robbing • **Greco-Roman** associated with Attis • **Hindu** punishment for urinating on a person of higher caste

cat domesticity; sensuality; desire; night; the waxing and waning of the moon; ease; cruelty; spite; salacity; independence; magical forces; guardian of marriage; love of freedom; self-indulgence; cleanliness; playfulness; grace; longevity; coquettishness; feminine energy; languor; melancholy; cunning; treachery; intuition; the subconscious; attribute of Eros/Cupid; a man between 70 and 80 years of age; disguise of witches; associated with Saturn (planet) • **black cat** death; darkness; evil; the lunar; unlucky, except in Britain; attribute of witches • **white cat** lucky, except in Britain • **Angora cat** expensive luxury; a pampered and spoiled person, especially a woman • **tortoise-shell cat** lucky • **Siamese cat** exoticism, at least in the West • **coat or cloak of cat skin** humility • **woman with a cat at her feet** Liberty personified • **Amerindian** *wild cat:* stealth • **British** *black cat:* lucky; *white cat:* unlucky • **Buddhism** a cursed animal • **Cambodian** drought; associated with primordial Chaos; *pouring water on a cat:* its howls were thought to awaken Indra who would give rain • **Celtic** underworld powers; a funeral animal • **Chinese** a yin animal; often a good omen; powers of evil; a shapeshifter; associated with witches; *strange cat:* omen of unfavorable change; *black cat:* misfortune; illness • **Christian** Satan; darkness; lust; laziness; attribute of Julian of Norwich, St. Gertrude of Nivelles; *cat at the foot of Christ:* sin overcome • **Egyptian** the lunar; salaciousness; sun rays; personification of Bast; attribute of Isis, Bast, the moon; associated with pregnant women, darkness; sacred to Set; *woman with a cat head or body:* Bast; *cat with a knife in its paw:* Bast's decapitation of Apep • **Finnish** sometime form of a para • **Greco-Roman** Galenthias; attribute of Artemis/Diana, and the goddess of liberty • **heraldic** courage; liberty; individualism; vigilance; indefatigability; cunning; strategy • **Hindu** the beatitude of the animal kingdom; steed of Shosti, Vidali • **Islamic** has seven lives; manifestation of a jinn; *black cat:* has magical properties; *cat flesh:* cure for bewitching; *cat's blood:* used to write powerful charms • **Japanese** peaceful repose; shape-shifter; associated with witches; evil omen; *sitting cat with raised paw:* maneko noko • **Kabalistic** emblem of sin; misuse of the good things of this world • **Mochican** *old man with cat whiskers and teeth:* Ai apaec • **Norse** attribute of Freyja; associated with wind; *chariot drawn by cats:* attribute of Freyja • **Persian** *black cat:* the alter ego, manifestation of a jinn • **Samian** sometime form of a smier-ragatto • **Sumatran** attribute of the guard on the bridge to the underworld • **Vietnamese** mandarins; rapacious government officials • **witchcraft** disguise of witches; *cats and dogs together:* rain makers • *see also* **wildcat**

catalpa • **Chinese** associated with Summer, South, filial piety, the paternal home

catastrophe the beginning of a transformation; the end of a cycle or period; violent change; destruction; loss; setbacks; broken relationships; there is often a positive aspect leading to rebirth, metamorphosis, social change

catchfly • **flower language** pretended love; snare; *red catchfly:* youthful love; *white catchfly:* betrayed

caterpillar parasite; man in this world; greed; ugliness • **Bantu** soul of the dead • **Hindu** transmigration • **Swiss** a tree spirit that would crawl into the brain and cause madness

catfish partial spiritual insight or development

cathedra • **Christian** episcopal dignity; authority; jurisdiction; knowledge; teaching • *see also* **throne**

Catherine wheel solar wheel; torture; great cruelty • **Christian** attribute of St. Catherine of Alexandria • **heraldic** one prepared to undergo great trials for the Christian faith

catnip excitement; used in spells for deception or paradox

Cato • **Roman** moral virtue

cat's eye (stone) platonic affection; longevity; the waning moon; charm against eye diseases, evil; stone for eighteenth and forty-fifth wedding anniversaries • **Assyrian** charm for invisibility • **Hindu** corresponds to the element air

cattail *see* **bulrush**

cattle emotions; desires; baser mental qualities • **cattle in pasture** agriculture; peace • **fat cattle** prosperity • **lean cattle** famine • *see also* **cow**; **bull**; **calf**

Caucasian the spiritual side of man; higher nature • *see also* **complexion**

caul lucky; affirmation of spirituality

cauldron martyrdom; witchcraft; the feminine principle; the Grail; mother; womb; resurrection; sustenance; abundance; fertility; magic vessel of rejuvenation; the underworld; realm of rebirth; inspiration; popularly associated with cannibals • **cauldron of boiling oil** punishment • **magic cauldron** the feminine power of transformation; fecundity; life and death; renewal and rebirth; transmutation and germination of the baser forces of nature; attribute of witches • **witch with a cauldron** Medea • **Celtic** abundance; corresponds to the cornucopia; resuscitation; reproductive earth powers; inexhaustible sustenance; rebirth; restores warriors to life; attribute of Bran, Dagda • **Chinese** receptacle for offerings; container for torture and capital punishment; *I Ching:* , plenty, lucky; *three-legged cauldron:* associated with divination, the Sages • **Christian** attribute of SS Boniface, Fausta, Vitus; *cauldron of boiling oil:* attribute of SS Ansanus, Cecilia, George, John; *eagle rising out of cauldron:* attribute of St. John • **Norse** *Roaring Cauldron:* the source of all rivers • **Welsh** attribute of Keridwen; *Cauldron of Keridwen:* inexhaustibility, regeneration, inspiration • *see also* **kettle**

caulking the limitation of ideas

cave the secretive; the universe; security; impregnability; the unconscious; the hidden; the womb; the womb of Mother Earth; mother; hell; resurrection; rebirth; place of initiation; place of earthly energy; burial; fertility; the human mind; primitive part of the self; the heart; place of union of Self and Ego; meeting place of the divine and human; refuge; passageway between Earth and heaven; primitive shelter; home of gnomes, robbers, monsters • **entering a cave** returning to the womb, one's beginnings • **passing through a cave** overcoming a dangerous obstacle, rebirth • **Amerindian** *series of caves one above the other:* the different worlds • **Celtic** entrance to the other-world; purgatory • **Chinese** the feminine; yin; gate to the Underworld • **Hindu** heart; center; *Cave of the Heart:* dwelling of Atma • **Jewish** *two caves:* associated with Obadiah • **Mithraic** place of worship of Mithras • **Platonic** worldly illusion and obscurity

cavern *see* **cave**

cedar constancy; virtue; strength; nobility; beauty; mystery; longevity; steadfast faith; incorruptibility; majesty; power; royalty; immortality; fertility; mercy; purification; vengeance; prosperity; growth; height; occasionally, God's power to weaken the strong; associated with the archangels Azrael, Michael • **cedar of Lebanon** emblem of Lebanon • **Chinese** fidelity • **Christian** majesty; stateliness; beauty; Christ • **Greco-Roman** emblem of Artemis/Diana • **flower language** strength; *cedar leaf:* I live for thee; *cedar of Lebanon:* incorruptibility, strength, constancy • **Hindu** fertility • **Jewish** incorruptibility • **Sumerian** Tree of Life; possessed magical powers; sacred to Tammuz

cedrela tree • **Chinese** the patriarch of a family

celandine • **flower language** joys to come

celery • **Greco-Roman** happiness; the triumph of youth; associated with funerals; *wild celery leaf crown:* awarded to winners in the Isthmian Games

celery-leaved crowfoot *see* **crowfoot**

celestial dog *see* **tengu**

cellar the unconscious; the subconscious; the instincts; childhood recollection; regression; the repressed; treasure chamber • **Christian** self-knowledge; the innermost heart where one may take stock of graces received • **Islamic** place of divine knowledge; sacred place of withdrawal where one may unite himself with God

censer purifying fire; prayer ascending to heaven; worship; the priesthood; flattery; attribute of Asia personified • **Celtic** attribute of the Lady of the Lake • **Christian** attribute of SS Laurence, Stephen, Maurus • **Jewish** attribute of Aaron, Levi; *censer and crown or scepter:* associated with Melchizedekffl *priests with censers, the ground opening at their feet:* associated with Aaron; *bull*

with censer: the Day of Atonement • *see also* **incense**

centaur domination by baser forces; animal nature; brute force; the superior force of the instincts; man torn between good and evil; the unconscious uncontrolled by the spirit; man's lower nature; a combination of blind power and guiding spirit; the conflict between the benign and savage aspects of nature; lechery; drunkenness; death; adultery; savage passions and excesses; vengeance; heresy; strength and nobility in the service of right • **centaur with bow and arrow** the fiery darts of the wicked • **Christian** heresy; incarnation of the devil; the dual nature of Christ; attribute of St. Anthony the Great; *centaur on a font:* overcoming original sin by baptism • **Greco-Roman** Chiron as the personification of Wisdom; teachers of the gods; occasional attribute of Dionysus/Bacchus • **heraldic** eminence in battle • *see also* **horse**

centaury • **flower language** felicity; delicacy

center the connection between heaven and earth; God; the genitals; going through death to eternity; the supreme being; unity; totality; wholeness; absolute reality; pure being; unmanifest being; the origin of all existence; World Axis; axis uniting all things vertically and horizontally; point of origin, departure, and return; the point where all emerges, revolves around it, and returns; eternity and perfect simultaneity; Paradise; potentiality; transcendence of time and space; the point of resolution and reconciliation where all opposites disappear; the law; associated with the archangels Metatron, Sandalphon • **moving from the center to the circumference** move from unity to manifestation and multiplicity • **moving from the circumference to the center** moving to the spiritual center, unity • **Aristotelian** the unmoved mover • **Buddhist** pure being; enlightenment; Nirvana • **Chinese** perfect peace; divine immanence; stillness; unity with divine will; the Pivot of the Law • **Hindu** pure being; unity; Ishvara; Brahman; point beyond time; the dark source of all light; place of the unconditioned • **Islamic** eye of the heart; the divine abode; the divine station of harmony, equilibrium, order; the incommunicable • **Jewish** the inward presence where God dwells; Shekinah; thought; the beginning of the universe • **North American Indian** the Great Spirit • **Taoist** the Tao; pure being; the "nought but infinity" which is neither this nor that

centipede regression; fragmentation of the psyche

Cerberus • **Greco-Roman** guardian of the underworld threshold; the underworld trinity; base life forces; the terrors of death; the spirit of evil; indwelling demon • **heraldic** past, present, and future; guardianship

cereal grains the seven gifts of the Holy Spirit

Ceres *see* **Demeter/Ceres**

cereus • **flower language** *creeping cereus:* modest genius, horror

chaff worthlessness; barrenness; the transitory; the ungodly; lower qualities

chain mail • **Tibetan** *gold chain mail:* attribute of Da

chains enthrallment; sin; slavery; binding; imprisonment; attachment of the mind to the lower world; the power of the devil; attribute of Vice personified; authority; dignity; unity; legal control; security; strength; matrimony; communication; command; link between heaven and earth; the Great Chain of Being • **multiple chains** usually punishment, suffering, slavery, hopeless misfortune • **broken chains** liberation • **golden chain** honor; dignity; respect; wealth; the spirit binding earth and heaven • **person in chains** enslavement by sin or earthly desires • **Buddhist** man's bondage to existence in the world of phenomena • **Celtic** communication of Ogmios to the ears of his listeners • **Christian** attribute of SS Balabina, Peter, the Flagellation of Christ; *demon in chains:* attribute of SS Bernard, Vincent; *broken chains:* attribute of St. Leonard • **heraldic** the refusal to be defamed or humiliated; honor; acceptable and weighty service; *chains with crowns and/or collars:* willingness to meet one's obligations for past services or favor • **Greco-Roman** ladder to heaven; attribute of Hermes/Mercury • **Islamic** the hierarchical universe; the Chain of Being • **Jewish** *chain and scepter:* Joseph's advancement

chair pause; rest; old age; authority; judgment; sovereignty • **empty chair** absence of authority; the deceased; undying hope • **occupied chair** implies the occupant's superior position to those who are standing • **raised chair** superiority; control; honor • *see also* **throne; cathedra**

chalcedony secret prayer; open righteousness; bodily vigor; charm against evil, sadness, phantoms, night visions, shipwreck; charm for political favor, victory, protection in revolution; associated with June • **Christian** a foundation stone of the New Jerusalem • **Greco-Roman** sacred to Artemis/Diana • *see also* **sardonyx**

chalice sacrifice; suffering; redemption; intuition; wisdom; prudence; the source of life; inexhaustible sustenance; abundance; holds the drink of immortality; associated with the heart (especially when filled with wine), the archangel Cassiel • **woman with chalice** Faith personified • **alchemic** *skull chalice:* immortality or knowledge bought by the death of the present state of existence, rebirth into a superhuman state • **Celtic** marriage; *chalice of an alcoholic drink handed to a king elect by a maiden:* sovereignty • **Christian** the blood of Christ; the New Testament; the cup of Salvation; the Eucharist; faith; the Last Supper; sacrifice; suffering; redemption; emblem of SS Barbara, Thomas Aquinas, Bonaventure, Bruno, Josaphat; *chalice with bread:* the Eucharist; *chalice with spider:* attribute of St. Norbert; *chalice on a closed book with a stole:* ordination; *chalice with serpent:* attribute of St. John; *chalice with wafer:* the sacrifice of Christ upon the cross; attribute of St. Barbara; *broken chalice:* attribute of St. Donatus; *chalice with rays of light:* the Holy Grail • **Egyptian** *basket chalice:* wholeness; togetherness under heavenly rule • **Hindu** *skull-chalice:* immortality or knowledge bought by the death of the present state of existence, rebirth into a superhuman state • **Jewish** attribute of Solomon; *chalice with staff:* attribute of the archangel Chamael; *chalice with bread:* associated with Melchizidek; *cup of salvation:* worship, thanksgiving • *see also* **cup; grail**

chalk attribute of an apprentice

chamber *see* **room**

chameleon adaptability; changeableness; betrayal; inconsistency; love; the element of air; attribute of Air personified • **African** rain-bringer • **Christian** Satan taking different forms to deceive mankind • **Dogon** associated with the rainbow • **Ela** fertility • **Pygmy** the demiurge; associated with thunder and lightning

chamomile love in adversity; cure for toothache, aches, pains, colds, weak stomachs, pleurisy • **flower language** energy in adversity • **heraldic** energy; action

chancel • **Christian** the Church Triumphant

chaos incipient creation; the unconscious; the earliest state of creation; death of religion and morality; man; absence of love; the incipient; the unformed; the human spirit overawed by the mystery of being; proto-matter

chaplet • **heraldic** (usually with green leaves and four roses) admiration; joy

charcoal • **piece of charcoal** attribute of an apprentice • **Oriental** prosperity; changelessness

chariot war; conquest; authority; the self; triumph; attribute of victors, heroes • **chariot**

wheels heaven and earth • **charioteer** the mind and/or spirit directing the body; reason controlling passions • **chariot team** indicates the qualities of the charioteer • **fiery chariot** the sun; ascent to heaven • **chariot bound in cord** associated with Alexander the Great • **chariot with three wheels** attribute of moon deities • **chariot drawn by angels** attribute of Eternity personified • **chariot drawn by an ass** attribute of the personifications of Idleness, Peacemaking • **chariot drawn by bats** attribute of Night personified • **chariot pulled by birds of prey** attribute of Greed personified • **chariot drawn by bulls** attribute of storm gods, sky gods, and solar gods • **chariot pulled by calves** attribute of Spring personified • **chariot drawn by cherubim** attribute of God • **chariot drawn by elephants** attribute of Fame personified • **chariot drawn by golden horses, griffins, or white horses** attribute of sky gods • **chariot drawn by black horses (usually two)** attribute of Night personified • **chariot pulled by winged horses** the dawn • **chariot drawn by mules** attribute of Poverty personified • **chariot drawn by oxen (usually black)** attribute of Death personified • **chariot drawn by roosters** attribute of Vigilance personified • **chariot drawn by stags** attribute of Chronos, Father Time • **chariot drawn by unicorns** attribute of Chastity personified • **Buddhist** *charioteer:* the spirit; *chariot team:* the senses; *chariot drawn by a white ox:* in Zen Buddhism, attribute of Buddha • **Celtic** *chariot drawn by deer:* attribute of Flidas; *chariot drawn by swans:* the solar chariot • **Chinese** the world • **Christian** the Church; conveyance of the faithful to heaven; *fiery chariot:* the Ascension of Christ • **Greco-Roman** the vehicle of all sun gods; *shell chariot:* attribute of Poseidon/Neptune, Galatea; *fiery chariot:* attribute of Phaeton; *black bearded king carrying off a maid in his chariot:* the rape of Persephone/Proserpine by Hades/Pluto; *chariot with a body dragging behind:* Achilles' victory over Hector; *chariot drawn over a corpse:* associated with Tullia; *chariot drawn by an ass:* attribute of Silenus; *chariot drawn by bulls:* attribute of Zeus/Jupiter; *chariot drawn by centaurs:* attribute of Dionysus/Bacchus; *chariot drawn by dogs:* attribute of Hephaestus/Vulcan; *chariot drawn by doves:* attribute of Aphrodite/Venus; *chariot drawn by dolphins:* attribute of Galatea; *chariot drawn by dragons:* attribute of Demeter/Ceres, Medea; *chariot drawn by eagles:* attribute of Zeus/Jupiter; *chariot drawn by goats:* attribute of Dionysus/Bacchus, Eros/Cupid; *chariot*

drawn by four hinds: attribute of Artemis/Diana; *chariot drawn by one white horse and one black horse:* attribute of Selene/Luna, Artemis/Diana; *chariot drawn by horses:* attribute of Ares/Mars, Eos/Aurora; *chariot drawn by black horses:* (usually three) attribute of Hades/Pluto; *chariot drawn by leopards:* attribute of Dionysus/Bacchus; *chariot drawn by lions or peacocks:* attribute of Hera/Juno; *chariot drawn by seahorses:* attribute of Poseidon/Neptune, Galatea; *chariot drawn by stags:* attribute of Artemis/Diana; *chariot drawn by swans:* attribute of Aphrodite/Venus; *chariot drawn by tigers:* attribute of Dionysus/Bacchus; *chariot drawn by Tritons:* attribute of Poseidon/Neptune; *chariot drawn by wolves:* attribute of Ares/Mars; *chariot drawn by two youths:* the youths are Kleobis and Biton; *woman with torch and bloody whip driving the chariot of Mars:* Bellona • **Hindu** the being in manifestation; the ego; the vehicle of the soul in a state of travail; *charioteer:* the Self; *reins:* intelligence and will of the driver; *axle:* World Axis; *wheels:* heaven and earth; *revolution of the wheels:* the cycles of manifestation; *golden chariot:* attribute of Indra; *three-wheeled chariot:* attribute of Soma, the Ashvins; *chariot drawn by antelopes:* attribute of Chandra, Shiva, Soma; *chariot drawn by red cows:* attribute of Ushas; *chariot drawn by gazelles:* occasional attribute of Shiva; *chariot drawn by luminous horses:* attribute of Savitri; *chariot pulled by red or purple horses:* attribute of Vayu; *chariot drawn by ten white horses:* attribute of Soma • **Italian** *chariot drawn by horses:* attribute of Armida • **Jewish** *fiery chariot and horses:* attribute of the ascension of Elijah, Elisha at Dothan; *four chariots:* associated with Zechariah • **Norse** *chariot drawn by cats:* attribute of Freyja; *chariot drawn by goat or rams:* attribute of Thor; *chariot pulled by seven oxen:* the sun • **Persian** *chariot drawn by four white horses:* attribute of Anahita • **Phrygian** *chariot drawn by lions:* attribute of Cybele • *see also* **quadriga**

Chariot (tarot) progress and victory; triumph; success; majesty; charity; universal love; the need for self-discipline; careful diplomacy; the man who has overcome opposition and brought together conflicting forces by strength of will

charoset • **Jewish** a reminder of Jewish slavery under the Egyptians

Charybdis • **Greco-Roman** desire for immediate fruits of an action as an impediment to moral progress; difficult passage

chaste tree • **flower language** indifference; coldness; chastity

chasuble vulva; originally an attribute of priests of goddesses • **Christian** the seamless garment of Christ for which the soldiers cast lots; celebration of the Eucharist; Christian charity; attribute of SS Ignatius of Loyola, Martin of Tours, Philip Neri; *the Virgin Mary robing a man in a chasuble:* St. Ildefonso; *purple chasuble:* the mocking robe of royalty for the King of the Jews; *stripe on the front:* the pillar where Christ was scourged; *Y design on chasuble:* Christ's arms on the cross; *red chasuble over Benedictine habit:* attribute of St. Thomas Becket

checkerboard the alternating pull of all fundamental dualities positive/negative, sun/moon, time/space, etc.; the criss-cross patter of life; alternation between good/bad, fortune/misfortune, etc.; the fundamental form of the city or temple; cosmic perfection; the battlefield of cosmic forces • **Hindu** the mandala of Shiva; Shiva the transformer

checkers (game) the effort to control irrational impulses by containing them in a given order; duality, light/dark, day/night, etc.; reason; intellect; the diversity of dualism in the manifest world • *see also* **checkerboard**

cheek • **pale cheek** melancholy • **rosy cheek** youth

cheetah speed; focus

chequers (game) *see* **checkers (game)**

chequy • **heraldic** constancy

cherry (fruit) virginity; merriment; fruitfulness; sweetness; attribute of Demeter/Ceres • **cherry pits** used in witchcraft • **Christian** a fruit of Paradise and the blessed; good works; sweetness, especially sweetness of character derived from good works; attribute of the Christ child; *cherry in Christ's hand:* the delight of the blessed • **Japanese** the warrior's calling; the search for the inner life

cherry tree education; protection against evil; the Great Divine Spirit; good heart; chivalry; man born naked into the word without possessions, and his state at death when he returns to the earth; emblem of women; associated with Aquarius • **cherry blossoms** friendliness; spring; April; spiritual beauty; feminine beauty; short-lived pleasures • **American** emblem of Washington, DC; attribute of George Washington (especially with ax) • **Chinese** *cherry blossoms:* Spring; the feminine principle; feminine beauty; hope; youth; virility • **flower language** education; *white or Winter cherry:* deception • **heraldic** *cherry blossom:* humility; riches; hospitality; education; transience of life; feminine love • **Japanese** emblem of Japan; riches; *cherry blossoms:* Spring; feminine

beauty; prosperity; earthly bliss; prefiguration of eternal happiness; the perfect death; indifference to worldly things; the transience of life; the samurai's dedication to his way of life; *cherry blossom tea:* lucky

cherub second only to the seraphim in rank; religion; vigilance; keepers of the threshold; executors of God's will; messengers of divine wisdom; guardians of the sacred; purity; innocence; attribute of St. Matthew • **four cherubim** the four elemental powers guarding the center of Paradise; the four evangelists; the four corners of the earth • **throne mounted on cherubim** the throne of Yahweh • **two cherubim on a throne** attribute of the Temple of Jerusalem • **chariot drawn by cherubim** attribute of God • **heraldic** dignity; glory; high position; honor; missionary service; bearer of joyful news

chervil • **flower language** *garden chervil:* sincerity

chess life; war; conflict; the sexes meeting on equal terms; conflict between the powers of light and dark; existence as a field of action of opposing forces; manifestation and reabsorption • **king** sun; the heart; forces of law and order; the power of action limited by manifestation • **queen** the spirit, the moon; the mover at will • **bishop** ruler of the spiritual world; the diagonal movement is associated with the existential, the feminine, Jupiter (planet) • **rook** temporal power; rulers of this world; associated with matter, the earth, virility, masculinity, Saturn (planet), the roc • **knight** the initiate; intellectual and devotional, but lacking the power of the spirit; associated with the military, chivalry, Mars (planet) • **pawn** the ordinary man attempting to cross through the seven grades of initiation to reach Paradise, realization, enlightenment; associated with Venus (planet), Mercury (planet) • **heraldic** *rook:* strategic thinking • *see also* **checkerboard** • **chest (container)** feminine principle; containment; related to fertility • **money chest with metal bands** emblem of banking • **buried money chest** pirate booty • **closed chest** secrecy • **Christian** *money chest:* attribute of St. Matthew; *money chest containing a heart:* attribute of St. Anthony of Padua; *poor woman placing a coin in a chest:* the Widow's Mite • **Greek** *woman and infant in a chest:* Danae and Perseus • *see also* **casket**

chestnut foresight; sensuality; voluptuousness; obstinate durability; associated with Gemini; *chestnut tree:* associated with the archangel Zadkiel • **old chestnut** mustiness; the hackneyed •

horse chestnut luxury • **Chinese** corresponds to Autumn, West • **Christian** chastity; virtue; triumph over the temptations of the flesh • **flower language** *sweet chestnut:* do me justice • **Jewish** magic • **Roman** associated with the lower classes • *see also* **horse chestnut (buckeye)**

cheveril *see* **leather**

chevron first step in the ladder of command; unfinished movement; stability; worth; competence; experience • **heraldic** protection; builders or others who have accomplished work of faithful service

chevrotain • **African** trickster

chick rebirth; emblem of Easter • *see also* **chicken**

chicken cowardice; effeminacy • **Chinese** *on a rooftop:* unlucky • *see also* **capon; chick; hen; rooster**

chickweed • **flower language** rendezvous; *mouse-eared chickweed:* ingenuous simplicity

chicory attribute of Frugality personified; emblem of the sun • **Jewish** the bitterness of bondage • **flower language** frugality

chief • **heraldic** guardianship

child the future; innocence; purity; beginning; dawn; spring; unity with nature; one's inner self; conjunction of the conscious and the unconscious; harbinger of beneficent change; hope; ignorance; ingratitude; potentialities; natural simplicity; the higher transformation of the individual; forgetfulness; the preconscious; state prior to Original Sin; associated with the eternal • **child wrapped in a cloak** personification of Winter • **child being suckled by a woman** charity • **child with flowers and leaves** personification of Spring • **white child and black child** sleep and death respectively • **child with ears of grain** personification of Summer • **child with fruit** personification of Autumn • **naked child** new life; *when issuing from the mouth of a dying person:* the soul • **winged child's head** a cherub • **child playing with a snake** Paradise regained; freedom from conflict • **alchemic** *naked child:* the innocent soul; *child crowned and/or clothed in purple:* salt; the philosopher's stone • **Christian** perfect faith and belief; attribute of SS Augustine, Hilary; *child on the back or shoulders:* St. Christopher carrying the Christ child; *child in the arms:* attribute of St. Vincent DePaul; *dead child:* attribute of St. Zenobius; *child kissing the hand of a saint:* the saint is St. Nicholas of Myra • **Greek** *old man and child with mirror:* Socrates • *see also* **birth; boy; girl; Christ child**

chimera complex evil; cunning; drought; darkness; the underworld; alarm; the non-existent; danger on land and sea; storm clouds and wind; illusory fancy; a wild incongruous scheme; psychological repression that causes suffering • **Christian** the spirit of evil • **heraldic** impossible or difficult to believe

chimere • **Christian** dutiful perseverance

chimney passage of escape to the heavens; the solar gateway; escape from the temporal to the eternal; Santa Claus coming through the chimney indicates the gifts are from heaven; entrance for witches • **house chimney** peace; life; happiness • **factory chimney** power; industry; commerce • **chimney belching black smoke** pollution

chimney sweep lucky omen; the work of chimney sweeping is related to fertility

China ancient wisdom; the mysterious; the unknown

china (pottery) an attractive woman; delicate beauty; associated with 20th wedding anniversaries

Chinese evergreen longevity

chi-rho *see* **XP**

Chiron • **Greek** the personification of Wisdom

chisel education; distinctive knowledge in initiation; the cutting away of error; the active discrimination; distinction • **Chinese** *blue man with wings, claws, drum, mallet and chisel:* Lei-kung

chive related to Mars (planet)

chocolate self-indulgence; sensuality; aphrodisiac

chopsticks emblem of the Orient

chorten *see* **stupa**

chough prattle • **heraldic** martial strategy; watchful of friends • *see also* **crow**

chrism • **Christian** baptism; ordination; conformation; unction; dedication; attribute of St. Catherine of Siena

Christ child • **on a man's shoulders or back** attribute of St. Christopher • **in a man's arms** attribute of St. Anthony of Padua • **in the arms of a man with a lily** attribute of St. Joseph • **holding out a ring to a woman** St. Catherine of Alexandria • *see also* **Jesus Christ**

Christmas • **Christian** God's love; renewal of love and hope

Christmas tree rebirth; immortality; the New Year; Winter solstice; Tree of Paradise; the Cosmic Tree • **Christmas tree lights or candles** souls; heavenly bodies

Chronos • **Greco-Roman** the personification of Time • *see also* **Cronus/Saturn** although Chronos and Cronus are not the same

chrysalis resurrection; the soul leaving the body; valor; regeneration; balance; transformation; organization; passive and blind obedience to the laws of nature; metamorphosis; change; a fleeting state between two stages of being

chrysanthemum nobility; royalty; regal beauty; constancy; reliability; longevity; purity; perfection; abundance; associated with Scorpio, Autumn; emblem of the sun • **Chinese** Autumn; October; September; scholarship; wealth; joviality; retirement; cool splendor; the life of ease; emblem of China; *butterfly with chrysanthemum:* beauty in old age • **flower language** *Chinese chrysanthemum:* cheerfulness under misfortune; *red chrysanthemum:* I love; *white chrysanthemum:* truth; *yellow chrysanthemum:* slighted love • **heraldic** abundance; cheerfulness; optimism; truth; hope; rest; friendship • **Japanese** imperial pride; longevity; happiness; associated with October; emblem of Japan; *superimposed on the solar disk:* the Imperial Family • **Oriental** scholarliness; fullness; completeness; intermediary between heaven and earth; longevity; immortality • **Taoist** simplicity; natural and restrained spontaneity

chrysoberyl patience; patience in sorrow; stone for an 18th wedding anniversary

chrysolite wisdom; discretion; prudence; unrequited love; charm against evil

chrysoprase eloquence; confidence; gaiety; joy; associated with Cancer, the planets Venus, Mercury; charm for calmness, business success, financial gain, making new friends, happiness, lucky, healing, and protection against envy, selfishness, greed, stress, nightmares

chrysothamnus • **Amerindian** the masculine, solar, day; and life principles

church faith; the intersection of heaven and earth; mystic center; dwelling of spiritual wisdom; place where spiritual forces encounter the material world; the spiritual façade presented to the world • **Christian** the body of Christ; *church on a rock:* the whole Church, securely founded on the rock of faith; *church as an ark:* the salvation of its members; *church model being carried:* attribute of SS Gregory, Jerome; a particular church being carried may indicate that the person carrying it was its founder or first bishop; *toppling church being supported by a saint:* SS Dominic, Francis of Assisi • **heraldic** religion; faith; community

churning creation; masturbation; coition • **Hindu** the churning of the waters with the world axle produced creation

ciborium • **Christian** consecration; Ark of the Covenant; womb of the Virgin Mary; the Last Supper; the Eucharist; the grave of Christ; attribute of SS Oswald, Bonaventure; *ciborium on pillars as a canopy over an altar:* the Ark of the Covenant

cicada chatter; melody; resurrection; worldly grandeur; immortality; metamorphosis; eternal youth; happiness; evanescent worldly glory; restraint of vice and lasciviousness; demon of light and darkness; the discarded lover; cunning; improvidence; negligence; attribute of Dawn personified, bad poets • **Chinese** resurrection; immortality; eternal youth; happiness; restraint of cupidity and vice; *jade cicada in the mouth of the dead:* ensures immortality • **Greco-Roman** immortality; associated with Tithonus; attribute of Eos/Aurora, Apollo

cicatrix *see* **scar**

cider rural festivities

cincture chastity; self-restraint; continence; patient suffering; temperance; preparation for service; truth; humility; contempt for the world • **Christian** the scourging of Christ; attribute of the Virgin Mary • *see also* **belt; girdle**

Cinderella the realization of one's higher self; human metamorphosis; transformation; rebirth

cinnabar • **alchemic** the hardened habits and terrestrial unions of soul and spirit that must be broken in calcination to free the essences; drug of immortality

cinnamon • **Christian** attribute of the Virgin Mary • *see also* **cassia**

cinquefoil (plant) maternal affection; death • **flower language** maternal affection; beloved daughter • **heraldic** hope; joy

Circe • **Greek** enchantment; sorcery; dangerous attraction; feminine wiles; desire leading to good or evil • *see also* **siren (mythology)**

circle perfection; totality; wholeness; completeness; unity; primordial unity; celestial unity; fulfillment; eternity; heaven; simultaneity; the Self; the self-contained; a cyclic process; solar cycle; dynamism; the ultimate fate of oneness; the most natural shape; the infinite; time enclosing space; timelessness without beginning or end; spacelessness as having no above or below; the cyclic; recurrence; the unmanifest; never-ending existence; God whose center is everywhere and circumference is nowhere; the feminine principle; protection; containment; a monogram of God • **two circles** male and female; love and knowledge • **two circles intertwined** marriage • **three circles (may be interlocking)** a triad; movement; the dynamic in tension • **four circles in a cross pattern (may be linked by a fifth circle)** wisdom, fear, knowledge, and hope • **five circles intertwined**

the five continents of the Olympics— Asia, Europe, America, Africa, Australia; emblem of the Olympic Games • **seven circles** the All-Knower; perfection; the seven heavens • **small circles on a sacrificial vessel** the sacrificial wafer, cake, etc. • **circle with a dot in the center** cyclic perfection; a complete cycle; the resolution of all possibilities in existence; the sun; gold; emblem of solar gods • **concentric circles** the solar and the lunar; the heavens; different state of manifest existence • **three concentric circles** past/present/future; earth/air/water; heaven/earth/hell; the phases of the moon; the rising, midday, and setting sun; the dynamics and reconciliation of opposites • **circle enclosing an equilateral cross** lucky; cosmic solar wheel; the four corners of the earth, rivers of Paradise, cardinal directions, quarters of the earth, seasons, ages of man, divisions of a cosmic cycle • **circle surmounting an equilateral cross** union of the male and feminine principles • **circle surmounted by a cross** *see* **orb** • **circle within a square** heaven and earth; integration • **squaring a circle** transforming the heavenly into earthly as in a sacred building; bringing heaven to earth; uniting the four elements and returning to primordial simplicity in unity • **semi-circle** *horns up:* the Lower Waters, the ark; *horns down* the Upper Waters, the rainbow; *presented together:* completion, Cosmic Egg • **winged circle** the Primordial Cosmic Pair; the creative sky and fertile earth; power from heaven; the sun god and solar power • **alchemic** unity; the one mind of God; experience beyond the duality of reason; *serpent passing through a circle:* fusion; *circle with a dot in the center:* gold, the sun • **Amerindian** *circle radiating in and out:* the feathered sun, the universe; *circle within a square:* the Cosmic Center, sacred space, the four directions of space • **astrological** *circle surmounting an equilateral cross:* Venus (planet); *circle with a dot in the center:* the sun • **Buddhist** the Round of Existence enclosing all in the phenomenal world; *three circles in a triangular form:* the Three Jewels • **Chinese** the heavens; *square within a circle:* the union of earth and heaven respectively, yin and yang, the perfect man • **Christian** the Church Universal; *twin circles:* Christ and his dual nature; *three circles (may be interlocking or in a triangle):* the Trinity; *square within a circle:* eternity of life • **Egyptian** *winged circle:* the rising sun, emblem of Ra • **Greco-Roman** time; fate; *two circles:* Castor and Pollux • **Hindu** the Round of Existence; *flaming circle:* emblem of Prakriti • **Islamic** the vault of

heaven, divine light • **Jainism** *swastika surmounted by a single circle:* full consciousness, omniscience; *swastika surmounted by three circles:* the Three Jewels of Right Belief • **Kabalistic** *circle within a square:* the life-giving spark of divine fire concealed in matter • **Masonic** *rayed star in a circle:* guidance • **Mexican Indian** *circle within a square:* the peyotl cactus which gives the drink of immortality grows at the center point • **Norse** *staff with circle:* divine light, sun rays • **North American Indian** time; the Great Spirit; *bird with a broken circle around its head:* creation of life, opening of the gate of heaven • **Platonic** the moving image of an unmoved eternity • **Taoist** the Precious Pearl • **Zen** *empty circle:* enlightenment • **Zoroastrian** *bearded man in a winged circle holding a ring:* Ahura Mazda • *see also* **circumambulation; circumference; ring**

circumambulation fixing the World Axis in a particular sacred place; the relation of harmony and stillness or the manifest and the Supreme Reality; defining the boundary between the sacred and profane; imitation of the path of the sun; imitation of the path of the Great Bear constellation; taking ritual possession • **Buddhist** *processing clockwise around a sacred object:* circling the world and the All contained in the Self; pilgrimage to find the Self • **Celtic** *clockwise circumambulation:* friendly intent; *counterclockwise circumambulation:* hostile intent • **Christian** *censing an altar by circling around it:* marking the space as holy • **Hindu** *processing clockwise around a sacred object:* circling the world and the All contained in the Self; pilgrimage to find the Self • **Islam** making seven circuits of the Ka'aba represents the seven attributes of God • *see also* **procession**

circumcision *see* **clitoris; foreskin**

circumference objects contained within are limited, defined, and of the manifest world; viewed from without, the circumference is the defense of the conscious world against the unconscious or chaos; enclosure; rotation; movement; represented by -9- • **moving from the center to the circumference** moving into manifestation and multiplicity • **moving from the circumference to the center** moving to the spiritual center, unity, the One • *see also* **circle**

circus *see* **carnival**

cistern a wife who must be guarded you keep pure • **broken cistern** false doctrine; uselessness • **Jewish** associated with Jeremiah

cistus • **flower language** popular favor; *gum cistus:* I die tomorrow

cithara *see* **zither**

cithern *see* **zither**

citrine occasionally used for a November birth-stone; charm for equability, cheerfulness; stone for 11th and 13th wedding anniversaries; associated with the archangel Michael

citron fertility; antidote for seasickness; occasionally the forbidden fruit in Garden of Eden and Garden of the Hesperides • **Buddhist** one of the Three Blessed Fruits of China; *fingered citron:* the shape of the hand of Buddha • **Far Eastern** immortality • **flower language** ill-natured beauty • **Hindu** attribute of Shiva • **Jewish** love; emblem of Sukkoth; a holy tree • **Roman** love; ornament of the bridal chamber

city the feminine principle; mother; the society or the beliefs of the society of which it is a part; manifestation of a particular discipline or principle; loneliness; the self; refuge; lack of spiritual, natural, or emotional contact • **golden city** Babylon • **city with seven gates** Thebes • **Christian** *city on a hill:* the stability and prominence of the Church, the New Jerusalem • **Hindu** *city with 1,000 gates:* Amaravati • **Jewish** *blue city:* Luz; *walled city:* the heavenly Jerusalem, the transcendent soul, associated with Zechariah; *walled city beneath a sword:* associated with Zephaniah

clam withdrawal; self-satisfaction; silence

clarion • **heraldic** martial readiness

claw greed; ferocity; flattery; degenerate sexuality; tenacity; prowess; the law; ferality • **heraldic** *bird claw:* the preyer who has been preyed upon; *eagle claw:* one who preys

clay that which can be shaped or formed; the material from which something new can be made shapeless matter; the act of creation; material of the first man • **feet of clay** having human faults • **Babylonian** food of the damned in Aralu • **Jewish** material of which Goid made Adam

cleanliness purity; innocence

clematis gladness; emblem of the Virgin Mary • **flower language** mental beauty; artifice; *evergreen clematis:* poverty

Cleobis and Bito • **Greek** filial devotion

clever • **Roman** attribute of Intercidona

cliff • **Christian** attribute of St. Sylvanus

climbing *see* **ascending**

Clio • **Greek** Muse associated with history, lyre-playing

clitoris the male element in woman; *clitoridectomy:* confirming the sexual status of a woman

cloak protection; shelter; the outer bounds of the wearer's personality; mental covering, often revealing the wearer's principles of action, opinions, prejudices, associations, mental state, etc.; dignity; protection; righteousness; concealment; mystery; disguise; invisibility; villainy; infamy; withdrawal; obscurity; dissimulation; sleep; attribute of a pilgrim • **dark cloak** protection • **black cloak** attribute of Night personified; renunciation of worldly vanities • **ritual cloak** transformation • **sky blue cloak** attribute of the Great Mother; queens of heaven • **russet cloak** attribute of Dawn personified • **cloak enveloping a deity** the unrevealed aspect • **cloak trimmed with crimson feathers** characteristic fairy dress • **cloak lined with fur** rank • **cloak lined with ermine** attribute of royalty, Charlemagne • **child wrapped in a cloak** personification of Winter • **surrendering one's cloak** surrendering oneself • **giving one's cloak to a disciple** bestowing one's powers or wisdom • **Celtic** attribute of royalty; *feathered cloak:* attribute of priests, journey to the other world • **Christian** Christian charity; attribute of St. Angela Merici; *black cloak:* attribute of the devil; *cloak split in two with a sword:* attribute of St. Martin of Tours; *cloak lined with ermine:* attribute of St. Ursula; *green cloak:* attribute of SS Anne (especially over a red robe), John; *yellow cloak:* attribute of SS Joseph, Peter; *cloak on the ground:* attribute of SS Alban, Martin; *cloak floating on the sea:* attribute of St. Hyacinth; *cloak used as a sail:* attribute of St. Raymond; *gray cloak:* attribute of Christ at the Last Judgment • **Egyptian** *cloak of stars:* attribute of Nut • **Greco-Roman** *mourning cloak (usually black or dun colored):* worn at initiation ceremonies to mark the death of the child and birth of the adult; *fawn-skin cloak:* attribute of devotees of Dionysus/Bacchus, Orpheus • **Hindu** *blue rain cloak* attribute of Indra • **Jewish** *cast off cloak:* attribute of Hosea; *rolled up cloak:* attribute of the ascension of Elijah; *cloak split in two:* attribute of Elisha • **Norse** *falcon feather cloak:* attribute of Freyja • **Persian** *gold embroidered cloak:* attribute of Anahita • **Teutonic** *cape of invisibility (Tarnkappe):* owned by Alberich, worn by Siegfried • *see also* **tunic**

clock the universe; order; the march of time; cyclic existence; related to the magical creation of beings that pursue their own autonomous existence; attribute of Temperance personified; associated with 23rd wedding anniversaries • **stopped clock** death; end of a cycle • **Christian** attribute of St. Ursula • **heraldic** *clock tower:* integrity • **portraiture** the temperate nature of the subject

cloister the heavenly Jerusalem; Paradise; intimacy with the godhead • **well, tree, cross, column, or statue in the center** World Navel • **square or rectangular shape open to the sky** the union of heaven and earth • *see also* **monastery**

closet secrecy; the grave; the earth; passage into another existence

clotbur *see* **burdock**

clothes deception; concealment of reality or truth; indication of profession, mental state, beliefs, associations, etc.; intimately related to the owner's personality; distinguishing of rank, sex, mood; hiding of nakedness, vice • **new clothes** (particularly at Easter) renewal of the owner • **changing clothes** changing personalities, roles, opinions, loyalties, etc. • **black clothes** renunciation of worldly vanities • **Christian** *black garments:* renunciation of worldly vanities; *goat or camel's hair clothes:* attribute of John the Baptist • **Islamic** *black garments:* renunciation of worldly vanities • **Jewish** *goat or camel's hair clothes:* attribute of Elijah • **Persian** *woman with golden clothes:* Ardvi Sura Anahita • *see also* particular articles of clothing such as **cloak; hat; shoes**

clouds the intermediate world between the formal and non-formal; the transitory; death; illusion; the sky; air; mystery; fertility; sanctity; chastity; change; storm; evanescence; freedom; independence; sleep; betrayal; obscured truth; disgrace; providence; messenger • **lightning flash through a cloud** mythology • **hand emerging from a cloud** the omnipotent God • **dark, or storm clouds** portent of evil, trouble • **fleecy clouds** benignity • **cloud of light** theophany • **Amerindian** fertility • **Chinese** fertility; life force; visible breath; *rain clouds:* compassion; *cloud banks:* immortality; *green clouds:* a plague of insects; *red clouds:* a favorable omen; *cloud descending on a sacrifice:* acceptance by the gods; *cloud rising from the tomb of an Immortal:* ascension into heavens; *colored clouds:* attribute of Ho Hsien-ku • **Christian** the unseen God; the veil of God • **Greek** the flocks of Apollo • **heraldic** mystery; obscured truth • **Hindu** the primal embryo; the undifferentiated • **Islamic** the primordial and unknowable state of God before his manifestation • **Jewish** *feet emerging from cloud above a mountain:* Nahum's vision • **Norse** steeds of the Valkyries • **North American Indian** lightheartedness; *bird with its head surrounded by clouds:* rain

clove • **flower language** dignity

clover the Trinity; lucky; ease; freedom; luxury; fertility; abundance; divine triad; sunwheel; ardent, but humble love; emblem of Ireland, the Irish • **four leaf clover** lucky; sacred to the Druids • **Chinese** Summer • **flower language** *red clover:* industry; *four leaf clover:* be mine; *white clover:* think of me; *purple clover:* provident • **heraldic** sincerity; hope

clown *see* **jester**

club (bat) brute force; punishment; strength; intrepidity; victory through destruction; phallus; brutality; a royal weapon; attribute of Fortitude personified • **Buddhist** *club with heart-shaped head:* divine office • **Celtic** appetite; strength; attribute of Dagda • **Christian** betrayal of Christ; martyrdom; attribute of SS Gervase, Protase; *knotted club:* attribute of St. Jude; *club with spear and/or lance and/or inverted cross:* attribute of St. Jude; *fuller's club:* attribute of SS James the Less, Mark, Simon • **European medieval art** the Wild Man • **Gallic** attribute of Sucellus • **Greco-Roman** attribute of Hermes/Mercury; *oak club:* attribute of Heracles/Hercules • **Hindu** attribute of Kali, Yama • **Jewish** *knotted club:* attribute of Cain • **Sumero-Semitic** the thunderbolt of sky gods; attribute of Baal, Ninurta • *see also* **mace; scepter**

clubs (playing cards) will power; authority; command, glory; enterprise; energy; reason; associated with peasants, air, fire, matter in combustion, ideas, opposition, radiant energy, the archetypal world, the triangle, the threefold aspect of life, the pyramid, Winter, agriculture, government, -3- • **ace of clubs** associated with Summer, new beginnings, growth • **king of clubs** associated with Zeus/Jupiter, Alexander the Great, King Arthur • **queen of hearts** queen of the air; associated with Hera/Juno, Arsine • **jack (knave) of hearts** associated with Apollo, Aeneas, Lancelot • **cartomancy** associated with inner wisdom, industriousness, creative enthusiasm; *king of clubs:* a dark-haired man; *queen of clubs:* a dark-haired woman, an older married woman; *four of clubs:* unlucky • **tarot** the power of command • *see also* **playing cards**

coal (ember) *see* **ember**

coal (mineral) repressed energy; the negative side of energy; dirtiness; worthlessness

coast *see* **shore**

coat protection; self-nurturing; self-care • **covering much of the body** stealth; secret motives • **British** *red coat:* attribute of British soldiers •

Christian *coat without seams:* attribute of the Passion • **Irish** *old man in a green or red coat:* a leprechaun • **Jewish** *coat of many colors:* attribute of Joseph • *see also* **cloak; clothes**

cobia • **flower language** gossip

cobbler lust • **Christian** SS Crispin, Crispinian; *cobbler's tools:* attributes of SS Crispin, Crispinian • **Irish** *elfin cobbler:* a leprechaun

cobra • **Egyptian** Amunet; Buto; sovereignty; the generative power of the sun; associated with Meretseger • **Hindu** steed of Vishnu; knowledge; wisdom; eternity; *two cobra-headed humans:* Naga, Nagina; *cobra with seven heads:* Naga, Nagina • *see also* **Naga; uraeus**

cobweb *see* **web**

cochorus • **flower language** impatient of absence

cock *see* **rooster**

Cockaigne • **Medieval European** ridicule of poetic bliss, wishful thinking, monastic life

cockatrice *see* **basilisk**

cockle evil; wickedness invading the good field of the Church

cockleshell *see* **shell**

cockroach filth; heat; contamination; filth; associated with the devil, witches • **French, Russian** protective spirit

cocoa tree wisdom; love

coconut wisdom; love; fertility; abundance; endless Summer; emblem of the South Seas, tropical islands • **coconut palm tree** associated with the archangel Gabriel

cocoon the soul; the protection of the soul; the womb of the soul; magic power; the potential power of the wind

Cocytus • **Greco-Roman** the river of mourning in Hades

codfish productiveness; fishery • **American** emblem of Massachusetts

coffer *see* **box**

coffin death; the return to the womb; the mystic womb of rebirth; redemption; salvation; resurrection • **Christian** *man rising from coffin:* Lazarus; *woman rising from coffin:* Drusiana and St. John • *see also* **sarcophagus**

cogwheel fate; industry; mechanics

coins avarice; bribery; trade; the unfavorable aspects of money; attribute of Vanity personified • **coins at the feet of an old man** charity to the poor; renunciation of worldly goods • **Christian** *coins at the feet of a saint:* St. Onuphrius; *thirty coins (especially silver):* attribute of Judas; *gold and silver coins in a dish:* attribute of St. Laurence; *poor woman placing a coin in a chest in temple:* the Widow's Mite; *coin drawn from a fish's mouth:* St. Peter's payment of the Temple

tax • **heraldic** trustworthy with treasure • **still life painting** the power and possessions that death takes away

coins (playing cards) *see* **diamonds (playing cards)**

cola nut • **African** the trials of life; bitterness; firm friendship; faithfulness

cold (disease) inhibition of psychic powers

cold (temperature) silence; a spiritualized atmosphere; longing, especially for solitude; resistance to all that is inferior; death; lovelessness; sexual frigidity; heartlessness

collar (clothing) insignia of office; rank; occupation; modesty • **Christian** *clerical turned collar:* humility; meekness; *clerical collar with two tabs:* the tablets of the Ten Commandments

collar (restraint) slavery; restriction of freedom; bondage; restraint; servitude

college expansion of consciousness; provider of discipline to the untrained mind

colossus *see* **giant; statue**

colt *see* **horse**

coltsfoot maternal care • **flower language** justice shall be done

coluber • **Egyptian** Apep; discord; destruction; the scorching sun; destroyer of souls

columbine folly; desertion; inconstancy; marital infidelity • **Christian** humility; love; the Holy Spirit, especially prior to the 16th Century; *with seven blooms:* the seven gifts of the Holy Spirit • **English** *Elizabethan:* compassion • **flower language** folly; *purple columbine:* resolution; *red columbine:* anxious and waiting

column (architectural) *see* **pillar**

comb knowledge; sacrificial remains; associated with burials; sun rays; entanglement; fertility; rain; vanity; music; attribute of Aphrodite/Venus, sirens, lamia, mermaids • **when stuck in the hair** communication with the supernatural; cohesion of the personality • **finding the comb of another** may change the finder's personality • **Christian** *iron wool carding comb:* attribute of SS Blaise, Laurence • **Islamic** *comb with five teeth:* the Hand of Fatima

comet unrest; impending disaster or change; omen of war, famine, plague, fire, earthquake, drought, etc.; a brilliant, but short-lived career; messenger of sun gods • **Christian** emblem of the Nativity

communion rail *see* **railing**

compass guidance; navigation • **heraldic** direction

compasses the act of creation; the beginning of all things; right conduct; the limits and bounds of rectitude; transcendent knowledge; geometry; science; astronomy; architecture; navigation; measuring; reason; temperance; knowledge; thought; melancholy; the cyclic nature of existence; heaven; unerring and impartial justice; attribute of Euclid, the personifications of Architecture, Astronomy, Geography, Geometry, Maturity, Melancholy, Prudence, Justice, Temperance, Truth • **compasses and builder's square** heaven and earth respectively; sound morality; good order; harmony of the celestial and earthly; the feminine and masculine principles respectively • **Chinese** right conduct; attribute of Fo-hi; *square with compasses:* order, propriety, the laws of virtue, the path of wisdom, the true guide, yin and yang, harmony, earth and heaven respectively, the masculine and feminine principles respectively • **Greco-Roman** attribute of Cronus/Saturn; *compasses with a globe:* attribute of Urania • **Masonic** *compasses open at 45 degrees:* the eighth degree of attainment; *at 60 degrees:* the sixth degree; *at 90 degrees:* the fourth degree • **portraiture** may denote an architect, navigator, or artist (the latter especially in renaissance or baroque art)

complexion • **dark complexion** death; sleep; ignorance; mystery; fertility; attribute of villains, underworld deities • **light complexion** knowledge; wisdom; peace; purity; attribute of heroes, heroines, heavenly deities • **folkloric** The red is wise / The brown trusty / The pale envious / And the black lusty, *or,* To a red man give thy counsel / With a brown man break thy bread / At a pale man draw thy knife / From a black man keep thy wife. [**NOTE:** This entry is for Caucasian complexions, not for races.]

compony • **heraldic** constancy

computer *see* **engine**

concealment *see* **withdrawal**

conch wealth; learning; the feminine principle; vulva; primitive summons; the spiritual and natural means of development rendered active; associated with the sea, the waters, the moon, gestation, fertility; the convolutions are associated with the rising and setting sun, the lunar spiral; attribute of deities associated with the sea • **Buddhist** learning; sound; oratory; the voice of Buddha teaching the Law; victory over samsara; one of the Eight Emblems of Good Augury; emblem of the footprint of Buddha; *white conch:* temporal power • **Cambodian** yoni • **Chinese** royalty; a prosperous voyage • **Greco-Roman** attribute of Aphrodite/Venus, Poseidon/Neptune, Triton; tritons blow conch shells while pulling the chariot of Poseidon/Neptune; *winged and bearded man with conch:* Aquilo,

Boreas • **Hindu** attribute of Vishnu, Panchajana; the primordial creative word Aum; the Word was made manifest from a conch shell • **Islamic** the ear that hears the divine Word • **Mayan** associated with the waters, the underworld • **Tahitian** sacred to 'Oro • **Tibetan** the sound is used to produce mental confusion as a preparation to receive inward perception of the sound of Truth • *see also* **shell**

concrete inflexibility; permanence

condor eternity; strength • **Andean Indian** manifestation of the sun

conductor (musical) agent of harmony; control of emotions; power; authority

conductor (train) guide of souls; parent; power; authority

cone psychic wholeness; phallus; sun; attribute of fertility deities; vortex; generative force; creative force; ascension; the feminine principle; return to unity; gradual spiritualization • *see also* **pine cone**

coney *see* **rabbit**

confetti fertility; a substitute for rice • *see also* **rice**

Confucius wisdom, especially of the Orient; the Golden Rule; benevolence; peace

construction making the mental into the material; renewing the work of creation; creating order out of chaos

convent *see* **monastery**

convolvulus humility; uncertainty; clinging; coquetry; emblem of Insinuation personified • **Chinese** love and marriage; dependence; dawn; transitoriness; emblem of Autumn • **flower language** bonds; uncertainty; *great or major convolvulus:* extinguished hope; *blue, minor, or night convolvulus:* night, repose; *three-colored convolvulus:* coquetry; *pink convolvulus:* worth sustained by judicious and tender affection

coot beauty; courtliness; understanding; wisdom; a common or stupid fellow; something valueless • **chattering coots** warning of a storm

cope (vestment) innocence; purity; dignity

copestone contemplation; the head

copper firmness; strength; hardness; low value; money; Autumn; harvest; decay; metal of the common people; associated with Taurus, Libra, Venus (planet), Cyprus, 7th wedding anniversaries, the archangel Anael • **Bambaran** *copper necklace of Faro:* enables him to hear the everyday conversations of men • **Dogon** associated with water, light, speech, sperm • **Chinese** *three legged-copper pot:* attribute of Huang Ti • **Greco-Roman** associated with Demeter/Ceres, Aphrodite/Venus

copse *see* **grove**

coral (sea coral) marriage; lucky; blood; longevity; protection against evil; sea tree of the Mother Goddess; the giver of life; associated with the moon, 35th wedding anniversaries • coral necklace protection; healing; attribute of Africa personified • Chinese official promotion; longevity • Greek the growth from the blood of Medusa • Hindu celestial coral tree: Parijata

cord execution; union; bondage; limitation; security; force; sin • golden cord the sun and reason respectively; the link between heaven and earth; attribute of the archangel Metatron • silver cord related to Judgment Day; holds the soul to the body during incarnation • broken cord death; freedom • cord on garments chastity; temperance; self-restraint • military cords rank; binding to office • Christian attribute of the Passion of Christ, St. Lucy; worn around the waist of monastic: commitment to celibacy, binding to vocation • Greco-Roman attribute of Zeus/Jupiter • Hindu knotted cord: depicts the acts of devotion performed • Jewish seven cords: associated with Samson • Oceanic attribute of Vaerua and Akaanga • Persian wrapped around the waist three times: good thought, word, and deed • Sumero-Semitic attribute of Shamash

coreopsis • flower language always cheerful; arkansa coreopsis: love at first sight

coriander hidden worth • flower language concealed merit

cormorant vanity; instability; Winter; desolation • Japanese emblem of Kushi-yatama-no-kami

corn see grain; maize

corn bottle • flower language delicacy

corn cockle • flower language gentility

corn flower see cornflower

cornel tree • flower language duration

cornelian cherry see dogwood

corner trap; meeting place of divergent views or idea; opportunity for change

cornerstone foundation; something; fundamental, or of primary importance; Christ; remnant of a foundation sacrifice (originally a child was used, later, small animals) • see also stone; ashlar

cornet attribute of Notoriety personified • see also horn; trumpet

cornflower related to the heavens; associated with Cyanus; emblem of Prussia • flower language delicacy; devotion to an inferior

cornucopia abundance; liberality; the bounty of God; endless bounty; the Horn of Plenty; thanksgiving; agriculture; the gathered fruits of the earth; attribute of mother goddesses, fate deities, vegetation deities, harvest deities, the personifications of Autumn, Abundance, Charity, Concord, Earth, Europe, Fortune, Hope, Hospitality, Peace, occasionally Africa • Greco-Roman the Horn of Amalthea; attribute of Althaea, Demeter/Ceres, Priapus, Tyche/Fortuna, Zephyr; old woman and naked goddess with cornucopia: Vertumnus and Pomona respectively; woman with cornucopia in her left hand and an olive branch in her right: Concordia • heraldic the country of nature • Jewish associated with Asher • middle ages attribute of Justice personified

coronation achievement; victory; consummation • Italian coronation of a youth by a maiden, or vice versa, in a pastoral setting: Mirtillo and Amarillis • Macedonian coronation of a young woman by a soldier: the soldier is Alexander the Great • see also crown

coronella • flower language may success crown your wishes

corpse the personality in its lower aspect; the end of a cycle or idea • Christian hanged corpse with its entrails out: Judas Iscariot • Jewish highly unclean • Mayan bloated corpse: Ah Puch

corrosion destruction; infirmity; suffering

corset support; protection; society hampering development of the psyche

corundum stability of mind

cosmetics vanity; deceit; disloyalty; trickery; wantonness; foolishness; lust; sorrow; seduction; depersonalization; attribute of a loose woman • Hindu cosmetics jar: attribute of Devi

cotta • Christian innocence; purity

cottage the simple, carefree, country life; the humble life • cottage in a vineyard loneliness

cotton associated with 2nd wedding anniversaries • American emblem of the South, especially ante-bellum • cotton blossoms happiness; well-being

couch a place for reverie, languor, seduction

cougar see puma

courtesan see prostitute

cow mother; the Great Mother; Mother Earth; related to most mother goddesses; female sexual desire; plenty; procreation; the maternal instinct; associated with the earth and the moon, moon goddesses, the celestial, the underworld; attribute of many fertility gods • heifer a bride; fertility; sacrifice; wantonness; mildness; a young woman • red cow hope; related to the dawn • white cow rain; sacrifice • cow horns the crescent moon; associated with moon and earth goddesses • solar disk between cow horns unity; sacred marriage of divine pairs; joint moon and sun deities; the two-in-one • **Babylonian** Ishtar • **Celtic** provider of perpetual nourishment; *red cow with white ears:* related to the underworld • **Chinese** yin; the earth principle; *cow with horse:* yin and yang respectively • **Druidic** the earth • **Egyptian** love; joy; associated with Bat; *double-headed cow:* Upper and Lower Egypt; *cow with stars on her belly:* Nut; *seven cows with a bull:* fertility; *goddess with the head of a cow:* Hathor, Isis; *goddess with the horns of a cow:* Isis; *cow with a solar disk between her horns:* Ahet • **Germanic** Audumla • **Greco-Roman** a form of Hera/Juno, Io; attribute of Apollo, Hermes/Mercury, Zeus/Jupiter; *hollow wooden cow:* the cow Dedalus built for Pasiphae; *man carrying a heifer at the Olympic Games:* Milo of Croton; *cow with a crescent on each side:* associated with Cadmus • **Hindu** fertility; plenty; the earth; the source of life; Aditi, Nandini, Prithivi, Surabhi; *cow and bull together:* the earth; *four legs of the Sacred Cow:* the four castes; *black cow:* used in funeral processions; *barren black cow:* sacred to Nirriti; *spotted cow:* associated with androgyny; *white cow:* Dhol • **Irish** *gray cow:* Glas Gaibleann • **Norse** *monstrous cow:* Audhumla • **Sumero-Semitic** Astarte; associated with the moon • **Zulu** mankind was belched up by a cow • *see also* **cattle; calf; bull**

cowboy rugged individuality; guardian; controller of nature

cowherd honored in Greece, low work in Britain and Egypt • **Hindu** Krishna

cowhide fertility

cowry fertility; giver of life; the feminine principle; wealth; lucky; the Great Mother; childbirth; vulva; the feminine power of water; protects against the evil eye • **funeral art** life and death • *see also* **mollusk; snail**

cowslip rusticity; grace; comeliness; pensiveness • **flower language** pensiveness; winning grace; divine beauty; early joys (particularly of youth); *American cowslip* you are my angel, my divinity • **heraldic** young love; innocence; youth

coyote • **Aztecan** a form of Quetzalcoatl; *double coyote:* the underworld aspect of Quetzalcoatl • **North American Indian** trickster; demiurge; transformer; magician; lover; hero-savior; guide out of danger; flood-bringer; a lunar animal; *Californian tribes:* an unlucky animal; responsible for evil, Winter, and death entering the world; obstructs hero gods responsible for creation

crab aggressiveness; peevishness; regression; withdrawal; grossness; death; regeneration; repulsive sex; impenetrable emotions; emblem of the sea, Cancer; associated with June, dishonesty, money-changers, unreliability, crookedness, drought, the moon, the archangel Gabriel • **hermit crab** caution; foresight • **Buddhist** the sleep of death; the period between reincarnations • **Cambodian** lucky; *catching a crab:* sign that one's wishes will be fulfilled • **Chinese** associated with Nu Chou, drought • **Christian** *crab pincer:* attribute of St. Ottilia • **Hindu** associated with Cancer • **Incan** the Terrible Mother; the waning moon; the devourer of the temporal world • **Jewish** summer • **Machican** evil • **Melanesian** *red crab:* revealed magic to mankind • **Sumerian** associated with Nina Thai; used in rainmaking ceremonies • *see also* **Cancer**

crab apple irritability; foolish old people • **Chinese** perpetual peace; *blossoms:* feminine beauty

cradle birth; rebirth; new life; fresh beginning; shelter; protection; cosmic barque; womb; ship of life rocking on the primordial ocean; coffin; innocence; motherhood; the mother's breast; security; Nativity of Christ; emblem of the Cumean sibyl • **rocking cradle** the ups and downs of life

cranberry the divine seed present in all lower nature • **flower language** cure for heartache

crane (bird) justice; longevity; the good and diligent soul; vigilance; loyalty; good life and works; messenger of deities; communion with deities; ability to enter a higher state of consciousness; haughtiness; stupidity; clumsiness; pomp; justice; purity; dawn; happiness; inquisitiveness; regeneration; lust; a good omen; related to poetry; attribute of the personifications of Religion, Monastic Life • **Bambaran** *crested crane:* self-awareness; self-contemplation; associated with the birth of speech • **Buddhist** carries souls to the Western Paradise; *white cranes:* inhabitants of the Isles of the Blessed, sacred birds • **Celtic** parsimony; meanness; evil woman; herald of death, war; associated with solar gods; a form of Pwyll • **Chinese** immortality; longevity; old age; protective motherhood; vigilance; prosperity; happiness; associated with the sun, pine trees; messenger of the gods; *white heron and black crane:* yin and yang respectively; *fungus with crane:* longevity, happiness • **Christian** vigilance; the vigilance of God over his creatures; Christ; goodness; good struggling against evil; good order in monastic life • **Egyptian** *two-headed crane:* omen of prosperity • **Germanic** sacred to a messenger god •

Greco-Roman intelligence; vigilance; messenger of the gods; herald of Spring, light; sacred to Artemis/Diana, Athena/Minerva, Apollo, Hermes/Mercury, Thoth, Theseus • **heraldic** close parental bond; *with a stone in its mouth:* vigilance • **Hindu** treachery; *crane-headed goddess:* Balgala-mukhi • **Japanese** longevity; luck; fidelity; happiness; eternal youth; attribute of Fukurokuju, Jurojin • **Taoist** immortality; steed of the Immortals

crane's bill (flower) *see* **geranium**

cranium *see* **skull**

crayfish nonchalance; laziness; loss of faith • **Christian** attribute of the Synagogue as the Jewish faith personified

Creation the end of chaos • **Jewish days of Creation:** *Sunday* light; *Monday* division of waters; *Tuesday* dry land, pastures, trees; *Wednesday* heavenly bodies; *Thursday* sea beasts, birds; *Friday* land beasts, man and woman; *Saturday* rest

cremation sublimation; purification; resurrection; return to ashes; destruction the base to make way for the superior; freeing the soul to ascend to heaven

crescent moon sleep; womanhood; the feminine principle in general; the pure soul; chastity; virginity; the Great Mother; the Queen of Heaven; the lunar barque; the receptive cup; emblem of virgin goddesses, moon goddesses, Byzantium, Islam, Turkey • **crescents back to back or one above the other** the waxing and waning moon • **crescent on an outhouse door** use reserved for females • **crescent with rays** associated with funerals • **crescent with solar disk** unity; sacred marriage of divine pairs; joint moon and sun deities; the two-in-one • **Buddhist** the self, emblem of Avalokitesvara, Guanyin • **Celtic** immortality • **Chinese** attribute of Guanyin • **Christian** the Virgin Mary; *crescent and many stars:* God and the Heavenly Host • **Egyptian** attribute of Isis • **Greco-Roman** emblem of Artemis/Diana, Lucina, Selene/Luna; *crescent and seven-pointed star:* attribute of Cybele; *cow with a crescent on each side:* associated with Cadmus • **heraldic** high honors, especially in the Crusades; one who has been honored by a sovereign; change; sciences; hope for greater glory; *in modern times:* second sons and their families • **Hindu** the newborn, quick and eager growth, the cup of the elixir of immortality, associated with soma; *crescent on the forehead:* attribute of Sarasvati, Shiva • **Islamic** death, resurrection, divinity, sovereignty, emblem of Islam; *crescent with star:* divinity; sovereignty; Paradise; resurrection • **Jainism** *swastika sur-*

mounted by crescent: the state of liberation • **Japanese** attribute of Kannon • **Kalmyk** shape of the Eastern Continent and the shapes of the faces of its inhabitants • **Maori** light out of darkness • **Sumero-Semitic** attribute of Astarte, the moon god Sin • *see also* **lunel; moon**

cress old age; something small or worthless • **flower language** stability; power; *Indian cress:* éclat, warlike trophy • *see also* **watercress**

cresset the Gospel • **heraldic** watchfulness; one who signaled in time of danger

crest thought; the predominating characteristic of its owner

cricket (insect) Summer; lucky; unlucky if it leaves or is killed • **chirping crickets** twittering women; loquacity; harbinger of rain, death, approach of an absent lover • **hearth cricket** lucky • **Chinese** life, death, and resurrection • **Greek** Tithonus • **Nigerian** attribute of Oshun • **Occidental** house spirit • **Oriental** Summer; courage

criminal the villainous aspect of one's hidden self; force of chaos

crimson sin; royalty; love • **Greco-Roman** attribute of Pan/Faunus • *see also* **red**

criosphinx silence • **Egyptian** Khnemu • *see also* **androsphinx; heirocosphinx**

crippling *see* **lameness**

crocodile fury; evil; fecundity; power; viciousness; the devourer; the necessity of passing through death to life; dissimulation; knowledge; hypocrisy; the devil; lust; the dual nature of man; silence; a monster of chaos; associated with the archangel Cassiel • **crocodile with open mouth** liberation from the limitations of the world • **being swallowed by a crocodile** descent into hell • **crocodile with jaws bound** Fasting personified • **African** sometimes the home of dead ancestors • **Aztecan** the crocodile gave birth to the Earth • **Cambodian** Kron Poli; associated with jewels, diamonds, lightning, rain • **Chinese** the inventor of singing and the drum; associated with rhythm and harmony in the world • **Christian** the devil; *soldier with crocodile:* St. Theodore • **Egyptian** fury; evil; tyranny; death; voracity; divine reason; Apep; Souchos; emblem of Set; attribute of Ptah; associated with Cheti-Cheti; sacred to Serapis, Sebek; *hawk-headed crocodile or crocodile-headed god:* Sebek; vicious passions; deceit; treachery; hypocrisy; dissimulation; *lion with hippopotamus hindquarters and crocodile jaws:* Ammit • **Hindu** steed of Mantra Vam • **Mayan** associated with Itzamna, abundance; the great primeval crocodile bears the earth in a conch shell on its back; *two-headed crocodile:* guard at the end of the four roads • **South American Indian** powers of the underworld • *see also* **Ammit; caiman; makara**

crocus death; cheerfulness; illicit love; hardiness; joy; emblem of the Virgin Mary • **flower language** abuse not; *saffron crocus:* mirth; *spring crocus:* youthful gladness, pleasures of hope

Croesus • **Greek** immense wealth

cromlech sacred to the Great Mother; the Sacred Center; the solar; the cyclic; the womb • *see also* **column; dolmen**

Cronus/Saturn • **Greco-Roman** destructive and devouring time; fertility; agriculture; consciousness; man as an existential being; activity; communication; endurance; reserve; subjective evil; insatiable greed for life; fear of being replaced by an heir; a ruler unable to adapt to a changing society; associated with castration, Saturday; *Cronus/Saturn bound or asleep:* the suspension of time • **NOTE:** Cronus is essentially the Greek equivalent of Saturn, but *Chronos* is an entirely separate god

crook (shepherd's) *see* **crosier**

crookedness • **Chinese** a crooked line signifies insincerity, artificiality, showiness • *see also* **straightness**

crosier pastoral life; power; divine leadership; power; sovereignty; authority; jurisdiction; creative power; faith; power to draw souls to God and to goad the slothful (the hooked end is for pulling, and the pointed end is for prodding); the correction of vices; mercy; firmness; attribute of shepherds • **Assyrian, Babylonian** attribute of royalty • **Christian** Christ as the Good Shepherd; attribute of bishops, abbots, the Apostles, SS Benedict, Giles, Sylvester, occasionally SS Bernard, Bridget, Clare, Martin; *crosier with fish dangling from it:* attribute of St. Zeno; *crosier with white banner or veil:* attribute of an abbot or abbess; *crosier terminating with a cross with two cross pieces:* attribute of archbishops, St. Gregory; *crosier terminating in a cross with three cross pieces:* attribute of St. Peter, popes • **Egyptian** sovereignty; attribute of Anubis, Osiris, pharaohs • **Greco-Roman** attribute of Proteus, Orpheus, Apollo, Thalia, Pan/Faunus, Argus, Polyphemus, soothsayers • **heraldic** the shepherd's watchfulness; Christian faith; pastoral authority; episcopal jurisdiction and authority • **Jewish** attribute of Moses, Abel (especially when shown with lamb), Amos, David • *see also* **staff**

cross androgyny; union of opposites; the duality of nature; the Supreme Identity; the descent of spirit into matter; eternal life; the four rivers of Paradise; the four elements of the world united; the connection between heaven and earth; mystic center; Tree of Life; crucifixion; suffering; agony; struggle; martyrdom; the suffering of existence; man's longing for the higher world; occasional attribute of the Hellespontic sibyl, the Cimmerean sibyl • **vertical axis** the celestial; the intellectual; the positive; the masculine principle; the active; the axis of the solstice • **horizontal axis** the earthly; the rational; the passive; the negative; the feminine principle; the axis of the equinox • **Cross of Lorraine** emblem of the Free French in World War II • **Greek cross** the union of male and female; emblem of the Rosicrucians, Red Cross Society • **Maltese cross** emblem of Freemasons, Germany; *with triangles at the end of each arm:* power • **red cross** emblem of the Red Cross Society • **yellow cross** sign of the plague • **alchemic** the natural order of the elements; *the central point:* the fifth and highest element, the substance of heavenly bodies • **Amerindian** rain; stars; wood-fire; the human form; maidenhood; the Cosmic Tree; the Great Spirit; the four winds, cardinal directions • **Assyrian** the four directions in which the sun shines; *sun-cross pendant:* attribute of the aristocracy • **Babylonian** *cross and crescent:* associated with moon gods • **Buddhist** the axis of the Wheel of Law and Round of Existence • **Bushmen** divinity; protection in childbirth • **Celtic** life; fecundity; phallus • **Chaldean** *six-rayed cross:* the six days of creation; the six phases of time and of world duration • **Christian** salvation through Christ's sacrifice; martyrdom; suffering; humiliation; the Passion of Christ; the Atonement; finished redemption; attribute of SS Louis of France, John Berchmans; *with martyr's palm:* attribute of St. Margaret of Antioch; *with a saw:* attribute of St. Simon Zelotes; *above a pomegranate:* attribute of St. John of God; *with a chalice:* attribute of Faith personified, St. Bonaventure; *with instruments of the Passion:* attribute of St. Bernard; *with rope on it:* attribute of St. Julia; *with a lamb:* the Crucifixion of Christ; *with a winding sheet:* the Passion of Christ; *with an empty skin:* attribute of St. Bartholomew; *with a carpenter's square:* attribute of St. Philip; *on three steps:* finished redemption (the steps represent faith, hope, and love); Calvary; *on an orb or globe:* salvation, the gradual enlightenment of the world, the triumph of Christ, triumph of the Gospel; *with a banner:* attribute of the Phrygian sibyl; *five crosses:* the five wounds of Christ; *with heart or lily:* attribute of St. Catherine of Siena; *pointed cross emerging from a chalice:* Gethsemane; *processional cross:* the Church Militant, attribute of the Phrygian sibyl; *carried by a deacon:* the deacon is St. Stephen; *with monstrance:* attribute of St. Clare *Eastern cross (two arms at top, a slanted bar below):* the mercy shown the thief to the right of Christ, emblem of the Greek Catholic Church; *green cross:* regeneration; *flowering cross:* resurgent life, the rod of Aaron, Tree of Life, attribute of St. Anthony of Padua; *pectoral cross:* attribute of bishops, abbots; *serpent on a cross:* prototype of Christ raised on the Tree of Life; *serpent with a woman's head entwined on the Cross:* the Temptation of Christ; *red cross on a breastplate:* attribute of St. Maurice; *tall cross:* attribute of St. Matthias; *tall cross with book or scroll:* attribute of St. Philip; *St. Andrew's cross:* attribute of SS Andrew (often with boathook), Patrick; *papal cross:* the papacy, attribute of St. Peter and of popes (with the exception of SS Sylvester, Gregory the Great); *patriarchal cross (two arms at the top):* attribute of patriarchs, archbishops, SS Sylvester, Gregory the Great; *patriarchal cross with a spear:* attribute of St. Philip; *Latin cross:* the Passion of Christ; the Atonement; *Latin cross borne by a woman:* SS Reparata, Margaret; *Latin cross carried in the hand:* St. Philip; *Latin cross made of reeds:* attribute of John the Baptist; *Latin cross borne by angels:* attribute of St. Helena; *Latin cross with rays on a shield:* faith, attribute of St. Paul; *red Latin cross:* attribute of SS Ursula, George of Cappadocia; *Latin cross with a circle in the center:* immortality; *inverted cross:* attribute of SS Peter, Philip; *inverted cross with lance, club, or halberd:* attribute of St. Jude; *Jerusalem cross:* the five wounds of Christ; *knotted cross:* attribute of St. Philip; *Greek cross:* usually the Church of Christ, rather than Christ or Christianity, emblem of the Templars; *Maltese cross:* the eight Beatitudes, attribute of John the Baptist • **Gnostic** the balance of perfection • **heraldic** faith; Christianity; service in the Crusade; *dart or arrow with cross:* affliction; *Celtic cross:* unity of heaven and earth; *Constantine's labarum:* Christ; Christianity; good omen; *crosslet:* the fourfold mystery of the Cross; *crosslet fitcheé:* Cross and sword; unshakeable faith; *cross flory:* conqueror; *cross formeé:* military honor; *Maltese cross:* blessings; emblem of the Knights Hospitalier; *cross moline:* the converse of human society; *cross ragouly:* difficulties encountered; *cross roucy:* faith; *St.

Andrew's cross: resolution • **Hindu** the expansion of being; the rajas associated with the Ganges River; fire sticks of Agni • **Islamic** the Supreme Identity, perfect communion of all states of being • **Jewish** *made of faggots:* attribute of Isaac; *with scroll:* attribute of Jeremiah • **Kabalistic** *six-rayed cross:* the six days of creation, the six phases of time and world creation • **Khoisan** divinity; protection in childbirth • **Manichean** *Cross of Light:* the suffering Jesus, the light that penetrates all nature • **Maori** the moon goddess; the common good • **Mexican Indian** Tree of Life; the four winds; fertility; Tlaloc; Quetzalcoatl • **Phoenician** life; health • **Platonic** the Creator • **Roman** doom for the malefactor • *see also* **ankh; tau cross**

crossroads choice; union; the mother; intersection or conjunction of any binary form — space/time, body/spirit, etc.; mystic center; the union of opposites; meeting place of demons, witches, fairies, ghosts, etc.; place of magic power, manifestation, revelation; burial place for felons, suicides, vampires, murderers • **reaching a crossroads** facing the unknown, the necessity for making a decision, a parting of the ways • **African** a holy place; dwelling place of the gods; a place to safely dispose of possessions of the dead, illegitimate and deformed babies, anything that is unclean • **Aztecan** place where the spirits of women who died in childbirth appeared at dusk • **Greco-Roman** place of encounter with fate; associated with Janus; sacred to Hecate, Hermes/Mercury, the Lares • **Hindu** associated with Ganesha, Rudra

crow chatter; usually an unfavorable omen; death; piracy; Negro; the negative or occult; solitude; cunning; pride; untrustworthiness; plebian; longevity; hermit; the isolation of one who lives on a superior plane; messenger; prophet; possessor of mystic powers; demiurgic power; associated with the archangel Cassiel, beginning; attribute of Hope personified • **alchemic** first stage of the Great Work • **Celtic** *hooded crow:* Babd, Macha, Neman; *white crow:* Branwen • **Chinese** evil; unlucky; malice; associated with business; *red or black crow:* the sun, filial piety; *three-legged crow:* lives in the sun • **Christian** solitude; the devil; *plucking out eyes:* the devil blinding sinners; *two crows:* attribute of St. Vincent • **Egyptian** *pair of crows:* conjugal felicity • **Greco-Roman** death omen; sacred to Apollo, Athena/Minerva, related to Asclepius, Cronus/Saturn; *man with crow's head:* Cronus/Saturn • **heraldic** strategy in battle; watchfulness for friends; divine providence •

Hindu attribute of Varuna • **Iroquoian** Gagaah • **Japanese** misfortune; ill omen; although in Shintoism, holy crows (sometimes pictured as a crow in front of the sun) are considered messengers of the gods and are associated with temples • **Jewish** carrion; a corpse • **Mediterranean** *crow croaking a ship's rigging:* ill omen for a voyage • **North American Indian** keeper of the sacred law; messenger to the spirit world; change omen; trickster; occasionally the demiurge • **Oriental** ill omen; *pair of crows:* conjugal fidelity • *see also* **chough; tengu; raven**

crowbar a passive intermediary

crowd the unconscious; discordant actions in the unconscious (when the crowd is orderly, it loses its negative connotations)

crowfoot (plant) • **flower language** ingratitude (especially celery-leaved crowfoot); *aconite-leaved crowfoot:* luster

crown pre-eminence; success; honor; sun rays; spiritual enlightenment (especially a jeweled crown); rank; sovereignty; victory; reward of virtue; eternal life; union of heaven and earth; completeness; continuity; associated with funerals; attribute of royalty, gods, the Cuman sibyl • **two crowns attribute** of Liberty personified • **three crowns** attribute of King Arthur • **crown of flowers held in the hand** attribute of the personifications of Asia, the Golden Age • **crown of feathers** nimbus; sun rays; attribute of America (both continents) personified • **crown of reeds and rushes** attribute of river gods • **crown of olive branches** attribute of Peace personified • **crown of bay laurel** attribute of poets, Homer, Dante, Virgil, the personifications of Victory, Fame (with trumpet), Truth (naked) • **crown of grape vine** attribute of Gluttony personified • **crown of thorns** attribute of the Delphic sibyl • **turreted crown** attribute of Earth personified, the Great Mother, towns and cities personified, the holy dwellings of deities • **rayed crown** the energy and power contained in the head; attribute of sun gods • **evergreen crown** life; immortality; victory • **crown at the feet** renounced royalty • **alchemic** the successful completion of an alchemical operation; the perfection of a metal • **Buddhist** emblem of the footprint of Buddha; *crown of Buddha:* his realization of the five gyanas; *five-leaved chodpan:* the five celestial Buddhas • **Central American Indian** attribute of agrarian gods • **Chinese** imperial power; supremacy; *crown covering the ears:* hearing no slander; *crown with veil or jewels covering the eyes:* seeing nothing unworthy; *rooster with*

crown: the literary spirit • **Christian** blessing and favor; victory over death; attainment; reward of martyrs; reward righteousness; Christ's kingly office; attribute of the Virgin Mary as the queen of heaven, SS Margaret of Antioch (especially when shown with a dragon), Catherine of Alexandria (especially with book and martyr's palm), Sebastian (especially with arrows), Gertrude (especially with lily and/or taper), Josaphat (especially with palm and/or pallium); *crown of stars:* attribute of the Virgin Mary (especially with lilies), virgin martyrs (usually held in the hand); *crown at the feet of saints:* noble birth; *crown on the head of saints:* royal birth; *triple crown:* attribute of the pope, St. Elizabeth of Hungary; *crown of thorns:* the mocking of Jesus Christ, attribute of SS Catherine of Sienna, Mary Magdalene, John of God, Rose of Lima, Joseph of Arimathea, Louis IX, Veronica; *crown of roses:* attribute of SS Casimir, Cecilia, Flavia, Dorothea, Elizabeth of Hungary; *angel placing crowns of roses on a man and a woman:* Valerius and St. Cecelia; *three crowns:* attribute of St. Charlemagne; *three crowns with cross:* attribute of St. Helena; *crown with scepter:* Christ as king; *crown with scepter at his feet:* attribute of St. Louis of Toulouse; *crown of olive branches:* attribute of St. Agnes; *crown of bay laurel:* attribute of St. Paul; *Crown of Life:* perfection • **Egyptian** attribute of gods, pharaohs; *red crown:* emblem of the Lower Kingdom of Egypt, attribute of Neith; *white crown:* emblem of the Upper Kingdom of Egypt; *white crown with a streamer:* attribute of Resheph; *white crown with asps, horns, and plumes:* attribute of Thoth; *red and white double crown:* union of the North and South, the higher mind and lower mind, the higher world and lower world; attribute of Mut, other chief gods, the pharaoh; *crown of ten double ostrich plumes:* power to divide the heavens and enter them • **English** *crown with strawberry leaves:* attribute of a duke • **Greco-Roman** victory; attribute of soothsayers; *bay laurel crown:* attribute of Apollo, Roman emperors and governors of provinces, Calliope (when held in the hand), Clio, Arion (riding a dolphin), winner at the Pythian games; *parsley crown:* winner at the Menean games; *grape vine crown:* attribute of Dionysus/Bacchus; *pine crown:* sacred to Poseidon/Neptune; awarded to winners at the Isthmian games; *crown of poplar leaves:* attribute of Heracles/Hercules in his descent to Hades; *wild olive crown:* sacred to Zeus/Jupiter; awarded to winners at the Olympian games; *turreted crown:*

attribute of Tyche/Fortuna, Urania; *crown of flowers:* attribute of Flora; *crown of grain:* attribute of Demeter/Ceres; *rayed crown:* attribute of sun gods and other deities; *crown of flowers:* attribute of Euterpe, Terpsichore, Flora, Melpomene; *crown of stars:* attribute of Urania; *crown of roses:* attribute of Comus • **heraldic** prestige; royal or seigniorial authority; *muraled crown:* defender of a fortress; civic honor, one who first breached fortress walls; *naval crown:* distinguished naval service; *crown of thorns:* adversity • **Hindu** *crown on the central temple pillar:* divine glory, the passage to heaven, the celestial world • **Jewish** *priest's crown:* the splendor that pleases God; *crown and scepter:* attribute of David, Deborah, Melchizedek (at his feet) • **Kabalistic** the Absolute; the state of Non-Being • **Middle Eastern** *turreted crown:* attribute of mother goddesses • **still life** the earthly power that death takes away • **Sumero-Semitic** *feather crown:* authority, power, celestial power, attribute of Marduk, Shamash • *see also* **coronation; tiara**

crown imperial • **flower language** majesty; power

crowsbill (plant) • **flower language** envy

crozier *see* **crosier**

crucible place of severe testing; place of initiation, formation; attribute of the Alchemist personified; the feminine principle; womb • **alchemic** woman; the matrix

crucifix • **Christian** pain; suffering; humiliation; ridicule; the suffering Savior; the Passion of Christ; the Atonement; attribute of SS Frances Xavier, Francis of Assisi, Mary Magdalene, Catherine of Alexandria, Anthony of Padua (especially with an unclothed Christ); *crucifix with Christ dressed in vestments:* the Reigning Christ; *crucifix with the figure of Christ leaning toward a saint:* attribute of St. John Gualberto; *crucifix between the antlers of a stag:* attribute of St. Hubert; *crucifix held by martyr with a hatchet in his head:* St. Peter Martyr; *crucifix entwined with lilies:* attribute of St. Nicholas of Tolentino; *crucifix entwined with roses:* attribute of St. Therese of Lisieux; *crucifix with dove:* attribute of St. Scholastica; *praying desert hermit praying with a crucifix:* usually St. Jerome; *crucifix and skull:* attribute of St. Charles Borromeo

crucifixion of a lamb • **Christian** the crucifixion of Christ

cruet • **Christian** redemption; the Eucharist

cruse • **Christian** *cruse of wine with napkin:* attribute of the Good Samaritan • **Jewish** *endless cruse of oil:* the inexhaustible grace and mercy of God; attribute of Elijah and the Widow of Sarepta

crutch misfortune; moral shortcoming; temporary handicap; hidden or shameful support; assistance; great age; attribute of beggars, Father Time • **Christian** attribute of SS Anthony the Great (especially with a bell on it), John Gualberto, Romuald, Maurus; emblem of those who care for the aged or crippled • **Greco-Roman** attribute of Hephaestus/Vulcan, Cronus/Saturn • **Islamic** associated with Nasiree

crystal transparency; purity; wisdom; intuitive knowledge; the spirit; the intellect; spiritual perfection and knowledge; simplicity; the self-luminous; truthfulness; the Great Spirit; related to the eyes, water, baptism, ice, tears, the moon, 15th wedding anniversaries, magic powers, the archangels Gabriel, Metatron; charm for faith, clarity, and protection from homesickness, stress • **crystal ball** immortality; divine light; entrance to another world; attribute of fortune tellers • **crystal shoes, tower, boat, etc.** a means of transfer from one state or plane to another • **Buddhist** the state of transparency; the pure mind; perfect insight; the sphere of spiritual insight; the five aggregates of body and mind • **Christian** *crystal ball:* the world of the light of God • **Greco-Roman** sacred to Selene/Luna • **Ural-Altaic** celestial power and light

cube the earth; the solidity and persistence of virtues; stability; devotion; truth; associated with artificial or constructed objects; immobilization; the result of squaring the circle; perfection; static perfection; immaculate law; cornerstone; foundation stone; attribute of the personifications of Faith, History • **axe embedded in a cube** the revealing of secret or hidden knowledge • **alchemic** salt • **Chinese** the earth deity • **heraldic** constancy; truthfulness; devotion • **Islamic** stability; static perfection; the Ka'aba • **Jewish** the Holy of Holies • **Mayan** the earth; site of thee Tree of Life

cubit (measuring rod) • **Egyptian** order, justice, truth, attribute of Thoth

cuckoo cuckoldry; usurpation; parasitism; jealousy; herald of Spring; egoism; selfishness; infidelity; foolishness; deception; the frivolous; insanity; the eternal bachelor; the devil; associated with April • **European** *Southern:* Spring; *Northern:* Summer • **Finnish** tears; desolation; emblem of Aino • **Greek** wedlock; occasional attribute of Hera • **Hindu** the sun hidden by clouds; rain maker • **Japanese** unrequited love; messenger of night • **Phoenician** a kingly bird; emblem on the scepter of Kings • **Siberian** associated with Spring, the administration of justice, bringing the dead back to life; *two cuckoos:* sun and moon

cuckoo plant Spring • **flower language** ardor
cucumber • **flower language** criticism
cudweed • **flower language** never ceasing remembrance
cuirass *see* **breastplate**
cumin • **Greek** meanness; cupidity
cup friendship; temperance; renewed spiritual vigor; the moon; the passive element; vulva; consolation; blessing; prize; the feminine principle • **overturned cup spilling wine** death; the spilling of blood • **golden cup** virginity; prize • **silver cup** prize • **clay cup** man's life • **broken cup** broken life • **cup with two handles** the loving cup; brotherly love • **art** *overturned cup:* vanity; the emptiness of worldly things • **Assyrian** renewed spiritual vigor • **Celtic** life; the heart; *cup and mallet:* attribute of Sucellus • **Christian** human destiny; *broken cup:* attribute of St. Benedict; *cup with a serpent in it:* attribute of St. John; *broken communion cup:* attribute of St. Donatus of Arezzo; Christ's agony in Gethsemane; *communion cup with wafer:* the Eucharist; attribute of SS Barbara, Bonaventure; *baptismal cup:* attribute of St. Ansanus; *two doves on a cup:* the Eucharist • **Egyptian** renewed spiritual vigor • **Greco-Roman** attribute of Hebe, Juventas, Heracles/Hercules, Dionysus/Bacchus, Asclepius, Hygeia, Hermes/Mercury, Chthonius, Ganymede; *woman drinking from a cup:* Sophonsiba, Artemisia • **heraldic** liberality; purity; joy; bailiff; treasurer; archivist; royal cup-bearer or meat-carver; *covered cup:* king's butler • **Hindu** *four cups of the Vedas:* the four rivers of Paradise, elements, castes, seasons, etc.; *cup on top of a column or other support:* grace and abundance given to one offering himself up to heaven • **Islamic** the heart; intuition; *Cup of Jamishi:* mirror to the world • **Italian** *heart in a cup:* associated with Ghismonda • **Jewish** human destiny; *cup in a sack of grain:* attribute of Joseph (son of Jacob); *cup of salvation:* worship, thanksgiving • **Norse** life token; container of the soul; emblem of the gods • **Persian** *cup with seven rings:* the seven heavens, attribute of Jamshyd • *see also* **chalice**
Cupid *see* **Eros/Cupid**
cupola a phallic symbol; dome of the sky; celestial vault; celestial world • **Buddhist, Hindu** spiritual protection; royalty
cups (playing cards) *see* **hearts (playing cards)**
curlew • **Christian** the good Christian
currants • **flower language** your frown will kill me; you please all (especially a branch of currants)
curtain concealment; protection; privacy; veil of the future • **dropping or closing a curtain** completion, death, concealing • **opening or raising a curtain** joining, revelation, beginning
cuscuta • **flower language** meanness
cushion comfort; wealth; authority; ease • **heraldic** authority • *see also* **pillow**
cuttlefish *see* **squid**
Cyanean Rocks *see* **Symplegades**
Cybele • **Roman** energy entombed in the earth; fertility through death
cyclamen • **Christian** attribute of the Virgin Mary • **flower language** diffidence; distrust; voluptuousness
Cyclops • **Greco-Roman** brute strength; demoniacal strength; stubbornness; abrupt emotion; low level of understanding; primitive and regressive force; forgers of the thunderbolts of Hephaestus/Vulcan, Zeus/Jupiter; *Arges:* brightness of lightning; *Brontes:* thunder; *Steropes:* lightning
cygnet *see* **swan**
cylinder material thoughts; the mechanistic intellect
cymbals vanity; religious ardor; dance (especially two cymbals); the two hemispheres of the earth; motion of the elements; attribute of Petulance personified • **Greco-Roman** associated with orgies, Dionysus/Bacchus, Cybele, Attis; *drinking from a cymbal:* part of a rite of Attis
cypress sorrow; death; immortality; eternity; mourning; Tree of Life; phallic; associated with cemeteries, funerals, the archangels Azrael, Chamuel; attribute of many underworld, nature and fertility deities • **cypress coffin** resurrection • **cypress chest** preservation • **cypress and marigolds** despair; melancholy • **cypress surmounted by the sun or moon** androgyny • **cypress wreath** mourning • **Chinese** grace; happiness; death • **Christian** endurance; perseverance in virtue; the Christian; the just man occasionally; the righteous man who preserves his faith; death; mourning; *cypress of Zion:* attribute of the Virgin Mary; *palm, olive, and cypress together:* attribute of the Virgin Mary • **Greco-Roman** attribute of the Erinyes/Furies, the Moirae/Fates, Heracles/Hercules, Zeus/Jupiter, Apollo, Aphrodite/Venus, Artemis/Diana, Hermes/Mercury; emblem of Hades/Pluto, Dis • **heraldic** death; eternal life • **Mithraic** residence of Mithras • **Phoenician** Tree of Life; sacred to Melcarth • **Sumero-Semitic** sacred to Astarte • **Zoroastrian** Tree of Life; emblem of Ormzud

D

D associated with adversity; material barriers; equity; justice; tolerance; limitation; the supreme being; the square; the geometric; Roman numeral for 500; corresponds to the blood, -4-, Jupiter (planet) • **tarot** the Empress

dabchick weakness; a sensitive purpose; a parasite; a girl; hiding; a seeker of the wisdom of the deeps

daffodil unrequited love; herald of spring; courage; dancing; short-lived beauty; death; mourning; spiritual rebirth; gracefulness; associated with Aquarius, -6-; emblem of Wales • **flower language** regard; *great yellow daffodil:* chivalry • **heraldic** chivalry; courage; regard; sunshine; respect

dagger danger; treachery; weapon of a traitor or assassin; phallus; protection against a foe; masculine principle; attribute of Wrath personified, the archangel Zadkiel • **wooden dagger** attribute of Vice personified • **Christian** attribute of SS Thomas the Apostle, Lucia (piercing her neck) • **Greco-Roman** attribute of Hecate, Melpomene (from the 17th Century on), Lucretia, Ares/Mars • **heraldic** military honor; justice • **Mithraic** attribute of Mithras • *see also* **knife**

dahlia elegance; the dignity of the lower, or lower-middle class; vulgar ostentation; instability; pomp; health • **blue dahlia** impossibility • **flower language** instability; my gratitude exceeds your care • **heraldic** dignity; elegance; together forever

daisy innocence; virginity; purity; adoration; dissembling; fidelity; resurrection; the silence of death; youth; the Sun of Righteousness; the solar; hope; humility; related to pearls; emblem of the nymph Belides • **art** a flower of Paradise • **Christian** the innocence of the Christ child; attribute of Christ, the Virgin Mary; *English daisy:* attribute of St. Margaret of Antioch; *ox-eye daisy:* attribute of SS John, Mary Magdalene • **flower language** innocence; *double daisy:* participation; *field or wild daisy:* considering a suit (particularly in the days of chivalry, when turned in a wreath and worn in the hair by a woman); *garden or small double daisy:* I share your sentiments, I reciprocate your affection (both, especially in the days of chivalry); *Michaelmas daisy:* farewell, an afterthought; *ox-eyed daisy:* a token; *parti-colored daisy:* beauty • **heraldic** innocence; gentleness

dakini • **Buddhist** female energy

Dalmatian (dog) associated with luxury, wealth, horses, heraldic ermine, horses, firehouses, fire fighters

dalmatic • **Christian** joy; salvation; justice; the Passion of Christ; attribute of deacons in the Western Church and bishops in the Eastern Church (although Western bishops and abbots may wear it under a chasuble), SS Laurence, Leonard (with a fleur-de-lis and/or broken fetters), Stephen (especially with three stones), Vincent of Sargossa

dam repression; restraint; reservoir of hope

damsel the anima • *see also* **woman**

dance creation; cosmic creative energy; a process; harmonious cooperation; desire for escape; passage of time; transformation of space into time; reinforcement of strength, emotion, and/or activity; fertility; release from disagreeable circumstances; war; victory; orgy; joy; gratitude; sex; protection; black magic; manifestation of the spirit of Life; the attempt to throw off duality and rediscover primeval oneness; seeking freedom in ecstasy; throwing off bonds • **chain dance** linking male and female, heaven and earth, etc. • **labyrinth, troy dances** strengthening the center object; *with a maiden in the center:* completing initiation, attaining a goal, attaining Paradise; • **round dances** imitation of the sun's course in the sky; enclosing a sacred space; angels dancing around God's throne • **sword dances, morris dances** sympathetic magic to help the sun in its course • **thread, rope dances** secret knowledge to get in and out of a maze; associated with Ariadne, the umbilical cord • **Asian** *belly dance:* mimicry of childbirth • **Greco-Roman** *belly dance:* promotion of fertility, sexual stimulation; *Dionysian/Bacchanalian dances:* emotional chaos • **Hindu** associated with Vishnu, Krishna, Shiva; *dancing man with multiple arms:* Shiva; *Dance of Shiva:* the eternal movement of the universe; *post-Vedic:* death, aging, *Upanishads:* death; liberation • **Islamic** *dervishes:* the cycles of existence and their circling by the Spirit, the whirling of a planet on its axis and around the sun • **Mediterranean** *dancing aboard ship:* unlucky • **North American Indian** *stick dance:* war rite, fertility rite; *sun dance:* regeneration of the sun, union with solar power • **witchcraft** *dancing in a circle nine times counterclockwise:* casting a spell

dancer death; seduction

dandelion coquetry; grief; bitterness; the sun; wisdom; the Passion of Christ; associated with Sagittarius, Leo, Jupiter (planet) • **seeds floating free** gossip • **flower language** love's oracle; *all seeds removed when blown:* a lover is faithful;

few seeds remain: a lover is unfaithful; *many seeds remain:* a lover is indifferent • **Jewish** a bitter herb of the Passover; the bitterness of bondage

dangling unfulfilled longing

daphne odora • **flower language** painting the lily

darkness spiritual darkness; evil; primeval chaos; the unconscious; the unknown; ignorance; the germinant; undeveloped potentialities; the maternal or feminine; the source of existential dualism; terrible judgment; misfortune; mystery; sin; error; associated with states of germination, germination, creation • **darkness appearing after light** regression • **darkness and light** the two opposing aspects of the Great Mother — creator/destroyer, birth/death, etc. • **Chinese** yin • **Christian** the devil; captivity; spiritual darkness • **Hindu** the dark aspect of Kali as Time the destroyer; associated with Durga • **Islamic** indiscretion • **Persian** associated with Angra Mainyu, Ahriman

darnel misfortune • **flower language** vice

dart sun ray; phallus; evil words; attribute of Eros/Cupid • **dart with flaming tip** attribute of St. Teresa (usually piercing her breast) • **dart and egg** male generation and female productiveness • **heraldic** readiness for battle; justice; military honor; *dart with cross:* affliction

Daruma • **Japanese** patience, tenacity

date (fruit) fecundity • **Chaldean** food for the soul • **Christian** *bunch of dates:* attribute of St. Ansanus • **Taoist** offspring • *see also* **palm tree**

David, King • **Jewish** victory over tremendous odds; divine love manifested on earth; emblem of Israel's golden age; associated with music, the Psalms

dawn creation; youth; beginning; a new start; regeneration; enlightenment; the unconscious broadening into consciousness; the beginning of salvation • **red dawn;** sailor's warning; emblem of Chinese communism • **Buddhist** the clear light of the Void • **Christian** the Advent of Christ; the Resurrection; *red dawn:* the blood of Christ • **Greco-Roman** youth; purity; freshness; emblem of Eos/Aurora • **Hindu** blessing; a bride; emblem of Ushas • **Jewish** God's power over darkness • *see also* **twilight**

day lily *see* **lily**

Day of Judgment (tarot) *see* **Judgment (tarot)**

day star Christ

days *three days:* the dark of the moon, days of death of an initiate or harvest god before rebirth • *see also* **birth; Creation; gods; marriages; sneezing; works; zodiac**

deacon • **Christian** *winged deacon:* St. Josaphat; *deacon with stones:* St. Stephen; *deacon carrying processional cross:* St. Laurence; *deacon with broken fetters:* St. Leonard

deafness inability to hear the conscience or spirit; may imply the person has a compensatory power • *see also* **hearing**

death end of an epoch; escape from unendurable tension; means of gaining immortality; omniscience; the unseen aspect of life; forerunner of spiritual rebirth; reunion of the body with the earth and the soul with the spirit; harbinger of revelation; liberation from negative and regressive forces; dematerialization; unleashes ascensional powers of the spirit • **little death** euphemism for orgasm • **Islamic** associated with the archangel Azrael • **Mongolian** the dead are associated with North

Death (personified) an old man or old woman, 90 to 100 years old in particular

Death (tarot) abandonment of earthly desires; ambivalence; creation; death of the old self (not necessarily physical death); decomposition; dematerialization; destruction; melancholy; strength; the progress of evolution; transformation; associated with the process of change, rebirth, regeneration

decagon • **Christian** the ten disciples who did not betray or deny Christ • *see also* **-10-**

decapitation *see* **beheading**

December coldness; gloom; peace and quiet; old age; associated with Capricorn, Saturn (planet)

decoration glorification; sublimation

Dedalus • **Greek** craftsmanship; cleverness; inventiveness; ingenuity; practical intelligence

deepness chaos; hell • *see also* **abyss**

deer timidity; fleetness; gentleness; the soul; aspiration of the soul (especially a jumping deer); longevity; Autumn; vanity; associated with the Tree of Life • **doe** timidity; fidelity; wildness • **fawn** flattery; subservience; innocence; defenselessness • **Aztecan** *two-headed deer:* associated with Mixcoatl • **Buddhist** meditation; meekness; gentleness; love-sickness as one of the Three Senseless Creatures of Chinese Buddhism; *deer on either side of the Wheel of Law:* Buddha's preaching in the park at Sarnath • **Celtic** supernatural animal of the fairy world; fairy cattle; divine messenger; guide of souls to the underworld; *chariot drawn by deer:* attribute of Flidas; *deer skin and/or antlers:* ritual vestments; *god with deer antlers:* Cernunnos • **Chinese** longevity; high rank; honor; official success; wealth • **Christian** a Christian searching after truth; a catechumen; attribute of St. Francis of Assisi; *fawn:* attribute of St. Jerome •

Egyptian sacred to Isis at Phocis • **Greco-Roman** sacred to Artemis/Diana, Athena/Minerva, Aphrodite/Venus, Apollo • **heraldic** peace; harmony • **Hindu** steed of Vayu; *deer skin:* attribute of Shiva • **Japanese** attribute of Fukurokuju, Jurojin; *deer with maple:* solitariness; melancholy • **Mayan** *dying deer:* drought • **Mexican Indian** bearer of the sun • **Mongolian** *yellow doe:* mother of Genghis Khan • **North American Indian** swiftness • **Panche** reincarnated human souls • **Ural-Altaic** conductor of souls of the dead • *see also* **stag; hart; hind**

defile (topography) *see* **gorge**

delta (Greek letter) feminine generative power; the door of life; fertility

deluge destruction and regeneration; the final stage of a cycle; purification; awakening of the mind from ignorance and error • *see also* **rain**

Demeter/Ceres • **Greco-Roman** agriculture; *with a torch and/or chariot drawn by dragons:* search for Persephone/Proserpine; *with a sickle, cornucopia, and/or wreath of grain:* earth's abundance personified • **Middle Ages** the Church

Demogorgon a fertility spirit; an evil spirit; an underground demon; chaos personified; the creative spirit

demon agent of the devil; a soul of the dead; intermediary between mortals and immortals • **demon underfoot** attribute of SS Norbert, Geminianus, Catherine of Siena • **demon emerging from victim's mouth** exorcism • **demon whispering in man's ear** the man may be Judas • *see also* **devil; monster**

Demos • **Greek** panic

dervish • **Islamic** the cycles of existence and their circling by the Spirit; the whirling of a planet on its axis and around the sun

descending failure; loss of control; searching for mystic wisdom, rebirth, immortality; overcoming death; entrance into primordial darkness prior to rebirth and regeneration; journey taken in initiatory rites and by dying gods; journey to understand and overcome the dark side of one's nature • *see also* **ascending**

desert a place of divine revelation; a spiritual and holy place; a place where one has to be dependent wholly on the grace of God; abandonment; bleakness; contemplation; primordial undifferentiated state; desolation; failure; quiet; the realm of abstraction, spirituality, truth, purity, ascetic spiritualism • **vast and unknown desert** may represent chaos • **desert animals** evil and the forces of destruction

desk authority; reflection of the self • *see also* **writing table**

devastation barrenness and unproductiveness in the spirit

devil the unrealized dark side of man; sin; the forces of regression; the center of darkness; evil; evil personified; sin personified; wickedness; separation from God; associated with temptation • **devil underfoot** attribute of St. Romuald • *see also* **Beelzebub; Belphegor; demon; Lucifer; Mephistopheles; Satan**

Devil (tarot) domination of the soul by matter; overindulgence in the material world; black magic; disorder; perversion; regression or stagnation of all that is fragmentary, inferior, or discontinuous; the instincts and desires; the half-knowledge of the senses

devil ray *see* **ray**

devouring acquisition of the powers of that which is eaten burial; assimilation; dissolution of the body after death; fear of castration; fear of death; fear of incest (especially maternal); fear of the Terrible Mother; mystery

dew spiritual illumination, refreshment; grace; purity; purification; divine blessing; peace; prosperity; freshness; youth; evanescence; change; illusion; fertility; remembrance; the light of dawn; related to nightfall, sleep, the moon, dawn • **Buddhist** ephemerality of material things; the world of appearances; brevity of life • **Chinese** immortality; the Sweet Tree of Dew; food of the Immortals on Ho-chu Island; the peaceful marriage of heaven and earth • **Christian** Christ; benediction • **Greco-Roman** semen of Zeus/Jupiter; associated with Aphrodite/Venus, Dionysus/Bacchus, fertility • **Kabalistic** resurrection; the Dew of Light from the Tree of Life • **Neo-Platonic** generation; the natural envelope of souls • **Norse** *dew of honey:* emblem of Servitur • **North American Indian** regenerated soil ruined by evil spirits • **Oriental** delicacy; fragility • **Sumero-Semitic** associated with Astarte

dew plant • **flower language** a serenade

diadem *see* **crown**

diamond (gem) absolute truth; fearlessness; fortitude; universal sovereignty; invincible constancy; purity; sincerity; incorruptibility; strength; durability; light; the sun; brilliance; moral and intellectual knowledge; sanctity; perfection; hardness; pride; intelligence; hardness of heart; invulnerable faith; innocence; lucidity; frankness; joy; life; dignity and wealth, especially royal; associated with Aries, Taurus, April, 10th, 50th, 75th wedding anniversaries, the archangels Metatron, Michael, Samael; charm for spirituality, protection, healing, reconciliation, sexual function • **yellow diamond** stone for 20th wedding anniversaries • **Buddhist** *Diamond Mace:* resolution; *on the Footprint of Buddha:* thunder striking at the passions of mankind; *Diamond Throne or Seat:* the place of enlightenment • **Christian** Christ; constancy; love • **French** constancy; strength; charm to banish anger, strengthen the bonds of marriage, promote reconciliation • **Jewish** *on vestments:* Winter, sun, light • **Renaissance art** equanimity; courage in adversity; integrity of character; freedom from fear; good faith • **Russian** charm for controlling lust and encouraging chastity • *see also* **diamonds (playing cards)**

diamond (shape) vulva • **heraldic** merchant; escutcheon of women

diamonds (playing cards) material force; eternity; trade; industry; justice; silence; associated with merchants, wealth, -4-, material possessions, education, physical well-being, world of the senses, material earth, physical form, the feminine, vulva, provisions, solid matter, Summer, the cube, the square, commerce, the intelligentsia • **ace of diamonds** associated with Winter, material gain, wealth • **king of hearts** associated with the fire king, Caesar, the arrowhead • **queen of diamonds** associated with fire and fuel, Nephthys, Persephone/Proserpine • **jack (knave) of diamonds** associated with warriors • **cartomancy** a woman with red or light-brown hair, also a young married woman; *nine of diamonds:* deadly fortune • *see also* **playing cards**

Diana *see* **Artemis/Diana**

dianthus divine love

dice chance; risk; divination; debauchery; vice; falseness; fickleness; foolish or wasteful action; fortune; gambling; fate; the irrevocable; attribute of Fortune personified, the Three Graces • **Buddhist** the four-square of the sacred four, the cycles of the yugas • **Christian** the casting of lots for Christ's garment • **heraldic** equity; constancy; fickleness of fortune

Dido tragedy

digestion mastery; assimilation (especially spiritual); dissolution; good digestion is a sign of congruence with nature, and vice versa • *see also* **eating; devouring**

digging examining or mining the unconscious; searching for information, knowledge; low work

dill cleansing • **heraldic** harmony; irresistible

dimple love; attribute of attractive children and maidens • **dimple in the cheek** misfortune • **dimple in the chin** lucky • **dimple when smiling** sign of loose character

dinosaur extinction; primitive nature; superannuation

Diomedes • **Greek** bravery

Dionysus/Bacchus • **Greco-Roman** the uninhibited unleashing of desire; sin; corruption; debauchery; the antithesis of Apollo; sexual passion; the attempt to spiritualize life forms; regressive forces; drowning of the conscious in the unconscious; the life force that tends to break restraints

diosma • **flower language** uselessness

dirt (earth) *see* **earth**

dirtiness accumulation of error, prejudice, sin

disability defect in the soul; indication that a person may a compensatory power

discus • **Greek** associated with Hyacinth

disease divine displeasure; malady of the soul; ailment of the psyche; pathway to heaven; natural or spiritual disorder or disharmony

disguise assumption of a different personality; entrance into a new stage of life • *see also* **mask**

dish limitation; the feminine principle; family; martyrdom • **washing dishes** doing away with old ideas • **eating off another's dish** borrowing another's ideas; presumption; intimacy • **Christian** *alabaster dish:* attribute of Mary Magdalene

disk sun; renewal of life; perfection divinity; power • **disk with a hole in the center** the cosmos surrounding the Void; transcendent and unique essence • **twirling disk** revolution of the universe • **winged disk** fire or power from heaven; a solar god; divinity; transfiguration; immortality; the generative power of nature; the dual life and death powers of nature; charm against evil • **Assyrian** *eagle-headed god with wings and disk, or just a winged disk:* Ashur • **Babylonian** *winged disk:* Shamash • **Buddhist** attribute of Vairocana; *circumference:* the round of creation; *center:* the Void • **Chinese** sun; heaven; divinity; spiritual and celestial perfection; *with encircling fighting dragons:* the Void • **Egyptian** Ra; power; fame; *disk of the rising sun:* renewal of life, life after death, resurrection; *winged disk:* the solar power of Aton, Ra, renewal of life; *disk with two falcon feathers:* attribute of Amen-Ra; *disk with goat horns:* life, strength, attribute of Isis; *lion-headed woman with solar disk and uraeus:* Bast • **Hindu** *flaming disk:* attribute of Krishna, the disk of Brahma; *twirling rayed disk:* revolution of the universe on its axis, revolution of the chakras, weapon of Vishnu • **Persian** *winged disk:* Ahura Mazda, Ormzud, the power of light • **zodiac** *disk on the horns of a ram:* Aries

dismemberment being possessed by the unconscious, unconscious mania, or unconscious obsessions; degeneration; destruction; disintegration, especially mental; death of the self before reintegration and rebirth; unity giving way to fragmentation; the many arising from the One • **dismemberment and reintegration** the multiplicity of the manifest world and the restoration of primordial unity; associated with Dionysus/Bacchus, Osiris, Zagreus, Orisha, the initiation of a shaman • *see also* **maiming; beheading**

dispersal *see* **dismemberment**

distaff time; the continuity of creation; weaving; spinning; industry; cosmic time; creation; woman; the domestic role of women; may have sexual significance; attribute of goddesses of spinning, weaving, fate • **Christian** attribute of the Virgin Mary at the Annunciation, St. Genevieve • **Greco-Roman** attribute of the Moirae/Fates (especially Clotho) • **Jewish** attribute of Eve after the expulsion from the Garden of Eden

ditch pitfall; the grave • **ditch digging** low work

dittany associated with childbirth, Venus (planet) • **flower language** *white dittany:* passion; *dittany of Crete:* childbirth • **Greco-Roman** associated with Hera/Juno, Artemis/Diana

dividers *see* **compasses**

divorce separation of love from wisdom, emotion from reason, or goodness from truth • **divorce for the purpose of marrying another** leaving higher nature for lower desire

dock (plant) changeableness; shrewdness; patience; attribute of Affection personified • **flower language** patience

doctor an agent promoting growth of the spirit, or treating its ailments • **Mochican** Ai apaec (especially with lizard and dog)

dodder (plant) • **flower language** meanness; baseness

dodecagon • **Christian** the 12 disciples • *see also* -12-

dodo extinction; stupidity; worthlessness

doe *see* **deer; hind**

dog flattery; contempt; impurity; depravity; envy; fury; heresy; prowling enemies; scavenger; paganism; war; greed; voracity; irritability; egotism; folly; faithfulness; companion of the dead; obedience; science; the will; flattery; bootlicking; fertility; cunning; watchfulness; courage; protection; a man 60 to 80 years old; dawn; healing; orthodoxy; married fidelity (especially when shown in a woman's lap or at her feet); emblem of the Great Mother, moon goddesses; associated with fire, death, hell, the underworld, the archangel Gabriel; attribute of nobles, hunting goddess, mother goddesses, witches, the personifications of Smell, Fidelity, Envy • **puppy** empty-headedness; a male child up to 10 years of age • **black dog** connected with sorcery, death, the diabolical, the damned • **dog hair** cure for dog bite, hangover • **two dogs fighting** quarreling theologians • **dog with prey in its paws** all-devouring death • **African** inventor and bringer of fire • **alchemic** primitive nature; natural sulfur; *dog and wolf:* the dual nature of Mercurius, the nous; *dog being devoured by a wolf:* the purification of gold using antimony • **Amerindian** rain bringer; fire inventor; mythical ancestor; intercessor; messenger; guardian; interchangeable with the coyote • **Aztecan** conductor of souls to the afterworld; fire; end of the year; death; chaos; resurrection and rebirth; emblem of Huehueteotl; *man with dog's head:* Xotl • **Baltic** *half-dog/half-man with one eye:* a koerakoonlased • **Buddhist** *lion dogs:* guardians of the Law • **Celtic** attribute of Nodens, Sucellus, war gods, hunter gods, heroes, warriors; associated with healing waters • **Chinese** fidelity; unswerving devotion; companion of the Immortals; *arrival of a dog:* omen of prosperity; *red dog:* tengu; *huge shaggy dog:* chaos • **Christian** fidelity; watchfulness; conjugal fidelity; the devil; attribute of SS Bernard, Roch, Sira, Tobias, Wendelin; *spaniel:* attribute of St. Margaret of Cortona *black and white dogs:* Dominicans; *herding dog:* the Good Shepherd, a bishop, a priest; *dog with a flaming torch in its mouth or spitting fire:* attribute of St. Dominic • **Egyptian** guide to the solar god to keep the sun on its path; attribute of Anubis, the Great Mother, Amenti; *dog-headed god:* Anubis • **German** a low animal; *three dogs:* the mercy, justice and truth of Christ; *four dogs:* the mercy, justice, truth and peace of Christ • **Greco-Roman** impudence; flattery; cynicism; shamelessness; conductor of souls; vigilance; healing by rebirth into a new life; sacrificial offering to Hecate; attribute of Hermes/Mercury, Orion, Asclepius, Heracles/Hercules, Artemis/Diana, Hephaestus/Vulcan, Hecate, Eileithyia; *dogs of Hades:* the gloom of dawn and dusk which are dangerous and demonic times; *three-headed dog:* Cerberus; *Sirius:* all-seeing vigilance; *young man with Phrygian cap, dog, and eagle:* Zeus/Jupiter; *two-headed dog:* Orthos; *two-headed dog with a normal dog:* Orthos and Gargittios respectively; *bitch:* occasional form of Hecate; *hunter eaten by his own* dogs: Actaeon • **heraldic** courage; vigilance; loyalty • **Hindu** *hunting dog:* companion of Indra; *dog with four eyes:* Yama, the gloom of dawn and dusk; *two dogs:* attributes and messengers of Yama • **heraldic** vigilance; faithfulness; affection • **Inuit** *big house with big guard dog:* dwelling of Sedna in Adlivun • **Iroquoian** *white dog:* sacrifice to the gods • **Islamic** a low animal; impurity; greed; gluttony; acceptable only as a guard; *as a motif in a carpet:* charm against evil, disease, sorcerers; *black dog:* brings death in a family, a jinn; *dog howling near a dwelling:* death omen; *black dog with white patches above the eyes:* the devil • **Japanese** protection; a guardian • **Jewish** impurity; a low animal; evil; thief; scavenger • **Mayan** guide of the sun on its journey underground • **Mexican Indian** buried with their masters to guide their souls after death • **Mithraic** conductor of the souls of the dead; associated with bull sacrifice • **Mochican** *old man with lizard and dog:* Ai apaec • **Norse** associated with rain, Brimo; *two dogs, especially with two ravens:* counselors, messengers for Odin; *Garmr:* guardian of the underworld; *bloodstained watchdog:* Gamr • **Oceanic** inventor and bringer of fire • **Parsi** accompanies funeral processions; *white dog with yellow eyes or with four eyes:* conductor of the souls of the dead • **Persian** drives away evil spirits; *bridge guarded by two dogs:* the Cinvat Bridge; *bird with a dog's head:* a simurg • **Phoenician** accompanies the sun; emblem of Gala • **Serbian** *one-eyed dog-headed man with horse legs and iron teeth:* a psoglav • **Siberian** dogs were buried with the dead to guide their souls after death • **Slavic** *large winged dog:* Simargl • **Sumero-Semitic** evil; the demonic; the baleful; Belit-ili; attribute of Astarte • **Tibetan** sexuality; jealousy; *black dog:* attribute of Da • **witchcraft** *cats and dogs together:* rain makers • **Zoroastrian** one of the cleanest animals, to kill one is sinful • *see also* **bulldog; Cerberus; greyhound; simurg; spaniel**

dog rose *see* **rose**

dog star *see* **Sirius**

dogfish the lowest kind of fish

dogsbane • **flower language** deceit; falsehood

dogwood faithfulness; durability; charm; finesse • **Christian** *dogwood blossoms:* the Crucifixion of Christ • **Far Eastern** the life-giving power of blood • **flower language** duration; durability; *dogwood blossoms by themselves* am I perfectly indifferent to you? • **heraldic** love; adversity

doll the soul; an ancestor; fertility; external beauty with no feelings; means of harming a person through magic or witchcraft; agricultural charm against witches, fairies, malevolent influences until the next harvest • **corn doll** the Corn Goddess

dolmen the feminine principle; entrance to the underworld • **Druidic** sun altar • *see also* **menhir**

dolphin woman; mother; womb; fertility; mystic center; fecundity; love; society; water; sea; swiftness; youth's pleasant wantonness; safety; warning of danger; harbinger of rain; the highest order of fish; sea-power; regeneration; resurrection; salvation; bearer of souls to the next world; divination; wisdom; prudence; related to death and homage to the dead, the archangel Asariel; sacred to moon goddesses; attribute of sea deities, the personifications of Water, Fortune, Youth (both the latter usually shown riding a dolphin) • **two dolphins swimming in the same direction** equipoise, or, sometimes merely ornament • **two dolphins swimming in opposite directions** involution and evolution; the duality of nature • **dolphin with trident** freedom of commerce; supremacy of the seas • **dolphin with anchor** swiftness and slowness; the prudent middle way • **dolphin with a boat** prudence • **woman riding a dolphin** Fortune personified • **pillar with a dolphin** male and female powers, respectively, combined; love • **Amerindian** messenger between worlds • **Celtic** associated with the powers of water, well-worship • **Christian** Christ as a savior and guide of souls over the waters of death; the Christian faith (used primarily in the early Church); salvation; rebirth; attribute of St. Matthew; *dolphin with anchor or boat:* the Christian soul, the soul of the Church, the Church being guided to salvation by Christ; *dolphin speared by a trident or on an anchor:* the Crucifixion • **Egyptian** marriage; attribute of Hathor, Isis • **French** emblem of the oldest son of the king of France • **Greco-Roman** souls of reformed pirates; conductor of souls to the Isles of the Blessed; attribute of Dionysus/Bacchus, Apollo, Aphrodite/Venus, Eros/Cupid, Poseidon/Neptune, Ulysses, Telemachus, Arion; Oceanus; *woman riding a dolphin:* Thetis; *man with a lyre riding a dolphin:* Arion; *dolphin pulling a chariot:* attribute of Galatea; *pirates leaping overboard and turning into dolphins:* the kidnapping of Dionysus/Bacchus • **heraldic** affection; charity; love of music; sea towns; seafarers; pugnacity; swiftness; diligence; love • **Japanese** fecundity • **Jewish** attribute of Jonah • **Minoan** sea power • **Mithraic** associated with

Mithras as the god of light • **Norse** attribute of Freyja • **South American Indian** *river dolphin:* shape-shifter • **Sumero-Semitic** Ea-Oannes; attribute of Ishtar, Atargatis, Astarte • *see also* **porpoise**, with which it was often confused, especially in classical times

dome canopy of heaven; the love of God; mystic center • **Hindu** Yama • *oculus in a dome* access to heaven; World Navel

dominoes scholarship; learning; emblem of the medieval period

donkey *see* **ass**

door the feminine; the sheltering aspect of the Great Mother; vulva; hope; opportunity; change; salvation; beginning; death; passage from one world or state to another; protection • **closed door** secrecy; prohibition; mystery; barrier • **open door** opportunity; hospitality; liberation • **house without doors** rumor • **front door** honest entry • **back door** subterfuge; dishonest entry • **trap door** the unexpected; pitfall • **Christian** Christ; attribute of St. Anne; *three doors on a cathedral:* faith, hope, and charity • **Hindu** *deities carved on door jambs:* the means through which man enters the Supreme Presence • **Indonesian** opening all the doors of a house eases childbirth • **Jewish** opened on Seder night to allow entrance for Elijah announcing the Messianic Age; *blood on doorposts:* the Passover; Atonement • **Mithraic** the entrance to the seven zones of Paradise; entrance to the cave of initiation • **Norse** *540 doors:* attribute of Valhalla • **Roman** associated with Janus • **Sumerian** *rope passing through a winged door:* the mystic link binding God and man • **zodiacal** *in Cancer:* associated with the Summer solstice, the "door of men," the dying power and descent of the sun; *in Capricorn:* associated with the Winter solstice, the "door of the gods," the ascent and rising power of the sun • *see also* **gate**

Dorothy (Wizard of Oz) the seeking soul; the seeker's journey; related to the Prodigal Son

dot the residual state after the removal of mass; the termination of return; source of expansion • **Chinese** the changeless mean; point of balance and harmony; source of meditation • **Hindu** seed of manifestation; undifferentiated Brahman • **Tibetan** the seed of manifestation

doubling two objects where one is normal usually indicate bipolarity, opposing forces such as good/evil, male/female, night/day

dough an early stage of a process; potential; naiveté; immaturity; *kneading dough:* preparing for change; fondling; masturbation

dove the soul; the life spirit; divine agent; the spirit of light; aspiration; gentleness; the All Mother; maternity; femininity; truth; wisdom; divination; amorous delight; lasciviousness; love; mourning; melancholy; timidity; humility; innocence; purity; simplicity; guilelessness; a dupe; sacrifice; cowardice; simpleton; longevity; peace; a peacemaker; pride; constancy; a girl 10 to 20 years of age; attribute of Great Mothers, queens of heaven, the Tiburtine sibyl, the personifications of Peace, Chastity; associated with the archangel Anael • **two doves** attribute of the personifications of Concord (when facing each other), Lust, Chastity • **dove embedded in lead** the spirit embedded in matter • **dove with date tree** earthly fertility • **dove with olive branch** the Deluge; peace; eternal life; victory; new life; *funeral art:* eternal peace • **dove with palm branch in funeral art** eternal peace • **white dove with changeable tints** chastity fighting and surmounting the passions of life • **white dove with blue wings** celestial thoughts • **gold and silver plumed dove** the treasures of purity and innocence • **dove meat** aphrodisiac • **billing and/or cooing doves** love • **dove with ark** the Deluge; peace; glad tidings • **dove on one's shoulder** creative imagination • **dove on a pillar** the Great Mother • **alchemic** renewed spirit; an infusion of energy from heaven; the change from the Black Stage to the White Phase of transformation • **Babylonian** a dove was sent forth from the Ark on the seventh day of the voyage • **Chinese** longevity; good digestion; faithfulness; impartial filial duty; orderliness; Spring; lasciviousness; associated with the Earth Mother • **Christian** the Holy Spirit; faithful marriage; attribute of SS Ambrose, Augustine of Hippo, David, Catherine of Sienna, Benedict, Gregory the Great, John Chrysostom, Teresa, Thomas Aquinas; *gold and silver dove with many wings:* the Church; *purple dove:* Christ; *white dove:* a departed soul, the Holy Spirit (particularly when shown descending), associated with John the Baptist; *two doves in a dish:* attribute of St. Nicholas of Tolentino; *seven doves:* the Seven Gifts of the Holy Spirit; *twelve doves:* the 12 Apostles; *dove with lily:* the Annunciation; *dove perched on the shoulder:* divine enlightenment; *doves in a basket:* the Presentation of Christ at the Temple (usually the basket is carried by St. Joseph); attribute of St. Joachim; *dove with three-rayed nimbus or stars around its head:* the Holy Spirit; *dove issuing from one's mouth:* the soul escaping at death, attribute of St. Reparata; *dove flying over the water:* Creation (especially when dove has a three-rayed nimbus around its head); *dove on a font cover:* regeneration through the Holy Spirit; *dove on a pyx:* the Reserved Sacrament; *dove on a wand or rod (the wand or rod may be flowering):* attribute of St. Joseph; *dove with a vial in its beak:* attribute of St. Remigius; *dove carrying an ampulla:* the baptism of Clovis; *dove hovering around a man's ear:* attribute of St. Bernardino; *dove drinking from a cup or eating bread:* the soul being fed by the Eucharist; *two doves on a cup:* the Eucharist; *lamb and dove:* the body and soul of Christ, his human and divine nature; *dove projecting rays of light:* spiritual blessing; *dove with a palm branch in its mouth:* victory over death; *dove with a serpent's tail:* the combination of wisdom and peace • **Egyptian** innocence; attribute of the Tree of Life and the vases of the waters of life; *black dove:* a woman who remained a widow until death • **Greco-Roman** love; heavenly messenger; renewal of life; voluptuousness; emblem of Dodona; *dove with star:* emblem of Venus Mylitta; *dove with olive branch:* emblem of Athena/Minerva, renewal of life, attribute of Zeus/Jupiter, Adonis, Dionysus/Bacchus, Aphrodite/Venus; *two doves:* attribute of Aphrodite/Venus • **heraldic** peace (especially when it carries an olive branch); loving constancy; eternal life; simplicity; the Holy Spirit • **Hindu** messenger of Yama • **Islamic** *three stones or pillars with doves on top:* the Three Holy Virgins • **Japanese** longevity; deference; sacred to Hachiman; *dove bearing a sword:* the end of war • **Jewish** simplicity; innocence; meekness; harmlessness; guilelessness; incubation; embodies the souls of the dead; *white dove:* purity, Temple offering, emblem of Israel; *dove with a twig:* signal of land to Noah on the Ark; *two-headed dove:* attribute of Elisha • **Minoan** attribute of the Great Mother • **North American Indian** (prairie tribes) *turtle dove with willow leaves in its beak:* messenger of the cycle of rebirth • **Parsee** the Supreme Being • **Sumero-Semitic** divine power; sacred to Astarte; attribute of Ishtar; *scepter tipped with a dove:* attribute of Atargatis, associated with flood myths • *see also* **pigeon**, with which the dove is frequently confused

dovecote • **Egyptian** *bat's head on a dovecote:* charm to keep doves from leaving • **Gallic** *dovecote on a pole:* attribute of Nantosuelta • **medieval European** associated with status, power, wealth, the nobility

dragon adversary; evil; the unconscious; a plague

or sickness; fear of incest; the enemy of truth; the devil; sin; idolatry; ignorance; pestilence; the bad element in nature; fertility; wisdom; prophecy; nature; chaos; the instincts; darkness; impurity; heresy; guardian of fertility; the Terrible Mother; attribute of the personifications of Strength, Vigilance, Prudence, Error, Heresy, Paganism; associated with Summer, Saturn (planet) • **dragon slain, bound, or chained** paganism or sin overcome; overcoming one's own dark side; attaining self-mastery • **rescuing a maiden from a dragon** releasing pure forces after overcoming evil • **dragon with two heads** an amphisbaena • **winged dragon** emblem of astrology • **two dragons drawing a chariot** attribute of Demeter/Ceres • **tattoo of a dragon in the 19th Century** a sailor who had been to China • **dragon biting its own tail** time • **dragon biting the hilt of a sword** emblem of Mars (planet) • **winged dragon with eagle's legs** a wyvern • **dragon with a knotted tail** evil defeated • **defeated dragon** sin, heresy overcome • **lion and dragon devouring each other** union without loss of identity • **green dragon** the young grain god • **dragon and lantern** attribute of the Persian sibyl • **alchemic** *winged dragon:* emblem of alchemy; *Chinese alchemy:* Mercurius, blood, semen; *winged dragon:* the volatile; *wingless dragon:* the fixed; *dragon in flames:* fire, calcination; *fighting dragons:* putrefaction; *dragon biting its tail:* the fundamental unity of all things • **Buddhist** *dragon with a ball under its foot:* the pearl of perfection, wisdom, enlightenment, the spiritual essence of the universe, the Bodhisattva of instantaneous enlightenment; *water dragon:* Apalala • **Celtic** sovereignty; emblem of a chief; *red dragon:* emblem of Wales • **Chinese** guardian; vigilance; the highest spiritual power; the supernatural; infinity; sun; light; life; the heavens; rhythms of nature; yang; the spirit of change; strength; indistinguishable from the serpent; emblem of China; *blue dragon:* East; *azure dragon:* vital spirit, celestial power, infinite supernatural power, the Emperor; *five-clawed dragon:* East, fertilizing rain, imperial authority, bearer of the imperial dead to Paradise; *four-clawed dragon:* lesser authorities, temporal power; *three-clawed dragon:* increasing prosperity; *Li the hornless dragon:* the scholar, controls the deep seas; *Chiao the dragon:* the statesman; *dragon in the clouds:* thunder, fertilizing rain, waters of the deep, Spring; *two contending dragons facing each other:* yin and yang, all opposites and complements; *two dragons back to back:* yin and yang, eternity; *two dragons biting each other's tails:* the reciprocal creative action of yin and yang; *dragon with a ball under its foot:* rolling thunder, the rain-bringing moon; *dragon and phoenix:* Emperor and Empress, union of heaven and earth, divine potential containing all opposites, androgyny, involution and evolution, birth and death, macrocosm and microcosm; *dragon and tiger:* lustfulness • **Christian** heresy; error; paganism; envy; the devil; temptation; evil; enemy of God; death; darkness; attribute of SS Theodore, Cado, Clement of Metz, Keyne, Samson, the Apostle Philip; *dragon underfoot:* evil defeated, attribute of SS George, Margaret of Antioch, Bernard of Clairvaux, Martha; *dragon thrown into a pit by an angel:* the Apocalypse; *chained dragon:* attribute of St. John of Rheims; *dragon led by a cord or transfixed with a spear:* attribute of St. Margaret of Antioch; *woman emerging from the stomach of a dragon:* St. Margaret of Antioch; *winged dragon:* attribute of St. Sylvester • **Egyptian** emblem of Osiris as god of the dead; Apep; the dragon of darkness and chaos was overcome each morning by Ra • **Finnish** Ajatar (especially nursing serpents) • **Greco-Roman** attribute of Heracles/Hercules; *two dragons drawing a chariot:* attribute of Demeter/Ceres, Medea; *dragon's teeth:* warfare, seeds of dissension, associated with Cadmus; *dragon guard:* Ladon; *dragon chained to a rock:* associated with Andromeda, Perseus • **heraldic** vigilance; valor; protection; charitable fervor; valiant defender of treasure; *seven-headed dragon:* terror, destruction; *winged dragon:* guardianship • **Hindu** manifest power; the uttered word; attribute of Soma, Varuna, Indra • **Japanese** steed of Benzaiten; *three-clawed dragon:* the Mikado, imperial and spiritual power • **Jewish** desolation; dweller in the wilderness; associated with places of shadow, death, destruction, desolation; *dragon underfoot:* paganism or sin overcome, attribute of the archangel Michael • **Lithuanian** *flying dragon:* outdoor form of an aitvaras • **Norse** *wingless dragon:* Fafnir • **Occidental** generally destructive, evil, infernal • **Oriental** generally beneficent, celestial; attribute of a beneficent deity; associated with the element water • **Persian** attribute of Haoma • **Sumero-Semitic** the adversary; the power of evil; Tiamat • **Taoist** *dragon with a ball under its foot:* the pearl of perfection, wisdom, enlightenment, the spiritual essence of the universe • *see also* **amphisbaena; Chimera; Hydra; lindworm; wyvern**

dragon plant • **flower language** snare

dragonfly male dominance; soul of the dead; regeneration; immortality; infernal agent of mischief • **Amerindian** whirlwind; swiftness; activity • **Chinese** instability; weakness; Summer • **Japanese** unreliability; irresponsibility; martial success; courage; strength; happiness; emblem of Japan, Summer • **Navajo** clean water • **Zuni** has supernatural powers

dragonwort • **flower language** horror

drain loss; elimination

drawbridge defense; repression; regression

dream message from the unconscious or a deity; precognition; expression of the dreamer's repressed wishes or subconscious; communion with spirits; absence of the consciousness of reality; premonition • **Egyptian** premonition • **North American Indian** final proof of anything under dispute

dregs the lower instincts that remain unpurified

dress external sign of spiritual potency; the outward shape of the inner being; membership within a group • **red dress** festivity; vivacity • **black dress** mourning • **white dress** purity; marriage • **Celtic** *feathered dress:* attribute of fairies • **Phrygian** *green dress with flowers:* attribute of Cybele

drilling coition

drinking the soul acquiring truth; acquiring divine life and power • **drinking from the same cup** marriage; ritual union; the end of the single life for newlyweds • *see also* **intoxication**

drops • **heraldic** one who has been subjected to torrents of liquid; *yellow drops:* gold; *blue drops:* tears; *green drops:* oil; *black drops:* pitch, tar; *red drops:* blood; *white drops:* water

drought an inert spiritual condition; loss of contact with God; temptation in the wilderness; testing by fire to prepare the way for union with God; divine punishment

drowning being overwhelmed by the conscience or subconscious; loss of self or ego

drugs desire; ignorance; warring against right and truth; escape; running away from reality

drum call to war; warning; primordial sound; the mediator between heaven and earth; communication, especially of word or tradition; a vehicle for magic; attribute of Ares/Mars • **beating a drum** the passage of time • **muffled drum** death; funeral • **kettle drum** emblem of Denmark • **war drum** associated with thunder and lightning • **African** the heart; magic power • **Buddhist** voice of the Law; joyous tidings; *beating the Dharma drum:* awakening the ignorant and slothful • **Chinese** voice of heaven; associated with the sun's passage across the heavens; emblem of Chang-Kuo-lao; *blue man with wings, claws, drum, mallet, and chisel:* Lei-kung; *rooster on a drum:* peace • **Greco-Roman** associated with ecstatic dancing, orgies; attribute of Ares/Mars • **heraldic** martial readiness • **Hindu** attribute of Kali, Durga, Indra, Karttikeya; emblem of Sarasvati; *Shiva's drum:* the primordial sound of creation; *hourglass drum:* attribute of Shiva • **Japanese** *rooster on a drum:* summons to prayer at the Shinto temple; *monster beating drums:* Raiden • **Phrygian** attribute of the Great Mother; associated with ecstatic dancing • **Tahitian** sacred to Tane • **Ural-Altaic** magic power to summon spirits; symbolically made from the Cosmic Tree; repeat of the primal sounds of creation; creator of religious ecstasy

drummer death; messenger

drunkenness *see* **intoxication**

dryness truth; immortality; the solar; the masculine principle • *see also* **drought**

duality ambivalence; the physical and spiritual nature of all things

duck connubial love; fidelity; love of knowledge of profound mysteries; freedom from worry; superficiality; idle chatter; volubility; deceit; lying; its meat was considered an aphrodisiac • **Amerindian** mediator between earth and sky • **Chinese** felicity beauty; *pair of mandarin ducks:* conjugal fidelity; *duck and drake together:* the union of lovers, fidelity, mutual consideration • **Egyptian** associated with Isis bringing forth the sun • **heraldic** resourcefulness • **Japanese** felicity beauty; *pair of mandarin ducks:* conjugal fidelity; *duck and drake together:* the union of lovers, fidelity, mutual consideration • **Jewish** immortality

ducking stool *see* **stool (furniture)**

dumbness (inability to speak) the early stages of creation; inability to express love from within; sometimes an indication that a person has compensatory powers; a prophet • **being struck dumb** regression; divine punishment • *see also* **silence**

dummy (mannequin) an image of the soul; false belief; false representation; alter ego

dung an equalizer of various classes; worthlessness; offensiveness, especially to ghosts • **Greenland Inuit** *piece of dried fox dung:* charm to give a boy cunning • *see also* **excrement**

dung beetle *see* **beetle**

Durga • **Hindu** life in constant and violent regeneration

dusk death; end of a cycle • *see also* **twilight**

dust the beginning and the end of man; the unstable lower mind; death; mourning; decay; disintegration; return to the primordial state; drought; famine; the passage of time; the great equalizer; something forgotten or neglected; worthlessness • **dust and ashes** deep humiliation; mourning; penitence • **shaking the dust from one's sandals** complete rejection of one's past; a renunciation • **Babylonian** food of the damned in Aralu • **Egyptian, Jewish** associated with mourning

dwarf hidden forces of nature; the Father Spirit; the unexpected; the unconscious; uncontrolled outburst of the unconscious; the instincts; amoral forces of nature; ignorance; inferiority; abnormality; possessor of supernatural powers; unpredictability; the underdeveloped; a good omen; associated with caves, blacksmithing, gods of the underworld, speaking the truth, frank speech, instinct, intuition • **Chinese** *dwarf standing on one foot:* attribute of Wen Chang • **Egyptian** Bes • **Greco-Roman** occasional depiction of Hephaestus/Vulcan • **Hindu** Vamana; *dwarf under the foot of Shiva:* human ignorance • **Japanese** the malignant river god; *ugly dwarf with writing brush:* Kuei Hsing • **Lithuanian** a kaukas • **Norse** *four dwarves:* support of the world; *dwarf king:* Andvari, Hreidmar; *dwarf blacksmith:* Regin • **Teutonic** Fialar • *see also* **jester; midget; Nibelungen**

dynamo power; energy; technology • *see also* **engine**

E

E associated with hope, munificence, logic, intellectual character, energy, excitement, catalysis, the Autumnal equinox, the liver, -5-, Aries, Mercury (planet) • **medieval** occasional Roman numeral for 250 • **tarot** the Archpriest

eagle height; the father; the solar; daring; speed; heroic nobility; sovereignty; imperial power; royalty; fertility, especially male; victory; pride; regeneration; longevity; protection of young; vigilance; mystic center; generosity; carrion eater; strength, but occasionally, impotence; the spiritual principle in general; prayer; resurrection; a divine messenger; divine grace descending; new life; the just; faith; contemplation; the mid-day sun; day; thunderbolt; the heavens; air; the spirit of prophecy; attribute of the personifications of Pride, Power, Strength, Youth, Victory, Geometry, Sight; associated with war gods, sky gods, South, fire, air, youth, noon, air, Scorpio, Cancer, the constellation Aquila, the archangel Zadkiel; emblem of the US, Germany, and other countries • **golden eagle** East • **white eagle** emblem of Poland • **head of an eagle** center point of the universe • **eagle's scream** battle; challenge; fury • **double-headed eagle** omniscience; doubled powers; supreme power; the union of two countries; creative power; emblem of Czarist Russia, the Holy Roman Empire, Flanders, Austro-Hungary, Gemini • **eagle holding a thunderbolt** vigilance; majesty • **lion-headed eagle** conflict between heaven and hell • **eagle and globe or orb** consecration of power • **eagle atop a column** emblem of sun gods • **eagle staring at the sun** mental enlightenment; direct perception • **eagle and owl** day and night respectively, beginning and end respectively, alpha and omega respectively • **eagle as a bird of prey** the demon that ravishes souls; rapacity; the sins of worldly power and pride • **eagle carrying a victim** victory of the superior over the inferior; augury • **eagle carrying a flaming pentagram** Jupiter (planet) • **eagle devouring a lion or bull** victory of the evolutive over the involutive; the triumph of the spirit or intellect over the physical • **eagle with a serpent in its talons or devouring it** spiritual victory; evil defeated by good; the victory of the spirit over sin • **tiger fighting an eagle** the instincts fighting higher consciousness • **eagle and serpent** light and dark respectively; cosmic unity; totality; the union of spirit and matter respectively • **alchemic** *soaring eagle:* volatilization, the liberated spiritual part of Prime Matter; *double eagle:* Mercurius; *crowned eagle and lion:* wind and earth respectively, Mercurius and sulfur respectively, the volatile and fixed respectively; *eagle devouring a lion:* a volatile component volatilizing a fixed component • **Assyrian** lightning; fertility; sacred to Ashur; emblem of Nisroch; *eagle-headed god with wings and disk:* Ashur • **Australian aboriginal** the deity • **Aztecan** celestial power; the luminous sky; the rising sun that devours the serpent of darkness; the imperial bird • **Babylonian** Marduk; *golden eagle:* emblem of Babylon; *double-headed eagle:* Nergal • **Buddhist** vehicle of Buddha; attribute of Amoghasiddhi • **Celtic** associated with healing waters • **Chinese** authority; the sun; yang; warriors; courage; tenacity; keen vision; fearlessness; *eagle and raven:* associated with war gods • **Christian** the soul renewed by grace; inspiration of the Gospels; aspiration; spiritual endeavor; renewal of youth; resurrection; Christ; Christ as mediator between God and man; the Christian soul strengthened by grace; Mary leading people to true light; the inspiration of the Gospels; emblem of St. John; attribute of SS Wenceslas, Medard, Prisca, Servatius; one of the four beasts of the Apocalypse; *eagle staring at the sun:* Christ gazing at the glory of God; *carrying it's young to the sun:* Christ bearing souls to God; *taking a fish from the sea:* Christ rescuing souls from sin; *holding book and/or pen and/or inkhorn:* attribute of St. John; *rising from a cauldron:* attribute of St. John; *grasping a serpent in its talons:* victory over sin; *tearing its victim apart:* the devil ravaging a soul; *double-headed eagle:* the Holy Spirit; *eagle's scream:* the Apocalypse; *flying eagle:* one of the guardians of the Throne of God; *eagle flying upward:* the Ascension; *eagle plunging into water:* regeneration by baptism • **Egyptian** the soul; the sun; the sons of Horus *golden eagle:* emblem of Egypt, the Nile • **Gnostic** *eagle atop a ladder:* The Way • **Greek** the solar; spiritual power; royalty; victory (especially with a serpent in its talons); favor; attribute of Zeus, Pan; emblem of Troy; sacred to Aphrodite; *youth borne aloft by an eagle:* Ganymede; *eagle and jug:* attribute of Hebe; *being given water by Ganymede:* victory over death; *young man with Phrygian cap, dog, and eagle:* Zeus; *eagle pecking at titan's liver:* Prometheus • **heraldic** a man of action; high position; lofty spirit; wisdom; nobleness; strength; bravery; alertness; high-spirits; ingenuity; quick-wittedness; judiciousness; true magnanimity; strength of mind; *eagle with spread wings:* protection; *eagle's claw:* tenacity, defense of freedom and justice, free hunting rights (in some parts of Germany) • **Hindu** the Garuda Bird; emblem of Indra; storm cloud • **Hittite** omniscience; solar power; *double-headed eagle:* attribute of Nergal • **Japanese** *white eagle:* divine right of kings, emblem of Jimmu Tenno • **Jewish** God's providential care over Israel; the divine spirit; renewal; East; *double-headed eagle:* associated with Elisha • **Mexican Indian** war • **Mithraic** attribute of the solar Mithras • **North American Indian** revelation; day; mediator between earth and sky; the greatest of birds; the Thunderbird; the Great Spirit; *eagle-feather head-dress:* Thunderbird, the Universal Spirit • **Norse** wisdom; emblem of Odin; associated with the North wind; *in the branches of Yggdrasil:* light, wisdom; *eagle and wolf:* emblem of the elect part of Valhalla • **Pawnee** *male white eagle:* associated with the

Father of All Things, daylight, the sun, South, man, tyranny; *female brown eagle:* associated with the Mother of All Things, night, the moon, North, temptation • **Persian** associated with Mithras, augury, military might • **Phrygian** emblem of Sabazios; *double-headed eagle:* doubled vision • **Roman** the solar; the Emperor; dignity; victory; favor; perceptiveness; lightning bearer of Jupiter; attribute of Jupiter, Faunus; emblem of Roman legions; *wand tipped with a globe surmounted by an eagle:* attribute of Jupiter, Roman Legions • **Sumero-Semitic** mid-day sun; attribute of Minute, Ningvisu; *double-headed eagle:* the heat of the Summer and mid-day sun, solar power, omniscience • **Syrian** *eagle with human arms:* sun worship • *see also* **allerion; griffin**

eagle owl *see* **owl**

earring amulet; talent for listening; associated with female sexuality • **earring of gold** sun worship; sailor's devotion to the sea, protection from drowning • **earring of silver** moon worship • **earring falling off** your sweetheart thinks of you • **single earring on a sailor** devotion to the sea • **Islamic** *earring on a Dervish:* celibacy • **Mochican** *old man with serpent earrings:* Ai apaec

ears inquisitiveness; eavesdropping; gossip; advice; temptation through flattery; vulva; conception; associated with the breath of life • **pointed ears** attribute of fairies, devils • **ears with long lobes** royalty; spiritual authority • **long ears** associated with an ass; connected with dwarves • **small ears** shyness; introversion • **large ears** adaptive ease; extroversion • **ear being cut off** defamation • **ass ears on a human** stupidity; a buffoon; folly; attribute of jesters • **burning or tingling ears** someone is talking about you; evil gossip; *left ear only:* your sweetheart is thinking of you; *right ear only:* someone is speaking spitefully of you • **pierced ears** blood sacrifice for the protection of a child • **Babylonian** *four ears:* attribute of Marduk • **Chinese** *long ears:* wisdom, longevity • **Christian** *dove entering the Virgin Mary's ear:* the Immaculate Conception, the attentive hearing of the word of God; *ear of slave being cut off:* St. Peter at the betrayal of Christ • **Egyptian** *right ear:* receives the air of life; *left ear:* receives the air of death • **Greco-Roman** *old woman with pointed ears and serpent:* Bona Dea; *pointed ears:* attribute of Pan/Faunus, satyrs; *ass ears on a human:* King Midas; *fat old man with horse ears:* Silenus • **Indic** *long ears on a man:* licentiousness; *amputated ears:* punishment for a thief • **Jewish** *pierced ear:* mark of a slave in voluntary servitude

earth the Great Mother; motherhood; the womb; fertility; regeneration; the origin of mankind; the passive; submission; sustainer of material life; the end of material life; the great sepulcher; the moral opposite of the heavenly or spiritual; humility; associated with the stomach, the archangels Lumiel, Metatron, Sandalphon, Zerachiel; corresponds to Taurus, Virgo, Capricorn • **handful of earth** death and mortality • **Chinese** *as an element:* associated with sweet taste, holiness, wind, white millet, oxen, the heart, yellow, muscles, love, -5- • **Christian** the Church • **Greco-Roman** Antaeus had to be touching the earth to have strength • **Kabalistic** associated with the archangel Lumiel • **Masonic** corresponds to the body, physical life • **Swiss** witches must be touching the earth to have strength • **Tungun** associated with North

earthenware humanity; mortality; associated with 9th, 24th wedding anniversaries

earthquake a sudden change in a process; upheaval in the unconscious; female orgasm; fertility; omen of divine birth, anger, intervention; omen of death, sacrifice, sudden cosmic change • **folkloric** a man born during an earthquake will be the ruin of a country

earthworm *see* **worm**

East illumination; the future; infancy; childhood; spring; the fount of life; dawn; rebirth; sunrise; resurrection; the mystic point of reference; wisdom; associated with Aries, Leo, Sagittarius, Spring, sky gods, the right half of the body, Christ, the archangel Raphael • **East wind** an ill omen • **Bambaran** land of the dead, associated with wild and domestic animals, white • **Buddhist** associated with Akshobhya • **Congolese** home of good spirits, Paradise • **Dogon** Associated with birds, Venus (planet) • **Mexican Indian** home of Tialoc and the quetzal; land of birth, rebirth, the sun; associated with renewal, youth, feasting, song, love, the sprouting of maize, red, Venus (planet) • **Mongolian** associated with air • **Siberian** direction of the living • **Tungun** associated with iron, air

eating the acquisition of knowledge; material existence; fertility; equivalent to the sowing of seed; imparts the quality of what it eaten; eating the food of another world binds one to that world • **eating fish** imparts fecundity • **eating a sacrificed god** imparts holiness and spiritual power • **eating oysters** imparts sexual potency • *see also* **cannibalism; devouring; digestion**

ebony death; melancholy; gloom; skepticism;

charm against fear; associated with 22nd wedding anniversaries • **flower language** blackness; you are hard • **Greco-Roman** *ebony couch:* bed of Hypnos/Morpheus; *ebony throne:* attribute of Hades/Pluto

echidna • **Australian aboriginal** initiation; death and resurrection

Echidna (mythology) • **Greek** destruction; the mother of all monsters; the libido which consumes the flesh; insatiable lust

echo thesis and antithesis; many of the same qualities as a mirror • **Mayan** attribute of the great underworld god

Echo (mythology) • **Greek** regression; passivity

eclipse omen of a cataclysmic event, such as war, plague, the death of the kings; the Day of the Lord is at hand • *see also* **devouring**

edelweiss purity; chastity; noble memories; ostentatious or feigned mountaineering skill or courage; sentimental, but dangerous good fellowship; emblem of Switzerland, the Alps • **heraldic** purity; noble courage; purity; immortality

eel slipperiness; elusiveness; enmity; nimbleness; phallus; augur of a storm; stealth • **electric eel** lurking threat • **Chinese** carnal love • **Japanese** messenger of the gods; disguised dragon • **Egyptian** the rising sun • *see also* **serpent**

effigy the psychic aspect of a person; contains a person's powers; has magical properties for warding off evil spirits, for fertility, for placating the gods; an image of the soul

egg Cosmic Egg; immortality; potentiality; creation; the germ of all creation; all seminal existence; the universe; the mother; the womb; the primordial matriarchal world of chaos; cosmic time and space; sanctuary; resurrection; hope; the perfect state of unified opposites • **golden egg** the sun, laid on the waters of Chaos by the primeval goose • **silver egg** the moon • **ostrich or porcelain egg in holy places** creation; life; resurrection • **egg with broken shell** resurrection • **egg surrounded by serpent** the eternal germ of life encircled by creative wisdom • **egg and dart design** male generation and female productiveness • **sulfur and eggs** purification; cure for unrequited love; worship of Isis • **two infants hatched from eggs** Castor and Pollux • **egg white** tastelessness • **egg shell** worthlessness • **alchemic** hermetically sealed vessel; container in which the Great Work is accomplished; source of the white flower (silver), the red flower (God), and the blue flower (wisdom); *philosopher's egg:* creation • **Buddhist** *eggshell:* the shell of ignorance, to break the

eggshell is to attain enlightenment and transcend time and space • **Chinese** totality; the origin of earth and sky; the universe; *yolk:* sky; *white:* the earth • **Christian** resurrection; hope; re-creation; *ostrich egg:* virgin birth; *red Easter egg:* the blood of Christ • **Coptic** creation • **Druidic** the Cosmic Egg laid by a serpent • **Egyptian** Cosmic Egg; *egg laid by the Nile Goose:* produced Ra, the sun; *laid by Kneph the serpent:* produced the Word • **Greek** *surrounded by Ouroboros:* Cosmic Egg, the mystery of life, creation, resurrection; *twins with eggshell caps:* Castor and Pollux • **Hindu** yoni; *golden egg:* Hiranyagarbha • **Japanese** the universe • **Jewish** *burned eggs:* burnt offering, the ancient glory of the Temple • **Persian** creation; the life principle • **Near East** creation • **Oceanic** *bird's egg:* sometimes the origin of the first man • **still life** resurrection (especially when it has a broken shell) • **Sumero-Semitic** Cosmic Egg

eglantine *see* **sweet brier**

Egypt the animal in man; bondage; idolatry; concern with life after death; ancient wisdom; antiquity

Eiffel Tower • **French** emblem of France in general, Paris in particular

eight ball willingness to take risks for gain; unlucky; occasionally, a willingness to engage in homosexual activities • **behind the eight ball** poor position

Einstein, Albert genius; eccentricity; creativity

elder tree zeal; death; related to witches; magic; ghostly powers; compassion; associated with Walpurgis night, the archangel Anael • **dwarf elder** *in Ireland:* power; *in the ancient Eastern Mediterranean area:* royalty • **Celtic** evolution; transition; continuation; associated with Saturn (planet), jet, November/December • **Christian** the tree of the Cross; the tree Judas hanged himself on • **flower language** zeal; compassion

Electra • **Greek** vengeance

electricity energy; excitement • **electrical appliances** associated with 8th wedding anniversaries

elephant strength; wisdom; memory; moderation; the power of the libido; puissant dignity; eternity; pity; stability; care; caution; the Self; chastity; priestly chastity; firmness; longevity; self-restraint; meekness; piety; religion; pride; purity; clumsiness; ponderousness; the earth; insensibility; the rising sun; attribute of the personifications of Fame, Africa, India, Instinct, Pity, Meekness, Piety, Religion; the mount of kings, deities; associated with Hannibal, the circus, military victory, the archangel Zadkiel; emblem of Judea • **winged elephant** clouds • **elephant's head** attribute of Africa personified • **trumpeting elephant** truth • **pink elephant** popular emblem of delirium tremens • **elephant with trunk drooping** sorrow; failure; defeat • **elephant with trunk held up** cheerfulness; success; victory • **African** vigilance; wariness; royal power and wisdom • **American** the Republican Party • **Baulé** strength, prosperity, longevity, wisdom • **Buddhist** compassion; kindness; love; Buddha's conception; steed of Akshobya; *white elephant:* reincarnation of Duggha, sacred to Buddha, Jewel of the Law, steed of Samantabhadra; *dark elephant:* reincarnation of Indra; *elephant hide:* ignorance, insensitivity; *elephant on a pillar:* enlightenment; *Nalagiri:* brute strength • **Chinese** strength; sovereignty; energy; sagacity; prudence; steed of P'u Hsien • **Christian** chastity; benignity; *elephant trampling a serpent:* Christ defeating evil • **Denmark** emblem of Denmark, a royal traveler to the East • **Ekoi** violence, ugliness • **folkloric** an elephant would not kill a virgin • **Greco-Roman** longevity; immortality; victory over death; a religious animal; attribute of Mercury (god) personifying Intelligence; *elephant in a tent:* associated with Fabricus Luscinus • **heraldic** power; cunning; ambition; lucky; sagacity; wit; happiness; royalty; longevity; willingness to be guided; chastity; courage; a person who has made distant journeys • **Hindu** longevity; intelligence; spirituality; wisdom; the strength of sacred wisdom; prudence; kingly rank; the support of the world; steed of Ganesha, Indra; attribute of Shiva; corresponds to ochre, the element earth; *four-armed man with an elephant head:* Ganesha; *white elephant:* can produce clouds; *elephant carrying off women:* Naraka; *elephant skin:* attribute of Shiva; *elephant goad:* attribute of Ganesha • **Kalmyk** *elephant head:* East • *see also* **proboscides**

elf enchantment; mischief; the joys of the natural life; powers of darkness • **light elf** generally favorable to man • **dark elf** generally unfavorable and may kill babies • **Norse** *dark elves:* Dokkalfar, Svartalfar; *light elves:* Ljosalfar

Elijah • **Christian** a forerunner of Christ • **Jewish** spiritual power but only human wisdom

Elizabeth of Hungary, St. • **Christian** female charity

elk nobility; graceful strength • **North American Indian** supernatural power; whirlwind • *see also* **deer**

ellipse the superconscious; Cosmic Egg; yoni; *the two sides:* ascent and descent, involution and

evolution • **Egyptian** the universe; the world of the dead

elm patriotism; dignity; longevity; beauty; grace; stateliness; justice; darkness; depression; related to burial places, fertility, the archangel Asariel • **elm with vine on it** the ideal husband and wife relationship; natural sympathy; unity; benevolence; marriage • **Christian** dignity; the strength derived by the devout from their faith in Scripture; *elm in leaf:* attribute of St. Zenobius • **flower language** dignity; *American elm:* patriotism • **Greek** sacred to the Ephesian Artemis • **heraldic** dignity • **Teutonic** origin of Embla

embalming purification of the soul through faith and trust in the ideal

ember old age; gloom; dying passion; the sun; purification; fertility; anger; warmth; the hearth; vengeance; martyrdom; a concentrated expression of fire; hidden power; occult forces • **ember held in tongs** associated with Isaiah

embrace coition; affection; concord

emerald victory over the flesh; hope; rebirth; youth; fertility; immortality; true love; the overcoming of temptation; associated with May, Gemini, Spring, the seasonal renewal of nature, the archangels Anael, Asariel, Lumiel, the waxing moon, 20th and 35th wedding anniversaries • **alchemic** associated with Hermes/Mercury • **Aztecan** associated with Spring, Quetzalcoatl • **Central American Indian** pledge of fertility; associated with rain, blood, the lunar cycle • **Christian** faith; purity; chastity; associated with the pope, hell, the most dangerous inhabitants of hell; the Holy Grail was carved from a single emerald • **folkloric** aphrodisiac; charm for love, money, mental powers, psychic powers, protection, exorcism, eyesight, true love, easing childbirth, and protection from eye diseases, epilepsy, poisoning; helped to foretell the future or converse with evil spirits when held under the tongue; protection against witchcraft when bound on the left arm, would set prisoners free if it had been consecrated • **Greco-Roman** associated with Aphrodite/Venus • **heraldic** freedom; happiness; beauty; friendship; health; hope • **Hindu** imparted immortality; could so frighten a viper or cobra that its eyes would drop out of its head • **Islamic** *emerald mountain range:* Kaf • **Jewish** *on vestments:* Spring

emperor absolute rule; tyranny; incarnation of the sun god • **Chinese** the Son of Heaven; the spiritual power of heaven • **Japanese** descendant of Amaterasu

Emperor (**tarot**) absolute power; authority; control; magnificence; energy; empire; good counsel; power; dominion; hostile prejudice; law; rule; severity; domination; subjection; success; initiation; intellectual supremacy; obstinate opposition; order; protection; thought; reason; solidity; sterile regulation and power; the demiurge; tradition; tyranny; universal sovereignty; associated with reason, experience, personal knowledge

Empire State Building • **American** emblem of New York City

empress • **Chinese** the earthly; supreme perfection and wisdom

Empress (**tarot**) comprehension; discrimination; the subconscious; the soul; production; growth; universal fertility; idealism; gentleness; the emotional; sweetness; dominance by persuasion; lack of refinement; pretentiousness; vanity; seduction; fecundity; the Word; personal growth; sovereign intellect; success; associated with love, beauty, understanding, the archangel Anael

emu emblem of Australia

enchantress the binding and destroying of the feminine principle; the spellbinding power of life; self-delusion • **Hindu** the illusion of Maya

endive • **flower language** frugality

endurance long endurance implies living in concord with God

Endymion • **Greek** man trespassing in a woman's realm

enemy the forces threatening a person from within

engine the inhumane forces of modern society; a magical invention which has an autonomous existence and will; technological power; the heart

entanglement ensnarement; submission; slavery; vassalage; imprisonment; the unconscious; the repressed; the forgotten past; being caught in the universe and being unable to escape; immobilization through sin or evil; man tied irrevocably to the Creator and the universe • **Babylonian** the cosmic principle uniting all things; the law which supports and holds all things together • **Buddhist** binding of offenders; attribute of Yama • **Christian** the bonds of sin and death; God's victory over Satan who is ultimately bound and cast out • **Greco-Roman** Saturn is kept bound except during the Saturnalia when chaos is loosed; attribute of Uranus/Caelus, Cronus/Saturn, the Moirae/Fates • **Hindu** attribute of Varuna • **Sumero-Semitic** associated with Tammuz,

Marduk, Shamash, Ea, Nisaba, Minute, Enil and his wife Ninkhursaq • *see also* **chains; cord; fasces; net; rope; sheaf; string**

entombment detention of the spirit in the world

Ephesus, Church of • **Christian** associated with patience, abandonment, the gonads, the white horse, the first seal

ephod • **Jewish** the universe compounded of the four elements; the splendor of enlightenment; *breastplate in the middle of the ephod*: the Cosmic Center

epigonation • **Christian** dignity; attribute of St. Gregory Nazianus and of bishops of the Eastern Church

epileptic seizure communion with a god; possession by evil spirits

epimacus *see* **griffin**

equinox the point of balance and change in the soul's development when a new stage is begun

Erato • **Greek** muse associated with love poetry, hymns, lyre-playing, pantomime

erica aborea • **Egyptian** enclosure of the coffin of Osiris

Erinyes/Furies • **Greco-Roman** anarchy; remorse; guilt turned to destructiveness; guilt turned upon itself to the destruction of the guilty; involutive fragmentation of the unconscious; disputation; instruments of divine vengeance; the conscience; impersonal justice; *Alecto*: implacability; *Megara*: disputation; *Tisiphone*: blood vengeance

ermine honor; purity; nobility; justice; teaching; moderation; chastity; attribute of royalty, judges, lawyers, and the personifications of Touch, Chastity • **Christian** attribute of aristocratic virgin saints (St. Ursula in particular, occasionally St. Mary Magdalene) • **heraldic** prudence; courage; cleanliness; dignity; sovereignty • **portraiture** alludes to the subject's virtue

Eros/Cupid • **Christian** *amethyst ring with a carved Eros/Cupid*: attribute of St. Valentine • **Greco-Roman** romantic love

eryngiurn • **Jewish** the bitterness of bondage

escarbuncle • **heraldic** supremacy; brilliant gem

escutcheon • **heraldic** defense; *escutcheon of pretense*: marriage to an heiress, claim of a prince to sovereignty

estoile • **heraldic** nobleness; celestial goodness

Ethiopia a "far away" land

Ethiopian *see* **Negro**

eucalyptus protection; nurture; sloth; prudence; associated with Australia • **Christian** associated with the archangel Anael

Eucharist • **Christian** attribute of SS Charles Borromeo, Ignatius of Loyola; *monk celebrating mass on board ship as fish gather to listen:* St. Brendan • *see also* **Host**

Eumenides • **Greek** guilt leading to compunction; a positive sublimation of guilt that turns one toward the good • *see also* **Erinyes/Furies**

eupatorium • **flower language** delay

Euphrates River the great fertilizer; the irreversible process of nature; the fourth river of the Garden of Eden

Euphrosyne *see* **Three Graces**

Eurydice • **Greek** the poet's anima escaping; half-formed intuitive vision; undeveloped imaginative or intuitive sensibility

Euterpe • **Greek** muse associated with dramatic tragedy, flute-playing, lyric poetry

evaporation transformation; passage from a lower state to a higher

Eve artlessness; guilelessness; beauty; gentleness; pride; the material and formal aspect of life; the mother of all things; emotionality; instinctiveness; inconstancy; lower nature; dissembling; that which diverts man from spiritual progress • **Christian** the inversion of the Virgin Mary

evening peacefulness; dead quiet; involution; return to chaos; middle or old age; Autumn or Winter • *see also* **night**

evergreens permanence; eternity; immortality; youth; vigor; poverty; generative power; associated with fertility and funeral rites, the archangel Cassiel • **evergreen crown or wreath** life; immortality; victory

everlasting (plant) • **flower language** never ceasing remembrance

ewer refreshment; purity • **ewer and basin** purity; innocence • **Christian** *ewer and basin:* refers to Pontius Pilate washing his hands • **Greco-Roman** emblem of Dionysus/Bacchus • *see also* **pitcher**

excrement allied with what is highest in value; it was thought to have magical powers over a person; evil; may carry the life force of the organism that produced it; foulness; related to gold • **alchemic** putrefaction; decomposition • *see also* **dung**

exile banishment of a principle or ideal; purification; ostracism

extraterrestrial unknown part of the self; unknown threats

eyebright clearness of vision • **folkloric** aid in seeing truth, fairies

eyebrows defense; the abode of pride • **eyebrows set far apart** cold-heartedness • **eyebrows set close to eyes** gravity • **long eyebrows** attribute of a sage • **bushy eyebrows** attribute of a su-

perstitious person • **eyebrows that meet** deceit; attribute of a vampires, werewolves, witches

eyelids vigilance; observation; lidless eyes show regression • **Finnish** *ugly man with lopsided eyes and no eyelids:* Hiisi

eyes the sun; sun gods; divine omniscience; omniscience; intuitive vision; knowledge; understanding; enlightenment; judgment; authority; stability; intellectual perception; fixity of purpose; the limitation of the visible; abode of the mind; window to the outer world; solar door to heaven; guardian of the inner man; vigilance; protection; mystic center; female genitals; testicles; care; the world; expressive of mood or character; androgyny • **blue eyes** innocence; sign of being in love; attribute of good fairies, sky deities, Northern Europeans • **green eyes** jealousy; hope; untrustworthiness • **red eyes** weeping; sorrow; demonic fury • **cross-eyes** an unlucky omen • **one eye** divine omniscience; the self-contained; the eye of God; subhumanity; extra human effort devoted to one aim, usually unfavorable; may imply the possession of second-sight • **one eye in a triangle** omnipresence; omnipotence; the All-Seeing Eye • **two eyes** physical and spiritual normality; binary functions such as male/female, sun/moon • **one open eye with one closed eye** happiness and sorrow • **three eyes** superhuman; divine attribute; attribute of Prudence personified • **four eyes** pejorative term for someone who wears glasses • **multiple eyes** usually associated with evil • **thousands of eyes on sky gods** the stars; infallibility; watchfulness • **closed eyes** death; avoidance of unpleasantness • **squinting eyes** poor vision; ignorance; meanness; attribute of Envy personified • **winking eye** seduction; joking; secrecy; mockery • **bandaged eyes** blindness; ignorance; slavery; impartiality; attribute of Justice personified • **owl eyes** blindness; ignorance • **eagle eyes** sharpness of vision • **mole eyes** intellectual and spiritual blindness • **right eye** *Occidental:* the sun, day, future; *Oriental:* the moon, night, past • **left eye** *Occidental:* the moon, night, past; *Oriental:* the sun, day, future • **double pupils** attribute of a witch • **eye of the heart** spiritual perception; illumination; intellectual intuition • **eye on a scepter** omniscience; temperance; modesty • **eyes in odd places of the body** clairvoyance • **Armenian** *fiery-eyed demon:* an al • **Ashanti** *hairy giant with bloodshot eyes:* Sasabonsam • **Assyrian** *two eyes:* the sun and the moon • **Babylonian** *four eyes:* attribute of Marduk • **Buddhist** light; wisdom; *third eye of Buddha:*

spiritual consciousness, transcendent wisdom • **Celtic** evil eye; ill-will; envy; *giant with one eye in the front of his head and one in back:* Balor • **Christian** the all-seeing God; omniscience; power; light; *one eye:* God the Father; *one eye in a triangle:* the Trinity; *two eyes (may appear with crab pincer):* attribute of St. Ottilia; *two eyes on a platter, or carried:* attribute of St. Lucy; *lamb with seven eyes:* the seven gifts of the Holy Spirit; the Apocalypse; *woman with veiled or bandaged eyes:* the Synagogue; *two eyes, one opened, one closed:* Church and Synagogue respectively; *eyes of flame:* perception • **Egyptian** *single eye:* emblem of Osiris; *left eye:* the moon and its phases; *right eye:* the sun, Ra, Osiris; *eye of Horus (includes eyebrow):* the eye of the mind, the Pole Star, illumination, omniscience, offerings to the gods, strength, power, associated with the moon and its phases; *two winged eyes:* North and South, the sun and moon, celestial space, the two divisions of heaven; *one white eye, one black eye:* night and day, emblem of Horus • **English** (Elizabethan) *blue eyes:* a sign of pregnancy; *green eyes:* valued for their rarity; *eyes with dark rings around them:* a sign of debauchery • **Estonian** *half-dog/half-man with one eye:* a koerakoonlased • **Finnish** *ugly man with lopsided eyes and no eyelids:* Hiisi • **Greco-Roman** the sun; Apollo; the eye of Zeus/Jupiter; *red eyes:* attribute of Dionysus/Bacchus, Charon, Erinyes/Furies • **heraldic** providence in government • **Hindu** *eye of Varuna:* the sun; *third eye of Shiva:* spiritual consciousness; transcendent wisdom; *four-armed man with four or five faces and three eyes:* Shiva; *man struck in the eye by an arrow:* the impact caused to the senses by what was seen; *red eyes or eyes that are vertical slits:* attribute of a rakshasa • **Islamic** illumination; *eye of the heart:* the spiritual center, the seat of Absolute Intellect • **Jewish** *prophet with one eye:* Balaam • **Khoikhoi** *people with eyes in the back of their feet:* Aigamuxa • **Latvian** *half-dog/half-man with one eye:* a koerakoonlased • **Lithuanian** *red eyes:* attribute of Baubas; *half-dog/half-man with one eye:* a koerakoonlased • **Masonic** the sun; the source of light and life; the Word, Logos, First Creative Cause; the Great Architect of the Universe • **Norse** *god with one eye:* Odin • **Phoenician** *four eyes of Cronus:* perpetual watchfulness • **Serbian** *one-eyed dog-headed man with horse legs and iron teeth:* psoglav • **Slavic** *one-eyed old woman:* Likho • **South American Indian** *jaguar with four eyes:* second sight • **Sumero-Semitic** Ea, Enki; wisdom; om-

niscience; vigilance • **Taoist** *square pupils:* attribute of the Immortals
eyesight mental perception

F

F associated with domestic felicity, protection, responsibility, fire, sun, life, the father, fertility, feelings, the protection of law and trial, failing (especially in education); corresponds to -6-, the ears and heart, Taurus, Virgo • **Anglo-Saxon** associated with money • **Celtic** associated with the alder tree • **medieval** occasional Roman numeral for 40 • **tarot** the Lovers
fabric the transitoriness of this world
Fabricus Luscinus • **Roman** abstinence; continence
face mirror of man's character (sometimes false); the outward personality; the sun; a deity; authority; power; part of the ego exposed • **two faces** dissembling • **three faces of the devil** *red:* anger; *yellow:* impotence; *black:* ignorance • **woman with two or three faces** Prudence personified • **shining face** enlightenment; innocence; ingenuousness; holiness • **dark face** associated with evil, the devil • **painted face** charm against the evil eye; seduction; depersonalization; vanity; deceit; disloyalty; trickery; foolishness; wantonness; lust; sorrow; attribute of a loose woman • **veiled face** inscrutability; secrecy; hidden knowledge; protection of the inner life • **Chinese** *ritual face-blackening:* self-abasement, appeal for pardon; *black face on stage:* a humble but honest person; *white-faced long-bearded man with bow and arrows and small boy:* Chang Hsien • **Greco-Roman** *two-faced god:* Janus; *three faces in the moon:* Kore, Artemis, and Hecate • **Hindu** *multiple faces on gods:* their different aspects, powers, or functions; *four-armed man with four faces:* Brahma, Shiva; *four-armed man with five faces and three eyes:* Shiva; *four faces on Shiva or Brahma:* the elements; *god with six faces:* Karttikeya • **Jewish** God's face is identical with his essence making it impossible to gaze upon • **Kalmyk** *oval face:* attribute of an inhabitant of the Southern Continent; *square face:* attribute of an inhabitant of the Northern Continent; *round face:* attribute of an inhabitant of the Western Continent; *crescent-shaped face:* attribute of an inhabitant of the Eastern Continent • **Mesopotamian** *two-faced god:* Isimud • *see also* **complexion**
factory industry; drudgery; low work; regularity; predictability

faggots *when burning:* martyrdom by fire • **Chinese** fleeting human nature • **Jewish** *when formed in a cross:* associated with Abraham, Isaac, Elijah, the Widow of Sarepta

fainting inability to express one's feelings; being overwhelmed; weakness; sign of sickness, pregnancy, hunger, fatigue

fairy supra-normal powers of the human soul; latent possibilities; personification of stages in the development of the spirit; the lesser spiritual moods of the universal mind; processes of adaptation to the real world and acceptance of the true self • **legendary or forgotten fairies** frustrated acts • **fairy land** escape or regression to childhood; the real joys of natural life

falcon fire; the sun; the hunt; nobility; pride; death; wind; storm; clouds; freedom; confidence; hope for release from bondage; aspiration; victory; ascension; modesty; noble servitude; wildness; evil thought or action; an evil person; predation; immortality (especially when spiraling upward); associated with Sagittarius • **tamed falcon** a holy man; attribute of the personifications of Logic, Touch, Taste, Speed • **hooded falcon** the hope for light of those who live in darkness; esoteric knowledge; stifled spiritual ardor; light hidden under a bushel • **falcon-headed sphinx** a hieracosphinx • **falcon tearing a hare to pieces** the conquest of lust; victory of the masculine principle over the feminine principle, light over dark, sun over the moon, etc. • **Celtic** a primordial manifestation; victory over lust • **Chinese** the destructive force of war • **Christian** attribute of SS Baldric, Julian the Hospitator; *tamed falcon:* a Gentile convert to Christianity; *soldier with falcon on wrist:* St. Bavo • **Egyptian** light; King of the Birds; the heavenly principle; hunting; the flight of the soul after death; Horus; Monthu; associated with Hemon, Seker; *falcon-headed god:* Horus, Ra; *disk with two falcon feathers:* attribute of Amen-Ra • **heraldic** chivalry; eager quest; untiring in reaching an objective; hunting skill (especially when hooded); *peregrine falcon with a raven:* emblem of the Isle of Man • **Incan** the solar; guardian spirit • **Mexican Indian** *falcon with agave cactus:* the power of the sun, the liberation of the new moon • **Norse** Odin could travel to earth as a falcon; attribute of Frigg; associated with Loki, fire; *falcon feather cloak or robe:* attribute of Freyja • **Taoist** associated with birds and flight as a means of liberation from the world into the realm of the Immortals; emblem of Chung-li Chuan • *see also* **hawk**

with which falcons are often confused; **hieracosphinx**

Fall *see* **Autumn**

Fall of Man • **Jewish** the incarnation of the Spirit

falling loss of control; failure; loss of position, reputation, innocence

family qualities in close connection to one another, and attached to a single center

famine mental and spiritual inertia or hunger; spiritual yearning

fan wind; the imagination; the moon; change; femininity; coquetry; fickleness; power; rank; dignity; celestial air; purification; separation; the spirit; related to the phases of the moon • **winnowing fan** associated with fertility rites • **African** royal dignity • **Buddhist** emblem of Buddhism • **Chinese** authority; dignity; delicacy of feeling; breath of life; power of the air; fanning oneself with the hands invited evil spirits; *Autumn fan:* a deserted wife • **Hindu** attribute of Agni, Vishnu; *winnowing fan worn on the head:* attribute of Sitala • **Japanese** authority; power; protection from evil spirits; *white-feather fan:* power of the winds

fanlight the rising or setting sun

farm *see* **agriculture; farmer**

farmer catalyst of the forces of regeneration and salvation in harmony with nature; a simple but honest person • **Mochican** Ai apaec (especially with lizard and dog) • *see also* **agriculture**

fasces authority; justice; punishment; controlled power resulting in unity (especially in marriage); strength in unity; the personifications of Concord, Justice • **Greco-Roman** attribute of Eros/Cupid, higher Roman magistrates with the power to scourge and behead • **heraldic** judge; magistrate

fasting self-mortification; penance; token of sanctity; seeking favor, contact or forgiveness from a deity; mourning; saintliness; drawing attention to a grievance

fat (animal fat) affection; love; plenty; riches; the seat of life; contains the powers of the animal from which it was taken • **fat in a sacrifice** the choicest morsel being offered to a deity • **covering one's face, heart, or flanks with fat** hubris; hardheartedness; presumption

father authority; the masculine principle; the sun; the spirit; courage; heaven; dominion; the conscious; force; ownership; procreation; repression; tradition; wisdom; moral commandments; the supreme deity; the Creator; death; prohibitions; protection; law and order; physical, mental, and moral superiority • *see also* **man**

Father Time the personification of Time; Chronos

Fatima • **Islamic** a perfect woman

faun lasciviousness; revelry

Faunus *see* **Pan/Faunus**

Faust, Johann the relentless pursuit of knowledge

fawn weakness; gentleness • **Greco-Roman** attribute of Apollo, Artemis/Diana; *fawn-skin cloak or sandals:* attribute of Maenads/Bacchantes, Orpheus

fear lack of intellectual will

feast a completed period or stage of development; membership; communion; communal worship

feather wind; air; ascension; fertility; lightness; purification of evil; pride; ostentation; charity; faith; truth; contemplation; thoughts; the heavens; the soul; the spiritual principle; flight to other realms; abundance; dryness; power; strength; triumph • **two feathers** light and air together; height; the North and South Poles; resurrection • **three feathers** light; the end of nurse's training; good thought, word, and deed; *passing through a ring:* faith, hope, charity • **white feathers** cowardice; sea foam; clouds • **crimson feathers** cloak trimming for fairies • **black feathers** sleep; mourning • **ostrich feathers** distinction • **feathered serpent** duality (good/bad, rain/drought, etc.) • **feathered crown** sun rays; a nimbus • **feathered helmet** honor; triumph; defiance • **wearing feathers** taking on the powers of birds including transcendent and instinctual knowledge, flight • **feathered serpent with horns** opposite forces in conflict • **feather quill pen** poetry; literature; the scribe • **horse feathers** nonsense • **Amerindian** *eagle feathers:* light rays, the Thunderbird, the Great Spirit, universal spirit; *feathered sun:* majesty, the universe, solar power, radiation of power, the Center • **Aztecan** celestial power; the soul; *feathers surmounted by a blue bird:* emblem of Huehueteotl • **British** *three feathers:* emblem of Wales, the Prince of Wales • **Celtic** *feathered cloak:* attribute of priests, journey to the other world; *feathered dress:* attribute of fairies • **Christian** faith; contemplation attribute of St. Gregory; *peacock feathers:* attribute of St. Barbara • **Druidic** *three feathers:* power, light, the Light of the World • **Egyptian** sovereignty; the sun; light; air; dryness; weightlessness; flight; truth; attribute of Amsu, Anheru, Hathor, Horus, Mentu, Nefertium, Osiris, Shu, Ra; *single feather:* attribute of Maat; *feathers in a scale:* Osiris weighing the soul against the feathers of truth; *disk with two falcon feathers:* attribute of Amen-Ra; *bearded man wearing a cap with two tall plumes:* Amen-Ra;

white crown with asps, horns, and plumes: attribute of Thoth • **European** dying on feathers was unlucky • **heraldic** (usually ostrich feathers) obedience, serenity; *peacock feather:* power and distinction, knowledge, beauty, royalty, pride of nation, attribute of a troubadour • **Mexican Indian** *house of green feathers:* home of the quetzal • **Norse** *falcon feather robe or cloak:* attribute of Freyja • **Tahitian** *red and yellow feathers:* attribute of 'Oro • **Taoist** communication with the next world; attribute of priests; *green feathers:* attribute of workers and officials in the Crimson Slenderness celestial palace • **Toltec** *feathered stick:* prayer, contemplation • **Ural-Altaic** *feathered robe:* communication between this world and the spirit world

feces *see* **excrement**

feeding dispensing truth and goodness to the mind and soul

feet the soul; humility; lowliness; stability; seat of power; magic power; genitals, especially the phallus; freedom of movement; associated with Neptune (planet) • **deformity or injury of the foot** weakness of the soul • **washing feet** ritual purification; humility; penitence; willing servitude • **bare feet** poverty; humility; direct contact with Mother Earth; attribute of Poverty personified • **flat feet** misfortune • **crown at one's feet** renounced royalty • **cloven foot** sin; attribute of the devil, unclean animals • **absence of feet on a fire god** the instability of flame • **stamping the foot** frustrated anger • **deity treading people underfoot** tamping down worldly passions; the illusory nature of existence • **feet of clay** having human faults • **Afghani** *woman with feet reversed:* an al • **Ashanti** *giant with feet that point both ways:* Sasabonsam • **Aztecan** *obsidian mirror as a foot:* attribute of Tezcatlipoca • **Chinese** *red and yellow bird with six feet and four wings:* chaos • **Christian** *washing feet in a basin:* humility, attribute of St. Lioba; *feet of brass:* understanding • **Egyptian** *winged foot crushing a butterfly:* Hapi • **folkloric** *itching foot:* you will journey to somewhere new; *flat feet:* sign of a bad temper; *entering a building left foot first:* unlucky • **Fulani** *god with 30 feet:* Kaydara • **Greco-Roman** *purple foot:* associated with Demeter/Ceres, Hecate; *monster with 12 feet:* Scylla; *winged foot crushing a butterfly:* Serapis; *child with serpents for feet:* Ericthonius; *man with serpents for feet:* Cecrops; *giant with serpents for feet:* Enceladus • **heraldic** discovery of an important track or fact which gains lasting merit • **Indic** *woman with reversed feet:* a churel;

ghost without hands or feet and his head tied to the pommel of a saddle: a dund • **Jewish** *bare feet:* mourning, respect, willingness to serve; *feet above a mountain:* Nahum's vision; *prophet with lame foot:* Balaam; *skull, feet, and palms of the hands:* the remains of Jezebel • **Khoikhoi** *ogres with eyes in the back of their feet:* Aigamuxa • **Slavic** *hut spinning on the feet of fowl:* dwelling of Baba Yaga • *see also* **footprints; heel; shoe; toes**

female *see* **woman; maiden; virgin**

fence barrier; protection; separating of thoughts, ideas, beliefs • **Slavic** *hut surrounded by fence of bones or skulls:* dwelling of Baba Yaga

Feng-huang • **Chinese** the Chinese phoenix; harbinger of peace, benevolent rule, a great sage, luck; associated with the sun, fire, warmth, summer, justice, obedience, fidelity; one of the Four Spiritually Endowed Creatures; *two Feng-huang:* the combination of Emperor and Sage • *see also* **Ho-o**

fennel dissembling; flattery; stimulant; spiritual rejuvenation • **garland of fennel** crown of a victorious gladiator • **Christian** attribute of the Virgin Mary • **flower language** worthy of all praise; force; strength • **Greek** sacred to Sabazios

Fenrir • **Norse** bringer of evil

fermentation the spirit surpassing ordinary limitations; associated with excrement, decomposition • **alchemic** transformation; transmutation; regeneration; the passage from death to life; cyclic ideas; eternal return

fern solitary humility; frankness; sincerity; endurance; confidence; fascination; ancient knowledge; archaism; Christ (although sometimes considered the devil's plant); associated with serpents; emblem of colonizers • **fern leaf** victory over death • **flower language** sincerity; fascination; *flowering fern:* reverie • **folkloric** favored by pixies; hated by witches and evil spirits • **heraldic** magic; confidence; shelter; fascination • *see also* **bracken**

ferret bloodthirstiness; fiery temper; cunning; restlessness; mischievousness; inquisitiveness for hidden things

ferry • **Greek** attribute of Charon

ferule attribute of the personifications of Grammar, Geometry

fess • **heraldic** service in the army; anyone ready to work for the public good; solidity; support; power; strength of character; guardianship

fetterlock • **heraldic** victory; one who has taken or rescued prisoners of war

fetters *see* **chains**

fever excitement; passion; restlessness; love; stress; frustration; anger • **Jewish** punishment for disobedience to God

fibula (clasp or buckle) virginity; restricted virility

ficoides • **flower language** your looks freeze me

fiddle, fiddler freedom from care; gaiety

field limitless possibility; fertility; space; freedom from restraint; physical creation; related to death • **field flowers** modesty • **Christian** *field flowers:* the Virgin Mary; the Church

fife • **American** associated with the Revolutionary War • **heraldic** martial readiness

fig (fruit) piece of dung; worthlessness; death; woman; breasts; testicles; phallus; sex in general; purgation • **opened fig** vulva • **eating a fig** erotic ecstasy • **basket of figs** fertility • **Christian** good works; occasionally used instead of the apple from the Tree of Knowledge • **Greco-Roman** phallus • **Mandaean** *fig and grape:* masculine and feminine fertility respectively

fig tree fertility; abundance; prosperity; luxury; longevity; spring; rejuvenation; truth; peace; fidelity; religious knowledge; sometimes the Tree of Knowledge; associated with the archangel Zadkiel • **fig tree and vine** male and female, respectively • **fig leaf** lust; sex; phallic • **sitting under a fig tree** the peaceful life • **withered fig tree** evil • **Buddhist** the bo tree of Buddha • **Chinese** immortality • **Christian** attribute of Nathaniel, St. Bartholomew; *withered fig tree:* the synagogue, a church in decline because of heresy, the tree Christ cursed • **flower language** argument; longevity; profuseness; profligacy • **Greco-Roman** sacred to Dionysus/Bacchus, Priapus, Zeus/Jupiter, Silvanus • **heraldic** peace; plenty • **Islamic** the Tree of Heaven • **Jewish** peace; prosperity; plenty; *fig tree and vine:* emblem of Israel, peace and plenty; *fig leaf:* attribute of Adam and Eve after The Fall • **Oceanic** often a Tree of Life • *see also* **Bo tree**

filbert (plant) *see* **hazel**

file (rasp) refined ideas or expressions; ideas free from superstition

fillet death; sacrifice; related to the gods • **white fillet** attribute of the dead in the Elysian Fields • **purple fillet** victory in sports • **German** attribute of an unmarried woman • **Roman** *slender fillet:* modesty, attribute of a married woman

fingernails *see* **nails (body)**

fingers the forces of the unconscious that can emerge without warning and hinder efforts of the conscious; phallus, especially a single finger extended • **index finger** direction; command; rule; fortunate guidance; delivery from evil; associated with character, materialism, law, order, the vernal equinox, Jupiter (planet); unlucky to administer medicine with • **index finger when upraised** warning; lesson; -1-, superiority; *when the finger is to the lips:* silence, vow of silence • **middle finger** related to death, humanity, system, intelligence, Summer solstice, Saturn (planet) • **middle finger upraised** coition; penetration; contempt; cuckoldry • **ring finger** linked directly to the heart; associated with truth, economy, energy, autumnal equinox, a sage, betrothal, marriage, the sun • **little finger** related to inspiration, divination, the phallus, goodness, prudence, Winter solstice, Mercury (planet) • **extra fingers** the luck of the extraordinary; sometimes a sign of evil • **long fingers** improvidence; musical or artistic ability; sometimes, a thief • **crooked fingers** a crabbed disposition • **crooked little finger** you will die rich • **short thick fingers** silliness; intemperance • **index finger as long as the middle finger** dishonesty • **fingertips** divination; poetic inspiration • **rubbing the fingertips** money; carefulness • **pointing a finger** insult; magic power • **two fingers raised** teaching; judging • **index and middle finger in a vee** victory; peace • **index and little finger extended** the horns of the moon; aversion of danger, bad luck, or the evil eye; the devil; *when pointed at someone:* insult, a curse, cuckold • **finger to the mouth** silence; thought; warning • **finger in the mouth (occasionally the thumb)** wisdom, coquetry • **crossed fingers** hope; untruth (especially when the fingers are hidden) • **cutting off a finger** mourning; atonement; ritual castration • **finger snapping** disdain; peremptory command; the beginning or end of an idea, cycle, or process • **American** *index and little finger raised:* bull horns, bull excrement, a lie; *index, little finger and thumb extended:* "I love you" in American Sign Language • **Christian** *three fingers in a blessing:* the Trinity; *index finger:* associated with the Holy Spirit; *index finger upraised:* Jesus Christ as the one way to salvation; *middle finger:* associated with the hope in the salvation of Christ; *ring finger:* associated with the divine nature of Christ, hope of resurrection; *little finger:* associated with the human nature of Christ; *crossed fingers:* the sign of the Cross • **Egyptian** *two fingers raised in blessing:* help and strength, the two fingers of Horus extended to help mount the ladder from this world to the next; *first finger:* divine justice; *middle finger:*

the Spirit; the Mediator; *infant with a finger in his mouth:* Horus • **Greco-Roman** *index finger:* associated with Zeus/Jupiter; *middle finger:* associated with Cronus/Saturn; *ring finger:* associated with Apollo; *little finger:* associated with Hermes/Mercury; *finger on the mouth:* silence, meditation, attribute of Polyhymnia, Nemesis/Invidia • **heraldic** *pointing finger:* direction, correct route • **Jewish** *raised hand, vee between the middle and ring fingers:* blessing • **Maori** *three fingers:* mind, character, and body • **Tinguinian** *half-man/half-bird with toes and fingers reversed:* an alan • *see also* **hands; thumb**

fir fervor; power; boldness; patience; patience; choice; elevation; constancy; immortality; regeneration; fidelity; integrity; purity; regal beauty; pride; fire; sun; hope; androgyny; the elect in heaven • **Celtic** energy; clarity; achievement • **Chinese** patience; the elect • **Egyptian** sex • **flower language** time; elevation (especially Scotch fir) • **Finnish** a sacred tree • **Greco-Roman** related to birth; sacred to Pan/Faunus, Artemis/Diana • **Jewish** related to birth, youthful strength, patience; used in the ceiling of Solomon's Temple • **Near East** sex • **Phrygian** Attis • **Teutonic** Tree of Life; sacred to Odin; *lights and/or luminous balls on a fir tree:* celestial bodies • *see also* **pine**

fire spiritual energy; power; the active principle; strength; protection; visibility; creation; fusion; destruction; immolation; purification of evil; the soul; the creator god; the sky father; essence of life; the sun; authority; power; spiritual enlightenment and zeal; passion; martyrdom; transformation; the means of transmitting messages or offerings to heaven; the means of changing from one state to another; regeneration; the libido; fecundity; impregnation; forbidden passions; war • **baptism by fire** restoration of primordial purity • **hearth fire** home; familial loyalty; the feminine aspect of fire • **beacon fire** communication between men • **fire and brimstone** hell; the vengeance of God • **circle or wheel of fire** chastity; magic spell; inviolability • **kindling a fire** birth; resurrection; sexual creation • **arson** regression (especially male) • **fiery serpent** purification; transcendence of the earthly state • **archangel covered in fire** Camael • **alchemic** the central element; unifier; stabilizer • **Aztecan** ritual death; redemption; penitence • **Buddhist** wisdom that burns away all ignorance; *fiery pillar:* Buddha • **Chickasaw** Ababinili • **Chinese** danger; anger; ferocity; speed; both yin and yang; corresponds to South, red, Summer, the heart; *as an element:*

associated with bitter taste, methodicalness, yang, beans, hens, lungs, red, breath, pleasure, -2-, Aries, Leo, Sagittarius • **Christian** religious fervor; the voice of God; divine revelation; Pentecost; the torments of hell; attribute of SS Anthony of Padua, Anthony the Great, Agnes, Florian (usually extinguishing a fire); *fire and a serpent:* attribute of St. Paul; *tunic on fire:* attribute of St. Laurence • **Egyptian** the active principle; associated with Thoth as inspiration • **Fulani** *rooster and/or fire:* a secret told to an enemy and causing ruin • **Greco-Roman** associated with Prometheus; attribute of Hephaestus/Vulcan, Hermes/Mercury, Hestia/Vesta • **heraldic** zealousness; *fire-fighting:* zealousness • **Hindu** transcendental light and knowledge; the vital energy of wisdom; Krishna; associated with Shiva; attribute of Agni, Kali, Durga; *kindling a fire:* re-enactment of creation; integration and reunion by means of sacrifice; *Agni's column of flame and smoke:* World Axis; *altar fire:* consecration, sacrifice; *three fires on a Vedic altar:* the earth, sun and sky, ether and winds • **Islamic** *fire and flame:* light and heat respectively, divinity and hell respectively • **Japanese** attribute of Fudo • **Jewish** divine revelation; the voice of God; *fiery chariot and horses:* attribute of the ascension of Elijah, Elisha at Dothan • **Masonic** corresponds to the spirit, initiation • **Mongolian** associated with South • **Norse** dwelling of Muspel; *circle or wheel of fire:* attribute of Brunhild • **North American Indian** intermediary between god and man; *in a medicine lodge:* dwelling of the Great Spirit • **Persian** the sacred Center of the temple; the solar; emblem of Atar; the life of the soul; *three fires:* Anaid, Mihr, and Berisov • **Pythagorean** associated with the tetrahedron • **Sumero-Semitic** emblem of Marduk; *altar fire:* consecration, sacrifice • **Tungun** associated with South • **Zoroastrian** the godhead • *see also* **flame,** with which fire is imperfectly distinguished

firebrand life; associated with Melager

firefly Summer; a spirit; a memory; ghost of the dead • **Buddhist** shallow knowledge • **Chinese** companion of poor students • **Japanese** ghost of a slain warrior • **Montagnard** the soul of a hero

fireplace *see* **hearth**

fireworks fertility; warding off of evil spirits; purification; celebration • **American** associated with Independence Day (July 4th)

fish phallus; wisdom; freedom; purity; sexuality; faith; folly; greed; the self hidden in the unconscious; the soul; fecundity; procreation; vulva; emblem of woman; sexual coldness; sacrifice; attribute of marine deities, Tobias, associated with the Great Mother, the archangels Asariel, Zadkiel • **fish with a bird's head (usually a swallow)** bringer of cyclic regeneration • **two fish** marriage; domestic felicity; sexual indifference; frigidity; the joy of union; a charm to avert evil; emblem of Pisces • **three fish with one head** all holy trinities • **fish swimming upward** evolution of spirit; return to unity • **fish swimming downward** involution of the spirit in matter • **alchemic** the arcane substance • **Bambaran** *man with a fish tail:* Faro • **Buddhist** one of the Eight Emblems of Good Augury; emancipation from desires and attachment; happiness; freedom; emblem of the footprint of Buddha • **Celtic** associated with Nodon; *salmon, trout:* associated with sacred wells • **Chinese** wealth; regeneration; harmony; the Emperor's subjects; emblem of the Guanyin and T'ang dynasties; *single fish:* orphan, widow, bachelor, the solitary person; *pair of fish:* fertility, connubial bliss, the joys of union • **Christian** Christ (Western church only); Christianity; Christians; baptism; immortality; resurrection; attribute of SS Anthony of Padua, Chrysogonus, Congall, Corentin, Francis of Assisi, Mauritius, Neot, Ulrich; *fish in a net or on a hook:* attribute of St. Peter; *fish and wallet:* attribute of the archangel Raphael; *fish and loaves of bread:* attribute of St. Jude; *fish with a key in its mouth:* attribute of St. Benno; *fish dangling from a crosier:* attribute of St. Zeno; *fish with a ring in its mouth:* attribute of St. Mungo; *fish on a confessional:* penitence; *fish with ship and windmill:* associated with St. Mary of Cleophas; *man with a fish in his hand:* St. Andrew; *two fish, crossed:* baptism; attribute of SS Simon, Andrew; *two fish on a hook, with a pitcher:* attribute of the Virgin Mary; *three fish:* the Trinity, Trinity Sunday, and baptism; *three fishes with one head:* the Trinity; *three intertwined fishes:* baptism in the Trinity; *three fish forming an equilateral triangle:* the Trinity, the equality of the Trinity; *fish with anchor:* hope in Christ; *fish swimming into a whale's mouth:* unsuspecting souls trapped by the devil; *monk celebrating mass on board ship as fish gather to listen:* St. Brendan • **Egyptian** phallus of Osiris; *two fish:* the creative principle; fertility; prosperity of the Nile; emblem of Isis, Hathor; associated with Hatmehit, Rem; *barbel:* an unclean fish, hatred, emblem of Typhon • **Greco-Roman** love; fertility; attribute of

Aphrodite/Venus, Poseidon/Neptune; offering for the dead; *half-fish/half-man:* a triton; *half-fish/half-man with horse forelegs:* an icthyocentaur • **heraldic** Christianity; unity with Christ; spiritual nourishment; taciturnity; secrecy; humility; temperance; health; vigilance; free-fishing rights; a true and generous mind; virtue for one's own actions, not because of heritage • **Hindu** wealth; fertility; Matsya; attribute of love divinities; *golden fish:* Varuna; *two fishes touching nose to tail:* yoni; *four-armed man with fish bottom:* Matsya • **Japanese** love; attribute of Kannon • **Jewish** food of the blessed in Paradise; eaten at a holy meal before the Sabbath; the faithful swimming in the waters of the Torah; attribute of Tobias; *twin fish:* emblem of February, Pisces • **Mandaean** eaten sacramentally at feasts for the dead • **Norse** love; fertility; adaptability; determination; attribute of Frigga • **Sumero-Semitic** lucky; love; fertility; emblem of love divinities; eucharistic food of priests of Atargatis; associated with Ea, Oannes, Tammuz, Ishtar; *seven fish-like men:* the Abgal • **zodiacal** the arcane substance; associated with Capricorn • *see also* **Capricornus (mythology); mermaid;** and specific kinds of fish: **carp; sturgeon,** etc

fisherman spiritual seeker; giver of spiritual insight; seeker of spiritual disciples • **Buddhism** Buddha • **Babylonian** Adapa • **Celtic** Nodon • **Christian** St. Peter; Christ; the Apostles • **Japanese** attribute of Ebisu • **Mochican** Ai apaec (especially with lizard and dog)

fishhook perfidy; faithlessness; deceit; means of investigation for esoteric knowledge, or of the unconscious • **Christian** *large fishhook:* attribute of St. Andrew • **heraldic** riches gotten from fishing; honor; patience; virtue; confidence; important fishing rights

fishing communion with nature; quietness; contemplation; exploration of the unconscious; searching for deeper wisdom; the act of cuckolding; seeking wisdom; introspection; seeking regeneration or spiritual rebirth • **Christian** bringing converts to the church • **Chinese** the art of good governance

fishing pole the means of spiritual seeking or development • **Japanese** attribute of Ebisu

fishnet *see* **net**

fist power; resistance; deterrent capability; threat; repressed emotions; anger; tension • **fist placed over the heart** tearing out one's heart as an offering • *see also* **hand**

fit *see* **epileptic seizure**

flag victory; self-assertion; thought or ideal; iden-

tification; nationalism • **lowering or striking a flag** defeat • **dipping a flag** salute • **flag at half-mast** mourning • **flag flown upside down** distress • **white flag** surrender; truce; peaceful intent • **white flag with red cross** attribute of the Phrygian sibyl • **black flag** pirates; death; execution of criminals; success in battle • **red flag** danger; revolution; anarchy; socialism; communism • **yellow flag** disease; quarantine • **green flag** seafaring wreck • **Christian** *white flag with red cross:* resurrection; victory over death; attribute of SS Ansanus, George, Reparata, Ursula • **Hindu** *white flag:* attribute of Vayu

flagellation *see* **whipping**

flagpole androgyny (the pole is masculine, the ball at the top is feminine)

flail the harvest; sovereignty; rule; dominion; supreme power; associated with August, sometimes September; attribute of Suffering personified • **Christian** attribute of St. Jude • **Egyptian** emblem of the king; attribute of Osiris

flak trouble; criticism

flame transcendence; illumination; wisdom; truth; inspiration; enlightenment; the soul; the supreme deity; charity; love; spiritual power, zeal; the manifestation of a divinity; religious zeal; martyrdom; attribute of Choler personified • **archangel holding flame** Uriel • **flame on the forehead** attribute of Fire personified • **flame on the head** divine inspiration; divine power; attribute of the personifications of Charity, Piety • **flaming mountain** divine inspiration • **flaming heart** attribute of Charity personified • **flaming pillar or tree trunk** the god of light and wisdom • **flaming sword** sun rays; protection; • **woman with flame in her hand or out of a vase** attribute of Charity personified • **flames surrounding a woman** Choler personified • **sea of flames** life as an infirmity • **wall of flame** initiation; magic protection • **Babylonian** *god with flame issuing from mouth:* Marduk • **Buddhist** *lion with flaming tail:* temple guardian • **Christian** the Holy Spirit; *six flames:* the six gifts of the Holy Spirit; *seven flames:* the seven gifts of the Holy Spirit; *nine flames:* the nine gifts of the Holy Spirit; *flaming tunic:* attribute of St. Laurence; *man with flames underfoot:* St. Anthony the Great; *flame on the head:* attribute of the Apostles at Pentecost; *eyes of flame:* perception; *flaming heart:* spiritual zeal, attribute of SS Anthony of Padua, Augustine; *flames at the feet of a bishop:* St. Januarius • **folkloric** *blue flame:* a spirit is passing, witches are present • **Hindu** Krishna; *ring of flame around Shiva:* cosmic cycle of creation and destruction; *white horse with flaming mane:* the sun • **Japanese** *tortoise with a flaming tail:* longevity • **Jewish** *flaming sword:* the Torah; attribute of the cherubim protecting the Garden of Eden • **Zoroastrian** *man covered with flame:* Ahura Mazda • *see also* **fire,** with which flame is imperfectly distinguished

flamen • **Roman** the spiritual flame in the individual and society

flamingo beauty; balance; grace • **American** *plastic flamingo:* kitsch • **Hindu** the soul migrating from darkness to light; the initiator into light

flanchi • **heraldic** royal recognition of virtue, learning

flask • **Christian** attribute of St. Omobuono

flax domestic industry; fertility; simplicity; fate; gratitude; life; vigorous growth • **flower language** I am sensible of your kindness; *when dried:* utility

flea parasite; pettiness; pest; despicability

fleece alluring desire; closely guarded wealth; life force of the sheep • **fox fur on a fleece** attribute of usurers • **Greek** *hanging from a tree, guarded by a dragon:* associated with Jason • **Jewish** *with bowl:* associated with Gideon; *warrior kneeling beside a fleece:* Gideon • *see also* **golden fleece; sheep; wool; sheep**

flesh lower nature; diabolical force dwelling in the body; enemy of the spirit • **Tungun** associated with North

fleur-de-lis androgyny; purity; light; life; spirit and power; emblem of France, royalty (especially French) • **Christian** the Trinity; the Annunciation; purification through baptism; attribute of Christ, the Virgin Mary, SS Jean d'Arc, Louis of France, Louis of Toulouse; *fleur-de-lis with letters IHC, or HIS:* the dual nature of Christ; *fleur-de-lis on a halo or book:* attribute of St. Zenobius • **flower language** flame; I burn • **heraldic** France; French royalty; purity; light; sixth son; *when red:* Florence • *see also* **jessant-de-lis**

flight *see* **flying**

flint fire; indifference to insult; everlastingness; hardness of heart; the spark of love; procreation • **thrown on a grave** a suicide • **flint arrowhead** charm against evil; attribute of fairies • **heraldic** zeal to serve

floating regression; return to the womb; passivity; refusal to explore the subconscious; sexual ecstasy (especially female); witches float on water and cannot drown

flock disordered or semi-ordered forces of the cosmos; a church congregation • **orderly flock** co-ordinated desires and emotions working for the evolution of the soul; prosperity; rural tranquility • **disorderly flock** loss of unity; disintegration; degeneration; regression

flogging *see* **flagellation**

flood punishment, as opposed to complete destruction; regeneration and purification; rebellion; end of a cycle; inundation of the spirit or emotions • **Jewish** the Flood

Flora's bell • **flower language** you make no pretension

flour truth; goodness; abundant life; the finest extract of something (as opposed to bran); the result of purification, discernment • *see also* **bread, grain**

flower-of-an-hour • **flower language** delicate beauty

flowers spring; transitoriness; beauty; the soul; the work of the sun; festivity; joy; the cycle of life (birth, coition, death, regeneration); virtue; purity; goodness; mystery; victory; temptation; deceit; love (especially female); vulva; virginity; woman; the feminine principle; passivity; balance; justice; the finest product; associated with 4th weeding anniversaries; attribute of the personifications of Spring, Smell, Logic, sometimes Hope • **when opening** development in manifestation particularly with the lotus in the Orient and the rose and lily in the Occident • **blooming out of season** unlucky omen • **vase of flowers** spiritual beauty; the fertility of the waters • **scattered flowers** joys • **field flowers** modesty • **flower gardens** associated with Paradise, the Fields of the Blessed, the abode of souls, etc.• **plucking flowers** innocent joys; sexual indulgence; coition • **flower bud** potentiality • **five-petaled flower** the microcosm • **six-petaled flower** (especially the lotus) the macrocosm • **red flower** love; passion; blood; dawn; the rising sun; animal life • **orange or yellow flower** the sun • **blue or golden flower** the impossible; the unattainable • **white flower** innocence; purity; blamelessness; love; coition; death; heroism; attribute of the Great Goddess • **red and white flowers together** death • **child with flowers and leaves** personification of Spring pleasures • **alchemic** *white flower:* silver; *red flower:* gold; *blue flower:* wisdom that grows from the Cosmic Egg; *five-petaled flower:* the quintessence • **Aztecan** *butterfly among flowers:* soul of a dead warrior • **Buddhist** transitory life; worship offering • **Celtic** the soul; the sun; spiritual blooming • **Chinese** the feminine; yin; *basket of flowers: basket of flowers:* longevity, happiness in old age, attribute of Lan

Ts'ai Hok, attribute of Han Xiang • **Christian** the result of charity and other good works; attribute of St. Elizabeth of Hungary; *white flower:* attribute of the Virgin Mary; *flowers in a field:* the Virgin Mary and the Church; *basket of flowers and fruit:* attribute of St. Dorothea of Cappadocia; *three flowers held in the hand:* attribute of St. Hugh of Grenoble • **Greco-Roman** continuing life in the next world; associated with funerals, Flora, Eos/Aurora, Zephyr; attribute of Artemis/Diana, Hera/Juno • **heraldic** hope; joy • **Hindu** corresponds to the Ether • **Mexican Indian** associated with Xochiquetzal, Xochipilli • **still life** decay; brevity of life (especially when shown with dewdrops) • **Taoist** *Golden Flower:* the Tao, attainment of immortality, spiritual rebirth, transcendent power, the crystallization of light • *see also* specific kinds of flowers, such as **lily; lotus; rose**

fluorite associated with the archangel Gabriel

flute dance; love; delight; lust; lasciviousness; phallus; erotic anguish or joy; wind; fertility; praise; attribute of Flattery personified • **Babylonian** *lapis lazuli flute:* attribute of Tammuz • **Chinese** harmony; *jade flute:* attribute of Han Xiang • **Greco-Roman** associated with funerals; attribute of Dionysus/Bacchus, Apollo, Euterpe, Marsyas, Hermes/Mercury, Adonis, sirens; *bird with a woman's head and a flute:* a siren • **Hindu** attribute of Krishna • **Phrygian** attribute of Cybele

fly (insect) pestilence sin; annoyance; minor trouble; impurity; lust; greed; filth; squalor; disease; a dandy; deceit; diminutive life; sin, leading to redemption; the priest, or other inhibitor of the preconscious who taints innocent joys; commonly associated with demons and evil gods; erratic thoughts or behavior • **Lord of the Flies** Beelzebub • **Christian** the devil; evil; pestilence; sin; *goldfinch and fly:* Christ and disease respectively • **Egyptian** protection • **European 15th, 16th century painting** often not a symbol, but a superstition that the painted fly would keep real flies from landing on the fresh paint • **Greek** a sacred creature • **Jewish** the fourth plague visited upon Egypt • **Phoenician** Beelzebub; destruction; putrefaction • *see also* **water fly**

fly trap (plant) • **flower language** deceit

fly whisk authority; command • **Buddhist** associated with the sparing of life • **Chinese** leadership; authority • **Hindu** *with a golden handle:* spiritual and temporal power

flying thought; imagination; spiritual elevation; ascension; spiritual release; speed; avoidance; escape; escape of the spirit of the dead; transcendence; passing from one plane of being to another; success; the release of the spirit from the limitations of matter; joy; euphoria; the desire for sublimation; the search for inner harmony; the resolution of conflict • **Mediterranean** *dreaming of flying on one's back:* good omen for a sea voyage • *see also* **ascending**

flying saucer message from another realm; fear of the unknown

foam body moisture, especially milk, semen, sweat, saliva, tears

fog dimness of vision; isolation; transformation; the unreal; confusion; lack of spiritual insight • **biblical** precursor of great revelation

foghorn danger; spiritual message

Fomorion • **Celtic** counteragent of initiation and psychic development

font • **Christian** baptism; rebirth; admission to the Church by baptism; attribute of Faith personified, St. Patrick; *circular:* the womb, especially the immaculate womb of the Virgin Mary; *square:* the Holy City; a sepulcher; *five-sided:* the five wounds of Christ; *eight-sided:* regeneration; the seven days of creation and the eighth day for resurrection • *see also* **baptism**

food truth; the real as opposed to the illusory; knowledge feeding the soul; the visible form of divine life; eating the food of another world binds one to that world • **sharing food** kinship; friendship; bonding • **Greece** *red food:* reserved for the dead • *see also* **eating; digestion**

fool inversion of the king; sacrificial victim; scapegoat; chaos; willful involution; inversion of the normal order; repressed unconscious urges; the inner personality; unregenerate man; absolute innocence; a critic of Church and Establishment practices; may personify Folly; related to seers, the abnormal, the unformed

Fool (tarot) the irrational; blind impulse; the unconscious; a choice of vital importance; Absolute Zero, from which all proceeds and returns; associated with being at a crossroads, the possibility of discovering one's true fate, the possibility of great luck; associated with the archangel Lumiel

foot *see* **feet**

footprints funereal implications; they leave the magic powers of the maker; evidence of divine visitation • **lack of footprints** sign of a fairy • **footprints going in opposite directions** past and present; past and future; coming and going

footstool *see* **stool (furniture)**

forceps attribute of a surgeon • **forceps holding a tooth** attribute of a dentist, St. Apollonia • *see also* **pincers**

ford marks a decisive stage in action, development; the dividing line between two states such as consciousness/unconsciousness, sleeping/waking, time/eternity • **Celtic** place of single combat; *woman washing bloody clothes at a ford:* death omen

forehead intelligence; the intellect; knowledge; wisdom; reflects character or feelings; piety; the noblest part of the body; related to the head • **high forehead** intelligence; refinement • **low forehead** lack of intelligence; ignorance • **blazing star on forehead** attribute of the archangel Lumiel • **Egyptian** *hand above the forehead:* attribute of Resheph • **Hindu** *blue bees on the forehead:* Krishna, the Ether; *crescent on the forehead:* attribute of Sarasvati, Shiva • **Indic** a man with two lines on his forehead will live 40 years, three lines will live 75 years, four lines will live 100 years • *see also* **head**

foreigner *see* **stranger**

forelock the point of control • **grasping a forelock** gaining control; grasping an opportunity • **grasping one's own forelock before a superior** subservience; acknowledgement of fealty

foreskin the female element in males; *circumcision:* confirming the sexual status of males, sublimated castration, spiritual purification, initiation (into the Jewish faith in particular), dedication, purity, religious or tribal membership rite, repetition of cutting the umbilical cord, birth into a new stage of life • *see also* **castration**

forest the feminine principle; the Great Mother; realm of the psyche; the unconscious; danger; mistakes; problems; obscurance of reason; fertility; enchantment; hunting; the home of outlaws, fairies, supernatural beings; a place of testing and initiation • **dark or enchanted forest** the realm of death; the spiritual world; unknown perils; lack of spiritual knowledge or spiritual light; place of initiation or spiritual death and rebirth • **Australian aboriginal** place of initiation; the Beyond; the realm of shades • **Buddhist** a natural shrine • **Celtic** a natural shrine • **Druidic** *sun and shade:* male and female, light and darkness • **Hindu** dwelling place for the contemplative life • **Ural-Altaic** the dwelling place of spirits • *see also* **grove**

forge the brain; thought; poetic inspiration; attribute of blacksmiths, alchemists • **alchemic** transmutation; the masculine principle; the infliction of force • *see also* **blacksmith**

forget-me-not ingenuous simplicity; constancy; true love • **flower language** remembrance; true love; forget me not

fork (implement) spitefulness; torture; a large fork may indicate martyrdom • **two-pronged** death; attribute of Hades/Pluto • **three-pronged** Caduceus; attribute of sea deities • *see also* **pitchfork**

fork (in a road or path) choice; parting of the ways; division of the whole; point where beliefs diverge

fornication the primacy of base desires • *see also* **sexual intercourse**

fort strength; bulwark; protection; defense; the sheltering and enclosing aspect of the feminine principle

Fortitude (tarot) *see* **Strength (tarot)**

Fortuna *see* **Tyche/Fortuna**

fortune-teller *see* **soothsayer**

fossil time; eternity; life and death; evolution; threshold; a link between two worlds; extinction

fountain rejuvenation; regeneration; purification; the soul; the life-force; the waters of life; life; spiritual energy; totality; the unconscious; birth; resurrection; divination; wisdom; truth; consolation; refreshment, both spiritual and physical; woman; related to death and future life • **flowing fountain** eternal life • **fountain in a square, cloister, courtyard, walled garden, etc.** the Cosmic Center; living waters; immortality; Earthly Paradise • **fountain issuing from the mouth of a figure** instruction; refreshment; the Word; the power of speech • **sealed fountain** virginity • **alchemic** *three fountains:* sulfur, Mercurius, and salt; *king and queen in a fountain:* the water operations of Dissolution and Distillation • **Christian** Christ as the fountain of life; the flow of the Word; redemption and purification by living waters; attribute of SS Clement, David; emblem of Christ, the Virgin Mary; *sealed fountain:* the Virgin Mary, the virginity of Mary; *fountain of life:* immortality, the Holy Spirit; *three fountains:* associated with St. Paul; *four fountains:* the four Evangelists • **heraldic** water; a spring • **Islamic** spiritual truth; grace; the knowledge of God • **Jewish** *fountain of living waters:* God • *see also* **spring (water)**

four o'clock (flower) timidity; rest

fox base desires or instincts; craft; cunning; slyness; intemperance; sensuality; mischief; guile; bucolic lust; thieving; flattery; fertility; sexuality; hypocrisy; a false preacher; solitariness; ingratitude; hiding; carrion eater; a man 40 to 50 years old; a solar animal; Protestantism; attribute of Intemperance personified; associated with Saturn (planet), the archangel Azrael • **meeting a fox** lucky • **meeting several foxes** unlucky • **fox fur on a fleece** attribute of usurers • **fox tail** badge of a jester • **African** boldness and cowardice; independence and gregariousness; sinfulness and righteousness • **Amerindian** craftiness; trickery; shape-shifter • **Chinese** longevity; cunning; mischief; the transmigrated soul of a deceased person; possessor of supernatural powers, such as shape-shifting • **Christian** the devil; deceit; cunning; guile; fraud; *spoiling a vine:* the actions of heretics and enemies of the Church • **Greco-Roman** protector of vines; *fox skin:* attributes of Maenads/Bacchantes • **heraldic** slyness; strategic cunning; sagacity or wit used in one's own defense • **Japanese** longevity; fertility; messenger; attribute of Inari; *black fox:* lucky; *white fox:* unlucky; *three foxes:* disaster • **Jewish** rapacity • **Siberian** messenger from hell (often black) • **Sumerian** associated with Enki • *see also* **Reynard the Fox**

foxfire a forest spirit; elusiveness; a wild scheme pursued • **Japanese** the deceptive and falsely alluring

foxglove youth; associated with Taurus • **foxglove and nightshade** together pride and punishment • **flower language** insincerity; a wish

fracture/fragmentation destruction and disintegration of the spirit; the disabling or altering of whatever the broken object symbolizes; ritual killing

France associated with wine, fine food, romance

Francis of Assisi, St. • **Christian** mastery over animal instincts; personal spirituality and faith; kindness to animals

frangipani • **Mayan** fornication

Frankenstein's monster base instincts; lower nature; perversion of nature

frankincense wisdom; purification of the mind; divine love • **Christian** adoration; attribute of the Nativity; Christ's priestly office; *casket of frankincense:* gift of Melchior the magus • **flower language** faithful heart • **Jewish** the priesthood; *frankincense smoke:* emblem of the race of Japhet

Franklin, Benjamin • **American** invention; patriotism; youthful spirit in old age; joy of life; ribaldry

fraxinella • **flower language** fire

freckles the gods do not obey or see people with freckles; youth, especially bucolic

freezing impenetrability; emotional detachment; the static; immobility of the soul or spirit

Freud, Sigmund the higher self; wisdom; psychiatry

Freyja • **Christian** a witch • **Norse** associated with Friday, love, beauty, fertility, gold, war, death

friars *see* **monks**

Friday a day of melancholy, fecklessness; related to the Great Mother, Venus (planet), Taurus, Freyja, the archangel Anael, works of love • **cutting one's nails on Friday** unlucky • **birthday** Friday's child is free and giving, or, Born on a Friday, worthily given (or, is loving and giving) • **marriage** Friday for losses • **sneezing** You sneeze for sorrow • **Christian** an unlucky day, especially on the 13th day of a month • **Jewish** *Creation:* land beasts, man and woman • **Roman** a lucky day • *see also* **days**

fritillary persecution; emblem of Power personified

frog fecundity; unconscious knowledge; inspiration; lasciviousness; eroticism; resurrection; renewal of life; evil; sin; the repulsiveness of sin; heresy; uncleanliness; worldly things and those who indulge in them; vanity; coldness; related to the moon, rain, creation; attribute of Laziness personified • **Amerindian** rain bringer; has cleansing power • **Australian aboriginal** Tiddalik • **Aztecan** *frog-monster:* Tlaltecuhtli • **Celtic** the Lord of the Earth; associated with healing waters • **Chinese** the lunar, yin principle; rainmaker; *frog in a well:* a person of limited vision and understanding • **Christian** resurrection; the Resurrection; the devil; evil; heretics; envy; avarice; worldliness; the repulsiveness of sin • **Egyptian** Heqet; new life; abundance; fertility; prolific generation; longevity; strength out of weakness; attribute of Heqet; emblem of Isis; *frog-headed god:* Kuk; *frog-headed goddess:* Heqet • **Greco-Roman** fertility; licentiousness; romantic harmony; attribute of Aphrodite/Venus; *peasants by osiers, changing into frogs:* associated with Leto • **Hindu** *Great Frog:* support of the universe, primordial substance, the basis of created matter, water, primordial slime • **Japanese** *tortoise with monkey head and frog legs:* Kappa • **Jewish** neophyte; a lower order aspiring to become higher; uncleanliness • *see also* **toad**

front the conscious; the right side

frost death; Autumn; friendliness • *see also* **ice**

fruit abundance; spiritual abundance; wisdom; immortality; heavenly bliss; the culmination of one state and the beginning of the next; earthly desires; ripeness; funeral offering • **fruit in a basket** temptation; fertility; women's quarters; women's housework; attribute Taste personified • **fruit in a bowl** attribute of Chastity personified; *when shown with a fat figure:* Gluttony personified • **fruit in a cornucopia** attribute of the personifications of Abundance, Summer •

child with fruit personification of Autumn •
Christian the Virgin Mary; *fruit in a basket:*
attribute of St. Dorothea of Cappadocia (especially when fruit is with flowers) • **Greco-
Roman** attribute of Priapus personifying fertility; *fruit in a basket:* attribute of Pomona; *fruit
in a cornucopia:* attribute of Demeter/Ceres •
heraldic felicity; peace

fuchsia taste; gentleness; grace; faithfulness;
confiding love • **flower language** taste

Fudo • **Buddhist** decision making energy; the
strength needed to lead a life of compassion

fuller's bat *see* **club**

fuller's teasel • **flower language** importunity; misanthropy

fumitory • **flower language** spleen; hatred

fungus • **Chinese** longevity; immortality; persistence; *fungus with crane (bird) or bat (animal):*
longevity; happiness • **Taoist** food of the immortals • *see also* **agaric; mushroom**

Furies *see* **Erinyes/Furies**

furnace the mother; spiritual gestation; uterus;
creative faculty; emotional frustration; extreme
trial; associated with smelting, pottery, alchemy
• **Jewish** *furnace full of inferior metal:* Jerusalem;
iron furnace: Egypt as a place of bondage and
oppression • *see also* **athanor**

furniture ideas; opinions; beliefs; that which fills
one's mind • **new furniture** new ideas; immature beliefs • **old furniture** old or tired ideas

furze anger; Spring equinox

fusil • **heraldic** labor, travel; *fusil of yarn:* negotiation

G

G associated with introspection, mediation, intuition, action, knowledge, Jesus, Gemini, Sagittarius; equivalent to -7- • **Masonic** a center of
enlightenment or direction • **medieval** occasional Roman numeral for 400 (P was also
used) • **tarot** the Chariot

Gabriel, Archangel divine messenger; associated
with truth, strength, the moon, silver (metal),
West, -1-, -2-, -7-, -12-, -18-, crystal, clear
quartz, aquamarine, fluorite, moonstones,
pearls, geodes, the 1st heaven, Cancer, Monday,
almond trees, bay laurel, coconut palms, hazel,
papaya trees, willows, crabs, dogs, seagulls,
owls, white peacocks, occasionally Mars
(planet) • **Christian** messenger of the Day of
Judgment, the Annunciation, the Resurrection
• **Islamic** conductor of souls; protector of Islam;

deliverer of the Koran to Mohammed • **Jewish**
protector of Israel; angel of judgment

Gabriel Hounds death omen • **Christian** the lost
souls of unbaptized infants

gadfly (insect) a pest; punishment for pride; noi-
some lust; war; attribute of Bellona

Galahad, Sir • **Celtic** the best knight in the world;
purity

galbanum • **Arabian** protection from jinns • **European** protection from gnomes • **Jewish** divine
wisdom

gall bitterness; bravery; nerve; misery; punishment; poison words; rancor; the bitterness of
injustice; seat of vitality; consecrated to Posei-
don/Neptune • **wormwood and gall** punishment

gallows sacrifice; disgraceful death; typical execution of lower class criminals, especially
thieves • **Chinese** valor • **Christian** associated
with the Crucifixion • **Jewish** death of the soul;
utter deprivation of God • *see also* **liver**

Gandhi, Mahatma associated with nonviolence,
peace, passive resistance, religious tolerance

Ganesha • **Hindu** wisdom; sound judgment; discretion; learning

Ganges River • **Hindu** the Upper Waters; connection between heaven, earth, and the underworld; all-cleansing; associated with Shiva; attribute of Varunna

gangrene spiritual decay

gannet • **heraldic** one who subsists on virtue and
merit without material help • *see also* **duck**

Ganymede • **Greek** male beauty; allegory of the
progress of the human soul toward God

garbage • **Babylonian** food of the damned in
Aralu

garden the conscious; the soul; nature subdued;
feminine fertility; Paradise; the fields of the
blessed; the abode of souls; happiness; salvation; purity; the world; vulva; place of mystic
ecstasy; place of inner spirituality, growth, and
peace; pure desire freed from all anxiety; attribute of Spring personified • **garden gate** vulva •
walled or closed garden virginity; the
feminine; the protective principle • **watering a
garden** nurturing spiritual growth • **garden
with water in the center** Paradise • **Chinese**
rooster and hen in a garden: rural pleasures •
Christian *walled or closed garden:* emblem of
the Virgin Mary • **Incan** *Garden of the Sun:* the
world • **Islamic** a state of bliss; *four gardens of
Paradise:* the soul, heart, spirit, essence; the
mystic journey of the soul • **Roman** *funerary
gardens:* the earthly counterpart of Elysium •
Taoist Paradise • *see also* **sowing; weeding**

gardener the Creator; Adam; Priapus; Mohammed; a cultivator of his soul; the higher self; the farmer raised to a higher or more spiritual plane

gardenia refinement; chastity; femininity • **Chinese** feminine grace; subtlety; artistic merit; emblem of November

gargoyle forces of the cosmos; evil forces made to serve good; evil spirits; objectified powers of evil; scarecrows for evil spirits; fertility enslaved by superior spirituality; evil passions • **on the outside of a church** evil passions driven out of man by the Gospels

garland fellowship; merit; ephemeral beauty; honor; dedication; holiness

garlic protection against the evil eye, vampires, serpents, plague, madness, scorpions, colds; magic protection; associated with lightning • **English** *Elizabethan:* associated with the lower classes • **heraldic** protection; strength; courage • **Roman** charm against witches

garment the body; knowledge; evanescence; reflection of the inner man; lack of innocence as a result of The Fall • **rending garments** grief; penitence; anger • **seamless garment** Christ's garment at the Crucifixion; purity, unity, divinity • **white garment** attribute of heavenly beings, important people, festivity, virginity, Egyptians • **multi-colored garment** diverse possibilities; disharmony; diverse and wide knowledge; attribute of Israelites, Free Will personified • *see also* **clothes**, and specific garments **cloak, trousers,** etc.

garnet deep affection; devotion; loyalty; energy; grace; strength; associated with Aquarius, blood, the archangels Azrael, Cassiel, Samael; birthstone for January; stone for a 2nd wedding anniversary; charm for healing, protection, healthy joints, protection from evil spirits • **almandine garnet** stone for a 19th wedding anniversary • **green garnet** stone for a 25th wedding anniversary • **rhodolite garnet** stone for a 15th wedding anniversary

garters sexuality • **red garters** attribute of the devil

Garuda • **Hindu** the sun; the sky; victory; the Bird of Life; enemy of the Nagas; steed of Vishnu • *see also* **phoenix**

gasoline energy; volatility

gate opportunity; the feminine principle; death; departure from this world; entrance into heaven or hell; a dividing barrier; communication between one world and another; commerce; power; fortification; protection; safety; justice; mercy; praise; salvation; vulva • **closed gate** restraint; expulsion; war; misery; inhos-

pitality • **open gate** hospitality; peace • **garden gate** vulva • **horn gate** entrance for prophetic dreams • **brass gate** entrance to Hades, hell • **pearl or gold gate** entrance to heaven, knowledge • **ivory gate** entrance for deceptive dreams • **arched gate** entrance to knowledge, or the way to knowledge • **Babylonian** *seven gates:* attribute of Aralu • **Buddhist** *four gates:* the four travels of Buddha • **Christian** *closed or turreted gate:* emblem of the Virgin Mary • **Egyptian** *15 or 21 gates:* attribute of Aalu • **Hindu** *city with 1,000 gates:* Amaravati • **Japanese** *torii gate:* emblem of Amaterasu, Inari • **Jewish** *closed or turreted gate:* emblem of Ezekiel; *twelve gates of Jerusalem:* the zodiac signs, the Twelve Tribes, the cardinal directions • **Norse** *540 gates:* attribute of Valhalla • *see also* **door; portcullis**

gauntlet protection; power; challenge; punishment • **heraldic** reward and elevation; justice; challenge; readiness for combat • **Norse** attribute of Thor

gavel law; order; discipline; attribute of a judge, chairman, president • **heraldic** justice; legal authority

gazelle graceful speed; the soul; struggle; gentleness; grace; innocence; the beloved; beauty; keen sight; the contemplative life • **biblical** gentleness; grace • **Christian** the soul fleeing from earthly passions • **Egyptian** associated with storms; attribute of Set; *Horus trampling on a gazelle:* quelling a storm; *gazelle-headed goddess:* Anuket; *gazelle horns:* attribute of Resheph • **Greco-Roman** attribute of Artemis/Diana • **Hindu** Ishvara; associated with Vayu; corresponds to the element air; steed of Chandra; emblem of Capricorn; *chariot pulled by gazelles:* occasional attribute of Shiva • **Sumero-Semitic** attribute of Astarte, Mullil • see also **antelope; deer**

geese fertility; the sun; creative energy; inspiration; breath; wind; truth; love; constancy; vigilance; providence; foolishness; conceit; silliness; stupidity; wind; snow; speech; eloquence; soul; Winter; conceit; innocence; cowardice • **goose** earth mother; maternity; a woman 50 to 60 years of age; female sexuality • **gosling** a young fool • **eating a goose** a sun sacrifice • **goose pursued around the table by an old man** the man is Philemon (of Philemon and Baucis) • **flock of geese** Autumn • **barnacle goose** the unhallowed soul of a dead person; immortality; augur of trouble or storm • **Celtic** attribute of war gods • **Chinese** *wild goose:* the bird of heaven, messenger between heaven and earth, masculinity, light, inspiration, swiftness, good omen, seasonal change, Autumn, the yang principle; *art*: associated with the Autumn moon; *pair of geese*: conjugal fidelity • **Christian** vigilance; providence; attribute of St. Martin of Tours; *goose with flames coming from its mouth*: the Holy Spirit • **Egyptian** love; messenger between heaven and earth; attribute of Geb, Thoth, Isis, Osiris, Horus; sacred to Amen-Ra; *Nile Goose*: creator of the world, laid the Cosmic Egg from which the sun was hatched; *god with the head of a goose*: Geb • **Greco-Roman** love; watchfulness; the good housewife; associated with Hera/Juno, Apollo, Hermes/Mercury, Ares/Mars, Priapus, Eros/Cupid, Aphrodite/Venus, Dionysus/Bacchus, Peitho • **heraldic** resourcefulness; vigilance; self-sacrifice • **Hindu** *wild goose*: freedom, self-existent being, spirituality, devotion, learning, eloquence; *gander*: the hamsa • **Japanese** Autumn; swiftness; messenger of good tidings; *wild goose flying*: manhood • **Norse** emblem of Freyja • **Sumerian** sacred to Bau • see also **swan**, with which the goose shares much symbolism

Gehenna • **Jewish** hell; eternal; punishment; eternal torment; complete destruction

gelatin instability; shakiness; fear; insecurity

Gemini the dual physical/spiritual, mortal/immortal nature of all things; creative and created nature; thesis and antithesis; opposites; inversion; Castor and Pollux; brotherly love; associated with air, Mercury (planet), versatility, intelligence, skillful communication, inconsistency, gossip, instability, the archangel Raphael

gems *see* **jewels**

genie the magical part of oneself; boundless creativity or manifestation of ideas; assistance from magic or one's higher self

genitals associated with Mars (planet)

gentian Autumn; loveliness

geode associated with the archangel Gabriel

geranium conjugal affection; melancholy; stupidity; foolishness; a bourgeois plant; associated with Aries • **flower language** envy; *fish geranium*: disappointed expectation; *ivy geranium*: bridal favor, I engage you for the next dance; *lemon geranium*: unexpected meeting; *night smelling or dark geranium*: melancholy; *nutmeg geranium*: an expected meeting; *oak geranium*: true friendship, lady deign to smile; *penciled geranium*: ingenuity; *pink or rose geranium*: preference; *scarlet geranium*: comfort, stupidity, folly; *silver-leaved geranium*: recall; *sorrowful geranium*: melancholy mind; *wild geranium*: steadfast piety • **heraldic** true friendship

Germany associated with rashness, subservience to authority, crudity, beer drinking

ghetto isolation; hopelessness; shunning

ghost psychic dissociation; disembodied spirit; lack of substance; one's true nature or inner self; unresolved past issues; messenger from the spirit world; generally considered unhealthy to meet one; a repressed feature of the ego returning to the conscious • **ghost dance** communication with the dead • **Indic** *ghost without hands or feet and his head tied to the pommel of a saddle*: a dund

giant the unconscious; the forces of dissatisfaction; everlasting rebellion; despotism; evil; impending evil; the Terrible Father; Universal Man; the father principle; quantitative simplification; man before The Fall; the id; tyranny; the brute force of nature; primordial power and forces; the elemental; innate regressive tendencies; protector of the common people; associated with darkness, cannibalism, Winter • **Ashanti** *hairy giant with bloodshot eyes*: Sasabonsam • **Australian aboriginal** *one-eyed giant*: Papinijuwari; *cannibal giant*: Thardid-Jimbo • **Burmese** *hideous giant with long slimy tongue*: a thaye; *hideous giantess with long slimy tongue*: a thabet • **Celtic** *giant with one eye in the front of his head and one eye in back*: Balor • **Chinese** *8 ft. tall man with a sparse beard*: Lu Tung-pin • **Christian** *giant carrying a baby on his back*: St. Christopher • **Dahomean** *giant with 30 horns*: Yehwe Zogbanu • **Finnish** Antero Vipunen; a nakki • **Greco-Roman** *one-eyed giant*: Polyphemus; Cyclops; *Heracles/Hercules holding a giant aloft*: the giant is Antaeus; *giant hunter*: Orion; *vulture pecking at giant's liver*: the giant is Tityus; *giants with serpents for feet*: Gigantes, Enceladus; *bronze giant*: Talos • **Jewish** Og; Rephaim; *Philistine giant*: Goliath • **Mayan** Chilmamat • **Norse** Bor; *giant woman*: Angurboda, Bestla • **Sumero-Semitic** *giant scorpion men*: sons of Tiamat, guardians of Shamash • *see also* **colossus; Cyclops; Titans**

gibbet disgraceful death

Gibil • **Sumerian** destruction; fire; associated with metallurgy

Gigantes • **Greek** associated with earthquakes, volcanoes

gilding associating an object with solar power, divine power and/or the power of fire • *see also* **gold**

gillyflower natural beauty; sweetness; chastity • **Christian** attribute of the Virgin Mary, the Annunciation • **flower language** unfading beauty; bonds of affection • **heraldic** hope; joy

gingerbread a burial or deity offering; Christ's body (especially at Christmas time)

gingko tree • Japanese eternal life; emblem of the gods

ginseng virility; immortality • **heraldic** passion; prosperity; health; permanence

giraffe lofty thoughts; eloquence; gentleness; coquetry; speed; ambition; the will • **biblical** timidity; fleetness • **Renaissance art** often depicted because of its unusual appearance rather than for any symbolic value

girdle (cincture) strength; sovereignty; righteousness; faithfulness; truth; wisdom; gladness; pilgrimage; protection; virginity; chastity; readiness to meet challenge; protection from evil spirits; binding to an oath or belief; marital fidelity; fertility; invisibility; spiritual purity invigorating the soul; strict attachment; assiduousness; the circle of life; attribute of love and fertility goddesses • **starred girdle** the heavens; the zodiac • **straw girdle** fertility; aid to childbirth • **girdle of a virgin, saint, or goddess** a protective talisman; inhibits the power of monsters • **turning one's girdle** preparing to fight • **woman loosening her girdle** sexual surrender • **removing a girdle** surrender; renouncing rights, office, beliefs • **serpent as a girdle** succession; dissolution and reintegration; the eternal cycling of the ages • **Christian** attribute of the Virgin Mary; *gold girdle:* attribute of Jesus; *girdle with locust:* attribute of John the Baptist; *leather girdle:* attribute of John the Baptist; *girdle with arrows and stones:* attribute of St. Thomas; *monastic's girdle:* continence, humility, the cords with which Christ was bound and scourged, spiritual watchfulness; *three knots on a girdle:* faith, hope, and love, or the vows of poverty, chastity, and obedience • **Egyptian** *Girdle of Isis:* immortality • **Greco-Roman** attribute of Hippolyta; *Aphrodite's girdle (Cestus):* fertility; inducer of love in all who saw it; *red girdle with black clothes:* attribute of Erinyes/Furies • **Hindu** wheel of the cosmic order; given at initiation; attribute of the twice-born; *multicolored girdle:* the cycles of time • **Islamic** *snapping a girdle:* a Christian converting to Islam • **Jewish** *vestment girdle:* the ocean; *leather girdle:* attribute of Elijah • **Norse** *girdle of strength:* attribute of Thor • *see also* **belt; cincture**

girl *see* **child; maiden; virgin; woman**

gladiolus abundance; generosity; readiness to fight • **Christian** the Incarnation

glass purity; peace; virginity; revelation; brittleness; delicacy; rigidity; transparency; unchanging emotion; short-lived beauty • **rose-colored glass** optimistic or unrealistic view • **blue-colored glass** pessimistic view • **stained glass** spiritual vision; attribute of churches • **breaking a glass** the transitoriness of human life • **glass shoes, tower, boat, etc.** a means of transfer from one state or plane to another • **basket of glassware** Alnaschar's dream (Arabian Nights) • **Christian** *sea of glass:* stilled emotions; *drinking glass:* the Immaculate Conception; *drinking glass with a serpent in it:* attribute of St. Benedict; *broken drinking glass with wine running from it:* attribute of St. Benedict • **European** *glass mountain:* divides this world from the otherworld

glasses *see* **spectacles**

glasswort • flower language pretension

Glastonbury thorn • Christian associated with the Nativity of Christ, St. Joseph of Arimathea

gleaning *see* **harvest**

globe wholeness; unity; perfection; imperial dignity; the head; the world soul; mystic center; eternity; the earth; felicity; travel; power; dominion over the earth; attribute of Charlemagne, the personifications of Fortitude, Fame, Abundance, Truth, Justice (especially when accompanied by scales and a sword) • **underfoot** attribute of the personifications of Philosophy, Fortune, Opportunity • **kicking a globe** disdain of the world • **celestial globe** attribute of Astronomy personified • **globe held in the left hand** far-reaching authority of a deity or ruler • **alchemic** *crowned globe:* the philosopher's stone; *black globe:* prime matter • **Christian** *globe underfoot:* attribute of Christ; God the Father; *globe surmounted by a cross:* the dominion of Christ • **Egyptian** *woman with the head of a lion, globe, ankh, and staff:* Tefnut • **Greco-Roman** fortune; fate; attribute of Apollo, Cybele, occasionally Eros/Cupid; *globe with compasses and/or or in a tripod:* attribute of Urania; *celestial globe:* attribute of Urania; *wand tipped with a globe surmounted by an eagle:* attribute of Zeus/Jupiter, Roman legions; *terrestrial globe:* attribute of Democritus; *globe underfoot:* attribute of Nemesis/Invidia • **heraldic** world travel; worldliness • *see also* **orb; sphere; ball**

glory (luminous glow around the body) the supreme state of divinity; attribute of God the Father, Christ, Christ as Judge • *see also* **nimbus**

glory flower • flower language glorious beauty

gloves power; protection; have some of the powers of their owners; nobility (especially the left glove); evidence of good faith; attribute of God in medieval plays, but also witches, thieves, and

other mysterious characters • **removing a glove (especially the right)** salutation; respect; candor; disarming oneself before a superior • **iron glove** tyranny; attribute of smith gods • **throwing down a glove** challenging someone • **rawhide gloves** attribute of a boxer in ancient times • **glove and ring (or gloves alone)** a traditional courting gift • **white gloves** innocence; elegance; good taste; a pure heart; formality; cleanliness; immunity to bribery • **black gloves** sorrow; grief; mourning • **kid leather gloves** gentleness • **Christian** attribute of the pope, cardinals, bishops • **Norse** *iron glove:* attribute of Thor • *see also* **fingers; hand**

glow worm resurrection; the soul of someone departed; harbinger of mourning; related to stars • **Chinese** industry; perseverance; beauty

glycine • **flower language** your friendship is pleasing and agreeable to me • **Chinese** tender and delicate friendship

gnat torment; irritation; insignificance; triviality; related to slander, sunshine, Autumn

gnome flash of knowledge, inspiration, enlightenment, intuition; knowledge held in secret; associated with mining • **male and female gnomes together** the conjunction of opposites; ignorance co-existing with knowledge, ugliness with beauty, light with dark, good with evil, etc. • **Kabalistic** dwellers in the center of the world

goad action; control; movement • **Buddhist** emblem of Buddhism • **Chinese** power; spiritual authority • **Greco-Roman** *ox-goad:* attribute of Lycurgus • **Hindu** attribute of Vayu; *elephant goad:* attribute of Ganesha • **Jewish** *ox-goad:* attribute of Cain, Shagmar

goat dishonor; materialism; desires; instincts; passions; abundant vitality; creative energy; evil; repression of one's conscience; lust; fertility; agility; elegance; inelegance; stupidity; stubbornness; freedom; fever; messenger of the gods; associated with Love personified, Lust personified, witches, tragedy; occasionally shows moral superiority, usually shows moral inferiority • **billy goat** a male child 10 to 20 years old; masculinity; *billy goat with a human head:* depravity • **nanny goat** caprice; vagabondage; feminine generative power; poor man's cow; wet nurse • **riding a goat** an initiation rite; inversion of the normal order • **goat with a spiral tail** Capricorn; December; occasionally, Winter • **goat's milk** error; desire; milk of the poor • **scapegoat** vicarious atonement • **half- goat/half-lion** duality (love/hate, good/evil, etc.) • **lion lying with kid** peace; Paradise regained; primordial unity; the Golden

Age; the end of the temporal world • **cheveril** conscience; elasticity; flexibility • **Babylonian** Ea; Anshar as the Pole Star; attribute of Marduk; emblem of Ningirsu; *god with goat's horns:* Ea-Oannes • **Chinese** the masculine principle; peace; goodness; *nanny goat:* associated with lightning; *goat's head bonnet and/or goat skin:* attribute of Yang Ching • **Christian** Satan; carnal love; lubricity; lust; a sinner, the damned; avarice; the Synagogue; *billy goat:* the devil; *goat feet:* attribute of the devil; *nanny goat:* the Christian searching for perfection, the penetrating perception of Christ; *goat hair shirt:* mortification, penance; attribute of John the Baptist • **Egyptian** a sacred animal; *disk with goat horns:* life, strength, attribute of Isis • **Germanic** *flock of sheep:* attribute of Holda • **Greco-Roman** lust; virility; creative energy; steed of Aphrodite, emblem of Pan/Faunus; associated with Eros/Cupid, Zeus/Jupiter, Athena/Minerva, Silvanus, Dionysus/Bacchus, Artemis/Diana; *kid:* sacrifice to Pan/Faunus, Silvanus; *half-goat/half-man:* Pan/Faunus; a satyr; *nanny goat:* associated with lightning • **heraldic** striving after higher things; victory through cunning rather than force • **Hindu** fire; creative heat; *billy goat:* steed of Agni; *nanny goat:* immanent primeval matter; *red, white, and black nanny goat:* Prakti • **Jewish** fraud; lust; lewdness; cruelty; *goat's hair shirt:* attribute of Elijah • **Mediterranean** *dream of goats:* omen of sea storms; *dream of black goats:* omen of huge waves at sea • **Mesopotamian** *goat-headed goddess:* Mamitu • **Norse** emblem of Odin, Thor; *chariot pulled by goats:* attribute of Thor; *goat with mead:* Heidrun • **Sumero-Semitic** attribute of hunting goddesses; sacred to Marduk; *kid:* sacrificed as a substitute of the dying god in death and resurrection rituals • **Syrian** *goat hair prayer garment:* union with the godhead • **Tibetan** *nanny goat:* associated with lightning • *see also* **Capricornus (mythology); Chimera; ibex**

goblet the feminine principle; the Eucharist; vagina; the human heart (especially when covered); attribute of Ares/Mars, Artemisia • **goblet filled with liquid** the non-formal world of possibilities • *see also* **cup**

goblin malice; terror; mischief; evil; Halloween • **Slavic** Likho

gobony *see* **compony**

Godiva, Lady • **English** fertility; *with Peeping Tom:* lechery

gods the supernatural; one's higher self; ultimate authority, power, wisdom; manifestation of the ineffable • **days associated with gods** *Sunday:* Helios/Sol; *Monday:* Selene/Luna, Artemis/Diana; *Tuesday:* Tiu, Ares/Mars; *Wednesday:* Hermes/Mercury, Woden, Odin; *Thursday:* Thor, Zeus/Jupiter; *Friday:* Freyja, Aphrodite/Venus; *Saturday:* Cronus/Saturn

gold (**metal and color**) solar light; the sun; fire; radiance; divine intelligence; virtue; superiority, especially on a spiritual plane; pure light; heaven; worldly wealth; prosperity; the highest value; worth; idolatry; the id; divinity; the glory of God; God as uncreated light; the splendor of enlightenment; sacredness; revealed truth; marriage; fruitfulness; glory; the glory of faith triumphant; endurance; the masculine principle; mystic center; spiritual truth or insight; associated with Leo, 1st wedding anniversaries; attribute of sun, grain, and harvest gods, the First Heaven • **gold and silver** the sun and moon respectively; two aspects of the same cosmic reality • **golden apple** discord; immortality • **golden ball** the sun; *atop a flagpole:* union of the masculine and feminine principle, androgyny • **golden chain** honor; dignity; respect; wealth; the spirit binding earth to heaven; high office • **golden cord** the sun and reason respectively; the link between heaven and earth • **golden cup** prize • **golden egg** the sun (laid on the waters of chaos by the primeval goose) • **golden horse** the sun • **converting base metal into gold** transmutation of the soul; regaining the primordial purity of human nature • **golden hair** sun rays; purity; wisdom; virtue; immortality; attribute of love goddesses, sun heroes, royalty • **alchemic** the sun; the essence of the sun; congealed light; durability; the equilibrium of all metallic properties; the perfection of mind, spirit, soul, matter; the Great Work • **Amerindian** associated with West • **Bambaran** *gold necklace of Faro:* enables him to hear the innermost thoughts of men • **Celtic** fire • **Christian** *golden casket:* the Epiphany, attribute of Gaspar the magus; *golden cup:* the Eucharist; the Holy Grail; the Immaculate Conception; *golden house:* the Virgin Mary • **Egyptian** Horus; Ra; maize; flesh of the sun • **Greco-Roman** *golden apple:* discord, attribute of Discordia, Eris; *golden apples:* attribute of the Hesperides; *three golden apples:* attribute of Atalanta; *golden chain:* attribute of Hermes/Mercury; *golden cord:* attribute of Zeus/Jupiter; *blizzard of gold:* fell on Athens at the birth of Athena; *golden antlers:* attribute of the Arcadian Hind captured by Heracles/Hercules • **heraldic** excellence; intelligence; respect; virtue; nobility; elevation of mind; generosity; dignity; sincerity; piety; *golden lyre:* attribute of Amphion (son of Zeus and Antiope) • **Hindu** light; life; truth; immortality; the seed; joy; the fire of Agni • **Irish** *pot of gold:* attribute of a leprechaun • **Islamic** *gold carpet:* rank, power, attribute of palaces and mosques • **Jewish** divine, mystic power • **Mesopotamian** *golden saw:* the sun cutting the darkness, emblem of Shamash • **Norse** associated with Freyja; *boar with golden bristles:* Gulliburstin, the bristles represent sun rays • **Persian** *white, red, and gold:* purity, love, and revelation, emblem of the Persian trinity; *bull with golden horns:* incarnation of Verethraghna • **Tinguinian** *house of gold:* dwelling of an alan • *see also* **gilding; yellow**

golden bough the rays of the setting sun needed by a sun hero to enter the underworld; the link between this world and the next; initiation; magic wand; rebirth; immortality; strength; wisdom; knowledge; the light that enables exploration of the underworld without harm to the soul • **Greco-Roman** *golden bough:* safe passage through the underworld for Aeneas, the priest of Diana on Lake Nemi won his office by killing his predecessor with a golden bough

golden calf • **Jewish** wealth; materialism instead of spirituality, the recurring temptation to worship wealth, power, sensuality; associated with Aaron, Baal

golden fleece conquest of the impossible; spiritual knowledge; supreme strength through purity of soul; wisdom; hidden treasure; the elusive; attribute of royalty

Golden Gate Bridge • **American** emblem of San Francisco, California

goldenrod precaution; encouragement

goldfinch gallantry; fruitfulness; the Passion of Christ; occasional attribute of Christ

goldilocks (**plant**) languishing passion • **flower language** *flax-leaved goldilocks:* tardiness

golem • **Kabalistic** matter artificially brought to life; warning against the unthinking use of magic; conflicting and destructive emotions; slavery to the passions; human creativity aping God and the evil that results; creation that escapes control of the creator

Gomorrah • **Jewish** carnal passion

gonads associated with Saturn (planet), the Church at Ephesus • **Hindu** associated with sustenance and physical survival

gong honor; announcement; associated with the Orient • **Greek** a bronze gong was sounded at the death of a king or a lunar eclipse

goose *see* **geese**

goose foot (plant) • **flower language** goodness; *grass leaved goose foot:* I declare war against you (especially when the stems alone are presented)

gooseberry anticipation; regret; worthlessness; the sun; attribute of Wisdom personified

gopher hiding of thoughts, emotions

Gordian knot • **Phrygian** the labyrinth

gorge the maternal; female sexuality; the unconscious; the forces of evil; danger; inferiority in the face of overwhelming odds; the part of the conscious through which parts of the unconscious may be glimpsed • **river or gorge crossed by a bridge** the two sides represent different worlds—mortality/immortality, unreality/reality, body/spirit, etc.

Gorgon • **Greek** fusion of opposites; a condition beyond the endurance of the conscious mind; the infinite forms in which creation is manifested; terror; an ugly or repulsive woman; the Terrible Mother • *see also* **Medusa**

gorilla low intellect; irrational behavior; primitive manhood

gorse roughness • **Celtic** transmutation; resourcefulness; exposure • **flower language** enduring affection

gosling *see* **geese**

gourd fertility; plenty; the creative power of nature; blessing; death; resurrection • **double gourd** yin and yang • **gourd rattle** creation; resurrection; rainmaker • **gourd cup** the feminine principle • **Amerindian** nourishment; the female breast • **Bambaran** Cosmic Egg • **Buddhist** emblem of Buddhism • **Chinese** longevity; mystery; necromancy; the cosmos in miniature; the creative power of nature; the original unity of the primordial parents; *smoke rising from a gourd:* the spirit escaping the body • **Christian** pilgrimage; pride; adaptability; the Resurrection of Christ; attribute of Christ, St. James the Great; *gourd and apple:* the Resurrection of Christ as an antidote for sin; *gourd with pilgrim's staff and wallet:* attribute of the archangel Raphael • **flower language** extent; bulk • **Jewish** attribute of Jonah • **Taoist** immortality; emblem of Li T'ieh-kuai • *see also* **pumpkin**

Graces *see* **Three Graces**

grafting artificial interference with the natural order; unnatural sexual intercourse; mankind gaining the power of the demiurge • **Jewish** grafted fruit is unclean

grail source of happiness, life; the waters of life; immortality; the Holy of Holies; God; Cosmic Center; the heart; spiritual knowledge; mystery; elusive quest; salvation; attainment of perfection; source of abundance; fertility; the inner wholeness which mankind desires; the futility of employing the material in the search for the spiritual; associated with King Arthur and the Knights of the Round Table • **loss of the grail** loss of Paradise, the Golden Age, primordial spirituality, purity, innocence • **search for the grail** search for redemption, the spiritual Center, Paradise, salvation • **Christian** the sacred heart of Christ; the cup of the last Supper; the cup in which Joseph of Arimathea caught the blood of Christ on the Cross; attribute of St. Joseph of Arimathea

grain fertility; abundance; awakening life; life springing from death; germination and growth through the sun; potentiality; the seed of life; cultivated higher emotions in the soul; associated with Autumn; attribute of Agriculture personified • **cereal grains** spermatic images • **ears, stalks, heads, sheaves** attributes of grain deities • **sheaf of grain** attribute of Concord personified • **sheaf of grain shown with a plough** attribute of the Silver Age personified • **grain and wine together** provision for life • **grain measure** abundance • **funeral grain** the abundance of the next world • **Chinese** justice; the mercy due all humans; empire; the earth • **Christian** human nature of Christ; the Eucharist (especially when shown with grapes); *seven grains:* the seven gifts of the Holy Spirit • **Egyptian** attribute of Osiris; *ear of grain:* attribute of Isis; *grain measure:* emblem of Serapis • **flower language** riches; *grain straw:* agreement; *grain straw:* argument • **Gnostic** *rooster with ear of grain:* vigilance producing plenty • **Greco-Roman** fertility; abundance; creation; life springing from death; attribute of Adonis, Demeter/Ceres, Gaia, Virgo; offering to Artemis/Diana; *ear of grain:* associated with the Eleusinian Mysteries; Attis; *planting grain on graves:* securing the power of the dead for the living • **Jewish** attribute of Ruth • **Phrygian** attribute of Attis • **Sumero-Semitic** sacred to Cybele • *see also* **barley; maize; oats; wheat**

grandparent wisdom or insight from experience; one's higher self; karmic memory

granite hardness of heart; death; power; intransigence

grapes fertility; sacrifice; the spiritual nature of love and wisdom; chastity; intoxication; wine; fruitfulness; blood • **harvesting of grapes** associated with September • **grapes with wheat** agriculture; fertility; attribute of many earth goddesses • **bunch of grapes** immorality; unity; attribute of many earth, agricultural, and fertility deities • **wild grapes** charity • **Christian** the Eucharist (especially when shown with wheat or bread); the blood of Christ; attribute of St. Vincent of Saragossa; *grape leaves or vine:* Christ; *workers in a vineyard:* the work of good Christians for the Lord; *birds feeding on grapes:* the faithful gathering sustenance from the blood of Christ; *twelve clusters of grapes:* the Apostles • **Greco-Roman** attribute of Dionysus/Bacchus, Cronus/Saturn • **heraldic** liberality; felicity; peace; abundance; wine-making; *grape leaves:* plenty, freedom, rebirth • **Hittite** *bunch of grapes:* attribute of a masculine divinity • **Jewish** attribute of Moses, Caleb, Joshua, the Tribe of Ephraim; *grapes borne on a staff by two men:* entry into Canaan, the Promised Land • **Mandaean** *fig and grape:* masculine and feminine fertility respectively • **Persian** attribute of Mithras • *see also* **wine**

grass humble usefulness; the common people; growth; submission (especially a lawn); hardiness; resilience; *handful of grass:* victory, conquest of land; *surrender of a handful of grass:* defeat • **Assyrian** *king on all fours eating grass:* Nebuchadnezzar • **flower language** utility; submission; *mouse-eared scorpion grass:* forget-me-not; *ray grass:* vice; *rye grass:* changeable disposition; *vernal grass:* poor, but happy • **Roman** *crown or wreath of grass:* awarded to life saver or military hero • **Jewish** the fleeting quality of life

grasshopper timidity; fear; old age; meaningless chatter; weakness; carefree life; improvidence; bad poets • **Chinese** abundance; virtues; lucky; omen of having many sons • **Christian** conversion • **European** irresponsibility; improvidence • **Greco-Roman** nobility; sacred to Apollo • **heraldic** nobility; home-bred • **Jewish** judgment of God; a scourge • *see also* **locust**

grave *see* **sarcophagus; tomb**

gravestone mortality

gray discretion; penitence; humility; barrenness; grief; egoism; neutralization; depression; half-mourning; inertia; indifference; the undifferentiated; asceticism; renunciation; vagueness; concealment; associated with ashes, mist, clouds, the second heaven • **pale gray** associated with Virgo • **silver gray** associated with the moon • **alchemic** earth • **Christian** death of the body and immortality of the soul; resurrection of the dead; often used by religious communities • **heraldic** tribulation • **Kabalistic** wisdom, associated with the archangel Uriel

grayhound *see* **greyhound**

Great Priest *see* **High Priest (tarot)**

Great Priestess *see* **High Priestess (tarot)**

Greece reason; intellectual keenness; hedonism • **American** sometimes associated with sodomy • **English** cunning; wantonness • **Jewish** paganism; idolatry • **Roman** the highest culture

green fertility; life; growth; rebirth; immortality; spiritual integrity; gladness; victory over the flesh, the vicissitudes of life; youth; eternal youth; hope; spring; regeneration of the spirit; freshness; innocence; liberty; peace; inexperience; folly; naïveté; sympathy; charity; vegetation; spiritual initiation; expectation; obedience; a feminine color; neutrality; passivity; indecision; decay; jealousy; envy; change; transitoriness; associated with Spring, water in pagan rites, young lovers, gladness, confidence, nature, Paradise, abundance, Libra, -5-; attribute of Nature personified, Mercury (planet), fairies, Venus (planet) • **yellow-green** associated with Virgo • **bluish-green** associated with Scorpio • **dark green** associated with Saturn (planet) • **green changing to gold** young corn changing to yellow corn • **green knight** an apprentice; impartial death; treason slaying youth and beauty • **green flag** seafaring wreck • **green dragon or lion** the young corn god; *alchemic:* beginning of the Great Work • **alchemic** growth; hope; *green lion:* beginning of the Great Work • **Buddhist** attribute of Amoghasiddhi • **Buddhist** associated with North, freedom from fear; *vernal green:* life; *pale green:* death • **Celtic** associated with the Emerald Isle, Tir-Non-Og; attribute of Bridget • **Chinese** the Ming dynasty; interchangeable with blue; associated with Spring, East; the Green Dragon, wood, water; *green clouds:* plague of insects; *green sedan chair:* attribute of a lower government official • **Christian** *vernal green:* immorality, hope, life, the triumph of life over death and Spring over Winter, initiation, good works, the Epiphany, the Trinity, St. John the Evangelist; *pale green:* evil, death, Satan; *green mantle:* attribute of SS Anne, John; *green cross:* regeneration • **Egyptian** Osiris as unripe corn; victory; decay • **heraldic** abundance; freedom; beauty; civility; happiness; love; joy; health; hope; meadows; mildness; a feminine color; woods; youth • **Hindu** attribute of Ganesha; *vernal green:* life; *pale green:* death; *green four-armed man:* Yama • **Islamic** a sacred color; a lucky color; Islam; Shiites; knowledge of Allah; associated with vegetation, peace, rebirth, resurrection, salvation; *from the 14th century:* worn by pilgrims to Mecca and descendants of Muhammad • **Kabalistic** victory; associated with the archangels Anael, Azrael • **North American In-**

dian (*prairie tribes*) associated with East • **Russian** *green eyes:* attribute of the Mistress of the Copper Mountain; *green lizard:* sometime manifestation of the Mistress of the Copper Mountain • **Tierra del Fuegan** associated with the Earth, South • *see also* **turquoise**

greenhouse the inner spiritual garden; growth impervious to outside influence; unnatural or artificial growth

grenade • **heraldic** one who has been subjected to attack by grenades

grey *see* **gray**

greyhound speed; hunting; elegance; sharp-sightedness; grace; fawning; attribute of the personifications of Lust, Envy, Sickness, Care • **heraldic** courage; loyalty; vigilance • **Islamic** a clean creature, while other dogs are considered unclean • *see also* **dog**

gridiron martyrdom • **Christian** attribute of St. Laurence, occasionally, St. Vincent of Saragossa

griffin the sun; the wealth of the sun; sacred to the sun; strength; invincibility; watchfulness; vengeance; the relationship between psychic energy and cosmic force; eternal vigilance; victory; emblem of Alexander the Great; associated with the archangel Michael • **two griffins** enlightenment and wisdom • **griffin with a ball underfoot** enlightenment protecting wisdom; supporter of a water goddess • **chariot drawn by griffins** occasional attribute of sky gods • **Christian** the dual nature of Christ; the Incarnation; Christ's kingdom on earth; Christ's omnipotence and omniscience; attribute of Christ; those who oppress and persecute Christians; the devil flying away with souls; *medieval:* the spiritual and temporal power of the pope • **Greco-Roman** strength; vigilance; obstacle to be overcome on a quest; attribute of Athena/Minerva, Dionysus/Bacchus, Nemesis/Invidia; steed of Apollo • **heraldic** watchfulness; courage; guardian of treasure • **Jewish** emblem of Persia • **Oriental** wisdom; enlightenment • *see also* **eagle; lion**

grill *see* **gridiron**

groom *see* **bridegroom**

grotto • **Greco-Roman** associated with Artemis/Diana and her nymphs

grouse (bird) uncontrolled passion; love that risks death; emblem of Scotland • **grouse feather in a hat** challenge to a duel • **heraldic** a forbearer who fought a gallant duel or was a great hunter

grove the cosmos

gryphon *see* **griffin**

Guanyin • **Buddhist** mercy; compassion; contemplation

guard force gathered on the threshold of transition

gudgeon credulity

guelder rose *see* **snowball (plant)**

guide one's higher self; wisdom; spiritual mentor

guillotine martyrdom; terror; the Reign of Terror in France

guinea hen a low woman; attribute of Artemis/Diana

guinea pig experiment

Guinevere, Queen • **Celtic** beauty; the anima; the feminine principle; sometimes betrayal, duplicity

guitar the masculine principle and the feminine principle • **Buddhist** excellence in the arts and sciences; harmony of existence in the deva world • **Chinese** *four-stringed guitar:* attribute of Virupashka

gull (bird) foil; victim; gullibility; voluptuousness; usefulness; plaintiveness; versatility; travel; adventure; emblem of the sea; associated with the archangel Gabriel; attribute of Aphrodite/Venus, Athena/Minerva, Leucothea • **Liloet** first owner of daylight

gum (plant gum) related to tears, semen; the seminal substance

gun power; violence; aggression; the threat of violence; phallus; the masculine principle; force; imposition of the will on others

guru *see* **poet**

guttees *see* **drops**

gypsophila • **heraldic** breath of the Holy Spirit; innocence; purity of heart

gypsum initiation; disguise; resurrection; slavery

Gypsy primitive man; seer; insight; intuition; the magical, enchanted, mysterious; the footloose life

H

H associated with rise and fall, -8-, Cancer, Libra, Mercury (planet), binary or complementary functions (such as justice/mercy) • **medieval** occasional Roman numeral for 200 • **tarot** associated with Justice, the High Priest

haberdasher a person of small wit

habit (monastic) humility • **black habit** attribute of Benedictines • **white habit with black scapular** attribute of Dominicans • **brown habit with white scapular** attribute of Carmelites • **brown habit with a rope around the waist** attribute of Franciscans • **saffron habit** attribute of Buddhist monastics • **soldier receiving monk's**

habit from abbot conversion of St. William of Aquitaine • *see also* monks; nuns

haddock • American, Canadian folkloric associated with the devil • Christian associated with St. Peter

Hades/Pluto • Greco-Roman personal inner darkness; primordial night of the soul; sadism; death; anguish; annihilation; ugliness; blackness

hag the Terrible Mother; famine; misfortune; associate of the devil • Burmese *hideous giantess with long slimy tongue:* a thabet • Celtic *hag washing bloody clothes at a ford:* death omen • Greco-Roman *three ugly old hags:* occasionally the Moirae/Fates • *see also* old woman

Hagar • Christian the church in bondage • Jewish a bondswoman unjustly oppressed; the synagogue

hail divine retribution; the assault of an enemy; destruction; a terrible judgment • hail destroying crops falsity destroying truth and goodness • hail stones evanescence

hair energy; life-force; strength; magical power; the external soul; God's providence; related to fire, sun rays, rain, love, fertility, ideas, thoughts, creativity, intellect, state of mind • gray hair old age; retrospection; wisdom; relativism; tenderness • golden hair sun rays; purity; wisdom; virtue; immortality; attribute of love goddesses, sun heroes, royalty • red hair connected with the underworld; a Venusian, satanic or demoniacal characteristic; attribute of smith gods • green hair attribute of mermaids • violet hair attribute of goddesses having a Spring festival • body hair irrational power; the instincts; virility • hair on the head spiritual powers; inspiration • braided hair profane love; attribute of courtesans, young girls • curly hair one who follows the arts; facility with foreign languages • dark hair terrestrial energy • short hair euphemism for pubic hair • lock of hair a love fetish; part of the virtues of whom it came from • disheveled hair involution; bereavement; madness; attribute of underworld deities • long hair worn by a man strength; attribute of a hermit • bound or covered hair subjection; attribute of a married woman • loosely flowing hair freedom; attribute of an unmarried woman • long, flowing hair penitence; sexuality • knotted hair confusion • hair covering the face equivalent to a veil • full, thick head of hair vitality; sexuality; lust; wildness • loose hair over brow attribute of Opportunity personified • letting normally short hair grow mourning • baldness a syphilitic; a

fool • loss of hair failure; poverty; rebirth • cutting the hair asceticism; purification; disgrace; mourning; humility; surrender; substitute for human sacrifice, castration • hair standing on end panic; magic power; divine possession • woman with serpents for hair Envy personified • brushing, combing, or delousing someone's hair mark of respect, welcome • allowing another to brush, comb, or delouse the hair sign of trust, intimacy • Assyrian *maid tending a woman's hair amid war preparations:* the woman is Semiramis • Buddhism *curled hair of Buddha:* serenity; tranquility; control of the life-force • Celtic *long hair:* attribute of royalty, aristocracy; *short hair:* attribute of commoners, slaves • Chinese *cutting the hair:* surrender, renunciation of office, privileges, even personality, also believed to stop rainfall; *shaved head:* mutilation; *disheveled hair:* mourning • Christian *long, flowing hair:* penitence; attribute of unmarried women, virgin saints, SS Mary Magdalene, Mary of Egypt and virgin saints; *long unkempt hair:* attribute of hermits; *man covered by long hair:* St. Onuphrius; *woman covered by long hair:* St. Agnes; *red hair:* attribute of Judas; *tonsure:* attribute of monks, early priests; *shaved head:* penitence, repentance; *goat or camel's hair shirt:* attribute of John the Baptist • Egyptian *heavy tress on the right side:* attribute of royal children; *shaved head:* attribute of devotees of Isis, Serapis • English *woman covered by long hair:* Lady Godiva • Finnish *beautiful woman with long curly hair and enormous breasts:* a nakinneito • Greco-Roman *cutting the hair:* for Greeks, a sign of mourning; *letting the hair grow:* for Romans, a sign of mourning; *violet hair:* attribute of Aphrodite/Venus, the Graces, the Muses, Eurydice; *wet hair:* attribute of Aphrodite/Venus; *serpents for hair:* the baleful aspects of feminine power, attribute of Gorgons, Medusa • Hindu *disheveled or matted hair:* attribute of Shiva, demon gods; *disheveled or matted hair of Shiva:* asceticism; *hair braided in a spiral:* attribute of Pushan, Rudra; *topknot:* connection with the superhuman; *river of blood, hair, and filth:* Vaitarani • Islamic *woman covering the hair:* modesty • Italian *maiden cutting her hair with a sword:* Erminia • Jewish strength; vitality; *white hair:* the Son of Man and the eternity of his existence; *hair being cut off a sleeping man:* Samson; *woman covering the hair:* modesty; *man covering his hair or head:* submission to God; *infant born with hair:* Esau; *goat or camel's hair shirt:* attribute of Elijah • Mediterranean *cutting hair at sea in good weather:* unlucky; *tossing hair clippings overboard during a storm:* appeasement • **Norse** *golden hair:* abundance • **Russian** *hair in a single plait:* attribute of an unmarried woman; *hair in two plaits:* attribute of a married woman • *see also* **tonsure; shampooing**

halberd • **Christian** attribute of SS Jude, Matthew, James the Less, Matthias (especially with a book) • **Greco-Roman** attribute of Athena/ Minerva • **heraldic** military service

Halloween return of Winter; chaos; the breakdown of the boundary between the living and the dead • **Halloween candle** *going out between 11 and midnight:* evil omen; *staying lit between 11 and midnight:* one year free from witchcraft

hallway passage to deeper consciousness, experience

halo *see* **nimbus**

halter (for an animal) the power of control over the intellect

Hamlet introspection; hastiness; rashness; tragedy; revenge

hammer power; destruction; fertility; immortality; divine vengeance; justice; physical power and strength; persistent thought; manual labor; industry; creation; fecundation; the masculine principle; phallus; attribute of thunder gods, blacksmiths, carpenters • **hammer and chisel** will; discrimination; distinction • **hammer and anvil** the masculine and feminine principles respectively, the active and passive respectively, the positive and negative respectively • **Babylonian** attribute of Ramman • **Celtic** attribute of Sucellus • **Chinese** sovereign power; divine shaping of the universe; *blue man with wings, claws, drum, mallet and chisel:* Lei-kung; *hammer-shaped tablet in the emperor's hand:* power • **Christian** attribute of St. Helena (especially with nails), St. Eloi; *hammer and nails:* emblem of the Crucifixion • **Etruscan** attribute of Charun • **Greco-Roman** thunder; vengeance; attribute of Hephaestus/Vulcan, Zeus/Jupiter, Castor, Pollux • **heraldic** honor; emblem of a smith • **Hindu** thunder; *stone hammer:* attribute of Parashu-Rama • **Japanese** wealth; lucky; creation; the masculine and feminine; *mallet:* attribute of Daikoku • **Masonic** discernment; the powers of the intellect directing the thoughts and animating meditation; attribute of the Worshipful Master • **Norse** thunder; attribute of Thor (may be shaped like a tau cross) • **Russian** *hammer and sickle:* emblem of the Soviet Union

hand flower tree • **flower language** warning

handcuffs imprisonment; death; sin; bad habits

• **broken handcuffs** death and sin overcome; release; freedom

handicap *see* **disability**

handiwork • **English** *Elizabethan:* euphemism for sexual activity

handkerchief seduction; jealousy; flirtation • **Chamian** *one red and one white handkerchief:* attribute of Aribada

hands protection; justice; power; authority (especially of the father, emperor, deity, etc.); emblem of the Tiburtine sibyl • **right hand** aggressiveness; associated with the rational, virility, logic, the conscious • **left hand** death; decay; associated with the subconscious, weakness, irrationality, the instincts • **God's left hand** associated with justice • **God's right hand** associated with mercy • **open hand** beneficence; generosity; *when fingers are extended:* sun rays, protection against the evil eye • **black hand** threat; vendetta; impending death • **white hand** Spring • **red hand** violence; murder; warning of death; the sun; guilt • **ivory hand** attribute of Fortune personified • **gilded hand** bribery • **golden hand** attribute of Fortune personified • **iron hand** harshness; ruthlessness; strength; tyranny • **raised open hands** prayer; swearing truth; voice and song; distress; surrender; death; dismay • **hand raised with palm outward** peace; a blessing; swearing truth • **hands clasped and raised overhead** union; victory • **hands placed together** submission; inferiority; respect; prayer; greeting; allegiance • **two hands clasped in a handshake** treaty; peace; concord; love; alliance; friendship; union; virile fraternity; solidarity; mystic marriage; individuation; *on a tombstone:* farewell and welcome • **folded hands** repose; intransigence • **one hand clasped between two others** swearing allegiance; pledge of service • **clapping hands** rainmaking; applause; unwillingness • **hands on hips** challenge; arrogance; independence; impatience; exasperation • **hands loose at sides** defeat; resignation • **washing hands** purification; repudiation; innocence; attribute of Innocence personified • **folded hands** composure; obedience; complacence • **folded hands with fingers interwoven** intransigence • **hands clasped behind the back** harmlessness; innocence • **veiled hands** a token of respect • **branded hand** attribute of a sheep thief • **laying-on of hands** transferring power; confirmation; ordination; death; a blessing • **hands on one's own head** mourning; grief; helplessness • **hand on the mouth** secrecy; member of a secret cult; a vow of silence • **hand flat on the**

breast pledge; a sage; love; adoration; salutation; submission; servanthood • **hand extended**
protection; invitation • **hand with palm upward** invitation; bribe; payment • **hand raised
over the head** victory; seeking attention •
hands crossed at the wrists bondage • **hand
with money** bribery; wealth • **laying on of
hands** transference of grace, healing, power •
hand with thumb and forefinger touching approval; vagina • **hands behind the neck** sacrifice; surrender • **wringing the hands** grief;
lamentation • **hand with three fingers extended** the phases of the moon • **woman holding
flame** Charity personified • **archangel holding
flame** Uriel • **Aztecan** emblem of -5- • **Buddhist**
Buddha's hand: protection, when the hand is
turned up it is unlimited giving; *finger and
thumb of Buddha's hand touching each other:* the
perfection of his action, thought, plan; *right
hand of Buddha touching the earth:* lordship, the
active principle; *Buddha holding an alms bowl
in his left hand:* receptivity, surrender; *closed
hand:* lying; secrecy • **Celtic** *long hand:* sun rays
• **Chinese** *clasped hands:* friendliness allegiance;
concealing the hands: deference; *right hand:*
yang, strength, generally corresponds with action; *left hand:* yin, weakness, generally corresponds with wisdom • **Christian** *hand descending from heaven:* God the Father; *two hands
clasped beneath the hand of God:* the blessing of
marriage by the Church; *hand with thumb and
last two fingers touching:* blessing, eternity, the
grace of Christ, the love of God and Communion with the Holy Spirit; *open hand:* the
slapping and mockery of Christ in the Passion;
hand with money: Judas' betrayal of Christ;
hand with straws: the drawing of lots for Christ's
garment; *washing hands:* Pontius Pilate; *hand
pierced with arrows:* attribute of St. Giles of
Provence; *hand holding three flowers:* attribute
of St. Hugh of Grenoble; *hand with thumb and
first two fingers extended:* the Trinity • **Greco-
Roman** *Roman soldier with his hand in a brazier:*
Mucius Scaevola; *woman with cupped hands before Apollo:* the Cumean sibyl • **heraldic** pledge
of faith; sincerity; justice; blessing; protection;
power; diligence; concord; innocence; *red hand:*
baronet, rank; *in armor:* leadership; *bare hand:*
industry • **Indic** *ghost without hands or feet and
his head tied to the pommel of a saddle:* a dund
• **Islamic** *open hand:* benediction, adoration,
hospitality, power, attribute of Mohammed;
Hand of Fatima: the hand of God, divine power,
providence, generosity, longevity • **Jewish**
might; justice; God; *upraised hands with middle*

finger and ring finger separated: Jewish blessing,
when on a tombstone it indicates the grave of
a Jewish priest; *first three fingers extended:* Was,
Is, and Is to Come • **Mandaean** *joining of the
hands:* truth and faithfulness • **Sumero-Semitic**
attribute of the Great Mother, Sabazios • **Toltec**
long hand: sun rays • *see also* **fist; fingers; palm
(hand); thumb**

handsaw *see* **saw**

handshake contract; friendship; connection

Hanged Man (tarot) mysticism; sacrifice; self-
denial; continence; the utopian dream world;
teaching; a public lesson; an example; detachment from materialism; a flight to overcome
evil; power derived from charity, wisdom,
fidelity and other higher virtues; reversal of
one's way of life by surrender to higher wisdom;
spiritual self-sacrifice; a suspended decision;
the need to move beyond one's usual thoughts
and activities; expiation; renunciation; enslaved
passions; end of a cycle; purification by reversal
of the normal order; associated with using the
higher levels of spirituality, wisdom, meditation

hanging (execution) ignominious death; death of
a common criminal; sacrifice to a sky god •
hanged man Despair personified • **Christian**
hanged man: Judas • **Jewish** *hangman:* Joshua •
see also **noose**

hanging (suspension) unfulfilled longing; sus-
pense

Hapi • **Egyptian** North; guardian of the North,
lungs of the dead; associated with the Nile

harbor the mother; the Church; Christ; security;
refuge; comfort; eternal life • **young man bearing a maiden off to a harbor** the abduction of
Helen of Troy • *see also* **bay**

hare a lunar animal; procreation; fertility; lust;
fleetness; diligent service; fecundity; resourcefulness; generally a male figure, but may be a
woman of loose morals; vigilance; timidity;
cowardice; curiosity; love of learning; melancholy; life; elemental existence; resurrection;
rebirth; rejuvenation; craftiness; servant or
companion of witches; emblem of Easter; attribute of moon deities, the personifications of
Lust, Fasting, Vagrancy; associated with Autumn • **white hare** snow • **March hare** madness
(especially youthful madness) • **hare's head or
foot** charm against evil • **knight pursued by a
hare** timidity; cowardice • **falcon tearing a hare
to pieces** the conquest of lust; victory of the
masculine principle over the feminine principle, light over dark, sun over the moon, etc. •
Amerindian demiurge, trickster, personifica-

tion of Light • **Anglo-Saxon** attribute of Eostre; *goddess with a hare's head:* Eostre • **Buddhist** total sacrifice; reincarnation of Buddha; moon-dweller; *moon and hare:* emblem of Buddhism • **Celtic** attribute of lunar and hunter deities • **Chinese** longevity; a supernatural creature; untiring industry; an auspicious omen; associated with the moon; yin; the imperial female consort; guardian of wild animals; *white hare:* divinity; *red hare:* lucky, peace, prosperity, virtuous rulers; *black hare:* lucky, a successful reign • **Christian** fecundity; lust; the rapid course of life; the Church persecuted; a Christian's haste to obtain divine gifts; those who put their hope in Christ; attribute of St. Jerome; *white hare at the Virgin Mary's feet:* her triumph over lust; *three hares turned so they appear to have one pair of ears:* the Trinity • **Egyptian** dawn; beginning; opening; uprising; periodicity; emblem of Thoth, Osiris; associated with the moon • **Greco-Roman** fertility; lubricity; messenger; attribute of Hermes/Mercury, Aphrodite/Venus, Eros/Cupid; emblem of Autumn • **heraldic** one who enjoys a peaceful, retired life; hunting skill; speed; vigilance; fertility • **Hindu** attribute of the crescent moon, Chandras • **Jewish** contemplation; intuition; the unclean • **Khoisan** associated with the moon • **Mayan** moon-dweller; inventor of writing • **Middle Ages** emblem of Spring • **Norse** attribute of Freyja; *hare with three legs:* the hare in the moon • **Persian** *message discovered in a hare's body:* associated with Cyrus the Great • **Teutonic** attribute of Eostre; *hare-headed goddess:* Eostre; *hares holding torches:* attribute of Holda

harebell • **flower language** grief, submission

harlequin mischievous intrigue; trickery; magic transformations; the discordant elements in life; inconsistency; lack of character, ideals, principles; detachment from desires; one who has not achieved individualization; related to underworld deities, fertility gods, gods of destiny

harlot *see* **prostitute**

harp bridge between heaven and earth; prayer; contemplation; joy; praise; poetry; music; worship in heaven; sadness; human stress; suffering; religious music; related to heaven; the mystic ladder to heaven; longing for love or death; soothing of strained nerves; related to blindness in conjunction with cunning or aristocracy; instrument of a harlot; attribute of Terpsichore • **harpist** the death wish; fascination with death • **Aeolian harp** conceit; self-

confidence; associated with those given to wine, women, luxurious living • **Celtic** emblem of Wales, Ireland • **Christian** attribute of SS Alfred, Cecilia, Patrick • **heraldic** contemplation; elevation; chastity; tempered judgment; composure; bridge between heaven and earth • **Jewish** contemplation; associated with the Psalms; attribute of David (especially with a lion) • *see also* **lyre**

harpoon fecundation; destruction; emblem of whalers and the whaling industry

harpy evil harmonies of cosmic forces; whirlwinds; storms; vice; guilt and punishment; involutive fragmentation of the subconscious; evil; rapacity; plunder; torment; voracity; the dark destructive aspect of the Great Mother; contamination; sensation and desire using knowledge to promote their own ends; vicious passions; obsessive torments of lust; remorse; emblem of Virgo, Music personified; associated with sudden death • **blindfolded harpy** attribute of Avarice personified • **heraldic** faithfulness and compliance with power and wisdom; ferocity under provocation

harrow (plant) • **flower language** rest; obstacle

harrow (tool) tribulation; agriculture; fertility; martyrdom

hart grace; nimbleness; resurrection; the morning star; immortality; piety and aspiration of the soul; solitude; purity; a substitute for the unicorn • **Christian** persecution of Christians; the catechumen; associated with Christ; *hart trampling a serpent:* Christ overcoming the power of evil • **Greco-Roman** associated with Artemis/Diana • **heraldic** harmony; peaceful unless provoked • **Jewish** thirst for salvation; religious aspiration and fervor; the faithful partaking of the waters of life; associated with Esther • *see also* **deer; hind; stag**

harvest the Last Judgment; associated with the months of June, July, August, and the personifications of Summer, the Silver Age • **Jewish** *woman gleaning:* Ruth

hat authority; power; thought; personality; freedom; nobility; related to the head; the color of the hat may reveal the wearer's primary characteristic; attribute of pilgrims, missionaries • **hat that confers invisibility** repression; regression • **changing hats** changing attitudes, opinions, and/or roles • **raising one's hat** salute • **removing one's hat** homage; subservience • **tall conical black hat** attribute of witches • **Christian** *cardinal's hat:* attribute of SS Vincent Ferrer, Jerome (although he was not a cardinal); *lying on the ground or hanging in a tree:* attribute of St. Bonaventure • **Middle Ages** *yellow hat:* attribute of a Jew • **Tibetan** *conical hat topped with a skull:* attribute of Nag-pa • *see also* **cap; turban**

hatchet execution; treachery; attribute of carpenters, woodsmen, SS Joseph (especially with saw and plane), Matthias • **American** *hatchet and cherry tree:* attribute of the young George Washington • **heraldic** military service • **North American Indian** war; *to bury a hatchet:* peace • *see also* **axe**, with which the hatchet is often imperfectly distinguished

hawk the evil mind of the sinner; fire; sun; the solar; the heavens; vision; the spirit; nobility; immortality; longevity; vengeance; ferocity; a swindler; brute force; violence; warmonger; freedom; fierce nobility; power; royalty; nobility; predation; watchfulness; a wild and intractable woman; attribute of sun gods • **hawk eating a hare** the triumph of the mind over the flesh • **Amerindian** helped recreate the world after the Flood • **Australian aboriginal** the deity • **Aztecan** messenger of the gods • **Egyptian** royal bird; the spirit; the soul; inspiration; Kensu; Ra; the sun; attribute of Ptah, Horus, Mentu, Rehu, Sokay, Kebhsenuf, Amenti; *hawk-headed god:* West; *hawk-headed crocodile:* Sebek-Ra • **Greco-Roman** messenger of Apollo; attribute of Circe • **heraldic** one who will not rest until objectives are achieved; *hawk's bells:* fearless of signaling approach; *hawk's lures:* fondness of hunting and falconry • **Hindu** bringer of soma from heaven; steed of Indra • **Jewish** the providence of God • **Mithraic** attribute of Mithras • **Persian** attribute of Ahura Mazda, Ormzud • **Polynesian** had the powers of prophecy and healing • *see also* **sparrow hawk**, and **falcon**, with which the hawk is frequently confused

hawk's eye stone for 13th wedding anniversaries

hawkweed • **flower language** quick-sightedness

hawsers *see* **moorings**

hawthorn death; purification; sexuality; fertility; indulgence; prudence; fairy-flower; associated with the archangel Samael; attribute of Servitude personified • **garland** virginity; chastity; virgin conception • **trained over a bench to make a bower** associated with old men, lovers • **Celtic** union of opposites; contradiction; associated with the hypothetical planet Vulcan, topaz, May, June, unluckiness • **Christian** associated with the Nativity • **flower language** hope; May, May Day in particular • **Greco-Roman** bridal flower; sacred to Hymen, Chloris, Hecate, Flora, Maia; attribute of

Carnea; *wreath:* marriage • **heraldic** a Tudor prince

hay *buttered hay:* deceit, cheating

hazel knowledge; wisdom; poetic art; love and fertility; healing; reconciliation; death; associated with Virgo, Mercury (planet), the archangels Gabriel, Raphael • **hazel nut** hidden wisdom; mystery; peace; lovers; associated with the Mother goddesses • **hazel wand** finds water, buried treasure, murderers, thieves; makes rain • **Babylonian** *hazel rod:* divination • **Celtic** a sacred tree; wisdom; creativity; purity; honesty; inspiration; magic; divination; underworld powers; Tree of Life; associated with milk goddesses, fire gods, amethysts, Mercury (planet), August/September; *hazel wand:* makes a person invisible • **Christian** *hazel nut:* attribute of Julian of Norwich • **flower language** reconciliation; peace; healing • **Germanic** associated with Idun; *cracking hazel nuts:* euphemism for coition • **Greco-Roman** *hazel wand:* communication; reconciliation; poetic inspiration; the caduceus; attribute of Hermes/Mercury, heralds • **heraldic** hope; joy; communication; reconciliation; peace • **Jewish** *hazel twigs:* associated with Jacob • **Norse** attribute of Thor • *see also* **witch hazel**

head the mind; spiritual life; wisdom; the sun; kingship; authority; the universe; oneness; virility; the masculine; fertility; the world; the spiritual principle as opposed to the body, which represents the physical principle; seat of the life-force, soul, folly; associated with Mars (planet) • **two heads** beginning and end; past and future; yesterday and present; choice; departure and return; the power of opening and closing doors; judging and discerning; cause and effect; inward and outward vision; Winter and Summer solstice; the solar and lunar; the ascending and descending sun • **three heads** past present, and future; three phases of the moon; rising, mid-day, and setting sun • **woman with two or three heads** Prudence personified • **winged head** life force; the soul; supernatural wisdom • **head on a tomb** the life force or genius of the person therein • **multiple heads** deterioration; fragmentation, however, it can sometimes indicate a positive intensification • **severed head** wisdom; life of the soul after death; proof of death • **severing the head of an enemy** capturing his strength, powers • **severed head held over an urn** Tomyris • **head-hunting** seeking the vital force or fertility of the victim • **veiled head** inscrutability; secrecy; hidden knowledge; protection of the inner life

• **bowing the head** submission • **nodding the head** pledging the life force; assent; greeting • **severed head pierced by an arrow** attribute of America personified (both continents) • **head as a fountain** the power of speech • **Celtic** the solar; divinity; associated with the phallus; *god with three heads:* Cernunnos • **Christian** *head of Judas:* the Betrayal of Christ; *Christ's head on a cloth:* attribute of St. Veronica; *sword or knife in the head, or just a head wound:* attribute of St. Peter Martyr; *severed head, blindfold, on a horse:* St. Paul; *severed head on a horse, or on a platter:* John the Baptist; *severed head:* attribute of SS Alban, Claire, Denis, Peter, Valerie; *severed head at the feet or in the hand or being put in a bag:* attribute of Judith; *winged head:* occasional early Christian symbol of Christ • **Egyptian** *three heads:* attribute of Serapis; *winged ram with four heads:* the North wind, Qebui; *man with four ram's heads:* the North wind, Qebui, Amen-Ra; *four-winged serpent-headed man:* the East wind, Henkhisesui; *lion-headed man with four wings:* Shehbui • **Fulani** *god with seven heads:* Kaydara • **Germanic** *severed head held by a woman before a king:* the king is Otto III • **Greco-Roman** *headless men:* the Libyan Acephali; *three heads:* attribute of Cerberus, Hecate; *head with two faces:* Janus; *monster with six heads:* Scylla; *serpent with three heads (man's, bull's, lion's):* Chronos; *dragon or serpent with seven heads:* Hydra; *severed head with serpents for hair held by youth:* Perseus with Medusa's head; *severed head at the feet of a winged god:* Hermes/Mercury; *heads of Castor and Pollux looking up and down:* day and night; the rising and setting sun; *severed head at the feet or in the hand:* attribute of Julius Caesar; *severed head together with the body:* Manlius Torquatus • **heraldic** honor for special services; power; *moor's head:* service in the Crusades, or the East India Company • **Hindu** *four heads of Brahma:* source of the four Vedas; *cobra with seven heads:* Naga, Nagina; *two humans with cobra heads:* Naga, Nagina; *three heads:* attribute of Indra • **Indic** *ghost without hands or feet and his head tied to the pommel of a saddle:* a dund • **Islamic** *angel with 70,000 heads each of which had 70,000 mouths:* Mohammed's vision • **Jewish** *head of a giant:* attribute of David; *winged head:* a cherub; *man covering his head:* submission to God • **Norse** *boar's head:* emblem of Freyja, in Yuletide it was abundance and good fortune; *three-headed deity:* Thor • **Persian** *bird with a woman's or a dog's head:* simurg, the Persian phoenix • **Phrygian** *double-headed eagle:* doubled vision • **Slavic** *triple-headed god:* the moon god • **Sri Lankan** *ten heads:* attribute of Ravana • **Sumero-Semitic** *two-headed god:* Sel, Marduk • *see also* **beheading; forehead; hair; scalp**

headband *see* **fillet**

healing the spiritual process by which certain qualities are harmonized and spiritualized

hearing intuitive perception of the truth in the soul; reception of divine wisdom • *see also* **deafness**

heart (organ) love; love as the center of illumination and happiness; love of God; romantic love; compassion; charity; will power; the center of being; the seat of true intelligence; understanding (as opposed to reasoning) • **heart of gold** a perfect person • **flaming heart** intense zeal; emblem of Charity personified, Aphrodite/Venus • **heart pierced with arrow** contrition; deep repentance or devotion; romantic love • **heart with cross and anchor** love, faith, and hope, respectively • **heart in a woman's hand** the woman is Charity personified • **stake driven in the heart** nailing the soul in a particular place; death for a vampire • **woman gnawing on her own heart** Envy personified • **missing heart in a sacrificial animal** portent of evil • **Aztecan** the center of man, religion, and love; the unifying life-principle; **heart sacrifice:** liberating the seed of life to germinate and flower; *pierced heart:* penitence • **Buddhist** essential nature of Buddha; *diamond heart:* purity, indestructibility, the man whom nothing can destroy • **Celtic** generosity; compassion; antithesis of the evil eye • **Chinese** one of the Eight Precious Organs of Buddha • **Christian** courage; love; understanding; joy and sorrow, attribute of SS John of God, Valentine; *heart in the hand:* love, piety; *heart pierced by a spear:* the Passion of Christ; *heart pierced with sword (sometimes the heart has wings):* the Virgin Mary; *heart with a cross:* attribute of SS Bernardine of Siena, Catherine of Siena, Teresa of Avila; *heart on a tablet or sun:* attribute of St. Bernardine; *heart crowned with thorns:* attribute of St. Ignatius of Loyola, emblem of the Jesuits; *heart pierced with arrow:* contrition, repentance, an occasional attribute of St. Augustine (usually with two arrows); *flaming heart:* Christian love, religious fervor, zeal, devotion, attribute of SS Anthony of Padua, Augustine (especially when transfixed with two arrows) • **Greco-Roman** emblem of Eros/Cupid • **heraldic** sincerity; reason; charity; *flaming heart:* intense, burning affection • **Hindu** Divine Center; dwelling of

Brahma • **Islamic** illumination; center of being; spiritual center; absolute intellect • **Jewish** Temple of God; *heart pierced with arrow with a woman's head shown on the heart:* sin against the 9th Commandment; *heart pierced by an arrow with a coin on the heart:* sin against the 10th commandment; *five hearts:* Judah's five sons • **Taoist** seat of understanding • **Tungun** associated with East • *see also* **hearts (playing cards)**

hearth the center of the home; love; filial loyalty; community; marriage; family life; altar for home gods (penates, lares, etc.); fertility; hospitality; sanctuary; temperance; conjunction of the masculine (fire) and feminine (hearth) principles; mystic center; interior spiritual center; World Navel • **hearth fire** home; familial loyalty; the feminine aspect of fire; androgyny • **blazing hearth** associated with Winter • **extinguishing a hearth fire** mourning • **Celtic** center of the cult of the dead • **Hindu** *round hearth:* the earth, the realm of man • **South American Indian** the point of communication with subterranean powers

hearts (playing cards) [Also known as cups] life center; source of life; world center; associated with knowledge, the mind, the creative world, the formal world, creative waters, cooperation, matter in liquid form, the chalice, the silver crescent, knowledge, friendship, Spring, hospitality, pleasure, happiness, romance, the clergy, two, emotion, water • **ace of hearts** family ties; Spring; productivity; fresh starts • **king of hearts** the water king; Poseidon/Neptune; Charlemagne • **queen of hearts** love; roses; Hathor; Sekhet; Semiramis; Aphrodite/Venus, Helen • **jack (knave) of hearts** Mars; war; agriculture; Parasurama • **cartomancy** love, emotion, spirituality; *ace of hearts* family ties; *queen of hearts:* an unmarried woman, a blonde woman • *see also* **playing cards**

heart's ease (plant) peace of mind • *see also* **pansy**

heat source of life; libido; motivation; vitality; passion; intuitive knowledge • **Celtic** valor • **Hindu** cosmic power; ascetic discipline • **Tungun** body heat is associated with South

heath • **Egyptian** *tree heath:* enclosure of the coffin of Osiris

heather humility; solitude; sympathy; allegiance; emblem of Scotland; attribute of Aphrodite/Venus, Isis • **red heather** mid-Summer; when shown with mountains and bees, associated with Cybele • **white heather** protection against acts of passion • **Celtic** feelings; dreams; romance • **flower language** *white heather:* lucky • *see also* **erica aborea**

heaven spirituality; the masculine principle; spiritual reward; union with God; the higher self; bliss; joy; father of earthly rulers; superhuman power; abode of the blessed • **Egyptian** matter; the feminine principle • **Jewish** the godhead • **Oceanic** matter • **Teutonic** matter

heavenly dog *see* **tengu**

Hecate • **Greco-Roman** the Terrible Mother; the evil side of the feminine principle responsible for madness, obsession, lunacy; the unconscious swarming with dangerous energy that must be tamed; associated with fertility, crossroads

Hector • **Greek** bragging

hedge privacy; secrecy; illicit love; prohibition; defense; *privet hedge:* implies a lack of means of enforcement; *thorn hedge:* implies a means of enforcement

hedgehog self-defense; rascality; cunning; greed; gluttony; strong defense; emblem of the sun; the critical aspect that destroys error; related to witches and demonic possession; attribute of the personifications of Touch, Fury, Slander, Gluttony • **Christian** the devil; evildoing • **heraldic** resistance; provident provider; *hedgehog surmounted by a crown:* Louis XII of France • **Sumerian** the Great Mother; emblem of Ishtar

heel vulnerability; the lower nature of the soul; subduer of the serpent, evil • **light heels, round heels** immorality; unchasteness; loose morals • **Greek** *warrior with an arrow in his heel:* Achilles • **Jewish** *one twin born clutching the heel of another:* Jacob and Esau respectively • *see also* **feet**

heifer *see* **cow**

Helen • **Greek** the instinctive and emotional aspects of woman; the transitory, inconsistent; unfaithfulness; dissembling; lower nature; that which diverts man from the path of spiritual progress

helenium • **flower language** tears

Helios/Sol • **Greco-Roman** the sun in its astronomic and spiritual aspect

heliotrope (flower) love; intoxication with love; eternal devotion; zeal; strength in sweetness; perfection; prayer; associated with the sun; *white heliotrope:* associated with Saturn (planet) • **Christian** attribute of the Trinity, angels, prophets, apostles, saints • **flower language** devotion; faithfulness; *Peruvian heliotrope:* devotion • **Greco-Roman** sacred to Apollo, Clytie • **heraldic** eternal love and devotion; pleasure • *see also* **sunflower**

heliotrope (stone) *see* **bloodstone**

hell punishment; evil; abode of the devil; turmoil; anguish suffering; separation from God

hellebore the Nativity of Christ • **flower language** scandal; calumny

helmet courage; lofty thoughts; salvation; protection of the soul from passions and desires; hidden thoughts, beliefs; invisibility; invulnerability; power; preservation; elevation; wisdom; attribute of a soldiers, heroes, the personifications of Faith, Fortitude; the color of the helmet often represents the wearer's thoughts, *see* specific colors (red, black, blue, etc.) • **crested helmet** a victor • **winged helmet** flight; swiftness; poetic thought • **closed helmet** hidden or suspect thoughts, dissimulation • **soldier pouring water from a helmet on a dying woman** Tancred and Clorinda • **Christian** attribute of St. George • **Greco-Roman** attribute of Hades/Pluto, Athena/Minerva, Hephaestus/Vulcan, Ares/Mars; *winged helmet:* attribute of Mercury, Perseus • **heraldic** martial prowess; lofty thoughts; hidden thoughts; *surmounted by a fleur-di-lis:* salvation; *surmounted by a wolf's head:* courage supplanted by astuteness; *surmounted by any kind of strange crest:* imagination, restless exhilaration; *helmet on a shield:* wisdom; security in defense • **Mycenian** *boar's tusk helmet:* attribute of a warrior • **Norse** *golden helmet:* attribute of Odin; *boar mask or helmet:* put the wearer under the protection of Frey and Freyja

helmet flower • **flower language** chivalry; knight errant

hem • **touching the hem of someone's garment** submission, allegiance • **cutting off the hem of a garment** taking power from that person

hematite vivacity; wifehood; associated with Pisces

hemlock death; punishment for unpopular beliefs; deceit; evil; unlucky; weakness; emblem of Fragility personified; attribute of Socrates • **flower language** you will be my death

hemp the rustic life; narcotic; attribute of Recognition personified • **flower language** fate

hen maternity; procreation; providence; the female; maternal care; vigilance; solicitude; a woman 40 to 50 years old; idle chatter; attribute of Grammar personified; associated with death • **hen with chicks** protection; providence • **hen on its nest** perseverance • **crowing hen** a bold woman; feminine dominion; an unlucky omen • **Chinese** *crowing hen:* the ruin of a family; *rooster and hen in a garden:* rural pleasures • **Christian** *hen with chicks:* the solicitude of Christ; Christ with his flock; *black hen:* a diabolical agent, an aspect of the devil • **Islamic** *black hen:* used in witchcraft • **Jewish** *rooster and hen:* a bridal couple • *see also* **chicken; chick**

henbane opiate; emblem of Imperfection personified • **flower language** defect; fault; imperfection

hepatica the liver • **flower language** confidence

Hephaestus/Vulcan • **Greco-Roman** intellect rebelling against the soul; the demiurge; the creative mind captured by the lower qualities; a weak, materialistic, and corrupt soul; associated with cuckolds

heptagon • **Christian** the seven early churches, seven angels, seven lamps, seven seals • **Hindu** divine abode; Brahma's palace • *see also* **-7-**

Hera/Juno • **Greco-Roman** wisdom; jealousy; the Terrible Mother

Heracles/Hercules • **English** *Elizabethan:* a ridiculous, brawny, boisterous tyrant • **Greco-Roman** strength; the quest for immortality; nobility; the fight against the Terrible Mother, the unconscious; the individual fleeing himself in the quest for immortality; expiation of sins through heroic striving and heroism; the personification of physical strength and courage; *holding a giant aloft:* the giant is Antaeus; *wrestling with a lion:* the solar hero overcoming death; *crown of poplar leaves:* attribute of his descent to Hades; *bloodstained tunic given to him by Deianira:* the tunic of Nessus • **tarot** related to the Emperor

herb natural forces; magic; healing; primitive desires and ambitions aroused by the senses; nobility; rural life; appetizer; poor man's food; the means by which fertility deities make themselves visible • *see also* specific herbs: **dill, sage,** etc.

Hercules *see* **Heracles/Hercules**

herd a perversion of man's socialization • **orderly herd** coordinated desires and emotions working for the evolution of the soul; prosperity; rural tranquility • **disorderly herd** loss of unity; disintegration; degeneration; regression

hermaphrodite *see* **androgyne**

Hermes/Mercury • **Greco-Roman** manly grace; messenger of heaven; the Holy Spirit; conscience; intellectual contemplation; intellectual energy; potentialities; occasionally, intelligence; conductor of the souls of the dead; personification of Reason, Eloquence

hermit solitude; contemplation; asceticism; emotional isolation; spiritual safety • **hermit on all fours** St. John Chrysostom, occasionally St. Onuphrius

Hermit (tarot) tradition; study; reserve; patient and profound work; tedium; taciturnity; worldly detachment; the philosopher; wisdom; good; morality; meticulousness; the successful union of personal will with cosmic will; prudence; solitary vigilance; withdrawal to discern wisdom; emblem of Diogenes; related to Leo, Uranus (planet), Neptune (planet); associated with the archangel Lumiel

hermitage withdrawal from worldliness; attribute of St. Giles

hero the union of heavenly and earthly powers; the human soul in its battle with perversion

Herod, King • Christian aggression; domination; betrayal; authority

heron morning; generation of life; regeneration; parental providence; longevity; silent memory; vigilance; quietness; danger overcome; indiscretion; melancholy; duality; attribute of February personified; usually a good omen; associated with water • **African** nosiness; indiscretion • **Chinese** seriousness; silence; tact; delicacy; can cause pregnancy by a glance; associated with the willow tree in art; *white heron and black crane or crow:* yin and yang, solar and lunar, light and darkness, respectively • **Christian** the Christian who turns away from false doctrine; the unfavorable aspects of the priesthood • **Egyptian** the first transformer of the soul after death; the Bennu bird; the rising sun; regeneration; associated with the flooding of the Nile, the return of Osiris, the renewal of life • **Greco-Roman** sacred to the Muses • **heraldic** prudence in danger; possession of free and rich fishing rights • *see also* **crane (bird)** with which the heron shares much symbolism

Hesperides • Greek treasure hunt; death

Hestia/Vesta • Greco-Roman purity; virginity; the demands of absolute purity

hexagon the six attributes of God (power, wisdom, majesty, love, mercy, justice) • *see also* -6-

hexagram the human soul; the union of opposites; male and female; union of the masculine and feminine principles; positive and negative; fire and water; evolution and involution; good and evil; the upper and lower worlds; God the Creator; the androgynous nature of the deity; the natural and supernatural; the celestial and terrestrial; lucky amulet; androgyny; "as above so below" • **alchemic** the union of opposites, fiery water, watery fire • **Hermetic** the synthesis of evolutional and involution forces through interpenetration • **Jewish** the six days of Creation; the six flats indicate the omnipresence of God; the 12 corners signify the 12 tribes of Israel; emblem of Israel, the Jewish faith, King David

hibiscus short-lived glory; frailty; conservativeness; fertility; beauty • **flower language** delicate

beauty hiding the period of life before and after its involution as matter, or before and after the manifest life of appearances • **heraldic** delicate beauty

hiding shame; safety; protection; duplicity

hieracosphinx • Egyptian Horus •

Hierophant (tarot) *see* **High Priest (tarot)**

High Priest (tarot) external religion; traditional teaching suitable for the masses; bondage to convention; information; philosophy; proof; religion; the man of knowledge; intercessor between man and the universe; the possibility of change, personal healing; associated with the search for truth, advice, knowledge

High Priestess (tarot) a balance between initiative and resistance; unrealized potential; duality; hidden influences; sanctuary; the law; knowledge; wisdom; wealth; self-control; stability; woman; the mother; the Church; associated with inspiration, intuition, introspection, contemplation

hill aspiration; constancy; stability; place of worship, meditation, innocent pleasures, freedom from care; eternity; fertility; the female; obstacle • **Celtic** location of the Otherworld • **Egyptian** the first manifestation of the creation of the world; the beginning of differentiation • **Norse** entrance to Valhalla • *see also* **mountain**

hind (deer) grace; elegance; acute hearing; timidity; sensitivity; cowardice; innocence; purity; charity; one's own wife; motherly love; surefootedness; wisdom; low birth; search for immortality; emblem of dawn • **Celtic** *hunting a hind:* the pursuit of wisdom • **Christian** *hind shot with an arrow:* attribute of St. Giles • **Greco-Roman** attribute of Hera/Juno, Artemis/Diana; *hunting a hind:* associated with Heracles/Hercules • **heraldic** peace; harmony • **Jewish** *running hind:* associated with Naphtali • *see also* **deer**

hippalectryon • Greek a solar animal; protection against evil, disease • *see also* **horse; rooster**

hippocampus • Greco-Roman healing; attribute of Poseidon/Neptune, Galatea, sea deities in general; safe travel, especially by sea • **heraldic** water power

hippogriff a spiritual, solar mount; combines the favorable aspects of both horse and lion

hippopotamus insensibility; duality; strength and vigor; impiety; craft; hate; intellectual pride; the mother principle; gross materialism; attribute of the personifications of Behemoth, Impiety • **Egyptian** *female:* the Great Mother, bounty, protection; *male:* the perverse forces in the world; *red hippopotamus:* Set, power and virility, the North Pole; *hippopotamus standing on hind legs:* Taueret; *lion with hippopotamus hindquarters and crocodile jaws:* Ammit • **Greco-Roman** murder; impudence; violence; injustice • **Jewish** Behemoth; brute strength; the vices and impulses man cannot master alone • *see also* **Ammit; Behemoth**

hitchhiker an unknown part of oneself

hive *see* **beehive**

hobby horse folly; drudge; a loose woman

hobo *see* **tramp**

hoe diligence; agriculture; fertility; election of the chosen; attribute of farmers, Spring personified • **heraldic** a right to part of the common ground • **Jewish** attribute of Adam after the Fall

hog *see* **swine**

hold (of a ship) the unconscious; experience on the lower plane

hole the Void; emptiness; the feminine principle; vagina; the passage between worlds or existences; mystic center; trap • **round hole** the heavens • **square hole** the earth • **hole in the roof of a sacred structure** passage to heaven; access to the spiritual world

Holland *see* **Netherlands**

hollow (topography) the abode of the dead; memories; the past; the unconscious; the mother; abstract form of a cave; inverse form of a mountain

holly a holy tree; mid-Winter; the second half of the year; eternal life; hospitality; harvest; domestic happiness; good will; joy; prickliness; associated with Green Knight, the archangel Samael • **Celtic** protection; associated with Earth (planet), red carnelians, July, August • **Christian** Christ's crown of thorns; charm against evil; occasional attribute of SS John the Baptist, Jerome; emblem of the Crucifixion (said to have been the tree of the Cross, as were other trees), Christmas • **flower language** foresight; Am I forgotten? • **Greco-Roman** health; happiness; related to Saturnalia; sacred to Cronus/Saturn • **heraldic** truth; penitence; foresight; defense • **North American Indian** vagina

holly oak the Great Spirit • **Greco-Roman** longevity

holly thorn *see* **hawthorn**

hollyhock ambition; fecundity • **flower language** fecundity; *white hollyhock:* ambition. especially female

Holmes, Sherlock investigation; close inspection, scrutiny; logic

Holy Grail *see* **grail**

holy oil *see* **oil**

holy water *see* **water**

homa • **Persian** lucky; glory; nobility of soul; mystical master

honesty (plant) • **flower language** honesty; sincerity; fascination

honey wisdom; food of the gods; food from heaven; eternal bliss; poetic ecstasy; spiritual wisdom; eloquence; sweetness; abundance; honor; chastity; virginity; flattery; deceit; lust; slumber; initiation; the higher Ego or Self • **astrological** associated with the moon, increase, growth • **Buddhism** associated with teaching • **Chinese** *honey and oil:* false friendship • **Christian** the Eucharist; the earthly ministry of Christ; the divine word; Paradise; the work of God; Christ and his work; religious eloquence; the spiritual exercise of soul-improvement; *bee and honey:* the Virgin Mary and Christ respectively • *locusts and honey:* food of John the Baptist • **Greco-Roman** poetic genius; eloquence; wisdom; food of the gods; associated with funerals • **Hindu** food of the Hamsa; fertility; source of life, immortality • **Hopi** purification; fertility • **Islamic** transcendental reality; charm to restore sight, preserve health, restore the dead to life • **Jain** forbidden food; offering to fertility gods • **Jewish** associated with the Promised Land; *honey and apples:* eaten on the New Year to symbolize the hope for sweetness and joy respectively • **Minoan** ritual food for the living and the dead • **Mithraic** offering to Mithras; poured on the hands and feet of initiates • **Norse** *dew of honey:* emblem of Servitur • **Sumerian** food for the gods

honey flower • **flower language** sweet and secret love

honeycomb labyrinth; confusion; foresight • **Christian** attribute of John the Baptist • **Greco-Roman** attribute of Eros/Cupid

honeysuckle love; fraternal love; generosity; emblem of the South in the US; associated with Aries; related to the lotus • **flower language** generous and devoted affection; *coral honeysuckle:* the color of my fate; *French honeysuckle:* rustic beauty; *monthly honeysuckle (woodbine):* bond of love, fraternal love, I will not answer hastily, domestic happiness; *wild honeysuckle:* inconstancy in love

Ho-o • **Japanese** the Japanese phoenix; emblem of the empress; associated with the sun, fire, rectitude, fidelity, obedience, justice • *see also* **Feng-huang**

hood repression; invisibility; death; detachment from the material world; spiritual blindness; regression; withdrawal; mysticism; thought;

spirit; shares in the symbolism of the head and hat • **black hood** attribute of an executioner • **Celtic** attribute of Cernunnos • **Greco-Roman** attribute of Cronus/Saturn • **heraldic** *falcon hood:* hunting prowess • **Jewish** *pointed hood:* associated with Joel

hoof • **cloven hoof** mark of the devil; separation; treachery • **Greco-Roman** *bronze hooves:* attribute of the Arcadian Hind captured by Heracles/Hercules

hook attraction; captivity; punishment; related to love, the male, fishing • **Christian** Christ; the Word; *hooked grill:* attribute of St. Vincent • **Egyptian** attribute of Osiris • **Greco-Roman** attribute of Dionysus/Bacchus, Priapus • **Hindu** *iron hook:* death; attribute of Devi, Kali

hoopoe parental care; ostentation; vanity; poverty; filth; attribute of royalty, Baseness personified • **Arabian** sagacity; personal internal inspiration; uncovers buried treasure; guards against ambush; messenger from the invisible world • **English** harbinger of evil • **Islamic** messenger between King Solomon and the Queen of Sheba • **Jewish** wisdom • **Persian** a wise and righteous man • **Swedish** associated with war

hops beer; mirth; injustice; passion; overwhelming pride; trust • **flower language** injustice

Horeb, Mount • **Jewish** seat of the sun

horehound • **flower language** fire

horizontal the plane of existence; lack of spiritual progress • *see also* **vertical**

horn (musical) call to arms; invocation of help; melancholy; the outside shape is phallic, the hollow inside is feminine, Fame personified • **Christian** *hunting horn:* attribute of St. Hubert • **Greco-Roman** attribute of Melpomene, tritons • **heraldic** *hunting horn:* fondness for hunting, high pursuits • *see also* **bugle; trumpet**

Horn of Plenty *see* **cornucopia**

hornbeam • **flower language** ornament

hornet evil; viciousness • **biblical** plague; punishment

horns (animal) power; supernatural power; strength; victory; virility; abundance; fertility; dignity; divinity; manifestation of the spirit; protection; defense; phallus; salvation; immortality; madness; rage; intelligence; the outside shape is phallic, the hollow inside is feminine; attribute of royalty, mother goddesses, queens of heaven, the Erythraean sibyl • **horns on a person's head** regression; evil; a cuckold • **breaking a horn** sapping strength, power • **horns with a ribbon** attribute of storm gods • **Assyrian** *horned headdress:* attribute of Ashur

• **Babylonian** *horn on the head:* material strength, attribute of Bel • **Celtic** fecundity • **Chinese** *man with horns on his head:* Chennung, Ch'i-You • **Christian** omniscience; power; attribute of the devil; *two horns:* the Old and New Testament; *lamb with seven horns:* the seven gifts of the Holy Spirit, the Apocalypse; *horned man:* the devil, a demon; *ten horns:* attribute of the Beast of Revelation • **Dahomean** *giant with 30 horns:* Yehwe Zogbanu • **Egyptian** *cow horns:* lunar, attribute of Hathor, Isis, Nut; *bull horns:* solar; *ram's horns:* attribute of Ammon; *horns with a long ribbon:* attribute of Set; *disk with goat horns:* life, strength, attribute of Isis; *gazelle horns:* attribute of Resheph • **Greco-Roman** attribute of Dionysus/Bacchus, Pan/Faunus, satyrs; *lobster-claw horns:* attribute of icthyocentaurs • **heraldic** *bull horns:* strength, fortitude • **Hindu** *four horns of the Rig Veda:* the four cardinal points • **Islamic** strength; victory; success • **Jewish** power; attribute of Asher; occasional attribute of Moses; *four horns:* associated with Zechariah; *seven horns:* entry into Jericho; *raising horns:* victory; *breaking horns:* defeat; *horn of oil:* associated with David; *ram's horn:* see **shofar** • **Minoan** power; divinity • **Norse** power; virility; hospitality; attribute of warriors • **Persian** *bull with golden horns:* incarnation of Verethraghna • **Sumero-Semitic** divinity; power (both solar and lunar); *horned headdress:* attribute of Anu, Bel; *horns with a ribbon and crown:* attribute of Adad • *see also* **antlers; cornucopia; shofar; tusk**

horse lust; fertility; selfishness; fidelity; vanity; stubbornness; stupidity; the unconscious; the self; war; the sun; occasionally clairvoyant; associated with the funerals, archangel Samael; attribute of kings, nobles, warriors, Europe personified • **colt** friskiness; wantonness • **white horse** innocence; intellect; reason; celestial knowledge; spirituality; a solar animal; the Divine Word; the pure and perfect higher mind; the hero's steed; imagination; dawn; manhood • **white horse with flaming mane** the sun • **horse without any white** viciousness • **black horse** famine; error; false knowledge; death; steed of a villain • **horse feathers** nonsense • **gray horse** the devil • **pale gray horse** dissolution • **golden horse** the sun • **red horse** war; the mind energized by the spirit; danger; desire • **grazing horse** peace and freedom • **double horse head** protection • **winged horse** poetry; the flight of the imagination; imagination itself • **chariot pulled by winged horses** the dawn • **three-legged horse** attribute of Death personified in time of pestilence • **ship with a horse's head** the sun chariot • **wooden horse** a ruse • **hobby horse** folly; a drudge; a loose woman • **wild horse** the blind forces of primeval chaos; the instincts; the baser forces in man; uncontrolled passions • **grazing horse** peace • **Buddhist** indestructibility; hidden nature of things; *winged horse:* Avalokitesvara; *white horse:* steed of Buddha leaving home; *horse-headed deity:* Hayagriva • **Celtic** messenger of the gods; guide for the dead; virility; fecundity; attribute of Epona (sometimes riding a white horse sidesaddle), Mebd of Tara, Macha of Ulster • **Chinese** yang; the heavens; fire; South; the earth; speed; lucky; perseverance; fertility; ruling power; *horse hoof:* lucky; *winged horse:* bearer of the Buddhist Book of the Law; *white horse:* avatar of Guanyin; *cow with horse:* yin and yang respectively • **Christian** the sun; courage; generosity; lust; the faithful Christian racing toward salvation; attribute of SS Eustace, George, Hubert, Martin, Maurice, Victor; associated with the Ascension of Christ; *four horses:* the Apocalypse; *white horse:* the conquering Christian, male virginity; *horse with sword coming from its mouth:* the Apocalypse; *horse with its leg removed for shoeing:* attribute of St. Eloi; *wild horses:* attribute of St. Hippolytus; *catacomb art:* the swift passage of life; *three-legged horse:* attribute of the devil; *gray horse:* the devil • **Finnish** *half-man/half-animal with horse feet:* a nakki • **Greco-Roman** attribute of Boreas, Casto, Artemis/Diana, Dionysus/Bacchus, Hades/Pluto, Ares/Mars, Zeus/Jupiter, the Muses; *winged horse:* Pegasus; *white horse:* attribute of Helios/Sol, Poseidon/Neptune, Castor, Pollux; *chariot with white horses:* attribute of Apollo; *horse attacked by a man with a club:* the man is Heracles/Hercules; *wooden horse:* the Trojan War; *horse, chariot, and rider falling from the sky:* the rider is Phaeton; *fat old man with horse ears:* Silenus • **heraldic** readiness for action; Master of the Horse; *white horse:* emblem of the House of Hanover • **Hindu** guardian of the South; *black horse (Vedic):* Dyaus; *winged white horse:* Devadatta, steed of Kalki; *white horse with flaming mane:* the sun; *Manu's mare:* deified earth; *horse-headed deity:* Hayagriva; *man with a horse head:* a kinnara; *horse with human head:* a kimpurusha; *half-man/half-horse (gandharva):* fecundity and abstract thought; intelligence and music; *horse and rider:* body and spirit respectively; *stallion (Aryan):* supremacy, aggressive masculinity, the solar; *mare (Vedic):* holder of the fire of destruction

at the end of the world; *Cosmic Horse:* Varuna • **Irish** *gray horse:* Liat Maca; *black horse:* Dub Sanglainn • **Islamic** happiness; wealth; steed of Mohammed ascending into heaven from the Dome of the Rock • **Japanese** *white horse:* avatar of Kannon ; *black horse:* attribute of the rain god • **Jewish** *red horse:* associated with Zechariah; *fiery chariot and horses:* attribute of the ascension of Elijah, Elisha at Dothan • **Kalmyk** *horse head:* West • **Lithuanian** *small twin horses pulling the carriage of the sun:* the Asvieniai • **Mithraic** *chariot with white horses:* attribute of Mithras • **Norse** sacred to Odin; attribute of Frey, Vanir; *eight-legged mare:* Sleipnir • **Persian** *stallion:* solar power; fire; attribute of warriors; *chariot with four horses:* attribute of the Magi; *chariot with four white horses:* attribute of Anahita; *white horse:* incarnation of Verethaghna • **Russian** emblem of marriage • **Scottish** *horse galloping its rider into a lake or river:* a kelpie; *horse galloping its rider into the sea:* an each uisage • **Serbian** *one-eyed dog-headed man with horse legs and iron teeth:* a psoglav • **Spanish** *tall thin knight on a gaunt horse:* Don Quixote • **Sumero-Semitic** *chariot with four horses:* attribute of Marduk; *horse head:* emblem of Carthage • **Taoist** attribute of Ch'ang Kuo • **Ural-Altaic** *winged horse:* guide of the dead; passage to the next world; *horse head:* the life principle • **Tibetan** *flying white horse:* attribute of Da • **Welsh** *gray horse:* emblem of Satan • *see also* **centaur; hippalectryon; hippogriff; horse rider; mare; Pegasus**

horse chestnut (buckeye) the sun; emblem of Ohio; associated with the archangel Samael • **flower language** luxury

horse rider triumph; the Ego trying to control the Id; the mind and/or spirit directing the body; bearer of immortality of prophecy; the horse being ridden indicates the qualities and intentions of the rider • **fallen rider** Pride personified • **headless horseman** the devil; death • **Christian** Christ; *rider on a white horse:* the word of God, Christ's spiritual conquest, Christ; *rider on a red horse:* war as a punishment of God; *rider on a black horse:* starvation; *rider on a pale horse:* death; *four horsemen charging:* the Apocalypse; *rider with white banner:* St. James the Greater; *riders on horseback in the sky:* revelation • **English** *nude woman on a horse:* Lady Godiva • **Greek** *rider on a winged horse:* Perseus, Bellerophon • **Hindu** *horse and rider:* body and spirit respectively • **Jewish** *soldiers on horseback in the sky:* portent of war • **Roman** *nude woman on a horse:* Cloelia • *see also* **horse**

horseradish • Jewish the bitterness of bondage

horseshoe protection; vagina; related to a horse's vitality and sexual potency; emblem of blacksmiths • **turned up** power; protection; the crescent moon • **turned down** unlucky • **heraldic** good luck; defense against evil spirits; *ostrich with a horseshoe in its mouth:* endurance • **American** *ring made from a horseshoe nail:* lucky charm

hortensia • flower language you are cold

Host (Eucharist) the sacrifice of Christ upon the Cross, especially when shown with a chalice; the body of Christ • **breaking the Host** the death of Christ's body

hound seeker of truth; inquisitiveness; intelligence; the hunter; pursuit; male desire; attribute of Artemis/Diana • *see also* **dog; Gabriel Hounds**

hourglass the transience of life; time; inversion; evanescence; creation and destruction; perpetual inversion of the upper and lower worlds; cyclic recurrence of life and death; death; night time as opposed to the sundial which symbolizes daytime; attribute of Temperance personified, the Grim Reaper, Father Time, alchemists • **hourglass with sand running out** the end of a cycle • **winged hourglass** fleeting time • **skeleton with sword, sickle, scythe, and/or hourglass** death; Death personified; the King of Death • **Greek** attribute of Chronos • **heraldic** mortality; evanescence

house tradition; one's life; the psyche; the feminine aspect of the universe; shelter; security; hospitality; World Center; the body, with the roof and attic corresponding to the mind, the basement to the unconscious, the kitchen as a place of transmutation, the windows and doors as body openings, etc. • **cedar house** incorruptibility • **clay house** evanescence • **sacred house** (church, mosque, temple, etc.) Cosmic Center • **Christian** *house on a rock:* the Church securely founded on the rock of faith • **Inuit** *big house with big guard dog:* dwelling of Sedna in Adlivun • **Mexican Indian** *house of green feathers:* home of the quetzal • **Roman** *golden house:* Nero's Palace of the Sun • **Tinguinian** *house of gold:* dwelling of an alan

House of God (tarot) the power of the heavenly over the earthly; spiritual truth breaking down ignorance; involution; materialism struck down by spiritual light to render regeneration possible; the dangerous consequences of overconfidence; the sin of pride; megalomania; wickedness; the wild pursuit of fanciful ideas; small-mindedness; sudden subversion; inevitability of change; associated with the archangels Samael and Uriel, the need to let go of the past and trust in the awakening of one's intuition

housefly *see* **fly**

houseleek vitality; attribute of Printing personified • **flower language** vivacity; domestic economy • *see also* **leek**

houstonia • flower language contentment

hoya • flower language sculpture

huitfoil • heraldic ninth son

humble plant • flower language despondency

hummingbird gaiety; courage; jealousy; love; joy; beauty • **Aztecan** Quetzalcoatl; the soul of a dead warrior • **folkloric** can stop time • **Nahua** Quetzalcoatl • **Toltec** Quetzalcoatl

hunchback sins of the past; nature perverted; regression; a good omen

hundred *see* **-100-**

hunger spiritual or mental craving; deprivation of one's desires; suffering

hunter action for its own sake; repetition; pursuit of the transitory; the devil; killer; pursuer; searcher for truth; desire; pursuit of worldly ends • **hind protected from a hunter** attribute of St. Giles • **Greco-Roman** *hunter restrained by nude woman:* Adonis; *hunter turning into a stag or observing a nude woman:* Actaeon; *hunter eaten by his own dogs:* Actaeon; *hunter grieving over a woman shot by an arrow:* Cephalus and Procis; *huntress:* Artemis/Diana, Atalanta, Erinyes/Furies • **Mochican** Ai apaec (especially with lizard and dog)

hurricane regeneration; fecundation; a hole through which one may pass out of space and time

husband and wife mind and emotion respectively

husk lower qualities

hut shelter; temporary shelter, associated with nomads, travelers, pilgrims, hermits • **Jewish** Feast of Sukkoth; reminder of the time in the wilderness • **Slavic** *hut surrounded by fence of bones or skulls:* dwelling of Baba Yaga • *see also* **house**

hyacinth (flower) sorrow; sport; game; play; diversion; resignation; faith; peace of mind; resistance to adversity; love and its woes; prudence; wisdom; kindliness; high estate; pride; exclusiveness; associated with Capricorn, April; attribute of Benevolence personified • **Christian** attribute of the Virgin Mary • **flower language** sport; play; *blue hyacinth:* constancy; *white hyacinth:* unobtrusive loveliness • **Greco-Roman** emblem of Cronus/Saturn; associated with Hyacinth, Apollo • **heraldic** games; playfulness; sports • **Middle Ages** mourning

hyacinth (stone) Christian prudence; peace of mind; the desire for heaven; fidelity; second-sight

Hyades (stars) tearfulness

Hydra • **Christian** the prolific nature of heresy, sin, false doctrine; the devil • **Greco-Roman** multifarious evil; blind animal life force; the whole catalog of vices; sordid vices • **heraldic** terror; destruction; victory over a very powerful enemy

hydrangea remembrance; frigidity; coldness; massive beauty • **flower language** boastfulness; heartlessness; you are cold

hyena falseness; duplicity; fickleness; avarice; ghoulishness; impurity; evil; cowardice; one who thrives on false doctrine; derisiveness • **Christian** the devil; the devil feeding on the damned • **Jewish** purification

hymn spiritual harmony; praise; aspiration

hyssop cleanliness; purification; freshness; penitence; Winter; decency • **Christian** penitence; humility; purgation; innocence regained; baptism; *hyssop and reed:* associated with the Passion of Christ

I

I the axis of the universe; the Roman numeral for one; associated with the Winter solstice, the liver, indestructibility, tolerance, sympathy, sensitivity, travel, Leo, Neptune (planet); the equivalent of -9- • **tarot** associated with the Hermit, Wheel of Fortune

ibex • **Egyptian** sacred to Set, Reshep • *see also* **goat;** ibex also share in the symbolism of the **gazelle**

ibis wisdom; perseverance; aspiration; morning; protector; dawn; spiritual awakening; occult art; regeneration; gratitude; a favorable omen; associated with moon goddesses, the arch-angel Raphael • **Christian** carnal desires; filth; laziness • **Egyptian** the soul; aspiration; perseverance; the morning; purification; guide of souls to heaven; incarnation of Thoth; sacred to Isis, Aah; *ibis-headed god:* Thoth; *as a killer of reptiles:* the solar; *crested ibis:* the sun; *with crescent moon on its head:* the lunar • **Greco-Roman** carnal desires; filth; laziness • **Jewish** wisdom; foreknowledge

Icarus • **Greek** the limitation of ideas; the intellect in the merely technical and non-spiritual sense; man's questing intellectual spirit; the danger of going to extremes; overweening ambition; failure to heed a parent's advice; the intellect trying to escape the world; intellect rebelling against the spirit; *wings of Icarus:* functional insufficiency

ice Winter; death; smoothness; feminine chastity; frigidity; rigidity; brittleness; impermanence; the rigid dividing line between the conscious and unconscious, or any other dynamic levels; stultification of potentialities; latent truth; inertness; resistance to the inferior • **melting ice** release of old thoughts or beliefs; an opening of the emotions; harbinger of Spring

ice plant • **flower language** rejected addresses; your looks freeze me

Iceland moss • **flower language** health

icicle chastity; frigidity

icon a window to heaven

iconostasis • **Orthodox Christian** the division between heaven and earth, the sacred and profane, the divine and human

idol apostasy; paganism; the heathen world; fixed ideas which bar the way to truth; outward observances regarded as true spiritual exercise; image without substance • **idol underfoot** denial of paganism; paganism overcome • **man with a cord around his neck tied to an idol** Idolatry personified • **Christian** Mammon worship; *shattered idol:* attribute of St. Philip; *fallen idol:* associated with the Flight into Egypt • **Jewish** Solomon's apostasy; *shattered idol:* associated with Hosea

IHC *or* **I.H.C.** • **Greek** the first three letters of Jesus' name; *see also* **I.H.S.,** below

IHS *or* **I.H.S.** • **Christian** an adaptation of IHC that came into use as Latin became the dominant language of the Church; the understanding was that it meant *Iesus Hominum Salvator* (Jesus, savior of men) or *In haec salus* (In this [cross], salvation); *IHS on a tablet, sun, or heart:* attribute of SS Bernardino of Siena, Ignatius Loyola, Teresa of Avila • **Greco-Roman** Latin initials for *in hoc signo,* or *in hac salus,* or derived from the ritual cry "Iacchos" and associated with Dionysius, Bacchus

illness *see* **disease**

immersion baptism; the return to the primordial waters of life and pristine innocence; transformation; renewal; rebirth; purification; revitalization; protection • **immersion while tied down** punishment through social humiliation

imp disorder; torment • **Christian art** a devil's helper in hell

imperial montague • **flower language** power

incendiarism *see* **arson**

incense homage to a deity; dawn; morning; spiritual goodness; prayer; fumigant to scare off evil spirits; sacrifice for thanksgiving or for a favor; atonement; flattery; purification by fire; inspiration; transmutation of the physical into the spiritual; communication with heaven; substitute for a burnt offering; related to the phoenix • **incense burner** emblem of Buddhism • **Central American Indian** an emanation of the divine spirit • **Hindu** the perception of consciousness • *see also* **censer**

incest longing for union with one's own self; reuniting original unity by marriage of the separate parts; individuation; corruption or perversion of the natural order; conflict with parts of oneself; regression

India ancient wisdom, spirituality

Indians *see* **American Indians**

indigo (color) associated with Taurus, Saturn (planet), Jupiter (planet); night; evil • *see also* **blue**

infant new beginning; new era; the New Year; innocence; helplessness; faith; hope • **winged infant** the soul • **infant suckled by a woman, with another infant nearby** attribute of Charity personified • **Christian** *infant in a manger:* Jesus Christ; *infant in a cradle:* attribute of SS Vincent DePaul, Anthony of Padua • **Egyptian** *infant with a finger in his mouth:* Horus • **Greco-Roman** *infant suckled by a goat:* Zeus/Jupiter; *infant suckled by a wolf:* Romulus (Remus is often represented with him); *infant fed by a satyr:* Dionysus/Bacchus; *infant discovered by shepherds:* Paris; *infant in the path of a plow:* Heracles/Hercules; *infant held by the ankle over a river:* Achilles; *infant eaten by an old man:* the old man is Cronus/Saturn; *infant holding a serpent in both hands:* Heracles/Hercules; *winged child:* Eros/Cupid, *infant in the arms of Hermes/Mercury:* Dionysus/Bacchus; *infant in a tree trunk:* Adonis; *woman and infant in a chest:* Danae and Perseus • **Jewish** *infant placed before a king and offered two dishes:* the infant is Moses; *infant held by a king:* the king is Solomon; *one infant born clutching the heel of another:* Jacob and Esau respectively; *infant born with teeth and hair:* Esau • *see also* **child; Christ child**

ink implies permanence • **purple ink** blood; in Byzantium, reserved for use by the imperial chamberlain • **red ink** deficit • **Islamic** the reflection of all existential potentialities

inkhorn attribute of authors • **Christian** attribute of SS Augustine, Matthew, Mark, Luke, John (often the evangelists' inkhorns are held by angels) • **heraldic** writing skill; education

inkwell *see* **inkhorn**

inn place of freedom, conviviality, protection; power without pomp

inn keeper *see* **tapster**

INRI *or* **I.N.R.I.** • **Christian** Latin initials for *Iesus Nazarenus Rex Iudaeorum* (Jesus of Nazareth, King of the Jews), a title originally given by Pontius Pilate

insanity a disordered condition in the soul

insect short life; a reduced primeval monster; semen; in swarms they have a negative connotation, such as forces in the process of dissolution, plague • **Central American Indian** the souls of the dead revisiting the earth; associated with the stars • *see also* specific insects, such as **mosquito, moth**

intercourse *see* **sexual intercourse**

intersection conjunction; communication; choice; union of opposites; the point at which change is sought or induced; a point of special power • *see also* **crossroads**

intestines the lower qualities; intuition; seat of the emotions • **Chinese** compassion; affection; the mystic knot • **Christian** *saint with his intestines wound around a capstan:* St. Erasmus • **Egyptian** believed to have magical powers; removed during the embalming ritual and put in a jar • *see also* **viscera**

intoxicant the libido; fornication

intoxication religious frenzy; elevation of normal powers; conviviality; loss of control; libido symbol; revelation of inner thoughts or feelings; escape from reality; release of truth; the overwhelming power of divine possession; means of contacting the Otherworld

invisibility regression; the repressed; dissociation; death; magic powers

iolite stone for 21st wedding anniversaries

iopode *see* **centaur**

Ireland associated with drunkenness, laziness, superstition, querulousness

iris (flower) hope; light; purity; power; royalty; eloquence; messenger of good news • **Chinese** grace; affection; beauty is solitude • **Christian** attribute of the Immaculate Conception (especially in Spanish art), the Virgin Mary, the Passion of Christ; *sword lily:* the sorrow of the Virgin Mary • **Egyptian** power • **flower language** my compliments; I have a message for you; *German iris:* archer, flame; *yellow iris:* flame, passion • **Greco-Roman** emblem of Iris (goddess); sacred to Hera/Juno • **heraldic** valor; faith; wisdom; friendship; hope • **Japanese** betrothal; purification; preservative against fire, disease, external evil; associated with June; *purple iris:* mourning

Iris (goddess) • Greek personification of the rainbow; messenger; the link between heaven and earth

iron (metal) war; strength; machinery; mental power; the mind; hardness; durability; strength; firmness; inflexibility; constancy; cruelty; bondage; patience; force; punishment; fetters; associated with Aries, Scorpio, the Father-Spirit archetype; Mars (planet), the archangel Samael • **white iron** associated with 6th, 10th wedding anniversaries • **Armenian** charm for protection from an al; *demon with iron teeth and scissors:* an al • **biblical** solidity • **Chinese** strength; firmness; determination; integrity; justice • **Egyptian** evil; attribute of Set • **Greco-Roman** attribute of Ares/Mars; *iron ring:* attribute of Prometheus after he was freed • **Hindu** the fourth and final age of the cycles of manifestation • **Islamic** the power of evil • **Kenyan** *women's iron necklace:* stimulates pregnancy, cures children's diseases • **Malian** associated with darkness, barrenness, drought, disorder, pollution, death • **Mexican Indian** the masculine principle • **Minoan** the masculine principle; *funerary art:* the feminine principle • **Norse** *iron or thick leather shoes:* attribute of Vidar • **Teutonic** slavery • **Tungun** associated with East

irrigation the bestowing of truth upon the lower qualities

Isis • Egyptian hope; faithfulness; devotion; the feminine principle; source of fertility, transmutation

island isolation; solitude; loneliness; death; the conscious; stability; superiority; refuge from the unconscious, mediocrity, the passions, chaos; safety; sanctuary; the synthesis of consciousness and will; spiritual center • **enchanted island** Paradise; abode of the Blessed • **desert island** isolation; abandonment

Israfel, Archangel *see* **Raphael, Archangel**

Issachar • Jewish agriculture

itching desire, especially sexual • **itchy palm** mercenary intent • **itchy elbows** joy • **itching nose** you will kiss a fool • **itching foot** you will journey to somewhere new

ivory purity; incorruptibility; moral fortitude; hardness; resistance; wealth; associated with 14th wedding anniversaries • **ivory tower** retreat from the world, especially by an intellectual or academic; shutting one's eyes to reality; the inaccessible; the feminine principle • **Christian** Christ; attribute of the Virgin Mary; *ivory tower:* the Church, emblem of the Virgin Mary • **Greco-Roman** *ivory scepter:* attribute of

Zeus/Jupiter, Aeetes; *ivory shoulder:* attribute of Pelops; *ivory quiver:* attribute of Atalanta

ivy longevity; despondency; dependence; trustfulness; wedded love; fidelity; immortality; tenacity; friendship; death; love; tenacity of memory; ambition; lyric poetry; parasite; intoxicant; ingratitude; attachment; undying affection; associated with Capricorn; attribute of Industry personified • **Celtic** associated with the moon, opals, September, October • **Christian** fidelity; everlasting life; death and immortality • **Egyptian** immortality; associated with Osiris • **flower language** friendship; fidelity; matrimony; *ivy sprig with tendrils:* eagerness to please • **Greco-Roman** revelry; conviviality; sacred to Dionysus/Bacchus; attribute of satyrs • **heraldic** strong and lasting friendship; constant love • **Semitic** immortality; sacred to Attis; *ivy leaf:* phallic, the male trinity

I.X. • Greek initials for Jesus Christ, often shown with the I bisecting the X

Ixion • Greek spiritual perversion; sexual perversion; pride; megalomania; deceit

J

J associated with leadership, an elevated station, gain, intellect, culture; corresponds to the lungs, Virgo, Capricorn; symbolically the same as the letter I (this is especially true in any but modern times); equivalent to -1-, especially multiplied ten times • **tarot** associated with the Wheel of Fortune

jacinth modesty • **British** regal temperance and sobriety • **Jewish** fidelity

jackal death; intellect; keenness of smell; cowardly service; ill omen • **Buddhist** a person rooted in evil • **Egyptian** associated with cemeteries, Wepwawet; *jackal-headed god:* Anubis, Khentimentiu • **Hindu** lust; greed; cruelty; sensuality; attribute of Kali; steed of Devi

jackdaw ignorance; vanity; empty conceit; stupidity; a thief; shares the unfavorable symbolism of kites and crows

Jacob • Jewish father of the 12 tribes; trickery; associated with Jacob's ladder

Jacob's ladder • Jewish communication with heaven

Jacob's ladder (plant) • flower language come down

jade power; perfection; purity; immortality; virtue; charm for good luck, health, protection from evil spirits, wisdom, healing, abundant crops, fertility, prosperity; associated with Venus (planet), 3rd and 12th wedding anniversaries • **Aztecan** associated with offerings to Huitzilopochtli, Tlaloc; *green jade skirt:* attribute of Chalchiutlicue • **Chinese** yang; eternity; righteousness; strength; perfection; excellence; virtue; emblem of the emperor, China; *jade cicada:* placed in the mouth of the dead to ensure immortality; *jade ring:* attribute of Mo-li Ch'in; *jade flute:* attribute of Han Xiang • **Mayan** rain; blood; the New Year • **Mexican Indian** water; fertile plant life

jadeite associated with 29th wedding anniversaries • often confused with **jade**

jaguar • **Aztecan** the powers of darkness; Tezcatlipoca • **Bororo** *jaguar and monkey teeth:* charm for strength and skill • **Central American Indian** Master of the Animals • **Mexican Indian** messenger of forest spirits • **Mochican** *old man with jaguar headdress:* Ai apaec • **South American Indian** familiar of shamans; a shape-shifted shaman; *jaguar with four eyes:* second sight

jail *see* **prison**

James the Great, St. • **Christian** *at the feet of a winged woman with hands raised heavenward:*

Janus • **Roman** wholeness; the past and the future; history and prophecy; the desire to master all things; priest and monarch; all pairs of opposites; change; beginnings; vigilance

japonica • **Chinese** married happiness

jar the feminine principle; womb; womb of the Great Mother; inner values; shelter; protection; preservation; nourishment; fertility; a place for the intermingling of forces; rain charm; source of plenty; still movement • **jar of water** cleansing of the soul; attribute of Penitence personified • **jar with water flowing from it** attribute of the Sea personified • **alchemic** *hermetic jar:* container of opposites; the receiver and nourisher of that which is to be transformed • **Buddhist** spiritual triumph; triumph over birth and death; an auspicious sign on the footprint of Buddha • **Chinese** heaven; *rapping on a jar:* thunder; *cracked jar:* storm • **Christian** *jar of ointment:* attribute of Mary Magdalene • **Egyptian** *Hopi with two jars:* the Upper and Lower Nile • **Far Eastern** *jar of vinegar:* life • **Greco-Roman** the grave; burial; the underworld; *eagle and jar:* attribute of Hebe, Juventas • **Hindu** inexhaustible plenty; *cosmetics jar:* attribute of Devi • **Mayan** *overturned jar:* attribute of Ixchel • see *also* **urn; vase**

jasmine delicate beauty; love; grace; fragrance; elegance; amiability; memory; separation; divine hope; heavenly felicity • **palm and jasmine** adoration of God • **Chinese** sweetness; grace; attraction; femininity • **Christian** grace; elegance; attribute of the Virgin Mary • **flower language** deception; despair; a lie; *cape jasmine:* transport of joy, I am too happy; *Carolina jasmine:* separation; *Indian jasmine:* I attach myself to you; *Spanish jasmine:* sensuality; *white jasmine:* amiability; *yellow jasmine:* grace and elegance • **heraldic** attachment • **Hindu** love

Jason • **Greek** opponent of degeneration into the commonplace; the flawed hero; moral compromise; the hero who fails to realize the means must be compatible with the ends; unfaithfulness; youth of failed promise

jasper joy; happiness; beauty; wisdom; pride; friendship; second sight; associated with Libra, the archangel Samael; charm for healing, health, childbirth, protection from women's diseases • **black jasper** charm for the capture of fleets and cities • **brown jasper** charm for centering, grounding • **mottled jasper** charm against drowning • **red jasper** associated with Aries; charm for healing, protection, beauty • **yellow jasper** charm for healing, compassion, sleep • **Gnostic** *sardonyx, jasper, and amethyst:* attribute of Abraxus • **Mithraic** friendship; attribute of Mithras

jaundice envy; jealousy

javelin kingly force; martial readiness • **Greek** *grieving hunter with javelin-pierced woman:* Cephalus and Procris respectively • **heraldic** courage; martial readiness; defense of honor; devotion to honor; speed; freedom; knightly service • **Jewish** martial readiness; kingly force • *see also* **lance; spear**

jaw • **Jewish** *jawbone of an ass:* the slaying of Abel by Cain; attribute of Samson • **Toltec** *sun god looking out of a serpent's jaws:* the sky

jay mischief; unlucky; generally unfavorable; loose or flashy woman; simpleton; bumpkin; senseless chatter

jelly human fear; spinelessness

jellyfish • **Greek** sacred to Medusa • **Japanese** attribute of Ebisu

jerkin ambiguity of thought

Jerusalem freedom; peace; justice; heaven; the Church • **Jerusalem with a sword above it** associated with Zephaniah • **New Jerusalem** the final transformation of the world; Paradise regained • **twelve gates of Jerusalem** the zodiac signs, the tribes of Israel, the cardinal directions

jessamine • **heraldic** hope; joy

jessant-de-lis • **heraldic** dominion over France

Jesse tree • **Christian** the human or royal genealogy of Jesus

jester *see* **fool**

Jesus Christ religion; Christianity; the Church • **Christian** human perfection; salvation; di-vine messenger; *napkin or veil with the picture of Jesus:* attribute of St. Veronica; *Jesus in a gray cloak:* the Last Judgment • *see also* **Christ child**

jet (stone) mourning; grief; wisdom; charm for safe travel, protection from the evil eye • **British** charm against storms, evil spirits, demonic possession, serpent bites, poison • **Hindu** protection from the evil eye • **Mediterranean** protection from the evil eye

Jew • **Christian** avarice; *Wandering Jew:* the imperishable side of man which cannot die

jewels spiritual knowledge; earthly success; the transience of earthly possessions (especially in a still life); may have infernal implications; attribute of the personifications of Vanity, Asia, Profane Love • **jewels guarded by a dragon or by other obstacles** the difficulty encountered in obtaining spiritual knowledge • **jewels hidden in caves or underground** the intuitive knowledge of the unconscious • **jewelry** associated with 17th wedding anniversaries • **Assyrian** *luminous gem tree of Paradise:* the great light of God • **Buddhist** attribute of Ratnasambhava • **Christian** *woman casting off her jewels:* Mary Magdalene • **Egyptian** *golden sycamore of jewels, fruits, and flowers in Paradise:* sacred to Nut • **heraldic** supremacy • **Hindu** *gem tree of Paradise:* sacred to Buddha; *container of jewels:* attribute of Varuna • **Jewish** *jewels offered to a woman at a well:* the woman is Rebecca; *twelve jewels on vestments:* the zodiac, the 12 months • *see also* specific stones such as **diamond; ruby**

Jezebel • **Jewish** misdirection of creative energies; false prophet

Job • **Jewish** faithfulness; patience; perseverance; enduring determination; acceptance of fate; victim of misfortune

John the Baptist • **Christian** associated with baptism, religious conversion, the wilderness; a forerunner

Jonah • **Christian** precursor of the resurrection of Christ; the Resurrection • **Jewish** resurrection; a reluctant prophet; misfortune

jonquil vanity; imprudence; uncontrolled affection • **flower language** desire; *from the 19th Century on:* I desire a return of affection

Jophiel, Archangel associated with the beauty of God, driving Adam and Eve out of Eden

Jordan River • **Christian** the River of Life; the flow of life essence from heaven to Earth; an aspect of the cosmic river from which all comes and all returns; associated with John the Baptist, the baptism of Christ

Joseph • **Jewish** self-realization; a favorite son; rising above adversity through initiative; reception of insight through dreams

journey adventure; spiritual pilgrimage; flight from the mother for fear of incest; aspiration; unsatisfied longing; desire for change; evolution; enquiring; studying; desire to undergo profound spiritual experience; search for the lost Mother, Paradise, perfection, the spiritual center, adventure, change, peace, truth, immortality • **journey into hell or caverns** exploration of the unconscious • **heroic journey** transformation; attaining perfection • **journey abroad** may represent the cutting of family ties • **moving from the center to the circumference** a journey into manifestation and multiplicity • **moving from the circumference to the center** a journey to the spiritual center, unity, the One

Joy (tarot) *see* **Sun (tarot)**

jubilee return to the beginning; return to the primordial state; a hallowed and fresh start

Judas • **Christian** disloyalty; betrayal; lack of wisdom; one who takes a bribe

Judas tree • **flower language** unbelief, betrayal

judge restorer of natural balance; oracle; worldly authority; inner wisdom; the superego

Judgment (tarot) the mystery of birth in death; awakening; renewal; the need to break free of old thought patterns; personal consciousness starting to blend with the universal; healing; illumination; regeneration; hot-headedness; Bacchanalian/Dionysian ecstasy; associated with the need for personal discernment, introspection, reflection, objectivity

jug *see* **jar**

Juggler (tarot) *see* **Magician (tarot)**

jujube tree • **European** *jujube berries:* cure for chest diseases • **Islamic** the limits of space and time; charm against attack; *jujube thorns:* charm against the evil eye • **Taoist** *jujube berries:* food of the Immortals

Julian, Saint • **Christian** bounty; liberality

jumping joy; escape; ritual ascension • **Celtic** violent anger; insult; combat; escape • **Chinese** grief • **Egyptian** grief

jungle primitive life; basic instincts; unruliness; the unconscious; lurking danger

juniper resilience; longevity; remembrance; immortality; soporific; protection from evil; chastity; associated with gin, the archangels Raphael, Zadkiel • **juniper wood** eternity • **flower language** succor; protection; asylum • **Greco-Roman** protection; confidence; initiative; sacred to Hermes/Mercury; associated with Erinyes/Furies

Juno *see* **Hera/Juno**

Jupiter *see* **Zeus/Jupiter**

Jupiter (planet) associated with reason, the soul, understanding, perfected emotions, decision, intellectual will, courage, energy, expansion, bulk, benevolence, -5-, blue, violet, orange, the thighs, tin, Thursday, maturity, agrimony, East, Sagittarius, Capricorn, Pisces, maturity, the archangel Zadkiel • **Babylonian** associated with Marduk • **Chinese** associated with East, wood • **Kabalistic** associated with organization, East, judgment, command

jury conscience; the higher self; inner wisdom

justica • **flower language** the perfection of female loveliness

Justice (tarot) spiritual justice; balance of opposites; active administration of law; harmony; firmness; strict and correct behavior; restriction; pettiness; craft; associated with the need for caution in accepting advice; human conscience

K

K associated with personal magnetism, force, strength, sensitivity, cooperation, martial qualities, theater; nervousness, vitality; corresponds to the nerves, Leo, Mars (planet), -2- • **medieval** occasionally the Roman numeral for 151

Ka'aba • **Islamic** World Navel; the essence of God; the point of communication between man and God; the heart of existence; *seven circuits around the Ka'aba:* the seven attributes of God • *see also* **cube**

Kaf, Mount • **Islamic** the mother-mountain of all mountains, the boundary between the visible and invisible worlds, home of the simurg

kangaroo gregariousness; peacefulness; sportiveness; lack of intelligence; emblem of Australia

Kannon *see* **Guanyin**

katydid *see* **cicada**

keel stability; the lower instincts and desires

kennedia • **flower language** mental beauty

kerchief *on the head:* sickness, attribute of a housewife • *see also* **handkerchief**

Keridwen, Cauldron of • **Celtic** inexhaustibility, regeneration, and inspiration

kestrel Christ's image in the world

kettle *see* **cauldron**

kettle drum emblem of Denmark

key authority; mystery; secrecy; discretion; release; knowledge, especially forbidden knowledge; scholarship; education; initiation; enigma; the door to the underworld or heaven; a task to be performed and the means for carrying it out; the threshold of the unconscious; spiritual power; the power of opening and closing, binding and losing; attribute of the initiated, wardens, the Terrible Mother, Faithfulness personified • **bunch of keys** attribute of Fidelity personified • **two keys crossed** home rule; the keys of Parliament on the Isle of Man • **gold key** philosophical wisdom; the key to the gate of heaven, or superconsciousness; perfection; spiritual power • **silver key** psychological knowledge; material power; discernment; understanding; power of the subconscious; earthly power • **diamond key** the power to act • **iron key** locks up the gates of heaven; prevents entry of witches, demons, etc. into keyholes • **finding a key** the stage prior to finding treasure • **alchemic** the power of opening and closing; dissolution and coagulation • **Celtic** attribute of Epona • **Christian** attribute of the Church, the pope, SS Peter, Genevieve, pilgrims to Rome; *bunch of keys:* attribute of the Virgin Mary, SS Martha (usually attached to her girdle), Peter; *two keys crossed:* confession and absolution, excommunication and restoration, attribute of St. Peter; *gold key:* the authority or material power of the Church; *a silver key and a gold key:* the power of the Church to bind and to loose; *iron key and gold key:* attribute of St. Peter, the gold key opens heaven's gate, the iron key locks it; *angel with a key, descending into a pit with a dragon:* the Apocalypse; *soldier with keys:* St. Hippolytus • **Greco-Roman** attribute of Hecate, Persephone/Proserpine; *antique key:* associated with Hades/Pluto; *bunch of keys:* attribute of Cybele; *two keys:* attribute of Janus • **heraldic** trust; guardianship; violence; dominion; faithfulness; readiness to serve; attribute of chamberlains, masters of the cellar, etc • **Japanese** prosperity; *three keys of the granary:* love, wealth, happiness • **Jewish** power; trust; *keys of God:* the raising of the dead, birth, fertilizing rain; *bunch of keys:* attribute of Adam • **Mithraic** attribute of Mithras • **Teutonic** attribute of Frigga

keyhole vulva; place of entrance for demons, witches, etc.

Khamsin God's punishment • *see also* "east wind" under **wind**

kid *see* **goat**

kidneys bodily constitution; sexual pleasure; power; strength to suffer adversity; seat of feelings; associated with Venus (planet) • **Chinese** associated with water, sacred fish, the emotions • **Jewish** sacrifice; seat of hidden desire, the emotions

kimono emblem of Japan • **Japanese** *red kimono:* worn on the 61st birthday

king universal and archetypal man; the grandeur of universal and abstract man; stability; self-control; dalliance; protection; divine right; sovereignty; temporal power; supreme consciousness; elegance; the father; seat of life, energy and power; the supernatural; a concentrated father and hero image; the nation; the ideas of a nation • **crowned king** the consummation or victory of the supernatural • **aged king** the collective consciousness; world memory • **sick king** sterility of the spirit; the negative aspect of man; punishment for sins • **king and queen** the union of heaven and earth, the conscious and the unconscious, the masculine and feminine principles; the perfect whole; completeness; androgyny; the sun and the moon; heaven and earth; gold and silver; day and night • **alchemic man**; solar consciousness; sulfur; *naked king:* the early stage of transformation; *clothed king:* completed transformation; *king and queen:* sulfur and Mercurius, Conjunction; *king and queen in a fountain:* the water operations of Dissolution and Distillation • **Assyrian** *king on all fours eating grass:* Nebuchadnezzar • **Chinese** intermediary between heaven and earth • **Norse** *dwarf king:* Andvari, Hreidmar; *dwarf blacksmith:* Regin • *see also* **chess**

kingcup • **flower language** ingratitude; childishness; desire for riches

kingfisher quiet; connubial faith; mourning • **Chinese** gaudy raiment, especially female; beauty; dignity; calm; speed; retiring nature; faithfulness; happy marriage • **Greco-Roman** associated with Alcyone, Hera/Juno, Athena/Minerva, Thetis

kiss veneration of holy objects; peace; reconciliation; good will; good faith; fellowship; love; affection; power to break a spell; joining together; mutual adherence; unity; usually has more to do with membership than sex • **kissing a serpent's head** fellatio • **kissing the hand or foot** humility; solicitation of protection • Christian peace; *kiss of Judas:* betrayal

kite (bird) pride; scavenging; death; cruelty; senseless killing; cowardice; meanness; despicability; a false servant • **Chinese** raucousness; a coarse bird • **Greco-Roman** second sight; sacred to Apollo; associated with augury • **Japanese** a divine bird; attribute of the emperor

kite (toy) venture; theory; experiment; idle recreation • **American** associated with Benjamin Franklin • **Vietnamese** drives away evil spirits

kitten playfulness; wantonness; helplessness • *see also* **cat**

kneading fondling; masturbation

knee seat of power; moral strength; generative force; vitality • **placing someone on the knee** recognition of paternity; maternal care; adoption

kneeling prayer; submission to the laws of order; reverence; respect; humility; petitioning; progress by restraining the lower qualities; associated with Saturn (planet)

knife vengeance; death; sacrifice; circumcision; severance; freeing; division; phallus; the instinctive forces in man; a base, secret weapon, the inversion of the sword; the instinctive forces in man; the dark part of the ego; attribute of hunters • **Buddhist** deliverance; releasing the bonds of ignorance and pride • **Chinese** emblem of the moon • **Christian** martyrdom; attribute of SS Crispin; Crispianus; James the Less, Lucy; *flaying knife:* attribute of. St. Bartholomew (especially three knives); *knife in the hand or the head:* attribute of St. Peter Martyr • **Greco-Roman** *flaying knife:* attribute of the satyr Marsyas; *pruning knife:* attribute of Pomona • **Hindu** associated with cruelty; attribute of cruel and angry gods • **Jewish** associated with circumcision; attribute of Abraham, Isaac, the archangel Zadkiel; *knife with starry blue shield:* emblem of Abraham • *see also* **dagger**

knight the spirit controlling the instincts and desires; a spiritually developed or chivalrous person; noble manhood; spiritual struggle, quest • **green knight** apprentice; squire; initiate; beginner; impartial death; treason slaying youth and beauty • **giant green knight** the powers of nature and sometimes death as well • **red knight** virility; passion; blood; wounds; sublimation; the ability to overcome all trials and baseness through sacrifice; conqueror • **white knight** purity; innocence; illumination; gladness; the hero; the one chosen to conquer; open-heartedness • **black knight** sinfulness; powers of evil; expiation; sacrifice involution; penitence; the hidden; sorrow; reclusiveness • **knight errant** one who has not completed his spiritual development initiate • **knight on a horse** the spirit guiding the body • **knight on a goat** superiority; a saint • **heraldic** (especially on horseback) the soul guiding the body; the journey through life • **Spanish** *tall thin knight on a gaunt horse:* Don Quixote • *see also* **chess**

knitting related to weaving, spinning

knocking aspiration; death; birth; coition; heartbeat

knot an unchanging psychic situation; attachment to a previous position or belief; restraining; the inescapable; difficulty; entanglement; binding; union; interdependence; intimate relationship; intermingling streams; virginity; agreement; marriage; love; infinity; enclosure; protection • **loosening or untying a knot** freedom; salvation; solving a problem; death; liberation; loosening earthly bonds to live on a higher plane • **cutting a knot** taking a short, steep step toward salvation; the overcoming of difficulty by force • **tying a knot** marriage; compact; contract; casting a spell • **Gordian knot** mystic center; the labyrinth; *cutting the Gordian knot:* short-lived victory • **knot interlaced with initials** marriage • **Chinese** longevity; binding the good and an obstacle to evil • **Christian** *three knots in a ecclesiastical girdle:* faith hope and love, or the vows of poverty, chastity, and obedience, attribute of Franciscans; *runic knot:* love of God • **Egyptian** life; *Knot of Isis:* immortality • **Hindu** *untying a knot:* attaining immortality • **Islamic** protection; *tying a knot in a beard:* charm against the evil eye; *tying knots in clothes:* charm for protection for pilgrims caught in a sea storm; *knotted clothes:* forbidden in Mecca • **Jewish** *Solomon's knot:* wisdom, divine inscrutability • **Russian** *knot in the village priest's girdle becoming undone:* harbinger of a birth • **witchcraft** obstruction; curse • *see also* **mystic knot**

koala emblem of Australia

Kokopelli • **Pueblo** fertility; seduction; trickster

Koran sacred wisdom; spiritual insight; associated with Muslims

Krishna • **Hindu** the personification of the fully realized, perfected self; androgyny

Kshatriya caste *see* **caste**

kundalini • **Hindu** latent energy; pure and creative energy; path to enlightenment

ky-lin • **Chinese** the union of yin and yang; benevolence; good will; fertility; herald of the birth of a sage or wise emperor; *riding a ky-lin:* attaining fame

L

L Roman numeral for 50; associated with success, popularity, versatility, intuition, activity, beauty, violent death, the divine Word; corresponds to the throat, Libra, Uranus (planet); equivalent to -3- • **tarot** associated with the Hanged Man

labarum *see* **XP**

label • **heraldic** first-born son

labradorite subtlety; hidden beauty

laburnum • **flower language** forsaken; pensive beauty • **Slavic** associated with marriage rites

labyrinth the world; the underworld; mystic center; divine inscrutability; the wind; pain; mental torture; a complex problem; confusion; fury; vulva; the subconscious; loss of the spirit in creation and the necessity of finding it again; the difficulty uniting oneself with God; error; separation from one's spirit and from God; initiation, death, and rebirth; return to the womb; spiritual journey • **Christian** originally the path of ignorance with hell at the center; trap for devils; the perplexities and problems encountered in the world; pilgrimage of the soul from earth to heaven • **Greco-Roman** the hero-savior Theseus followed Ariadne's golden thread of divine instinct to slay savage nature represented by the Minotaur; the subconscious; secrecy; inscrutability • **Minoan** the solar masculine principle surrounded by the lunar feminine principle; together it is the sun taking up the mists or miasma • **Oceanic** the journey of the soul in the realms of the dead • **Sumero-Semitic** an imitation of the lower world

lace attribute of females; associated with 13th wedding anniversaries

ladder ambition; ascension; the connection between heaven and earth; conjunction of heaven and earth; World Axis; passage from one world to another • **rungs** the years of human life • **seven or 12-runged** the degrees or stages of initiation • **climbing a ladder** success; achievement; the gradual acquisition of knowledge; the ceaseless striving of man; overcoming the difficulties of the material world; coition • **descending a ladder** demotion; failure; leaving the higher world for a lower one; abandonment of standards, beliefs • **Buddhist** attribute of Sakya-muni • **Christian** the Ascension of Christ; attribute of the Crucifixion, SS Benedict, Angela Merici, John Climacus; *ladder to heaven, or monks in white habits on a ladder:* associated with St. Romuald; *nuns observing soldiers scaling city walls on ladders:* associated with St. Clare; *people climbing up ladders against a house:* associated with St. Andrew; *brazen ladder:* associated with St. Perpetua • **Egyptian** attribute of Hathor, Horus, Set • **Gnostic** *eagle atop a ladder:* The Way • **heraldic** fearlessness in attacking; *ladder against a tower:* wariness of spiritual and bodily attack • **Islamic** leads the faithful to God; associated with the ascent of Mohammed • **Japanese** communication between heaven and earth; attribute of Amaterasu • **Jewish** means of communication between God and man; attribute of Jacob (especially with angels on the ladder) • **Mithraic** *seven-runged ladder:* passage of the soul through the seven heavens • **Montagnard** connection between heaven and earth; Cosmic Tree • **North American Indian** access to the other world • **Ural-Altaic** communication with the spirit world

ladle attribute of housewives • **Christian** attribute of St. Martha • **Hindu** *ladle and bowl:* attribute of Kali

lady slippers • **flower language** fickleness, capricious beauty

ladybird *see* **ladybug**

ladybug lucky; delight; trust; associated with red in the beneficial sense; connected with the scarab • **German** child-bringer • **Middle Ages** associated with the Virgin Mary

Lady's bed straw (plant) • **Christian** associated with the manger of Christ

lady's mantle (plant) • **flower language** fashion

lagerstraemia • **flower language** eloquence

lake prime matter; the occult; the mysterious; giver of fertility; uterine waters; source of creative power; transition of life and death, often in a destructive sense; the unconscious; the feminine principle; the humid; an eye of the earth • **reflection in a lake** the conscious; revelation; self-contemplation • **Celtic** abode of supernatural beings; access to other worlds; otherworld wisdom; location of Tir-nan-og • **Chinese** receptive wisdom; absorption; the humid and the passive • **Egyptian** the Lower Waters • **Gallic** deities; abode of deities

lamb sweetness; tranquility; refreshment; peace; forgiveness; meekness; docility; weakness; innocence; sacrifice; temperance; frolic; purity; the just man; neophytes; mystic rebirth; associated with Spring; attribute of the personifications of Innocence, Gentleness, Patience, Humility, Phlegmatic Man • **lion lying with calf** peace; Paradise regained; primordial unity; the Golden Age; the end of the temporal world • **Chinese** filial piety • **Christian** sacrificial victim; Christ; God's love; attribute of SS Agatha of Sicily, Catherine of Alexandria, Colette, Francis of Assisi, Genevieve, Joachim, Joanna, Regina, sometimes SS Clement, John the Baptist; *crucifixion of a lamb:* the crucifixion of Christ; *lamb with nimbus:* Christ, often shown on a hill (the Church) with four streams running down it (the Gospels); *lamb with banner:* attribute of St. Agnes; *lamb with cross:* Christ; the Crucifixion; *lamb lying down:* the suffering of Christ; *Christ carrying a lamb:* Christ bearing the sins of mankind; *lamb standing up:* the triumphant, risen Christ; *lamb with white flag with a cross on it:* the body of Christ, that is, the Church (if the flag is on a cruciform staff, it indicates the way in which Christ died); *lamb with book with seven seals:* Christ as judge at the Second Coming; *lamb with seven horns and seven eyes:* the seven gifts of the Holy Spirit; the Apocalypse; *lamb and dove:* the body and soul of Christ; his human and divine nature; *lamb with a row of sheep:* Christ leading his disciples • **folkloric** *black lamb:* a flock cannot prosper without one, but more than one is unlucky • **Greco-Roman** *lamb skin:* the Golden Fleece, attribute of Jason • **heraldic** patience in suffering; gentleness; *lamb with staff, banner, and/or cross (paschal lamb):* faith; innocence; bravery; purity; gentleness; resolute spirit • **Islamic** sacrificial victim • **Jewish** sacrificial victim; the coming messiah; the child of Israel who belongs to God's flock; *slain lamb:* the Passover; *lamb on an altar as a sacrifice:* associated with Abel • *see also* **fleece; sheep**

lambstongue (plant) associated with Mars (planet)

lameness a weak or corrupt soul; defect or imbalance in the soul or spirit; castration; the imperfection of the demiurge who makes the imperfect world; an indication that the person may have a sixth sense or other compensatory power; the brand left upon people who have come near to the power of a supreme deity; attribute of smith gods, lightning gods • **Greco-Roman** attribute of Hephaestus/Vulcan, occasionally the Moirae/Fates • **Jewish** Jacob; *prophet with lame foot:* Balaam

Lamia • **Greek** the Terrible Mother; cruelty; infanticide; an evil woman; the jealousy of a childless woman

lamp intelligence; learning; wisdom; the word of God; life; immortality; remembrance; guidance; light; the stars; goodness; good works; vigilance; purity; virginity; love; piety; charity; beauty; self-sacrifice; attribute of Florence Nightingale, the Persian sibyl, the personifications of Night, Vigilance • **oil lamp** intelligence; learning; the Word of God • **extinguishing a lamp** death; abandonment of hope • **lighting a lamp** creating hope, understanding • **old man with a lamp** Diogenes • **genie issuing from a lamp** magic source of wealth; male masturbation and its objectified emotional consequences • **Chinese** *red lamp:* allows truth to be distinguished from falsity • **Christian** sacrifice; love; divine presence; attribute of SS Agatha, Brigit, Gudula, Genevieve, Hugh, Hiltrudis, Lucy; *abbot anointing a boy's lips with lamp oil:* the abbot is St. Nilus; *seven lamps:* the seven gifts of the Holy Spirit, the seven early churches; *five maidens with lit lamps:* the five wise virgins; *five maidens with extinguished lamps:* the five foolish virgins; *sanctuary lamp in Anglican and Roman Catholic churches:* the presence of the reserved sacrament • **Egyptian** attribute of Isis • **folkloric** *blue flame:* a spirit passing; the presence of witches • **Greco-Roman** attribute of Hestia/Vesta; *naked maiden with a lamp, standing over a sleeping god:* Psyche standing over Eros/Cupid • **heraldic** transitoriness; life; light; spirituality • **Hindu** emblem of Ketu; *oil of a lamp:* devotion; the ocean; *lamp wick:* earth; mind; *lamp flame:* love • *see also* **lantern**

lamprey phallus; voracity; ingenuity; evil; sin; the debilitating effect of sin • **alone, or entwined with a serpent** adultery

lance war; a kingly weapon; an earthly weapon as opposed to the spiritual implications of the sword; truth; discretion; phallus; the solar; sun rays; World Axis; attribute of the lower form of knighthood; associated with the primitive unconscious • **sheaf of lances** a thunderbolt • **Christian** the Passion of Christ, attribute of SS Barnabas, Jude, Longinus, Matthew; *lance with three stones:* attribute of St. Matthias; *broken lance:* attribute of St. George of Cappadocia; *lance with spear and arrows:* attribute of St. Thomas; *lance piercing a heart:* the Passion of Christ *saint in armor with shield and lance:* St. Demetrius • **Greco-Roman** war; the solar; attribute of Artemis/Diana, Athena/Minerva, Ares/Mars, Achilles • **heraldic** courage; martial readiness; defense of honor; devotion to honor; speed; freedom; knightly service • **Hindu** strength; power; victory over evil; divine wisdom; attribute of Indra • **Japanese** attribute of Izanagi • **Jewish** *lance with broken sword:* attribute of Micah • **Mongolian** *blue lance:* attribute of Er Toshtuk • **Sumero-Semitic** *pillar topped with lance:* Marduk; *pillar topped with ram's head:* Ea-Oannes • *see also* **javelin; spear**

Lancelot, Sir • **Celtic** bravery; male beauty; deception; human passion; that which appears to be flawless but is not

lancet attribute of a doctor, SS Cosimas, Damian • **doctor cutting a patient's forehead with a lancet** a quack operation for stones in the head

lantana • **flower language** rigor; sharpness

lantern transitory life in the face of the eternal; transitory truth; distraction; individual light (as opposed to cosmic light); attribute of St. Christopher, Diogenes, Judas in the betrayal of Christ, hermits • **lantern and dragon** attribute of the Persian sibyl • **heraldic** watchfulness; service giving an alarm • *see also* **lamp; torch**

Laodicea, Church of • **Christian** associated with lukewarmness, silence, the pituitary gland, the seventh seal

lap (human) procreation; protection; flirtation; euphemism for female genitalia

lapis lazuli nobility; success; divine favor; ability; joy; love; fidelity; courage; stone for 9th wedding anniversaries; charm for healing, protection, psychic power; associated with the archangels Anael, Zadkiel • **Amerindian** the starry night • **Babylonian** *palm tree with lapis lazuli branches:* Tree of Life; *lapis lazuli flute:* attribute of Tammuz • **Chinese** success; ability • **Christian** chastity; part of a bishop's ring • **Greco-Roman** love; emblem of Aphrodite/Venus • **Mesopotamian, Persian** the starry night • **Sumerian** the firmament and its power; attribute of temples

Lapland land of witchcraft and sorcery

lapwing royalty; craftiness; deceit; a stupid, conceited fellow who thinks he knows better than his elders; treachery; ill omen • **Greco-Roman** a disguise Zeus/Jupiter • **Islamic** a prophetic bird of Solomon • **Jewish** a sacred bird

larch impregnability; stability; independence; boldness; immortality; associated with the archangel Raphael • **flower language** audacity; boldness • **Siberian** Cosmic Tree

lark dawn; gaiety; cheerfulness; youthful enthusiasm; ardor; recklessness; activity; alertness; joy; wisdom; connection between heaven and earth; natural art; visionary inspiration; the humility of the priesthood; treason; evolution and involution; of manifestation; associated with heaven, love, Spring • **lark's song** pure and happy prayer • **Gallic** a sacred bird; good omen; *lark's legs:* charm against harassment, evil • **Greco-Roman** disguise for Athena/Minerva

larkspur • **flower language** swiftness; lightness; levity; *double larkspur:* haughtiness; *pink larkspur:* fickleness

larvae • **Roman** evil souls

lash *see* **whip**

lasso knowledge; attribute of a cowboy in the American West

latch *door latch:* the ability to resist change

laurel *see* **bay laurel**

laurestina • **flower language** a token; I die if neglected

lavabo cleansing; purity

lavender (color) associated with Neptune (planet)

lavender (plant) virtue; industry; acknowledgment; precaution; associated with Gemini • **French lavender** emblem of Distrust personified • **sea lavender** sympathy • **flower language** distrust; *sea lavender:* dauntlessness • **heraldic** constancy; loyalty

laver of brass Old Testament worship

lawn (grass) submission; emblem of suburbia

Lazarus • **Christian** resurrection; rebirth; healing

lead gravity; weight and density; especially in a spiritual sense; a base metal; stubbornness; ignorance; inertness; death; torture; hypocrisy; matter; associated with Capricorn, Saturn (planet), the archangel Cassiel • **dove embedded in lead** the spirit embedded in matter • **alchemic** baseness; unregenerate man; opaque consciousness

leaf happiness; transitoriness; fertility; growth; renewal; a true fact or idea; people coming and going • **dead leaf** sadness; death; decay; Autumn • **fallen leaves** discarded ideas • **raking leaves** remembrance • **green leaf** nobility; sound judgment; hope; revival; renewal • **yellow leaf** old age • **crown of leaves** divinity; triumph; victory • **five-pointed leaf** the microcosm • **oak leaf** bravery • **fig leaf** shame; obscuring an unpleasant fact • **branch with green leaves** friendship; protection; a tavern pleasures • **Chinese** *leaves of the Cosmic Tree:* all beings in the universe • **Christian** the result of charity and other good works; *girdle of leaves:* attribute of St. Onuphrius • **Jewish** *fig leaf:* attribute of Adam and Eve after eating the fruit of the Tree of the Knowledge of Good and Evil

Leah • **Jewish** the active life

leash restraint; control; the law

leather resistance; lack of sympathy; stupidity; insensitivity; faithlessness; associated with 3rd wedding anniversaries • **leather medal** farcical award for stupidity or inferiority • **cheveril** conscience; elasticity; flexibility • **Jewish** *leather girdle:* attribute of Elijah

leaven spiritual nature permeating lower nature; the Kingdom of Heaven; the Word; Christian influence; increasing corruption; malice; wickedness • *see also* **yeast**

lectern education • **Christian** *lectern with eagle:* the Gospel taking flight; *lectern with pelican feeding her young:* the atoning work of Christ;

double-headed lectern: the Old and New Testaments; the Law and the Gospels; the Epistles and the Gospels

ledge danger

leech avarice; intemperance; grandiloquence; emblem of a physician • **horse leech** unending greed

leek victory; protection; liveliness; emblem of Wales • **Celtic** attribute of Aeddon • **Christian** attribute of St. David • *see also* **houseleek**

lees the lower instincts of man that remain unpurified

left side associated with the past, the sinister, the repressed, the illegitimate, the abnormal, involution, death, the unconscious, the feminine, introversion, the magical, the lunar, clumsiness, awkwardness • **Chinese** yin; the side of honor except in wartime, when it became the right side • **Japanese** associated with wisdom, loyalty, instinct, the sun, the male • **Occidental** the side of honor • **political** associated with dissatisfaction with the social order, demand for one's rights, dynamism, liberation, risk-taking, innovation, the quest for greater justice and progress, liberalism, progressivism • *see also* **right side**

legs firmness; foundation; nobility; elevation; erection; founding; motion; speed; energy; victory; support of the soul; euphemism for genitals; supremacy (especially when bestriding something) • **knees and calves** associated with Saturn (planet) • **very long legs** stirring emotions; love of excitement • **short legs** often a characteristic of sun deities • **one-legged god** the phallic; the lunar • **art** *crossed legs, right over left:* the posture of Crusaders, Knights Templar, kings, noblemen • **Chinese** *bird hopping on one leg:* rain omen • **Christian** *crossed legs, right over left:* prayer; the position of Christ's legs on the cross; *youth's severed leg restored:* associated with St. Anthony of Padua; *patient with one black leg and one white leg:* attribute of SS Cosmas and Damian; *horse's leg removed for shoeing:* attribute of St. Eloi • **Egyptian** lifting • **Gallic** *lark's legs:* charm against harassment, evil • **heraldic** strength; expedition; stability; *three legs joined at the thigh:* emblem of the Isle of Man; *three legs joined at the thigh with Medusa's head in the middle:* emblem of Sicily, Palermo • **Hindu** *three-legged man with eight teeth:* Kubera • **Kabalistic** firmness; glory • **Norse** *three-legged hare:* the hare in the moon • **Serbian** *six-legged monster with gnarled horns:* Bukavac

lemon sourness; sharpness grief; mockery; enthusiasm; pleasant thoughts; discretion; barrenness; failure; defeat; *lemon tree:* associated with the archangel Sandalphon • **Christian** fidelity in love; emblem of the Virgin Mary • **flower language** zest; *lemon blossoms:* fidelity in love; discretion • **Jewish** harvest; occasionally the fruit of the Tree of Knowledge; *carried in the left hand:* attribute of the Feast of Tabernacles • **Semitic** associated with Dionysus

lemur (spirit) *see* **ghost**

Lent • **Christian** suffering and sacrifice, particularly of Christ; austerity; penance

lentil humbleness; poor man's food

Leo (zodiac) associated with reproduction, vital forces, solar power, the will, feelings and emotions, generosity, magnanimity, organization, clear judgment, perception, the spiritual beginnings of man, aggressiveness, intolerance, opinionation, fire, the sun, lust for life, the archangel Michael

leogriff illusion; the Terrible Mother

leopard ferocity; aggression; cruelty; valor; stealth; bravery; destruction; fraud; jealousy; dark force; lust; sin; pride; the opinionated lower mind full of errors that are mingled with truth; attribute of Fury personified • **leopard lying with lamb or kid** peace • **crouching leopard** jealousy • **African** attribute of storm gods • **Chinese** bravery; ferocity; *leopard skin bag:* attribute of Vaisravenna • **Christian** the devil; the duplicity of the devil; sin; the Antichrist; concupiscence; *leopard with Christ and the Magi:* the incarnation of Christ that was necessary for the redemption of sin • **Dahomean** attribute of royalty • **Egyptian** the dignity of the High Priest; attribute of Osiris; associated with Set • **Greco-Roman** attribute of Artemis/Diana; *chariot pulled by leopards:* attribute of Dionysus/Bacchus • **heraldic** bravery; a valiant warrior who has engaged in hazardous undertakings; power and pride; freedom; cunning; impetuosity; activity • **Hindu** occasional attribute of Shiva • **Ibo** associated with fertility • **Jewish** swiftly striking disaster • **Middle Ages** Christ • *see also* **jessant-di-lis; panther**

leper the unclean; the outcast; the spiritually and morally fallen; the lower mind troubled with conflicting emotions, desires, and confused ideas

leprosy rotting of the spirit from lack of moral progress; divine punishment, especially for pride; punishment for eating tabooed food

Lethe • **Greek** oblivion; forgetfulness of the past

letter (epistle) communication; an ill omen; opportunity; new idea; insight

lettuce temperance • **Egyptian** fertility • **flower language** coldness; cold-heartedness • **Jewish** return of spring; resurrection; redemption; a characteristic food of feasts • **Phoenician** sacred to Adoni; ephemeral existence

level (tool) equality; temperance; justice; transcendent knowledge • **Chinese** the just man; attribute of a magistrate • **heraldic** virtue; equity

Levi • **Jewish** priest; priesthood without land

Leviathan envy; the waters of Chaos; the power of the deep; a primordial monster of the ocean and chaos; rebellion against the creator; God's playfulness; duality; Evil personified; a totalitarian state • **Jewish** will be served as food at the End Time • **Phoenician** a monster of primeval chaos • *see also* **whale**

Leydig cells • **Hindu** associated with sexuality and propagation

liana • **Thai** the original link between heaven and earth • *see also* **vine**

Libra associated with cosmic and psychic equilibrium, fairness, diplomacy, idealism, legality, justice, harmony, communication, indecision, changeability, air, Venus (planet), the archangel Anael

library the higher mind; the soul; intellectual knowledge; reservoir of knowledge

lichen hardship • **flower language** dejection; solitude

licking flattery; subservience; affection; cleansing; healing

licorice (plant) • **flower language** I declare against you

light the spirit; manifestation of divinity; virtue; intellect; creative force; cosmic energy; cosmic creation; the Word; encounter with the ultimate reality; purity; moral value; source of goodness; knowledge; wisdom; primordial intellect; truth; illumination; the nous; evolution; ascension; the masculine principle; creative force; optimism; the past; discovery; understanding; truth; divine revelation; divine love • **darkness and light** the two opposing aspects of the Great Mother — creator/destroyer, birth/death, etc. • **sunlight** direct knowledge • **moonlight** analytical knowledge • **Christmas tree lights** souls; heavenly bodies • **Buddhist** truth; liberation; direct knowledge; transcendence of the world; identification with Buddha; *pure light:* ultimate reality; the Void; *impure light:* rebirth into the world of phenomena; *boundless light:* associated with Amitabha • **Chinese** yang; heavenly power • **Christian** belief; grace; charity; Christ • **Egyptian** *Anubis:* life-giving, favorable, uplifting light; *Set:* evil light from dark places • **folkloric** when lamps burn blue there are witches about • **Greco-Roman** Zeus/Jupiter; carried in Eleusinian rites • **Hindu** the self; Atman; cosmic creation; progenitive power; spirituality; wisdom; wisdom; sanctity; the manifestation of Krishna • **Islamic** pure being; the heavens; air; the manifestation of divine knowledge; majesty; beauty; the intellect; the Word; the godhead; the illumination of Allah • **Persian** pure being; pure light • **Taoist** the Tao; Light of Heaven; unity; manifestation of non-being • **Zoroastrian** Ormuzd, Ahura Mazda • *see also* **darkness**

lighthouse *see* **beacon**

lightness indicates an advanced spiritual state; wisdom

lightning enlightenment; spiritual illumination; revelation; producer of inward light; descent of power; speed; sudden realization of the truth; masculine power; manifestation of a deity's power; divine message; phallus; fecundity; the male orgasm; brevity; an act of God; attribute of storm and thunder gods • **death by lightning** immediate transmission to heaven • **lightning through clouds** mythology • **Australian aboriginal** a tumescent penis • **Christian** *lightning striking a tree near a monk*: the monk is St. Philip Benizzi • **Greco-Roman** attribute of Zeus/Jupiter • **heraldic** swiftness; power • **Hindu** Agni; truth; the flash of the third eye of Shiva; attribute of Rudra • **Manichean** the Virgin of Light • **North American Indian** revelation by the Great Spirit • **Ural-Altaic** *being struck by lightning*: immediate initiation

Lightning Struck Tower (tarot) *see* **House of God (tarot)**

Liguria, Italy lying; deceit; abnormal coition

lilac (color) friendship; fraternal love; sometimes, male homosexuality

lilac (plant) youth; first love; spring; fastidiousness; mourning; associated with Libra • **flower language** *field lilac*: humility; *purple lilac*: the first emotions of love; *white lilac*: purity, modesty, youthful innocence • **heraldic** beauty; youth; pride; innocence

Lilith • **Jewish** the Terrible Mother; temptress; the discarded mistress taking revenge; hatred of family life, children, marriage • **Kabalistic** wife of Satan

lily purity; virginity; the purified soul; heavenly bliss; peace; connubial chastity; mystic center; majesty; queenly beauty; grace; immortality; chastity; showiness; fertility; phallus; the masculine principle; desire; repentance; grief; sorrow; danger; caution; deadly beauty; attribute of virgin goddesses • **day lily** fleeting beauty •

tiger lily female courage; fertility; productivity; pride • **alchemic** *white lily*: the feminine principle • **Chinese** *day lily*: dispels care • **Christian** purity; innocence; the Virgin Mary; emblem of the Annunciation, the Immaculate Conception, Easter; attribute of virgin saints (especially in the early Church), the archangel Gabriel, the Erythraean sibyl, Christ, the Virgin Mary, SS Anthony of Padua, Casimir, Catherine of Siena (usually surmounting a cross), Clare, Dominic, Euphemia, Francis of Assisi, Francis Xavier, Gertrude, Joachim, Joseph (may also be with carpenter's square), Louis of Toulouse, Philip Neri (usually he is also praying before an image of the Virgin Mary), Scholastica, Thomas Aquinas; *flag lily*: attribute of St. Louis of France; *lily with a dove*: the Annunciation; *lily entwined around a crucifix*: attribute of St. Nicholas of Tolentino; *lily with IHC in a triangle*: the dual nature of Christ; *rose and lily*: emblem of the Virgin Mary; *lily among thorns*: the purity of the Immaculate Conception taking place in the sinful world; *sword on one side, sword on the other in art*: innocence and guilt respectively • **Egyptian** emblem of Upper Egypt; fruitfulness • **flower language** majesty (especially the imperial lily); *day lily*: coquetry; *yellow lily*: falsehood, gaiety; *white lily*: purity, sweetness • **Greco-Roman** purity; emblem of Hera/Juno, Artemis/Diana • **heraldic** magnificent beauty; purity; chastity; *tiger lily*: wealth; pride • **Italian** *flag lily*: emblem of the Medici • **Jewish** trust in God; emblem of Judah • **Minoan** attribute of Britomartis • **Sumero-Semitic** fruitfulness • *see also* **lotus** which is the symbolic equivalent in the East; **lily of the valley; water lily**

lily of the valley daintiness; sweetness; humility; virginity; return of spring; return of happiness; modesty; associated with Gemini • **Christian** attribute of the Virgin Mary, Christ, the Immaculate Conception, Advent, St. Leonard • **flower language** the return of happiness • **Jewish** emblem of Israel

Limbo place of waiting • **Christian** place of those who lived good lives but are unbaptized • **Greek** abode of stillborn or prematurely dead babies

lime tree (genus Tilia, not the citrus tree) *see* **linden**

Lincoln, Abraham • **American** honesty; freedom; martyrdom; equality

linden gentleness; modesty; sweetness; beauty; happiness; a feminine tree; feminine grace; hospitality; judgment; protection; associated with Sagittarius • **leaf** lightness • **flower lan-**

guage conjugal love; *American linden:* matrimony • **Greco-Roman** *oak and linden:* Philemon and Baucis respectively; conjugal happiness • **heraldic** (often the leaf or branch only) tenderness; life; resurrection; vitality; energy; charm; grace • **Teutonic** Tree of Life; *lights and/or luminous balls on a linden tree:* celestial bodies

lindworm war; pestilence

line (geometric) division; boundary; limitation; measurement; *straight line:* light; rectitude; undeviating conduct; infinity; freedom; *horizontal line:* the passive; the temporal; *vertical line:* the active; the spiritual; the cosmic axis; *wavy line:* heat; motion • *see also* **zigzag**

linen purity; destiny; homage; divine truth; priestly dress; ultimate reality; wisdom; goodness; love; related to music, burial shrouds; associated with 12th wedding anniversaries • **woman in linen** a virtuous woman • **Christian** *linen altar cloth:* the winding sheet of Christ; *fine linen:* purity; righteousness; associated with the Church Triumphant • **Greco-Roman** *linen thread:* attribute of the Moirae/Fates • **Jewish** *linen vestments:* the earth

lingam • **Hindu** Shiva; the phallus; creativity; the masculine generative principle; cosmic creation; renewal of life; energy; strength; spiritual virility; World Navel • *see also* **yoni**

linnet courtship; motherly love

lint (plant) • **flower language** I feel all my obligations

lion the king; King of the Beasts; King of the Jungle; majesty; nobility; royal dignity; the sun; the masculine principle; the spirit; continual struggle; mystic center; victory; index of latent passions; depraved social drive; the danger of being devoured by the unconscious; gold; blood; earth; fertility; the underworld; time; valor; virility; strength; health; compassion; aloofness; generosity; gratitude; an avenging god; guardianship; wildness; ferocity; cruelty; rage; ambition; melancholy; a sinner; pride; a man between 30 and 40 years of age; male sexual desire; courage; associated with Summer, Leo, July, the archangel Michael; attribute of the personifications of Africa, Pride, Wrath, Choler, Victory; emblem of England, the United Kingdom • **two lions back to back** sunrise and sunset • **lion's mane** fire • **lion skin** attribute Fortitude personified, sun heroes; *lion's skin on an ass:* a coward who hectors; a fool who apes a wise man • **bull and lion** death • **lion with prey in its paws** all-devouring death • **eagle devouring a lion** victory of the evolutive over the involutive respectively • **lion fighting**

a serpent higher consciousness fighting lower desires respectively • **tiger fighting a lion** the instincts fighting higher consciousness respectively • **woman wrestling with a lion** Fortitude personified • **half-lion/half-goat** duality (love/hate, good/evil, etc.) • **lion eating straw** peace • **winged lion** androgyny; union of two natures • **lion and unicorn** two contending powers of the universe, such as positive/negative, male/female • **old lion** the setting sun • **young lion** the rising sun • **victorious lion** the exaltation of virility • **tamed lion** the subjugation of virility • **lion and unicorn** contending solar/lunar, male/female forces • **lion killing a boar** the sun overcoming Winter • **lion and dragon devouring each other** union without loss of identity • **lion lying with calf, lamb, or kid** peace; Paradise regained; primordial unity; the Golden Age; the end of the temporal world • **hero slaying a lion** taming the heat of the midday sun • **lion throne** subjugation of cosmic forces • **green lion** the young corn god; *changing to gold:* green corn changing to the yellow corn of the harvest • **alchemic** *red lion:* sulfur; the masculine principle; *green lion:* the beginning of alchemical work; the all-transmuting elixir; *two lions:* the dual nature of Mercurius; the nous; *eagle devouring a lion:* a volatile component volatilizing a fixed component respectively • **Buddhist** defender of the law; wisdom of Buddha; spiritual zeal; bravery; advancement and cognizance; steed of Ratnasambhava; *lion throne:* occasional attribute of Buddha; *lion cub:* new initiated Bodhisattva; *lion with a cub underfoot:* compassion; Buddha ruling the world; *lion's roar:* Buddha's fearless teaching of the Dharma; *lion with flaming tail:* temple guardian • **Chaldean** Nergal; the hostile aspect of the sun; the fierce heat of the solstice; *lion with two lion's heads back to back:* Nergal as god of the sun and the underworld • **Chinese** valor; energy; strength; warrior form of Chiu-shou; *lion with ball underfoot:* duality; sun; Cosmic Egg; *lion with horse:* the man in marriage; *lion with flowers:* the woman in marriage • **Christian** vigilance; fortitude; spiritual watchfulness; imperious will; uncontrolled strength; tyrannical domination; solitude; the Resurrection; the devil; Christ as king; a hermit; one of the guardian of the Throne of God; emblem of contemplation; attribute of SS Adrian, Euphemia, Germanicus, Natalia, Prisca, Thecla; *old lion:* attribute of St. Jerome; *lion with thorn in paw:* attribute of St. Jerome; *winged lion:* emblem of St. Mark; *lion scratching out graves in the desert:*

associated with SS Anthony the Great, Mary of Egypt, Onuphrius, Paul the Hermit; *two lions:* attribute of SS Onuphrius, Paul the Hermit; *rooster and lion:* good and evil respectively; *lion at the feet of saints and martyrs:* magnanimity; *roaring lion:* occasionally, the devil; *lion's body with human head and hands:* the Beast of the Second Coming; *winged lion:* emblem of St. Mark • **Egyptian** protection; guardian; occasionally, Ra; solar when shown with a sun disk; lunar when shown with a crescent moon; *lion or lion-headed man with four wings:* the South wind, Shehbui; *lion with human head:* union of the intellect with physical power; *lion with a human head holding up the sky:* Shu; *two lions back to back with solar disk:* past and present, yesterday and tomorrow; *lion with solar disk:* Ra; the solar; *lion with crescent moon:* the lunar; Osiris; *lion-headed serpent:* protection against evil; *lion-headed man:* Maahes; *lion-headed woman with solar disk and uraeus:* Bast; *woman with the head of a lion, globe, ankh, and staff:* Tefnut; *lion with hippopotamus hindquarters and crocodile jaws:* Ammit; *dwarf wearing a lion's skin:* Bes • **Greco-Roman** royalty; solar fire; the ravening power of death; man's victory over death; attribute of Apollo, Artemis/Diana, Tyche/Fortuna, the Gorgons, sometimes Dionysus/Bacchus; *lion skin:* attribute of Heracles/Hercules; *Heracles/Hercules wrestling with a lion:* the solar hero overcoming death; *half-lion/half-goat:* Pan/Faunus; *man attacked by a lion, hands trapped in an oak tree trunk:* Milo of Croton; *chariot drawn by lions:* attribute of Hera/Juno; *lion with head and breasts of a woman:* inscrutability, pestilence; *humans changed into lions:* Atalanta and Hippomenes • **heraldic** courage; valor; a soldier; dauntlessness; strength; ferocity • **Hindu** Supreme Lord of rhythm; guardian of the North; attribute of Devi, Durga; steed of Sitala; *lion and lioness:* shakta-shakti; *half-lion/half-man:* Agni, Narasimha; *lion face by itself:* Kirttimukha • **Indic** *three lions seated back to back:* emblem of the state of India, King Ashoka • **Iranian** emblem of Iran • **Islamic** protection against evil; *Lion of Judah:* Ali, son-in-law of Mohammed • **Italian** emblem of Venice; attribute of Venice personified • **Japanese** the King of Beasts; *lion and peony:* attribute of the Queen of Flowers • **Jewish** mightiness; cruelty; attribute of Hosea; emblem of the tribe of Judah; *winged lion:* South, the Lion of Judah; *man wrestling with a lion:* Samson, David; *lion and harp:* attribute of David; *unharmed man in lion's den:* Daniel,

God's redemption of his people • **Kalmyk** *lion head:* North, Northeast • **Middle Ages** watchfulness; the Resurrection • **Mithraic** the solar; the 4th grade of initiation; solar fire; *lion and bull:* death; *lion and stag:* the moment of death; *lion-headed deity:* Mithras • **Persian** royalty; solar power; light; *lion with sun:* emblem of Persia • **Phrygian** *chariot pulled by lions:* attribute of Cybele • **Sumero-Semitic** sovereignty; strength; courage; solar fire; *two lions:* attribute of Inanna, Ishtar as the Great Mother; *lion with a bough in its paws or with two heads:* Ninib; *pillar topped with lion's head:* Nergal; *woman warrior seated on a lion:* Anath • **Tibetan** attribute of Tara • *see also* **Ammit; Chimera; griffin; hippogriff; jessant-di-lis; leogriff; lioness**

lioness the solar; female sexual desire; protection; maternity; emblem of goddesses of Crete, Mycenae, Phrygia, Sparta, Syria, Thrace; attribute of the Great Mother, virgin warrior goddesses, love goddesses, earth goddesses • **lionesses pulling a chariot** attribute of the Great Mother • **Buddhist** attribute of Tara • **Egyptian** maternity; attribute of Sekmet, mother goddesses; personification of Bast • **Greco-Roman** attribute of Artemis/Diana, Cybele, the Gorgons; Hecate, Ops; Rhea, Tyche/Fortuna; *chariot drawn by lionesses:* attribute of Cybele, Hera/Juno; *lioness and bees:* Demeter/Ceres and her priestesses respectively • **Hindu** the Word; the power of manifestation; *lion and lioness:* shakta-shakti; attribute of Tara • **Tibetan** attribute of Tara

lips associated with sexuality, language, the Word, eloquence, desire for knowledge • **art** the wind • **sealed lips** repression; secrecy • **thin lips** cruelty; frailty • **thick lips** crudity; grossness

liquor the desire to escape reality

lisping infanthood; voluptuousness; associated with homosexuality • **Spanish** associated with royalty, nobility and upper classes

liver seat of passion, the soul; lust; strength; power; feeling; the baser qualities of the personality; seat of outbursts of rage, spiteful thoughts • **Chinese** the source of strength; *eating an enemy's liver:* assimilating the victim's valor • **Greco-Roman** *vulture pecking at giant's liver:* Tityus; *eagle pecking at titan's liver:* Prometheus • *see also* **gall**

liverwort • **flower language** confidence

livery subservience; the body

lizard evil; piety; impiety; religion; spring; health; security; inactivity; immobility; regeneration; guardianship; divine inspiration; wisdom; military strategy; the Word; idolatry; malice; shyness; silence; disrespect for elders; the power of evil; a lunar animal; the humid principle; attribute of the personifications of Logic, Affection • **African** invocation of protective spirits; fertility; household tranquility • **Australian aboriginal** Tarrotarro, Mangar-kunjer-kunja; *pair of lizard men:* Wati-Kutjari • **Christian** evil; the devil; rejuvenation; rebirth; resurrection; the illuminating influence of the Gospel; God's word; contemplative ecstasy; attribute of the Virgin Mary • **Egyptian** kindliness; benevolence; divine wisdom; lucky; fecundity; devouring heat; attribute of Serapis • **Greek** divine wisdom; lucky; attribute of Hermes, Sabazios (usually on his hand) • **Mochican** *old man with lizard and dog:* Ai apaec • **Polynesian** Moko • **Russian** *green lizard:* occasional manifestation of the Mistress of the Copper Mountain • **Roman** death and resurrection • **South American Indian** Master of Animals and Fish; messenger of the gods • **Zoroastrian** Ahriman; evil • *see also* **skink**

loaves *see* **bread**

lobelia • **flower language** malevolence

lobster an unfeeling, grasping monster; bigotry; chaos; lechery; escape; attribute of Inconstancy personified • **Greek** *lobster-claws horns:* attribute of icthyocentaurs **Japanese** longevity; congratulations; associated with the New Year festivities, happy events • **Oriental** longevity • **Sumerian** associated with Nina

lock *see* **padlock; latch**

locomotive sexuality; the libido; unconscious forces that threaten to overrun the conscious; the conscious ego • *see also* **train**

locust (insect) scourge; appetite; force of destruction; wisdom; heathen; heretic; false prophet; seduction • **Chinese** associated with seasonal fertility rites, the well-balanced family and society; *horde of locusts:* cosmic disorder; blessing of heaven • **Christian** *locusts and honey:* food of John the Baptist; *locust held by Christ:* the conversion of the nations to Christianity; *horde of locusts:* divine wrath; a nation without Christ; spiritual and moral torment • **Jewish** divine wrath; the judgment of God • *see also* **grasshopper**

locust tree • **flower language** elegance; friendship; secret love; *green locust tree:* affection beyond the grave

lodestone attraction; guidance; emblem of the sun

lodge retreat from the world; solitariness; melancholy; integrity; honesty; virility; associated with the archangel Cassiel • **North American Indian** the opening in the top is access to the heavens; *sweat lodge:* purification, rebirth, the body of the Great Spirit; *sun dance lodge:* sacred Center

loincloth of leaves • **Christian** attribute of SS Onuphrius, Paul the Hermit and other anchorites

loins procreation • **girding of the loins** the restraint of passion and the turning toward the spirit loitering spiritual inertia

Loki • **Norse** trickster; the triumph of expediency over conscience; lying that depraves the spirit

London pride • **flower language** frivolity

longevity implies living in concord with God

loom industry; the mysterious strands of life woven into one span; fortune; chance; fate; time; the weaving of destiny • **Greco-Roman** attribute of Arachne, Penelope; *spider's web with woman at loom, or woman weaving watched by the goddess Athena/Minerva:* Arachne • **Islamic** the structure and motion of the universe • *see also* **weaving**

lords and ladies (plant) *see* **arum**

Lorelei *see* **siren (mythology)**

loss guilt; death; spiritual bankruptcy; prelude to rebirth sign of final purification • **searching for a lost object** quest for life, immortality, enlightenment, Paradise, the Holy Grail • **dreaming of loss** longing for a treasure; the desire to rid oneself of something

lote tree • **flower language** concord • **Islamic** the impassable boundary

lotus the sun; the solar matrix; associated with the solar wheel; light; spiritual evolution; life; immortality; the supremely sacred flower of the East; perfection; perfect beauty; the soul transcending the flesh; the cosmos rising from chaos; mystic center; resurrection; superhuman or divine birth; human rebirth; the heart; purity; creative power; fire; renaissance; repose; fecundity; the feminine principle; androgyny; the sexual prison of marriage; spirit and matter; intellect; mental energy; illumination • **lotus blossom** beauty; self-fructification • **lotus root** indissolubility • **lotus stem** umbilical cord • **lotus seed pod** the fecundity of creation • **five-petaled lotus** birth; initiation; marriage; retirement; death • **thousand-petaled lotus** the sun; the skull; the dome of the firmament; final revelation • **two lotuses** the upper and lower waters • **flaming lotus** divine revelation; the union of fire and water, sun and moon, male and female • **lotus throne** spiritual perfection; perfect harmony in the universe • **lotus and cobra** the duality of manifestation; the tension of opposites in the process of unity; the dual nature of the

Great Mother • **Buddhist** primordial waters; spiritual flowering and unfolding; the potentialities of the manifest world and man; one of the Eight Emblems of Good Augury; wisdom; nirvana; sacred to Buddha; peace; harmony; union; attribute of Amitabha; *lotus in full bloom:* Amitabha, Guanyin, the Maitreya Buddha; *book resting on lotus:* attribute of the white Tara; *lotus stem:* World Axis • **Chinese** Summer; offspring; July; a sacred flower; purity; perfection; spiritual grace; fecundity; feminine genius; past, present, and future; a gentleman from low beginnings but uncontaminated by them; attribute of Ho Hsien-ku • **Christian** the Christian • **Egyptian** creation; fecundity; rebirth; immortality; royalty; royal power; the fire of intelligence; emblem of the Upper Nile; sacred to Horus; attribute of Hapi, Isis, Osiris; *lotus scepter:* virility • **flower language** eloquence; *flower alone:* estranged love; *leaf alone:* recantation • **Greco-Roman** dreaminess; indolence; emblem of Aphrodite/Venus; associated with funerals • **heraldic** mystery; perfection; purity; truth • **Hindu** purity; beauty; longevity; health; fame; fortune; the self-generative; eternal regeneration; superhuman origin; the passive aspect of manifestation; the highest aspect of the earth; the world; the procreative power of the eternal substance; the mover on the face of the waters; the immortal and spiritual nature of man; the unfolding of all possibilities; throne of Brahma; origin of Agni; emblem of Surya, Vishnu, Sri Lakshmi, Padma; *lotus on a temple threshold:* the dwelling of divinity; the purity and dispassion demanded of the faithful; *lotus resting on water:* the interaction of Purusha and Prakriti; *lotus on a triple stem:* the triple aspect of time; *bee on a lotus:* Vishnu; *thousand-petaled lotus:* the Sahasrara chakra (above the crown of the head); *goddess on a lotus:* Lakshmi; *woman with a crescent on her forehead reclining on a lotus:* Sarasvati • **Japanese** *lotus blooming on muddy waters:* morality unsullied by sordid surroundings • **Mayan** the earth; the manifest universe • **Persian** the solar; light • **Sumero-Semitic** creative generative power; resurrection; immortality; life and death; solar with sun gods; lunar with Great Mothers and moon goddesses; associated with funerals • **Taoist** the Golden Flower; cosmic wheel of manifestation; spiritual unfolding; the heart; emblem of Ho Hsien-ku

louse (insect) a pest; filth; disease; plague; accusation; shame; love

lovebird conjugal affection; associated with the archangel Anael

love-in-a-mist • **flower language** perplexity

love-in-a-puzzle • **flower language** embarrassment

love-lies-bleeding • **flower language** hopeless, not heartless

Lovers (tarot) the right choice; moral beauty; integrity; uncertainty; temptation; antagonistic but complementary forces creating an equilibrium; union; harmony of inner and outer life; human love; the tension between sacred and profane love; associated with deciding what one's soul truly desires

lowness humility; inferiority; submissiveness; associated with evil

lozenge (shape) the feminine principle; the mother; vulva; attribute of fertility goddesses • **lozenge-shaped ornaments on a serpent** male-female unity; dualism and reintegration; the reconciliation of opposites; androgyny • **Chinese** victory • **Christian** attribute of the Virgin Mary • **heraldic** an unmarried woman; a widow; noble birth; justice; honesty; constancy • *see also* **fusil; mascle**

lozenges (playing cards) *see* **diamonds (playing cards)**

lucerne • **flower language** life

luggage past experiences, ideas, emotions • **losing luggage** helplessness; inferiority; fragmentation of the psyche • **heavy or excessive luggage** self-imposed obligations; unconscious fixations; desire to be noticed; unwillingness to change • **disposing of luggage** gaining freedom; unburdening the unconscious

Lumiel, Archangel associated with the Earth, quartz, emerald, -0-, -9-, -20- • **Kabalistic** associated with Earth, brown, -10- • **tarot** associated with the World, Fool, Hermit

Lunacy *see* **insanity**

lunel • **heraldic** honored by the sovereign; hope of greater glory

lungs • **Buddhist** one of the Eight Precious Things • **Chinese** seat of consciousness; origin of inner thoughts

lupin sensitivity; endurance; generosity; associated with the underworld • **flower language** voraciousness; imagination • **heraldic** imagination

lute marital bliss; friendship; lasciviousness; androgyny; instrument of troubadours, lovers, divine praise; attribute of the personifications of Music, Hearing, the Lover • **lute with a broken string** discord • **Chinese** governmental harmony; friendship; married bliss; the scholar •

Christian followers attracted by Christ and the Gospel; passions subdued by Christ • **Egyptian** attribute of Nefer-Hetep • **Greco-Roman** mediation; harmony; reconciliation of natural forces; occasional attribute of Apollo, Orpheus, Polyhymnia • **Japanese** *woman with ten arms holding a lute:* Benzaiten

lycanthrope *see* **werewolf**

lychnis • **flower language** *meadow lychnis:* wit; *scarlet lychnis:* sunbeaming eyes

lying down safety; female sexual surrender • **lying prone** mourning; humility

lynx ferocity; deceit; ingratitude; forgetfulness; cleanliness; keen vision; vigilance; suspicion • **Christian** the vigilance of Christ • **heraldry** vigilance; keen vision; courage; liberty; individualism; indefatigability; cunning; strategy

lyre the relationship between heavens and earth; the harmonious union of cosmic forces; poetry; song; concord; emblem of conjugal love; attribute of Poetry personified • **four-stringed lyre** the four ancient elements (fire, water, earth, and air) • **seven-stringed lyre** the seven planets known to the ancients, the seven tone musical scale, etc. • **twelve-stringed lyre** the zodiac, the 12 tone musical scale, etc. • **Christian** active participation in beatific union • **Egyptian** harmony of the gods • **Greco-Roman** triumph of the intellect; realism; attribute of Apollo, Hermes/Mercury, Orpheus, Harmonia, Aeolus, Urania, Erato, Arion (usually riding on a dolphin), occasionally Terpsichore; *bird with a woman's head and a lyre:* a siren; *blind man with broken lyre sitting in Hades:* Thamyris; *golden lyre:* attribute of Amphion (son of Zeus and Antiope) • **heraldic** poetry; contemplation; tempered judgment • **Jewish** the constellation Vega; active participation in beatific union

M

M the Roman numeral for 1,000; associated with strength of character, orderliness, concentration, enlightenment of the soul and spirit, work, nobility, indomitability, transformation, change, -4-, Saturn (planet), masculinity when printed angularly, femininity when printed rounded • **as a monogram** the Virgin Mary (especially when shown with a crown); attribute of the archangel Gabriel • **as a brand on the thumb** a murderer • **tarot** associated with Death

macaroni foolishness; rashness; insolence; lying; immorality

macaw • **Mayan** fire; solar energy • **Mexican Indian** emblem of South

mace (weapon) royal office; divine office; annihilation or destruction as opposed to simple victory; the subjective assertive tendency in man; authority, especially of the state; battle weapon of medieval bishops • **Buddhist** *Diamond Mace (Ju-i):* Buddha; the Doctrine; resolution; supremacy; conquering power; on the Footprint of Buddha it is thunder striking at the passions of mankind; *mace with heart-shaped head:* divine office • **Egyptian** the creative Word • **Greco-Roman** attribute of Heracles/Hercules • **Sumerian** *seven-headed mace:* battle • *see also* **club; scepter**

machines that which has no independent will or thought; their symbolism derives from their particular shapes, functions, or other dominant characteristics; they commonly have ingestive, digestive, reproductive, or sexual meanings, and have infernal implications, or are connected with soulless technology

madder (plant) talkativeness • **flower language** calumny

madwort • **flower language** tranquility

Maenads/Bacchantes • **Greco-Roman** storm spirits; involutive fragmentation of the unconscious; women given to debauchery and sin; demonic possession

magenta associated with Mars (planet)

maggot immorality; death; decomposition; decay; filth

magic inner and unobserved processes within the soul by which the lower qualities are raised to a higher level (especially in white magic); black magic has infernal implications

magician *see* **sorcerer**

Magician (tarot) personal will in union with the divine; gifts of the spirit; occult wisdom; consciousness; inquiry; man in his struggle with occult powers; associated with the search for knowledge

magnet *see* **lodestone**

magnolia magnificence; fecundity; love of nature; feminine sweetness and beauty; beauty; love; perseverance; pride; dignity; respectability; power; the lofty soul; sensuousness • **American** emblem of the South • **Chinese** ostentation; self-esteem; Spring; *magnolia blossoms:* feminine beauty, May • **flower language** love of nature; *laurel-leaved magnolia:* dignity; *swamp magnolia:* perseverance • **heraldic** love of nature; perseverance; nobility • **Japanese** associated with May

magpie mischief; chattering; thievery; tattling;

indiscretion; destroyer of vermin and insects; generally an evil omen; a woman 20 to 30 years old; dissimulation; attribute of Dissimulation personified • **Chinese** lucky; the imperial rule of the Manchu dynasty; omen of an impending visitor • **Christian** the devil; dissipation; vanity; attribute of St. Oda • **Greco-Roman** envy; presumption; idle chatter; snobbery; attribute of Dionysus/Bacchus; *nine magpies:* the Pierides • **Mediterranean** *magpie perching in a ship's rigging:* ill omen

Maia • **Greek** externalization of the Ego

maiden virginity; innocence; dawn, spring, new start; grace; gentleness • **maiden slaughtered by tyrant** fertility conquered • **maiden killed by a natural calamity** flood, frost, etc. • **Christian** *five maidens with lit lamps:* the five wise virgins; *five maidens with extinguished lamps:* the five foolish virgins • **Greco-Roman** *maiden abducted by a black bearded king in a chariot:* rape of Persephone/Proserpine; *maiden abducted by a white bull:* rape of Europa; *maiden abducted to ships in harbor by a young man:* abduction of Helen of Troy; *two maidens with two soldiers on horseback:* the soldiers are Castor and Pollux • *see also* **virgin; woman**

maidenhair fern pubic hair • **flower language** discretion

maidenhead secrecy

maidwort *see* **madwort**

mail *see* **letter (epistle)**

maiming a weakness or defect in the soul; revenge for maiming shows some vestige of moral strength remains • **Celtic** *king with missing or artificial arm:* Nuada • *see also* **mutilation**

maize fertility; germination and growth; development of a potentiality; health; plenty; peace; prosperity; nourishment; a spermatic image • **child with ears of maize** personification of Summer • **American** emblem of agriculture, the Midwest • **Amerindian** *ear of maize:* all the people and things of the universe; life • **Aztecan** attribute of Chalchiutlicue; *ear of maize:* attribute of Cinteotl, Chicomecoatl • **Mexican Indian** awakening vegetation; *maize with hummingbird:* attribute of a sun hero • **Peruvian Indian** *large or oddly shaped ears:* Saramama

makara • **Cambodian** temple guardian • **Hindu** water; aphrodisiac; steed of Varuna, Ganga, emblem of Kamadeva; astrological sign of Capricorn; attribute of Vishnu • **Tibetan** strength; tenacity

malachite prosperity; longevity; health; love; peace; power; charm for business success, pro-

tection • **Russian** *malachite dress:* attribute of the Mistress of the Copper Mountain

male *see* **man; boy**

mallet *see* **hammer**

mallow beneficence; rankness; attribute of Benevolence personified • **Chinese** humility; peace; quietness; rustic life; associated with September • **flower language** mildness; *marsh mallow:* beneficence; healing; *Syrian mallow:* consumed by love, persuasion; *Venetian mallow:* delicate beauty

Maltese cross *see* **cross**

Mammon • **Christian** avarice; temptation

man the conscious; the spirit; heaven; fire; the imagination • **young man** the governed; the hero; subversion; boldness; intuition; the primitive mind; new ideas; the rising sun • **muscular and/or hairy man** energetic and strong mental qualities • **man's head on a woman's body** solid and profound judgment • **bull-man** guardian protection; guardian; wards off evil • **green man changing to gold** green corn changing to the yellow corn of the harvest • **Bambaran** *man with a fish tail:* Faro • **Chinese** *man with horns on his head:* Chen-nung, Ch'i-You • **Christian** one of the guardians of the Throne of God; *winged man:* St. Matthew (especially with book and/or pen, especially with an angel dictating or pointing toward heaven); *twelve men:* (often each with a sheep) the Apostles; *man with bat wings:* the devil, a demon; *man with goat feet:* the devil, a demon; *man with horns:* the devil, a demon; *man with a monkey tail:* the devil, a demon • **Hindu** *man with the head of a buffalo or bull:* Yama; *half-lion/half-man:* Agni • **Islamic** the link between God and nature • *see also* **boy; old man; wild man**

manchineal tree • **flower language** hypocrisy; falsehood; duplicity

mandala world image; totality; microcosm; enclosure of sacred space; penetration to the sacred center; cosmic intelligence; the presence of the godhead at the center of all things • **mandala center** the sun; a sky door; access to the heavens

mandorla divinity; holiness; spiritual glory; virginity; vulva; perpetual sacrifice and regeneration; perfect blessedness; birth into the next world; gateway to the two sides of duality; flame

mandrake fertility; the Great Mother; the soul in its negative and minimal aspects; associated with magical powers • **Christian** emblem of the Virgin Mary • **flower language** horror; rarity • **folkloric** screams when uprooted; grows under the gallows of murderers • **Greek** emblem of

Circe • **Jewish** conception; fertility • **witchcraft** used for curses and other negative spells

manger • **Christian** ignorance from which wisdom rises; humility from which charity rises; envy; attribute of the Nativity of Christ, the Cumean sibyl; *manger with enthroned lamb:* the humiliation and exaltation of Christ, respectively

mani • **Chinese** richness; benefaction; the Buddhist trinity (Buddha, his Word, the priesthood)

maniple • **Christian** spirituality; purification; good works; vigilance; repentance; penitence; strength; endurance; the order of subdeaconship; the bands that held the wrists of Christ in the Garden of Gethsemane, when he was scourged, and dragged through the streets

manna goodness; truth; spiritual sustenance; God's word; poetic inspiration; the Eucharist; the Bread of Life; a free and valuable gift; God's grace; said to be exuded from the tamarisk • **Sumerian** associated with Anu

mantelleta • **Christian** worn as a sign of limited jurisdiction or authority, red for a cardinal, purple for a bishop

manticore a storm demon; the personification of a Sirocco; a beastly rationalist • **heraldic** a soldier

mantis courage; persistence; voracity; cruelty and greed camouflaged by a hypocritical attitude of prayer or religiosity; female viciousness • **Bushmen** a trickster • **Chinese** pertinacity; greed • **Christian** prayer; adoration • **Greek** divination

mantle (clothing) *see* **cloak**

manure fertility; fertilization • *see also* **excrement**; **dung**

maple retirement; conjugal love; earthly, bourgeois happiness; reserve • **in the Autumn** past happiness; transitoriness • **sugar maple** success; abundance • **Canadian** emblem of Canada • **Chinese** *maple leaf:* emblem of lovers, Autumn • **flower language** reserve • **heraldic** *maple leaf:* bestowing honor, gift-giving • **Japanese** *deer with maple:* solitariness, melancholy; *maple leaf:* emblem of lovers, Autumn

marathon endurance; an arduous task

marble cold beauty; death; authority; inflexibility; durability; eternity

mare fertility; witchcraft; erotic madness; the Mother; the mother as protector; the Terrible Mother • **Greco-Roman** occasional form of Hecate • *see also* **horse**

marguerite (flower) emblem of the sun; innocence

marigold the sun; constancy; fidelity; worth; endurance in love (especially of women); grief; misery; mercy; incorruptibility; innocence; comeliness; despair; associated with Leo; attribute of Despair personified • **marigolds and cypress** despair and death respectively • **Chinese** longevity • **Christian** attribute of the Virgin Mary • **flower language** grief; sorrow; pain; chagrin; despair; *African marigold:* a vulgar mind; *corn marigold:* comeliness; *French marigold:* jealousy; *fig marigold:* idleness; *garden marigold:* uneasiness; *prophetic marigold:* prophecy; *small cape marigold:* omen; *marigolds mixed with roses:* love's sweet sorrows; *marigolds mixed with red flowers:* the varying course of life • **heraldic** devotion; piety; sweetness; splendid beauty • **Hindu** associated with Krishna • **Oriental** *marigolds and poppies:* soothing of grief

marjoram grief; marriage • **flower language** beneficence; blushes

marking *see* **tattooing**

maroon • **heraldic** patience and victorious in battle

maror • **Jewish** a reminder of the bitterness of their history

marriage union of the discrete; union of the conscious and unconscious; union of the masculine and feminine principles; spiritual union; attainment of perfection • **days associated with marriage** Monday for wealth/ Tuesday for health/ Wednesday the best of all/ Thursday for crosses/ Friday for losses/ Saturday, no luck at all • **alchemic** union of sulfur and Mercurius, sun and moon, gold and silver; king and queen, etc.• **Christian** union of the soul with Christ

marrow manly prowess; semen; strength; life-force; vitality; lust; center of being

Mars *see* **Ares/Mars**

Mars (planet) war; action; energy; aspiration; enthusiasm; destruction; objective evil; the sacrifice necessary in creation; striving; aggression; associated with things martial, the driving force, passions, activity, movement, self-confidence, courage, fire, iron, bloodstones, asbestos, brimstone, red, South, the prime of life, -3-, Tuesday, tigers, panthers, wolves, sharks, head, genitals, Aries, Scorpio, lambstongue, butterbur, the archangel Samael • **Babylonian** associated with Nergal • **Chinese** associated with South, fire • **Hindu** associated with the third chakra (adrenals) • **Kabalistic** associated with destruction, South, action

marsh sloth; idleness; the unconscious; place where matter germinates in secret • **Buddhist** sensual pleasures that are obstacles on the Eightfold Path • **Chinese** concord; fulfillment;

wealth • **Sumerian** the feminine principle; undifferentiated matter

marsh mallow (plant) *see* **mallow**

Martha, St. • **Christian** personification of the busy housekeeper

martin (bird) domestic happiness; dupe

martlet • **heraldic** the fourth son; cunning; alertness; good reputation; subsisting on merit and virtue

martyrdom self-sacrifice; sacrificing the material for the spiritual

marvel of Peru (plant) • **flower language** timidity

Mary *see* **Virgin Mary**

Mary Magdalene, St. • **Christian** human metamorphosis; self-sacrifice; service; forgiveness

mascle • **heraldic** persuasiveness

mask dissimulation; ambiguity; equivocation; transformation; indication of what the wearer would like to be or to control; protection; hypocrisy; concealment; hollowness; nonbeing; attribute of the personifications of Deceit, Vice, Night • **mask with a frown** tragedy; *17th Century on:* attribute of Melpomene • **mask with a smile** comedy; *17th Century on:* attribute of Thalia • **animal mask** access to animal or instinctual wisdom; understanding or communication with animals • **carnival mask** usually represents the lower aspects of nature • **Norse** *boar mask or helmet:* put the wearer under the protection of Frey and Freyja • *see also* **disguise**

mason *see* **stone mason**

mast aspiration; belief; the connection between heaven and earth; Tree of Life; World Axis; pride; energy • **mast on a ship** androgyny • **lowered mast** a change in belief or opinions • **broken mast** submission; defeat

mat the unrolling of a mat signifies the unfolding of life • **prayer mat** a place apart from the profane world; Paradise

match (fire) uprightness; hope

mathematics the creation of order; precision; calculation

matron the domineering mother; protection; the Church; personification of a city

mattock toil; attribute of Adam after the Fall

matzoth • **Jewish** suffering; affliction; hope

mausoleum *see* **sarcophagus**

maypole Tree of Life; World Axis; union of opposites; sexual union; the phallic reproductive powers of nature together with the vulva-circle regulation of time and motion; renewed life; Spring; resurrection • **Greek** the sacred pine of Attis

maze *see* **labyrinth**

mead drink of the gods • **Celtic** drink of immortality • **Norse** *mead with goat:* the goat is Heidrum

meadow unlucky; sadness; peace; humbleness; patience; dreaminess; gladness; limitation; uniformity; lust; connected with the river of life

meadowsweet • **flower language** uselessness

measuring • **Christian** *measuring with a line:* associated with Zechariah • **Sumero-Semitic** *measuring rod with line:* attribute of Marduk, Shamash, sometimes Ea

medal honor; glory; victory; prize • **leather medal** a farcical award for stupidity or inferiority

meditation the process of integration of the self; listening to the higher mind, the voice of a deity

Medusa • **Greek** the Terrible Mother; primal sexuality; sin; the dangerous female; annihilation • **heraldic** *three legs joined at the thigh with Medusa's head in the middle:* emblem of Sicily, Palermo • *see also* **Gorgon**

Megara *see* **Erinyes/Furies**

Melchizedek • **Christian** righteousness; peace; priesthood

melody *see* **music**

Melpomene • **Greek** muse associated with lyre-playing, dramatic tragedy

melting the gradual release of old ideas, thoughts, emotions

Melusina • **European** intuitive genius; virginity; motherly love; the destruction of love through lack of trust; failure to accept the limitations of the unconscious and the hidden • **heraldic** seafaring ancestors • *see also* **mermaid**

men *see* **man**

menhir the masculine; the phallic; World Axis; vigilance; protection; place of sacrifice • **Jewish** the altar of Jacob

menorah (nine-branched) • **Jewish** emblem of Chanukah • *see also* **candelabrum; -9-**

menorah (seven-branched) • **Hindu** the seven chakras • **Jewish** emblem of Judaism; Tree of Life; World Axis; the divine presence; Old Testament worship; the Church; attribute of the Temple in Jerusalem; the seven gifts of the Holy Spirit; the seven Patriarchs of Mankind; the seven Righteous Men; the seven celestial spheres; the six days of creation, with the center light as the Sabbath • *see also* **candelabrum; -7-**

Mephistopheles • **German** craftiness; cynicism; the negative aspect of the psychic function which has broken away from the spirit to acquire independence; the deceived deceiver; merchant avarice • *see also* **devil**

Mercurius • alchemic the beginning and end of the work; the prima materia; the caput corvi; the nigredo; androgyny; *outwardly:* mercury (metal); *inwardly:* the world-creating spirit concealed or imprisoned in matter

Mercury *see* **Hermes/Mercury**

mercury (metal) speed; adaptability; inconstancy; uncertainty; the unconscious; the soul; the dominant feminine principle; associated with Gemini, Virgo, Mercury (planet), the archangel Raphael • **alchemic** Mercurius • **Chinese** corresponds to dragons, blood, semen, the kidneys, the element Water • **Hindu** the concentration of solar energy underground; Shiva's semen • *see also* **Mercurius**

Mercury (planet) associated with the intellect, the nervous system, the stomach, Gemini, Virgo, communication, reason, calculation, -4-, intuition, duality, free will, rhythm, trial, initiation, communication, movement, adaptation, mediation, purple, deep blue, Wednesday, childhood, valerian, hazel, the archangel Raphael • **Babylonian** associated with Nabu • **Chinese** associated with North, water • **Hindu** associated with the sixth chakra (pineal) • **Jewish** associated with the archangel Michael • **Kabalistic** associated with the center, the archangel Raphael, civilization, the intuition

Merihim pestilence

Merlin • Celtic enslaved imagination; inner wisdom

mermaid sensual pleasure; fatal allurement; the unconscious; the power of song magic; the power of seduction; transformation; water divinity; the understanding of the ancients that humans were both one with and different from animals; integration of the physical and the spiritual; the feminine energy that arises from the unconscious • **British** usually an unlucky omen; *Elizabethan:* a courtesan • **Christian** the dual nature of Christ; attribute of SS Christopher, Margaret • **heraldic** eloquence; sea-faring ancestors • **West African** occasional depiction of Yemaya • *see also* **Melusina**

merman similar in most respects to mermaids • **Greek** *merman pursing a sea nymph:* Glaucus and Scylla respectively

mesembryanthemum • flower language idleness

messenger insight; inspiration; intuition; the higher or inner self; the archangel Raphael

metal wealth; war; the senses; eternity; the libido; energy solidified; strength; endurance; connected with the underworld • **base metals** associated with the flesh, desires • **precious metals** associated with the spirit • **molten metals** conjunction of opposites—fire/water, solid/liquid, etc. • **metal worker** *see* **blacksmith** • **Chinese** *as an element:* associated with pungent taste, friendliness, cold, oil seed, dogs, the liver, white, the nails, sorrow, -4-; *smelting:* the acquisition of immortality • *see also* **blacksmith**, and specific metals, such as **copper; gold; silver**

Metatron, Archangel celestial scribe; associated with the Earth, diamonds, crystal, mistletoe, almond trees, the center • **Kabalistic** associated with -1-

meteor usually an unfavorable omen

meteorite heavenly creative fire; revelation; seed; spiritual messenger; spiritual life descended to earth; heavenly vestments

Methuselah • Jewish extreme age, wisdom; renewal; quick thought

mezerion • flower language the desire to please

mezuzah • Jewish emblem of Judaism; reminder of devotion to God

mica • Chinese food of immortality

Michael, Archangel messenger of divine judgment; warrior; guardian of the Jewish nation; associated with the -11-, -19-, gold, brass, amber, carnelians, diamonds, rubies, topaz, West, 4th heaven, Leo, Sunday, acacia, beech, cedars, bay laurel, lions, wolves, griffins, sparrowhawks • **Christian** associated with the sun • **Jewish** guardian angel of Jacob; associated with Mercury (planet) • **Kabalistic** associated with -6-, yellow • **tarot** associated with the Sun

midget the undeveloped; germination phase • **midget monk** St. Neot • *see also* **dwarf**

midnight gloom; solitude; mortification; the witches' hour; a magical or mystical time; beginning of the ascendant part of day • **Chinese** the most favorable time for conception • **Hindu** the condition of absolute repose in a state of beatitude • **Islamic** entanglement; confusion • *see also* **noon**

mignonette • flower language your qualities surpass your charms

milfoil *see* **achillea millefolium**

milk the elixir of life; regeneration; abundance; fertility; nourishment; wisdom; concord; kindness; truth; semen; food of initiates; natural religion and knowledge • **milk and honey** abundance; heavenly food; associated with Canaan • **milk and water** spirit and matter, respectively; weakness • **goat's milk** error; desire • **mother's milk or cow's milk** higher nature; innocence • **Buddhist** the nourishment of the Buddha Dharma • **Christian** the Word; the Church; the simple food given to those who do not yet receive the wine of Communion; *milk pail:* the spiritual nourishment of Christ and the Church • **Greco-Roman** *milk, water, and honey:* drink of the Muses • **Islamic** brings good luck • **Jewish** *afterbirth ashes and milk:* charm against wasting disease in children • **Norse** *four rivers of milk:* attribute of Asgard • **Zoroastrian** sacred food • *see also* **breast**

milkmaid a robust, but not too discriminate woman • **Norse** disguise of Loki

milkvetch • **flower language** your presence softens my pain

milkwort associated with hermits

Milky Way infinitude • **Australian aboriginal** the river of heaven • **Celtic** the chain of Lug • **Chinese** the celestial river • **Norse** the pathway to Valhalla • **North American Indian** the pathway of ghosts

mill place of transformation; fate; fertility; the revolving heavens; time; greed; habitual and uncreative thinking; logic as a feeble protection against passion • **Christian** the Church; the Gospel • *see also* **water mill**

millet • **sheaf of millet** attribute of Preservation personified • **Chinese** reaping; harvesting; fertility of the soil

millipede regression; fragmentation of the psyche

millstone heavy burden; hardness; punishment; gravity; martyrdom • **two millstones** mutual converse of human society; will and intellect • **ass with a millstone** Obedience personified • **Buddhist** samsara • **Christian** attribute of SS Aurea, Callixtus, Christina, Florian, Quirinus, Victor, Vincent of Saragossa • **heraldic** determination; going one's own way; the miller's trade; the mutual converse of human society • **Norse** the revolving universe

mimosa sensitiveness; fastidiousness; exquisiteness; associated with Sagittarius; emblem of Australia, South Africa • **flower language** sensitivity; bashfulness; delicate feelings; security; certainty

minaret • **Islamic** torch of spiritual illumination; mystic center

miner extraction of spiritual values; shares in much of the symbolism of the blacksmith • **Greco-Roman** related to Hephaestus/Vulcan, Ares/Mars

Minerva *see* **Athena/Minerva**

minnow insignificance

Minotaur • **Greek** miasma; savage passions of nature; a solar personification; a psychic state of perverted domination; sins repressed in the subconscious; *fighting against the Minotaur:* spiritual struggle

Minstrel (tarot) *see* **Magician (tarot)**

mint (plant) virtue; attribute of the Virgin Mary • **flower language** virtue • **heraldic** virtue; warm feelings • **Jewish** the bitterness of their bondage

mirror imagination; thought; unconscious memories; consciousness; self-consciousness; self-realization; the ego; the mind; introspection; truth; wisdom; fertility; love; the soul; virginity; reflection of one's inner self; feminine pride; seduction; retrospection; prophecy; door to another world; thesis and antithesis; magical in that it may remember what it sees; associated with divination; attribute of the personifications of Truth (especially a hand mirror), Prudence, Pride, Vanity, Sight, Lust • **two lovers in a mirror** Rinaldo and Armida • **mirror and serpent** attribute of Prudence personified • **dirty mirror** the spirit darkened by ignorance • **mirrored glasses** hiding of thoughts or emotions; deceit • **Aztecan** *obsidian mirror as a foot:* attribute of Tezcatlipoca • **Buddhist** purity; the soul in a state of purity; the enlightened mind; sincerity; samsara; one of the Eight Precious Things of Chinese Buddhism • **Chinese** sincerity; harmony; happy marriage; emblem of the queen; *square mirror:* the earth; *round mirror:* the heavens; *octagonal mirror:* intermediary between heaven and earth; *central boss in a mirror:* Gate of Heaven; Sun Door; *broken mirror:* separation • **Christian** *spotless mirror:* the Immaculate Conception, attribute of the Virgin Mary; *mirror with the image of the Virgin Mary in it:* attribute of St. Germinianus • **Greco-Roman** truth; attribute of Aphrodite/Venus; *old man and child with mirror:* Socrates • **Hindu** unreality; contrivance of thought • **Hittite** attribute of feminine divinities • **Japanese** sun; truth; revelation of truth; perfect purity of soul; the unsullied spirit; one of the Three Treasures; attribute of Amaterasu, the emperor; *sacred mirror:* entered by a deity to reveal himself; *octagonal mirror:* harmony, perfection • **Mexican Indian** attribute of Tezcatlipoca • **Nigerian** attribute of Oshun (usually on her belt) • **Phoenician** attribute of Ishtar • **Taoist** mechanism of self-realization; the calm mind of the sage • **Tibetan** *metal mirror breastplate:* attribute of Nag-pa

miscarriage a failure of order, natural or proper development

mist things indeterminate; illusion; confusion; error; the intermediate world between the formal and non-formal; care; prelude of revelation or manifestation; associated with the distant past, memory • **rising mist** the feminine principle in nature desiring the male • **Irish** associated with the music of the Otherworld • *see also* **clouds**

mistletoe fertility; regeneration; life; protection; immortality; atonement; good will; reconciliation of opposites; freedom from limitation; witchcraft; paganism; sacred to the Druids; associated with Christmas, witchcraft, paganism, the Winter solstice, the archangels Metatron, Samael • **Celtic** *oak and mistletoe:* male and female powers respectively • **Druidic** equivalent to the gold bough; a sacred plant • **flower language** I surmount all obstacles • **Norse** *mistletoe spear:* associated with the death of Baldur

miter authority • **Babylonian** attribute of Ea-Oannes • **Christian** the flame of the Holy Spirit; associated with Pentecost; attribute of St. Sylvester, popes, cardinals, bishops, abbots; *white miter:* now worn by bishops, but once also worn by cardinals and some abbots (an abbot's miter was usually unadorned); an occasional attribute of St. Benedict; *three miters on the ground:* attribute of SS Bernardino of Siena, Bernard of Clairvaux; *triple miter:* attribute of the pope; *miter lappets (fanons):* the letter and the spirit of the Old and New Testaments • **heraldic** authority • **Jewish** the two rays of light that came from the head of Moses when he received the Ten Commandments; attribute of the high priest; *miter and censer:* attribute of Melchizedek • **Mithraic** attribute of the high priest

mock orange • **flower language** counterfeit; brotherly love

mocking bird mimicry; courage

Mohammed • **Islamic** human contact with the divine; one who brings order out of chaos

moistness falsity

mold (plant) decay

mold (tool) nature; mother

mole (animal) blindness; obtuseness; idolatry; lies; avarice; timidity; industry; keen hearing; wisdom from the underworld; the powers of darkness; destruction; death; misanthropy; attribute of Avarice personified • **Hindu** associated with Rudra

mole (body) • **right side of body** usually lucky •**left side of body** usually unlucky • **face, chin, or neck mole** wealth omen • **mole on the arm** have a rich farm • **chest or stomach mole** strength • **mole on the nose** lechery • **English** *woman with a mole on her upper right temple:* omen of a good marriage; *on her thigh:* unfaithful, spendthrift; *on her breast:* irresistible • **Indic** *mole on a woman's left breast:* good omen

molehill insignificance

Moloch • **Jewish** associated with child sacrifice; a vengeful and pitiless tyrant; tyranny of the state

monastery spiritual haven; withdrawal from the material world; place of spiritual seeking and development • **Christian** *man holding a model of a monastery:* St. Gerald of Aurillac • *see also* **cloister; monks; nuns**

monastics *see* **monks; nuns**

Monday associated with the moon, Selene/Luna, Artemis/Diana, the archangel Gabriel, works of divination, Cancer • **birthday** Born on a Monday, fair of face, or, Monday's child is fair in the face (or, full in the face) • **marriage** Monday for wealth • **sneezing** you sneeze for danger • **Jewish** *Creation:* division of waters • *see also* **days**

money value; bribery; lucky • **money bag** attribute of Avarice personified • **open money bag** charity to the poor • **Christian** *man with money in two hands:* Judas; *woman giving money away:* St. Elizabeth of Hungary; *dish of money:* attribute of St. Laurence; *money bag:* attribute of Judas, SS Cyril, Laurence, Nicholas of Myra; *money bag with thirty pieces of silver:* attribute of Judas; *three money bags:* attribute of St. Matthew

monkey sexual desires; lasciviousness; obscenity; impudent self-satisfaction; imitation; mischief; maliciousness; unconscious activity; pettiness; the sanguine temperament; flattery; hypocrisy; melancholy; inquisitiveness; impudence; base instincts; pride; idle foolishness; agility; attribute of the personifications of Dissimulation, Inconstancy, Avarice; associated with the archangel Raphael • **man worshipping a monkey** Idolatry personified • **Aztecan** incarnation of the Blacksmith who stole fire; associated with cheerfulness, an equable nature, lovability • **Buddhist** greediness; a grasping person; one of the Three Senseless Creatures of Chinese Buddhism • **Cambodian** hunting monkeys brings rain • **Chinese** trickery; ugliness; charm against evil; bringer of success, health, protection; 9th animal of the Twelve Terrestrial Branches; associated with Sagittarius in the zodiac; *three monkeys:* attribute of Koshin — the monkeys are Mi-Zaru, Kiki-Zaru, Iwa-Zaru, • **Christian** the devil; vanity; luxury; humanity degraded by sin, especially lust and malice; *man with the monkey tail:* the devil, a demon • **Hindu** attribute of Hanuman; *monkey-headed deity with yellow face and an endless tail:* Hanuman • **Japanese** *monkey doll:* drives off evil spirits, eases childbirth; *tortoise with monkey head and* *frog legs:* Kappa • **Mayan** associated with promiscuity; *monkey-headed god:* god of the North Star • **Quechuan** *monkey-headed god:* God of the North • **Tibetan** consciousness of the material world that hinders spiritual development; Mani bka'bum; *man-monkey:* attribute of Da • *see also* **ape; baboon**

monkey puzzle tree associated with the archangel Samael

monks solitude; contemplation; asceticism; silence • **Christian** *monk with claw or cloven hoof showing from under the habit:* the devil tempting Jesus; *monk offering a stone to Jesus:* the devil tempting Jesus in the wilderness; *monk with a book:* the book is usually the rule of the order; *monks in white habits on a ladder:* associated with St. Romuald; *monk with white scapular, arms crossed on breast:* St. Bruno; *monk with tau cross and/or raven and/or pig and/or bell:* St. Anthony the Great; *monk with sword through head or hand:* St. Peter Martyr; *monk celebrating mass on board ship as fish gather to listen:* St. Brendan; *monks in a small boat:* St. Brendan; *midget monk:* St. Neot; *beggar kneeling before a monk:* the monk is St. John of God; *lightning striking a tree near a monk:* the monk is St. Philip Benizzi; *friar in black and white habit with lily and book:* St. Dominic; *Benedictine monk with broken fetters:* St. Leonard; *Benedictine monk with red chasuble over his habit:* St. Thomas Becket; *Benedictine monk with armor and crown lying beside him:* St. William of Aquitaine; *Camaldolese monk with white beard, sometimes holding a crutch or skull:* St. Romuald; *Capuchin monk receiving bread from a child:* St. Felix of Cantalice; *Carmelite monk with books at his feet:* St. John of the Cross; *Carmelite monk in brown and white habit:* may be Elijah; *Dominican monk carrying a monstrance and/or statue of the Virgin Mary:* St. Hyacinth; *Franciscan with a short scapular rounded at the corners:* St. Francis of Paola; *Franciscan preaching to fish or with the Christ child seated on a book:* St. Anthony of Padua • **Japanese** *tall monk in a straw hat:* Raiden • *see also* **habit (monastic); monastery; nuns**

monkshood (plant) • **flower language** chivalry; knight errant

monolith resurrection; eternal life; unity counterbalancing multiplicity; solidarity; strength; primitive life; associated with Osiris; related to the solar, masculine, and procreative principles • *see also* **menhir**

monster primordial life; cosmic forces one step removed from chaos; the libido; the unconscious; instincts that hinder man in his search for truth; an unbalanced psyche; base forces; irrational thought or behavior; repressed parts of the self; guardian of treasure, immortality; difficulties to be overcome on a quest • **fighting a monster** the struggle to free the conscious from the unconscious; the spirit battling base forces • **monster ravaging the countryside** a bad king • **man-eating monster** the unconscious threatening to devour the conscious • **aquatic monster** a cosmic or psychological situation at a deeper level than land monsters • **underground monster** danger from the subconscious • **Japanese** *monster beating drums:* Raiden • **Jewish** the forces of chaos, darkness; disorder preceding creation • **Serbian** *six-legged monster with gnarled horns:* Bukavac

monstrance • **Christian** attribute of the Eucharist, SS Clare, Hyacinth (often with a statue of the Virgin Mary), Thomas Aquinas, Norbert

moon the feminine principle; passivity; pensiveness; the maternal; the soul; the psyche; the unconscious; involuntary and instinctual action; intuition; irrationality; inner knowledge; resurrection; abode of the dead; inconstancy; regenerative receptacle of the soul; the mutable; the cyclic; passing time; perpetual renewal; enlightenment; the transitory; potential evil; serene loveliness; chastity; virginity; imagination; lunacy; magic; death; silence; coldness; isolation; regulator of water, rain, the fertility of women, animals, plants; associated with emotion, femininity (usually), -2-, the sea, mother goddesses, queens of heaven, the archangel Gabriel, Pisces, Scorpio, Cancer, Monday • **changing moon** change in the world of phenomena • **sun and moon together** heaven and earth; king and queen; etc. • **full moon** wholeness; completion; strength; spiritual power • **red moon** indication of the activity of witches • **blood on the moon** evil omen • **moonlight** distorted truth; associated with romantic love • **African** Ashang; time; death; occasionally associated with trees • **alchemic** purified affections • **astrologic** the seat of sensation; related to the animal soul, sexual life, impulse, life-style, early childhood • **Aztecan** daughter of Tlaloc • **Buddhist** *moon and hare:* emblem of Buddhism, peace, serenity, beauty; *full moon, new moon:* times of spiritual power • **Chinese** heaven's beauty; yin; the passive; the transient; immortality; fertility; the hare in the moon mixes the elixir of immortality with a mortar and pestle • **Christian** the physical nature of Christ; the Church reflecting the light of Christ, however, sometimes the Synagogue, with the Church represented as the sun; *moon and sun in scenes of the Crucifixion:* allusion to the convulsions of the heavens • **Egyptian** associated with Hathor, Thoth • **Eskimo** the sender of snow • **Greco-Roman** associated with trees, the liver, the Moirae/Fates, Selene/Luna, Artemis/Diana, Hecate, Janus • **heraldic** serene power over the mundane • **Islamic** *cloven moon:* the duality of manifestation that will return to unity • **Japanese** Tsukiyomi, emblem of Susano-o, the hare in the moon mixes the elixir of immortality with a mortar and pestle • **Jewish** the Children of Israel, attribute of Rachel, abode of the archangel Gabriel; *full moon and the sun surrounded by 12 stars:* Jacob's wife, Jacob, and their 12 sons respectively • **Kabalistic** associated with the nadir, imagination, archangel Gabriel, the sending of dreams, the strengthening of hopes • **Manichean** Jesus • **Maori** the father god; husband of all women • **Mayan** idleness; sexual laxity; associated with Ixchel • **Mexican Indian** emblem of Metzli • **Norse** attribute of Freyja • **North American Indian** light of the Great Spirit; associated with trees, maize, occasionally evil • **Oceanic** eternal youth; associated with Hina • **Persian** Mah; chastity • **Sumero-Semitic** associated with trees, bushes; emblem of Ashtaroth, Astarte, the moon god Sin; *full moon:* time of prayer, rejoicing, sacrifice • **Taoist** truth; yin; *moon and sun:* all radiance, supernatural being • **Teutonic** masculine divine power • **Ural-Altaic** magic power • *see also* **black moon; crescent moon; lunel**

Moon (tarot) intuition; imagination; magic; reflection; objectivity; error; loneliness; disease; deceptive appearances; treachery; bigotry; arbitrary fantasy; imaginative sensitivity; the path of mystic enlightenment; upward progress of man; the acquisition of truth by hard experience; the spiritual sullied by the material; neurasthenia; depression; the descent of the life force from the heavens; involution; regression in order to make a fresh start; the rejection of reason; associated with uncertainty, the possibility of change, the need for caution, the use of one's own intuition

moonstone thoughtfulness; tenderness; youth; associated with lovers, the archangel Gabriel; charm for love, divination, psychic power, gardening success, protection, dieting, sleep, equability, reducing the effects of the moon on the wearer; stone for 13th wedding anniversaries

moonwort • **flower language** forgetfulness

moorings the higher self; God; the attachment of the physical and spiritual, or spiritual and instinctual • **Christian** the Church

moose largeness; clumsiness; self-esteem; assertiveness; longevity • **North American Indian** supernatural power; whirlwind • **Senecan** Oyandone, the East Wind

Mordred • **Celtic** traitor

morning childhood; youth; any propitious time; pristine happiness; Paradise; purity; promise; renewal of love; bringer of health, freshness, wealth; release of treasures locked in darkness or myth; trust in oneself; new beginning • **red sky at morning** sailor take warning • *see also* **dawn**

morning glory associated with Virgo • **flower language** affectation • **heraldic** affection • **Japanese** associated with July

Morning Star the perpetual rebirth of daylight; the life principle • **Christian** the state of perfection before the Fall • **Islamic** serene beauty • **Mayan** elder brother of the moon; associated with forest animals and hunters • **Mexican Indian** bringer of evil • **North American Indian** *Great Plains:* the life principle; a trinity with the sun and moon

mortar and pestle the feminine principle and masculine principle respectively; the small factors that influence events; attribute of SS Cosmas and Damian; emblem of pharmacy; pharmacology, alchemy • **Chinese** attribute of the hare in the moon

moschatel • **flower language** weakness

Moses • **Jewish** emancipation; law-giver; spiritual messenger; associated with the Ten Commandments

mosque • **Islamic** emblem of Islam

mosquito unrest; disquietude; wickedness; rebellion; annoyance; aggressiveness • **Chinese** rebellion; wickedness • *see also* **insect**

moss humility; service; friendship; boredom; parasite • **flower language** maternal love; *Iceland moss:* health; *mosses gathered together:* ennui

moth corruption; parasite; decay; destruction; the soul seeking God; being consumed by mystical love; faithless frivolity • **Greek** a form of Psyche • **Turkic** reincarnation of the dead • *see also* **insect**

mother material life; the unconscious; the collective unconscious; strength; the feminine principle; unconditional love; shelter; tenderness; warmth; nourishment; comfort; wisdom; the earth; the life principle, but may be indifferent to individual human suffering; the containing principle • **Christian** the Church • *see also* **stepmother; virgin mother; woman**

motherwort • **flower language** secret love; concealed love

motor *see* **engine**

motorcycle often has a sexual connotation • *see also* **steed; vehicle**

mould *see* **mold**

mound Earth Mother; dwelling of the dead; entrance to another world

mountain loftiness of spirit; spiritual elevation; connection between heaven and earth; passage from one plane to another; realm of meditation; communion with the spirit, deities, wisdom; solitariness; resurrection; mystic center; World Axis; World Navel; home of deities; freedom; peace; majesty; constancy; stability; changelessness; firmness; eternity; stillness • **mountain peak** meditation; achievement; victory; oneness; full consciousness; the bounds of human development; the supraconscious; associated with rain, sun, thunder gods • **twin mountain peaks** duality; seat of solar, or astral divinities; seat of the sun and the moon • **pilgrimage up a sacred mountain** aspiration; renunciation of worldly desires • **mountain climbing** inner elevation; spiritual ascent • **snow-covered mountain** nobility; cold reason; abstract thought • **two brass mountains** the gates of heaven • **mountain interior** sometimes the abode of the dead • **African** abode of the gods; the longing for and dangers of initiation • **Amerindian** abode of the gods • **Christian** attribute of St. David; *mountain with four rivers:* the throne of God • **European** *glass mountain* • **Hindu** *blue sapphire mountain:* the southern face of Mount Meru • **Islamic** *Mount Kaf:* the mother-mountain of all other mountains, the boundary between the visible and invisible worlds, home of the Simurg; *emerald mountain range:* Kaf • **Jewish** place of proximity to God; *mountain with temple on top of it:* associated with Micah; *mountain with feet above it protruding from a cloud:* Nahum's vision; *Mount Horeb and Mount Sinai:* seat of the sun and the moon respectively • **Sumerian** an undifferentiated mass of primal matter • **Taoist** place where Immortals descended and left messages for mankind; place where Immortals ascended into heaven; *Mountain in the Middle of the World:* home of the Immortals

mountain lion *see* **puma**

mourning bride (plant) • **flower language** unfortunate attachment; I have lost all

mouse timidity; senseless agitation; turbulence; poverty; humility; insignificance; quietness; domesticity; untidiness; madness; silence; cleverness; vanity; gratitude; fecundity; decay; passing time; destruction; the powers of darkness; evil; associated with Saturn (planet) • **mouse skin coat or cloak** humility • **Christian** the devil; the devourer; a soul in purgatory; attribute of SS Fina, Gertrude of Nivelles • **Greco-Roman** attribute of Apollo, Sabazios, Zeus/Jupiter • **Hindu** steed of Ganesha • **Jewish** duplicity; hypocrisy

mouth creation; destruction; the creative Word; gateway to another state or realm; the power to control the use of reason; the gates of hell; the doors of Paradise • **open mouth** the female • **closed mouth, or with tongue sticking out** the male • **gagging the mouth of initiates** the need for secrecy and not speaking without permission • **Aztecan** the all-consuming earth • **Egyptian** *opening the mouth of the dead:* enabling the dead person to speak the truth to his judges in the underworld; *infant with his finger in his mouth:* Horus • **Estonian** *water-spirit with enormous mouth:* a nakk • **Indic** *woman with no mouth:* a churel • **Islamic** *angel with 70,000 heads each of which had 70,000 mouths:* Mohammed's vision

moving plant • **flower language** agitation

mozzetta • **Christian** a non-liturgical garment worn by popes and cardinals when not in Rome, and by bishops, archbishops, and abbots within the limits of their jurisdiction

MR *or* M.R. stands for *Maria Regina* in Latin; monogram of the Virgin Mary, especially when shown with a crown • **on a shield** attribute of the archangel Gabriel

mud the emergence of matter; a nascent state; evil; primordial slime; excrement; the receptive earth impregnated by fertilizing water; source of fertility and growth; primitive and unregenerate man; the opposite of marble; the lower level of existence; retrogression • **sinking in mud** fear of maternal incest; devouring

mugwort clumsiness; awkwardness; ugliness; beer flavoring • **flower language** tranquility; happiness • **folkloric** used for love potions

mulberry kindliness and sharpness combined; slowness; wisdom; tragic love; related to silk, war (especially the juice); associated with initiation, the archangel Raphael; the three stages of life — white for innocence, red for activity, black for old age and death • **Chinese** industry; filial piety; the comforts of home; emblem of East; Tree of Life; *mulberry staff:* mourning for a mother; *bow of mulberry wood:* used to shoot arrows in the four directions to destroy evil; *mulberry tree that appears miraculously at a dy-*

nastic event: a evil omen • **Greek** misfortune in love; the mingled blood of Pyramus and Thisbe • **heraldic** liberality; peace; felicity

mule perversity; stubbornness; pride; hypocrisy; heresy; sterility; mutual help among underdogs; durability; a faithful worker; mount of a king or cardinal • **chariot drawn by mules** attribute of Poverty personified • **heraldic** abbot or abbess with pastoral jurisdiction only • **Tibetan** *woman on a white-faced mule:* Lha-mo • *see also* **ass**

mullein • **flower language** *white mullein:* good nature

mullet (bird) lasciviousness; stupidity; swiftness

multiplicity intensification; disintegration; regression; loss of unity

mum *see* **chrysanthemum**

mummy life; magic beyond the grave; associated with curses, ancient Egypt • **Jewish** attribute of Joseph, Jacob

murder to remove an idea or principle from one's mind, or from existence

mushroom suspicion; the ephemeral; rapid growth; bad news; lucky; a wanderer; related to fairies; connected with ecstatic visions, death • **American** popular emblem of Bohemian-Americans • **Chinese** longevity • **Bantu** the soul • **Dogon** associated with the coating of the stomach, musical instruments • **Tungun** reincarnated souls of the dead • **Taoist** image of primeval heaven • *see also* **fungus**

music order; harmony; a general restorative; related to fertility; harmony arising from chaos; the harmony of the universe; will; mockery; generally indicative of the prevailing atmosphere (chaotic, erotic, somber, etc.); the spiritual made manifest • **Celtic** *apple tree branch:* has the power to erase sad memories with its magic music • **Christian** *music written on a scroll:* attribute of SS Ambrose, Cecilia, Gregory the Great • **Pythagorean** the harmony of numbers with the cosmos

musical instruments • **angels with instruments** praise of God • **stringed instruments** usually associated with joy; the feminine • **metal instruments** usually associated with warriors, nobles, pageantry, war • **wooden instruments** usually associated with the common folk • **pipe instruments** phallic • **Christian** attribute of St. Cecilia • **Indic, Tibetan** *musical instrument of bone:* asceticism, access to immortality • *see also* specific instruments such as **drum; flute**

musician the fascination with death; harmony with divine nature; the mind which fosters higher emotions • **Mochican** Ai apaec (especially with lizard and dog)

musk female sexuality • **Christian** attribute of the Virgin Mary

musk plant • **flower language** weakness

mustard (plant) fertility; abundance; patience; faith; the Church; indifference • **mustard seed** great growth from small beginnings; fire

mutilation fertility rite; proof of courage at puberty; mourning; grief; covenant of friendship; appeasement of a deity; gaining power over a deity; often regarded as a disqualification for office • *see also* **maiming**

myrobalan • **flower language** privation; bereavement

myrrh a sacred ointment; embalming; purification; chastity; gladness; higher qualities; peace; bliss; truth; logic; natural good and wisdom; power; strength; vitality; mysticism; suffering; sorrow • **Christian** attribute of the Nativity of Christ, the Virgin Mary, Nicodemus; *casket of myrrh:* attribute of Balthazar the magus; *myrrh and aloes:* the Passion of Christ, martyrdom, sorrow, pity, Christ's priestly office • **flower language** gladness • **Greek** *myrrh tree:* mother of Adonis • **Jewish** *myrrh smoke:* associated with the race of Ham

myrtle love; victory; amicability; constancy; immortality; humaneness; virginity; messianic promises; everlasting love; conjugal fidelity; supplication; life; nature; happiness; peace; joy; triumph; justice; prophecy; pastoral poetry; tranquility; purity; mastery of impulses; connected with the underworld, death, immortality, resurrection; attribute of Academy personified • **myrtle wreath** attribute of initiates, brides • **burnt myrtle** envy • **Christian** attribute of Christ, the Virgin Mary, gentiles converted by Christ • **Egyptian** love; joy; sacred to Hathor • **Greco-Roman** love and marriage; marital bliss; childbirth; sacred to Adonis, Aphrodite/Venus, Poseidon/Neptune, Artemis/Diana, Europa, the three Graces, Dionysus/Bacchus; associated with Bona Dea • **heraldic** love; joy; mirth • **Jewish** marriage; the flower of the tabernacle • **Mandaean** rebirth; renewal of life; vehicle of the breath of life; attribute of priest, marriage, baptism, death • **Roman** *myrtle with sleeping soldier:* Scipio the Younger

mystic center *see* **center**

mystic knot infinity; everlasting life; never-ending wisdom and awareness • **Buddhism** continuity of life; infinity and eternity; one of the Eight Treasures • **Chinese** longevity; compassion • **Hindu** *mystic knot of Vishnu:* continuity; immortality; infinity

N

N associated with alertness, inconstancy, imagination, water, the ash tree, entrance, initiation, physical existence, the liver, the nerves, Saturn (planet), Aquarius, Scorpio; equivalent to -5- • **medieval** occasionally the Roman numeral for 90 • **tarot** associated with Temperance

naga, nagina • **Buddhist** temple guardians; givers of the begging bowl; protector of the Buddha • **Hindu** fertility; rejuvenation; guardians of thresholds, treasure, spiritual knowledge, and cattle; the life force; passionate nature; possessors of the elixir of life and immortality; connected with rain and water; *two nagas intertwined:* the fertilized waters from which the earth goddess arises • **Nepalese** connected with rain

naiad oracle; prophecy

nails (body) • **long nails** attribute of a seductress, an evil being, an aristocrat, the leisure class • **clipping** purification • **clippings** magically charged; part of the soul • **Armenian** *demon with brass fingernails:* an al • **folkloric** *white specks on nails:* sign of lies, or good luck; *yellow specks:* death omen; *black specks:* unlucky; *cutting nails on Friday or Sunday:* unlucky • **Mediterranean** *cutting nails at sea in good weather:* unlucky; *tossing nail clippings overboard during a storm:* appeasement

nails (hardware) phallus; World Axis; tenacity; binding; support; attribute of the Hellespontic sibyl • **iron nails** protection against evil • **finding a nail** (especially rusty) lucky • **American** *ring made from a horseshoe nail:* lucky charm • **Christian** attribute of Christ's crucifixion (early use was four nails, later, three nails became customary), also of SS Helena, Joseph of Arimathea, Bernard, Louis IX; *nails protruding from fingers:* attribute of St. Erasmus • **heraldic** suffering • **Tibetan** *ritual nail (phurbu):* impales or drives off demons

nakedness *see* **nudity**

Nalagiri • **Hindu** brute strength

name the soul; key to power; renaming a ship is unnatural, or unlucky, occasionally this belief is carried over to other objects or beings

Nandi • **Hindu** justice; strength; dharma; the cosmic order; steed of Shiva

Naonhaithya • **Zoroastrian** Discontent personified

napkin • **Christian** *with Christ's likeness on it:* attribute of St. Veronica; *napkin with cruse of wine:* attribute of the Good Samaritan

Narcissus • **Greek** grace; self-consciousness; self love; the death of youth; egotism; introspection

narcissus (flower) attribute of Revenge personified; shares in the symbolism of Narcissus in mythology • **Arabian** the righteous man • **Chinese** introspection; self-esteem; lucky omen for the coming year • **Christian** triumph of divine love over worldliness and the triumph of sacrifice over selfishness • **flower language** egotism; *poet's narcissus:* egotism, selfishness, self-love; *yellow narcissus:* disdain • **Greco-Roman** attribute of Erinyes/Furies, Persephone/Proserpine; sacred to Demeter/Ceres, Hades/Pluto, Narcissus, Nemesis/Invidia, Selene/Luna; *narcissus fumes:* producer of madness • **Japanese** joy; silent purity • **Jewish** associated with Spring, the end of the world

nard *see* **spikenard**

nasturtium • **flower language** patriotism; trophy of war

navel origin; midpoint; mystic center; World Axis; fertility; order; peace; the point on the mental plane midway between higher and lower nature; vulva; related to prophecy

navigator conductor of the soul

Nazareth • **Christian** a point of progress on the path to perfection

Nazi domination; fascism; slaughter; tyranny

Nebuchadnezzar (tarot) *see* **Wheel of Fortune (tarot)**

Necessity (tarot) *see* **Strength (tarot)**

neck purified emotions; strength; stubbornness; willpower; execution; has a sexual and phallic connotation; communication of the soul with the body • **Christian** *wound on the neck:* attribute of St. Lucy; *three wounds on the neck:* attribute of St. Cecilia • **Hindu** *blue neck usually with entwined serpents:* attribute of Shiva

necklace unification of diversity; order from chaos; fertility; riches; light; protection; willpower; rank; office; dignity; cosmic and social ties and bonds; an erotic bond (especially on females); attribute of sky goddesses • **broken necklace, with scattered beads** psychic dismemberment; universal upheaval • **Bambaran** *Faro's copper necklace:* enables him to hear the everyday conversations of men; *Faro's gold necklace:* enables to him to hear the innermost thoughts of men • **Greek** *Harmonia's necklace:* unlucky • **Hindu** *necklace of skulls:* attribute of Shiva • **Roman** *gold necklace:* attribute of a foreign soldier; *silver necklace:* attribute of a soldier who was a Roman citizen • **Yoruban** *amber necklace:* sacred to Oshun

necktie cohesion; social bonds; phallus; male energy

nectar the soul's entire service to the highest ideals

needle marriage; the intellect; repression; phallus; attribute of a tailor, housewife • **being pricked on the finger by a needle** ill omen • **threading a needle** passing through the gateway of the sun; escaping the cosmos

Negro child of darkness; the primitive and emotional self; the collective unconscious; the Terrible Father; base passions; dark side of the personality; the instincts; the soul before entering on the path of spiritual evolution • *see also* **complexion**

neighbor associated with the masculine or feminine aspects of one's self

neighing an expression of lust, pride, bragging

Neptune *see* **Poseidon/Neptune**

Neptune (planet) associated with intuition, spiritual aspirations, extrasensory perception, treacherous tendencies, mysticism, genius, sensitivity, the deepest layers of the soul, nine, the feet, the primordial ocean, Pisces, regeneration, the subconscious, the cosmic, passive receptivity, conscience, the subconscious, universal integration, wholeness, the Bronze Age, Poseidon/Neptune, the archangel Asariel • **Hindu** associated with the second chakra (Leydig cells)

Nereids • **Greco-Roman** personification of the waves of the ocean

nerve • **nervous system** associated with Mercury (planet) • **Roman** euphemism for phallus

nest heaven; haven for growth of the spirit; home; protection; comfort • **Chinese** *bird destroying its own nest:* harbinger of disorder and trouble in the empire • **Hindu** Paradise

Nestor • **Greek** justice; eloquence; wisdom

net entrapment; ensnarement; entanglement; death; fertility and love; craftiness; repression; the negative aspect of feminine power; attribute of supreme deities, Great Mothers • **fishnet** searching the waters of the unconscious; associated with fishing, fisherman • **dragnet** the police • **Chinese** net of heaven; the stars • **Christian** the Church; the unbreakable bond of the Church; ensnarement by the devil; attribute of the disciples, St. Andrew (usually has a fish in it); *dragnet:* the Church • **Egyptian** associated with the underworld • **Greco-Roman** attribute of Hephaestus/Vulcan; *lovers under a net:* Venus and Mars • **Jewish** anguish • **Norse** attribute of Ran • **Oceanic** attribute of Vaerua, Akaanga • **Sumero-Semitic** the Word of deities; attribute of Marduk, Enil, Ninkhursaq; associated with Bel, Ishtar, Tiamat • **Taoist** *heaven's net:* unity • see also **entanglement**

Netherlands associated with sailing, drinking, gluttony, stinginess, rudeness, the Renaissance

nettle annoyance; distress; envy; slander; cruelty; death; repentance; danger; an aphrodisiac • **flower language** cruelty; *stinging or burning nettle:* slander; *nettle tree:* concert, plan • **heraldic** pride; vanity; sting of death to foes

New Jerusalem *see* **Jerusalem**

New Testament • **Christian** spiritual truth; emblem of Christianity, the Gospel

New Year starting anew; renewal; cosmic regeneration; the promise of new growth; the increasing power of the sun

Nibelungen • **Germanic, Norse** the megalomania of the petty mind; subconscious forces that provoke insatiable greed and ruin; doomed human ambitions

niche dwelling of the divine presence

Nidhogg • **Norse** malevolent forces of the universe

night the unconscious; the feminine principle; death; madness; disintegration; regression; evil; Winter; germination; gestation; dormancy; potentiality; darkness; the disappearance of all knowledge that may be defined; deprived of all psychological support; the wiping clean of the intellect; passivity; involution; precursor of creation; the subconscious; the lustful female; feminine fertility; the womb; chaos; pre-natal darkness preceding rebirth, initiation, illumination • **night birds** associated with Saturn (planet)

night blooming cereus • **flower language** transient beauty

nightingale harmony; exclusiveness; passion; unrequited love; night love; worldly love; herald of spring; wakefulness; purity; poetic escape or ecstasy; the tragic victim; forlornness; rape; superstition; betrayal • **Christian** the soul who waits for God at the darkest times; the devil's deceit • **Greek** Procne

nightjar (bird) an ill omen; the soul of an unbaptized child nightmare the longing of man for God; an ill omen; the unconscious threatening the conscious; sexual repression, especially of incest

nightmare the unconscious erupting into the conscious; unmet fears; inability to handle one's current fears; warning; evil omen

nightshade death; darkness; witchcraft • **deadly nightshade (belladonna)** death • **nightshade and foxglove** together punishment and pride, respectively • **flower language** *deadly nightshade (belladonna):* silence; *enchanter's nightshade:*

sorcery, witchcraft, skepticism, dark thoughts; *woody or bittersweet nightshade:* truth

Nike/Victoria • Greco-Roman victory; strength; progress; freedom; triumph; courage

Nile River emblem of Egypt; *sailboat on the Nile:* attribute of St. Athanasius

nimbus (radiance surrounding the head) supreme power; solar power; divine energy; genius; virtue; the vital force of wisdom; transcendental light of knowledge • **circular nimbus** attribute of dead sacred persons, the personifications of fundamental virtues (Faith, Hope, Charity, etc.) • **polygonal nimbus** sometimes used for allegorical figures • **hexagonal nimbus** used for a figure considered one degree below a saint; attribute of the personifications of fundamental virtues (Faith, Hope, Charity, etc.) • **square, rectangular, or hexagonal nimbus** attribute of a person honored while still living • **double nimbus** the dual aspect of the divinity • **blue nimbus** celestial joy • **Buddhist** *red nimbus:* solar, dynamic activity; attribute of Buddha • **Chinese** sun rays; sanctity • **Christian** holiness; saintliness; sanctity; divinity; note that in the Eastern church, the nimbus originally signified power and as such might be part of representations of Satan; *gold or white nimbus:* attribute of the Virgin Mary, members of the Trinity; *triangular or diamond-shaped nimbus:* God the Father; *three-rayed nimbus:* member of the Trinity; *black nimbus:* (usually polygonal) occasional attribute of Judas • **Greco-Roman** attribute of Helios/Sol, demigods, deified Roman emperors; *blue nimbus:* attribute of Zeus/Jupiter, Apollo • **Hindu** sanctity; sun rays; *flaming nimbus:* attribute of Shiva; *trefoil nimbus:* Hindu triad • **Japanese** sun rays; sanctity; *god with a boat-shaped nimbus:* Amida • **Jewish** *nimbus of Moses with two rays or horns:* truth and justice • **Mithraic** attribute of Mithras • *see also* **glory**

Niobe • Greek pride humbled

Nirvana • Buddhist extinction of the Ego within the Self

Noah • Jewish overseer of cleansing, transformation; one who is ready to undergo transformation or change

nobles dignity; fame; pride; one's higher self; the high point of existence

noise punishment; chaos; associated with hell

noon the opposite of darkness; corresponds to Summer, to middle age in man • **Islamic** the zenith of spiritual light • **Jewish** light at its fullest; a pause in time; eternity • *see also* **midnight**

noose knowledge; the captive; death by hanging; despair; death; threat of death • **Hindu** knowledge; intellectual power; the force to seize and hold firm; death; attribute of Devi, Kali, Varuna, Yama • **Sumero-Semitic** attribute of Marduk (may also have a net) • *see also* **hanging (execution); rope**

North coldness; Winter; old age; wisdom; that which does not change; the new moon; the home of the gods; land of the dead; night; darkness; obscurity; barbarianism; the furthest bounds of the universe; associated with Saturn (planet), the archangels Cassiel, Raphael • **facing North** posing a question • **Bambaran** home of Faro, associated with the seventh heaven, kingship, water creatures • **Buddhist** associated with Amoghasiddhi • **Chinese** cold; Winter; water; yin; fear; day; light; associated with the Black Tortoise • **Christian** darkness; night; barbarianism; evil; the region of Lucifer; *reading the Gospel from the North end of a church:* the desire to convert barbarians, the heathen • **Egyptian** day; light; the masculine • **Dogon** associated with the Pleiades, humans, fish • **Hindu** light; day; the masculine • **Persian** evil; the powers of darkness; associated with Ahriman • **Jewish** associated with evil, unrighteousness, idolatry; *North wind:* associated with destruction • **Mayan** associated with red • **Mexican Indian** home of the moon, the Milky Way, Texctlipoca; associated with the Underworld, darkness, cold, hunger, drought, darkness, the eagle, black • **Mongolian** associated with the dead • **Tungun** associated with earth, flesh, bone • **Ural-Altaic** home of the World Mountain, home of the supreme deity

North Star the unmoved mover; a hole in space and time; spiritual guidance; the highest ideal

Northeast • Hindu the heavenly home of demons

nose inquisitiveness; meddling; snobbery; clarity; phallus; intuition discernment • **hooked nose** attribute of the White Goddess • **Chinese** *long nosed man:* may be a tengu • **Far Eastern** *amputated nose:* punishment for a faithless wife • **folkloric** *itching nose:* you will kiss a fool • **Japanese** *long nose:* attribute of the proud, boastful; *long-nosed man:* may be a tengu • **Middle Eastern** *amputated nose:* punishment for a faithless wife

nosegay *see* **bouquet**

nostrils seat of the breath of life, anger, passion

nothingness annihilation; chaos

nourishment *see* **food**

nudity natural state; birth state; resurrection in rebirth; throwing off of worldly ambition and wealth; renunciation; shame; protest; related to madness, the dead; loss of one's worldly pretensions; return to the primeval state • **nuditas naturalis** the natural state of man • **nuditas virtualis** purity; innocence; sinlessness; self-abnegation before deities • **nuditas temporalis** lack of worldly goods, especially when abandoned in service to God; penitence; contempt for worldly things • **nuditas criminalis** lust; vanity; the absence of all virtues; lasciviousness • **deity god naked to the waist** the top half represents the sky, the bottom half the earth • **naked deity or hero** freedom from worldly taint • **Christian** holy renunciation of worldliness; penitence; pagan or demonic shamelessness • **Roman** shame; poverty

number the farther a number is from -1-, the more deeply involved it is in the world; the first ten numbers refer to the spirit; repetition of a number stresses its quantitative power, but detracts from its spiritual dignity • **even numbers** associated with the soluble, ephemeral, feminine, earthly, negative and passive principles • **odd numbers** associated with the insoluble, masculine, celestial, positive, and active principles • **Chinese** *even numbers:* yin; associated with night, cold, Winter, earth, black, the terrestrial, the mutable, the inauspicious; *odd numbers,* yang; associated with clay, fire, heat, sun, white, the celestial • *see also* specific numbers: -0-, -1-, -2-, etc.

nunnery • **English** *Elizabethan:* euphemism for a whorehouse

nuns contemplation; the higher virtues; chastity • **nun with a book** the book is usually the rule of the order • **nuns watching soldiers scale city walls** associated with St. Clare • **nun in gray Franciscan habit** St. Clare (often holding monstrance or crozier) • **candle held by a nun, blown out by a demon** St. Genevieve • **Franciscan nun with roses in her lap and/or a crown** St. Elizabeth of Hungary • **Carmelite nun being presented a white veil by the Virgin Mary** St. Mary Magdalene of Pazzi • *see also* **habit (monastic); monastery; monks**

nurse a promoter of spiritual growth; comforter; caregiver

nursing new birth; charity; adoption • **woman nursing a child** motherhood; love; charity; Charity personified; the Mother Goddess • **woman nursing more than one child** Charity, Earth personified • **Finnish** *dragon nursing serpent:* Ajatar • **Roman** *woman nursing an old man:* Cimon and Pero • *see also* **breasts**

Nut (goddess) • **Egyptian** personification of the sky

nut hidden wisdom; fertility; hidden riches; testicles; the soul; reincarnation; mystery (especially a hazel nut) • **nut cracking** coition, especially between a small man and a large overbearing woman • **Christian** Christ (especially a split walnut) — the outer casing being his flesh, the hard shell the wood of the Cross, and the kernel his divine nature • *see also* specific kinds of nuts: **walnut; chestnut**, etc.

nutmeg thought to have been an aphrodisiac, an abortive

nymph the unconscious; license; lawlessness; soulless beauty; pleasure of the world; the lure of heroic madness manifested in erotic or warlike feats; temptation; transitoriness; multiplicity and dissolution; the independent and fragmentary characteristics of the feminine unconscious; the feminine productive powers of the universe; guardians of chastity, groves, fountains, springs, and mountains; associated with the fertility of nature • **nymphs as companions of a god** expression of the god's ideas • **Christian** *nymph with St. John:* his victory over worldly temptations • **Greek** *merman pursing a sea nymph:* Glaucus and Scylla respectively • *see also* **Ondine**

O

O associated with the cosmos, material responsibility, balance, intellect, the home, business, children, affection, restriction, fertility, perfection, eternity, corresponds to Virgo, the liver, -6-, the heart • **medieval** occasionally the Roman numeral for -11- • **tarot** corresponds to the Fool

oak strength; longevity; liberty; hospitality; fertility; thunder; majesty; endurance; eternity; force; virtue; forgiveness; fire; World Axis; turning point; faith; courage; a door; durability; steadfastness; protection; man; the human body; great growth from a small beginning; a tree of the first rank; emblem of sky, thunder, fertility deities; associated with Sagittarius, the archangels Cassiel, Zadkiel • **oak leaf** bravery; regeneration • **oak wreath** strength; hospitality; victory on the seas • **Celtic** a holy tree; strength; hospitality; stability; nobility; sacred to Dagda; associated with Jupiter (planet), diamonds, June/July; *oak and mistletoe:* the masculine and feminine respectively • **Chinese** masculine strength; the fragility of unyielding strength • **Christian** Christ; the Virgin Mary; the endurance of the Christian against adversity; forgiveness; eternity; a tree of the Cross; *bishop with foot on fallen oak:* St. Boniface; conversion of pagans • **Druidic** the sacred tree; the masculine principle; emblem of Druidism • **flower language** hospitality; *live oak:* liberty; *white oak:* independence; *oak leaf:* bravery, humanity • **Greco-Roman** majesty; tree mother; World Axis; Cosmic Tree; emblem of Cybele, Silvanus, Philemon; sacred to Zeus/Jupiter, Hera/Juno, the Ephesian Artemis; *crown or wreath of oak leaves:* award for victory in the Pythian Games, lifesaving; attribute of Zeus/Jupiter; *man attacked by a lion or wolves, hands trapped in an oak tree trunk:* Milo of Croton; *oak club:* attribute of Heracles/Hercules; *oak spear:* attribute of Quirinus • **heraldic** pride; beauty; strength; victory; great age; power; *oak leaves:* military distinction; *oak with acorns:* continuous growth and fertility; *oak leaf and acorn wreath:* service saving a life or in homeland defense • **Jewish** the Tree of the Covenant; the Divine Presence; place of angelic visions; emblem of Abraham • **Norse** Thor's Tree of Life; *oak grove:* a place of worship; *oak at Volsung's palace:* Branstock • **North American Indian** sacred to Mother Earth • **Prussian** associated with Ramow • **Slavic** associated with Perun • **Yakut** World Axis, Cosmic Tree

oar creative thought; knowledge; skill; power; navigation; progress; punishment; slavery; attribute of river gods • **steering oar** skill; knowledge; bravery • **Christian** the Word; attribute of St. Julian the Hospitator; *oar with saw or battleaxe, or two oars crossed:* attribute of St. Simon • **Egyptian** sovereignty; rule; action; *boat with eight oars:* Tchetetfet • **Greco-Roman** attribute of Cronus/Saturn, *oars turning into serpents:* the kidnapping of Dionysus/Bacchus • **Jewish** attribute of Noah

oats food of the lower classes; youthful excesses • **flower language** music; the bewitching soul of music

obelisk aspiration; regeneration; eternal life; fertility; phallus; may generative power; sun ray; a penetrating spirit; a stabilizing force; solar ascension; finger of a god; support of the sky; World Axis; Tree of Life; protection against evil spirits; mystic center • **Egypt** Ra; sun ray; solar generative power

obesity gluttony; prosperity; attainment; high standing; importance

oboe plaintiveness; phallus; the masculine principle

obsidian peace; charm for protection, grounding,

divination • **Aztecan** the source of life; healing; bringer of both life and death; *obsidian mirror as a foot:* attribute of Tezcatlipocal • **Central American Indian** charm against black magic, evil spirits

ocean grandeur; dynamic force; universal life; immense illogic; the generative source of life; the collective unconscious; the Great Mother; the mother; woman; separation of the heaven and earth; unbounded desolation; death and regeneration; the Abyss; primordial creation; the source of life; related to sexual desire, amniotic waters, longing for adventure, spiritual exploration, conscience, time, eternity; liberty; untamable wildness; loneliness; formlessness; chaos; purification; the mediating agent between life and death; the deepest reaches of the soul or psyche • **ocean swells, or a stormy sea** activity or disturbance in the unconscious • **sea of flames** life as an infirmity • **return to the sea** death • **Christian** *sea of glass:* stilled emotions • **Islamic** infinite divine wisdom; exoteric wisdom • **Sumero-Semitic** primordial waters; wisdom; the feminine principle; blind forces of chaos; associated with Apsu, Tiamat • **Taoist** the Tao; inexhaustibility; primordial life • *see also* **salt water; voyage; waves**

ocelot • **South American Indian** the solar; female sexual desire; protection; maternity; attribute of the Great Mother, virgin warrior goddesses, love goddesses, earth goddesses

ochre deceitfulness; earth • **African** associated with earth

Ocnus • **Greek** a man with a demanding wife; hesitation; frustration; delay; the wasting of time and effort

octagon regeneration; renewal; rebirth; baptism; the halfway point in squaring the circle • **Chinese** path of life; *octagonal mirror:* intermediary between heaven and earth • **Japanese** emblem of the palace of heaven; *octagonal mirror:* harmony; perfection • *see also* **eight; circle**

October associated with harvest, sowing, Autumn

octopus existentialism; malignancy; craftiness; the unfolding of creation; associated with Cancer, Summer Solstice, deep waters; shares in the symbolism of the dragon, spider, and spiral • *see also* **squid**

oculus *see* **dome**

Odin • **Norse** blind violence; the internal contradictions of power; success doomed to destruction

odor *see* **smell**

Odysseus/Ulysses • **Greco-Roman** cleverness; versatility; perseverance; adventure; courage

odyssey *see* **journey**

Oedipus • **Greek** fixation of the son on the mother; the individual wavering between the neurotic and the commonplace; overattachment to earthly things; achieving self-mastery by acceptance of death

offering sacrifice of lower values for higher ones

ogre pre-human savage life; blind, greedy force; tyranny; stupidity • **male ogre** the Terrible Father • **female ogre** the Terrible Mother; fear of incest

oil divine love; the grace of God; fertility; mercy; consecration; dedication; riches; light; preservation against corruption; joy; peace; cunning; dedication; incentive; calmness; healing; spiritual illumination; cunning • **olive oil** the grace of God • **alchemic** intermediary bond; cleansing; protection • **Christian** *oil in a cauldron:* attribute of St. John • **Jewish** *horn of oil:* attribute of David; *endless cruse of oil:* the inexhaustible grace and mercy of God, attribute of Elijah and the Widow of Sarepta • **Japanese** primeval water • *see also* **chrism**

ointment love; divine love; coition; purity; heroism; hospitality; luxury • **Christian** attribute of the burial of Christ; *box of ointment:* attribute of SS Mary of Bethany, Mary of Egypt, Mary Magdalene, Cosmas, Damian • **Greek** *box of ointment:* attribute of Phaon

old man the father; the master; tradition; contemplation; justice; mortality; wisdom; insight; one's higher self; old and/or tired ideas; the setting sun; the waning moon; the old year; Saturn (planet) • **naked or half-naked old man, especially bald or with a single lock of hair, and/or with an hourglass** Father Time; Chronos; the personification of Time • **old man with a scythe and hourglass, sometimes on crutches** the Grim Reaper; the personification of Death • **Aymaran** an achachila • **Finnish** Ahti • **Greco-Roman** *old man with a scythe:* Cronus/Saturn; *old man with wings carrying off a girl:* Boreas; *old man with serpent tails for feet:* Boreas; *old man and child with mirror:* Socrates; *old man with an hourglass:* Chronos • **Irish** *old man in a green or red coat:* a leprechaun • **Kabalistic** esoteric and occult wisdom • **Mochican** Ai apaec (especially with cat whiskers and teeth, and/or lizard, dog) • **Russian** *gray-haired old man living behind a stove:* a domovik • *see also* **man**

Old Testament pre-Christian religion • **Jewish** spiritual truth; wisdom; emblem of Judaism

old woman • **old woman, 90 to 100 years old** Death personified • **Buddhist** *blind old woman in the Round of Existence:* absence of knowledge, ignorance leading to death • **Greco-Roman** *old woman with pointed ears and serpent:* Bona Dea; *old woman and naked goddess with cornucopia:* Vertumnus and Pomona respectively • **Slavic** *one-eyed old woman:* Likho • *see also* **hag**

oleander danger; deadly beauty

olive immortality; fertility; peace; plenty; courageous love and faith • **olive tree** dwelling place of the moon; emblem of the moon • **olive branch** reconciliation between God and Man • **olive branch** peace; deliverance; concord; charity; prosperity; wisdom; fertility; faith; righteousness; victory; dedication; anointing; beauty; the new year; attribute of the personifications of the Golden Age, Peace, Concord, Wisdom • **olive wreath** peace • **wild olive** bitterness • **dove with olive branch** divine peace; attribute of the personification of the Golden Age • **Chinese** delicacy; grace; quiet; persistence; *olive wreath:* literary merit • **Christian** peace; Christ's peace, healing, faith, and beauty; the Church; the fruit of the Church; the faith of the just; attribute of St. Agnes; Gethsemane (especially a gnarled olive tree); *palm, cypress, and olive trees together:* Gethsemane; *dove arising with an olive branch in its mouth:* a soul that has made its peace with God; *olive branch:* occasional attribute of the archangel Gabriel at the Annunciation • **flower language** peace • **Greco-Roman** achievement; victory; peace; emblem of Zeus/Jupiter, Athena/Minerva, Heracles/Hercules, Cybele, Hermes/Mercury, sometimes Apollo; *olive wreath:* prize for winners at the games of Athena/Minerva, Hera; *crown of wild olives:* prize for winners at the Olympic Games, attribute of Zeus/Jupiter; *crown of olives with crown of wild olives:* the sacred marriage of Zeus and Hera, Jupiter and Juno, the sun and the moon; *woman with cornucopia in her left hand and an olive branch in her right:* Concordia • **heraldic** *olive branch or leaves:* peace, concord, reconciliation • **Islamic** *olive tree:* World Axis, the Tree of Blessing which gives spiritual blessing and illumination • **Japanese** friendship • **Jewish** strength; beauty; safe travel; attribute of Noah, Abraham, the Paradise of the chosen

om *see* **aum**

omega (Greek letter) end; finality • **alpha and omega** the beginning and the end; creation and destruction; Christ; totality; infinity • *see also* **alpha**

onager a wild man; one who is very difficult to tame • **Christian** reluctance to accept the yoke of God • **Jewish** Ishmael; nomad; adventuresomeness • *see also* **ass** which the onager is frequently confused

Ondine • **German** the perilous nature of water; the perils of unconditional surrender to seduction

onion unity; the many in one; the cosmos in equilibrium; deity emblem; light; aphrodisiac; immortality; revelation; protection against evil spirits, especially lunar • **Egyptian** *onion stalk:* charm against disease • **Hindu** the ego which must be stripped away layer by layer • **Roman** avoided because it weakened the life force

onyx dignity; sincerity; clearness; perspicacity; quarrel; reciprocity; charm for marital happiness, friendship, spiritual thoughts, curbing passions, changing bad habits, protection against nightmares and evil spirits; thought to cause stillbirths, discord, nightmares; stone for 7th wedding anniversaries; associated with the archangel Cassiel • **Indic, Persian** charm to ease childbirth and protect from the evil eye • *see also* **sardonyx**

opal lucky; prayers; assurance; religious fervor; associated with Scorpio, October, 12th, 14th, 26th wedding anniversaries, the archangel Raphael; charm for hope, self-confidence, prophetic powers, increasing faithfulness, tenderness, and happiness in love, purifying thoughts, driving out grief, protecting innocence, preventing heartache, fainting, and evil affections • **Greco-Roman** charm for foresight, prophecy, protection from disease

ophrys *spider ophrys:* associated with Arachne • **flower language** *bee ophrys:* error; *frog ophrys:* disgust; *spider ophrys:* adroitness; skill

opinicus *see* **griffin**

opium dissipation; evil • *see also* **poppy**

opossum strategy; diversion; deceit

oppressors prejudices; opinions that oppose truth

orange (color) fire; flame; the Holy Spirit; pride; ambition; heat; lust; marriage; hospitality; benevolence; luxury; health; vigor; passion tempered by earthly wisdom; balance between spirit and libido; endurance; flame; associated with the House of Orange, the sun, protestants in Northern Ireland, Jupiter (planet) • **impure orange** malevolence; egoism; cruelty; ferocity; the devil; desperation • **Buddhist** attribute of Buddha • **Chaldean** emblem of Jupiter (planet) • **Chinese** love; happiness • **Greco-Roman** *orange bridal veil:* permanence, fidelity; *orange clothes:* occasional attribute of Dionysus/Bacchus • **heraldic** endurance; strength; worthy ambition • **Japanese** love; happiness • **Kabalistic** splendor • **Oriental** associated with convicted criminals in ancient times • **zodiacal** associated with Gemini, Leo; *red-orange:* associated with Taurus; *yellow-orange:* associated with Cancer

orange (fruit) life; fecundity; generosity; jealousy; love; purity; chastity; the world; the feminine • **orange blossom** fecundity; exuberance; attribute of a bride • **cinnabar orange** lucky; immortality • **Chinese** immortality; lucky; an imperial sacrifice to heaven; fertility • **Christian** attribute of the Virgin Mary; *orange in the hand of the Christ child:* alludes to him as the future redeemer of mankind from original sin; *orange in representations of Paradise:* the fall of man and his redemption • **Greek** the Golden Apples of the Hesperides • **heraldic** marriage; fecundity; innocence; virginity • **Jewish** occasional substitute for the apple as the fruit of the Tree of Knowledge • **Kabalistic** associated with the archangel Raphael

orange tree generosity • **Arabian** *blossom wreath:* fertility, attribute of brides • **Christian** *blossom:* purity, chastity, virginity • **Greco-Roman** *blossom:* emblem of Artemis/Diana • **flower language** *blossom:* chastity, your purity equals your loveliness • **Japanese** *blossom:* pure love • *see also* **mock orange**

orant prayer

orb the world; sovereignty; completeness; perfection • **with serpent around it** sin encircling the earth • **with a spread eagle** devotion • **with an orrery** sovereignty at sea • **with wings** spiritual evolution • **British** attribute of kings • **Christian** *with serpent around it at the feet of the Virgin Mary:* her role as the second Eve; *peacock surmounting an orb:* rising above worldly things; *orb with a cross on it:* Christian dominion over the world, God's ultimate dominion over the world, salvation, gradual enlightenment of the world • **Germanic** attribute of Holy Roman emperors • *see also* **globe**

orchard death; opportunity; spiritual cultivation • **Christian** *pomegranate orchard:* attribute of the Virgin Mary

orchestra activity of the corporate whole; cooperation of the discrete toward a given end; social harmony

orchid luxury; love; beauty; magnificence; purity; perfection; spiritual perfection; fertilization; nobility; vulva; associated with Aquarius • **purple orchid** euphemism for phallus • **Chinese** refinement; harmony; fragrance; love; beauty; fecundity; the perfect or superior man; feminine charm; the secluded scholar; stimulant for procreation; associated with Spring festivals • **heraldic** magnificence

orchis • **flower language** a beauty; a belle; *bee orchis:* industry; *butterfly orchis:* gaiety; *fly orchis:* error

ordeal trial by a deity; test of authenticity, truth

Orestes • **Greek** revenge

organ (instrument) the universe; harmony; attribute of the personifications of Hearing, Music • **Christian** the praise of God from the Church; attribute of St. Cecilia • **Greek** attribute of Polyhymnia

orgasm voluntary return to primordial chaos from which life proceeds

orgy return to chaos; cosmic night; dissolution; regression; involution; invocation of primordial chaos; the lower potentialities of man; excessive self-gratification; misuse of one's talents; escape from time to pre-time • **Spring orgies** the union of the sun god with mother earth; encouragement of the forces of nature; regeneration; the sowing of seed; imitative fertility • **Winter orgies** return of chaos; celebration of the rebirth of the dying god • **Babylonian** duel between chaos and cosmos

Orient illumination; the fount of life

oriole • **American** *Baltimore oriole:* emblem of Maryland • **Chinese** marriage; gladness; emblem of Spring • **North American Indian** *golden oriole:* harmony, equilibrium

Orion • **Greek** the hunter

orle • **heraldic** protection; preservation • *see also* **annulet**

Orpheus • **Christian** Christ • **Greek** song; music; enchanter; seducer; one who can suppress but not destroy evil; pursuer of the ideal who makes no real sacrifices to attain it

orrery • **on an orb** sovereignty at sea

osier freedom; sincerity without finery or dissimulation • **flower language** frankness • *see also* **willow**

Osiris • **Egyptian** the inexhaustible power of plant life; the continuance of birth and rebirth; the universal life force; *mutilation of Osiris:* dissociation; *restoration of Osiris:* reintegration in a higher form

osmunda • **flower language** dreams

osprey sovereignty; cause of sorrow

ostensorium *see* **monstrance**

ostrich cowardice; shame; forgetfulness; lack of understanding; justice; cruelty; intemperance; inconstancy; heresy; sinful man; hypocrisy; man deserted by God; one who trusts in God; speed; stamina; foolishness; stupidity; a monster of Chaos • **ostrich feathers** truth and justice; knightly dignity; justice; distinction; fertility • **British** *three ostrich feathers:* emblem of the Prince of Wales • **Christian** *ostrich feather:* attribute of St. Bessus • **Coptic** *ostrich egg:* creation, life, resurrection, vigilance • **Dogon** light; water • **Egyptian** *ostrich feathers:* truth, justice, righteousness, sound judgment of the dead, attribute of Mat, Bes, Ament, Shu, Osiris, Anat; *crown of ten double ostrich plumes:* power to divide the heavens and enter them • **heraldic** endurance (often with a horseshoe in its mouth); *ostrich feathers:* obedience, serenity • **Islamic** *ostrich egg:* creation, life, resurrection, vigilance • **Semitic** a demon • **Zoroastrian** divine storm

otter transitory fertility; a lunar animal; playfulness; free spirit; balanced feminine energy • **Celtic** guide of the dead • **Christian** Christ's descent into hell; attribute of St. Cuthbert • **heraldic** prudence; free fishing rights; one who lives life to the fullest • **North American Indian** messenger of the gods; initiating spirit than kills and restores to life • **Persian** *thirty otter skins:* attribute of Anahita • **Romanian** guide of the dead • **Zoroastrian** a clean animal, to kill one is sinful

Ouranos *see* **Uranus/Caelus**

Ouroboros continuity of life; cosmic unity; primordial unity; time and eternity; cyclic time; spatial infinity; self-fecundation; self-sufficiency of nature; disintegration and reintegration; totality; truth and cognition in one; androgyny; the darkness before creation; immortality; eternity and wisdom; associated with funerals, alpha and omega • **alchemic** latent power; the unredeemed power of nature; unformed matter • **Buddhist** wheel of samsara • **Egyptian** circle of the universe; path of the sun god • **Greek** *surrounding an egg:* creation, resurrection, Cosmic Egg, mystery of life • **Hindu** wheel of samsara; latent energy • **Sumero-Semitic** the All One

oval the female; vulva; earth; suggests a natural (biological) object; attribute of a sacred figure • **Kalmyk** shape of the Southern Continent and the faces of its inhabitants

oven the womb; feminine transforming power; lust; unrevealed sorrow; a crucible; pure spiritual gestation

owl death; night; darkness; cold; passivity; knowledge; wisdom; ingratitude; darkness; vigilance; prophecy; loneliness; solitude; associated with hermits; despair; mourning; an object of ridicule; lack of nobility; desolation; related to witches, the archangel Gabriel, mourning; attribute of the personifications of Night, Wisdom, Sleep, Avarice • **owl screeching in daylight** unlucky omen • **screech owl** ill omen;

disaster; misfortune • **Ainu** *eagle owl:* messenger of the gods, a divine ancestor; *screech owl:* omen of danger; *barn owl, horned owl:* demonic, evil • **Amerindian** wisdom; divination; attribute of sorcerers • **Arabian** omen of bad luck • **Australian aboriginal** a woman's soul; messenger of Muurup • **Aztecan** the god of hell; the embodiment of rain, darkness, storm; associated with death, the lunar-terrestrial powers of the unconscious governing plants and the waters • **Bantu** associated with sorcery • **Celtic** associated with the underworld, corpses; attribute of Gwynn • **Central American Indian** death • **Chinese** evil; crime; death; an ungrateful child; horror; a sign of too much yang; cause of drought; associated with lightning, thunder, the Summer Solstice, drums, death; emblem of Huang Ti • **Christian** the devil; the powers of darkness; mourning; desolation; omen of misfortune, death; solitude; Jews who preferred the darkness to the light of Christ; pejorative emblem of the Synagogue; associated with Christ; *eagle and owl together:* day and night respectively, beginning and end respectively, alpha and omega respectively • **Egyptian** death; night; coldness; emblem of Amen-Ra • **Etruscan** attribute of the god of darkness • **Greco-Roman** emblem of Athens; sacred to Minerva, Athena/Minerva, Demeter/Ceres; *screech owl:* wisdom • **heraldic** vigilance; acute wit; the retired life • **Hindu** death; messenger and emblem of Yama; attribute of Karachi • **Islamic** an unclean animal • **Inuit** helper; guide • **Japanese** death; omen of misfortune; filial ingratitude; crime; an ungrateful child • **Jewish** a good omen; blindness; desolation; an unclean animal • **Lithuanian** sacred to Gilding • **Maori** unlucky • **Mayan** death omen • **Mexican Indian** night; death • **North American Indian** death; dominion over the night; conductor of souls • **Persian** bringer of bad luck • **Phoenician** Moloch • **Siberian** a helpful spirit; *eagle owl:* the soul of a woman who died in childbirth • **Sumerian** attribute of Lilith • **Ural-Altaic** *eagle owl:* wards off evil spirits; *eagle owl head:* charm to protect livestock; *eagle owl feathers on a cloak:* attribute of shamans who metamorphosed into birds; *eagle owl disguise at a bear feast:* kept away the dead bear's soul • **Welsh** emblem of Blueweed; *owl hoot:* an unmarried girl has lost her virginity • **Zulu** associated with sorcery

ox suffering; sacrifice; patience; labor; agriculture; wealth; submissiveness; stolidity; patient toil; cosmic forces; the solar; fertility; strength; kindness; tranquility; peaceful strength; humility; antithesis of the bull; those who labor for the good of others; wealth; attribute of the personifications of Sloth, Patience • **castrated ox** the lunar • **black ox** death • **lion-headed ox** abundance and earthly power • **ox head with crown** regeneration • **ox skull** death; mortality • **ox skull adorned and with horns** immortality • **coat or cloak of ox skin** fertility • **Buddhist** *chariot drawn by a white ox:* attribute of Buddha (Zen Buddhism); *white ox:* contemplative wisdom (Chinese Buddhism) • **Celtic** Hun • **Chinese** fertility; Spring; agriculture • **Christian** patience; strength; Christ; associated with the nativity of Christ; Christ's sacrifice (especially in the Early Church); attribute of SS Ambrose, Juliet, Leonard, Lucy, Medard, Sylvester, Thomas Aquinas; *winged ox:* emblem of St. Luke; *ox, eagle, lion, and angel:* SS Luke, John, Mark, Matthew respectively; *brass ox:* attribute of St. Antipas; *ox with ass in Nativity scenes:* Gentiles and Jews respectively • **Greco-Roman** a sacred animal; agriculture; sacrifice; *ox yoked with ass:* attribute of Heracles/Hercules; *ox-goad:* attribute of Lycurgus • **heraldic** valor; generosity; magnanimity; *ox head alone:* power guided by reason • **Jewish** the Jewish nation; *winged ox:* North; *ox-goad:* attribute of Cain, Shagmar • **Kalmyk** *ox head:* South • **Norse** *seven oxen:* pull the chariot of the sun • **Taoist** *black ox:* untamed animal nature; *white ox:* tamed passions

ox-eye (plant) • **flower language** patience

oxlip (plant) boldness

oyster silence; stupidity; the lowest form of animal life; lust; vulva; the womb; feminine creative power; birth and rebirth; initiation; folly; imbecility; considered an aphrodisiac • **oyster maid** a low trade • **Chinese** cosmic life; the power of waters; fertility; yin

P

P associated with preservation, precaution, foresight, intellect, curiosity, ego, potential for good and evil, prudence, success followed by ruin, the shepherd's crook; corresponds to Mars, Capricorn, -7-, the brain • **medieval** occasionally the Roman numeral for 400 (G was also used) • **tarot** corresponds to the House of God

padlock silence; security; virginity; prudence; secrecy • **Chinese** *worn as an amulet:* longevity; good health

pagoda an image of the Sacred Mountain as a World Axis; the levels indicate the degrees of ascent to heaven • **Cambodian** Buddhism • **Japanese** *model of a pagoda carried in the hand:* attribute of Bishamon • **Taoist** attribute of Li, a celestial guardian • **Thai** Buddhism

pain mental or spiritual disharmony or disorder • **sudden unaccountable pain** a portent

painting • **painted face** vanity; deceit; disloyalty; trickery; foolishness; wantonness; lust; sorrow; seduction; protection against the evil eye; attribute of a loose woman • **wall painting** absolute knowledge • **Christian** *painting of the Virgin Mary:* attribute of St. Luke • *see also* **picture**

pairs the union of opposites (male/female, sun/moon, night/day, etc.)

palace mystic center; the three levels of the psyche; authority; power; lucky; knowledge; riches; honor; the unmoved mover • **palace of mirrors, crystal, or glass that suddenly appears by magic** ancestral memories of mankind; unconscious memories; primitive awareness of the Golden Age • **secret chambers in a palace** the unconscious • **treasures hidden in a palace** spiritual truths; fertility • **Buddhist** *underwater jewel-studded palace:* home of a naga • **Christian** *floating palace with banners:* attribute of St. Francis of Assisi • **Greco-Roman** *bronze palace:* attribute of Pheme/Fama • **Hindu** *underwater jewel-studded palace:* home of a naga • *see also* **castle**

pale • **heraldic** valor; military strength

paleness fear; maidenhood; lovesickness; envy; sickness

palette art; attribute of painters, St. Luke

pall • **Christian** *as a chalice cover:* the linen in which the body of Christ was shrouded; *covering a monastic with a pall at final vows:* death to the world; withdrawal into God

pallium • **Christian** crucifixion of Christ; papal authority

palm (hand) • **oily or wet palm** wanton disposition • **itchy palm** avarice; bribery • **palm held up** peace; friendship; innocence • **palm held out** bribery; payment; demand for possession • **Jewish** *skull, feet, and palms:* the remains of Jezebel

palm (tree) victory; military victory; fecundity; the solar; elevation; exaltation; fame; blessings; abundance; ascension; androgyny; immortality; joy; prosperity; regeneration; Tree of Life; virility; the masculine; associated with Leo; attribute of the anima, the personifications of Chastity, Abundance, Abstinence,

Victory, Fame, Asia • **palm with dates** the feminine • **date palm with doves** earthly paradise • **coconut palm tree** associated with the archangel Gabriel • **Assyrian** emblem of Ishtar; a sacred tree • **Arabian** Tree of Life • **Babylonian** emblem of Ishtar; *palm tree with lapis lazuli branches:* Tree of Life • **Chaldean** Tree of Life • **Chinese** retirement; dignity; fecundity • **Christian** the righteous; immortality; divine blessing; Paradise; the martyr's victory over death; victory over the flesh; the Resurrection; the Virgin Mary, SS Barbara, Sergius, Bacchus, Peter; *palm, cypress, and olive:* the Virgin Mary; *palm and jasmine:* adoration of God; *garment of palm leaves:* attribute of SS Apollonia, Catherine of Alexandria, Clare of Assisi, Euphemia, Justina of Padua, Justina of Antioch, Laurence, Margaret of Antioch, Stephen, Vincent, Paul the Hermit, sometimes also St. Onuphrius and other desert hermits; *children holding palms:* the Holy Innocents; *woman with seven children holding palms:* St. Felicity and her children; *palm tree staff:* attribute of St. Christopher; *palm branch:* Christ's entry into Jerusalem, glory, triumph, resurrection, victory over death and sin, attribute of one who had made a pilgrimage to the Holy Land, the archangel Gabriel; *dove with a palm branch in its mouth:* victory over death; *date palm:* the tree under which may gave birth to Jesus • **Egyptian** Tree of Life; life in the abstract; the residence of the gods; the tree of the calendar with one branch for each month • **Greco-Roman** sacred to Leto; emblem of Apollo; attribute of Nike/Victoria • **heraldic** righteousness; victory; resurrection; peace; creative power; *palm branch:* victory; royal honor; life; fecundity; wisdom; conquest; success; generosity; justice; peace; friendship • **Jewish** the righteous man; emblem of Judea; attribute of Asher • **Phoenician** *palm tree:* Tree of Life • **Sumero-Semitic** Tree of Life; emblem of Baal-Tamar, Astarte • **Taoist** Tree of Life • *see also* **coconut; date (fruit)**

Pan/Faunus • **Greco-Roman** nature; the vitality of base forces; base or involutive life; animal cunning; insatiable sexuality; paganism

pancake • **Christian** emblem of Shrove Tuesday, Mardi Gras

panda emblem of China

Pandora, Pandora's Box • **Greek** the wicked temptations besetting mankind; the irrational; the unconscious; the wild tendencies of the imagination; female masturbation and its objectified emotional consequences; rebelliousness against divine order; that which is better left untouched; the fire of lust which brings misfortune to mankind

pansy remembrance; meditation; reverie; marriage; man; trinity and unity; the sun; humility; thought; an effeminate homosexual; associated with Capricorn · **Christian** emblem of Trinity Sunday · **flower language** thoughts · **heraldic** thoughtful recollection

panther night; martial ferocity; bravery; rejuvenation; luxury; maternity; associated with Mars (planet) · **hart and panther** opposites · **panther skin** the overcoming of low desires · **Chinese** bravery; ferocity; *panther-headed god:* Chang Fei · **Christian** the sweet influence of Christ; the ability to save people from the devil · **Greco-Roman** attribute of Dionysus/Bacchus · **heraldic** fierceness; impetuosity; fury; remorselessness; a beautiful woman, normally tender, but fierce in defense of her young · *see also* **leopard**, with which the panther is frequently confused; **puma**

papaya love; protection; associated with the sex drive · **papaya tree** associated with the archangel Gabriel

paper transitoriness; lack of durability; emblem of bureaucracy; associated with 1st wedding anniversaries

papyrus knowledge; omniscience; love; the hidden; the occult; the world in gestation · **rolled papyrus** knowledge; progress; omniscience; efflorescence · **unrolling papyrus** the unfolding of life · **Egyptian** attribute of Amon; *papyrus with red crown:* emblem of the Lower Kingdom of Egypt; *papyrus scepter:* youth, eternal youth, vigor, learning

paradise mystic center; heaven; the heart of the world; beatitude; union with the spirit; primordial perfection; pristine innocence; the Golden Age; the place of immortality; the innermost soul · **paradise lost** the descent from unity to multiplicity · **paradise regained** return to unity

parasol World Axis; a solar wheel; sun emblem; protection; authority; dignity; irradiation; emblem of divinity, royalty; dome of the sky · **Buddhist** protection; the state of Nirvana; one of the Eight Emblems of Good Augury · **Chinese** *state parasol:* authority, respect, protection of the throne, high rank, dignity, good fortune · **Egyptian** honorable distinction · **Hindu** protection; royalty; universal spiritual rule · **Maya** royalty; rank; dignity; attribute of Queen Moo · *see also* **umbrella**

parchment · **heraldic** academic success; scholarship

Parjanya · **Hindu (Vedic)** personification of the rain cloud

park beauty; fertility; wealth; paradise · *see also* **garden**

Parnassus · **Greek** excellence

parrot prophecy; foolish chatter, imitation; repetition; laughter; verbosity; greed; docility; attribute of the personifications of Eloquence, Docility · **Amerindian** (Pre-Columbian) oracle; bringer of rain · **Chinese** brilliance; warning to unfaithful wives · **heraldic** far travels · **Hindu** oracle; bringer of rain; attribute of Kama · *see also* **lovebird**

parsley fecundity; death; promiscuity; spring; hope of redemption; the feminine; a mystic plant · **flower language** feasting; useful knowledge; festivity; *fool's parsley:* silliness · **Greco-Roman** sacred to the dead; *crown or wreath of parsley:* increased cheerfulness and appetite, victory at the Nemean Games, attribute of Pan/Faunus

partridge lasciviousness; fertility; deceit; cunning; disloyalty to one's own kind; parental affection; the hopelessness of worldly endeavor; preservative against poison · **Christian** the Church; the truth of Christ; the devil; deceitfulness; temptation; damnation; theft; cunning · **Cretan** associated with Zeus, Talos · **Greek** associated with Aphrodite, Talos

Pasiphae · **Greek** the deliberate flouting of natural and divine law; the overthrow of reason by animal passion; sexual guilt; unnatural lusts

pasque flower *see* **anemone**

passion flower · **Christian** the Passion of Christ (specifically, the ten petals are said to represent the ten apostles who did not deny or betray Christ, or the ten apostles who fled; the rays within the flower represent the crown of thorns; the five stamens represent the five wounds; the three styles represent the nails; the leaf represents the spear; the tendrils represent the cord used to bind Christ; the ovary represents the hammer; and the central column represents the pillar before the Praetorium); Christ's suffering · **flower language** belief; susceptibility; Christian faith; religious superstition

paste *see* **mud**

paten · **Christian** the dish used at the Last Supper; attribute of the Eucharist

path life; experience; learning

patience dock *see* **dock**

paulownia · **Japanese** rectitude; attribute of the emperor

pavement humility; foundation

pavilion · **heraldic** martial readiness

pawn (chess) *see* chess

pawning exchanging something of greater value for something of lesser value

pea love; respect • flower language *everlasting pea:* an appointed meeting, lasting pleasure; *sweet pea:* departure, delicate pleasures

peace union or conjunction of the higher and lower planes • Christian *peace of Christ:* a state of spiritual contemplation

peach (fruit) marriage; longevity; vulva; the feminine principle; luxury; the fruit of salvation; the silence of virtue; perfection; attribute of the personifications of Silence, Truth • peach with leaf attached the heart and tongue • Buddhist one of the Three Blessed Fruits • Chinese fairy food; good wishes; immortality; longevity; attribute of Ho Hsien-ku; *peach pit:* charm against evil spirits • Christian the fruit of salvation; attribute of the Virgin Mary; *peach with leaf attached:* virtue of heart and tongue, the virtue of silence • Egyptian sacred to Athor, Harpocrates • Japanese immortality; fertility; protection against thunder; attribute of Momotaro • Taoist food of the immortals; *peach and phoenix:* emblem of Si Wang Mu; *peach pits:* ward off evil

peach tree immortality; associated with Aquarius • peach blossom emblem of February, Spring • Chinese Spring; immortality; longevity; marriage; preservative against evil influences; Tree of Life; *peach blossom:* emblem of brides, Spring; *peach wood staff:* used for exorcism; *peach wood:* charm against evil spirits • flower language I am your captive; your qualities, like your charms, are unequalled • Japanese purity; faithfulness; Tree of Immortality; *peach blossom:* Spring, feminine charm, marriage, virginity • Taoist Tree of Life

peacock immortality; longevity; the incorruptible soul; love; the apotheosis; resurrection; eternal life; royalty; vanity; pride; the solar; stars; vanity; wholeness; attribute of the personifications of Pride, Transitoriness, Disobedience; associated with rain, the peony, tree and sun worship • white peacock associated with the archangel Gabriel • Babylonian the royal throne • Buddhist compassion; watchfulness; *peacock fan:* attribute of Avalokitesvara, Amitabha • Burmese emblem of the monarchy; sacrifice to bring rain • Cambodian sacrificed to bring rain; steed of Skanda • Chinese beauty; dignity; a sacred bird; attribute of Si Wang Mu; emblem of the Ming dynasty; *peacock feather:* imperial favor, official rank, attribute of Guanyin; *half-pheasant/half-peacock:* Feng-huang, the Chinese

phoenix • Christian Easter; Christ; the ever-vigilant Church; immortality; resurrection; the glorified soul; incorruptibility; attribute of St. Liborius; *peacock surmounting an orb:* rising above worldly things; *peacock feather:* attribute of St. Barbara • Egypt occasional companion of Isis • folkloric fidelity; dies of grief or remains single if it loses its mate; dances when rain is coming • Greco-Roman the solar; emblem of Phaon, Roman empresses, and princesses; attribute of Pan/Faunus, Hera/Juno • heraldic *peacock or peacock feather:* power and distinction; knowledge; beauty; royalty; pride of nation; attribute of troubadour • Hindu steed of Lakshmi, Skanda-Karrtikeya, Sarasvati, occasionally Brahma; *peacock ridden by Kama:* desire • Islamic incorruptibility; light; *peacock's eye:* associated with the Eye of the Heart • Japanese seat of Kujaku-mayoo; *peacock feather:* attribute of Kannon; *half-pheasant/ half-peacock:* Ho-o • Nigerian attribute of Oshun • Persian a sacred bird; attribute of the Tree of Life, royalty, the royal throne • see also Feng-Huang; Ho-o

peahen a woman 30 to 40 years old • dancing peahen dawn

pear the human heart; generosity; affection; hope; good health; sensuality; attribute of personifications of Affection, Hope • Chinese good health; justice; companionship; felicity; *pear tree:* longevity; *pear blossoms:* sometimes mourning, emblem of August; *wild pear tree:* wise administration, good government • Christian felicity; Christ's love for mankind; attribute of St. Catherine, occasionally of the Virgin Mary • flower language affection; comfort; *prickly pear:* satire • heraldic peace; felicity • Japanese felicity; companionship • Jewish occasionally, the fruit of the Tree of Knowledge

pearl enlightenment; the human soul; the lunar; innocence; purity; innocence; chastity; virginity; longevity; fertility; incorruptibility; tears; mystic center; parthenogenesis; faith; esoteric wisdom; hidden knowledge; wealth; health; self-sacrifice; the union of fire and water; birth and rebirth; initiation; justice; the sublimation of instinct; matter; spiritualization of matter; salvation; in large numbers they lose their favorable significance and become mere beads; attribute of Eloquence personified; associated with Cancer, the moon, the waters, the embryonic, the feminine principle, the life-giving power of the Great Mother, 3rd, 30th wedding anniversaries, the archangel Gabriel; charm for love, wealth, protection, luck •

British *Victorian:* euphemism for clitoris • **Chinese** yin; the feminine principle; immortality; good omen; potentiality; purity; beauty; obscure genius; protection against fire; treatment for eye diseases; attribute of Vaisravenna; *pearl tree of Paradise:* purity in eternity • **Christian** salvation; baptism; virgin birth; purity; spiritual grace; the Word of God; attribute of Christ, the Virgin Mary, St. Margaret of Antioch • **Egyptian** attribute of Cleopatra • **European** used to treat melancholy, madness, epilepsy • **Gnostic** the Fall and subsequent salvation • **Greco-Roman** love and marriage; emblem of Aphrodite/Venus • **heraldic** (usually on a ring) high grace • **Hindu** spiritual consciousness; transcendent wisdom; enlightenment; the crystallization of light; corresponds to the element water; *powdered pearls:* health tonic, aphrodisiac; *pearl in the forehead of Shiva:* the third eye • **Indic** used to treat bleeding, jaundice, madness, poisoning, eye and lung diseases • **Islamic** heaven; the Divine Word • **Persian** longevity; the Savior; primeval manifestation; celestial semen; a subtle thought; *threading pearls:* versification; *unflawed pearl:* virginity • **Sumero-Semitic** the generative power of the waters • **Taoist** *Pearl of Effulgence, Pearl of Potentiality, Night-Shining Pearl:* yin powers of the waters, lunar powers of the waters; *Flaming Pearl:* spiritual unfolding, man's search for reality, the experience of Light

peasant ignorance; a personification of Sloth

pebble justice; eloquence; thrown on the graves of suicides • **white pebble** not guilty; a graveside gift to provide resurrection or rebirth • **black pebble** guilty • **Christian** attribute of St. Liborius

Peeping Tom • **English** lechery; Lechery personified

Pegasus • **Greco-Roman** poetry; poetic inspiration; the poet; intellect and morality; heightened natural forces; creative imagination; sublimated imagination; fame; innate capacity for changing evil into good and for spiritualization; Fame personified; lower nature striving for the higher; passage from one plane to another; bearer of the thunderbolt of Zeus/Jupiter; a solar animal; a cloud of fructifying rain • **heraldic** energy leading to honor; messenger of God; poetry; inspiration; the Inner Temple of the Inns of Court

pelican loneliness; melancholy; parental love and sacrifice; gregariousness; greed; charity; piety; resurrection; proof of the possibility of virgin birth; attribute of Penitence personified; emblem of Louisiana • **Christian** an allegory of Christ and his atonement on the cross (especially when feeding its young with its own blood); the suffering Christ; the Eucharist; the Crucifixion • **heraldic** (usually with wings spread) filial devotion; self-sacrifice; charity; Christian readiness to sacrifice

pelt *see* **skin**

pen (writing instrument) learning; phallus; attribute of writers, scholars • **Christian** attribute of Doctors of the Church, SS Matthew, Mark, Luke, John, Augustine, Bernard of Clairvaux, Ambrose, Cyril of Alexandria, Isidore, John Chrysostom, Leander of Seville; *pen with three books:* attribute of St. Hilary of Poitiers • **Egyptian** attribute of Logios, Theut, scribes; *pen and staff:* awakening of the soul • **heraldic** writing skill; educated employment • **Islamic** universal intellect; the Essence; the first thing of created Light; *book with pen:* static being and the creative principle respectively

penance aspiration implying discontent with the worldly conditions one is bound to

pendulum time; balance of judgment

Penelope • **Greek** faithfulness

penis the masculine principle; generative power • **Egyptian** *man with an erect penis:* Min • **Greco-Roman** *man with an erect penis:* Priapus • **Mayan** *god with an erect penis:* Backlumchaam • *see also* **phallus**

pennyroyal • **flower language** flee

pentacle wholeness; the godhead; marriage; meditation; religion; versatility; the five senses (except in the East); spiritual aspiration; protection from sorcery • **eagle carrying a flaming pentacle** emblem of Jupiter (planet) • **inverted pentacle**; the manifested nature of God; the infernal; witchcraft; black magic • **alchemic** the quintessence • **Christian** the five wounds of Christ; *inverted pentacle:* Epiphany; the Virgin Mary • **Egyptian** *inverted pentacle:* Horus • *see also* **-5-**

pentagon heavenly wisdom; guidance; perfection; divination

Pentagon • **American** the US military establishment; war; military force

pentagram *see* **pentacle**

pentangle *see* **pentacle**

Pentecost • **Christian** descent of the Holy Spirit to the Apostles in particular, and mankind in general

peony healing; shame; feminine loveliness; anger; indignation; spring; regal power; affluence; prosperity; stability; associated with Leo, the moon • **Chinese** love; affection; wealth; honor;

feminine loveliness; light; glory; the imperial flower; emblem of Summer; associated with the peacock; *tree peony:* yang, youth, lucky, royalty, happiness, emblem of March • **flower language** shame; bashfulness • **Greek** healing; *peony tea:* charm against sorcery • **heraldic** healing • **Japanese** Spring; fertility; marriage; riches; glory; gaiety; dignity

pepper satire; temper; aphrodisiac

peppermint wealth • **flower language** warmth; cordiality; the combination of the coldness of fear with the warmth of love

perch (fish) • **Chinese** aphrodisiac • **Egyptian** sacred to Neith • **Far Eastern** sexual appetite

Pergamum, Church of • **Christian** associated with faithfulness, challenges, the red horse, the adrenal glands, the third seal

perfume memories; emotions; nostalgia; reminiscences; amorousness; love-sickness; presence of a deity; the perception of consciousness

peridot happiness; simplicity; modesty; friendship; hope; emblem of a thunderbolt; associated with Virgo, Leo, Pisces, 1st and 16th wedding anniversaries; birthstone of August; charm for the strengthening of vision, heart, and the respiratory system; charm against depression

periphery *see* **circumference**

periwinkle love; aphrodisiac • **crown of periwinkle** death • **flower language** *blue periwinkle:* pleasures of memory, early friendship; *red periwinkle:* early friendship; *white periwinkle:* pleasant recollections, pleasures of memory • **heraldic** hope; joy

Persephone/Proserpine • **Greco-Roman** Spring; the earth; unconscious repression

Perseus • **Greek** attainment of an ideal through courage, struggle, and careful choice

persicaria • **flower language** restoration

persimmon wisdom; joy • **Chinese** joy • **Far Eastern** good luck in business • **flower language** bury me amid nature's joys • **Japanese** victory

pestle *see* **mortar and pestle**

Peter, Saint • **Christian** betrayal; inversion

petrel presage of a storm; the soul of a dead mariner

petrifaction detention of moral progress

petticoat emblem of woman • **English** (Elizabethan) *red petticoat:* attribute of prostitutes

petunia demonic powers; Satanism; anger; resentment • **flower language** soothing presence • **heraldic** soothing presence

peyote *see* **cactus**

Phaeton • **Greek** aspiration beyond ability

phallus nature's regenerative forces; penetration; World Axis; the self; the libido; sexuality; active power; the perpetuation of life; the propagation of cosmic forces; related to oaths or covenants; attribute of sun heroes • *see also* **penis**

pheasant vigilance; activity; resurrection; the sun; beauty; luxury; motherly love; lasciviousness; attribute of the personifications of Simplicity • **Chinese** yang; light; virtue; lucky; prosperity; beauty; emblem of the Emperor Yu; *half-pheasant/half-peacock:* Feng-huang; *rooster comb and pheasant's plume together:* bravery, prosperity; *marsh pheasant:* an unhampered but careworn toilsome existence • **Christian** Christianity; attribute of the personification of Christianity • **Far Eastern** *cock's call:* cosmic harmony; *hen's answering call:* related to thunder, Spring, cosmic disturbance, Ch'en, conception • **heraldic** hunting; resourcefulness • **Japanese** maternal love; *half-pheasant/half-peacock:* Ho-o; *hen pheasant:* emissary of Amaterasu Ame-wakahiko • *see also* **Feng-Huang; Ho-o**

pheasant's eye (plant) *see* **Adonis (plant)**

phial *see* **vial**

Philadelphia, Church of • **Christian** associated with expectation, faultlessness, earthquake, the pineal gland, the sixth seal

Phlegethon • **Greco-Roman** the river of burning in Hades

phlox • **flower language** unanimity

Phobos • **Greek** fear

phoenix resurrection; immortality; eternal youth; eternity; chastity; temperance; gentleness; royal succession; faith; constancy; augur of a storm; the cycle of destruction and recreation; death and rebirth by fire; the power to overcome death, change, or tragedy; attribute of the personifications of Justice, Chastity (usually on a shield), occasionally Perseverance; associated with the rose in gardens of paradise • **alchemic** the consummation of the Great Work; regeneration • **Aztecan** the solar; blessings; happiness; companion of Quetzalcoatl • **Chinese** Feng-huang (shown as half-peacock/half-pheasant) • **Christian** Easter; Christ's suffering and the Resurrection; triumph over death; faith; constancy • **Egyptian** Bennu; the sun; the solar; resurrection; immortality; associated with Ra • **heraldic** resurrection • **Japanese** Ho-o (shown as half-peacock/half-pheasant) • **Mayan** the solar; blessings; happiness; companion of Quetzalcoatl • **Persian** simurg (shown as a bird with a woman's or a dog's head); prosperity; steed of Mohammed •

Roman the rebirth and perpetuity of the Roman empire; imperial apotheosis • **Taoist** *peach and phoenix:* emblem of Si Wang Mu • **Toltec** the solar; blessings; happiness; companion of Quetzalcoatl • *see also* **Bennu; Fenghuang; Ho-o; simurg**

photograph has magical powers of access to the soul of the subject

Phrygia love; fertility; liberty; wisdom; eroticism in a superior form

Phrygian cap phallus; obsessive eroticism; sacrifice; self-immolation, or that of others; freedom; liberty • **Egyptian** attribute of Osiris • **French** attribute of Republicans in the French Revolution • **Greco-Roman** attribute of Ganymede, Castor, Pollux, Paris, freed slaves; *young man with Phrygian cap, dog, and eagle:* Zeus/Jupiter • **Mithraic** attribute of Mithras • **Persian** attribute of magi

physician *see* **doctor**

picture has magical powers of access to the soul of the subject • **picture falling off the wall for no apparent reason** unlucky • **Christian** *picture of SS Peter and Paul:* attribute of St. Sylvester; *picture of Christ on a cloth:* attribute of St. Veronica • *see also* **painting**

Pierrot • **French** the masculine principle still in a state of innocence

pig *see* **swine**

pigeon purity; aspiration; gentleness; cowardice; homebody; a dupe • **modern urban use** a nuisance; a low bird • **wood pigeon** monotonous chanting; victim of the cuckoo; a cuckold; vanity • **pair of pigeons** love • **Chinese** longevity; good digestion; faithfulness; impartial filial duty; lasciviousness; emblem of Spring • **Christian** *two pigeons on a plate:* attribute of Nicholas of Tolentino • **Hindu** messenger of Yama • **Islamic** a bird of ill omen • *see also* **dove**, with which the pigeon shares much symbolism and is frequently confused

pigeon berry • **flower language** indifference

pike (fish) • **heraldic** a true and generous mind; unity with Christ; spiritual nourishment; virtue for oneself, not because of heritage

pike (weapon) *see* **spear**

pile • **heraldic** tenacity

pilgrim man in his journey toward salvation; the lover; cleansing; expiation; the human being on earth, traveling toward mystic center; the human soul; renunciation; inner detachment from the world • **Christian** Christ at Emmaus, SS James the Greater, Bridget, and Roch are often portrayed as pilgrims; *ragged pilgrim:* may be St. Alexis, or the archangel Gabriel

pilgrimage the journey toward salvation; the process of spiritual evolution and growth

pillar the connection between heaven and earth; power; World Axis; support of heaven; phallus; the masculine principle; strength; stability; steadfastness; power; Tree of Life; mystic center; the upward impulse; boundary marker; attribute the personifications of Fortitude, Constancy • **two pillars** the point at which the sun god re-enters the inhabited world; Heaven's Gate; *when shown together:* binary combinations such as love/knowledge, beauty/strength, justice/mercy, etc. • **half-white/half-black pillar or one white pillar with one black** bi-polarity; divine duality; bisexual or androgynous divinity; the Tree of Life and the Tree of Knowledge (death); complementary opposites • **three pillars** any triad, such as goodness/wisdom/power, etc.; the phases of the moon; lunar goddesses; the Great Mother; equilibrium; wisdom, beauty, and strength; wisdom and power united by goodness • **four pillars** the supports of heaven; the points of the compass • **seven pillars** wisdom; sanctity; extreme riches • **twelve pillars** creation; the planets; the months • **broken pillar** death; mortality; broken faith; defeat; frustrated hope; unfinished work; attribute of Strength personified • **free-standing column** sky god or other deity; glory; achievement; honor • **woman holding a column** Fortitude personified • **horizontal pillar** inertia • **soldier sleeping by a pillar, woman kneeling beside him** Rinaldo and Armida • **bird on a pillar** union of spirit and matter; a sun god • **dove on a pillar** the Great Mother • **pillar with a dolphin** male and female powers, respectively, combined; love • **Corinthian column** the degeneration of primitive force • **Doric column** primitive force • **Ionic column** the influence of education on primitive force • **Babylonian** *pineapple atop a column:* attribute of Marduk • **Buddhist** *fiery pillar:* Buddha • **Carthaginian** *three pillars:* the Great Goddess, the moon • **Chinese** the way; uprightness • **Christian** attribute of the Passion, SS Sebastian, Simon Stylites; *three pillars:* the Trinity; *flaming pillar:* attribute of St. Hecla; *angel with flaming pillars as legs:* the Apocalypse; *broken column:* attribute of St. Titus; *tau column:* attribute of St. Philip • **Egyptian** the pillars of heaven; attribute of Osiris, Neith, Nut *Djed pillar:* the resurrection of Osiris, stability • **Greco-Roman** Zeus/Jupiter; *two pillars:* Castor and Pollux; *three pillars:* the Great Goddess, the phases of the moon; *silver pillars:* attribute of Styx's dwelling; *dove on a* *pillar:* prophetesses of Dodona • **heraldic** fortitude; constancy; *pillar with serpent wrapped around it:* wisdom with fortitude • **Hindu** *elephant on a pillar:* enlightenment • **Islamic** *five pillars:* the five strengths of Islam; *seven pillars:* wisdom • **Jewish** *two pillars shown apart:* Jachin and Boaz, strength and stability, king and priest; *broken pillar:* attribute of Samson; *two pillars:* attribute of Samson; *twelve pillars:* the tribes of Israel; *pillars of fire and smoke:* the presence of God, the sustaining power of God; *two pillars of Enoch:* the brick pillar is proof against fire, the stone pillar is proof against water; *Egyptian column:* attribute of Joseph • **Kabalistic** Yahweh; Abraham; *three pillars:* wisdom, strength, beauty • **Masonic** *red pillar:* Jachin of Solomon's Temple, the masculine principle, fire; *white pillar:* Boaz of Solomon's Temple; the feminine principle, air • **Mithraic** *two pillars:* Cautes and Cautopates, the bull and the scorpion, light and darkness • **Phoenician** *three pillars:* the moon • **Sumero-Semitic** World Axis; *wood pillar:* Astarte; *pillar topped with lion's head:* Nergal; *pillar topped with lance:* Marduk; *pillar topped with ram's head:* Ea-Oannes • **Taoist** the Tao; the way • **Tuareg** *whirling pillars of sand in a sandstorm:* Ahl attrab • *see also* **maypole; menhir**

pillow security; mercy; comfort; trust; hospitality; peace; love; anguish; luxury; mute audience of confession • **Jewish** *stone for a pillow:* attribute of Jacob • *see also* **cushion**

pilot divine messenger or guide; the higher self; authority

pimpernel fruitfulness; childhood; the poor man's weatherglass • **flower language** assignation; change; cheerfulness

pin love; marriage; restraint; excitement (often sexual); something of value up to the middle of the 18th century, something valueless after

pincers • **doctor holding a stone with a pincers** quack operation for stones in the head • **Christian** attribute of St. Agatha; **pincers with tooth:** attribute of St. Apollonia • **heraldic** smith's profession; honor • *see also* **tongs**

pinching wantonness; return to reality or wakefulness; connected with fairies, death, and night symbols such as the owl, cat, mouse, etc.

pine immortality; longevity; virility; vitality; victory; grief; endurance; strength of character; pity; philosophy; gloominess; silence; solitude; punishment; uprightness; straightness; associated with Saturn, Capricorn, the archangels Asariel, Azrael • **fallen pine** a man fallen in misfortune • **Akkadian** sacred to Zeus • **Assyrian**

a tree of the gods; *pine with seven branches and seven buds:* Tree of Life, completeness • **Chinese** faithfulness; constancy; longevity; courage; emblem of Confucius, Lao Tzu, Winter; *bamboo, plum, and pine:* the Three Friends of Winter • **Egyptian** a tree of the gods; emblem of Serapis • **flower language** *black pine:* pity; *pitch pine:* time, philosophy; *spruce pine:* farewell, hope in adversity • **Greco-Roman** virginity; emblem of Zeus/Jupiter, Aphrodite/Venus, Artemis/Diana; associated with Asclepius, Mithras, Cybele • **heraldic** death; eternal life • **Hindu** Tree of Life; fertility • **Japanese** longevity; conjugal affection; lucky; irresistible strength tempered by daily struggle; those who hold their opinions despite criticism; emblem of Suminoye, Takasago; one of the Three Trees of Good Omen; *in art:* the life force • **Mithraic** *pine tree:* Tree of Life • **Phrygian** *pine tree:* sacred to Attis, Cybele • **Taoist** *pine nuts, needles, resin:* food of the Immortals • *see also* **fir; evergreens**

pine cone fertility; spiritual fertility; phallus; masculine creative force; conviviality; healing; lucky • **two cocks fighting over a pine cone** truth made manifest • **Egyptian** attribute of Serapis • **Greco-Roman** attribute of Dionysus/Bacchus; emblem of Cybele, Sabazios, Artemis/Diana; *white pine cone:* attribute of emblem of Aphrodite/Venus; *wand tipped with pine cone:* attribute of Dionysus/Bacchus, satyrs • **heraldic** life • **Sumero-Semitic** life; fertility; attribute of Astarte

pineal glands associated with self-realized individuals, Mercury (planet) • **Christian** associated with Christ, the Church at Philadelphia • **Hindu** associated with light and the higher mind, the 6th chakra

pineapple fertility; emblem of the Hawaiian Islands • **flower language** perfection; you are perfect • **Mesopotamian** *pineapple atop a column:* attribute of Marduk • **Phrygian** emblem of Cybele

pink (color) sensuality; the emotions; the flesh; femininity; effeminacy; homosexuality; joy; youth; good health • **Gnostic** resurrection

pink (flower) associated with Sagittarius • **flower language** boldness; *carnation pink:* woman's love; *Indian single pink:* aversion; *Indian double pink:* always lovely; *mountain pink:* aspiring; *pink pink:* newlyweds; *red single pink:* pure love; *red double pink:* pure and ardent love; *variegated pink:* refusal; *white pink:* ingenuity, talent

Pinocchio • **Italian** the immature, undeveloped self; the soul's journey through life; the process of self-realization

pipal *see* **bo tree**

pipe (musical) harmony; allurement; a religious instrument; peace; phallus, especially when played by a male lover; lust; attribute of Dionysus/Bacchus, Euterpe, Hermes/Mercury, Pan/Faunus, shepherds, Marsyas, satyrs, Vice personified • **pipes of Pan** universal harmony • **heraldic** festivity; rejoicing • **Islamic Dervish** *reed pipe:* the soul separated from the Divine and the yearning to return to it • **Taoist** *Pipe of Iron:* fertility • *see also* **syrinx; flute**

pipe (smoking) *smoking a pipe:* monotony; idle filling of time • **North American Indian** (Great Plains) Pipe of Peace; reconciliation; conciliation humility; sacrifice; purification; union with the fire of the Great Spirit; *pipe bowl:* center of the universe, the heart; *pipe stem:* spinal column, channel of the vital spirit, World Axis; *the smoke:* transport to heaven; *red pipe:* war

piranha the misery caused by a tormented imagination; unconscious terrors; aggressive hostility; attribute of the Amazon River

pirate the villainous self • **Greco-Roman** *pirates leaping overboard and turning into dolphins:* the kidnapping of Dionysus/Bacchus

Pisces associated with humbleness, intuition, spirituality, impracticality, vagueness, secrecy, defeat, failure, exile, seclusion, the final stage of a cycle, Neptune (planet), water, the inner shadowy world, lack of firmness, the archangel Zadkiel

pismire *see* **ant**

pit hell; euphemism for vagina • **Jewish** associated with Joseph

pitch (pine) evil; punishment in hell • *see also* **caulking**

pitcher (vessel) refreshment; recognition; election; something of low value; the feminine principle; attribute of Aquarius, Temperance personified • **woman watering plants from a pitcher** Grammar personified • **Christian** attribute of St. Florian; *pitcher with basin:* attribute of Pontius Pilate; *pitcher with rays above:* attribute of St. Bede; *pitcher with dish and two fish:* attribute of the Virgin Mary • **Greco-Roman** attribute of Hebe, Juventas; *pitcher overturned with Naiads embracing a youth:* the youth is Hylas; *pitcher overturned with corpse entwined by a serpent:* Cadmus • **heraldic** service worker • **Jewish** *water pitcher and sword:* emblem of Levi; *pitcher with loaves of bread:* attribute of Obadiah; *pitcher with light:* attribute of Gideon • **still life** *pitcher overturned:* the emptiness of worldly things • *see also* **ewer**

pitchfork ambivalence; typical implement of a man; weapon of rebellious peasants; attribute of the devil, farmers; • *see also* **fork**

pituitary gland associated with Jupiter (planet) • **Christian** associated with God's will, the Church of Laodicea • **Hindu** associated with universal love and oneness; the seventh chakra

placenta *see* **afterbirth**

plague marriage; vices; God's judgment • **love's plague** pejorative for pregnancy, children

plaid associated with Mercury (planet), Scotland

plain (topography) the land of reality, truth; boundless space

plait intimate relationship; intermingling streams; interdependence; continuity; involution • *see also* **knot**

plane (tool) attribute of Melancholy personified • **Christian** attribute of St. Joseph (especially with saw and hatchet)

plane tree charity; firmness of character; moral superiority; protection; friendliness; grandeur; magnificence • **Christian** charity; moral superiority; the all-covering love of Christ; the charity of Christ • **flower language** genius; cultivation of the mind; associated with the Greek philosophers • **Greek** learning; scholarship; love of nature; associated with Helen of Sparta; emblem of Xerxes • **Minoan** sacred to Zeus • **Persian** magnificence; learning

plant life; death and resurrection; cycle of life; life-force; mythical ancestor; usually connected with fertility deities such as Osiris, Adonis, Demeter/Ceres; the healthy growth of plants signifies cosmic, spiritual, material fecundity • **withered plant** death • **aquatic plant** creation arising out of the primordial waters; the nascent character of life • **plant growing from the body or blood of a dead deity** life flowing from one state to another; mystic union between man and plant • **heraldic** hope; joy

plantain morning; the food of the pilgrim, of the multitude seeking Christian growth or salvation • **Chinese** self-education; fertility; *picking plaintains:* charm to promote pregnancy

plate containment; sacrifice; the feminine principle

platinum associated with Aquarius, the archangel Uriel

platypus ridiculousness; silliness

playing cards gambling; idle pastime; attribute of Vice personified; the 52 weeks of the year; the 13 cards in each suit represent the lunar months; the four suits represent the four worlds, elements, cardinal directions, winds, seasons, castes, corners of the Temple • **red suits**

the powers of light; the two warm seasons • **black suits** the powers of night; the two cold seasons • **ace** the monad • **king** spirit; essence; father • **queen** soul; personality; mother • **jack** (knave) ego; energies; the messenger • **two black jacks** omen of poverty and unhappiness • **two red jacks** hidden enemy • **jack, queen, king together** spiritual triad • **joker** the non-material world; *alchemic:* the quintessence; *Hinduism:* the ether • **pair of aces and pair of eights** the dead man's hand • *see also* **clubs** (playing cards); **diamonds** (playing cards); **hearts** (playing cards); **spades** (playing cards); **tarot**

playwright the demiurge

Pleiades completeness; order; since there are seven of them, they share in the symbolism of that number • **rising of the Pleiades** start of the navigation season; the early or Spring harvest; beginning of a new year • **setting of the Pleiades** new sowing; Fall

plough *see* **plow**

plover greed; warns sheep of approaching danger; its song is a death omen • **Christian** *golden plover:* the soul of a Jew who crucified Christ and is doomed to forever lamenting the act

plow fertility; fertilization; agriculture; the masculine principle; phallus; the earthly side of man's consciousness; peace; abundance; diligence; labor; attribute of Cincinnatus, Cain, agricultural deities, the personifications of Lust, the Silver Age • **heated plow** martyrdom; lust • **two wheeled plow** emblem of consecrations; royal dignity; has divine associations • **plowing** coition; fertilization of the virgin soil; deflowering; servile work; associated with writing • **Amerindian** plowing is a violation of Mother Earth • **Buddhist** spiritual exertion; self-denial • **Christian** the Cross; *stags pulling a plow:* attribute of St. Neot; *heated plow:* attribute of St. Cunegunda • **Chinese** attribute of Shen Nung • **Greco-Roman** *plow drawn by both an ox and an ass:* attribute of Heracles/Hercules • **heraldic** agriculture; dependence upon providence • **Hindu** attribute of Bala-Rama • **Islamic** low-mindedness; impudence; vanity • **Jewish** creation

plowman obeyer of natural law; provider of society; Christ; the Christian community • **Roman** *plowman approached and/or offered a sword by Roman soldiers:* Cincinnatus

plum prize; a valuable object or situation • **Chinese** *butterfly with a plum:* longevity; *unripe plum:* a student • **Christian** independence; fidelity

plum tree fertility • **plum blossoms** spring; chastity; fidelity • **Chinese** longevity; purity; the universe; birthplace of Lao-Tzubeauty; a recluse; strength; endurance; triumph; Tree of Life; emblem of Winter, January; *bamboo, plum, and pine:* the Three Friends of Winter • **flower language** keep your promises; *Indian plum tree:* privation; *wild plum tree:* independence • **Japanese** sacrifice rewarded; emblem of the Samurai; *plum blossom:* Winter; Spring triumphant over Winter; virtue and courage triumphant over difficulties; marriage, happiness; feminine purity; one of the Three Trees of Good Omen • **Oriental** Winter; emblem of Confucius • **Pawnee** fertility • **Taoist** food of the Immortals

plumb bob *see* **plummet**

plume *see* **feather**

plummet righteousness; justice tempered by mercy; punishment; transcendent knowledge; attribute of the personifications of Architecture, Geometry • **Christian** attribute of St. Thomas • **heraldic** equity; virtue; upright action

Pluto *see* **Hades/Pluto**

Pluto (dwarf planet) associated with the negative aspect of the spirit, Scorpio, elimination or destruction, renewal, regeneration, explosive forces, unpredictability, zero, providence, radical restructuring, invisible forces, actors, the will to exercise power, transformation, new birth self-centeredness, the potential for growth, the archangel Azrael

poet a spiritually advanced person capable of leading others to higher qualities

poinsettia fertility; eternity • **Christian** Christ's nativity; Christmas • **heraldic** purity; Christmas

point unity; center; origin; that which has no magnitude

pointing an ill omen; an affront

poison harmful emotions, actions, ideas

poison ivy ridicule; yearning

pole creative energy; Tree of Life; stability in the midst of flux • **bent pole** old age • **alchemic** *serpent on a pole:* the fixation of Mercurius; the subjugation of vital force • **Christian** *serpent on a pole:* prototype of Christ raised on the Tree of Life • **Sumero-Semitic** *serpent on a pole:* god of healing

Pole Star the ideal; throne of the Supreme Being; eye of heaven; World Axis; World Navel; the hole between space and time; the Gate of Heaven; constancy • **Babylonian** personification of Anshar • **Christian** Christ • **Egyptian** the dead Pharaoh

police the censorious super-ego inhibiting forces of the pre-conscious; the conscience; regulation

pollen • **Apache, Navajo** charm for peace, prosperity, happiness

polyanthus • **flower language** pride of riches; *crimson polyanthus:* the heart's mystery; *lilac polyanthus:* confidence

Polyhymnia • **Greek** muse associated with hymns, pantomime, religious dance

polyp collector; cunning; cruelty

pomegranate fecundity; immortality; perennial fertility; plenty; wealth; royalty; womb; the feminine principle; sanctity; multiplicity in unity; concord; love; truth; frankness (usually shown open); love; God's gifts; the return of Spring; rejuvenation of the earth; attribute of the personifications of Sufficiency, Victory • **pomegranate flower** hope; immortality; the sun • **bursting pomegranate** resurrection; the fertility of the Word • **Buddhist** *peach, citron, and pomegranate:* the Three Blessed Fruits • **Chinese** abundance; fertility; posterity; many and virtuous offspring; a happy future; *blossoms:* June • **Christian** Christ; the Church; eternal life; spiritual fecundity; hope; attribute of the Virgin Mary; *bursting pomegranate:* Easter; *pomegranate topped by a cross:* attribute of St. John of God • **Egyptian** fertility • **flower language** foolishness; foppishness; *the flower alone:* mature elegance • **Greco-Roman** abundance; rejuvenation; immortality; fertility; attribute of Hera/Juno, Aphrodite/Venus; associated with Dionysus/Bacchus, Demeter/Ceres, Persephone; *crown of pomegranate leaves:* attribute of married Roman women • **heraldic** the perfect kingdom; prosperity; fertility; abundance • **Indic** *pomegranate juice:* cure for barrenness • **Jewish** regeneration; fertility; sometimes the fruit of the Tree of Knowledge; emblem of the High Priest; traditional food of Rosh Hashanah; *bells and pomegranates on vestments:* fecundating thunder and lightning • **Persian** fertility; abundance; the female breast • **Vietnamese** *pomegranate flower:* emblem of Summer

pond corruption; stagnation; reflection; a wife • *see also* **pool**

poniard *see* **knife**

Pontius Pilate • **Christian** disavowal of responsibility; betrayal

pool (body of water) wisdom; cosmic knowledge; universal consciousness • **Greco-Roman** *youth gazing into a pool:* Narcissus; *man in pool reaching up for dangling fruit:* Tantalus; *lovers in a pool:* Hermaphroditus • **Italian** *nymphs bathing observed by soldiers:* Rinaldo and Armida • *see also* **pond**

poor people *see* **poverty**

pope spiritual authority, control, discipline; emblem of the Roman Catholic church

Pope (tarot) *see* **High Priest (tarot)**

popinjay amusement; wantonness

poplar Tree of Life; sympathy; lamentation; grief; tremulousness; the regressive powers of nature; victory; the duality of all things; associated with the archangel Zadkiel • **black poplar** despair • **Celtic** transformation; victory; vision • **Chinese** yin-yang; duality • **flower language** *black poplar:* courage; *white poplar:* time • **Greco-Roman** sacred to Sabazios; emblem of Zeus/Jupiter; associated with the Heliades, Leuce; *black poplar:* associated with Heracles/Hercules, Hades/Pluto; *white poplar:* associated with the Elysian Fields; *crown of poplar leaves:* attribute of Heracles/Hercules in his descent to Hades • **heraldic** (often just the leaf) hope; joy; a flourishing family; firm faith; aspiration; emblem of Lombardy

poppy sleep; heavenly sleep; rest; peace; oblivion; fecundity; the Great Mother; fertility; death; chastity; extravagance; ignorance; indifference; idleness; consolation; resurrection; Autumn; intoxication; evanescent pleasure; commemoration of the dead on Armistice Day; associated with Taurus, attribute of lunar and nocturnal deities, the personifications of Sleep, Night, Cunning, Lethargy • **Chinese** retirement; rest; beauty; success; associated with December • **Christian** sleep; ignorance; indifference; *blood-red poppy:* the sleep of earth, occasional attribute of the Passion of Christ • **flower language** evanescent pleasure; *red or corn poppy:* consolation; *scarlet poppy:* fantastic extravagance; *white poppy:* sleep, my bane, my antidote • **Greco-Roman** sleep; the time of sleep and death of vegetation; attribute of Hypnos/Somnus, Morpheus, Demeter/Ceres, Persephone, Aphrodite/Venus, Circe • **heraldic** hope; joy; dreaminess; imagination • *see also* **opium**

porcupine blind anger; defensiveness • **East African** associated with fire • **Nigerian** associated with divination • *see also* **hedgehog**

porpoise lust; presage of a storm • *see also* **dolphin**, with which the porpoise is frequently confused, especially in classical times

port *see* **harbor**

portcullis • **heraldic** protection, especially in an emergency

portrait *see* **picture**

Poseidon/Neptune • Greco-Roman the negative aspect of the spirit and of humanity; the regressive and evil side of the unconscious; enemy of spiritualization; the perverted satisfaction of desire; the active force that stirs the receptive; creational powers of the Underworld; associated with earthquakes, the lower primeval waters

post *see* pillar

pot (usually earthen) dullness; stupidity; connected with rain, fertility, the Great Mother, the womb, Nature's inexhaustible womb, rejuvenation, the underworld, any body moisture (blood, sweat, semen, tears, urine, saliva); emblem of Aquarius • broken pot uselessness • African the womb • Bambaran knowledge • Chinese *three legged-copper pot:* attribute of Huang Ti • Christian attribute of SS Justina, Ruffina; *water pots:* the first miracle of Christ at Cana; *water pot with asperges:* attribute of St. Martha • Egyptian attribute of Nut; *god pouring water from two pots:* Hapi • Hindu water; the female; *trident driven in the ground and a pot:* attribute of Manasa; *pot in left arm:* attribute of Sitala • Irish *pot of gold:* attribute of a leprechaun • Nigerian attribute of Oshun • Sumero-Semitic *watering pot:* attribute of Ea-Oannes • *see also* potsherd; potter; jar; urn; vase

potato tranquility; dullness; commonness; the ordinary; poverty; the subconscious; considered an aphrodisiac; fertility; emblem of Ireland • flower language benevolence

potsherd dryness; thrown on the grave of a suicide

potter a creator deity; connected with the womb • Egyptian Khnemu

potter's wheel the Christian's life shaped by divine influence • Egyptian intellect; attribute of Khnemu • Jewish attribute of Jeremiah

pottery *see* earthenware

poverty spiritual inessentials stripped away; a return to simplicity; detachment from the phenomenal world

prayer self-expression; opening of the higher self; an appeal to heaven • youth praying in a barnyard the Prodigal Son • praying saint before Saints Peter and Paul, receiving staff and book St. Dominic • saint praying before an angel and eating a scroll or book St. John • praying saint surrounded by angels St. Charles Borromeo • praying desert hermit with an erotic or monstrous vision St. Anthony the Great • saint praying in the desert or the wilderness SS Jerome, Bruno • saint praying in a hollow

tree St. Bavo • praying monk with a skull usually St. Francis of Assisi • praying monk among plague victims St. Frances of Rome • praying bishop attacked by soldiers St. Thomas Becket • praying pope with a monk, surrounded by flames the pope is St. Gregory the Great • several people praying before an altar on which wands are piled associated with St. Joseph • praying saint before an image or vision of the Virgin and Child *aged saint, X-shaped cross:* St. Andrew; *lily lying nearby:* St. Philip Neri; *Virgin presenting a scapular:* St. Simon Stock; *Virgin placing veil on the saint's head:* St. Mary Magdalene of Pazzi; *Virgin handing the Christ child to:* usually SS Mary Magdalene of Pazzi, Francis of Assisi; *Virgin and St. Joseph handing cloak to:* St. Teresa • praying saint before an image or vision of the crucified Christ with Christ reaching down SS Bernard of Clairvaux, Francis of Assisi; *Christ inclining his head to:* SS Margaret of Cortona, John Gualberto; *Christ presenting instruments of the Passion to:* St. Mary Magdalene of Pazzi; *Christ presenting the Crucifixion nails, or showing wounds:* St. Teresa; *Christ bearing a cross:* SS Gregory the Great, Ignatius of Loyola

prayer beads perpetual continuity; devotion; meditation; inane repetition; circle of perfection; futility of aspiration; prayer • Buddhist emblem of Buddhism; the Wheel of the Law; the Round of Existence; the 108 Brahmins present at the birth of Buddha; attribute of Brahma, Sarasvati • Christian emblem of Catholicism; the mystic rose garden of the Virgin Mary; attribute of SS Dominic, John Berchmans, occasionally Catherine of Siena • Hindu attribute of Brahma, Ganesha, Shiva, Devi, Kali; *thread:* the non-manifest; *beads:* the multiplicity of manifestation; *circular shape:* time; *Rosary of Shiva:* the berries of the Rudraksha tree • Islamic *first 99 beads:* the Divine Names; *100th bead:* the Name of the Essence, found only in Paradise

prayer book piety • Hindu attribute of Devi

prayer mat *see* mat

prayer wheel the active force of the word

praying mantis *see* mantis

precipice suggestive of the Fall of Man; euphemism for vulva

pregnancy expectation • Greco-Roman *goddess accusing a pregnant nymph:* Artemis/Diana and Kallisto/Callisto, respectively

president secular authority

press (tool) passion; harvest; Autumn; the wrath of God

pretzels a charm for luck, prosperity, spiritual wholeness • **Christian** associated with Good Friday; *folded arms of a pretzel:* a prayer posture; *three holes of a pretzel:* the Trinity

prickly pear • **flower language** satire

Pride of China • **flower language** dissension

priest spiritual mentor, authority; promoter of spiritual growth; emblem of the Church • **Chinese** *Taoist priest:* Han Chung-li • *see also* **flamen**

Priest (tarot) *see* **High Priest (tarot)**

Priestess (tarot) *see* **High Priestess (tarot)**

primrose youth; gaiety; dalliance; herald of Spring; death; inconstancy; innocence; purity; pertness • **Celtic** associated with fairies • **flower language** early youth; *evening primrose:* inconstancy; *red primrose:* unpatronized merit • **heraldic** young love; innocence; youth; good tidings; *black primrose:* hope, joy

prince rejuvenated form of the king; the hero; often has powers of intuition; sometimes has the powers of the demiurge; the untarnished self; the idealization of man; the promise of supreme authority • **prince rescuing a sleeping princess** conjunction; the sun awakening the Spring; the awakening of a girl's sexuality

princess the anima; the untarnished self; the idealization of woman • **princess sleeping or in a secluded palace** passive potential; purity; the individual unconscious that has not yet emerged from the collective unconscious • **wooing a princess** aspiring to a higher psychic or spiritual state

priory *see* **monastery**

prison crime; confinement; punishment; the early state of the soul in which the spirit is in bondage to the lower instincts and desires; trap of circumstance • **old man in prison, surrounded by youths** Socrates • **Christian** *imprisoned saint, aroused by an angel:* St. Peter; *imprisoned saint, released by an earthquake:* St. Paul; *imprisoned saint with a dog:* St. Roch • *Italian old man dying in prison with dead children:* Ugolina della Gherardesca

privet *see* **hedge**

proboscides • **heraldic** longevity; strength; royalty; dignity; patience; wisdom; happiness; lucky

procession a cycle; the passage of time; monsters carried or imitated in a parade indicates that they are dominated • **Christian** *procession in church:* Christ's entry into Jerusalem • **see also circumambulation**

Procrustes • **Greek** tyranny; perversion of idealism

Prodigal Son • **Christian** youthful foolishness; remorse; contrition

Prometheus • **Christian** prefiguration of Christ • **Greek** freedom; the artist; prophecy; the will to resist oppression; sublimation; the intellect in open rebellion against the soul; magnanimous endurance of unwarranted suffering

prophet the dawning of a higher consciousness; the beginning of a new era

Proserpine *see* **Persephone/Proserpine**

prostitute the spirit seeking satisfaction instead of wisdom; an idol worshipper; lower nature; instability which is caused by object interest; the allurement of sensation and desire, which capture the soul; Pride personified • **sacred prostitution** union with the godhead; divine marriage; the oneness of the living in the wholeness of being • **alchemic** the unredeemed; the body sunk in darkness; primordial state; primordial material

Proteus • **Greek** changeableness; evasiveness; the unconscious

prune prostitute, especially where stewed prunes are referred to; suggestive of constipation, both physical and mental

pruning hook peace• **Greek** attribute of Pomona

psaltery • **Jewish** attribute of King David

Psyche • **Greek** the soul; the mind

pulpit • **Christian** the Word of God; religious instruction; attribute of St. Vincent Ferrer

pulse passion; life; time

puma • **Iroquoian** Dajoji • **North American Indian** *western tribes:* trickster

pumpkin Autumn; feminine symbol of containment; the two worlds, earthly and celestial; stupidity; the head; related to the moon, witches; charm against evil spirits; emblem of Halloween • **African** *pumpkin seeds:* intelligence • **Chinese** fruitfulness; health; gain • **flower language** bulkiness • **Roman** stupidity; empty-headedness; madness • *see also* **gourd**

Punch and Judy • **Italian** the anti-hero overcoming learning, domesticity, death, and the devil; contagious humor and common sense overcoming all obstacles

puppet man as the plaything of fate or deities; the individual with no sense of purpose • *see also* **doll**

puppy *see* **dog**

purgative drives out evil spirits or ghosts

purple royalty; sacerdotal power; imperial power; pomp; pride; noble birth; dignity; mourning; wisdom; power; spirituality; penitence; sublimation; fasting; abstinence; love; justice; wisdom; temperance; knowledge; sorrow; associated with Sagittarius, Mercury (planet), underworld divinities, congealed blood • **purple-blue** tranquility • **purple-red** severity; anger • **Aztecan** majesty; sovereignty • **Chinese** attribute of an educated person • **Christian** truth; humility; penitence; Advent; Lent; attribute of God the Father, bishops, abbots; royal and sacerdotal power; *purple chasuble:* the mocking robe put on Christ as the King of the Jews • **Greco-Roman** royalty; secrecy; associated with Jupiter • **heraldic** dignity; justice; rank; rule; sovereignty; royal majesty; temperance in plenty; sometimes used in place of violet • **Incan** majesty; sovereignty

purse penury; charity; avarice; philanthropy; finance; scrotum; attribute of bankers, merchants, pilgrims, the personifications of Avarice, Melancholy, Vanity • **Christian** attribute of almoners, Judas, SS Matthew, Lawrence, Thomas of Villaneuva, Cyril of Jerusalem, Matilda; *three purses:* attribute of SS Matthew, Nicholas of Myra; *open purse:* charity to the poor; Christian benevolence; *purse with 30 coins:* attribute of Judas • **German** *self-replenishing purse:* attribute of Fortunatus • **Greco-Roman** attribute of Hermes/Mercury, Priapus • **heraldic** a liberal blessing; a treasurer • **still life** the possessions that death takes away • *see also* **wallet; bag; money bag**

pussy willow harbinger of Spring • **British** emblem of Palm Sunday • **heraldic** motherhood

putrefaction spiritual decay; dissolution and disintegration before reintegration and rebirth; death of the body and release of the soul

putto harbinger of profane love; angelic spirit; attribute of Erato, Aphrodite/Venus

Pygmalion • **Greek** inhibitions overcome; self-realization; personal transformation

pyramid firmness; strength; endurance; stability; the sun; eternal light; the abode of the dead; the whole work of Creation; composure; aspiration; death; immortality; princely glory; time; ancient wisdom; mystic center; androgyny; emblem of Egypt; attribute of Glory personified • **pyramid and star** the flight into Egypt; Israel in Egypt • **axe embedded in a pyramid** the revealing of secret or hidden knowledge • **Aztecan** the fifth sun of Quetzalcoatl

Pyramus and Thisbe • **Roman** perfect love

pyre • **death on a funeral pyre** associated with Dido, Heracles/Hercules, Petroclus

pyrus japonica fairies' fire

Pytho • **Greek** falsehood; the unconscious; instinct

python a demon; a soothsayer; the serpent of wisdom; the evil powers of darkness • **man shooting python with arrows** Apollo; the sun overcoming darkness • *see also* **serpent**

pyx • **Christian** the Last Supper; the Blessed Sacrament; attribute of St. Longinus, the archangel Raphael when accompanying Tobias; *pyx bearing the Host:* attribute of St. Clare of Assisi

Q

Q phallus and vulva; World Axis and universe; associated with fertility, happiness, digestive organs, Aries, Mercury (planet), mysticism, martial qualities, personal magnetism, -8- • **medieval** occasionally the Roman numeral for 500 (D is the letter normally used) • **tarot** associated with the Star

quadrant (**astronomy**) attribute of Astronomy personified

quadriga the sun; partakes in the symbolism of -4- • **Christian** attribute of the Magi • **Greco-Roman** attribute of Apollo, Eos/Aurora, Athena/Minerva, Phaeton; *drawn by four white horses:* attribute of Eros/Cupid • **Mithraic** *drawn by four white horses:* attribute of Anahita (usually accompanied by Mithras)

quail courage; poverty; resurrection; lasciviousness; heat; fertility; pugnacity; God's providence; a female child up to 10 years of age; attribute of Malignity personified; associated with night, good fortune; harbinger of Spring or Summer depending on location; an endearment; sometimes given as a gift from one lover to another • **Chinese** pugnacity; courage; poverty; fire; military zeal; South; *Red Bird:* Summer • **Greco-Roman** harbinger of Spring; renewal of life; associated with Asteria, Zeus/Jupiter, Latona, Apollo, Leto, Artemis/Diana • **Hindu** associated with the dawn; harbinger of Spring • **Jewish** miraculous food in the desert; the food of wrath and lust • **Roman** courage; victory in battle • **Russian** the sun; emblem of the sun, Spring, the tsars • **witchcraft** the devil's bird; diabolical powers; sorcery

quaking grass • **flower language** agitation

quamoclit • **flower language** agitation

quartz integrity; limited vision or insight; power; charm for protection, psychic power, healing, lactation; the celestial element in initiation • **rose quartz** remembrance in prayer; related to Taurus, the heart, healing; said to enhance inner and outer beauty; associated with the archangel Anael • **smoky quartz** associated with Libra, 70th wedding anniversaries, the archangels Lumiel, Sandalphon • **clear quartz** associated with the archangel Gabriel • **Australian aboriginal** celestial power of light

quatrefoil • **Christian** the four Gospels, Greek Doctors of the Church, Latin Doctors of the Church • **heraldic** good tidings; *black quatrefoil:* hope; joy; *double quatrefoil (huitfoil):* ninth son; *blue or white quatrefoil:* hope, joy; *sanguine quatrefoil:* hope, joy, dreaminess, imagination • *see also* -4-

queen the feminine principle; the Great Mother; the higher self • **alchemic** lunar consciousness; woman; Mercurius; *king and queen:* Conjunction; *king and queen in a fountain:* the water operations of Dissolution and Distillation; *naked queen:* early stages of transformation; *clothed queen:* completed transformation • *see also* **chess**

Queen (tarot) see **Empress (tarot)**

quetzal emblem of Guatemala • **Aztecan, Mayan** the god of air • **Latin American** freedom

quicksand enchantment; the obstruction of destiny; danger; the unconscious threatening to engulf the conscious; helplessness

quicksilver see **mercury (metal)**

quill see **pen**

quince fertility; marriage; disappointment; scornful beauty; attribute of Marriage personified; in hotter countries may partake of other symbolism of the apple • **quince tree** associated with the archangel Anael • **Arabian** virility • **Christian** Christ • **flower language** temptation • **Greco-Roman** associated with Aphrodite/Venus • **Jewish** may be used for the fruit of the Tree of Good and Evil • **Spanish** virility

Quisling, Vidkun • **Norwegian** traitor; collaborator with the enemy

quiver (archery) the feminine receptive principle but also may stand for the phallus as it contains the shooting arrows (semen); attribute of deities • **Cupid's quiver** euphemism for vagina • **Greco-Roman** *bow and quiver:* attribute of Orion • *see also* **arrows; bow (archery); bowstring**

quivering sexual excitement; timidity; apprehension

Quixote, Don • **Spanish** personal confusion; foolish questing; innate dignity; delusion; madness

R

R often stands for *rex* (king) or *regina* (queen); associated with Aquarius, Venus (planet), the heart, tremendous force for either good or evil, the occult, rapidity, regeneration, -9- • **medieval** occasionally the Roman numeral for 80 • **tarot** associated with the Moon

rabbi • **Jewish** spiritual authority, wisdom; the higher self; emblem of Judaism

rabbit gregariousness; timidity; skepticism; suspicion; wisdom; fecundity; uninhibited sexuality; euphemism for female genitals; speed; witty trickery; desultory reading and learning; wariness; cowardice; mildness; distraction; humbleness; a peasant; a victim; resourcefulness; connected with Easter; hope, life (especially the young); attribute of Lust personified; associated with the lunar, moon goddesses, earth mothers, the archangel Anael • **rabbit skin cap** attribute of a fool • **rabbit's foot** phallus; lucky • **African** trickster • **Aztecan** associated with the moon • **Chinese** associated with the moon • **Christian** *rabbit at the feet of the Virgin Mary:* the victory of chastity • **Greco-Roman** attribute of Aphrodite/Venus • **heraldic** a peaceful and retired life • **Mayan** attribute of Ixchel • **Mexican Indian** associated with South • **North American Indian** Manabozho; trickster; fecundity; lust; *rabbit skin in rituals:* docility and utility before the Great Spirit • **Orient** *on a gold or white disk:* the moon • **Teutonic** emblem of Eostre • *see also* **hare**, with which the rabbit is closely related and sometimes imperfectly distinguished

raccoon thievery; disguise; dexterity • **North American Indian** *Eastern woodlands:* trickster

Rachel • **Jewish** the contemplative life

radiance transfiguration; wisdom; sanctity; purity of heart; the supernatural; pure spirituality; related to fire and daylight in both the positive and negative aspects; suggests the supernatural or divine • *see also* **glory; nimbus**

radish thinness; redemption; dieting; Spring; supposed to be an aphrodisiac; related to Mars (planet); prevents poisoning, drunkenness

raft temporary safety

ragged robin • **flower language** wit

rags poverty; despair; self-deprecation; wound to the soul (the particular garment that is in rags gives a more precise meaning to this) • **rag hung on a tree** substitute for human sacrifice • **rag thrown in the water** substitute for drowning; an offense cast off

railing help; support • **broken railing** danger; loss of control; loss of support • **Christian** *communion rail:* the separation between heaven and earth, or between the Church Militant and the Church Triumphant

rain fertility; purification; the impartial grace of God; revelation; life; spiritual influences from heaven; an increase in spiritual energy; initiation; mercy; the inseminating power of a sky god • **rain of gold** sun rays • **wind and rain** physical love • **torrential rain** punishment; divine vengeance • **Greek** *rain of gold:* disguise of Zeus to seep into the underground chamber of Danae • **Hindu** *blue rain-cloak:* attribute of Indra • *see also* **deluge**

rainbow blessing; lucky; the bridge between heaven and earth; hope; God's mercy; heavenly glory; transfiguration; union; divine pardon and reconciliation; throne of sky gods; promise • **African** sometimes associated with the celestial serpent • **Australian aboriginal** *rainbow serpent:* Galeru, Jolunggul • **Buddhist** the highest state attainable in samsara • **Chinese** equated with the sky dragon; yin and yang; the union of heaven and earth; bridge to heaven; divine benevolence • **Christian** pardon; reconciliation between God and man; Christ; the throne of the Last Judgment; *tri-colored rainbow:* the Trinity • **folkloric** Rainbow in the morning, sailor take warning; / Rainbow at night, sailor's delight. / Rainbow to leeward, foul falls the day; / Rainbow to leeward, damp runs away. • **Greco-Roman** emblem of Iris; associated with Zeus/Jupiter, Hera/Juno; emblem on Agamemnon's shield • **heraldic** good times after bad • **Hindu** the highest yogic state in samsara; the bow of Indra; *rainbow-like archery bow:* attribute of Shiva • **Islamic** the four classical elements of earth, wind, fire, and water • **Japanese** bridge to heaven • **Jewish** God's covenant with Noah, man; *rainbow with ark:* end of the Deluge • **Norse** Bifrost • **North American** emblem of the lesbian /gay/bisexual/transgendered community • **Yoruban** *rainbow serpent:* Oshunmare

raincoat isolation from the emotions of others

rake (implement) avarice • **Norse** attribute of Hel

ram (sheep) resurrection; sacrifice; strength; virility; creative force; emblem of the Creator, Persia; associated with March, sun gods, sky gods, the archangel Samael • **ram as a sacrifice** peace • **ram with its pugnacity emphasized** power; war • **ram's horn** thunder; associated with sun gods, moon goddesses • **ram's head on a serpent** generative power; fertility • **sphinx with ram's head** a criosphinx • **Babylonian** *god with ram's horns:* Ea-Oannes; *pillar topped with ram's head:* Ea-Oannes • **Celtic** fertility; *serpent with a ram's head:* companion of Cernunnos • **Fulani** *rooster and/or ram in a yard:* a secret told to relatives of close friends • **Gallic** Belin; *serpent with a ram's head or horns:* Cernunnos • **Christian** the divine word; Christ • **Egyptian** procreation; solar energy; creative heat; the renewal of solar energy; attribute of Osiris; attribute or personification of Amen-Ra; associated with Banebdjet, Heryshaf; *ram-headed man:* Khnemu, Mendes; *man with four ram's heads:* North wind, Qebui; *winged ram with four heads:* the North wind, Qebui; *ram-headed man with four wings:* West wind, Hutchaiui; *beetle with a ram's head:* West wind, Hutchaiui • **Greco-Roman** fertility; generative power; sacred to Zeus/Jupiter, Sabazios, Dionysus/Bacchus; associated with Aphrodite/Venus, Pan/Faunus; attribute of Hermes/Mercury • **heraldic** patience; temperance; reconciliation; the right to keep sheep; a leader; a duke • **Hindu** the sacred fire, sacred to Agni • **Islamic** the sacrificial animal • **Jewish** *ram with four horns:* attribute of Daniel; *ram with its horns stuck in a bush:* the sacrifice of Isaac; *seven ram's horns:* the fall of Jericho • **Norse** *rams pulling a chariot:* attribute of Thor • **Persian** *wild ram:* incarnation of Verethaghna • **Phoenician** *god with ram's horns:* Baal, Hamon • **Sumero-Semitic** supporters of Rashap's throne; *ram's horns:* attribute of Rashap • **Tibetan** *ram's head:* Lak-Pa • **zodiac** associated with Aries; *disk on the horns of a ram:* Aries • *see also* **criosphinx; sheep; shofar**

Rama • **Hindu** the model son, brother, husband

ranunculus • **flower language** you are radiant with charms; I am dazzled by your charms; *Asiatic ranunculus:* your charms are resplendent; *garden ranunculus:* you are rich in attractions; *wild ranunculus:* ingratitude

Raphael, Archangel divine healing; divine restorer; pilgrimage; guardianship; messenger; associated with -1-, -6-, -13-, agate, opal, yellow topaz, aluminum, mercury (metal), 2nd heaven, Gemini, Virgo, Wednesday, ash, aspen, almond tree, bottle brush tree, hazel, larch, mulberry, rowan, silver birch, juniper, monkey, bird, ibis, North, East • **Christian** associated with Mercury (planet) • **Islamic** herald of the Resurrection • **Jewish** associated with the sun • **Kabalistic** associated with -8-, orange (color)

raspberry envy; the human heart; joy; kindly feelings; tender-heartedness; remorse; associated with the planet Venus • **flower language** remorse

rat decay; passing time; infirmity and death; has phallic implications; enmity; evil; disease; major troubles; plague; an infernal animal; meanness; slander; destruction; the devil; an informant; sneakiness; a ghoul• **black rat with white rat** day and night; attribute of Night personified • **Chinese** timidity; meanness; the first of the Twelve Terrestrial Branches • **Christian** evil; the devil; attribute of St. Fina • **Egyptian** utter destruction; wise judgment • **folkloric** rats will desert a ship that is going to sink • **Greco-Roman** associated with Apollo; *white rat:* lucky omen; *objects gnawed by rats:* omen of bad luck • **Hindu** prudence; foresight; steed and attribute of Ganesha; attribute of Shiva • **Japanese** *white rat:* attribute of the god of happiness and the god of wealth

ratsbane lechery leading to disease and death

rattle rainmaker; birth; protection against evil spirits, death

rattlesnake virulence; malignity; independence; danger • **Aztecan** attribute of Coyolxuahqui

Ravana • **Sri Lankan** the incarnation of wickedness, law-breaking, ravishing of women

raven solitude; self-isolation; melancholy; stubbornness; the lower mind; prophecy; materialism; wisdom; evil; bad tidings; sin; an ill omen; a messenger of the gods; dawn; trust in divine providence; unrest; death; the impenitent sinner; the dark side of the psyche; the passing of time; attribute of Rapacity personified (especially with a ring in its beak) • **alchemic** blackening; mortification; the nigredo; putrefaction • **Assyrian** messenger of the gods • **British** *ravens deserting the Tower of London:* omen of the death of the royal family and the fall of Britain • **Celtic** Morrigan; associated with augury; attribute of Benegeit Bran, Lugh, war and fertility goddesses; *two ravens:* attribute of Lugh; *Babd the raven:* war, bloodshed, panic, malevolence; *all-black raven:* ill omen; *raven with one white feather:* good omen • **Chinese** one of the Twelve Celestial Branches; associated with the sun; an ill omen; *eagle and raven:* associated with war gods; *three-legged red raven:* lives in the sun • **Christian** the devil; solitude; attribute of SS Boniface, Ida, Oswald, Vincent of Saragossa; *raven with a loaf of bread:* attribute of SS Anthony the Great, Benedict, Onuphrius, Paul the Hermit; *two ravens:* attribute of St. Meinrad • **Cornish** King Arthur lives on as a raven; *raven's caw by a house:* unlucky • **Egyptian** destruction; malevolence • **Gallic** attribute of Nantosuelta • **Greco-Roman** longevity; fertility; bearer of bad tidings; messenger of Apollo; prophetic; attribute of Helios/Sol, Athena/Minerva, Cronus/Saturn, Asclepius; *raven with pine cone and torch:* death • **heraldic** a man who has made his own fortune; divine providence; victory; courage; *peregrine falcon with a raven:* emblem of the Isle of Man • **Hindu** a manifestation of Brahma • **Indic** messenger of death • **Inuit** teacher of survival to the first humans • **Japanese** messenger of the gods • **Jewish** impurity; mortification; carrion; destruction; deceit; attribute of Noah; *Noah's raven:* wandering, unrest, the unclean; *raven with a loaf of bread:* attribute of Elijah • **Mayan** messenger of the thunder god • **Mithraic** servant of the sun; the first grade of initiation; attribute of Mithras • **Norse** emblem of the Danes, Vikings; *two ravens on the shoulder of Odin:* Hugin and Munin • **North American Indian** *Eastern forest:* trickster, demiurge, finder of lost things • **Scottish** *raven's caw:* omen of good hunting • **Taoist** *three-legged red crow:* the solar; yang; the Great Triad; the three great powers of the cosmos— Heaven, Earth, and Man • **Welsh** *army of ravens:* attribute of Owein • **witchcraft** the familiar of witches • **Zoroastrian** purity; remover of pollution • *see also* **crow**, with which the raven is closely related and imperfectly distinguished

ray • **devil ray** malignancy • **sting ray** cunning

rayonee • **heraldic** splendor; glory; enlightenment; intelligence; fountain of life

reaper a death figure

reaping harvest; reward or consequence; slaughter; castration; death

rear the unconscious; related to the left side

recessional • **Christian** going forth to work in the world

rectangle the most rational, secure, and regular of geometric forms • **rectangular nimbus** indicated the holiness of a person still living

red love; virility; courage; anger; war; divine zeal; passion; emotion; the sun; creative force; imperial power; supernatural power; solar power; sacredness; love of God; divine zeal; patriotism; sacrifice; revolution; charity; sentiment; sin; primitive wildness; disease; martyrdom; blood; loyalty; attribute of dawn deities, war gods, martyrs; associated with hell, the devil, the body of man, dedications, left-wing politics, revolutionaries, the Fifth Heaven • **painting or staining red** renewal of life; associating an object with solar power, divine power and/or the power of fire • **dark red** associated with Scorpio • **brilliant red** associated with Aries, Mars (planet) • **orange-red** associated with Taurus • **red-violet** associated with Pisces • **red and black** life and death; associated with Satan • **red and white** death • **red, white, and black** the three stages of initiation • **red rose** love; divine love • **red flag** danger; auction; provocation; revolution; socialism; communism; anarchy • **red cap** invisibility • **African** associated with life, young mothers, initiates, mature men • **alchemic** man; the masculine principle; the Red Lion or Red Dragon; the sun; gold; the third stage in the Great Work; the zenith point of color; associated with sulfur, blood, passion, sublimation • **American** associated with the Democratic party • **Amerindian** joy; fertility; daylight • **Andaman** associated with the soul • **Aztecan** fertility; blood; the desert; evil; misfortune • **Buddhist** activity; creativity; life; associated with West, meditation; attribute of Amitabha; *red, white, and blue:* Brahma, Vishnu and Shiva; intelligence, order, and unity • **Celtic** death; disaster; the red horseman • **Chaldean** emblem of Mars (planet) • **Chinese** joy; happiness; the yang principle; the sun; fire; the phoenix; the soul; lucky; the luckiest of colors; life; anything red had healing qualities; associated with Summer, South, the earth; *red cloud:* calamity and warfare; *red-faced person on the stage:* a sacred person • **Christian** Christ's passion; the blood of Calvary; the fire of Pentecost; zeal; love; power; priestly dignity; intrepidness; cruelty; charity; color of Pentecost, All Saints Day, feasts of martyrs; martyrdom; attribute of SS Anne, John, the Holy Spirit, cardinal's vestments; *red with white:* the devil, Purgatory; death; *red with black:* Satan; *black cassock with red trim:* attribute of a monsignor, dean; *red dates on a calendar:* holy days • **Egyptian** associated with virility, violence, harmfulness, wickedness, perversion; attribute of beneficent Genii; *red skin:* attribute of Set; *red letters in writing:* words of ill omen • **Greek** the active masculine principle as opposed to purple which is the royal and passive principle; associated with Apollo, Ares, Priapus, Sparta • **heraldic** victorious power; triumph; rule; courage; magnanimity; zeal; *blood red:* patriotism; military service; military strength and magnanimity; sacrifice; martyrdom • **Hindu** *red-painted woman, sometimes with four arms:* Sitala • **Indic** *red ribbon or thread around the neck:* protection from an acheri • **Islamic** gnosis • **Japanese** emblem of the Taira clan; *red cap and kimono:* worn on the 61st birthday • **Hindu** activity; creativity; life energy; human love; South; the rajas as expansion in manifestation; attribute of Vishnu • **Islamic** lucky; happiness • **Kabalistic** severity; associated with the archangel Samael • **Kalmyk** West • **Masonic** intelligence; discipline; glory • **Mayan** associated with victory, success, East, honey greed for power and wealth • **Mexican Indian** associated with East • **North American Indian** *prairie tribes:* associated with South • **Oceanic** divinity; nobility • **Persian** associated with rebellion; *white, red, and gold:* purity, love, and revelation; emblem of the Persian trinity • **Pueblo** associated with West • **Roman** divinity; associated with Apollo, Mars, Bacchus; attribute of Pollux • **Semitic** associated with Baal • **Tierra del Fuegan** associated with the rising sun, East • **Turkish** lucky; happiness; associated with the Ottomans, Seljuks

Red Sea • **Jewish** deliverance through God's protection; salvation; purification; baptism; rebirth

red snapper • **Japanese** attribute of Ebisu

reed weakness; fragility; indiscretion; wantonness; resilience; divine protection; fertility; transitoriness; docility; humility; quietness; vulva; woman; humiliation of greatness; humility; justice; attribute of river gods • **Aztecan** *green reed:* associated with East, the land of rebirth • **Celtic** health; harmony; growth; associated with the dwarf planet Pluto, jasper, October, November • **Chinese** prosperous administration; advancement; learning • **Christian** attribute of the Passion of Christ; humiliation; the faithful living by the waters of grace; *reed with hyssop and/or sponge, ladder, scarlet robe:* the Passion of Christ; *small cross of reeds:* attribute of John the Baptist; *reed surmounted by a Latin or tau cross:* attribute of St. Philip • **Egyptian** royalty; *flowering reed and white crown:* emblem of the Upper Kingdom of Egypt • **flower language** music; docility; *feathery or split:* indiscretion; *flowering reed:* confidence in heaven • **Greco-Roman** music; harmony; attribute of Pan/Faunus; *nymph hiding in reeds:* Syrinx • **Indic** World Axis • **Japanese** learning; associated with cleansing; *reed sprouting from the primeval waters:* manifestation • **Mexican Indian** fertility; plenty; wealth • **Sumero-Semitic** *two looped reeds:* attribute of Ishtar

reef the obstruction of destiny; danger lurking in the unconscious; regression; consciousness hardened into hostility; stagnated spiritual progress

reflection consciousness; the temporal, phenomenal world; truth

reindeer primitive life; steeds of Santa Claus; conductor of souls; emblem of the North polar region • **Norse** sacred to Disa

reins intelligence; will; power; law; the relationship between soul and body • **cutting reins** dying; liberation

relief • **weak relief** futility; falsity; equivocation •

powerful relief the nascent surge of an idea or emotion

remora an omen of disaster; the self contained in the unconscious s• **Christian** Christ • **heraldic** obstacle • **remora pierced by an arrow** attribute of Prudence personified

renaming see **name**

rending anger; grief; penitence; mourning; an irrevocable step; a break with existing order; an attempt to break through to another plane

reptile primordial life; cold-bloodedness; lack of human warmth; old age; materialism; sexuality; heresy; an infernal animal

rescue see **relief**

reseda tenderness; modesty

resin embalming; resurrection; incorruptibility; purity; immortality; regeneration; depilatory; the soul substance of a tree • **Chinese** *cypress resin:* charm to acquire weightlessness; *seeds and resin:* food of the Immortals • **Taoist** *pine nuts, needles, resin:* food of the Immortals • see also **sap; frankincense; galbanum; myrrh**

rest see **peace**

return fulfillment • **returning home or to one's birthplace** dying in the positive sense of reintegration of the spirit with God

Revelation, Book of • **Christian** Apocalypse; Judgment Day; the Second Coming of Christ

Reynard the Fox • **European** carnal appetite; cunning; the Church; trickster; amorality; antithesis of chivalry

rhinoceros bravery; victory; culture; short sighted passion; lack of sensitivity; materialism • **Chinese** *rhinoceros horn:* happiness, aphrodisiac • **heraldic** one who does not seek combat, but will defend to the death when attacked

rhododendron fire; danger of intoxication • **flower language** danger; beware • **heraldic** wariness; caution

rhomb vagina

rhubarb bitterness; brouhaha • **flower language** advice

ribbon award; distinction; sun-ray; pleasure • **blue ribbon** first prize; marriage • **red ribbon** second prize; Order of the Bath • **knotted ribbon** fraternity • **ribbon knotted to form a circle** immortality; an undertaking fulfilled; attribute of the hero • **ribbon tied in a bow** blossoming • **Indic** *red ribbon around the neck:* protection from an acheri

rice fecundity; wisdom; a spermatic image; productiveness; happiness; immortality; spiritual nourishment; knowledge; abundance; primordial purity • **Japanese** associated with 88th birthdays; *man standing on rice bales:* Daikoku

riches wisdom, especially when they are gifts from gods or fairies

riding (usually on an animal) adventure; triumph; supremacy; pride; coition • **fallen rider** Pride personified

right side associated with the felicitous, evolution, openness, the normal, the legitimate, life, birth, the higher virtues, the future, the forces of reason, action, extroversion, the solar, the masculine, the active, the conscious, extroversion • **Chinese** yang; strength; the side of honor only in war • **Hindu** a sacred object must be passed by keeping it at the right • **Japanese** associated with the female, water, the moon • **Jewish** the side of one's protector • **Occidental** the side of honor • **political** associated with order, stability, authority, hierarchies, complacency, conservatism, reactionarism

ring continuity; wholeness; marriage; an eternally repeated cycle; a contract; vow; group membership; union; the female genitals; power; bond; slavery; fertility; female love; authenticity; justice; legitimacy; invisibility; mourning; eternity; equated with the personality • **two linked rings, side by side** permanent marriage union • **two linked rings, one above the other** earth and sky; the physical and the spiritual • **five linked rings** emblem of the Olympics • **animal with a ring in its mouth** guardian of the way • **signet ring** delegation of authority • **Chinese** authority; dignity; eternity; *a perfect ring:* the emperor's pleasure; *an imperfect ring:* the emperor's displeasure; *jade ring:* attribute of Mo-li Ch'in; *half-ring:* banishment, exile; *broken ring:* rejection, disfavor; *ring sent by the emperor:* a summons to the court • **Christian** eternity; unity; faithful affection given freely; spiritual marriage; *wedding ring:* attribute of SS Catherine of Siena, Catherine of Alexandria (especially when held out to her by the Christ child); *three linked rings:* the Trinity; *amethyst ring with a carved Eros/Cupid:* attribute of St. Valentine; *fish with a ring in its mouth:* attribute of St. Mungo • **Greco-Roman** *iron ring:* attribute of Prometheus after he was freed • **Hindu** *ring of flame around Shiva:* the cosmic cycle of creation and destruction • **Islamic** *carnelian ring:* attribute of Mohammed • **Samiam** *brass ring on right arm:* charm for protection when handling the dead • **Sumero-Semitic** *triple ring (sometimes a single ring):* attribute of gods; *ring with crown, scepter and/or sickle:* attribute of royalty • **Zoroastrian** *bearded man in a winged circle holding a ring:* Ahura Mazda • see also **annulet; circle**

river fertility; the irreversible passage of time; the sense of loss; oblivion; life; peace; refreshment; the creative power of time and nature; rebirth; entrance to the underworld; obedience to time. life, the law • **river or gorge crossed by a bridge** the banks or sides represent different worlds life/death, mortality/immortality, body/spirit, etc. • **Buddhist** the flux of life • **Chinese** *crossing a river:* ritual cleansing • **Christian** *four rivers:* the four Gospels • **Hindu** *carved on a temple door:* ritual ablution, purification of the devotee; *four Rivers of Paradise:* the four cardinal directions, phases of cyclic development, yugas, sacrificial cups of the Vedas; *river of blood, hair, and filth:* Vaitarani • **Kabalistic** bringers of spiritual influences from the upper world to the lower world • **Norse** *four rivers of milk:* attribute of Asgard • **Persian** flowing of the sacred haoma • **Sumero-Semitic** *four Rivers of Paradise:* the four seasons, quarters of the earth, cardinal directions

river bank *see* **shore**

road life; potentialities; progress; adventure; experience; difficulty; associated with pilgrims, prostitutes • **one-way road** death

robber *see* **thief**

robe concealment; may reveal the wearer's inner personality, or only the personality shown to the world (especially a full robe) • **white robe** purity; chastity; innocence; virtue; triumph of the spirit over the flesh • **gold robe** the fire of the sun • **black robe** mourning; magic; sinisterness; night; judgment • **seamless robe** wholeness; that which is integrated • **flowing or full robe** righteousness; peace; wisdom; knowledge; beneficence • **rich robe** worldly pomp and vanity • **yellow robe** attribute of Jews • **velvet and ermine robe** rank; royalty • **Buddhism** *saffron-colored robe:* attribute of monks • **Chinese** *long blue robe:* attribute of Wen Chang • **Christian** *scarlet or purple robe:* the mock royal robe given to Christ; *seamless robe:* charity, unity, attribute of the Passion of Christ; *white robe:* innocence, triumph of the spirit over the flesh; *red robe under a green cloak:* occasional attribute of St. Anne • **Greco-Roman** mourning; *girls in yellow robes:* participants in rites of Artemis/Diana; *red robe:* attribute of soothsayers • **Mithraic** *robe with zodiac signs:* attribute of the initiate • **Norse** *falcon-feather robe:* attribute of Freyja • **Spanish** *yellow robe:* worn by those condemned by the Inquisition • **Ural-Altaic** *feathered robe:* communication between this world and the spirit world • *see also* **kimono**

robin harbinger of Spring; tameness; love; friendliness; trust; associated with May • **Christian** death and resurrection; attribute of St. Mungo • **Norse** sacred to Thor; associated with storm clouds

roc • **Arabian, Persian** storm bird; associated with wind and lightning; the sky; World Axis; a solar animal; a powerful king or emir famed for valor

rochet • **Christian** loving administration

rock solidity; permanence; changelessness; stability; reliability; cohesion; the source of human life; truth; the spirit as foundation; the Spirit; the Creator; hiding place; durability; immortality; constancy; justice; solitude; conservatism; rigidity; coldness; hardness • **being thrown from a rock** punishment of a traitor • **two rocks** doorway to another plane of existence • **hiding under a rock** trait of a low animal • **Christian** strength; steadfastness; the Church; Christ (especially when surmounted by a cross); St. Peter; *four rivers gushing from a rock:* the Gospels • **Greco-Roman** *man chained to a rock, attacked by eagles:* Prometheus; *woman chained to a rock, attacked by a monster:* Andromeda, Hesione; *man and woman (sometimes veiled) throwing rocks behind them:* Deucalion and Pyrrha; *rock of Sisyphus:* insatiable desire and the ceaseless fight against it • **heraldic** refuge; safety; protection • **Japanese** firmness • **Jewish** God's strength, faithfulness; *water flowing from a rock:* associated with Moses • **Mithraic** Mithras was born from a rock • *see also* **stone; Symplegades**

rocket (plant) in **flower language** rivalry; *queen's rocket:* fashionable, you are the queen of coquettes

rocking fertility; life's changing fortunes; mindless movement

rod punishment; official power; authority; dignity; correction; wickedness; liberty; phallus; light; World Axis; support; attribute of messengers, magicians, conductors of souls to the next world, the Tiburtine sibyl • **rod with rays** attribute of thunder and lightning gods • **measuring rod** attribute of Time personified • **flowering rod** the Cosmic Tree • **Babylonian** *hazel rod:* divination • **Buddhist** *rod with jingling rings:* kindness, mercy, attribute of pilgrims • **Christian** attribute of the Passion of Christ; *flowering rod:* attribute of the Virgin Mary, St. Joseph; *Rod of Jesse:* attribute of Christ, the Virgin Mary • **Greco-Roman** *measuring rod:* attribute of Chronos, Nemesis/Invidia • **Islamic** *rod with snake:* the unregenerate soul turned into spiritual power • **Jewish** *flowering rod:* attribute of Aaron; *rod with serpent:* attribute of Moses • **Sumero-Semitic** *measuring rod with line:* attribute of Marduk, Shamash, sometimes Ea • *see also* **staff**

roebuck nimbleness; speed; gentleness; Christ; love; wisdom; foresight • *see also* **deer**

roll *see* **scroll**

Roman associated with heroic death, suicide, holiness, past glory, greatness

Rome ancient civilization; past glory; the Vatican; the Roman Catholic imperium; mystic center

rood *see* **cross**

rood beam • **Christian** the necessity of the cross of Calvary in passing from the Church Militant to the Church Triumphant

rood screen the gates of heaven; veil of the Ark of the Covenant

roof protection; safety; hospitality; feminine sheltering principle; stage for preaching; peeping spot; place of idolatry, mourning, lamentation, hiding

rook (bird) dawn; April; Spring; gregariousness; a priest • **rooks flying in a great flock** presage of rain • **Egyptian** marriage; *dead rook:* sunset

rook (chess) *see* **chess**

room individuality; loneliness; privacy of mind and body • **closed room without windows** virginity; non-communication; place of initiation • **closed room with windows** the possibility of understanding and communication

rooster vigilance; the sun; the dawn; the Bird of Fame; supremacy; courage; vigilance; activity; resurrection; the masculine principle; incest; egotism; defiance; anger; insolence; inordinate and frustrated desire; self-confidence; emblem of France; attribute of the personifications of Lust, Adultery, sun gods except for Celts and Scandinavians • **young rooster** foolishness • **white rooster** lucky; dawn; a man of holy ways • **black rooster** unlucky; death; night; agent of the devil • **white tail on a rooster** disinclination to fight; cowardice • **rooster on a weathervane** vigilance watching for evil; guard of the steeple at night when the bells are silent; *when gilded:* solar power • **rooster crowing at night** unlucky • **chariot drawn by roosters** attribute of Vigilance personified • **two roosters fighting over a pine cone** truth made manifest • **alchemic** the three stages through which the work must pass • **Azande** associated with witchcraft • **Buddhist** carnal passion; pride; *rooster and sun:* emblem of Buddhism; *at the center of the Round of Existence:* carnal passion; *Tibetan Buddhism:* one of the Three Poisons • **Celtic** attribute of underworld gods, Bride • **Chinese** the yang prin-

ciple; courage; benevolence; the Five Virtues; tenth symbolic animal of the Twelve Terrestrial Branches; valor; faithfulness; funeral charm against evil spirits; war; aggression; associated with the sunset, October, the Pleiades; *red rooster:* the sun, protection against fire; *white rooster:* purity, protection against ghosts, evil, the only capable guide of transient spirits, occasional initiation sacrifice to indicate the death of the old life and the purity of the new; *rooster with crown:* the literary spirit; *rooster with spurs:* warlike character; *three-legged rooster:* lives in the sun; *rooster and hen in a garden:* rural pleasures; *rooster on a drum:* peace; *rooster comb and pheasant's plume together:* bravery, prosperity • **Christian** vigilance; liberality; Christianity; Christ putting evil and darkness to flight; herald of the dawn of Christ; attribute of the Crucifixion, St. Peter (especially when crowing); *red rooster:* emblem of Catholicism; *rooster and lion:* good and evil respectively; *two roosters fighting:* the Battle of Life, Christians fighting for Christ • **Egyptian** vigilance; foresight • **German** guide of the dead • **Gnostic** *rooster with an ear of grain:* vigilance producing plenty • **folkloric** buried under cornerstones to ward off evil • **Fulani** associated with secrecy, *rooster in a hut:* a secret told to no one; *rooster and/or ram in a yard:* a secret told to relatives or close friends, *rooster and/or bull in the streets:* a secret told to everyone, *rooster and/or fire:* a secret told to an enemy and causing ruin • **Gothic** war • **Greco-Roman** vigilance; pugnacity; sacred to Apollo, Asclepius, Athena/Minerva, Attis, Ares/Mars, Artemis/Diana, Hermes/Mercury, Leto, Priapus, Zeus/Jupiter; sacrifice to Lares, associated with Persephone/Proserpine in the Spring and the renewal of life • **heraldic** soldierly conduct; religious inspiration; courage; perseverance; heroism; ability in politics; *black rooster:* law, the legal profession • **Hindu** attribute of Skandha • **Islamic** announces the presence of an angel; the call to prayer; *white rooster:* the enemy of the enemies of God; *giant rooster of the first heaven:* when it ceases to crow the Day of Judgment has come • **Japanese** courage; summoner of Amaterasu; *rooster on a drum:* Shinto summons to temple prayer; *rooster on a gate:* emblem of Amaterasu • **Jewish** fertility; God-given intelligence; courtesy; *rooster and hen:* a bridal couple • **Lithuanian** *black or white rooster:* indoor form of an aitvaras • **Malian** associated with crossroads, the center, uncertainty • **Masonic** vigilance; the enlightenment of initiation • **Mithraic** sacred to

Mithras • **Norse** military vigilance; guard; *golden rooster:* Vithafmir; *Fralar:* calls the sleeping heroes of Valhalla for the last great battle • **Oriental** *rooster on a red or gold disk:* the sun • **Persian** *rooster on a scepter:* attribute of royalty • **Pueblo** associated with the sun • **Sumerian** *rooster-headed god:* occasionally Nergal • **Vietnamese** *boiled rooster's claw:* the microcosm • *see also* **alectorian stone; capon; chicken; chick; hen; hippalectryon; weather cock**

roots foundation, but they do not necessarily imply stability

rope mythic ascension; despair; betrayal; link; sun ray; the prerogative of power (especially a short piece); hanging • **rope around the neck** penitence, hanging • **putting a rope on one's head** repentance • **gold rope** divine power • **rope binding a chariot** the Gordian knot, associated with Alexander the Great • **knotted rope** fetters; entanglement; bondage • **Akkadian** *rope of the world:* the waters surrounding the world that binds heaven and earth • **Australian aboriginal** access to other worlds • **Aztecan** *rope hanging from the sky:* divine semen falling to the earth • **Bon** the connection between heaven and earth • **Buddhist** emblem of Buddhism • **Central American Indian** *rope hanging from the sky:* divine semen falling to the earth • **Christian** Christ's betrayal and Passion; attribute of St. Andrew; *rope around the neck:* attribute of Judas, SS Charles Borromeo, Mark • **Egyptian** *knotted rope:* an individual being, the stream of life reflected upon itself • **Greco-Roman** attribute of Fortune; *rope and vase:* attribute of Nemesis/Invidia; *rope-maker:* Ocnus; *ass eating a rope:* attribute of Ocnus • **Hindu** attribute of Varuna, Yama, Indra, Vritra, Nirrti; *invisible rope:* gnosis that gives the power of ascent • **Islamic** ascent • **Japanese** *rope held in the left hand:* attribute of Fudo-Myoo; *rice-straw rope (shimenawa):* charm against misfortune, injury, evil spirits • **Mayan** used by God to draw up the souls of the dead; *rope hanging from the sky:* rain • **Norse** attribute of Odin • **Sumerian** *rope passing through a winged door:* the mystic link binding God and man • *see also* **entanglement; cord; noose; hanging (execution)**

rosary *see* **prayer beads**

rose (color) associated with Libra; • **rose-colored glasses** make one see things in the best possible light, or better than they really are

rose (flower) completion; heavenly perfection; earthly passion; seduction; mystic center; the heart; God; the beloved; messianic hope; beauty; grace; happiness; vulva; integration of the personality; secrecy; discretion; associated with Taurus; attribute of the Samian sibyl; emblem of Iran • **blue rose** impossibility; unattainabilty; faithful unto death; martial honor • **gold rose** absolute achievement; fame; perfection • **purple rose** sorrow • **red rose** divine love; motherhood; desire; passion; joy; beauty • **white rose** inspired wisdom; joy; innocence; virginity; spiritual unfolding • **red and white rose together** the union of opposites; the union of fire and water • **yellow rose** infidelity; jealousy; emblem of Texas • **black rose** anarchy; death; mourning; impurity • **eight-petaled rose** regeneration • **rose with thorns** thesis and antithesis; conjunction of opposites; deadly beauty • **rose garland** reward of virtue • **wreath of roses** heavenly joy • **rose garden** regeneration; Paradise; place of mystic marriage, the union of opposites • **alchemic** virtue • **Chinese** fragrance; prosperity; sweetness in desolation • **Christian** Christ; the Virgin Mary; the flower of Paradise; attribute of SS Angelus, Elizabeth of Hungary, Elizabeth of Portugal, Rita, Rosalia, Rose of Lima, Rose of Viterbo; *red rose:* blood of Christ, charity, martyrdom; *white rose:* innocence, purity, chastity, emblem of the Virgin Mary; *golden rose:* papal benediction, emblem of the pope; *rose and lily:* emblem of the Virgin Mary; *rose entwined around a crucifix:* attribute of St. Therese of Lisieux; *roses in apron or lap:* attribute of St. Elizabeth of Hungary; *crown of roses:* attribute of SS Casimir, Flavia, Dorothea, Elizabeth of Hungary; *angel placing crowns of roses on a man and a woman:* Valerius and St. Cecelia; *basket of roses and apples:* attribute of St. Dorothea; *angels with rose garlands:* exultation of St. Dorothea; *roses springing from blood drops:* associated with St. Francis of Assisi; *rose on a corpse:* the death of Christ; *red and white roses together:* emblem of the Virgin Mary; *garland of roses:* heavenly bliss, the Virgin Mary as the Rose of Heaven, an allusion to the rosary; *garland of red and white roses:* attribute of St. Cecilia; *thornless rose:* associated with the Virgin Mary; *rose garden:* the new Jerusalem • **Egyptian** pure love without carnality; sacred to Isis, Osiris • **flower language** love; beauty; *Australian rose:* thou art all that is lovely; *bridal rose:* happy; *burgundy rose:* unconscious beauty; *cabbage rose:* ambassador of love; *campion rose:* only deserve my love; *Carolina rose:* love is dangerous; *Chinese rose:* beauty always new; *Christmas rose:* the Nativity of Christ, tranquillize my anxiety; *daily rose:* I aspire to your smile; *damask rose:* freshness, brilliant complexion, beauty ever new; *deep red rose:* bashful shame, martyrdom; *dog rose:* pleasure and pain, simplicity; *full red rose:* beauty; *hundred-leaved rose:* pride, dignity of the mind, emblem of the Three Graces; *Japan rose:* beauty is your only attraction; *Lancaster rose:* union; *maiden blush rose:* if you love me you will find it out, you will reveal it; *May rose:* precociousness; *moss rose:* love, voluptuousness; *moss rose bud:* confession of love; *full moss rose:* superior merit; *mundi rose:* variety, you are merry; *musk rose:* capricious beauty; *musk rose cluster:* charming; *pompon rose:* gentility, pettiness; *red rose:* love; *red-leaved rose:* beauty and prosperity; *red rosebud:* you are young and beautiful, pure and lovely; *rock rose:* safety; *unique rose:* call me not beautiful; *white rose:* silence, girlhood, heart of ignorant love; *dried white rose:* unfaithfulness, death is preferable to loss; *full white rose:* I am worthy of you; *withered white rose:* transient impression; *red and white roses together:* unity, warmth of hearth; *multiflora rose:* grace; *guelder rose:* Winter, age, good news, bound; *full-grown rose placed over two buds:* secrecy; *single rose:* simplicity; *thornless rose:* early attachment; *York and Lancaster roses together:* war; *rose in a tuft of grass:* there is everything • **Greco-Roman** joy; beauty; desire; love triumphant; resurrection; eternal Spring; emblem of Aphrodite/Venus, Eos/Aurora, Helios/Sol, Dionysus/Bacchus, the Muses, the Three Graces; associated with funerals, the blood of Adonis; *crown or wreath of roses:* attribute of the Roman emperor and Comus • **heraldic** seventh son; youth; beauty; charm; joy; hope; innocence; silence; gentleness; *white rose:* love, charm, innocence, faith, emblem of the House of Lancaster; *red rose:* love, desire, grace, beauty, emblem of the House of York; *yellow rose:* jealousy, infidelity; *chaplet with four roses:* joy, admiration • **Islamic** the blood of Mohammed, connected with the eyes of Mohammed • **Kabalistic** *center of the rose:* the sun; *rose petals:* the infinite but harmonious diversities of nature • **portraiture** *white rose:* purity; *red rose:* martyrdom • **Rosicrucian** divine light of the universe; associated with the Tree of Life, regeneration, resurrection

Rose of Sharon • Christian Christ's love for the Church

rose window eternity; mystic center • *see also* **lotus**

rosemary remembrance; devotion; constancy; madness; Nativity of Christ • **flower language** your presence revives me; memory; fidelity between lovers; remembrance; remembrance of the dead • **Greco-Roman** sacred to Ares/Mars • **heraldic** remembrance; enduring love; constancy; loyalty; fidelity

rosette *see* **lotus**

rotting *see* **putrefaction**

round • Kalmyk shape of the Western Continent and the faces of its inhabitants

roundel • heraldic *gold or yellow:* worthy of trust or treasure; *white:* generosity; *purple:* wounded; *blue:* hurt; *red:* communion wafer; *black:* cannon ball

rowan oracle; death; wisdom; immortality; protection from fairies; protection from witches, but also used by them; associated with the archangels Raphael, Samael • **Celtic** protection; connection; used in divination; source of the first woman • **Gallic** Tree of Life • **Norse** charm against sorcery; sacred to Thor • **Teutonic** charm against sorcery; sacred to Donar

rubber associated with 9th wedding anniversaries

rubber tree associated with Cancer

rubbing (motion) friction; impediment; difficulty; annoyance; transfer of magical power

Rubicon • crossing the Rubicon going past the point of no return; associated with Julius Ceasar

ruby zeal; divine zeal; human love; passion; charity; human love; majesty; beauty; dignity; divine power; royalty; light; elegance; happiness; lucky; longevity; rashness; invulnerability; stone for 15th, 40th 80th wedding anniversaries; birthstone for December; associated with Leo, July, the sun, the archangels Azrael, Michael, Samael, Capricorn, Cancer • **star ruby** stone for a 60th wedding anniversary • **ruby changing color** presage of mischief, evil • **ruby regaining color** the danger is over • **Arabian** associated with Taurus • **Chaldean** associated with Mars (planet) • **folkloric** charm to ward off evil thought, banish sorrow, restrain lust, resist poison, prevent plague, stanch bleeding • **Jewish** *on vestments:* Summer • **Russian** charm to promote health of the heart, brain, memory, vitality, blood

rudbeckia • flower language justice • **heraldic** encouragement

rudder safety; government; royalty; dignity; power; moral rectitude; prudence; wisdom; love; divine will; control; power; authority; zeal; skill; knowledge; intuition; navigation; responsibility; foresight; guidance; attribute of Nemesis/Invidia, Tyche/Fortuna, the personifications of Abundance, Chance, Fate, Fortune • **rudder on a globe** sovereignty • **rudder with a caduceus and cornucopia** the government of Caesar

rue (plant) grace; goodness; related to the sun; pity; mercy; repentance; sorrow; disdain; purification; virginity; bitterness; grief; antidote for madness, poison; associated with Leo • **flower language** disdain; *goat's rue:* reason • **Jewish** repentance

ruins life defunct; sentiments, ideas, or customs which are dead and irrelevant to present life, but which nonetheless persist • **columns in ruins** death; mortality; broken faith; defeat; frustrated hope; unfinished work; attribute of Strength personified attribute of St. Titus

rule (measuring) standard of morality; reason; choice; rectitude; attribute of the personifications of Geometry, Arithmetic, Melancholy • **Christian** attribute of St. Thomas • **Hindu** attribute of Vishvakarma • **Egyptian** attribute of Ptah

rune magic; ancient knowledge

rush *see* **reed**

russet (cloth) earth; filth; heat; violence; oppression; dawn; love of darkness and lies • **russet mantle** loss of good reputation; attribute of Dawn personified

Russia darkness; dreariness; communism; coldness; alcoholism

rust disuse; age; destruction; infirmity; suffering

rye connected with love

S

S associated with a new cycle, the wheel of fortune, the creative impulse for intangible things, incentive, unifying movement, the serpent, health, wisdom, the Holy Spirit, the lungs, Pisces, Cancer, -1- • **medieval** occasionally the Roman numeral for 7 or 70 (Z was also used) • **tarot** associated with the Sun

saber *see* **sword**

Sachiel, Archangel *see* **Zadkiel, Archangel**

sack attribute of Isaiah • **Japanese** attribute of Daikoku, Hotei

sackcloth sorrow; abject humiliation; mourning, penitence, affliction

sacrifice giving up something of lower value for something of value on a higher plane; restoring primordial unity; reuniting what is scattered in manifestation; submission to divine guidance through reconciliation • **animal sacrifice** bringing one's animal instincts under control • **human sacrifice** atonement for pride • **sacrifice of a king** restoration of fertility

saddle • **heraldic** martial readiness

saffron humility; renunciation; disinterestedness; magic; wisdom; love; charity; associated with the sun • **Buddhism** *saffron-colored robe:* attribute of monks • **Christian** attribute of the Virgin Mary (especially when with spikenard) • **flower language** beware of excess; do not abuse; *crocus saffron:* mirth; *meadow saffron:* my happiest days are past

sage (herb) remembrance; longevity; immortality; egotism; emblem of Health personified • **flower language** esteem; domestic virtues; *garden sage:* esteem • **heraldic** longevity; esteem; wisdom

sagebrush • **American** lucky; emblem of the West in the US

Sagittarius the complete man in both animal and spiritual nature; associated with sincerity, adaptability, optimism, carelessness, tactlessness, rebellion against power, an inflated self-importance, exaggeration, fire, Jupiter (planet), movement, nomadic instincts, independence, quick reactions, the archangel Zadkiel

sailboat • **Christian** the Church; attribute of SS Simon, Jude (especially when mast is cross shaped); *sailboat on the Nile:* attribute of St. Athanasius • *see also* **boat; ship; sail**

sailor conductor of the soul; pilgrim; coming to grips with the unconscious; partakes of the symbolism of the ocean, sails, sailboats, boats, ships

sails breath; venture; adventure; action; creative breath; fertility; the spur to action; the wind; related to boats, ships, sailboats, funeral shrouds; attribute of Fortune personified • **full sail** pregnancy; swelling powers; emblem of Air personified • **striking sails** defeat; surrender; humbleness • **black sails** an ill-fated ship • **Christian** *medieval:* the Holy Spirit • **Egyptian** breath; *purple sails:* attribute of Cleopatra's barge • **Islamic** 70 sails cover God's face

sainfoin • **flower language** agitation

Saint Elmo's fire • **Breton** a lost soul • **German** message from the soul of a lost comrade — good weather if it rises, bad weather if it lowers • **Mediterranean** the actual presence of St. Elmo

Saint John's wort • **flower language** animosity; superstition; you are a prophet

sakaki tree • **Japanese** Tree of Life, the mirror of Amaterasu, the holiest of all trees; regeneration; immortality

sakkos *see* **dalmatic**

salamander fire; immunity to fire; the ardent lover; chastity; virginity; baptism; enduring and triumphant faith; a soldier surviving a battle; associated with Winter; attribute of Fire personified • **Christian** the Christian who resists temptation by grace; enduring faith; the righteous man; the devil personified; Christ as the king of fire • **Egyptian** associated with the cold • **French** emblem of Francis I • **Greek** emblem of Winter • **heraldic** constancy; bravery; courage; protection

salmon fecundity; phallus • **Celtic** wisdom, knowledge; inspiration; prophecy; associated with sacred wells signifying the foreknowledge of the gods • **Norse** determination; Andvari • **North American** emblem of Alaska, the Pacific Northwest

Salome • **Jewish** wantonness; pleasure

salt strength; superiority; perpetuity; permanence; hospitality; wisdom; wit; piquancy; worth; preservation; incorruptibility; truth; immortality; fidelity; friendship; life; associated with the archangel Cassiel • **alchemic** rectification; clarification; the fixed; earthly nature; the body uniting spirit and soul, active and passive • **Celtic** the incorruptible Spirit • **Christian** the elect; superiority; divine wisdom; worth; purity; incorruptibility; strength; discretion • **Greco-Roman** literary wit; charm against evil • **Islamic** friendship • **Japanese** a cleansing agent • **Jewish** spiritual discernment; friendship; associated with Lot's wife; *communal eating of bread and salt:* friendship that cannot be broken

salt water sterility; truth; the ocean; tears; holy water • **Japanese** a cleansing agent • **Jewish** the tears shed by the race

Samael, Archangel associated with Mars (planet), bronze, iron, brass, -4-, -16-, bloodstones, diamonds, garnets, jasper, rubies, topaz, 5th heaven, Aries, Scorpio, Tuesday, sheep, rams, horses, bears, wolves, acacias, horse chestnuts, hawthorns, holly, mistletoe, rowans, thorn trees, monkey puzzle trees • **Jewish** the guardian angel of Esau • **Kabalistic** associated with -5-, red • **tarot** associated with the Lightning Struck Tower

Samson strength

sanctuary lamp • **Anglican, Catholic** the presence of the Host at the altar

sand barrenness; fruitless labor; endurance; time; instability; impermanence; the womb; connected with sleep • **Islamic** purity; substitute for water in ablutions • **Japanese** *ritual sprinkling sand:* rain, plenty • **Jewish** the descendents of Abraham • **Tuareg** *whirling pillars of sand in a sandstorm:* Ahl at-trab

Sandalphon, Archangel associated with earth, willows, -10-, lemon trees, the center, turquoise • **Kabalistic** associated with brown

sandals liberty; freedom; humility; the lowest material life; attribute of royalty, the wealthy (especially in ancient art) • **winged sandals** loftiness of spirit; fleetness; attribute of messenger gods • **golden sandals** attribute of royalty • **one sandal** attribute of a warrior • **carrying sandals** humility • **going without sandals** poverty; mourning • **shaking the dust from one's sandals** complete rejection of one's past; renunciation • **Christian** attribute of monastics, pilgrims • **Greco-Roman** *winged sandals:* attribute of Hermes/Mercury, Perseus; *fawn-skin sandals:* attribute of devotees of Dionysus/Bacchus, Orpheus; *sword and sandal under a rock:* associated with Theseus • **Jewish** *throwing down a sandal:* making a claim; *handing over a sandal:* relinquishing claim • **Persian** *woman with golden sandals:* Ardvi Sura Anahita • *see also* **shoes; feet**

sandalwood exoticism; sacredness

sap celestial milk of the mother goddess; life fluid (blood, semen, etc.); life force; strength; vitality • **Scottish** *ash sap:* protection of children from witches • *see also* **resin**

sapphire truth; heavenly virtues, truth, meditation, reward; sincerity; conscience; hope; purity; chastity; power; money; associated with, Libra, Virgo, Taurus, Gemini, 5th, 45th, and 70th wedding anniversaries, the archangels Cassiel, Zadkiel, the planets Saturn, Jupiter, Mercury, Venus; birthstone of April, September; charm for psychic power, meditation, peace, healing, the command of spirits, the understanding of prophecies; charm for protection from poison, plague, eye diseases, envy, harm • **blue sapphire** stone for a 10th wedding anniversary • **yellow sapphire** stone for a 7th wedding anniversary • **Christian** emblem of the Virgin Mary; a foundation stone of the New Jerusalem; *sapphire ring:* attribute of a cardinal • **Greek** associated with Apollo, September • **heraldic** piety; sincerity • **Hindu** prosperity; light of the gods; corresponds to the element earth; *sapphire mountain:* the southern face of Mount Meru • **Jewish** stone on which the Ten Commandments were etched; attribute of the High Priest's breastplate; *on vestments:* Autumn, truth, sincerity, chastity, constancy • **Persian** a sacred stone • *sometimes confused with* **hyacinth (stone), lapis lazuli**

Saracen • **heraldic** service in the Crusades

Sarah • **Jewish** patience; spiritual regeneration

sarcophagus the feminine principle of containment; death; mortality; earth as the beginning and end of material life

Sardis, Church of • **Christian** associated with imperfection, the souls of the perfect slain, the few undefiled, the thyroid, the fifth seal

sardony • flower language irony

sardonyx honor; renown; brightness; vivacity; self-control; conjugal fidelity; associated with Mercury (planet); charm for protection, courage, peace, good luck, legal success; charm for protection from witches, wicked thoughts, warts, boils, cramps, the evil eye • **Egyptian** blood of Isis, stone of August • **Gnostic** *sardonyx, jasper, and amethyst:* attribute of Abraxus • **Jewish** *two sardonyxes on priestly vestments:* the sun and moon • **Roman** *engraved with an image of Mars (Ares):* soldier's charm for bravery, fearlessness • *see also* **onyx**

sash (clothing) distinction; office; attribute of St. Monica; symbolically the same as the belt • **Tibetan** *sash of human bones:* attribute of Nag-pa

Satan anger; witchcraft; delusion; the dark side of one's own nature; a proud and evil adversary • **Catharistic** the demiurge • **Christian** *Synagogue of Satan:* unperfected aspects of the self; *Satan being held by the nose with a pair of tongs:* St. Eloi holds the tongs

satinflower • flower language sincerity

Saturday associated with the archangel Cassiel, Saturn (planet), Cronus/Saturn, Capricorn, works of mourning • **birthday** Saturday's child works hard for a living • **marriage** no luck at all • **sneezing** see your sweetheart tomorrow • **Jewish** *Creation:* rest • *see also* **days**

Saturn *see* **Cronus/Saturn**

Saturn (planet) reason and intellect; the contemplative and rational; associated with caution, conservatism, restriction, discipline, concentration, contraction, inertia, determination, perseverance, rebirth, sudden changes, Capricorn, Aquarius, -7-, black, lead, North, old age; senility; asphodels, white heliotropes, dragons, vipers, cats, mice, foxes, night birds, Aquarius, the knees and calves, Cronus/Saturn, the archangel Cassiel, Saturday • **Babylonian** associated with Ninib, righteousness, justice • **Chinese** associated with the earth, the Center • **Hermetic** associated with black, copper, a break or slowing in development • **Hindu** associated with the first chakra (gonads) • **Kabalistic** associated with North, patience, perseverance, the archangel Oriphiel • **Sumerian** associated with righteousness, justice

Saturnalia • Roman the invocation of primordial chaos; a desperate quest for a way out of time; the desire to concentrate all the possibilities of existence in a small period of time; the Winter solstice

satyr • Greco-Roman abandon; folly; lust; a child of the devil; revelry; license; lasciviousness; untamed nature; evil; fertility; an oversexed man; associated with Dionysus/Bacchus, Silvanus, Pan/Faunus; attribute of Lust personified; *satyr removing the robe of a sleeping woman:* Jupiter and Antiope respectively

saucer feminine symbol of containment; dish for bloodletting

Saul • Jewish perfect friendship

savage the darker side of the personality; the natural man; instincts; desires; parts of the self in conflict • **heraldic** service in the Crusades • *see also* **wild man**

saw (tool) attribute of Melancholy personified • **Christian** attribute of SS Euphemia, James the Less (especially with the handle upright), Joseph (often with plane and hatchet), Jude, Matthias, Simon Zelotes (especially a saw and/or one or two oars) • **heraldic** industry • **Jewish** attribute of Isaiah • **Mesopotamian** *golden saw:* the sun cutting the darkness, emblem of Shamash

scabbard feminine symbol of containment; vagina

scabious mourning • **flower language** unfortunate love; *sweet scabious:* widowhood

scaffold associated with hanging, building, and theater

scales (balances) *see* **balances**

scales (fish) spiritual defense; armor; related to water and the underworld; moral or cosmic inferiority; attribute of Ea-Oannes, priestesses of Great Mother cults • **scales on mermaids, dragons, the devil** the past continuing in the present; the inferior continuing in the superior

scallop shell *see* **shell**

scalp martial success; contains the power of a person • *see also* **head**

scapegoat vicarious atonement; escape from the consequences of sin; Christ

scapular • Christian the yoke of Christ; attribute of St. Simon Stock

scar remnant of mutilation, usually with a sinister connotation; inability to release past ideas or emotions • **Dahomean** *scarification:* making a child so ugly or unrecognizable that the possessing abiku would leave him • see also **mutilation**

scarab fertility; immortality; eternity; the rising sun; androgyny; reincarnation; resurrection; the creation and revival of life; related to the ladybug • **Congolese** eternal renewal; related to the moon • **Egyptian** the sun; the path of the sun; resurrection; immortality; divine wisdom; virility; generative power of life; self-creation;

Khepri; *scarab-headed god:* Khepri • **Mayan** the filth of the earth • *see also* **beetle**

scarecrow originally a fertility deity; powerlessness; old age; the soul; disguise of the self to avoid facing reality

scarf love; romance; false front; often related to middle age • **black scarf** death • **red scarf** socialism

scarlet energy; life; fire; fervor; worldliness; protection; jurisprudence; general virtue and merit; mutual love; sin; steady drinking; a loud color • **scarlet coat** attribute of huntsmen, British soldiers • **scarlet hat** attribute of a cardinal • **scarlet letter A** attribute of an adulterer • **scarlet robe** the mocking of Christ • **scarlet woman** prostitute; woman of loose morals • *see also* **red**

scepter fertility; power; phallus; fecundation; divine power; royal power; the creative power of the Word; the power of chastity; sovereignty; authority; military command; World Axis; high office; the connection between heaven and earth; magic wand; attribute of sky gods, monarchs, magicians, the personifications of Philosophy, Justice, Fortitude, Good Government, Europe • **split scepter** peace; reconciliation of opposites • **scepter of lead** night • **scepter tipped with a dove** peace and reconciliation; attribute of English kings • **scepter tipped with orb and cross** attribute of English kings • **scepter tipped with an eye** attribute of Modesty personified, signifying Temperance • **breaking one's scepter** abdication • **Buddhist** *diamond scepter:* the Dharma; the highest power; justice; authority; the seven positive and permanent virtues • **Chinese** supreme authority; the power of faith; attribute of the god of learning and literature • **Christian** authority; *scepter underfoot:* attribute of St. Louis of Toulouse (often also with crown); *scepter tipped with a cross:* temporal power; Christ as king; *scepter tipped with a fleur-de-lis:* attribute of the Virgin Mary; *scepter tipped with cross and lily:* attribute of Principalities • **Egyptian** attribute of Osiris; *papyrus scepter:* youth, eternal youth, vigor, learning; *lotus scepter:* virility • **French** *scepter tipped with a fleur-de-lis:* attribute of French kings • **Greco-Roman** attribute of Aphrodite/Venus, Demeter/Ceres, Artemis/Diana, Hades/Pluto, Kore, Persephone/Proserpine; *scepter tipped with a cuckoo:* attribute of Hera/Juno, Zeus/Jupiter, Cybele; *scepter tipped with eagle:* attribute of Roman consuls, triumphant generals; *scepter underfoot:* attribute of Melpomene • **heraldic** justice • **Hindu** the highest authority;

the Dharma; attribute of Indra, Vasu • **Japanese** authority; attribute of abbots • **Jewish** attribute of the archangel Gabriel; *scepter and chain:* Joseph's advancement; *scepter with scroll:* attribute of Solomon; *scepter and trumpet:* attribute of Joshua; *scepter with censer:* messianic hope; attribute of Melchizedek • **Mithraic** attribute of Mithras • **Norse** *scepter with circle:* divine light, sun rays • **Persian** *scepter tipped with a rooster:* attribute of royalty • **still life** the power that death takes away • *see also* **vajra**

scepters (playing cards) *see* **clubs (playing cards)**

schinus • **flower language** religious enthusiasm

scimitar emblem of Muslim countries, the Middle East • **American** emblem of the Shriners • **Christian** attribute of St. Bartholomew; *scimitar with book (usually closed):* attribute of St. Matthias

scissors creation; birth; destruction; death; conjunction of opposites; union; physical extermination; spiritual decision; fate; union; two independent entities working together; attribute of barbers, tailors, sheep shearers, Fury personified • **Armenian** *demon with iron scissors:* an al • **Christian** attribute of St. Agatha of Sicily • **Greco-Roman** attribute of Atropos • **heraldic** usually an occupational sign (barbers, tailors, sheep shearers, etc.) • **Jewish** attribute of Delilah

Scorpio related to sexual function, material life, persistence, discernment, powerful emotions, jealousy, introversion, stubbornness, Mars (planet), Pluto (dwarf planet), water, resistance, dynamism, endurance, struggle, the archangel Samael

scorpion the devil; sin; remorse; torture; evil; suffering; mischief and discord; contempt; treachery; flattery; Scorpio; unbending pride; defensive stewardship; fire; lust; death; disaster; destructive force; suicide; associated with October; attribute of the personifications of Envy, Dialectics, Hatred, Heresy, Africa, Earth, Logic • **Babylonian** *giant scorpion men:* sons of Tiamat, guardians of Shamash • **Christian** evil; treachery; torment; Judas Iscariot; a Jew • **Dogon** associated with a female's male soul, surgery (especially clitoridectomy) • **Egyptian** attribute of Isis (usually seven scorpions), Selket, Set; associated with Hedetet, Ta-Bitjet • **Greco-Roman** associated with the death of Orion • **Jewish** venom; death • **Mayan** repentance; associated with hunting, surgical bloodletting; *man with a scorpion tail:* Ekchuah • **Phrygian** attribute of Sabazios • **Sumero-Semitic** guardians of the Gateway of the Sun, the Mountains of the East, the Twin Gates; associated with Nina, Ishtar

Scotland associated with thrift, obstinacy, perseverance, roughness; Puritanism

scourge (whip) discipline; divine chastisement; form of penance, torture; a sharp tongue; promotion of fertility; related to hunting; remorse; persecution; attribute of the Agrippine sibyl • **two scourges and a pillar** persecution • **Christian** attribute of SS Ambrose (usually with three knots, sometimes two scourges with a beehive), Boniface, Gervase, Peter, Protase, Peter, the Passion of Christ (usually two, often crossed) • **Greco-Roman** attribute of Bellona, Erinyes/Furies • *see also* **whip**

scourging encouragement against spiritual laxity or inertia; punishment; casting out of devils • **Christian** *man being scourged:* SS Andrew, Laurence; *man scourged by angels:* St. Jerome • **English** *Elizabethan:* punishment for prostitutes • **Greco-Roman** punishment for debtors • *see also* **whipping**

scratch weed • **flower language** hardness

screech owl *see* **owl**

screw security; tightness; sexual activity

screwdriver phallus

scrip • **Christian** associated with pilgrimage

scroll wisdom; life; the passing of time; the extent of a life; prophecy; learning; knowledge; punishment of God; decrees of fate; destiny; divine revelation; writing skills; contract; legal document; sometimes merely ornamentation; attribute of writers, the personifications of the Logic (most common), Music, Astronomy, Arithmetic, Geometry, Rhetoric, Grammar • **unrolling scroll** the unrolling of life, the upper roll is the future, the lower roll is the past • **scroll with harp** music • **scroll with pencil or quill** literature • **Buddhist** the unfolding of the Law; emblem of Buddhism • **Chinese** longevity; scholarship • **Christian** Holy Scripture; attribute of saints, the Apostles, the Evangelists, St. James the Great; *twelve scrolls:* the 12 Epistles of St. Paul; *four scrolls:* the four Gospels; *bishop's miter on scroll:* attribute of St. Asaph; *winged scroll:* associated with Zechariah; *scroll with two keys:* attribute of St. Peter; *scroll with the word Theotokos:* attribute of St. Cyril; *scroll with tall cross:* attribute of St. Philip; *scroll with the words Ecce agnus Dei or Vox demantis in desetto:* attribute of John the Baptist; *scroll with the words Ora pro nobis Deum:* attribute of St. Gregory the Great; *scroll being eaten:* St. John at the Apocalypse; *scroll in the hands of a Patriarch:* the darkness faith was enveloped in before Christ; *scroll with Gregorian music:* attribute of SS Gregory the Great, Ambrose; *scroll with seven seals:* fate, destiny • **Egyptian** knowledge; emblem of Lower Egypt • **Greco-Roman** attribute of Asclepius, Clio, Calliope, Thalia • **heraldic** academic success; scholarship • **Japanese** *scroll tied to staff:* attribute of Jurojin • **Jewish** the Law; attribute of the prophets, the archangel Uriel; *five scrolls:* the Pentateuch; *scroll and red vestment:* attribute of Elijah; *scroll with a sheaf of wheat:* Old Testament Pentecost; *scroll with scepter:* attribute of Solomon; *scroll on a grave:* divine presence • **Mexican Indian** *god with scroll in mouth:* Tlaloc

Scylla • **Greek** the immediate expectation of the fruits of action as an impedance to moral progress; *Scylla and Charybdis:* difficult passage; the powers of water; two equal dangers

scythe time; death; Autumn; harvest; death of the old year; related to the moon; union of the male and the female; passivity; castration; phallus; the inexorable march of time; self-mutilation; instrument of castration; renewed hopes for rebirth; weapon of peasants; attribute of Father Time, the Grim Reaper, the personifications of Summer, Death • **skeleton with sword, sickle, scythe, and/or hourglass** death; Death personified; the King of Death • **Greco-Roman** attribute of Chronos, occasionally Demeter/Ceres; *old man with a scythe:* Cronus/Saturn • **heraldic** hope of a fruitful harvest

sea *see* **ocean**

sea bream • **Japanese** attribute of Ebisu

sea gull *see* **gull**

sea horse *see* **hippocampus**

sea lion boldness • **heraldic** dauntlessness at sea

sea serpent • **on old maps** unexplored waters • *see also* **ocean; serpent**

sea urchin sun emblem; life force; the primordial seed; resurrection; immortality; Cosmic Egg; latent force • **Greco-Roman** sacred to Aphrodite/Venus

seal (animal) the circus; exhibitionism; protection; steed of sea deities; a human being under a spell; virginity inspired by fear of self-surrender and/or lack of love; the unconscious, especially the part derived from repression • **heraldic** dauntlessness at sea

seal (stamp) ownership; individuality; security; secrecy; authenticity; authority; identity; power; authorization; individuation; preservation; virginity; love; possession; conclusion • **wax seal** virginity; repression; narrow-mindedness • **Abraham's seal** circumcision • **Christian** *seven seals:* the seven principal events in Christ's life (incarnation, baptism, the passion, the descent into hell, resurrection, ascension, descent of the Holy Spirit); attribute of the scroll of fate • *see also* **Solomon's seal**

seasons *see* **Autumn; Spring; Summer; Winter**

seat stability • **seated man or woman** supreme deity or the earthly representative thereof • **Buddhist** *Diamond Seat:* the place of enlightenment • *see also* **throne**

seaweed the eternal; bondslaves; maternal fertility; God; eternal life secret the power of the supernatural; boundless life; elemental life; primeval food • **heraldic** purity; leadership • **Japanese** charm to ease childbirth, safeguard sailors • **Scottish** *man with seaweed in his hair:* an each uisage

sedan chair • **Chinese** *blue sedan chair:* attribute of a high government official; *green sedan chair:* attribute of a lower government official

sedge refuge of the lover • **absence of sedge** desolation

see-saw balance; vacillation; choice; coition; attribute of wind deities

seed latent possibilities; hope; mystic center; fertility; growth; potentiality; children; divine instruction; sperm • **germinating seed** the mother • **African** *pumpkin seeds:* intelligence • **Hindu** Atman; the Divine Spirit; the heart; the center of being; *at the center of a temple:* life, consciousness • **Jewish** *three seeds of the Tree of Life:* associated with Seth • *see also* **mustard seed**

semen the purest part of an individual or of one's being; fertility; the life force

sensitive plant *see* **mimosa**

senvy flower language indifference

septfoil • **Christian** the Seven Gifts of the Holy Spirit, sacraments of Pre-Reformation times, etc. • *see also* **-7-**

sepulcher death; corruption • **whitened sepulcher** attribute of a hypocrite • **Christian** *red-hot sepulcher:* attribute of a heretic; *model of a sepulcher:* attribute of St. Helena

seraph guardianship; might; swiftness; heavenly messenger; wisdom; zeal; the spirit of love and imagination; divine love; divine heat • **heraldic** dignity; glory; honor; missionary; high position; purity; bringer of joyful news • *see also* **angel**

serpent evil; sin; energy; force; night; subterranean life; fertility; wisdom; power to heal; generative energy; regeneration; secrecy; hiding; danger; death; materialism; slavery; temptation; fascination; jealousy; wisdom of the deep; guardian of the springs of life, immortality, the superior riches of the spirit, treasure; great mysteries; forces of destruction; subtlety; seduction of strength by matter; the inferior within the superior; the evil inherent in all worldly things; the evil side of nature; the feminine principle; a phallic symbol; androgyny; the unconscious expressing itself suddenly and unexpectedly with terrible or frightening results; primordial instinctive nature; mediator between heaven and earth; attribute of the Great Mother, female deities, the personifications of Time, Earth, Logic, Innocence, Africa • **horned serpent** water; intensified duality; opposite forces in conflict • **feathered serpent** duality (good/evil, heaven/earth, etc.) • **plumed serpent** beneficence; reconciliation of opposites; the angel of dawn • **serpent with two heads** an amphisbaena • **serpent with head erect** human wisdom • **rising serpent** retrospection • **serpent in a circle, or biting its own tail** eternity; time; union of the sexes (has to have its tail in its mouth); the zodiac; an amphisbaena • **serpent encircling a globe** the spread of sin; the omnipresence of sin • **woman holding a mirror and a serpent** Prudence personified • **serpent with sheep's head** spring; initiation; spiritualization • **winged serpent with eagle's legs** a wyvern • **twin serpents** death; all binary opposites (good/evil, male/female, life/death, etc.) • **serpent sloughing its skin** rebirth; healing • **kissing a serpent's head** fellatio • **serpent with a woman's head** Deceit personified • **bird fighting with serpent** the conflict of solar and underworld powers respectively • **woman treading on serpent** the Persian sibyl • **image of a serpent with a human head on a shield** attribute of the Iron Age personified • **child playing with a serpent** Paradise regained; freedom from conflict • **serpent coiled around a woman** the male-female relationship • **serpent with stag or eagle** cosmic unity; totality; dark and light; the union of matter and spirit • **serpent in an eagle's talons or trampled underfoot by a stag** evil defeated by good; the victory of the spirit over sin • **lion or tiger fighting a serpent** higher consciousness fighting lower desires • **fiery serpent** purification; transcendence of the earthly state • **serpent as a girdle or bracelet** succession; dissolution and reintegration; the eternal cycling of the ages • **serpent with lozenge-shaped ornaments** male-female unity; dualism and reintegration; the reconciliation of opposites; androgyny • **serpent with a ram's head** generative power; fertility • **winged serpent** the union of spirit and matter • **serpent with its head erect** human wisdom • **two serpents entwining a tree or staff** the solstices; the spiral cycles of nature • **woman with serpents for hair, serpent for a tongue, or a serpent's tongue** Envy personified • **anchor with entwined serpent** union of the male and female • **African** royalty; vehicle of immortality; reincarnation of the dead; mythical ancestor; the rainbow; associated with water, fecundity; attribute of Mami Wata; *battle between a bird and a serpent:* the battle between life and death respectively; *serpent deity:* Da • **alchemic** *serpent on a pole:* the fixation of Mercurius, the subjugation of vital force; *serpent passing through a circle:* fusion; *two serpents:* the masculine and feminine properties of the Great Work; *three serpents:* the higher principles of sulfur, Mercurius, and salt; *winged serpent:* a volatile substance; *wingless serpent:* a fixed substance; *crucified serpent:* the fixation of a volatile substance • **Armenian** *demon with serpent hair:* an al • **Australian aboriginal** the masculine principle; lightning; associated with pregnancy; Ulanji; Wollunqua; Yurlungur; Akurra; Wagyl; Noongar; *rainbow serpent:* Galeru, Jolunggul • **Aztecan** mythical ancestor; *plumed serpent:* the sun; the spirit; ascension; rain; wind; thunder and lightning; knowledge; the breath of life; attribute of Quetzalcoatl, rain gods, wind gods; *skirt of woven serpents:* attribute of Coatlicue; *bird of prey gripping a serpent god:* the dismemberment of original unity; birth of mankind from the serpents blood; *serpent and maize:* attribute of Chalchiutlicue • **Babylonian** *Tiamat:* chaos; the undifferentiated; the undivided; guile; wickedness • **Buddhist** sometimes associated with Buddha; the serpent and the cat were the only two animals unmoved by the death of Buddha; *serpent with pig and rooster:* the center of the Round of Existence; *serpent at the center of the Round of Existence:* anger; *water serpent:* Apalala • **Celtic** associated with healing waters, wells; emblem of Bridget; *wreath of serpents:* fertility; charm against evil; *serpent wreath:* fertility, charm against evil • **Chinese** evil; cunning; sycophancy; deceit; malevolence; destructive force; attribute of Vaisravenna; 6th of the animals of the Twelve Terrestrial Branches; one of the Five Poisonous Creatures; *two serpents with human heads:* Fo-Hi and Niu-Kua • **Christian** the devil; guile; craftiness; the grave; evil; destruction; attribute of St. Patrick; *serpent battling a fish:* Satan tempting Christ; *serpent on a tau cross:* Christ; *brass serpent:* associated with the Crucifixion; *serpent at the foot of the Cross:* Christ's

overcoming evil; *hart trampling a serpent:* Christ overcoming the power of evil; *the Virgin Mary with a bruised serpent or a serpent underfoot:* her victory over sin; *serpent emerging from a cup or chalice:* the attempted poisoning of St. John; *serpent on a sword:* attribute of St. John; *serpent in a loaf of bread or in other food:* attribute of St. Benedict; *serpent over a fire or on a man's wrist:* associated with St. Paul; *three coiled serpents:* attribute of St. Hilda; *serpent entwined on the Tree of Life:* wisdom; beneficence; *serpent entwined on the Tree of Knowledge:* Lucifer, malevolence; *serpent on a cross or pole:* prototype of Christ raised on the Tree of Life; *serpent with a woman's head entwined on the Cross:* the Temptation of Christ; *dove with a serpent's tail:* the combination of wisdom and peace • **Egyptian** associated with Unet, Wadjet; *serpent-headed woman:* Amunet; Kauket; *serpents at the side of a sun disk:* the goddesses who drove out the enemies of Ra; *lion-headed serpent:* protection against evil; *woman with serpent to breast:* Cleopatra; *four-winged serpent-headed man:* the East wind, Henkhisesui; *serpent with many coils and/or a human head:* Apep • **Finnish** *dragon nursing serpent:* Ajatar • **Gallic** *serpent with a ram's head or stag's head:* attribute of Cernunnos • **Gnostic** author of divine gnosis; *winged serpent:* Phanes; *serpent with a nimbus:* knowledge; illumination; the Light of the World • **Greco-Roman** healing; renewal of life; the life principle; fertility; resurrection; wisdom; the soul; lares; penates; the dead, especially heroes; reincarnation of dead souls; attribute of Asclepius, Maenads/Bacchantes, Chronos, Athena/Minerva, Hermes/Mercury, Hippocrates, Hygeia, Janus, Salus, Cronus/Saturn, Erinyes; occasional form of Ammon, Zeus/Jupiter; sacred to Apollo; *infant wrestling with two serpents:* Heracles/Hercules; *man shooting python with arrows:* Apollo; *surrounding an egg:* Cosmic Egg; the mystery of life; creation; resurrection; vitality; the passions vitalizing the masculine and feminine principles; *three serpents:* emblem on Agamemnon's shield representing the rainbow; *woman with serpent hair:* enchantment; magic powers; guile; wisdom; attribute of Medusa, the Moirae/Fates, Gorgons, Graia; *serpent with three heads (man's, bull's, and lion's):* Chronos; *serpent with seven heads:* Hydra; *serpent entwined around a woman's arm or leg:* Eurydice; *two youths and a man wrestling with a serpent:* Laocoon and his sons; *serpent entwining a corpse, with other victims nearby:* Cadmus; *serpent with infant in a basket:*

Erichthonius; *child with serpents for feet:* Erichthonius; *man with serpents for feet:* Cecrops; *serpent with a man's head:* Erichthonius; *serpent with a woman's head:* a lamia; *oars turning into serpents:* the kidnapping of Dionysus/Bacchus; *old woman with pointed ears holding a serpent:* Bona Dea; *giant with serpents for feet:* Enceladus; *maiden feeding a serpent from a dish:* Hygeia • **Haitian** *serpent god:* Damballa • **heraldic** strategy; military fame; courage; vigilance; wisdom; instinct; the subconscious; *serpent wrapped around a column:* wisdom with fortitude • **Hindu** the shakti; nature; chaos; the amorphous; the non-manifest; cosmic power; fire; Agni; *driving a stake through a serpent's head:* subduing evil; creating order; *serpent with a human body:* Naga, Nagina; *serpent with many heads:* Naga, Nagini; *god with serpents entwined around his blue neck:* Shiva • **Incan** the beneficent aspect of Quetzalcoatl • **Islamic** the life principle • **Japanese** attribute and personification of Susano-o; steed of Benzaiten • **Jewish** evil; sin; temptation; sexual temptation; agent of the Fall; Leviathan; emblem of the tribe of Dan; *serpent encircling a tree:* the Fall of Man; *serpent with rod or staff:* the miracles of Aaron, Moses; *bronze serpent:* healing, God's protection, attribute of Moses • **Kabalistic** emblem of sin; misuse of the good things of this world • **Manichean** Christ • **Maori** earthly wisdom; irrigation; growth • **Mayan** *feathered serpent:* Gukumatz, Kulkulkan, Q'uq'umatz; *serpent on the head:* attribute of Ixchel • **Melanesian** *female serpent:* figona; *bat-winged serpent with human head, four teeth, four teeth, and breasts:* Hatuibwari • **Minoan** fertility; sacred to Eileithyia; incarnation of the dead; ancestor; ghost; resurrection; immortality; Asclepius; attribute of the Great Goddess • **Mochican** *old man with serpent earrings:* Ai apaec • **Norse** *serpent with his tail in his mouth forming a circle:* the universe, Jormungandr; *Nidhogg:* malevolent forces of the universe; *giant serpent:* Jormungandr • **North American Indian** eternity; harbinger of death; defiance; wisdom; the spear of war gods; mediator between men and the lower world; associated with thunder, lightning, rain, the moon, magic power; *horned serpent:* the water spirit, the fertilizing power of water, a form of the Great Manitou • **Oceanic** creator of the world; associated with pregnancy • **Persian** an aspect of Ahriman, Angra Mainu; *Azi-dahak:* enemy of the sun god • **Phrygian** attribute of Sabazios • **Sumero-Semitic** attribute of Ishtar; *Lakhmu, Lakhamu:* parents of heaven and earth; *serpents*

springing from shoulders: attribute of the Dying Sun god and Nidaba; *serpent on a pole:* a god of healing; *serpent with a human head:* Ningizzida • **Toltec** *sun god looking out of a serpent's jaws:* the sky • **Yoruban** *rainbow serpent:* Oshunmare • *see also* **amphisbaena; asp; coluber; cobra; Hydra; kundalini; leogriff; Naga; python; sea serpent; uraeus; viper; wyvern**

servant submission; devotion; service

service free • **flower language** prudence

sesame fertility • **Chinese** tonic; promotes longevity

Set • **Egyptian** evil light from dark places; primeval power directed to evil ends

Severn River • **English** an aspect of the cosmic river from which all comes and all returns

sewer the unconscious; the instincts; the base and the vile

sewing life; the temporal; the transitory; the cyclic; typical occupation of the housewife

sextant navigation; attribute of Astronomy personified

sexual intercourse union of the masculine and feminine principles; the conjunction of opposites; harmony; the union of heaven and earth; fertility; renewal; fecundation; the return of Spring • **Hindu** *coition of washerwoman and sage:* the union of opposites • *see also* **fornication**

shade the incompletely revealed; ease

shadow the evil or base side of the self; existence between the soul and the body; the alter ego; the soul; the primitive side of an individual; a departed soul; gloom; obscurity; the past; protection; a ghost; the negative principle; the repressed; half-truth • **Chinese** yin; *lack of a shadow:* attribute of one who has escaped the limits of bodily existence • **folkloric** ghosts have no shadows • **Hindu** a bhut casts no shadow

shaft *see* **column**

shaking sainfoin • **flower language** agitation

Shakti • **Hindu** the female element in all being; cosmic energy; manifestation; the Divine Mother

shala • **Buddhist** a royal tree; temporal power; the power of the Brahman; associated with the birth of Buddha and his escape from the cycle of rebirth

shampooing ridding oneself of old thoughts, emotions, ideas; preparation for reception of new thoughts, emotions, or ideas • *see also* **hair**

shamrock the Trinity; loyalty; emblem of Ireland; attribute of SS Patrick, Gerald • **flower language** light-heartedness • **heraldic** perpetuity

Shangri-la retreat from the world; eternal youth

shark danger; evil; rapacity; persistence; perseverance; associated with Mars (planet)

sheaf unification; agriculture; harvest; integration; unity; reduction of the many into one; strength; discipline; God's bounty; plenty; emblem of Thanksgiving; associated with Autumn • **sheaf with a sickle** death; harvest; Autumn • **sheaf of arrows or lances** a thunderbolt • **heraldic** *sheaf of wheat:* the harvest of one's hopes has been secured • **Jewish** Joseph's dream; *sheaf with scroll:* Old Testament Feast of the Pentecost; *fourteen sheaves:* Joseph, his wife, and their 12 sons • *see also* **wheat; entanglement**

shears *see* **scissors**

sheen time

sheep the higher qualities and virtues of the soul; innocence; simplicity; love; gentleness; charity; sacrifice; guilelessness; gregariousness; helplessness; obstinacy; stupidity; blind following; wiliness; straying; clouds; attribute of Usury personified; associated with the archangel Samael • **sheep with its feet bound** the sacrificial lamb • **sheepskin** connected with parchment; diploma • **coat or cloak of a sheep's skin** fertility • **Chinese** the retiring life; the eighth animal of the Twelve Celestial Branches • **Christian** the flock of Christ; the faithful; *sheep on a man's shoulders:* the Good Shepherd; *twelve sheep:* the Apostles *lamb with a row of sheep:* Christ leading his disciples • **Germanic** *flock of sheep:* attribute of Holda • **Jewish** attribute of Eve • *see also* **fleece; flock; lamb; ram; shepherd; wool**

sheet bed; coition; death; ghost; sail; garb of ghosts • **winding sheet** death • **Christian** *sheet with cross:* the Passion of Christ

Shekinah • **Jewish** God's presence

shell fertility; the feminine principle of containment; vulva; life; love; marriage; regeneration; alludes to the presence of water; related to the moon, woman, water, virgin birth; attribute of the personifications of Folly, the North Wind • **chariot of shell** the vehicle of Fortune personified • **shell dripping with water** baptism • **kneeling youth offering a shell as a cup to a maiden** Granida and Dafilo • **Chinese** the feminine; yin; a good life in the next world; lucky • **Christian** related to the Virgin Mary, baptism, resurrection, funerals; attribute of pilgrims (particularly to Santiago), SS Roch, Augustine of Hippo, James the Great, Michael; *shell-shaped stones:* attribute of St. Stephen; *scallop shell with a snail:* attribute of St. Lydia • **Greco-Roman** resurrection; sexual passion; emblem of sea voyagers; associated with funerals; attribute of Boreas, Aphrodite/Venus; *shell chariot:* attribute of Poseidon/Neptune, Galatea • **heraldic** pilgrimage, especially to Santiago in Spain; any successful distant journey; victorious naval commander • **Hindu** *shell trumpet:* attribute of Vishnu • *see also* **conch**

shellfish associated with the archangel Gabriel

Sheol • **Jewish** separation from God; abode of the dead; a diminished life of silence

shepherd the conductor of souls to the land of the dead; the priest; a protector; savior; God; guardian of ancient wisdom; the moon; the rustic lover; the nomad • **Buddhist** *Tibetan:* Chenrezig • **Christian** Christ; a bishop, abbot, or abbess; *twelve shepherds:* the Apostles • **Egyptian** Ra; kings • **Greco-Roman** Hermes/Mercury; Orpheus; Pan/Faunus • **Hindu** Shiva; associated with Krishna • **Italian** *female warrior among shepherds and basketmakers:* Erminia • **Jewish** God • **Sumero-Semitic** Tammuz; associated with Amynos, Magos

sheriff *see* **police**

shewbread • **Jewish** the dependence of man on God for spiritual and physical food; the operation of grace for the granting of things earthly; *twelve loaves:* the 12 months

shield defense; protection; faith; salvation; virtue; defense of the spirit; divine defense; attribute of the personifications of Rhetoric, Chastity, Virtue, Strength, Victory, Vigilance, the Church • **shield with an image of a lion or a ball** attribute of Fortitude personified • **shield with an image of a serpent with a human head** attribute of the Iron Age personified • **Christian** *saint in armor with shield and lance:* St. Demetrius; *blank or yellow shield:* attribute of Judas; *shield inscribed "Maria," "A.M.," or "AMGPDT":* attribute of the archangel Gabriel; *white shield with a red cross:* attribute of St. George of Cappadocia • **Egyptian** *figure-eight shield:* attribute of Neith • **Greco-Roman** attribute of Athena/Minerva, Ares/Mars, Artemis/Diana; *shield with an image of Medusa's head:* attribute of Athena/Minerva; *highly polished shield:* attribute of Perseus; *shield and spear:* attribute of initiation into adulthood • **heraldic** defense; *shield with a helmet on it:* security in defense, wisdom • **Mongolian** *blue shield:* attribute of father of Genghis Khan, and Er Toshtuk

Shiloah (Jerusalem) • **Jewish** God's Protection

ship consciousness; transcendence; safety; hope; confidence; the womb; a feminine symbol of containment; vehicle of the sun and moon; the earth floating upon the primordial waters • **ship with a horse's head** the sun chariot • **model of a ship in the hand of a woman** attribute of Fortune personified • **ship with a woman figurehead** the great Mother; womb; cradle; feminine vessel of transformation • **tattoo of a full rigged ship** attribute of a 19th century sailor who had sailed around Cape Horn • **ship plowing waves** joy; happiness • **ship sailing** living to transcend existence • **ship in full sail on a woman's head** Hope personified • **hold of a ship** the unconscious; experience on the lower plane • **ghost ship** impossibly idealistic dreams; the hopeless quest for fidelity in love • **monk celebrating mass on board ship as fish gather to listen** St. Brendan • **Buddhist** the Law that enables man to cross the ocean of existence • **Celtic** *ship without oars or sails:* attribute of Manannan • **Christian** the Church; attribute SS Julian, Francis Xavier, Nicholas of Myra, Ursula, Vincent, occasionally St. John; *twelve men rowing a ship:* the Apostles; *man preaching from the stern of a ship:* St. Peter leading the Church; *ship on the Nile:* attribute of St. Athanasius; *ship with windmill and fish:* attribute of St. Mary of Cleophus; *ship with a staff:* attribute of St. Wilfred; *bishop holding a ship model:* St. Erasmus; *ship on a stormy sea:* the Church surviving persecution, heresy, schism, allusion to Christ's calming of the Sea of Galilee • **Egyptian** vehicle of the sun and moon • **Greek** *young man bearing woman off to ships:* abduction of Helen of Troy • **heraldic** veteran of sea expeditions; merchant riches; happiness; power; succor in extremity; *sailing ship in particular:* ancient sea voyages; *dismasted ship:* disaster at sea • **Japanese** the ship of Kami-nari connects heaven and earth • **Jewish** Noah's ark; *ship in a harbor:* associated with Zebulun • **Roman** attribute of Janus • **Mediterranean** *sneezing going up a gangplank:* ill omen; *crow or magpie croaking in the rigging:* ill omen; *dancing on a ship:* unlucky; *bird perching in the rigging:* good omen • **Norse** associated with Vanir; attribute of Freyja • **Teutonic** *ship made of nail clippings:* Naglfar • *see also* **ark; boat**

ship of fools sailing as an end in itself without seeking a safe arrival in heaven

ship's wheel control

shipwreck tragic fortune • **Mediterranean** *glimpse of wreckage on the shore:* ill omen for a voyage

shirt protection • **shirtlessness** material deprivation; social abandonment; utter moral loneliness • **giving the shirt off one's back** unbounded generosity • **hair shirt** associated with

asceticism, penance • **silk shirt** associated with wealth • **Christian** *goat or camel's hair shirt:* attribute of John the Baptist • **Jewish** *goat or camel's hair shirt:* attribute of Elijah

shittim • **Jewish** associated with the Ark of the Covenant, the Burning Bush of Moses

Shiva • **Hindu** associated with fertility, reproduction, power, transition, destruction

shiver a sudden shiver for no apparent reason is considered a bad omen

shoes liberty; usefulness; utility; vagina; fertility; love; humility; pleasure; power; royalty (especially golden shoes); the soul • **removing one's shoes** sign of respect; first step in intimacy • **Armenian** *iron shoes:* footwear of the damned souls in Dzokhk • **Christian** attribute of SS Crispin, Crispinian • **Greco-Roman** attribute of a free man or woman; *winged shoes:* attribute of Hermes/Mercury • **Islamic** *removing one's shoes before entering a house:* sign that one acknowledges another's ownership • **Middle Eastern** *holding up a shoe to someone or throwing a shoe:* great disdain, disrespect, and insult • **Norse** *iron or thick leather shoes:* attribute of Vidar • *see also* **buskin; cobbler; feet; sandals**

shofar • **heraldic** call to repentance; admonitions of the prophets • **Jewish** the call of God; obedience to divine will; supreme loyalty to God; attribute of Abraham

shooting star a heavenly omen; related to angles; seed from the gods

shore safety; the dividing line between different worlds, such as life/death, body/spirit, conscious/unconscious, etc. • **Mediterranean** *glimpse of wreckage on the shore:* ill omen for a voyage

shoulders strength; responsibility • **Bambaran** the seat of strength and violence • **Christian** *giant with child on his shoulders:* St. Christopher carrying the Christ child • **Greek** *young man with old man on shoulders:* the young man is Aeneas; *ivory shoulder:* attribute of Pelops

shovel fertility; androgyny; labor; attribute of Adam after the Fall

showbread *see* **shewbread**

shower of gold sun rays • *see also* **ram**

shrimp smallness; shyness

shroud death; the robe of light for resurrection; associated with Theseus, sails, John Donne • **Christian** attribute of St. Joseph of Arimathea; *shroud with cross:* the Passion of Christ; *shroud pierced with knife and bleeding:* St. John's shroud (usually held by St. Gregory the Great)

shuttle (weaver's) man's life; transitoriness; lightness

sibyl the intuiting of higher truths; prophetic powers; the human being raised to a transnatural level allowing communication with the godhead; emanation of divine wisdom

sickle time; death; agriculture; the crescent moon; fertility; reaping; end of the world; instrument of castration; attribute of the archangel Azrael, the personifications of Hope, Summer • **hammer and sickle** emblem of the USSR, communism • **skeleton with sword, sickle, scythe, and/or hourglass** death; Death personified; the King of Death • **Celtic** *golden sickle:* used to harvest mistletoe • **Christian** *held by Christ enthroned with angels about:* the Apocalypse • **Greco-Roman** attribute of Perseus, Priapus, Silvanus, Cronus/Saturn, Demeter/Ceres, Erinyes/Furies; *three sickles of Megara:* lucky • **heraldic** hope of a fruitful harvest • **Japanese** *on a housetop:* charm against thunder • **Sumero-Semitic** *ring with sickle:* attribute of royalty

sickness *see* **disease**

sidra tree • **Islamic** the Celestial Tree, the center of Paradise, origin of the rivers of milk, honey, water, and wine

Siegfried • **Germanic, Norse** self-destructive violence; careless youth; the pitiless law of nature; elemental energy held prisoner by pagan cosmogony; the existence of opposites within the human psyche

sieve purification; perfection; separation of good from evil; pitiless choice; impartial and loveless judgment; wisdom; self-knowledge through action; rain clouds; fecundity; criticism; conscience; selection; choice; small talk; vanity; hope; chastity; vehicle for witches; attribute of Chastity, Prudence personified • **Christian** sifting the faithful from unfaithful; *broken sieve:* attribute of St. Benedict • **Egyptian** attribute of scribes • **Hindu** the sky through which soma juice falls as rain; the discretionary bounty of the gods • **Jewish** divine judgment • **Orphic** purifier; cradle • **Roman** attribute of Tuccia

sigma divine power; communication or connection with heaven

silence preface to revelation; spiritual progression; the voice of God; the state before Creation; the state of the end of the world; absence of life • *see also* **dumbness**

silk beauty; extravagance; luxury; upper classes; the bonds of social behavior; sensuality; purity; virtue; riches; associated with 4th, 12th wedding anniversaries • **woman in silk** a loose woman

silk worm • **Chinese** emblem of industry; attribute of Lei Tsu

silver (color and metal) purity; faith; chastity; eloquence; innocence; clear conscience; virginity; fidelity; object of desire and the harm it causes; associated with Cancer, the moon, the feminine principle, 25th silver anniversaries, the archangel Gabriel • **silverware** associated with 16th wedding anniversaries • **silver as payment** bribery; betrayal • **silver weapons** bribery • **silver doors** associated with the palace of the sun • **silver bough** the link between this world and the fairy world • **gold and silver** the sun and moon respectively; two aspects of the same cosmic reality • **alchemic** purified affections • **Chinese** brightness; purity; yin; protects children from evil influences • **Christian** chastity; purity; eloquence; divine wisdom; *thirty pieces of silver:* the betrayal of Christ by Judas • **Greco-Roman** associated with Selene/Luna; *silver bow and arrows:* attribute of Artemis/Diana • **heraldic** chastity; innocence; wisdom; sincerity; justice; peace; joy; victory; purity; faith

simpleton *see* **fool**

simurg • **Islamic** the hidden self; the quest for self; steed of Mohammed; *Sufi:* metaphor for God • **Persian** phoenix; prosperity; the union of earth and sky; messenger and mediator between earth and sky; bestower of fertility; *simurg perched on a cleric or would-be ruler:* acceptance of that person by Ormuzd as a divine representative

Sinai, Mount • **Jewish** seat of the moon

singing fostering and bring forth life • *see also* **music**

siren (mechanical) danger; a human cry; hysteria; psychic disturbance

siren (mythology) temptation; deception; a treacherous woman; feminine seduction; the base forces in woman; sensual pleasure; death bearer; death wish; corrupt imagination; seducer of seafarers; desire leading to self destruction; sensuality overpowering reason and leading to ruin; sorcery; empty or deceptive attraction; involutive fragmentation of the unconscious; the seductive powers of the senses and of illusion; entanglement; dangerous affection • **Egyptian** a soul separated form the body • **Greek** an evil soul hungry for blood • *see also* **Circe**

Sirius death; plague; Summer fever; war; wantonness; an evil omen

sistrum fertility; wedding; prostitution; war; the motion of the elements; the movement of angels' wings • **Egyptian** chastity; attribute of Hathor, Isis; *cat-headed woman with sistrum:* Bast • **Japanese** virtue; piety; call to the gods •

Sumero-Semitic associated with Ishtar • *see also* **tambourine**

Sisyphus • **Greek** senseless human endeavor; the rise and fall of the sun

sitting sovereignty; judgment; council; peace; leisure • **act of sitting down** acquiescence • **sitting on the ground** desolation; mourning; penance; leisure • **sitting at a window** mourning; yearning • **sitting in darkness** slavery

sixpence cleanliness; a lucky coin

skeleton death; mortality; the swift passing of time and life; vanity; usually has infernal implications; Death personified, sometimes the Devil personified • **skeleton at a feast** reminder of mortality • **skeleton with sword, scythe, sickle, and/or hourglass** Death personified; the King of Death • **smiling skeleton** one who has crossed the threshold of life and learned the wisdom of the other world • **returning an animal skeleton to the forest** ensures the continuance of the species • **alchemic** putrefaction; blackness • **France** (Brittany) *skeleton with revolving head:* Ankou • **Greco-Roman** associated with Cronus/Saturn • **Mayan** Ah Puch; associated with the underworld • *see also* **bones; skull**

skidding • **psychological** loss of control of the Id by the Ego and Superego

skin matter • **human skin** death by flaying • **animal skin** associated with death and rebirth • **coat or cloak of cat, mouse, or ass skin** humility • **coat or cloak of ox skin, sheep skin** fertility • **lion skin** attribute of Fortune personified, sun heroes • **wearing an animal mask or skin** access to animal or instinctual wisdom; understanding or communication with animals • **Central African** *wildcat skin:* used for medicine • **Chinese** *goat's skin:* attribute of Yang Ching • **Christian** *human skin:* attribute of St. Bartholomew; *animal skin:* attribute of John the Baptist • **Egyptian** *blue skin:* attribute of Amon; *yellow skin:* attribute of the immortals • **Greco-Roman** *lion skin:* attribute of Heracles/Hercules • **Hindu** *god with blue or black skin:* Krishna • **Jewish** attribute of Elijah • *see also* **complexion; fleece**

skink • **African, Arabian, Egyptian** a good omen; the beneficent aspect of serpents and reptiles • *see also* **lizard**

skirt a woman • **spreading a skirt over someone** coition; protection; taking possession • **Aztecan** *green jade skirt:* attribute of Chalchiutlicue; *skirt of woven serpents:* attribute of Coatlicue • **Greek** *woman with raised skirt:* Baubo

skull mortality; the worldly survival of the dead; death; the dying sun; the transitory nature of life on earth; the useless nature of earthly things; sin; the physical manifestation of life and continuance of the species; the seat of thought; attribute of Hamlet, the personifications of Old Age, Melancholy • **skull and crossbones** poison; the brevity of life; danger to life; spiritual perfection; emblem of pirates • **smiling skull** one who has crossed the threshold of life and learned the wisdom of the Beyond • **alchemic** dying to the world; the blackening and mortification of the Lesser Work; *skull chalice:* immortality or knowledge brought by the death of the present state of existence, rebirth into a superhuman state • **Blackfoot** carrying a skull would make one invisible • **Buddhist (Tantric)** *skull filled with blood:* renunciation of life, emblem of Tara, Yama • **Christian** the vanity of worldly things; contemplation of death; attribute of SS Francis of Assisi, Romuald, Mary Magdalene, Paul, Jerome, and other hermit and penitent saints; *skull with a cross:* the eternal life that comes after death; *skull at the foot of the Cross:* refers to the legend that the Cross rested upon the bones of Adam, with Adam's remains representing sin; *crucifix and skull:* attribute of St. Charles Borromeo • **heraldic** mortality • **Hindu** *skull filled with blood:* renunciation of life, attribute of Durga, Kali, Shiva, Yama, rakshasas; *skull of the first man:* the vault of heaven; *necklace of skulls:* attribute of Shiva • **Icelandic** *skull of Ymir:* the vault of heaven • **Jewish** the Fall of Man; attribute of Adam, Hosea; *skull, feet, and palms of the hands:* the remains of Jezebel • **Mayan** the god of death and the underworld • **Masonic** the cycle of initiation through the death of the body to rebirth at a higher level • **portraiture** a mark of piety; *with a bay laurel crown:* fame that will endure • **Russian** *animal skull:* protection against harm from that species • **Slavic** *hut surrounded by fence of skulls:* dwelling of Baba Yaga • **Tibetan** *woman drinking blood from a skull:* Lha-mo; *conical hat topped with a skull:* attribute of Nag-pa

skullcap dignity; reverence; distinction skunk offensiveness; obscenity; truculence; complete defeat • *see also* **cap**

skunk foulness

sky the active masculine principle; the father; holiness; purity; the supreme deity or his dwelling; transcendence; height; infinity; the heavens

skylark *see* **lark**

slavery subjection to lower nature

sleep ignorance; retreat; withdrawal; wisdom;

giver of prophetic dreams; connected with coition; opportunity for the soul to leave the body; susceptibility to evil

sleeping beauty passive potential; dormant ancestral memories in the unconscious; the anima; sexuality lying dormant in a woman until the right man appears; fertility awakened by the sun slime substance of Chaos; stagnancy; decay; inertia preceding rebirth; evil; sin

sling • **Incan** attribute of Illapa • **Jewish** the strength of the weak; resistance to established power structures; attribute of David in his battle with Goliath (especially with five stones)

slipper *see* **shoe; sandal; feet**

slithering things *see* **creeping things**

sloe difficulty; austerity; the berry of the blackthorn

slug (animal) the tendency of darkness to move toward light; attribute of Sloth personified • **Egyptian** the male seed; the origin of life; moisture

sluice euphemism for coition • **sluice gate** vagina

smell bridge to heaven • **evil smell** sin • **pungent smell** protection against evil spirits

smelling apprehension; discrimination; investigation

smith the Creator; the son of the supreme deity; controller of fire; associated with creation, magic, initiation • **pastoral societies** malevolence; a despised figure • **African** ancestor; guardian of tradition, the altar

smoke evanescence; all that is fleeting; the shortness of life; vanity; the anger and wrath of God; mental darkness; evil; love; protection; punishment; war; industrialization; illusion obscuring truth; the futility of earthly glory; the supernatural; the relationship between heaven and earth • **chimney belching black smoke** pollution • **smoke escaping from a sacred space** World Axis; communication to heaven • **column of smoke** World Axis • **Chinese** raises the soul to the other world • **Christian** shortness of life; the vanity of fame, anger • **Persian** *rising smoke:* retrospection • **Tibetan** raises the soul to the beyond

Smyrna, Church of • **Christian** associated with suffering, insincerity, the black horse, Leydig cells, the second seal

snail fruitfulness; resurrection; slowness; humility; the sinner; laziness; emergence of sexual power; voluptuousness; vulva; the regular cycle of rebirth; sensitivity; the self; tenderness; the lunar; attribute of Sloth personified • **sea snail** androgyny • **snails when eaten** sexual power • **snail's track** the Milky Way;

connection between heaven and earth • **Aztecan** *sea snail:* the moon god, pregnancy, parturition • **Aztecan** conception; pregnancy; birth • **Christian** sin; sloth; *snail with scallop shell:* attribute of St. Lydia • **Egyptian** the spiral • **heraldic** perseverance; deliberation; acquired possessions to be preserved and enlarged

snake *see* **serpent**

snake's foot • **flower language** horror

snake's lounge • **flower language** slander

snapdragon • **flower language** presumption, indiscretion • **Greek** *snapdragon tea:* charm against sorcery • **heraldic** graciousness; strength • **Jewish** *afterbirth, ashes, and snapdragons:* charm against bewitchment in children

snare sin; temptation; a strange woman

sneezing the soul trying to leave the body; generally an ominous sign, but in Greece and Rome, a good sign; confirmation of a prophecy • **sneezing on a ship's gangplank** ill omen for a voyage • **cat sneezing** harbinger of rain • **Monday**, you sneeze for danger • **Tuesday**, you kiss a stranger • **Wednesday**, you sneeze for a letter • **Thursday**, you sneeze for something better • **Friday**, you sneeze for sorrow • **Saturday**, see your sweetheart tomorrow • **Sunday**, for safety seek, the devil will have you the whole of the week • **African** *sneezing while talking to someone:* divine approval of what was said; *sneezing in a period of silence:* a good omen

sniffing *see* **smelling**

snipe a fool; a simpleton

snood virginity

snow death; blindness; nothingness; purity; chastity; impotence; frigidity, especially in women; virginity; euphemism for cocaine; overpowered emotions • **melting snow** the softening of the heart; augur of Spring • *see also* **ice**

snowball • **flower language** bound; age; Winter of age; good news

snowdrop friendship in adversity; consolation; purity; purity of heart; humility; hope; herald of Spring • **Christian** connected with Candlemas; emblem of the Virgin Mary • **flower language** consolation; hope

sock (stocking) comedy

Sodom • **Jewish** carnal passion

soil *see* **earth**

Sol *see* **Helios/Sol**

solar wheel life; fertility; the sun • *see also* **sun**

soldier bravery; defense; vigilance; service; devotion to a cause; striving mental qualities; ancestor; forces of consciousness warring within a personality; force; latent force in the personality ready to come to the aid of the conscious;

masculine aggressiveness • **several soldiers attacking women and children** the Iron Age • **soldier on a couch with a woman, his weapons aside** love conquering war • **warriors seen in the sky** portent of war • **female warrior** Fortitude personified • **Chinese** Han Chung-li • **Christian** SS Sergius, Bacchus; *soldier on a white horse, killing Saracens:* St. James the Greater; *soldier with anvil:* St. Adrian; *soldier with palm and banner of the Resurrection:* St. Ansanus; *soldier with falcon on wrist:* St. Bavo; *soldier with stag:* St. Eustace; *soldier with millstone, or bucket, or pitcher:* St. Florian; *soldier with crocodile:* St. Theodore; *soldier with keys:* St. Hippolytus; *soldier with lance on horseback:* St. Longinus; *soldiers scaling city walls observed by nuns:* associated with St. Clare; *woman being threatened by a soldier with an arrow:* martyrdom of St. Ursula; *soldiers killing babies:* slaying of the Holy Innocents; *soldier standing with sword, and shield or lance:* St. Demetrius; *soldier holding cloak and sword:* St. Martin of Tours; *soldier with palm, banner with eagle and red cross on breastplate:* St. Maurice; *soldier receiving monk's habit from abbot:* conversion of St. William of Aquitaine; *soldier with dragon:* SS George, Theodore, Angelica; *Moorish Roman soldier or soldier with a red cross on his breastplate:* St. Maurice • **Gallic** *soldier throwing his sword onto a scale pan:* Brennus • **Greco-Roman** *female soldier:* Athena/Minerva, Bellona; *soldier on a couch with a woman, his weapons aside:* Mars with Venus; *soldier kneeling before a fleece:* Gideon; *soldier accompanied by Hermes/Mercury:* Heracles/Hercules; *soldier on horseback, leaping into a pit:* Marcus Curtius; *soldier fighting enemy on bridge:* Horatio; *blind and begging soldier:* Belisarius; *soldier placing his hand into a brazier:* Mucius Scaevola; *soldier with dragon:* Perseus; *soldier stabbing a woman before a judge:* death of Virginia; *soldier before a tomb, woman at swordpoint:* the sacrifice of Polyxena; *soldier holding a naked woman at swordpoint in bedchamber:* the rape of Lucretia; *soldier slaying a sage:* death of Archimedes • **Hindu** Parashurama • **Italian** *soldier fighting with naked man on bridge:* Rodomont and Orlando respectively; *dying female warrior in armor attended by a male warrior:* Clorinda and Tancred respectively; *female warrior among shepherds and basketmakers:* Erminia; *soldier holding a mirror for his mistress:* Rinaldo and Armida • **Jewish** *winged soldier:* the archangel Michael; *woman hammering a tent peg into a soldier's head:* death of Sisera • **Sumero-Semitic** *woman warrior:* Anath

Solomon, King human wisdom combined with human weakness; justice • **Solomon's ring** wisdom and power • **Solomon's knot** wisdom, divine inscrutability • **woman with Solomon at her feet** Prudence personified

Solomon's seal the Bible; key to the kingdom of heaven; health amulet; inspiration; perfection

Solon • Greek humbleness; wisdom; happiness

solstice *see* **Summer solstice; Winter solstice**

solvent, universal the undifferentiated

Soma (plant and god) divine power and understanding; inspiration; nourishment; sacramental intoxication

son heir; rebirth; earthly spirit; beauty; sun-prince

soothsayer interpreter of messages from the gods; the predominance of the spiritual over the rational

Sophia wisdom of the universe; creative spirit of God

sorb prudence • *see also* **apple**

sorcerer the Terrible Father; the evil demiurge; the wise old man; the dark unconscious of man; manifestation of the irrational content of the psyche; bringer of an alternate level or reality; untamed creative energy; aberrant forces of power • **Christian** priest of the devil • *see also* **witch**

sores the suffering of lower nature

sorrel parental affection; purification; resignation to sorrow • **flower language** affection, especially parental; *wild sorrel:* ill-timed wit; *wood sorrel:* joy, maternal tenderness • **Japanese** *wood sorrel:* elegant beauty; comforting affection • **Jewish** the bitterness of their bondage

soul reason; aspiration; man's creative or immortal part

sound that which brought the universe into being; the being of the universe is sound; that which lacks sound is the First Cause itself; sound existed before sight

soup comfort; healing

South Summer; light; youth; midday; the full moon; warmth; sun; the infernal regions; escape; failure; spiritual light; to face South was to speak with the authority of the gods; associated with Mars (planet), the lower self, materiality, the archangel Zadkiel • **Bambaran** home of pollution; evil being destroyed by Faro at the beginning of time; associated with plants • **Buddhist** associated with Ratnasambhava • **Christian** the South wall of a church was often dedicated to defenders of the faith; associated with the New Testament, particularly the Epistles •

Dogon associated with Orion's Belt, domesticated animals • **Egyptian** darkness; hell; the feminine; region of Amset • **Indic** associated with night, the feminine • **Mexican Indian** home of Hitzilopochtli, Mictlantecuhtli; associated with thorns, fire, the mid-day sun, rabbits • **Mongolian** associated with fire • **Tungun** associated with fire, body heat

southernwood (plant) mockery; pleasantry • **flower language** jest; bantering

Southwest associated with the archangel Azrael

sow (swine) fecundity, especially of evil; brutalization; grossness; the feminine principle reduced to reproduction • **Celtic** Keridwen, Phaea • **Egyptian** sacred to Bes, Isis; *sow with piglets:* Nut • **Greco-Roman** associated with Zeus/Jupiter; sacrificed to Demeter/Ceres • **Hindu** *Adamantine Sow:* Vajravarahi • **Norse** *Black Sow:* coldness, death, evil • **Oceanic** fertility; the lunar • **Tibetan** *Diamond or Adamantine Sow:* Vajravarahi • *see also* **swine**

sowbread • **flower language** diffidence

sower October or November personified • **woman sower** the Silver Age personified • **Greek** *sower of dragon's teeth:* Cadmus

sowing dissemination; creation; insemination

spade (shovel) fertility; death; hatred; toil; the masculine principle; attribute of Spring personified • **Christian** attribute of SS Maurus, Phocas • **Jewish** attribute of Adam after the Fall

spades (playing cards) life; penetrating intellect; discrimination; associated with nobility, fire, war, -1-, high rank, blackness, the circle, sphere, daring, action, expression, air, matter in gaseous form, the astral world, death, thunderbolts, struggle, trouble, difficulty, leaves, Fall, warriors, kings • **ace of spades** high rank; conquest; harvest; blackness; disaster; death • **king of spades** earth king; associated with Cronus/Saturn, Hades/Pluto, King David • **queen of spades** war; lightning flash; associated with Athena/Minerva, Neith • **jack (knave) of spades** associated with Hermes/Mercury, Asclepius • **cartomancy** *ace of spades:* unlucky; *king of spades:* a widower; *queen of spades:* a widow; *jack (knave) of spades:* unlucky • *see also* **playing cards**

Spain associated with bragging • **Celtic** associated with the underworld • **Greek** associated with the underworld • **Roman** associated with thievery

spaniel fawning; subservience; faithfulness; emasculation • **Christian** attribute of St. Margaret of Cortona

spark fire; the soul; a soul scattering from mystic center into the world of phenomena; God; the heavenly father; the initiator; life; the spiritual principle giving birth to each individual

sparrow love; lasciviousness; lechery; fecundity; humility; pugnacity; boldness; chattering; melancholy; solitude; purification; the devil; vandalism; the traveler; insignificance; attribute of the personifications of Lust, Solitude, Wantonness; associated with the archangel Anael • **Christian** lowliness; insignificance; lewdness; lechery • **Greco-Roman** attribute of Aphrodite/Venus • **Japanese** loyalty

sparrow hawk sharp vision; brave warrior; jealousy, associated with the sun, the archangel Michael • **male and female sparrow hawk together** marriage dominated by the wife • **Egyptian** the sun; the bird of Horus; associated with Osiris • **Greco-Roman** associated with the sun, Apollo • *see also* **eagle; hawk**

Sparta obedience through custom; simplicity; frugality; courage; brevity of speech; diligence

spear sun ray; lightning; World Axis; knighthood; fertility; war; phallus; martyrdom; attribute of soldiers, warriors, hunters, the European sibyl, royalty in ancient times, the Bronze Age personified • **spear with pillar** attribute of Constancy personified • **African** *bundle of spears:* kingly power • **Buddhist** emblem of Buddhism • **Celtic** attribute of Lamfhada, Lug • **Chinese** attribute of Kwan-yu, Mo-li Ch'in and various minor gods • **Christian** attribute of the Crucifixion, SS Liberalis, Longinus, Michael; *spear with V-shaped frame:* attribute of St. Andrew; *spear with inverted cross and/or fuller's bat:* attribute of St. Jude; *man pierced with spears:* St. Thomas (especially when on a cross); *spear with builder's square, arrows or book:* attribute of St. Thomas; *spear with patriarchal cross or tau cross and long staff:* attribute of St. Philip • **Greco-Roman** attribute of Hera/Juno, Athena/Minerva, Ares/Mars, Minerva, initiates into adulthood; *blunt spear:* awarded to military heroes; *oak spear:* attribute of Quirinus • **heraldic** honorable warrior; valiant knight; *spear head:* honor; martial readiness, nimble wit, dexterity • **Japanese** World Axis; sun ray; the action of being upon undifferentiated matter; attribute of Hachiman, Izanagi, Izanami • **Norse** Gunginir, attribute of Odin; *mistletoe spear:* associated with the death of Baldur • **Tibetan** *blue-bladed flaming spear with two eyes:* attribute of Da • *see also* **javelin; lance**

spearmint burning love; severity • **flower language** warmth of sentiment

speckles • **Jewish** *speckled bird:* the Law; the Word of God • **Pueblo** associated with the center

spectacles (glasses) old age; bookishness; learning; enhanced comprehension; binary functions (love/knowledge, revelation/learning, illusion/clear sight, etc.); twin deities; attribute of Temperance personified • **rose-colored glasses** make one see things in the best possible light, or better than they really are • **blue-colored glasses** make one take a pessimistic view • **mirrored glasses** hiding of thoughts or emotions; deceit

speculum *see* **mirror**

speed *see* **swiftness**

speedwell • **flower language** female fidelity; *Germander speedwell:* facility; *spiked speedwell:* semblance

sphere the world; Cosmic Egg; intellectual life; thought; abstraction; perfection; unity; God; creative motion; a celestial or terrestrial form; the primordial form containing all possibilities of other forms; eternity; the vault of heaven; the world; the wheel of life; deity form • **alchemic** unity; the one mind of God; experience beyond the duality of reason • **Chinese** the pearl of wisdom • **Egyptian** the sun; the moon • **Islamic** the spirit; primordial light • **Japanese** the pearl of wisdom • *see also* **ball; orb; globe**

sphinx *sphinx with a human head:* see **androsphinx;** *sphinx with a ram's head:* see **criosphinx;** *sphinx with a hawk's head:* see **hieracosphinx** • **heraldic** secrecy; omniscience

spice love; fertility; sexual activity; sanctity; purification; rejuvenation; spiritual qualities which purify the mind

spider patience; subtlety; industriousness; ambition; cunning; presumption; temptation; envy; aggressiveness; malice; a miser; the supreme deity; the Creator; the Great Mother; the lunar; avarice; craftiness; deceit; entrapment; despair and hope; heaven; continuous sacrifice; repulsive sex; attribute of fertility, moon goddesses • **tarantula or black widow spider** repulsiveness; danger • **spider in the center of its web** the sun and its rays; the cycle of life and death with death at the center; the wheel of existence • **African** trickster • **Amerindian** wind and thunder; protection • **Ashanti** *spider, or a mix of spider and human parts:* Anansi • **Christian** the devil ensnaring sinners; the greedy bleeding the poor; *spider with a cup:* attribute of St. Norbert • **Egyptian** attribute of Neith • **Greco-Roman** attribute of Persephone/Proserpine, Harmonia, the Moirae/Fates; *woman turning into a spider:* Arachne • **heraldic** wisdom; prudence; labor • **Hindu** *spider on a thread:* deliverance; the means and support of spiritual self-realization

• **Montagnard** the soul of an ordinary person • **Norse** Holda; the Norns • **Roman** acumen; lucky • **Sumero-Semitic** attribute of Targatis, Ishtar • **Ural-Altaic** the soul freed from the body • *see also* **web**

spiderwort • **flower language** esteem, but not love; transient happiness • *Virginian spiderwort:* momentary happiness

spikenard perfume; allurement; purification; holiness; death • **Christian** humility; the ointment Mary (of Martha and Mary) used to anoint Christ's feet; *spikenard with saffron or camphor:* emblem of the Virgin Mary

spindle life; the temporal; transitoriness of life; mutual sacrifice; phallus; axis of the universe; coition; union of heaven and earth; attribute of mother goddesses, goddesses of the moon, earth, vegetation • **Greek** attribute of Lachesis, Atropos, Atropos; *golden spindle:* attribute of the Nereids • **heraldic** *spindle (fusil) of yarn:* negotiation • **Jewish** attribute of Eve after the fall

spindle tree associated with sculptors • **flower language** your image is engraved in my heart; your charms are engraved in my heart

spine firmness; stamina; courage; life; force; aspiration; World Axis • **Ainu** seat of life • *see also* **kundalini**

spinel charm for calmness, curing hemorrhaging and inflammatory diseases; stone for a 22nd wedding anniversary • **blue spinel** stone for a 65th wedding anniversary • **green spinel** stone for a 9th wedding anniversary • **red spinel** stone for a 16th wedding anniversary

spinning (thread) creation; fate; bringing forth and fostering life • **three spinners** goddesses of fate, representing birth, life, and death, or past, present, future • **Greco-Roman** attribute of the Moirae/Fates

spinning wheel the revolving heavens; emblem of femininity; vulva

spiral mystery; complexity; escape from the material to the spiritual; resurrection; the soul's journey after death; mystic center; immortality; breath; spirit; authority; mystery of life and death; evolution of the universe; growth; vulva; the development of strength; the spirit; the air; rolling thunder and lightning; vortex; generative forces; associated with the moon, water • **double spiral** life and death; evolution and involution; expansion and contraction; winding and unwinding; day and night; the two hemispheres; yin and yang; shakta and shakti; androgyny; DNA (deoxyribonucleic acid); emblem of Cancer • **African** the dynamic of life;

the movement of souls in the created universe • **clockwise spiral** creation; evolution; growth • **counterclockwise spiral** destruction; involution; death; decrease; whirlpool • **Celtic** flame; fire • **Chinese** *double spiral:* the union of heaven and earth, Emperor and Empress, divine potential containing all opposites, androgyny, involution and evolution, birth and death, macrocosm and microcosm, the manifestation of energy in the universe • **Greco-Roman** *clockwise spiral:* attribute of Athena/Minerva; *counterclockwise spiral:* attribute of Poseidon/Neptune • **Hindu** associated with Kundalini, *hair braided in a spiral:* attribute of Pushan, Rudra • **Maori** phallic; the masculine principle; vulva

spire heavenly aspiration; bridge to heaven; universal axis; mystic center; creative force; aspiration; purity; phallus • **Christian** *the largest spire:* God the Father; *the smaller spires* God's celestial offspring; *topped with a finger pointed to heaven:* one God, reminder of heaven; *topped with a weathervane:* a challenge to face difficulties and changing conditions

spitting disdain; regurgitation; idleness; indifference; a sign of truth; antidote to the evil eye; binding oneself to a bargain or bet • **spitting in the ocean** inconsequence

spittle contains the essence of the personality • **folkloric** has curative powers; *witch's spittle:* poisonous • **Indic** *Airi spittle:* poisonous

spittoon repulsiveness

spleen seat of emotions (sexual passion, mirth, impetuosity, capriciousness, but especially anger, ill-humor, melancholy) • **Arabian** cheerfulness; laughter • **Chinese** seat of terrestrial (yin) energy; one of the Eight Treasures; associated with the umbrella, the earth, yellow, sweetness, the center

sponge parasite; obliteration; attribute of the Crucifixion

spoon the maternal; feminine symbol of containment • **Hindu** *sacrificial spoon:* attribute of Agni, Brahma

spot the female; impurity; blemish

spread-eagle exaggeration; boastfulness; flogging; death; torture • **when lying down** surrender

Spring (season) regeneration; revival; youth; innocence, especially female; rebirth; sweetness; mildness; courtship; time; associated with early morning, the live, Aries, Taurus, Gemini, green, occasionally white • **Greco-Roman** sacred to Hermes/Mercury

spring (water) holy source of water; motherhood; channel of primary manifestation; the soul; freshness; living water; purification; regenera-

tion; beginning of life; genius; power; good fortune; grace; knowledge • **Christian** Christ as the fountain of life; the Virgin Mary • *see also* **fountain**

springwort fertility

sprinkling fertility; the cycle of impregnation, conception, gestation, birth, and baptism • **sprinkling with holy water** the blessing of God

sprite *see* **water sprite**

spruce pity; fidelity; boldness • **Norway spruce** associated with the archangel Zadkiel • **Shoshone** *powdered spruce needles:* charm against illness • *see also* **pine**

spurs stimulus to action; knighthood; qualification; attribute of cowboys • **Chinese** *rooster with spurs:* warlike character • **heraldic** martial readiness; fighting spirit; knightly dignity; willingness to press forward

spy limitation; the inclination to trust the flesh rather than the spirit

square (shape) firmness; stability; permanence; material things; the merely rational; the instinct; the earth; limitation; order; organization; man not yet at one with himself; tense domination; earthly existence; God manifest in creation; mortality; honesty; integrity; the perfect type of enclosure • **square nimbus** an indication of the holiness of a person still living • **circle within a square** heaven and earth; integration • **squaring a circle** transforming the heavenly into earthly as in a sacred building; uniting the four elements and returning to primordial simplicity in unity • **circling a square** transforming the earthly into the heavenly • **Buddhist** *at the base of a chorten:* the earth level in the planes of existence • **Chinese** the earth; *square within a circle:* the union of yin and yang, heaven and earth • **Christian** the new Jerusalem; the unwavering firmness of the Church; honesty; *square within a circle:* eternity of life • **Greco-Roman** feminine reproductive power; attribute of Aphrodite/Venus • **Hermetic** stability; *square standing on one corner:* movement; *square surrounding a circle:* the world soul • **heraldic** truth; equity; constancy; stability • **Hindu** pattern of perfect order in the universe; the standard of proportion and perfect measure; Purusha; essence; space; the four cardinal directions; the four castes; *square at the base of a stupa:* the earth plane; *square and circle:* the order of things in the cosmos, ornaments of the dharma • **Kabalistic** *circle within a square:* the spark of divine fire concealed in matter and giving it life • **Kalmyk** shape of the Northern Continent and the faces of its inhabitants • **Masonic** attribute of the Venerable Master • **Pythagorean** the soul • **Taoist** *square pupils:* attribute of the Immortals

square (**tool**) right conduct; truth; honesty; carpentry in particular, the building trades in general; attribute of the personifications of Melancholy, Geometry • **square and compasses** earth and heaven respectively • **T-square** attribute of Geometry personified • **Chinese** emblem of the emperor; attribute of Niu-kua; *square with compasses:* order, propriety, harmony, the laws of virtue, the path of wisdom, the true guide, yin and yang, heaven and earth, the masculine and feminine principles • **Christian** attribute of SS Matthias, James the Less; *square with cross:* attribute of St. Philip; *square with spear or arrows:* attribute of St. Thomas; *square with boat hook:* attribute of St. Jude; *square with lily:* attribute of St. Joseph • **heraldic** constancy

squid • **Greco-Roman** attribute of Aphrodite/Venus, Poseidon/Neptune; sacred to Hydra • **Nootkan** the first keeper of fire • **Polynesian** attribute of Fe'e • *see also* **octopus**

squill attribute of Envy and other vices personified

squinting skepticism; lack of understanding; attribute of Envy personified

squirrel forethought; nimbleness; playfulness; hoarding; greed; providence; thrift; heavenly meditation; the striving of the Holy Spirit • **American** *squirrel tail:* emblem of a scout in the Revolutionary War • **Celtic** emblem of Medb • **Chinese** avarice; greed • **heraldic** service as an important messenger; courage; impartiality; a great hunter; sylvan retirement; lover of the woods • **Japanese** fertility • **Norse** Ratatosk

Sraosha • **Zoroastrian** the personification of Divine Service, Obedience

stable • **Christian** the Nativity of Christ; a guarded place; light and revelation arising from ignorance; realm of darkness from which light emerges

staff support; blindness; old age; a royal weapon; authority; dignity; masculine power; magic power; an instrument of punishment; guidance; fertility; resurrection; the sun; phallus; the axis of the universe; faith; attribute of travelers, shepherds, Good Shepherds, the lover (especially with purse) • **broken staff** famine • **flowering staff** innocence; forgiveness • **budding staff** attribute of the Hellespontic sibyl • **staff surmounted by a crescent** conjunction of opposites • **two serpents entwining staff** the solstices; the spiral cycles of nature • **staff with**

gourd and/or wallet attribute of the archangel Raphael • **staff with cup** attribute of the archangel Chamael • **Buddhist** law and order; the teaching of Buddha • **Celtic** *staff topped with a beehive:* attribute of Nantosuelta • **Chinese** attribute of Wen Chang; *ash staff:* mourning for a father; *mulberry staff:* mourning for a mother • **Christian** attribute of abbots, bishops, Christ, the Nativity of Christ, pilgrimage; *staff crossed with sword:* associated with the Passion of Christ; *long staff and spear:* attribute of St. Philip; *staff surmounted by a Latin or tau cross:* attribute of St. Philip; *staff made of a palm tree:* attribute of St. Christopher; *staff and white banner with red cross:* attribute of SS Jerome, John the Baptist, Ursula; *staff with ship:* attribute of St. Wilfrid; *staff with wallet or hat, or letters "S.J." or crossed with a sword:* attribute of St. James the Great; *flowering staff:* attribute of SS Ethelreda, Joseph of Arimathea; *staff with scallop shell:* attribute of a pilgrim to Santiago • **Egyptian** attribute of Osiris (usually shown with a flail); *staff with pen:* the soul awakening, attribute of Logios, Theut; *woman with the head of a lion, globe, ankh, and staff:* Tefnut • **Gallic** *staff topped with a beehive:* attribute of Nantosuelta • **German** attribute of Tannhauser • **Greco-Roman** attribute of Asclepius, Dionysus/Bacchus, Hermes/Mercury; *staff striking rock and producing water:* Rhea; *staff topped with a beehive:* attribute of Mellonia • **heraldic** watchfulness; Christian faith; pilgrimage to Jerusalem; pastoral authority • **Hindu** *Vaishnava staff:* the sage's control of thought, word, and deed • **Japanese** *scroll tied to staff:* attribute of Jurojin • **Jewish** attribute of Abel, Amos, Moses, David; *staff with serpent:* attribute of Moses and Aaron before Pharaoh; *staff striking rock and producing water:* attribute of Moses • **Norse** *staff with circle:* divine light, sun rays • *see also* **crook; rod**

stag piety; religious aspiration; devotion; longevity; regeneration; growth; related to heaven and to light; a messenger of the gods; the life of solitude and of purity; agility; grace; fertility; sexual ardor; rejuvenation; swiftness; prudence; timidity; immortality; hearing; beauty; mildness; chastity; fertility; the cycle of growth and rebirth; Tree of Life; continual creation and rebirth; associated with the archangel Asariel; attribute of the personifications of Hearing, Prudence • **stags pulling chariot** attribute of Father Time • **serpent with stag** cosmic unity; totality • **serpent trampled underfoot by a stag** evil defeated by good; the victory of the spirit over sin • **winged stag** swiftness to act • **alchemic** Mercurius; *stag and unicorn:* Mercurius and sulfur respectively, the nous, the dual nature of Mercurius • **Cambodian** harbinger of disastrous fire; *golden stag:* a solar animal, bringer of drought • **Celtic** the solar; the therapeutic; fertility; virility; longevity; plenty; conductor of souls of the dead; attribute of Cocidus, Ossian, hunters; *stag's antlers:* attribute of Cernunnos • **Chinese** happiness; pecuniary gain; longevity; bringer of drought; *white stag:* Shou-hsien; *stag with dragon's head and lion's mane:* a ky-lin; *stag's antlers:* an aphrodisiac • **Christian** Christ; the Christian; the word of God; piety; purity of life; solitude; attribute of SS Aidan, Eustachius, Felix, Ida, Jerome, Julian the Hospitator; *stag with a crucifix between its antlers:* attribute of SS Eustace, Hubert; *hunted stag:* persecution of early Christians; *stag trampling on a serpent or dragon:* Christ's power over Satan; *two stags drinking:* baptism; *stags pulling a plow:* attribute of St. Neot; *four stags:* SS Matthew, Mark, Luke, John • **Gallic** attribute of Cernunnos; *serpent with a stag's head:* attribute of Cernunnos • **Greco-Roman** lyric poetry; music; attribute of Artemis/Diana, Adonis, Erato; *stags pulling a chariot:* attribute of Artemis/Diana, Chronos; *stag being torn apart by hunting dogs:* Actaeon • **heraldic** lover of justice and harmony; skill in music; mildness; kindness; political providence; lover of faith and trust; possessor of hunting rights; peaceful unless provoked; *stag's antlers:* strength; fortitude • **Hindu** *golden stag:* a bodhisattva who calms passions and saves mankind from despair • **Hittite** steed of protective male deities; *man standing on a stag:* the god of animals • **Japanese** attribute of Fukurokuju, Jurojin; *white stag:* longevity • **Jewish** the soul thirsting for God; slayer of serpents; associated with Susannah and the elders • **Mithraic** *stag and bull:* the moment of death • **Norse** *the four stags of Yggdrasil:* the four winds • **North American Indian** Tree of Life • **Pawnee** herald of dawn, guide to the light of the sun • **Siouan** guardian of the North • **Sumero-Semitic** *stag's head:* emblem of Reshep; *man dressed as a stag:* the fertility god prepared for sacrifice • *see also* **deer; hart**

stage (theater) the world

stain death; the passage of time; the transitory; the abnormal or defective; dishonor

stairs spiritual ascension; aspiration; transcendence; Christian pilgrimage; World Axis (especially when surmounted by a cross, fleur-de-lis, star, or angel); communication between different worlds; grades or ranks in the hierarchical world • **ascending stairs** journey to mystic center; pilgrimage; longing for the higher world; acquisition of learning; the quest for exoteric knowledge • **descending stairs** entry into the infernal world; knowledge of the occult, the subconscious; the quest for esoteric knowledge • **stairs up to an altar** ritual ascent • **spiral stairs** the movement of the sun • **winding stairs** the mysterious • **white stairs** higher knowledge • **black stairs** black magic • **Amerindian** the months of the year • **Buddhist** *seven stairs:* the seven cosmic stages; the seven heavens • **Egyptian** associated with Osiris and the stairs to heaven; *nine steps of the throne of Osiris:* the nine days of the ancient Egyptian week; *fourteen stairs:* the days of growth to the full moon • **Hindu** *three stairs:* the manifestations of light; the steps to the control of the universe • **Mithraic** *seven metal stairs:* the major planets, the grades of ascension for the initiate • **Parsee** *three steps of the altar:* the degrees of initiation • **Sumerian** *seven stairs of the Ziggurat:* the seven heavens

stake • **stake driven into the heart** nailing the soul in a particular place; the prescribed method for killing a vampire • **being bound to a stake** sacrifice of a fertility king • **Christian** torture or death by fire; martyrdom, particularly of SS Agnes, Sebastian, Dorothea • **Hindu** *driving a stake through a serpent's head:* subduing evil; creating order • **Jewish** *soldier being killed by a woman pounding a tent stake into his head:* the soldier is Sisera

stallion *see* **horse**

standing respect

Star (tarot) renewed hope; inspiration; discovery; the possibility of future rewards, accomplishments; the promise of help from one's higher self; center of light; the world in the process of formation; associated with sleep, darkness, materialized inspiration

Star of Bethlehem (plant) • **flower language** guidance; purity

Star of David *see* **hexagram**

Star of the Sea (usually seven-pointed) emblem of many mother or sea goddesses (Isis, Aphrodite/Venus, etc.); emblem of the Virgin Mary

starfish inextinguishable power of true love; the grace of God not quenched in a sea of sin; divine love; the everlasting power of love • **Christian** the Holy Spirit; religion, charity; the Virgin Mary as Stella Maris

starling connected with mid-Winter; life in death; a messenger • **American** an invasive species and a pest

stars the spirit; the forces of the spirit struggling against the forces of evil; destiny; supremacy in a particular area; the presence of a deity; disintegration; immortality; the soul; guidance (especially spiritual); hope; purity; constancy; vigilance; the eyes of the night • **five-pointed star** *see* **pentacle** • **six-pointed star** *see* **hexagram** • **seven-pointed star** cyclic progression; human skill; Star of the Sea • **eight-pointed star** baptism; regeneration; the rising sun; the Wheel of Fortune • **stars in a constellation** order • **cloud of stars** infinitude • **veil with stars on it** night • **blazing star on forehead** attribute of the archangel Lumiel • **Aztecan** *morning star ascending:* the spiritual, masculine power of the sun; *evening star descending:* the earthly, feminine power of the moon • **Chinese** *stars with the sun and moon:* the spiritual wisdom of rulers • **Christian** divine guidance and favor; the birth of Christ; attribute of SS Athanasia, Bruno, Humbert, Swidbert; *four-pointed star:* the Cross; *seven-pointed star:* the Holy Spirit; the seven gifts of the Holy Spirit; *nine-pointed star:* the Holy Spirit; the nine gifts of the Holy Spirit; *ten-pointed star:* the ten Apostles who neither denied nor betrayed Christ; *seven stars:* the seven gifts of the Holy Spirit; *seven falling stars:* the Apocalypse; *nine stars:* the nine gifts of the Holy Spirit; *twelve stars:* the Apostles; *star on the breast:* attribute of St. Nicholas of Tolentino; *crown of stars:* attribute of the Virgin Mary; *crown of stars with lilies:* attribute of the Virgin Mary at the Immaculate Conception; *star on the forehead or on a halo:* attribute of St. Dominic; *day star:* Christ; *morning star:* Christ • **Egyptian** *crown of stars:* attribute of Isis; *cloak of stars:* attribute of Nut • **Greco-Roman** drops of blood from Uranus/Caelus; attribute of planetary gods; *morning star/evening star:* Aphrodite/Venus; *seven-pointed star:* attribute of Cybele; *eight-pointed star:* attribute of Aphrodite/Venus; *crown of 12 stars:* attribute of Urania • **heraldic** the third son; divine grace; learning; virtue; *estoile:* nobleness; celestial goodness; excellence • **Hindu** *seven-pointed star:* the chakras • **Islamic** divinity; supremacy • **Jewish** the eternal life of the righteous; *twelve stars:* the 12 tribes of Israel; *twelve stars surrounding the sun and the moon:* Jacob, his wife, and their 12 sons; *stars and a knife on a blue shield:* attribute of Abraham • **Maori** guidance for the triumph of good over evil • **Masonic** *rayed star in*

a circle: guidance • **Mithraic** the all-seeing eyes of Mithras • **Oceanic** the children of Mother Sun and Father Moon • **Sumero-Semitic** *four-pointed star:* emblem of Shamash; *eight-pointed star:* Gula; *morning star/evening star:* Ishtar; *crown of stars:* attribute of Astarte, Ishtar • *see also* **hexagram; pentacle; Morning Star; Pole Star; Star of the Sea**

starwort • **flower language** afterthought; *American starwort* welcome to a stranger; cheerfulness in old age; *Christmas starwort* the Nativity of Christ

statue the desire to make an ideal or emotion immortal and unchanging; the lifeless part of the self; attribute of Idolatry personified • **colossus** supranormal power; the infinite; the absolute • **Christian** *statue of the Virgin Mary carried by a Dominican over water:* the Dominican is St. Hyacinth • **Greek** *life-sized female statue with sculptor:* the sculptor is Pygmalion; *life-sized male statue with a god:* the god is Prometheus

Statue of Liberty • **American** freedom; hope; emblem of the United States

steam the psyche; evanescence • **North American Indian** the life-giving power of the Great Spirit

steed the animal in man; the force of the instincts; the control of baser forces; the body • *see also* specific steeds (**ass, goat, horse,** etc.)

steel strength; war; industry; armor; weapons; the all-conquering spirit; cruelty; chastity; trustworthiness; associated with 11th wedding anniversaries • **heraldic** ready for zealous service

steelyard *see* **balances**

steeple *see* **spire**

steering wheel control

stem World Axis; the manifest world; the middle world between the underworld (roots) and heaven (flowers)

stepmother jealousy; cruelty; the Terrible Mother

steps *see* **stairs**

Steropes • **Greek** lightning

stick punishment; World Axis; leadership; death; starvation; wisdom; attribute of St. Hilary • **burnt stick** death and wisdom • **North American Indian** *stick dance:* war rite; fertility rite • **Toltec** *feathered stick:* prayer, contemplation • *see also* **staff**

stigmata attribute of SS Catherine of Siena, Francis of Assisi, persons of high religious character

stilts deceit; associated with wading birds

sting death; sexual appetite; the ploy of a confidence man

sting ray *see* **ray**

stirrup • **heraldic** readiness for active service

stock (plant) • **flower language** *ten week stock:* promptitude; lasting beauty

stockings • **Middle Ages** *green stockings:* worn at weddings by an older unmarried sister of the bride • *see also* **sock**

stocks (restraint) loss of liberty; confinement; marriage; constancy; a form of **entanglement**

stole (religious garment) • **Christian** willing servitude; innocence; the yoke of man's sin borne by Christ; the hope of immortality; a sign of ordination; priestly dignity and power; obedience; patience; submission to God's will; the reign of Christ; *when worn crossed:* celebration of the mass; *when worn on the left shoulder and across the breast:* attribute of a deacon

stomach seat of courage, anger, temper, resentment, nausea, disgust; endurance; learning and truth; associated with Mercury (planet) • **Chinese** one of the Eight Treasures • *see also* **belly**

stone cohesion; harmonious reconciliation with the self; the spirit; the spirit as a foundation; the first solid form of creation; firmness; hardness; unity; strength; stability; durability; witness; immortality; imperishability; silence; remembrance; blindness; martyrdom; punishment; testicles; emblem of the Creator, Mother Earth, earth mothers • **broken stone** dismemberment; psychic disintegration; death; infirmity; annihilation • **cubic stone** stability; static perfection • **round stones** the moon; the feminine • **female beggar holding a heavy stone** Poverty personified • **crane with a stone in a raised foot** Vigilance personified • **axe embedded in a stone** the revealing of secret or hidden knowledge • **black stone** sin; defeat; restraint • **white stone** victory; theater admission; virtue; resurrection; immortality; happiness • **baetylic stone** World Navel; dwelling of dead spirits; dwelling of a deity; marker of holy ground; prophecy; meeting place of heaven and earth • **alchemic** *hidden stone:* the prima materia; *Philosopher's Stone:* the supreme quest, the reconciliation of all opposites, the attainment of unity, perfection, absolute reality, wholeness • **Amerindian** the bones of Mother Earth • **Arabian (pre-Islamic)** Manat • **Buddhist** *black stones:* evil deeds; *white stones:* good deeds • **Celtic** *nine white stones:* attribute of Bridget; *rocking stones:* associated with prophecy • **Chinese** reliability; hardness; *stone chimes:* fertility, they warded off evil • **Christian** sure foundation; indestructibility; attribute of SS Alphege, Barnabas; emblem of Christ; *man carrying large stone:* St. Bavo; *monk offering a stone to Christ:* the devil tempting Christ in the wilderness;

stones on a book: attribute of St. Emerantiana; *stone with open Bible and whip:* attribute of St. Jerome; *stone held in hand of kneeling hermit:* the hermit is St. Jerome; *man at prayer, beating his breast with a stone:* St. Jerome; *stone held in the hand of a soldier with a falcon:* the soldier is St. Bavo; *two stones:* attribute of St. Matthew (especially with battleaxe); *three stones:* attribute of St. James the Less; *three stones with lance:* attribute of St. Matthias; *three stones with dalmatic:* attribute of St. Stephen; *stones with spear or girdle or arrows:* attribute of St. Thomas • **Egyptian** truth; *green stones:* youth; immortality • **Greco-Roman** the bones of Mother Earth; associated with Cronus/Saturn; *black stone:* Cybele; *conical stone:* Cybele; *square stone:* attribute of Aphrodite/Venus; *cairn of stones:* Hermes/Mercury; *black stone:* guilty vote; *white stone:* acquittal vote • **Hindu** stability; *conical stone:* Shiva • **Islamic** *Ka'aba:* World Navel, communication between God and man • **Irish** *perforated stone:* charm to prevent fairies from stealing milk • **Jewish** attribute of Jeremiah; *foundation stone of the Temple:* world center, support of the world; *five stones and sling:* attribute of David; *stone full of eyes:* associated with Zechariah; *placing a stone on a grave:* permanence, proof of visitation; *stone for a pillow:* attribute of Jacob • **Oceanic** parents to all things in the world • **Sumero-Semitic** *conical stone:* Astarte • **West African** *blue stone:* the power of the sky god • *see also* **alectorian stone; cromlech; dolmen; menhir; petrifaction; rock**

stone mason *see* **mason**

stonecrop • **flower language** tranquility

stool (furniture) • **ducking stool** punishment of a scold; implement for the punishment and/or shaming of women • **footstool** the earth; lowest subservience • **Christian** attribute of St. Mary of Bethany • **Greco-Roman** *three-legged stool:* attribute of Apollo • **heraldic** hospitality • **Sumero-Semitic** *footstool:* attribute of El, Baal

stork filial piety; parental affection; longevity; birth; domestic peace and happiness; obedience; fertility; vigilance; pretension; self-conceit; chastity; harbinger of spring; generally a good omen; emblem of the traveler; attribute of the personifications of Help, Commerce • **Britain (ancient)** adultery • **Chinese** longevity; dignity; the recluse; filial piety; contented old age • **Christian** chastity; purity; vigilance; prudence; piety; new life in the Annunciation and the coming of Christ • **Egyptian** filial piety • **folkloric** brings babies; can cause pregnancy with a glance • **Greco-Roman** archetypal woman; life-bringer; nourisher; piety; filial piety; attribute of Hera/Juno, Hermes/Mercury • **heraldic** close parental bond; *with a stone in its mouth:* vigilance • **Japanese** longevity; immortality • **Jewish** an unclean animal

storm creation; creative intercourse between the elements; unleashing of creative activity; passions of the soul; psychic disruption; theophany; manifestation of divine power or anger; divine punishment; herald of divine revelation; passions • *see also* **wind; hurricane; thunder,** etc.

stove • **Russian** *gray-haired old man living behind a stove:* a domovik

stramonium • **flower language** disguise stranger the possibility of unforeseen change; the future made present; mutation; the replacement of reigning power

stranger bringer of change; the coming power of the future; disguised deity or magician; incongruity; an unknown or unassimilated part of oneself; the human condition in the world

straw emptiness; death; weakness; worthlessness; the transitory; a sinner • **broken straw** quarrel; dissension; renunciation of an agreement or of allegiance • **making bricks without straw** punishment • **flower language** *broken straw:* the rupture of a contract; *whole straw:* union

strawberry good hidden under evil; love; temptation; passion; rewarded effort; emblem of love goddesses • **strawberry leaves** aristocracy • **Christian** righteousness; good works; fruits of the spirit; attribute of the Virgin Mary, John the Baptist; *strawberries and violets:* the humbleness of the truly spiritual; *strawberries with other fruit:* the good works of the righteous, fruits of the spirit • **English** *crown with strawberry leaves:* attribute of a duke • **flower language** perfect excellence • **Roman** *sprig of strawberry plant at a doorway:* prevented witches from entering

strawberry tree • **flower language** esteem and love

stream peace; righteousness; flow of divine power and/or munificence • **well fed by a stream** the union of male and female • **Buddhist** self-nature; *crossing a stream:* leaving the world of illusion to attain enlightenment

Strength (tarot) power through conscious awareness of eternity; the triumph of intelligence over brutality; insensitivity; fury; spiritual power; triumph of love over hate; the spirit ruling over matter; personal responsibility; the need for love, patience, and fortitude in meeting obstacles

string cohesion of all things in existence; World Axis; bondage • *see also* **entanglement; rope; cord; bowstring**

stubble (plants) transitoriness • *see also* **chaff**

stumbling losing sight of spiritual ascension through one's own fault; falling into sin

stupa • **Buddhist** Nirvana; enlightenment; the cosmos; the Doctrine; *stupa dome:* the heavens, the five dhyani Buddhas; *stupa base:* the earth; *stupa stairs:* the planes of existence

sturgeon preservation; security; longevity; wisdom; courage • **Chinese** literary eminence; scholarly excellence, particularly in examinations • **Greco-Roman** sacred to Aphrodite/Venus • *see also* **fish**

sty (animal pen) corruption; lowliness

Styx death • **Greco-Roman** the river of oblivion in Hades

submarine the irrational; the unconscious; a vehicle of the unconscious; the means of exploring the unconscious

subway the subconscious; a journey in understanding

succory *see* **chicory**

succubus the devil in female form; the anima

suckling *see* **nursing**

Sudra caste *see* **caste**

sugar sweetness; flattery; deceit; a plea for happiness; a palliative

suicide war within oneself

sulfur the desire for positive action; reason and intuition; vital heat; the passions; infernal fumes; punishment for sins; distraction; associated with Mars (planet); preventative for cramps • **sulfur and eggs** purification • **alchemic** the Spirit; the masculine, fiery, active principle; dryness; hardness; unification • **Christian** associated with hell, the devil, guilt, punishment • **Jewish** divine punishment

sumac resoluteness • **flower language** *Venice sumac:* splendor; intellectual excellence

Summer maturity; abundance; youth; love; extended peace or happiness; beauty anticipating decline; perfection; charity; innocence; heat; ripening; associated with Cancer, Leo, Virgo • **Greco-Roman** sacred to Apollo

Summer solstice gateway from which dark emerges • **Chinese** corresponds to fire, the sun, the head • **Hindu** inaugurates the Way of the Ancestors • **Pythagorean** gate of mortals

sun potential good; the will; the hero; eye of God; theophany; creative light; the spiritual; the source of light; blessing; youth; sovereignty; supreme cosmic power; fertility; active power of nature; promise of salvation; mystic center; center of intuitive knowledge; the heart; the power of feeling and believing; guiding light; the male; the creator; the mind; splendor; magnificence; authority; heaven; paradise; life and earth; renewal of life through death; associated with the heart, authority, domination, masculinity, young manhood, Sunday, Leo, -1-, the archangels Michael, Raphael, Zerachiel; attribute of solar gods, Truth personified • **sunrise** resurrection; the beginning of a cycle • **sunset** death; the end of a cycle • **eclipse of the sun** omen of the death of kings, the end of the world, the start of war or plague • **Amerindian** the universal spirit; the heart of the sky; *feathered sun:* majesty; the universe; solar power; radiation of power; the Center; *sun dance:* regeneration of the sun, union with solar power • **Ammonite** fierce heat; emblem of Moloch • **astrologic** life; vitality; one's incarnate character; the heart and its desires • **Assyrian** sovereignty; emblem of Ashur • **Aztecan** the air; pure spirit; Quetzalcoatl • **Buddhist** the light of Buddha; *rooster and sun:* emblem of Buddhism • **Celtic** feminine power • **Chinese** power; yang; the masculine principle; the heavens; *ten suns in a tree:* the end of a cycle • **Christian** the light and love of God the Father; the divine essence in man; the Logos; emblem of Christ (seldom used in modern times); *sunrise:* Christ; *eclipse of the sun:* the day of the Lord is at hand; *sun with the letters IHC in the middle:* Christ; *sun on the breast:* attribute of St. Thomas Aquinas; *sun and moon together:* attribute of the Virgin Mary; *sun and moon together at the Crucifixion:* the sorrow of all creation, the two natures of Christ • **Egyptian** sovereignty; *rising sun:* Horus; *midday sun:* Ra; *setting sun:* Osiris, location of Amenti • **France** emblem of Louis XIV of France • **Greco-Roman** light of the universe; the eye of Zeus/Jupiter; attribute of Apollo, Helios/Sol • **heraldic** authority; splendor; glory; magnificent example; fountain of life • **Hermetic** the Maker • **Hindu** the divine life-giver; the eye of Varuna; Shiva; world door; the entrance to knowledge, immortality; *triple tree with three suns:* the Trimurti; *tree with 12 suns:* the months, the zodiac signs, the Adityas • **Islamic** the eye of Allah; the heart of the universe • **Japanese** *rising sun:* emblem of Amaterasu, the emperor, Japan • **Jewish** divine will and guidance; *sun and full moon with 12 stars:* Jacob, his wife, and their 12 sons • **Kabalistic** associated with the will, the zenith, light of the world • **Lithuanian** *small twin horses pulling the carriage of the sun:* the Asvieniai • **Oceanic** Mother of All • **Persian** the creation of light;

lion with sun: emblem of Persia • **Mithraic** emblem of Mithras • **Phoenician** power; emblem of Baal • **Platonic** creativity, wisdom • **Pythagorean** *ten suns:* cyclic perfection • **Norse** blessing; fertility; the eye of Odin; emblem of Loki • **Shintoist** *crow before the sun:* a holy crow, messenger of the gods, associated with temple • **Sumero-Semitic** *winged sun disk:* Shamash • **Taoist** *sun and moon:* supernatural being

Sun (tarot) renewal of life; Mother Nature; the happiness of being at one with nature; balance between conscious and unconscious, physical and spiritual; liberation from physical limitations; associated with concord, clear judgment, happy marriage, fallacious appearance, pretence, brotherly love, enlightenment, the archangel Michael

Sunday associated with the archangel Michael, the sun, Helios/Sol, works of light, Leo • **cutting one's nails on Sunday** unlucky • **birthday** Sunday's child is full of grace, or, Born on a Sunday, you'll never want (or, lucky and happy and good and gay) • **sneezing** For safety seek, the devil will have you the whole of the week • **Jewish** *Creation:* light • *see also* **days**

sundial natural time, in the general rather than the personal sense; daytime as opposed to the hourglass which indicates night

sunflower (helianthus annuus) gratitude; affectionate remembrance; religious remembrance; worship; devotion; infatuation; homage; foolish passion; false riches; royalty; the sun • **American** emblem of Kansas • **Chinese** food of immortality; longevity; has magical powers • **Christian** the soul turning to Christ • **flower language** *dwarf sunflower:* adoration; *tall sunflower:* haughtiness • **Greek** Clytie; attribute of Daphne • **Mithraic** attribute of Mithras

sunrise *see* **sun**

sunset *see* **sun**

sunspurge emblem of the sun

surgical instruments attribute of SS Cosmas and Damian

surplice • **Christian** innocence; purity; man renewed in justice and in truth

suspension unfulfilled longing

swallow (bird) wandering spirit; spring; domesticity; harbinger of Spring; hunger; prayer; contentment in poverty; hope; diligence; obedience; sociability; equality; sunshine; wantonness; instability; chattering; the inexorable march of time; filial piety; attribute of Equity personified; emblem of Summer • **Bambaran** purity, attribute of Faro • **Chinese** daring; danger; fidelity; emblem of good luck; a woman's voice; *swallow nesting on a house:* success, prosperity; *swallow nest:* insecurity, danger • **Christian** the Incarnation of Christ; hope; resurrection; new life • **Egyptian** sacred to Isis; attribute of the Tree of Life • **Greco-Roman** sacred to Aphrodite/Venus • **heraldic** readiness to do business; promptness; bringer of good news • **Islamic** the renunciation of good fellowship; the Bird of Paradise • **Japanese** domesticity; maternal care; unfaithfulness • **Jewish** paternal inheritance • **Minoan** associated with the Great Mother • **Persian** *swallow song:* loneliness, separation • **Sumero-Semitic** Nina • *see also* **martlet**

swan grace; peace; tranquility; serenity; purity; poetry; music; solitude; beauty; the hypocrite; androgyny; mystic center; the union of opposites; chaste female nudity; time; transience; mortality; dignity; nobility; haughtiness; jealousy; the soul; eternity; wisdom; resurrection; return to the womb; incestuous maternal relationship; connected with prophecy, dawn, the solar, poets; emblem of virginity in general (usually a white swan) • **swan neck** phallus; masculine • **swan body** feminine • **red swan** sunset • **five swans** the five Scandinavian countries • **swan song** the desire which brings about self-destruction; melancholy; self-sacrifice; martyrdom; death; tragic art • **alchemic** Mercurius; the union of opposites • **Celtic** benevolence; love; purity; Fionnuala; *swan with a gold or silver chain around its neck:* a divinity • **Christian** Christ; Christian retirement; attribute of SS Cuthbert, Hubert of Lincoln, Hugh, Ludger; *white swan:* purity, grace, emblem of the Virgin Mary; *swan song:* Christian resignation, martyrdom • **Greco-Roman** amorousness; a happy death; poetry; a form of Zeus/Jupiter; attribute of Aphrodite/Venus, Clio, Apollo, occasionally Erato; *swan embracing a young girl:* Zeus and Leda, respectively; *youth changed into a swan:* Cygnus • **heraldic** a learned person; a lover of harmony; *swan with a crown on its neck:* dignity, high rank, liberal views • **Hindu** breath and spirit; steed and emblem of Brahma; layer of the Cosmic Egg from which Brahma sprang; *Supreme Swan:* the Self; *two swans:* Ham and Sa, perfect union, balance, life • see also **goose**, with which the swan shares much symbolism

swastika revival; prosperity; lucky; felicity; the sun; agriculture; the succession of generations; speed; rotation; mystic center • **swastika over a door** protection against fire • **swastika in a circle or triangle** cosmic harmony; *if the tops are curved:* death • **clockwise swastika** increase; growth; spring; sun; lucky; white magic; some-

times the masculine • **counterclockwise swastika** decay; darkness; death; the Autumnal sun; unlucky; black magic; sometimes the feminine; emblem of Nazi Germany • **Buddhist** the Round of Existence; the seal of Buddha's heart; the esoteric doctrine of Buddha; one of the Eight Auspicious Signs; attribute of the footprint of Buddha • **Celtic** lucky; attribute of thunder gods; associated with Bridget • **Chinese** lucky; perfection; movement according to the law; longevity; *blue swastika:* infinite celestial virtues; *red swastika:* infinite sacred virtues of the heart of Buddha; *yellow swastika:* infinite prosperity; *green swastika:* infinite virtues in agriculture; *clockwise swastika;* yang; *counterclockwise swastika:* yin; *swastikas in a border:* the Ten Thousand Things, perpetuity; *two swastikas:* yin and yang; *interlaced swastikas:* infinity, divine inscrutability • **Christian** *in the catacombs:* Christ as the power of the world; *medieval:* Christ as the cornerstone, the four Evangelists with Christ as the center • **Gnostic** resignation, the Seventh Tirthankara • **Greco-Roman** attribute of Zeus/Jupiter, Hera/Juno, Helios/Sol, Demeter/Ceres, Artemis/Diana • **Hindu** life; lucky; happiness; movement; Agni; Dyaus; the sacred fire of heaven; associated with Brahma, Ganesha, Shiva, Surya, Vishnu • **Islamic** the four cardinal directions, control of the seasons by angels • **Jainism** the divine force, the Creator, the four grades of existence; *swastika surmounted by a single circle:* full consciousness, omniscience; *swastika surmounted by three circles:* the Three Jewels of Right Belief; *swastika surmounted by a crescent:* the state of liberation • **Japanese** lucky; the heart of Buddha; good wishes • **Manichean** the Cross • **Norse** the hammer of Thor; thunder and lightning; lucky • **North American Indian** fertility; rain; lucky; the four winds; prosperity • **Sumero-Semitic** *swastika on a triangle:* the feminine generative power of Astarte

sweat toil; sin; venereal disease; anxiety • **sweat on the face** falsity; illusion • **sweating image** omen of danger

sweeping *see* **broom (for cleaning)**

sweet brier poetry; elegance; talent; funeral bouquet; related to fairies • **flower language** *American sweet brier:* simplicity; *European sweet brier:* I wound to heal, poetry; *yellow sweet brier:* decrease of love

sweet flag • **flower language** fitness

sweet pea • **flower language** departure

sweet sultan • **flower language** felicity; supreme happiness; *when the flower is alone:* widowhood sweet William • **flower language** gallantry; finesse; a smile

sweetbrier *see* **sweet brier**

swiftness energy; indicates an advanced spiritual state; intelligence

swimming being engulfed in emotions, ideas, spirituality

swine impurity; uncleanness; abomination; an unbeliever; gluttony; greed; lasciviousness; lethargy; grossness; lack of feeling; obstinacy; viciousness; desire that seeks sustenance in matter rather than in spirit; transmutation of the higher into the lower; the moral plunge into corruption; a pagan; sensuality; sloth; self-indulgence; filth; selfishness; voracity; ingratitude; corruption; lust; boorishness; attribute of the personifications of Lust, Sloth, Gluttony • **pigskin bag** attribute of a tinker • **Amerindian** rainbearer • **Buddhist** *at the center of the Round of Existence:* greed, ignorance, the sins that bind man to the world of illusion, senses, and rebirth • **Celtic** food for the gods in the otherworld; attribute of Manannan • **Chinese** untamed nature; greed; dirtiness • **Christian** Satan; gluttony; sensuality; attribute of St. Anthony the Great; *youth praying among swine:* the Prodigal Son • **Egyptian** *black swine:* Set • **Greco-Roman** sacred to Zeus/Jupiter; sacrificed to Cybele, Demeter/Ceres, Heracles/Hercules, Ares/Mars, Tellus, Aphrodite/Venus; attribute of Dionysus/Bacchus; *swine in a palace:* associated with Circe; *men turning into swine:* associated with Circe • **heraldic** fertility • **Islamic** an unclean animal • **Jewish** an unclean animal • **Sumero-Semitic** attribute of Timmon, Tiamat, Great Mother goddesses • **Tibetan** *Diamond or Adamantine Sow:* Vajravarahi • *see also* **boar; sow**

swineherd a low job

swinging life's changing fortunes; purification by air; coition; fertility • **Hindu** communication between heaven and earth; the fecundating power of breath; associated with rainmaking

sword liberty; strength; the higher form of knighthood; courage; strife; the Word; authority; power; protection; vigilance; the administration of justice; destruction of the physical; the masculine principle; conjunction of the physical and spiritual; purification; antithesis of the monster; a cross; spiritual evolution or ornament; leadership; a spiritual weapon; spiritual decision; discriminating intellect; sacred inviolability; death; war; attribute of soldiers, the European sibyl, the archangel Michael, the personifications of Jus-

tice, Fortitude, Wrath, Choler, Rhetoric, Constancy (with pillar), the city of Venice (with two lions), Temperance (with sword in a sheath and/or the hilt bound) • **straight sword** masculine; solar; attribute of Europeans • **curved sword** feminine; lunar; sometime attribute of Muslims • **crossed swords** battle; military strategy or power • **blunted sword** mercy • **obtusely pointed sword** religion • **pointed sword** justice • **flaming sword** the authority of God; ardent zeal • **two-handed sword** civil power; the state • **two-edged sword** duality; powers that are contrary in appearance but complementary in reality • **two-edged sword between a sleeping man and woman** chastity • **sword and scabbard** conjunction of the masculine and feminine principles • **sword hanging overhead** constant threat; immediate danger; vulnerability to fate; the suddenness of fate • **woman with scales and sword** Justice personified • **sword and children** charity • **sword with balances (scales)** justice • **broken sword** peace; defenselessness • **woman killing herself with a sword** Despair personified • **skeleton with sword, sickle, scythe, and/or hourglass** death; Death personified; the King of Death • **four swords at a coronation** the state, mercy, spiritual justice, and temporal justice • **alchemic** purifying fire • **Buddhist** the discrimination that cuts through ignorance; attribute of Amoghasiddhi, Manjursi • **Celtic** the active aspect of the will; associated with supernatural underwater powers; attribute of Nuada • **Chinese** penetrating insight; *sword with a wave-shaped blade:* a swimming dragon; *triangle with suspended sword:* regeneration • **Christian** martyrdom; the Crusades; attribute of Christ's Passion, SS Adrian, Agnes, Alban, Barbara, Catherine of Alexandria, Edmund, John Gualberto, Jude, Justin Martyr, Peter, occasionally Julian the Hospitator; *sword held with the hilt upward:* the Cross, consecration, allegiance; *crossed swords:* attribute of St. Paul; *sword and scabbard crossed:* attribute of St. Paul; *sword with serpent twined around it:* attribute of St. Paul; *sword behind a book:* attribute of St. Paul (the book is usually inscribed "Spiritus Gladius"); *sword on a book:* attribute of St. Matthias; *sword with an anvil:* attribute of St. Adrian; *sword and cloak:* attribute of St. Martin; *sword and broken lance:* attribute of St. George of Cappadocia; *two saints, one with a sword, one with a whip:* SS Protase and Gervase respectively; *sword and pilgrim's staff crossed, or sword with a scallop shell:* attribute of St. James the Great; *sword through* *the throat or breast:* attribute of St. Justina of Padua; *sword through the head or hand:* attribute of St. Peter Martyr (usually shown as a monk); *sword piercing a skull or hand:* attribute of St. Thomas Becket (usually shown as a bishop); *sword piercing a book:* attribute of St. Boniface (usually shown as a bishop); *sword piercing a woman's bosom with a lion present:* St. Euphemia; *sword piercing a woman's neck:* St. Lucia; *sword held by the point:* attribute of St. Matthias; *flaming sword and a shield:* Christian conquest; *sword and palm:* martyrdom; *sword and torch crossed:* the Passion of Christ; *sword and staff:* the Passion of Christ; *sword at the feet:* attribute of St. Pantalon; *saint in armor with hand resting on a sword:* St. Demetrius • **Greek** attribute of Melpomene; *sword hanging overhead:* associated with Damocles; *sword and sandals under a rock:* associated with Theseus • **heraldic** defense; justice; execution; a free man; military honor • **Hindu** the war-like nature of the Asuras, attribute of warriors, Shiva; *Vedic wooden sword:* lightning • **Islamic** holy war against infidels; holy war of man against his own evil; *curved sword:* associated with Muslim warriors • **Japanese** courage; strength; one of the Three Treasures; the soul of the Samurai; attribute of Susano-o; *two-edged sword:* rain prayer sword • **Jewish** the 10th Plague of Egypt; attribute of Elijah, Simeon, Melchizidek, the archangel Michael; *flaming sword:* attribute of the archangel Jophiel driving Adam and Eve from the Garden of Eden; *sword hanging over walled city (Jerusalem):* associated with Zephaniah; *sword and water pitcher:* associated with Levi; *sword and trumpet:* associated with Joshua; *broken sword with lance:* associated with Micah • **Norse** attribute of Freyr; *flaming sword:* attribute of Surtr • **Roman** *sword and book offered to a sleeping soldier:* Scipio; *sword offered to a plowman by a Roman soldier:* the plowman is Cincinnatus • **Taoist** victory over ignorance; penetrating insight; attribute of Ma; *two swords:* attribute of Cho

swords (playing cards) *see* **spades (playing cards)**

sycamore abundance; variety; curiosity; wisdom; love; growth; persistence; strength; endurance • **British** *acer pseudoplantanus:* fertility • **Christian** *sycamorous ficus:* the wood of the Cross, cupidity, the unbelieving Jew, associated with Zacchaeus • **Egyptian** *sycamorous ficus:* Tree of Life, residence of Hathor, Nut; *golden sycamore of gems, fruits, and flowers in Paradise:* sacred to Nut • **flower language** *acer pseudoplantanus:*

curiosity, reserve • **Greek** *sycamorous ficus:* associated with Artemis of Ephesus

symmetry achievement; triumph; equipoise; unity through the synthesis of opposites; the oneness of conception; rationalization that constrains or stifles

Symplegades • **Greek** difficulties that may be overcome by courage and intelligence; fear of failure; an expression of stress

synagogue Jewry; Judaism; the Old Testament personified • **Christian** *Synagogue of Satan:* unperfected aspects of the self

syringa • **flower language** memory; *Carolina syringa* disappointment

syrinx lust; attribute of shepherds, Pan/Faunus, Polyphemus, Daphnis and Chloe • *see also* **pipe (musical)**

T

T the first letter of the Greek word for God (*Theos*); God; the Cross; associated with cooperation, the feminine principle, following, indecision, devotion, -2- (especially magnified 10 times), generative power, change, perfection • **medieval** occasionally the Roman numeral for 160

tabernacle the body • **Christian** the Eucharist; *three tabernacles (usually on a mountain top):* the Transfiguration; *tabernacle on an altar:* the reserved Host; the Real Presence • **Jewish** worship; world center; the cosmos; the Holy of Holies; abode of Shekinah; *tabernacle in a tent:* worship in Old Testament times

table fellowship; banquet; conviviality; conference; memory; earth; an altar • **round table** the universe; the sun; heaven; wholeness; equality; cooperation; teamwork; attribute of King Arthur and his knights • **Christian** the Last Supper; Communion; *writing table, pen, and books:* attribute of St. Ambrose • **Jewish** *table with showbread:* the dependence of man on God for spiritual and physical food; the operation of grace for the granting of things earthly • **heraldic** hospitality

tablet justice; law; divine word, order; destiny; esoteric knowledge; divine knowledge • **tablet with stylus** attribute of the personifications of History, Arithmetic • **two tablets of stone with oak leaves** sturdiness; regeneration • **broken tablet** injustice • **breaking a tablet** breaking a contract or partnership; the rescinding of a debt • **Chinese** dignity; lucky; *green jade tablet:* Spring, East; *hammer-shaped tablet in the em-*

peror's hand: power • **Christian** *heavenly tablets:* the future of mankind • **Greco-Roman** *tablet with stylus:* attribute of Clio, Calliope; *old man beside youth who has tablet and stylus:* the old man is Homer; *tablet with the name of a person:* gave power over the person; control of the dead • **Hermetic** *Emerald Tablet:* reflection of the microcosm and macrocosm • **Islamic** medium of divine plans; *Guarded Tablet:* communication between heaven and earth, the fate of mankind; *pearl tablet:* the upper and lower waters; *tablet with ink:* all possibilities in manifestation • **Jewish** *two tablets of stone:* associated with Moses, the Ten Commandments • **Sumero-Semitic** attribute of Aldebaran, Nabu; *Tablets of Destiny:* confer omnipotence, attribute of Marduk

taboo moral consciousness, moral censorship; transference of law to conscience

tabor festivity; instrument of beggars • **Greco-Roman** associated with rites of Dionysus/Bacchus, Cybele • **heraldic** festivity; rejoicing; dangerous if aroused • *see also* **drum**

tabret religious ecstasy; ecstasy of victory; instrument of goddess feasts • *see also* **drum**

tail animal power; balance; guidance; judgment; adjustment; phallus; expression of an animal's mood; attribute of a devil, false prophet • **animal without a tail** may be a witch in animal form

tailor the Creator; sexual curiosity; impotence; imperfect humanity, or an incomplete person; coward; a bad shot with a weapon

tallit • **Jewish** *when worn by the entire congregation in a synagogue:* a sign that all men are equal before God

Talos • **Greek** debased energy

tamarind • **Indic, Laotian, Sri Lankan, Thai** home of maleficent influences

tamarisk fertility; resurrection; attribute of Crime personified • **Chinese** immortality; associated with sweet solitude, vast empty spaces • **Egyptian** residence of Osiris; associated with the sun • **flower language** crime • **Japanese** associated with forecasting and making rain • **Jewish** said to be the source of manna; associated with Abraham at Beersheba; a holy tree • **Sumero-Semitic** Tree of Life; sacred to Anu, Tammuz

tambourine joy; rejoicing in the Lord; attribute Vice personified • **Greco-Roman** associated with orgies, Dionysus/Bacchus, Cybele, Attis; attribute of Maenads/Bacchantes, occasionally of Erato, also of Heracles/Hercules when dressed as a woman; *eating from a tambourine:* part of a rite of Attis • **Jewish** attribute of Jepthah's daughter Miriam • *see also* **sistrum**

taming self-knowledge and/or self-mastery resolving conflict

tansy • **flower language** I declare against you

Tantalus • **Greek** self-infatuation; over-reaching pride; eternal frustration; the sin of offering a deity material things rather than spiritual things; the sin of trying to make oneself an equal to a deity

tanzanite stone for 8th, 24th wedding anniversaries

Taoism selflessness; simplicity; absence of emotion; contemplation

tapestry visual representation of a soul journey; the higher self; the subconscious mind

tapir • **Mayan** equivalent to a serpent

tapster false geniality; a very ignorant person; a falsifier of accounts

tar connected with sailors and ships; blackness; stickiness; sin that cannot be readily expiated; entrapment

tares • **Christian** inners; *wheat and tares:* the Church on earth

tarot deck comprises an image of initiation; portrays the complementary struggles in man's life (practical reason/pure reason, self/ others, reflection/intuition, physical/spiritual, etc.) • **gold suit** material forces • **suit of goblets** sacrifice • **sword suit** discernment and the meting out of justice • **club suit** power of command • **cards I to XI** the solar way — the active, conscious, reflective, autonomous • **cards XII to XXII** the lunar way — the passive, unconscious, intuitive, dependent • *see* specific cards, such as **Fool, High Priest, World**

tartan *see* **plaid**

tassel sun ray; friendliness

tattoo a rite of entry; declaration of allegiance to what is signified by the mark; a turning point in one's life; has magical properties; a cosmic activity; protection; sacrifice; mystic allegiance; counter-magic; adornment • **tattoo of a full-rigged ship on a 19th century sailor** a veteran of sailing around Cape Horn • **American** *blue star tattoo:* an urban legend that lick-and-stick blue stars laced with LSD were given to school children to get them hooked

tau cross life; Tree of Life; hidden wisdom; regeneration; the life to come; the hammer of thunder gods; divine power and rule; emblem of the Hellespontic sibyl; attribute of the archangel Lumiel • **Babylonian** attribute of Tammuz • **Christian** attribute of St. Anthony the Great; *tau cross on the end of a staff:* attribute of SS Philip, Anthony the Great • **Egyptian** the hammer; the Avenger; the grinder; hidden wisdom; emblem of early Egypt • **Judaism** Passover • **Mayan** Tree of Life; Tree of Nourishment • **Norse** Thor's hammer; thunder; lightning; storm; fertility; the power of storm gods • *see also* **cross**

Taurus associated with fecundation, creation, primordial sacrifice, invigoration, long-suffering, slowness to anger but furious once provoked, strength, dependability, endurance, practicality in business, stolidity, reliability, lack of intelligence, laziness, secretiveness; possessiveness, stubbornness, obsessiveness, April, May, Venus (planet), the archangel Anael

tea exoticism; the Orient; connected with amorous intrigue and scandal; sociable life; the brew of life; connected with the Britain, China, Japan • **Japanese** *tea plant and flower:* rank, riches; *cherry blossom tea:* lucky

teacher a spiritually advanced person capable of leading others to higher qualities; counselor

tearing (ripping) *see* **rending**

tears (weeping) sorrow; grief; weakness; suffering endured in pursuit of truth; ecstasy of joy; fertility • **Aztecan** *tears of child victims of rainmaking sacrifices:* rain • **Christian** attribute of St. Monica

teasel • **flower language** *fuller's teasel:* misanthropy

teat *see* **breast**

teeth primitive weapon; cruelty; power; transience; wisdom; divination; ingratitude; potency; an expression of activity, especially sexual activity; defense; guardian of the inner person; means of enforcement; attack • **loss of teeth** fear; castration; failure; frustration; inhibition, loss of youth, strength, life force • **false teeth** false words, worn out or false ideas • **vagina dentata** fear of castration • **baby teeth** immature words, ideas • **dragon's teeth** the aggressiveness of perverted lust for domination; associated with Cadmus, warfare, seeds of dissension • **African** children born with teeth sometimes killed at birth • **Armenian** *demon with iron teeth:* an al • **Asian** *child born with teeth:* evil omen • **Bororo** *jaguar and monkey teeth:* charm for strength and skill • **Celtic** *wisdom tooth:* connected within a spell for poetic enlightenment • **Chinese** warfare • **Christian** *tooth in pincers:* attribute of St. Apollonia • **Finno-Urgic** children born with teeth will become vampires or witches • **folkloric** *long teeth:* attribute of an ambitious person • **Hindu** *canines:* aggressive strength that needs to be controlled; *three-legged man with eight teeth:* Kubera • **Hungarian** children born with teeth

are changelings • **Jewish** *infant born with teeth:* Esau • **Slavic** children born with teeth will become vampires or witches • *see also* **braces (dental)**

telegram information; insight; intuition; telepathy

telephone information; insight; intuition; telepathy

telescope the ability to see into the future; clear insight; oversensitivity to the insignificant; attribute of astronomers, astrologers

Temperance (tarot) generally has a favorable significance; universal life; ceaseless cycling through formation, regeneration, purification; the flow of life; the cyclic; the seasons; that which is always different yet always the same; the union of the masculine and feminine principles; interaction of spirit and matter; adaptation and coordination; successful combination; perpetual evolutive movement from the past to a golden future; harmony; balance; associated with the need for patience, moderation, the mastery of desire, the archangel Asariel

temple (building) mystic center; the soul; the world; throne of the deity; the intersection of heaven, earth, and the underworld; one's spiritual life; the spiritual façade presented to the world; the place where spiritual forces impinge on the material world • **circular temple** the sun • **triangular temple** trinity • **cave temple** return to the Center • **Christian** *temple on a mountain:* the spiritual Zion, the Church • **Jewish** *temple under construction:* associated with Solomon, Haggai; *model of a temple:* attribute of Solomon, Habakkuk; *temple on a mountain:* the spiritual Zion, associated with Micah • *see also* **church**

tendrils • **flower language** ties

tengu • **Chinese, Japanese** destruction; catastrophe; mischief; war; hypocrisy; associated with eclipses; meteors

tennis ball *see* **ball**

tent protection; temple; tabernacle; the heavens; transitoriness; often has spiritual significance; place where the godhead is summoned to make itself manifest; often protects and hides something, such as the mystery of the universe; partakes of the symbolism of clothes; associated with shepherds, nomads • **round tent** the cosmos; the world • **heraldic** readiness for war or battle; hospitality • **Jewish** associated with Israel in the wilderness; *tent of boughs:* associated with Feast of the Tabernacles

termitary • **Cambodian** *plunging a staff into a termitary:* causes rain • **Indic** related to primeval matter, the underworld • **Malian** the earth's clitoris; oneness • **Montagnard** sometime home of Ndu

termite destruction from within; hidden danger; spiritual corruption; slow and secret destruction

tern *see* **gull**

Terpsichore • **Greek** muse associated with flute-playing, choral dancing and singing

terror lack of intellectual will

tetractys the beginning and the end; birth, growth, and death; perfect harmony

tetragrammatron • **Jewish** Yahweh

tetramorph the synthesis of four powers; the four winds, cardinal directions, corners of the earth, elements, etc. • **Christian** the Evangelists • **Egyptian** the sons of Horus • **Hindu** Brahma

Thalia • **Greek** muse associated with comedies, idylls • *see also* **Three Graces**

Thames River associated with London • **swimming the Thames** metaphor for converting to Anglicanism

thaw the return of fertility; corruption; dissolving of the flesh

theater the world of phenomena; this world and the next; social life • *see also* **stage; playwright**

theta • **Christian** *blue theta on the shoulder:* attribute of St. Anthony the Great

thief the lesser nature which robs the self of primordial wealth; time; death; the villainous aspect of one's self; a force of chaos; personification of natural calamities (flood, frost, drought, etc.); the villainous part of the self

thighs strength; firmness; dynamic support of the body; sexual vigor; euphemism for genitals; holy, sacrificial spot; oath; promise • **smiting one's thigh** mourning • **Christian** *plague spot on thigh:* attribute of St. Roch

thimble insignificance; femininity; vagina

thirst longing; spiritual deprivation; the blind appetite for life

Thisbe *see* **Pyramus and Thisbe**

thistle sorrow; austerity; rejection; vengeance; misanthropy; emblem of Scotland • **Christian** sin; earthly sorrow; evil; wickedness encroaching on virtue • **Chinese** plant for longevity and fortifying the body• **flower language** *common thistle:* austerity; *Scotch thistle:* retaliation • **heraldic** defiance; surliness • **Jewish** the Fall of Man

Thomas the Apostle, St. • **Christian** doubt; skepticism

Thor • **Norse** associated with Thursday

thorn error; evil; the flesh; suffering; grief; obstacle; sin, sometimes only minor; tribulation; austerity; remorse; materialism killing spiritual

aspiration; sharp intelligence; affliction; annoyance; deprivation; the horns of the crescent moon; temptation of the flesh; the road to salvation, fame, truth, chastity; associated with Aries • **branch with thorns** martyrdom • **crown of thorns** attribute of the Delphic sibyl • **roses and thorns** thesis and antithesis; conjunction of opposites (pleasure/pain, etc.) • **Chinese** flying thorns were used to drive out evil spirits• **Christian** sorrow; tribulation; sin; associated with empty untilled soil; *crown of thorns:* attribute of the crucified Christ, martyrs, SS Catherine of Siena, Ignatius Loyola, Louis of France, martyrs; *thorn bush:* SS Benedict, Francis of Assisi overcame sexual tension by throwing themselves on one • **Egyptian** *acacia thorns:* emblem of Neith • **flower language** *a branch of thorns:* severity, rigor; *evergreen thorn:* solace in adversity • **Greco-Roman** associated with Ares/Mars, war • **heraldic** *thorn leaf:* irritation; nuisance • **Jewish** associated with empty untilled soil • **Mexican Indian** used by priests to mortify their flesh • *see also* **brier; bramble**

thorn apple • **flower language** deceitful charms

thorn tree associated with the archangel Samael • *see also* **blackthorn; Glastonbury thorn**

thousand *see* **-1000-**

thread World Axis; ascension; the connection between planes (spiritual, biological, social, etc.); unity; binding; continuity; sublimation; escape; connection in general; life; destiny; semen • **threading a needle** passing through the gateway of the sun; escaping the cosmos • **Greco-Roman** *three women spinning thread:* the Moirae/Fates • **Indic** *red thread around the neck:* protection from an acheri • **Jewish** *thread wrapped three times around the thumb:* associated with Seth

three *see* **-3-**

Three Graces • **Greco-Roman** the personfications of Beauty, Love, and Pleasure; the personifications of Giving, Receiving, and Requiting; bestowers of beauty and charm • **Neo-Platonism** the three aspects of love • **Medieval art** Charity, Beauty, and Love personified

threshing harvest; fertility; destruction; involution • **threshing floor** World Navel; the universe; mystic center; fertility

threshold transition between two worlds; transcendence; separation; the reconciliation and separation of two worlds (sacred/profane, life/death, etc.) • **threshold monsters (lions, dragons, etc.) at entrance to holy place** warning against profanation

thrift (plant) • **flower language** neglected beauty

throat vagina; associated with Venus (planet), the thyroid, the fifth chakra

throatwort • **flower language** neglected beauty

throne support; exaltation; equilibrium; security; stability; unity; majesty; seat of a deity; mystic center; authority; justice • **ebony throne** attribute of Night personified • **lion throne** subjugation of cosmic forces • **Babylonian** *peacock throne:* the royal throne • **Buddhist** *empty throne:* Buddha; *Diamond Throne:* Cosmic Center, the place of enlightenment • **Christian** authority; *empty throne:* God, the Second Coming; *empty throne with dove and crucifix:* the Trinity; *throne with four rivers:* attribute of God; *burning throne:* attribute of the devil • **Greco-Roman** *ebony throne:* attribute of Hades/Pluto • **Islamic** *throne with eight angels:* the throne of Allah • **Jewish** *throne mounted on cherubim:* the throne of Yahweh; *two cherubim on a throne:* attribute of the Temple of Jerusalem • **Persian** *peacock throne:* the royal throne • *see also* **cathedra**

thrush bird of spring; love; shyness; wisdom; heavenly aspiration • **Greek** Philomela • **Tahitian** *light yellow thrush:* manifestation of 'Oro

thuja • **Chinese** immortality; associated with Spring, sunrise

Thule *see* **Ultima Thule**

thumb power; the transmission of power; awkwardness; phallus; related to Venus (planet), Heracles/Hercules, the will, logic, God the Father • **when up** phallus; mercy; favor; pleasure • **when down** no; disfavor; death • **thumb in mouth** infancy; regression; coition; penetration; coquetry • **thumb between closed first and second fingers** coition; penetration; contempt; lucky • **thumb to the nose, or biting the thumb** contempt; occasionally, wisdom • **cutting off thumbs and great toes** incapacitation of a warrior • **M branded on the thumb** a murderer • **Jewish** *thread wrapped three times around the thumb:* associated with Seth • *see also* **hand**

thumbscrews torture

thunder divine power or warning; threat or precursor of war; war itself; cosmic disturbance or upheaval; voice of supreme deities, storm gods; fertility • **Buddhist** *rolling thunder:* spreading of the teaching of liberation • *see also* **lightning; storm; thunderbird; thunderbolt**

thunderbird • **North American Indian** the Creator; dynamic sky power; guardian of the sky, heaven; bearer of happiness; associated with war, destruction; *thunderbird track:* good omen

thunderbolt supreme creative fire; dawn; illumination; sovereignty; action of the higher world upon the lower; divine wrath; the male orgasm; weapon of the supreme deity; divine power; the Word piercing the darkness; power or speed (especially with wings); union of the sky god and earth mother; attribute of the supreme deity, smith gods, Fire personified • **eagle holding a thunderbolt** vigilance; majesty • **Babylonian** attribute of Ramman • **Buddhist** transcendental truth; enlightenment; attribute of Aksmobhya; *double thunderbolt:* attribute of Amoghasiddhi • **Greco-Roman** attribute of Zeus/Jupiter, Hephaestus/Vulcan • **Hindu** divine force; enlightenment; destruction; generation; attribute of Indra, Krishna, Rudra • **Japanese** attribute of Aizen-myoo • **Phrygian** attribute of Sabazios • **Sumero-Semitic** attribute of Adad • *see also* **lightning; thunder**

thurible *see* **censer**

Thursday associated with Jupiter (planet), Zeus/Jupiter, Thor, the archangel Zadkiel, Sagittarius, works of politics and religion • **birthday** Thursday's child is inclined to thieving, or, Born on a Thursday, merry and glad (or, has far to go) • **marriage** Thursday for crosses • **sneezing** You sneeze for something better • **Jewish** *Creation:* sea beasts, birds • *see also* **days**

Thyatira, Church of • **Christian** associated with charity, fornication, the thymus, the pale horse, the fourth seal

thyme activity; courage; bravery; strength; the opposite of hyssop; attribute of Diligence personified • **flower language** activity • **heraldic** strength; bravery; courage

thymus • **Hindu** associated with self-gratification and human love

thyroid • **Hindu** associated with life and personal will

thyrsus life; fertility; regeneration; gaiety; ecstasy; the manifold nature of the inner being • **Greco-Roman** euphemism for phallus; attribute of Dionysus/Bacchus, satyrs, Maenads/Bacchantes

tiara temporal power • **Christian** *triple tiara:* the three estates of the Kingdom of God; the Trinity; attribute of popes, Aaron, SS Gregory the Great, Sylvester • **Greco-Roman** *triple tiara:* attribute of Demeter/Ceres, Cybele, Attis • **Mithraic** *triple tiara:* Mithras • *see also* **crown; coronation**

Tiber River • **swimming the Tiber** metaphor for converting to Roman Catholicism • **Italian** an aspect of the cosmic river from which all comes and all returns; associated with Rome

tickling expectancy; ignominious death; playfulness

tide balance of nature; bringer of the divine; the ebb and flow of fortune; reciprocity • **turning of the tide** changing of fortune • **ebb tide** finish; completion; low fortune; the soul leaving at death • **flood tide** success; high fortune

tie *see* **necktie**

t'ien-kou *see* **tengu**

tiger wrath; cruelty; bloodthirstiness; aggression; ferocity; courage; beauty; grace; deceit; cunning; brutality; jealousy; violent desires; repressed sex; treachery; martyrdom; energy; drive; strength; stalking; savagery; royalty; the drowning of consciousness in elemental desires; attribute of Asia personified, associated with Mars (planet) • **tamed tiger** strength and valor in the fight against evil; the defense of order against chaos • **riding a tiger** confronting dangerous forces; risk-taking • **tiger fighting a serpent or other low animal** higher consciousness fighting lower desires • **tiger fighting an eagle, lion, or other higher animal** the instincts fighting higher consciousness • **tigress** aggression; spite; gossip; sexual dominance • **alchemic** *Chinese:* lead, the body • **Aztecan** the setting sun • **Buddhist** anger; the power of the faith and spirit fighting through the Forest of Sin; one of the Three Senseless Creatures of Chinese Buddhism • **Chinese** fierceness; courage; military prowess; authority; one of the Twelve Terrestrial Branches; emblem of fourth class military officers, gamblers; steed of the god of wealth, goddess of the wind; guardian of graves; associated with the underworld, the earth, the material world; *dragon and tiger:* spirit and matter, lustfulness; *child escaping from a tiger's jaws:* the new moon; *white tiger:* associated with Autumn, metal, West; *blue tiger:* associated with plants, Spring; *red tiger:* associated with Summer, fire, South; *black tiger:* associated with Winter, water, North; *yellow tiger:* associated with the center, the sun, the emperor • **Christian** emblem of Christ • **Egyptian** attribute of Set • **Greco-Roman** sometimes tigers pull the chariot of Dionysus/Bacchus • **heraldic** fierceness; valor; strength; resentment; dangerous if aroused • **Hindu** emblem of Kshatriyas associated with the earth, the material world; steed of Durga; *tiger skin:* attribute of Shiva • **Japanese** courage; attribute of warriors; associated with the earth, the material world • **Ural-Altaic** messenger of forest gods; steed of gods, immortals, exorcists

tiger flower • **flower language** for once may pride befriend me

tightrope danger; instability; the need for extreme care

Tigris River fertility; refreshment; wisdom

tiller (boat) control

timbers • **Jewish** associated with Haggai

timbrel rejoicing; religious ecstasy; usually an instrument of women

time destroyer; revealer of truth • **cessation of time** eternity; breakthrough to enlightenment

tin dross; cheapness; malleability; changeability; associated with Sagittarius, Pisces, Jupiter (planet), 10th and 18th wedding anniversaries, the archangel Zadkiel

tinker a man living outside the conventions of society; an impressive drinker; a sexual freebooter; associated with eroticism

Tiresias • **Greek** androgyny; lunar knowledge

Tisiphone *see* **Erinyes/Furies**

Titans • **Buddhist** supermen with the failings of aggression, ambition, and envy which lead to their downfall • **Greco-Roman** wild and untamable forces of primeval nature; the force of manifestation; the brute strength of the earth; desire in rebellion against the spirit; *eagle pecking at titan's liver:* Prometheus • *see also* **giant; Prometheus**

titmouse imprudence

toad fertility; clumsiness; wisdom; inspiration; resurrection; evil; insensitivity; an evil spirit; an enchanted being; vice; connected with witches; the inverse and infernal aspect of the frog; loathsomeness; ugliness; death; attribute of the personifications of Injustice, Death (especially with skull and crossbones) • **bloated toad** attribute of Pride personified • **toad hanging from the breasts of a woman or eating female genitalia** attribute of Lust personified • **toad as a steed** attribute of Avarice personified • **alchemic** the dark side of nature; earthly matter • **Aztecan** the earth • **Celtic** evil power • **Chinese** yin; longevity; wealth; the unattainable; *three-legged toad:* the three phases of the moon • **Christian** avarice; the devil; sign of possession • **Egyptian** associated with the dead • **French** the sun; royalty; *three toads, erect, saltant:* an ancient crest of France • **Greek** sexual abandon; attribute of Sabazios • **North American Indian** the Dark Manitou; the moon waters; the powers of darkness and evil • **Oceanic** death • **Taoist** attribute of Hon Hsien-hsing • **Vietnamese** strength; harbinger of rain; *scarlet toad:* strength, valor, wealth • **witchcraft** lucky; form of a witch • *see also* **frog** with which the toad is often mistaken

toadstool *see* **mushroom**

tobacco ephemeral pleasure; forgetfulness • *see also* **smoking; pipe**

toenails *see* nails (body)

toes direction; way of life; phallus; light ray • **amputation of great toes and thumbs** incapacitation of a warrior • **extra toe** lucky • **second toe longer than the first toe** a sign of a cruel husband • **Tinguinian** *half-man/half-bird with toes and fingers reversed:* an alan • *see also* feet

toilet the lower self; moral depravity; uncleanliness; failure

tomahawk attribute of North American Indians • **North American Indian** related to war; *to bury a tomahawk:* to make peace

tomato love

tomb transformation; the unconscious; the feminine; the maternal; the womb; the body and its fleshly desires; the body imprisoning the soul; involution with the hope of regeneration; finality; the lower self; the subconscious; repressed desires • **bees carved on a tomb** immortality • **tomb shaped like a beehive** immortality • **alchemic** dying to the world; mortification of the first stage of the Lesser Work • **Christian** attribute of Lazarus, St. Joseph of Arimathea; *empty tomb:* the Resurrection of Christ • *see also* sarcophagus

tombstone mortality

tongs attribute of smith and thunder gods, Thor, Hephaestus/Vulcan, etc. • **Christian** attribute of SS Agatha, Eloi, *Satan being held by the nose with a pair of tongs:* St. Eloi holds the tongs • **Jewish** *tongs holding a glowing coal:* attribute of Isaiah • *see also* pincers

tongue speech; gossip; malicious talk; lasciviousness; eloquence; persuasion; inconstancy; perfidy (especially a double, or forked tongue); scandal; lies; blasphemy; the sense of taste; substitute for phallus • **blister on the tongue** sign of a lie • **animal with extended tongue** exhaustion; a supplication for water, rain • **silver tongue** persuasive speech • **woman with a serpent for a tongue, or a serpent's tongue** Envy personified • **Buddhist** *long tongue:* attribute of Buddha • **Burmese** *hideous giantess with long slimy tongue:* a thabet; *hideous giant with long slimy tongue:* a thaye • **Christian** *long fleshy tongue:* attribute of Satan; *speaking in tongues:* possession by the Holy Spirit • **Egyptian** *extended tongue:* attribute of Bes • **Hindu** *extended tongue:* attribute of Kali • **Oriental** *large protruding tongue:* attribute of a demon • **Sumerian** *extended tongue:* attribute of monstrous animals

tonsure asceticism; spiritual transformation; spiritual thoughts; renunciation of the generative forces of nature; consecration; humility; rejec-tion of the temporal; dedication to divine service • **Christian** Christ's crown of thorns; reminder of the perfect life (Christ's); attribute of a monk (although in the early Church, they were also worn by secular clergy)

tooth *see* teeth

toothwort • **flower language** secret love

topaz felicity; fruitfulness; friendship; fidelity; integrity; divine love and goodness; ardent love and gentleness; wisdom; associated with Sagittarius, the sun, the archangels Azrael, Michael, Samael; birthstone for November; attribute of cherubim; charm for protection, love, healing, money, peaceful sleep, equability, protection from evil magic, negative energy • **blue topaz** stone for a 4th wedding anniversary • **imperial topaz** stone for 23rd and 50th wedding anniversaries • **yellow topaz** associated with the archangel Raphael • **Arabian** associated with Leo • **Brazilian** emblem of dentists • **Christian** uprightness; a foundation stone of the New Jerusalem; attribute of SS Hildegard, Matthew • **Hindu** corresponds to the element ether • **Jewish** a stone of the High Priest's breastplate; *on vestments:* friendship, true love

Torah ancient wisdom; religious doctrine • **Jewish** associated with the Pentateuch; emblem of Judaism

torch the truth; progress; the sun; the active, positive power of nature; enlightenment; scholarship; life; fervor, especially religious; victory; high ideals; purification; spiritualization through illumination and guidance; vigilance; marriage; regeneration; life of tradition passed from one generation to another; the solar or masculine; phallus; anarchy; revolution and ultimate liberty; attribute of the Libyan sibyl, the personifications of Sight, Peace, Temperance, Fury, Lust, Slander • **flaming torch** hope of resurrection; anger • **upright torch** life • **inverted or extinguished torch** death • **inverted torch on a tombstone** end of a family line • **woman with a torch dragging a youth before a judge** the woman is Calumny personified • **Christian** Christ; Christian witness; the Gospel; attribute of St. Dioscurus; *two burning torches:* Christ as the light of the world; *torch in Nativity scenes:* Christ as the light of the world; *torch crossed with a sword:* refers to the Passion of Christ; *torch held in the hand:* attribute of St. Theodore; *torch held by a dog:* attribute of St. Dominic; *torch held by a woman tied to a stake:* St. Dorothea of Cappadocia; *monk driving off a young woman with a torch:* St. Thomas Aquinas • **Greco-Roman** life; progress; emblem of

Anaitis; attribute of Demeter/Ceres, Kore, Persephone/Proserpine, Aphrodite/Venus, Eros/Cupid, Eos/Aurora, Hecate, Hymen, Prometheus, Hephaestus/Vulcan, Heracles/Hercules, Comus, Erinyes/Furies; *woman on a seashore with a torch:* Hero (of Hero and Leander); *woman with torch and bloody whip driving the chariot of Mars:* Bellona • **heraldic** science; fame; truth; intelligence; life; zealousness in serving • **Hindu** the active power of nature • **Kabalistic** intelligence; equilibrium • **Mithraic** *torches held up and down by Cautes and Cautopates:* life and death, the rising and setting sun, morning and evening, Spring and Winter, lengthening and shortening days, etc. • **Slavic** rebirth of the sun; attribute of Svarog • *see also* **lamp; lantern**

tornado invincible power; destructiveness; violence; a hole through which one may pass out of space and time

torrent • **Christian** attribute of St. Christopher

tortoise longevity; time; fecundity; divination; the feminine principle; androgyny (the head is phallic, the body feminine); the moon; the Earth Mother; caution; foresight; apathy; insolence; Chaos with the hope of renewal of life; regeneration; chastity; sloth; withdrawal; silence; the earth; attribute of Industry personified • **African** trickster • **alchemic** creative chaos • **Amerindian** the Cosmic Tree is rooted in the back of a tortoise • **Chinese** strength; endurance; longevity; divination; oracle; yin; one of the Four Spiritually Endowed Creatures; *black tortoise:* primordial chaos, associated with Winter, North; *dragon and tortoise banner:* indestructibility; *tortoise and crane:* longevity • **Christian** married modesty; *early Christian:* evil • **Greco-Roman** the feminine principle; fertility of the waters; attribute of Aphrodite/Venus; emblem of Hermes/Mercury • **heraldic** steadfastness; invulnerability; glorious development of family • **Hindu** Kasyapa; the first living creature; the power of the waters; support of the elephant on whose back the world rests; *Akupara:* the tortoise upon whom the world rests; *man with four arms and tortoise bottom:* Kurma; *Kurma's upper shell:* the celestial world; *Kurma's lower shell:* the terrestrial world • **Japanese** lucky; support; emblem of Kumpira; attribute of Benten, Fukurokuju, Jurojin; support of the abode of the immortals and the Cosmic Mountain; *tortoise with a flaming tail:* longevity; *tortoise with monkey head and frog legs:* Kappa • **Mexican Indian** the Terrible Mother • **Sumerian** sacred to Ea-Oannes

• **Taoist** the great Triad; the entire cosmos; *upper shell:* the sky; *body:* the earth; *lower shell:* the waters • *see also* **turtle**, with which the tortoise is sometimes confused

touch transfer of power • **touching wood** touching the Cosmic Tree, which was a place of sanctuary and protection

touch-me-not • **flower language** impatient desire

tourmaline generosity; friendship; thoughtfulness; courage; inspiration; associated with Pisces, Libra; birthstone for October; stone for 8th, 28th wedding anniversaries; charm for friendships, business, social harmony, popularity, intuition, love, money, peace, health, courage, energy • **black tourmaline** charm for grounding, protection • **blue tourmaline** charm for peace, calmness • **green tourmaline** charm for money, creativity, success • **pink tourmaline** stone for a 5th wedding anniversary • **rainbow tourmaline** charm for astral projection • **red tourmaline** charm for energy, protection, courage

towel • **throwing a towel in a boxing ring** admission of defeat • **Christian** *spotless towel:* attribute of the Virgin Mary; *towel with pitcher:* refers to Pilate washing his hands during the Passion of Christ

tower ascent; the link between heaven and earth; man; strength; power; purity; aspiration, especially toward God; isolation; withdrawal from the material world; phallus; height; the supreme deity; salvation; World Axis; hope; virginity; watchfulness; refuge; hidden truth; conscience; the higher self; beauty; treasure • **round tower** connected with solar worship • **round tower surmounted by crescent** androgyny • **leaning tower** emblem of Italy in general, Pisa in particular • **ivory tower** inaccessibility; the feminine principle; virginity; philosophical retirement; scholarly retirement from the world • **Christian** the Virgin Mary; *ivory tower:* attribute of St. Barbara; *tower, usually with three windows:* attribute of St. Barbara; *two towers, one leaning:* attribute of St. Petronius • **Greek** *brass tower:* prison of Danae • **heraldic** grandeur; nobility; solidity; strategy; safety; protection; strength; *bell or clock tower:* integrity; *ladder against a tower:* wariness of spiritual and bodily attack • *see also* **Babel, Tower of**

Tower (tarot) *see* **House of God**

toy temptation; childhood

train (transportation) progress; life; human communication • **missing a train** missing an opportunity • **departure platform** the unconscious; the beginning of a quest, journey, new stage of life • **traveling without a ticket or in a higher class than paid for** fraud; self-deception • **crash and/or derailment** failure; neurosis; internal conflict • **crowded train** difficulty becoming part of society or being noticed • **fear of being run over by a train** extreme anxiety • *see also* **locomotive; luggage**

Trajan, Emperor • **Christian art** attribute of Justice personified (shown at her feet)

tramp (hobo) the primitive, instinctual, natural self; one who has lost his spiritual direction; detachment from the material world; laziness; fecklessness

transfiguration the visible form of divinity; manifestation of divinity or supernatural powers

transvestitism identification with a deity, parent, or ideal of the opposite sex; sign of homosexuality; overcoming a castration anxiety; androgyny; return to chaos; loss of identity; identification with the qualities of the original wearer • **man wearing women's clothing in an initiation** return to the womb

trapezium in comparison with a trapezoid, it shows a greater degree of abnormality, irregularity, incompletion • *see also* **trapezoid**

trapezoid sacrifice; abnormality; irregularity; incompletion; an inferior form • *see also* **trapezium**

trash discarded and worthless ideas, emotions, beliefs

traveler seeker after truth; someone engaged in personal development, especially spiritual or religious; a pilgrim

traveler's joy • **flower language** safety

treasure something of spiritual value • **treasure in a cave** mystic center; the self being reborn; the value to be found in the unconscious • **hidden treasure** the fruits of supreme illumination • **search for treasure** the search for spiritual evolution

tree immortality; stability; the life of the cosmos; the whole of manifestation; the universe; the link between the heaven, earth, the underworld; the synthesis of heaven, earth, and water; World Axis; World Navel; eternal life; longevity; fertility; mythic ascension; the slow process of individuation; diversity in unity; wisdom; divine wisdom; life, especially dynamic life; the home of spirits or the gods; the feminine; earth's fecundity • **felling a tree** castration • **tall tree** aspiration • **withered tree** death • **pearl or gem bearing tree** spiritual wealth • **flowering tree** life • **fruit tree** a sacred tree • **evergreen tree** immortality; undying spirit • **deciduous tree** constant renewal and regeneration • **inverted tree**

magic; illumination; sun rays upon the earth; the reflection of the terrestrial and celestial worlds on each other; the power of heaven descending to the earth; *in initiation ceremonies:* the death of the former self; *on funeral urns:* death • **tree with branches that divide and rejoin, two trunks with one root, or two trees with joining branches** the union of heaven and earth; manifestation cycling from unity to diversity and back again • **tree atop a mountain** World Axis; Cosmic Tree • **tree with ten or twelve birds** the solar cycle • **tree with three birds** the lunar phases • **serpent or dragon guarding a tree** the difficulty of attaining wisdom • **tree with a serpent entwined** World Axis and the cycles of manifestation, respectively • **two serpents entwining a tree** the solstices; the spiral cycles of nature • **tree, stone, and altar** the microcosm • **grove of trees** the cosmos • **climbing a tree** ascent to heaven, reality, the gods; passage between planes of existence; attaining esoteric knowledge by transcending the world • **alchemic** the primary substance of the world containing the potentiality for all forms, the processes of transformation; *tree of suns:* the Greater Work, solar work; *tree of moons:* the Lesser Work, lunar work • **Arabian** *tree with 12 branches with stars on them:* the zodiac • **Assyrian** *luminous gem tree of Paradise:* the great light of God • **Australian aboriginal** *tree with stars:* Cosmic Tree; *upside down tree:* magic • **Buddhist** the bo tree; *tree with four branches and four roots:* Damaba, the Tree of Life • **Celtic** *oak and mistletoe:* male and female powers • **Chinese** *trees with intertwining branches:* a pair of lovers; the union of pairs of opposites; *sun with a tree:* the end of day; *sun resting on a tree:* the end of a cycle; *sun at the roots of a tree:* darkness; *ten suns in a tree:* the end of a cycle; *tree atop a mountain:* Tree of Sweet Dew; *Tree of Sweet Dew:* World Axis; *pearl tree in Paradise:* purity in eternity • **Christian** the Cross; the Church; man; *flowering tree:* attribute of St. Zenobius; *man praying up in a tree, or in front of tree:* St. Bavo; *tree with robin:* attribute of St. Mungo; *tree with many branches:* the divisions of Protestantism • **Egyptian** Hathor • **Greco-Roman** *tree and pruning hook:* attribute of Silvanus; *gifts on a tree:* offerings to Attis, Cybele, Dionysus/Bacchus • **heraldic** justice; prosperity; life; constancy in faith; connection between heaven, earth, and underworld; possession of wooded land; *sprouting tree stump or branch:* new life springing from the old • **Hindu** the cosmos with branches in heaven, the trunk in the world, and the roots in the underworld; *triple tree with three suns:* the Trimurti; *tree with 12 suns:* the months, the zodiac signs, the Adityas; *gem tree of Paradise:* sacred to Buddha • **Islamic** *inverted tree:* Tree of Happiness with its roots in heaven and branches over the earth; *Cosmic Tree:* the universe • **Jewish** *three tree seeds:* attribute of Seth • **Persian** *seven-branched tree:* Cosmic Tree, the seven planets governing a millennium • **Sumero-Semitic** *seven-branched tree:* the Tree of Life, the seven planets, cosmic regeneration; *gifts on a tree:* offerings to Cybele, Atargatis; *tree trunk:* Astarte • **Taoist** *trees with intertwining branches or a common branch:* the unity of the Tao, opposite pairs, yin and yang • **Zoroastrianism** *Tree of the Solar Eagle:* origin of the primordial ocean; *Tree of All Seeds:* contains the germs of all living things • *see also* **Yggdrasil**, and specific kinds of trees (**bo tree, oak, pine, palm,** etc.)

Tree of Life mystic center; the cosmic axis; marks the center of Paradise; regeneration; eternity; the return to primordial perfection; the beginning and end of a cycle; place of death for the Dying God • **twelve (occasionally ten) fruits on the Tree of Life** forms of the sun, which will all appear together at the end of a cycle as manifestations of Unity • **eating the fruit or drinking the liquid of the Tree of Life** attaining immortality • **Egyptian** *pair of androsphinx with the Tree of Life:* fertility, conception • **heraldic** knowledge • *see also* **arbor vitae**

Tree of the Knowledge of Good and Evil • **Jewish** the Fall of man; death and resurrection; the lunar phases of decline and degeneration; associated with the first man, Paradise

trefoil (design) the Trinity; integration, but sometimes disintegration; equilibrium • **heraldic** perpetuity

trefoil (plant) foresight; inspiration • **flower language** revenge

tremella nestoe associated with alchemy; once thought to be an emanation from a star • **flower language** resistance; opposition

tressure • **heraldic** protection

trestle • **heraldic** hospitality

triangle (geometric form) three; the threefold nature of the universe • **triangle with apex up** the masculine principle; fire; sun; the active; the godhead; the spiritual world; aspiration of all things toward unity; the urge to escape from this world to the Origin; love, truth, and wisdom; royal splendor; associated with red • **equilateral triangle** the godhead; harmony; proportion • **triangle with apex down** the feminine

principle; the Great Mother; water; moon; the passive; the heart; underworld powers; associated with white • **triangle within a circle** man and woman; trinity and unity • **double triangle** *see* **hexagram** • **two horizontal triangles with apexes touching** the waxing and waning moon; death and life; death and resurrection; eternal return • **alchemic** sulfur, Mercurius, and salt; *two triangles:* essence and substance, spirit and soul, stability and volatility; *apex up:* fire; *apex down:* water; *double triangle (six pointed star):* the union of opposites, fiery water, watery fire • **Buddhist** pure flame; the Buddha, the Dharma, and the Sangha • **Chinese** *triangle with suspended sword:* regeneration • **Christian** *equilateral triangle:* the Trinity, and the equality of the Trinity; *triangle formed by three interlacing circles:* the Trinity, and the equality of the Trinity; *triangular nimbus:* attribute of God the Father • **Egyptian** *right triangle:* the base is the female, the perpendicular the male, the hypotenuse their offspring; *black bull with white triangle on the forehead:* emblem of Ptah • **Greek** *delta:* feminine generative power; the door of life; fertility • **Hindu** *apex up:* lingam, shakta, fire, emblem of Shiva; *apex down:* yoni, shakti, water, emblem of Vishnu; *upward and downward triangles:* shakta and shakti, lingam and yoni, Shiva and his shakti, the creation of fire and water; *bee surmounting a triangle:* Shiva • **Masonic** the cosmic triad • **Mayan** sun ray • **Pythagorean** *equilateral triangle:* Athena/Minerva • **Sumero-Semitic** *swastika on a triangle:* the feminine generative power of Astarte • *see also* **hexagram**

triangle (musical instrument) an occasional attribute of Erato

trident the sea; sin; the unconscious; lightning; thunderbolt; sun rays; the eternal; Tree of Life; destruction; the male as creator; the past, present, and future; attribute of sea deities • **Buddhist** the Buddha, the Dharma, and the Sangha; the destruction of anger, desire, and sloth • **Chinese** authority, power • **Christian** in ancient times, the Trinity or a disguised cross, later it was used as an inversion of the Trinity and an attribute of Satan • **Greco-Roman** attribute of Zeus/Jupiter, Poseidon/Neptune, sometimes Amphitrite • **heraldic** maritime dominion; upper class merchant • **Hindu** fire; attribute of Agni, Shiva (especially with a handbell); *trident driven in the ground and a pot:* attribute of Manasa • **Minoan** sea power

trillium • **flower language** modest beauty

triplets sometimes considered unlucky and abandoned at birth

tripod achievement in song or dance; the rising, noonday, and setting sun; past, present, and future; attribute of the Delphic oracle; associated with fire, heaven

triquetra renewal of life; the rising, noonday, and setting sun; the three phases of the moon; lucky; emblem of Sicily, the Isle of Man • **Celtic** Manannan; the Trinity • **Norse** associated with Thor

triskelion the sun; the revival of life and prosperity; motion; energy; victory; fertility

Tristan • **Celtic** self-sacrifice in an unendurable situation

trisula *see* **trident**

Trojan lower emotions; diligence; endurance; war

troll (folklore) malice; evil; sin

trombone voluptuousness • **being played** coition

Trophonius • **Greek** denial of the past to conceal feelings of guilt; fratricide

trousers superiority; adulthood

trout jealousy; sexual activity; adaptability; stubbornness in overcoming obstacles • **Celtic** foreknowledge of the gods; the wisdom and knowledge of the other world; associated with sacred waters and wells

truffle hidden revelation; associated with thunderbolts, lightning • **flower language** surprise

trumpet the call to action; the call of the spirit; power; glory; war; the yearning for power, glory, fame; praise; death; rallying cry; warning; resurrection; the call to worship; attribute of the archangel Gabriel, the personifications of Fame, Terror • **Christian** associated with Judgment Day, the Resurrection of Christ; attribute of angels in heaven, SS Jerome, Vincent Ferrer • **Greco-Roman** attribute of Clio, Calliope, occasionally Euterpe • **heraldic** martial readiness • **Hindu** *shell trumpet:* attribute of Vishnu • **Jewish** attribute of the archangel Gabriel and other angels; *trumpet with sword, pitcher, or scepter:* attribute of Joshua; *seven trumpets:* the fall of Jericho, the seven archangels; *Trumpet of Zion:* associated with Hosea • **Norse** attribute of Heimdall • *see also* **cornet; horn; shofar**

trumpet flower • **flower language** fame; *ash leaved trumpet flower* separation

tsavorite stone for a 25th wedding anniversary

tub • **Christian** *three children in a tub with a bishop:* the bishop is St. Nicholas of Myra

tuba tree • **Islamic** the Celestial Tree, the center of Paradise, origin of the rivers of milk, honey, water, and wine

tuberose • **flower language** dangerous pleasures; voluptuousness; *when received from the hands of a lady:* mutual affection

Tuesday associated with Tiw, Ares/Mars, Scorpio, the archangel Samael, works of wrath • **birthday** Tuesday's child is solemn and sad, or, Born on a Tuesday, full of (God's) grace • **marriage** Tuesday for health • **sneezing** You kiss a stranger • **Jewish** *Creation:* dry land, pastures, trees • *see also* **days**

tulip fame; charity; constancy; declaration of love; chalice of the Eucharist; eloquence; extravagance; renown; magnificence; spirituality; spring; separation; inconstancy; emblem of the Netherlands; associated with Pisces • **flower language** fame; *red tulip:* declaration of love; *variegated tulip:* beautiful eyes; *yellow tulip:* hopeless love; *Near East tulip:* inconstancy, violent love • **heraldic** dreaminess; imagination; perfect love; fame • **Islamic** ardent affection • **Persian** perfect love • **Turkish** emblem of the House of Osman

tumeric • **Hindu** *burning tumeric:* protection against a bhut

tuna wisdom; sagacity; sovereignty

tungsten associated with the archangel Azrael

tunic the soul; the inner self; clothing that reveals the true man, as opposed to a cloak which may be to hide the true man; attribute of monastics • **Christian** attribute of monastics; *soldiers gambling for a tunic:* associated with the Crucifixion • **Greco-Roman** *bloodstained tunic given to Heracles/Hercules by Deianira:* the tunic of Nessus • **Jewish** *bloodstained tunic presented to an old man:* Joseph's garment shown to Jacob • *see also* **cloak**

tunicle • **Christian** service; joy and contentment of heart; worn by a subdeacon at a high mass

tunnel hazardous passage; birth canal; vagina; associated with initiation • **entering a tunnel** coition • **exiting a tunnel** birth • **light tunnel** passage to a higher realm or level of consciousness • **dark tunnel** passage to the underworld or a lower level of consciousness • **underwater tunnel** spiritual passage • **tunnel through a mountain** finding one's way through a difficult situation

tunny *see* **tuna**

turban glory; the glory of the sun; attribute of Middle Eastern peoples, Saracens, the sibyls, Hittites, Babylonians, Egyptians, Sikhs, Incas • **Christian** occasional attribute of St. Veronica • **Islamic** spiritual authority; *black turban:* mission of vengeance; *green turban:* attribute of descendents of Mohammed; *yellow turban:* attribute of angels • **Jewish** attribute of Aaron, Old Testament priests and other Old Testament figures; *white Levite turban:* the full moon; the winding serpent of the moon god

turkey (**bird**) arrogance; pride; foolishness; lunacy; senseless anger; ostentation; vanity; • **American** traditional food for Thanksgiving, Christmas • **restless turkey** harbinger of storms • **North American Indian** *turkey cock:* virility; *turkey hen:* fecundity • **Toltec** a sacred bird

turnip associated with peasants • **flower language** charity • **Taoist** *turnip seed:* a food of the Immortals

turquoise sincere affection; courage; fulfillment; success; earth and water; associated with Capricorn, Aquarius, Sagittarius, Venus (planet), 6th and 11th anniversaries, the archangels Anael, Cassiel, Zadkiel, Sandalphon; birthstone for December; charm for balancing, healing energy, protection from evil • **American** associated with the Southwest • **Amerindian** the sky; the breath of life • **Aztecan** associated with the sky, fire, sun, rain, fertility, rebirth, Spring, the quetzal • **Central American Indian** related to fire, the sun • **Egyptian** *turquoise mask:* attribute of Nut; *turquoise on a bridle:* charm for sure-footedness

turtle lubricity; material existence; natural evolution as opposed to spiritual; longevity; obscurity; slowness; stagnation; highly concentrated materialism; involution; the marriage of heaven and earth; silence; safety; withdrawal; the body is maternal, the head phallic; androgyny • **Amerindian** cowardice; braggadocio; sensuality; the human; the obscene; emblem of Winter • **Chinese** attribute of the god of examinations • **Egyptian** drought; enemy of the sun god • **Maori** agriculture; harvest success • *see also* **tortoise**, with which the turtle is often confused

turtle dove fidelity; affection; love; purity; constancy; joy; plaintiveness; timidity; seclusion; gentleness; a victim; obedience to God's law • **Christian** Christ; *two doves:* Christ's presentation in the Temple • **Greco-Roman** constancy • *see also* **dove**

tusk phallus; an offensive weapon; spiritual power overcoming ignorance and evil; power; strength; an aphrodisiac • **tusk on a grave** immortality • **Mexican Indian** *god with tusks:* Tlaloc

tussilage • **flower language** *sweet scented tussilage:* justice shall be done to you

twilight dichotomy; the dividing line which both joins and separates pairs of opposites; lack of definition; ambivalence; uncertainty; threshold of day and night; end of a cycle; perception of a new state of being; associated with enchantment, mystery • *see also* **dawn; dusk**

twins opposites that have a complementary and opposing function (life/death, sunrise/sunset, etc.); Gemini; the duality of all things; ego and alter ego; sometimes considered unlucky and abandoned at birth • **twin lions back to back** sunrise and sunset • **twin archangels** Metatron and Sandalphon • **African** usually a bad omen • **Australian aboriginal** *twin sisters:* Mar'rallang • **Babylonian** Lachmu and Lachamu • **Christian** SS Cosmas and Damian • **Egyptian** Osiris and Set; *twin lions with human features:* Shu and Tefnut • **Greco-Roman** *twins with eggshell caps:* Castor and Pollux; *twins with she-wolf:* Romulus and Remus • **Hindu** *twin horsemen:* the Ashvins; *twin brother gods:* Nara, Narayana • **Jewish** Cain and Abel; Jacob and Esau; *one twin born clutching the heel of another:* Jacob and Esau respectively • **Lithuanian** *small twin horses pulling the carriage of the sun:* the Asvieniai • **Manichean** the Twin Spirit • **Mayan** *twin brothers:* Hunahpu and Xbalanque • **Mithraic** the dadophoroi • **Norse** Baldur and Loki • **Teutonic** the Alci

twisting deviation; abnormality; irregularity

Tyche/Fortuna • **Greco-Roman** the capricious and arbitrary forces that control human life

Typhon • **Greek** destruction; the father of all monsters; brute stupidity; regression

U

U World Pot; womb; the feminine principle; yoni; cauldron of plenty; the lunar; water; rain; receipt of a gift; associated with Pisces, charm, inspiration, profligacy, good but tenuous fortune, misery, grief, -3- • **tarot** associated with the Cup

Ultima Thule • **Greco-Roman** mystic center; the northern limits of the known world; consciousness; desire; limitation

Ulysses *see* **Odysseus/Ulysses**

umbrella protection; honor; position; mourning; dome of the sky; sun emblem; divine or royal power or protection; avoidance of reality; popular attribute of an Englishman • **Buddhist** (**Chinese**) *umbrella of chaos, darkness, and earthquakes:* attribute of Virudhaka • **Chinese** associated with the spleen • *see also* **parasol**

undertaker the death of an idea; the end of a cycle

unguent divine love and truth

unicorn feminine chastity; purity; virginity; the noblest of animals; uprightness; the word of God; high birth; peace; prosperity; solitude;

guardian of the Tree of Life; wariness; unified, absolute monarchy; sometimes considered an enemy of man; steed of Faith personified; attribute of moon goddesses, virgin goddesses, Chastity personified • **lion and unicorn** two contending powers of the universe, such as positive/negative, male/female • **two unicorns with joined horns** union of opposites • **alchemic** Mercurius • **Chinese** longevity; grandeur; felicity; gentleness; benevolence; good will; the wise administration of government; the illustrious offspring of a family; a good omen; prosperity; peace; an emblem of perfect good • **Christian** Christ; purity; feminine chastity; virginity; solitude; monastic life; attribute of the Virgin Mary, the Annunciation, the Incarnation of Christ, SS Justina of Antioch, Justina of Padua • **Egyptian** moral virtues • **Greco-Roman** the crescent moon; attribute of Artemis/Diana • **heraldic** royalty; knightly power; extreme courage; pugnacity; the word or spirit; virtue; strength; trademark of chemists or druggists signifying the purity of their goods • **Islamic** chastity • **Japanese** virtue; radiant beauty • **Jewish** royalty; power; strength • **Persian** moral virtues; perfection • **Sumero-Semitic** the lunar; attribute of the Tree of Life, virgin goddesses • **Taoist** the essence of virtues and the five elements • *see also* **kundalini; kylin**

United States associated with freedom, democracy, liberty

universal solvent the undifferentiated

Universe (tarot) *see* **World (tarot)**

uraeus • **Egyptian** fire; light; motion; sovereignty; royalty; power over life and death; protection; knowledge; gold; supreme divine and royal power and wisdom; Wadjet; the eye of Ra; created by Is; attribute of pharaohs, Horus, Set; *lion-headed woman with solar disk and uraeus:* Bast • *see also* **asp**

Urania Astronomy personified • **Greek** muse associated with astronomy, cosmological poetry

Uranus/Caelus the unconscious; man's ancestral memory; latent thought; the cycle of evolution; boundless, undifferentiated creative abundance that overwhelms what it creates; chaotic and undifferentiated effervescence

Uranus (planet) associated with originality, the unexpected, the unusual, intuition, insight, going to extremes, personal magnetism, eight, the ankles, Aquarius, boundless space, the will, the unmanifest, the thyroid, the fifth chakra, the archangel Uriel

urchin *see* **sea urchin**

Uriel, Archangel leader of the Seraphim; divine light; associated with the fire of God, prophecy, wisdom, Uranus (planet), platinum, -12-, -17- • **Kabalistic** associated with -2-, gray • **tarot** associated with the House of God

urn death; mourning; fate; the feminine principle; health; purification; cauldron of plenty; attribute of river gods (especially when lying on its side); emblem of Aquarius • **draped urn** death • **river god by urn** Water personified • **urn with a lid on it** the state of supreme enlightenment which triumphs over birth and death • **urn with flame issuing out** resurrection • **Christian** *urn of gold or silver with a white lily:* attribute of the Virgin Mary; *four urns with water flowing from them:* the four evangelists and the four Gospels • **Greco-Roman** *voting urn:* fate; *funeral urn:* attribute of Artemisia; *severed head placed in an urn by two women:* Tomyris with the head of Cyrus; *urn held by woman with boat:* Agrippina the Elder; *urn lying on its side pouring water:* attribute of Alpheus • *see also* **jug; pot; vase**

utensils their symbolism is derived from their practical function as applied to a spiritual plane; secondary implications are derived from shape, color, or material

uterus *see* **womb**

V

V joining; support; until modern times, identical with U; Roman numeral for -5-; associated with metaphysical gifts, earthly success with spiritual gifts, trial, hard work, losses, Taurus, Venus (planet), -4- • **tarot** corresponds to the Lovers

vagina gateway to secret wealth and hidden knowledge; that which takes and gives; gateway to life; the transmutation of opposites • **vagina dentata** fear of castration • **toad eating female genitalia** attribute of Lust personified • *see also* **womb**

Vaishya caste *see* **caste**

vajra • **Buddhist, Hindu** emblem of the footprint of Buddha; attribute of Akshobhya, Agni, Indra; *diamond vajra:* spiritual power; *double vajra:* thunder and lightning;

vale protected life; gloom; declension

valerian benevolence; dissimulation; formerly a perfume but now found offensive; sacred to Hermes/Mercury • **flower language** accommodating disposition; *blue flowered or Greek valer-*

ian: rupture, warfare; *red valerian:* readiness, thought to restore strength, sight, spirits • **Welsh** a girl who put valerian in her underwear would be irresistible to men

Valkyrie • **Norse** the intoxication of enthusiasm; the risks inherent in love conceived as a struggle

valley life; fertility; cultivation; flocks; shelter; neutrality; the soul's secret retreat; peace; security; peacefulness; protection; place of fecundating change • **Chinese** places from which the sun rose and set • **Islamic** place of spiritual passage • **Jewish** death; *valley of bones:* Ezekiel's vision

vampire sin; death; lust for life; turning of the psyche against itself; the devil; a harlot; the aftermath of orgasm • **Greco-Roman** lamia

vase feminine symbol of containment; womb; the Great Mother; fertility; the waters; the heart; acceptance; attribute of the personification of Smell; emblem of Aquarius, Virgo • **full vase** fertility • **empty vase** the body separated from the soul • **woman holding two vases** Temperance personified • **birds drinking from a vase** eternal bliss • **pottery vase** man • **vase of wine** inspiration • **vase with flowers or boughs** the fertility of the waters; spiritual beauty • **woman pouring water from a vase** a river goddess; the Great mother or a female deity pouring out the waters of life and fertility • **man with flowing vase** a river god; libation for a deity • **vase with flame coming from the mouth** the union of fire and water; attribute of the personifications of Charity, Sacred Love • **Buddhist** one of the Eight Emblems of Good Augury; emblem of the footprint of Buddha • **Celtic** healing waters; attribute of mother goddesses • **Chinese** *vase with flowers:* longevity, perpetual harmony; *vase with the waters of life:* attribute of Guanyin • **Christian** *lily in a vase:* attribute of the Virgin Mary at the Annunciation; *vase of ointment (usually with a lid):* attribute of SS Mary Magdalene, Irene; *alabaster vase:* attribute of Mary Magdalene • **Egyptian** life-giving powers of nature; the matrix; the waters; the heart; the Nile; emblem of Isis, Osiris • **Greco-Roman** wine vessel of satyrs; attribute of Hebe, Juventas, Pandora, Psyche; *rope and vase:* attribute of Nemesis/Invidia; *vase with flame coming from the mouth:* attribute of Aphrodite/Venus • **Hindu** the power of shakti • **Sumero-Semitic** • *see also* **jug; urn; pot**

vault the subconscious; hidden talents or wisdom

vegetation abundance; nourishment; immobility; inactivity; laziness; the cyclical existence of all being; the underlying oneness of life; unconscious life • **abundant vegetation** fecundity • **vegetation growing in cycles** death and resurrection

vehicle the ego; the vicissitudes of psychological development; being in a vehicle is the self; seeing a vehicle may indicate someone else's self; the type of vehicle reveals the character, the mind, or the ideas of the driver • **style of driving or piloting** how one controls one's life • **being in a vehicle one does not belong in** not being true to oneself • **running out of fuel** exhaustion, insufficient strength • **overloaded vehicle** too many concerns or too much work • **condition of the vehicle** reflects the condition of the driver or pilot • **crashing vehicle** the destructive power of conflict, an obstacle to development • *see also* specific types of vehicles or steeds (**chariot; horse; motorcycle**, etc.)

veil invisibility; concealment of certain aspects of truth or of the deity; a pre-enlightened state; hiding the self; ignorance; truth; protection from a deity; fertility hidden underground; mystery; inscrutability; secrecy; hidden or esoteric knowledge; chastity; modesty; virginity; death; darkness; separation; atonement; renunciation of the world; attribute of the personifications of Chastity, Prudence, Lust, Hypocrisy • **black veil** death; mourning • **blue veil** attribute of sky deities • **white veil** chastity; virginity • **painted veil** mystery; life and death • **veil with likenesses of animals on it** fecundity • **veil with stars on it** night • **veiled face** inscrutability; secrecy; hidden knowledge; protection of the inner life • **Buddhist** the obscurance of reality • **Christian** chastity; modesty; renunciation of the world; submission; attribute of nuns, St. Agatha; *veil with Christ's likeness on it:* attribute of St. Veronica; *veiled cross:* period when Christ was in the tomb; *Veil of the Temple:* the division of Jews and Gentiles which was rent at the Crucifixion of Jesus; *Carmelite nun being presented a white veil by the Virgin Mary:* St. Mary Magdalene of Pazzi; *woman with veiled eyes:* the Synagogue personified • **Egyptian** concealment; revelation; illumination; *veil of Isis:* the mysteries of all creation • **Greco-Roman** attribute of Hera/Juno; *orange bridal veil:* permanence, fidelity; *man and woman (sometimes veiled) throwing rocks behind them:* Deucalion and Pyrrha • **Islamic** hidden knowledge; attribute of Mohammed; *parting a veil:* revelation • **Hindu** the obscurance of reality; *veil of Maya:* fabric from which the world of phenomena is woven, the obscurance of reality • **Jewish** attribute of Moses after speaking with God; *Veil of the Temple:* the division between heaven and earth • **Phoenician** attribute of Tanit • **Sumero-Semitic** the world of manifestation woven by the Great Goddess

vein vital male energy; maternal links

velvet luxury

Venus *see* **Aphrodite/Venus**

Venus (planet) associated with sexual emotions, love of beauty, the arts and crafts, love in all forms, happiness, the waters, feminine passivity, the passions, desires, synthesis, companionship, music, sympathetic attraction, harmony, gentleness, imagination, green, pale yellow, turquoise (color), -6-, copper, West, Friday, white roses, verbena, woundwort, Taurus, Libra, the throat, back, kidneys, adolescence, the archangel Anael • **Aztecan** Quetzalcoatl • **Babylonian** associated with Ishtar • **Chinese** associated with West, metal • **Hindu** associated with the fourth chakra (thymus) • **Kabalistic** associated with love, West, the archangel Anael, love, fellowship • **Persian** associated with Anahita

Venus' car • **flower language** fly with me

Venus fly trap • **flower language** deceit

Venus' looking glass • **flower language** flattery; vanity

verbena marriage; faithfulness; fertility; sanctity; peace; lucky; used in amulets to bring protection and good luck • **Celtic** had magic properties; venerated by the Druids • **flower language** enchantment; reconciliation; prophecy • **Greco-Roman** sacred to Ares/Mars, Aphrodite/Venus; *verbena wreath:* marriage, protects against spells • **Persian** granter of wishes

veronica • **flower language** fidelity (especially female)

vertical transcendence; aspiration; elevation; progress; connection between heaven and earth • *see also* **horizontal**

vervain *see* **verbena**

vessel *see* **jar; pot; urn; vase; ship; boat**

Vesta *see* **Hestia/Vesta**

vestments attribute of priests • **Jewish** *vestments with bells on the hem:* attribute of Aaron, old Testament priests; *red vestments and scroll:* attribute of Elijah • *see also* **clothes**, and particular vestments (**cassock; surplice**, etc.)

vetch • **flower language** shyness

vial feminine symbol of containment • **Christian** attribute of St. Philip Neri; *dove with a vial in its beak:* attribute of St. Remigius; *two vials on a book:* attribute of St. Januarius

Victoria *see* **Nike/Victoria**

victory subduing of lower nature; that which is conquered often represents the very inferiority of the conqueror himself

Victory (personified) implies spiritual worth

vine Autumn; resurrection; safety; happiness; affection; an unfailing source of natural creation; foundation, root, or basis; associated with Libra; attribute of the personifications of Autumn, Gluttony • **vine wood staff** authority • **elm and vine** the ideal husband and wife (respectively) relationship • **Bulgarian** *crawling naked three times under a vine arch:* cure for scrofula • **Buddhist** covetousness • **Celtic** introspection; relaxation; depth; associated with Venus (planet), emeralds, September • **Christian** Christ; the Christian faith; *vine with branches:* Christ and his followers, Christ and the Church, the relationship between God and his people; *vine with 12 bunches of grapes:* Christ and the Apostles; *vine with wheat:* the Eucharist; *vine with doves resting in it:* spiritual fruitfulness, souls resting in Christ • **Egyptian** sacred to Osiris • **flower language** drunkenness; intoxication • **Greco-Roman** sacred to Apollo; attribute of Dionysus/Bacchus; *vine garland:* attribute of Silenus • **heraldic** hospitality; strong and lasting friendship; strength; peace; luck; plenty; liberality; happiness; truth; belief • **Jewish** the Israelites as the chosen people; attribute of Noah; *vine with fig tree:* peace and plenty, emblem of Israel • **Persian** the joy of life; the wisdom of materiality • **Sumero-Semitic** sacred to Baal, Tammuz; attribute of Geshtinanna • *see also* **vineyard**

vinegar bitterness; sadness; poor man's wine • **alchemic** *antimonial vinegar:* conscience • **Christian** attribute of the Crucifixion; *vinegar and gall:* attribute of the Crucifixion • **Far Eastern** *jar of vinegar:* life

vineyard a place of joy; the female body • **Christian** the Church; the Kingdom of God; a place where the children of God flourish; *work in a vineyard:* the work of good Christians for the Lord • **Jewish** Israel • *see also* **vine**

viol attribute of Music personified; instrument of a pagan feast • **Greco-Roman** attribute of Thalia, Terpsichore, Erato, Orpheus, Apollo, Arion (especially riding a dolphin); *old man playing a viol covered with bay laurel:* Homer • **Jewish** attributed of King David

violet (color) humility; secrecy; suffering; sympathy; fasting; nostalgia; grief; memories; repentance; love of truth; intelligence; knowledge; sanctity; purification; sickness; sadness; temperance; authority; balance between heaven and earth, sense and spirit, passion and reason, love and wisdom, clarity of mind; constancy; deliberate action; mourning; penitence; fasting; love of truth; preparation; a transitional stage (as between sleeping/walking, worldliness/spirituality); half-mourning; death as a phase not a state; a feminine color; associated with Cancer, Aquarius, religious devotion, old age, the archangel Zadkiel • **violet-blue** associated with Capricorn • **red-violet** associated with Pisces • **slate violet** associated with the planets Mercury, Jupiter • **Christian** sacerdotal rule and authority; truth; sadness; fasting; obscurity; fasting; associated with Advent, Lent, the Passion; attribute of St. Mary Magdalene • **Greco-Roman** the color of Apollo's cloak • **Kabalistic** foundation

violet (flower) modesty; sweetness; loyalty; humility; Spring revival; mourning; death; love; faithfulness; constancy; humble life; watchfulness; true virtue; chastity; transience; hidden virtue and beauty • **Christian** humility; the humility of Christ; *white violet:* attribute of the Virgin Mary; *white violets sprouting from death bed:* attribute of St. Fina • **flower language** *blue violet:* faithfulness, love; *dame violet:* watchfulness, you are the queen of coquettes; *purple violet* you occupy my thoughts; *sweet violet* modesty; *wild violet* love in idleness; *yellow violet* rural happiness • **French** emblem of Bonapartists • **Greco-Roman** grew from the blood of Attis; the flower of Ares/Mars, Io; *violet crown:* attribute of Eurydice, the Pleiades, occasionally Athena/Minerva • **heraldic** virtue; modesty; love; affection; faithfulness • **Islamic** *as a carpet motif:* lucky

violin passion; androgyny

viper unnatural treachery; evil genius; ingratitude; unconscious impulses not yet integrated into the conscious; the devil; sin; the undifferentiated; associated with Saturn (planet) • **Egyptian** a place of spiritual transformation; an agent of change; *horned viper:* Cerastes

Virgil worldly wisdom

virgin innocence; fear; wisdom; self love; purity; purified emotions; latency; the unrevealed; the soul emptied to receive the divine seed; Virgo; the soul in its primordial innocent state • **black virgin** the void; the darkness of the undifferentiated; two opposing aspects of the Great Mother —creator/destroyer, birth/death, etc. • **Christian** *five maidens with lit lamps:* the five wise virgins; *five maidens with extinguished lamps:* the five foolish virgins • *see also* **maiden**

virgin birth union of the divine and the human, union of heaven and earth; the birth of higher faculties in man • *see also* **virgin mother**

Virgin Mary • **Christian** virtuous womanhood; the Mother Church which Christ left in the world; the feminine aspect of Christ; the soul made perfectly one with God; a bridge between heaven and earth; *black Madonna:* virgin soil yet to be fertilized; the passive aspect of virginity; *Virgin Mary appearing to a bishop in a vision:* the bishop is St. Andrew Corsini; *image of the Virgin Mary being painted:* attribute of St. Luke; *Carmelite nun being presented a white veil by the Virgin Mary:* St. Mary Magdalene of Pazzi

virgin mother the primordial state; the matrix; light bearer; transforming power • *see also* **virgin birth**

Virginia creeper *see* **clematis**

virgin's bower (plant) • **flower language** filial love

Virgo hermaphroditism; the duality of all things; supreme expression of dynamic consciousness; associated with the birth of a demigod, Mercury (planet), modesty, analytic thought, harvest, work, cleanliness, neatness, worry, conventionality, criticism, retention, control, self-discipline, scrupulosity, attachment to rules and regulations, the archangel Raphael

viscera lower qualities • **hanged corpse with its viscera out** Judas Iscariot • **woman eating her own viscera** Envy personified • *see also* **intestines**

Vishnu • **Hindu** divine preservation; the supreme deity

voice unmaterial existence; conscience

volcano fertility; evil destruction; the fire of creation; primary forces of nature; divine destruction or punishment; tremendous passions; anger • **erupting volcano** the male orgasm; the sudden attack of the unconscious on the conscious • **dormant volcano** repressed emotions

volkemania • **flower language** may you be happy

vomit rejection; cleansing of the self; repulsiveness

vowel the masculine principle

voyage emotional or spiritual experience; searching the unconscious • *see also* **journey; pilgrimage**

Vulcan *see* **Hephaestus/Vulcan**

vulture a mother image; death; destruction; punishment; remorse; purification; compassion; portent of evil tidings, death, major troubles; protection; fertility; sun; wind; righteousness; Summer; heat; sedition; rapacity; robbery; gluttony; scavenger; hypocrisy; the devil; ruthlessness; revenge; evil; a woman 60 to 70 years old; attribute of a desolate place, Nature personified • **Dahomean** *bald-headed man with a vulture's* *body:* Suvinenge • **Egyptian** the Mother Goddess; maternity; maternal love; purification; good works; protection; the cycle of death and life in a ceaseless series of transmutations; a form of Isis; attribute of Neith, Nekebet, Mut; *vulture-headed goddess:* Hathor; *vulture headdress:* attribute of Hathor, Mut; *scarab and vulture:* attribute of Ptah; *vulture on a basket:* conception within the womb • **Greco-Roman** bird of augury; sacred to Apollo; steed of Cronos/Saturn; *vulture pecking at giant's liver:* Tityus; *scarab and vulture:* attribute of Athena/Minerva • **heraldic** purification; maternity; virginity • **Hindu** scavenger • **Mayan** death; an agent of regeneration; associated with water • **South American Indian** the first possessor of fire • *see also* **harpy**

vulva *see* **vagina**

W

W associated with wavering emotions, change, acquisition, adventurousness, words, travel, any twin formations (such as Gemini), surprises, things held in abeyance, the liver, -5- • **tarot** associated with the World

wading progressing with a certain degree of resistance; cautious progress; spiritual passage

wafer the sun; sacrifice to the moon goddess • **Christian** the Host of the Eucharist • *see also* **Host**

wagtail amorousness; attribute of Comeliness personified • **Greco-Roman** the enchantment of love; associated with Aphrodite/Venus, Jason, Medea • **Japanese** the demiurge; the teacher of sexual intercourse to Izanagi and Izanami

wake robin • **flower language** ardor

walking • **Mediterranean** *dreaming of walking on water:* good omen for a sea voyage • *see also* **circumambulation; procession**

wall defense; safety; sacred enclosure; prohibition; woman; wisdom; salvation; prosperity; impotence; delay; resistance; a limiting situation; the separation between worlds; protection (especially when the wall is viewed from the inside); limitation to communication • **city walls** the feminine principle; shelter; safety • **wall of flame** initiation; magic protection • **wall painting** absolute knowledge • **Babylonian** *seven walls:* attribute of Aralu • **Egyptian** rising above ordinary levels; *White Wall:* separation of the Upper and Lower Kingdoms • **Hindu** stability; comprehensiveness

wallet feminine containment; conservation; memory; attribute of merchants, messenger gods • **Christian** attribute of almoners, pilgrims, Judas Iscariot, SS Matthew, Nicholas; *beggar with wallet as shoulder bag:* St. Felix of Cantalice; *saint with wallet and staff, sword, or letters SJ:* St. James the Greater; *archangel with wallet, staff and gourd or fish:* Raphael • **Greco-Roman** attribute of Hermes/Mercury, Perseus, Priapus

wallflower (plant) • **flower language** shyness; fidelity in misfortune; *garden wallflower:* lasting beauty wallowing depravity; a sacrificial act to encourage inversion or change

walnut hidden wisdom; longevity; fertility; selfishness; strength in adversity • **flower language** intellect; strategy • **Christian** *split walnut:* Christ (the outer casing represents his flesh; the hard shell, the wood of the cross; the kernel, his divine nature) • **Greco-Roman** prophecy; longevity; *stewed walnuts:* fertility, served at weddings; *walnut tree:* sacred to the Laconian Artemis • **heraldic** *walnut leaves:* joy; hope • **Italian** *double walnut:* charm against the evil eye, witches, headache, and for good luck • *see also* **nut**

waltzing harmonious cooperation; blithe progress

wand intensity; authority; power; controller of supernatural force; direction; phallus; authority; conjuring; measuring; attribute of Grammar personified, musical conductors • **magic wand** attribute of magicians, sorcerers, shamans, medicine men, Circe, Hypnos/Somnus • **wand and staff** official authority • **Amerindian** punishment; pain • **Celtic** *golden wand:* attribute of a bard of the first rank; *silver wand:* attribute of a bard of the second rank; *bronze wand:* attribute of the third or lower rank • **Christian** *flowering wand:* attribute of St. Joseph • **Druidic** *magic wand:* power over the elements • **Greco-Roman** *magic wand:* attribute of Asclepius, Hermes/Mercury; *wand tipped with a globe surmounted by an eagle:* attribute of Jupiter, Roman Legions • **heraldic** authority • **Jewish** *flowering wand:* attribute of Aaron; *wand and staff:* attribute of Jeremiah

wandering aimless, pointless movement • **Buddhism** samsara

Wandering Jew • **Christian** the imperishable side of man which cannot die

wands (playing cards) *see* **clubs (playing cards)**

war the struggle of good against evil; disintegration and reintegration; the seeking of unity; conflict within oneself

warlock *see* **sorcerer**

warmth love; comfort; protection; maternal comfort • *see also* **heat**

warp *see* **weaving**

warrior *see* **soldier**

wart self-criticism; self-punishment; associated with the devil, sexual potency, boorishness, crudity

washerwoman • **Celtic** *hag or beauty washing bloody clothes at a ford:* death omen • **Hindu** a woman of low caste; sexual depravity; associated with wisdom; *coition of washerwoman and sage:* the union of opposites

washing purification from guilt, subjective and inner evils, ritual uncleanness • **washing in a stream** death omen • **washing hands** ritual purification; self-proclamation of innocence • **washing in sacred water** obtaining the virtues of the water • **Buddhist** in the initiation of a monastic, washing away one's lay past • **Islamic** the return to primordial purity

Washington, George • **American** honesty; patriotism

wasp evil; viciousness; irritation; petty danger; generally an unfavorable symbol, but it can mean love

watch *see* **clock**

watchtower consciousness; alertness • *see also* **tower**

water the source and grave of all things; the source of all potentialities in existence; mystery; fertility; the personal or collective unconscious; the Great Mother; the universal womb; innocence; sexuality; baptism; regeneration; refreshment • **immersion, or ritual immersion (baptism)** purification; rebirth; regeneration • **looking into water** contemplation • **drinking or drawing water from a well** the soul or mind acquiring truth • **African** attribute of Mami Wata • **alchemic** cleaning, purification, one of the four basic elements • **Aztecan** primeval chaos • **Buddhism** the perpetual flux of the manifest world • **Celtic** *lakes, sacred wells:* abode of supernatural beings, access to other worlds, other-world wisdom, location of Tir-nan-og • **Chinese** yin; the lunar; purity; the North region; *blood and water:* yin and yang; *as an element:* associated with, seriousness, salt taste, rain, yellow millet, pigs, the kidneys, black, blood, anger, -1- • **Christian** regeneration; baptism; cleansing; sanctification; *water mixed with wine at the Eucharist:* Christ's humanity and divinity respectively, the spirit acting upon acting upon the earthly, the mingling of the divine and the human; *holy water:* purification, expulsion of evil; *blood and water at the Crucifixion:* the life of the body and the life of the spirit respectively • **Egyptian** birth; growth; regeneration;

god pouring water from two pots: Hapi • **Incan** primeval chaos • **Islamic** mercy; life; purification; gnosis • **Jewish** the Deluge; attribute of Reuben; *water gushing from a rock:* associated with Moses • **Kabalistic** associated with the archangels Anael, Azrael • **Mandaean** *water and wine:* union of the Cosmic Father and Cosmic Mother • **Masonic** corresponds to the soul, religion • **Mediterranean** *dream of walking on water:* good omen for a sea voyage • **Mongolian** associated with West • **North American Indian** the flowing power of the Great Spirit • **Sumero-Semitic** *watering pot:* attribute of Ea-Oannes; *water flowing from the arms and/or hands of a god:* the god is Ea-Oannes • **Taoist** the strength of weakness; the power of adaptation and persistence; the fluidity of life; the doctrine of wu-wei • **Tungun** associated with West • **zodiacal** associated with Pisces, Cancer, Scorpio; *man pouring water:* emblem of Aquarius

water bouget • **heraldic** supplier of water to an army or a besieged place

water buffalo serenity; contentment; agriculture

water cress old age; renewal of life; rejuvenation; redemption • *see also* **cress**

water fly busy fertility; something small and unimportant; an effeminate homosexual

water jug *see* **pot; jug**

water lily eloquence; fertility; charity; companionship; companionability; beneficence; purity; stability in an unstable environment; associated with Pisces, the moon • **Egyptian** the loveliest of flowers; the cradle of the sun • **flower language** purity of heart • **heraldic** eloquence; persuasion • **Hindu** *four-armed woman sitting on a water lily:* Manasa • **Mayan** plenty; fertility

water mill time; the material world of phenomena; fertility • *see also* **mill; water wheel; water; wheel**

water pot *see* **pot**

water sprite • **Amerindian** tempter; seducer; associated with change, decay, supporters of the world

water wheel fate; time; industry • *see also* **water; wheel; water mill**

waterfall • impermanence; continuous evolution; continuous motion **Chinese** humility • **Japanese** *primary waterfall:* the masculine principle; *secondary waterfall:* the feminine principle

watermelon fertility • **American** associated with Negroes in a pejorative sense • **flower language** bulkiness

waves (ocean) regeneration; righteousness; the feminine principle; the passive; the female orgasm; maternity and death; the flux and reflux of life; dreams; the unconscious; purity; change; illusion; vanity; ceaseless motion; renewed spiritual vigor; associated with dancing; not to be confused with an ocean swell • **storm waves** the sudden inroads of the unconscious; mental or emotional turmoil • **diving into waves** a break in the normal lifestyle; a radical change in ideas, beliefs, behavior • **Jewish** insidious moral dangers • *see also* **ocean**

wax secrecy; elevation; pliability; insincerity; pure flesh; humanity • **melting wax** fear; hot love • **sealing wax** *see* **seal** • **Greek** associated with the wings of Icarus

wax plant • **flower language** susceptibility

weapon conflict; power; often supernatural; dominion; protection; destruction; the will directed toward a certain end; thesis and antithesis as the counterpart to monsters or enemies; the powers of spiritualization and sublimation; attribute of the personifications of Europe, the Iron Age • **woman reclining on weapons** Victory personified • **woman destroying weapons** Peace personified • **exchanging weapons** friendship • **sharp weapons** fire • **Greco-Roman** *weapon in a blacksmith's forge:* attribute of Hephaestus/Vulcan • **Japanese** *woman holding weapons in eight arms:* Benzaiten • *see also* specific weapons, such as **knife; lance; spear; sword;** etc.

wear signs of wear indicate weariness of spirit, poor health, or an extinct or outmoded idea

weasel vigilance; courage; slenderness; bloodthirstiness; arrogant quarrelsomeness; avarice; killer of vermin; squirminess; emblem of Christ

weather cock, weather vane inconstancy; frivolity; foolhardiness; versatility; showiness; vigilance; watching for evil; *gilded:* solar power • **Christian** *weather cock on a church:* guard of the steeple at night when the bells are silent; St. Peter (especially when crowing); his denial and subsequent repentance; a reminder to be humble; *red weather cock on a church:* an occasional emblem of Catholicism • *see also* **rooster**

weaving creation; life; snare; ladder to heaven; peace and concord; the union of opposites; the union of the masculine and feminine principles • **warp** the vertical plane joining all degrees of existence; immutability; the masculine; sunlight • **woof (weft)** the horizontal plane; manifest nature; instability; the human state; the feminine; moonlight • **weaving as a feminine activity** the world of matter; creation; life; vegetation; order and balance in nature; love; poetry • **weaving as a masculine activity** an incomplete man • **Chinese** alternation of yin and yang • **Christian** *warp:* the fundamental doctrine of Scripture; *woof (weft):* commentary on Scripture • **Egyptian** associated with Neith • **Greco-Roman** associated with Arachne, Athena/Minerva, Harmonia, the Moirae/Fates, Penelope • **Hindu** the breath of life • **Norse** associated with the Norns • **Sumero-Semitic** associated with Atargatis, Ishtar • **Teutonic** associated with Holda, the Valkyries • *see also* **loom; distaff; spindle; thread**

web destiny; entanglement; mystic center and the unfolding of Creation; illusion; the Labyrinth; rays of the sun; the world of phenomena; false trust or hope; the laws of man; sin; sorrow; despair; entrapment • **spider web** human frailty; the negative side of the universe; decay; desolation; fine work; transience; the laws of man that catch small transgressors but let the big ones escape; the cosmic plan • **spider in the center of its web** the sun and its rays; the cycle of life and death with death at the center; the wheel of existence • **Buddhist** maya • **Christian** snare of the devil; snare of human frailty; the malice of evil-doers • **Greek** *spider's web with woman at loom:* the woman is Arachne • **Hindu** maya • *see also* **net; spider; web**

Wednesday associated with Mercury (planet), Woden, the archangel Raphael, works of science, Gemini • **birthday** Wednesday's child is merry and glad, or, Born on a Wednesday, sour and sad (or, full of woe) • **marriage** the best of all • **sneezing** you sneeze for a letter • **Jewish** *Creation:* heavenly bodies • *see also* **days**

weeding discarding useless or negative ideas

weeds disorder; grossness; sin; carelessness; the lower qualities driving out the higher; negative thoughts, ideas

weeping grief; mourning; cleansing; associated with Tammuz

weft *see* **weaving**

weight the burden of sin • **lightness** indicates an advanced spiritual state; wisdom

well baptism; life; rebirth; refreshment, especially spiritual; fortune; plenty; secrecy; source of life; time; access to earth gods; the feminine principle; attribute of the Great Goddess; the womb of the Great Mother; the psyche • **well with trees** divine marriage; vulva and phallus • **well fed by a stream** the union of feminine and masculine respectively • **peering into a well** contemplation • **drawing water from a well** acquiring truth • **putting money or other offerings into a well** an offering to the gods, especially earth gods • **Well of Life** mystic center • **Celtic** *sacred wells:* abode of supernatural beings, access to other worlds, other-world wisdom, location of Tir-nan-og • **Chinese** sincerity; righteousness; lucky • **Christian** salvation; purification; the Gospel; typical meeting place; *sealed well:* the Virgin Mary • **Far Eastern** abyss of hell • **Islamic** *two angels hanging upside down in a Babylonian well:* Harut and Marut • **Jewish** the Torah; typical meeting place; *well with fruitful bough above:* attribute of Joseph • **Kabalistic** *well fed by a stream:* marriage

werewolf the irrationality latent in man and the possibility of its reawakening

West death; to turn West is to prepare to die; Autumn; middle age; evening; the waning moon; the setting sun; abode of evil; abode of demons; completion; darkness; associated with Venus (planet), the archangels Gabriel, Michael, Zadkiel • **Amerindian** home of the Thunderer • **Bambaran** associated with goodness, loveliness, birds • **Buddhist** attribute of Amitabha • **Chinese** Autumn; sorrow; dryness; associated with metal, white, the White Tiger • **Christian** the region of darkness • **Congolese** home of evil spirits • **Dogon** associated with plants, insects, wild animals • **Mexican Indian** land of the setting sun, old age, evening; gateway to the mysterious rain, fertility goddesses • **Mongolian** associated with water • **Siberian** direction of the dead • **Tungun** associated with water, blood

whale the world; cunning; deceit; lust; avarice; mystic center; the grave; brawn without intellect; regeneration; the power of the cosmic waters; associated with the archangel Zadkiel • **modern** the grandeur or nobility of nature and the need to conserve it • **Christian** the devil; Christ and his resurrection; *fish swimming into a whale's mouth:* unsuspecting souls trapped by the devil; *the open jaws of a whale:* the gates of hell; *the belly of a whale:* hell • **Jewish** attribute of Jonah; *belly of the whale:* place of death and rebirth; *emerging from the belly of a whale:* rebirth, emerging from initiation into new life • *see also* **Leviathan**

wheat prosperity; wisdom; the bounty of the earth; a spermatic image • **grain goddesses with wheat** agriculture • **wheat with grapes** agriculture; attribute of earth goddesses • **Christian** the bread of the Eucharist; the Body of Christ; bounty; the righteous; the godly; *wheat with grapes:* the Eucharist; *wheat with vine:* the bread and wine of the Eucharist respectively; *wheat with tares:* the believers and nonbelievers, respectively, in the Church that will be separated out at Judgment Day; *wheat with tares:* believers and nonbelievers who will be separated at Judg-

ment Day; *wheat stack:* the body of Christ • **flower language** prosperity • **Greco-Roman** attribute of Cronus/Saturn, Demeter/Ceres • **heraldic** *wheat ear:* faithfulness; *sheaf of wheat:* the harvest of one's hopes has been secured • **Jewish** *stalk of wheat:* associated with Ruth • **Sumero-Semitic** sacred to Cybele; attribute of Tammuz, Dumuzi, Dagon • *see also* **sheaf**

wheel the sun; solar power; the passage of time; the cycle of life; fortune; the zodiac; mutability; torture; transcendence; progress; the manifest world; the mutability of the manifest world; completion; power; dominion; nobility; associated with the lotus; attribute of sun gods, sun kings, the personifications of Fortune, Inconstancy • **chariot wheel** sovereignty; authority • **winged wheel** swiftness • **prayer wheel** the active force of the word • **wheels within wheels** male and female; complex influences at work • **ship's wheel, steering wheel** control • **Assyrian** *solar wheel:* emblem of Ashur • **Buddhist** time; sovereignty; destiny; the cosmos; the Wheel of the Law; the Round of Existence; the symmetry and completeness of the Dharma; the dynamism of peaceful change; Buddha; emblem of the footprint of Buddha; attribute of Vairocana • **Christian** attribute of SS Erasmus, Euphemia, Quentin; *candles set around a wheel rim:* attribute of SS Blaise, Donatian; *wheel with knives or spikes in it:* attribute of St. Catherine of Alexandria; *winged wheel:* the Holy Spirit • **Greco-Roman** fate; the cycle of generation; emblem of Dionysus/Bacchus; *wheel with six spokes:* attribute of Zeus/Jupiter; *solar wheel:* the sun chariot of Apollo, Helios/Sol; *fiery wheel:* the punishment of Ixion • **heraldic** cycle of life; fortune • **Hindu** unending and perfect completion; attribute of Varuna, Vishnu, Vayu • **Jain** time • **Jewish** attribute of the expulsion of Adam and Eve from the Garden of Eden; *wheel with eyes on rim:* Ezekiel's vision; *flaming wheels with wings or eyes:* the throne of God; *winged wheel:* associated with Cherubim; *winged wheels within wheels:* Thrones (angels) • **Mithraic** the sun • **Sumero-Semitic** *solar wheel:* attribute of Baal, Shamash, war gods • **Taoist** the world of phenomena; the sage; wu-wei

Wheel of Fortune (tarot) manifestation; fecundity; the equilibrium of contrary forces of expansion and contraction; the principle of polarity; the mystery of all things; the intermingling of the disparate; law of cause and effect; unchanging reality despite changing events; unexpected turn of luck; irreversible fate; divine will; evolution; progress; success; balance; associated with the archangel Zadkiel, the need to make prudent and wise decisions

wheelbarrow labor; poverty; suffering; drunkenness; enhancement of human strength

whetstone lying; wit

whin • *flower language* anger

whip domination; mastery; authority; rule; government; superiority; punishment; slavery; sovereignty by force; impetus; fertility; victory; hunting; phallus; penitence; remorse; conscience; lightning; attribute of Grammar personified, royalty, the Terrible Mother, the Agrippine sibyl • **Chinese** the power to drive away evil; happiness; attribute of Vaisravenna • **Christian** Christ's cleansing of the Temple, attribute of SS Vincent of Saragossa, occasionally Mary Magdalene; *whip with three knots:* attribute of St. Ambrose; *whip with stone and open Bible:* attribute of St. Jerome; *two saints, one with a whip, one with sword:* SS Gervase and Protase respectively • **Egyptian** authority; strength; the power to drive away care; happiness, pleasure; attribute of Menat, Osiris, Min • **Greco-Roman** attribute of Apollo, Cybele, Dionysus/Bacchus, Hecate, Poseidon/Neptune, Erinyes/Furies; *woman with torch and bloody whip driving the chariot of Mars:* Bellona • **Jewish** *whip with pile of bricks:* Israel in bondage • *see also* **scourge**

whipping initiation; purification; expiation; fertility; sexual stimulation; restoring of male vitality; promotion of fertility; introversion • *see also* **scourging**

whipping post • **Christian** attribute of the Passion

whirlpool passions; emotions; the source of life, natural energy, magic; female sexuality at its most frightening and mysterious level • *see also* **spiral**

whirlwind universal evolution; invincible power; violence; destruction; transcendence; ascent and descent; space; the angry voice of a deity; steed of souls to the next world, deities; associated with wind, rain, and thunder deities • **Aymaran** attribute of Anchanchu • **Egyptian** an aspect of Typhon • **North American Indian** the Great Spirit; the power of the Great Spirit • **witchcraft** steed of witches, wizards, evil spirits • *see also* **spiral; whirlwind**

whisk *see* **fly whisk**

whisky *see* **intoxicants**

whisper secrecy; witchcraft

whistling idleness; frittering away time; boredom; signal; a magical act; cleanness; pretense of in-

nocence; a typical male activity, sometimes considered a taboo for women

white the purest of all colors; attribute of creator deities; associated with sun, air, illumination, peace, purity, perfection, faith, timelessness, the undifferentiated, transcendent perfection, ecstasy, the moon, lividness, spiritual intuition, simplicity, cowardice, blandness, reason, amnesty, nobility, consummate wisdom, humility, integrity, light, joy, detachment from worldliness, glory, perfection, chastity, holiness, sacredness, spiritual authority, redemption, the First Heaven • **white in connection with death** birth into a new life; a loss that will be filled • **white in connection with matrimony** death to the old life and birth into the new life • **red, white, and black** the three stages of initiation • **white flag** surrender; truce; peaceful intent • **white rose** inspired wisdom; chaste love; purity • **white robe** purity; chastity; triumph of the spirit over the flesh; attribute of goddesses of death • **African** associated with healing, the dead, the first phase of initiation • **alchemic** associated with enlightenment, happiness, woman, the feminine principle, the White Lily, the moon, silver, Mercurius, the purity of undivided light, the second stage of the Great Work, innocence • **Arabian** associated with Arabs until the Umayyad dynasty • **Aztecan** the dying sun • **Bambaran** associated with East • **Buddhist** redemption; mastery of self; the Mother of all Buddhas; the White Tara; the highest spiritual transformation through womanhood; associated with the center, teaching; attribute of Vairocana; *red, white, and blue:* Brahma, Vishnu, and Shiva; intelligence, order, and unity • **Celtic** the terrestrial goddess • **Chinese** Autumn; West; metal; mourning; the White Tiger; *white face on an actor:* a cunning, treacherous, but dignified man; *white nose on an actor:* a comedian • **Christian** vestment color for matrimony, baptism, first communion, death, confirmation; associated with chastity, faith, joy, purity, virginity, holiness, light, integrity, Easter, Christmas, Epiphany, Ascension; attribute of the Creator, the Virgin Mary, St. John, saints who did not suffer martyrdom; *white with red:* the devil, Purgatory, death • **Druidic** worn by priests and at baptism • **Egyptian** associated with good luck, mourning, Osiris; *white and green:* joy • **Greco-Roman** mourning; love; live and death; divine purity; emblem of Zeus/Jupiter; *white robe:* attribute of Aphrodite/Venus • **heraldic** purity; faith; peace; sincerity • **Hindu** pure consciousness;

self-illumination; light, East; sattva; manifestation; the color of Shiva, Arjuna, Brahman, the Sudra caste, the priesthood • **Islamic** purity; light; peace; a lucky color; associated with light, sunshine, opposition groups, the Koran • **Italian** emblem of the Ghibellines • **Japanese** emblem of the Minamoto clan • **Jewish** joy; cleansing • **Kabalistic** the Crown • **Kalmyk** East • **Korean** mourning • **Maori** truce; surrender • **Masonic** associated with wisdom, grace, victory • **Mayan** associated with health, hope, North, peace, promise, the first man, the first tree • **Norse** *white robe:* attribute of Freyja, Hel; *half-white/half-black goddess:* Hel • **North American Indian** sacredness • **Oriental** mourning • **Persian** *white, red, and gold:* purity, love, and revelation; emblem of the Persian trinity • **Pueblo** associated with East

White House • **American** emblem of the American government, especially the presidency

Whitsunday *see* **Pentecost**

whore *see* **prostitute**

whortleberry • **flower language** treason

wick *see* **taper (wick)**

wig façade; false beliefs

wild man, wild woman primeval force; the primitive, instinctive, baser part of the personality; the unconscious in its perilous and regressive aspect; lust; aggression • **heraldic** *as supporters:* base forces of nature subjugated and transcended • *see also* **savage**

wildcat • **African** *wildcat skin:* used for medicine bags • **Amerindian** stealth; a hunter god • **Central African** clairvoyance • **heraldry** vigilance; keen vision; courage; liberty; individualism; indefatigability; cunning; strategy • **Pawnee** cunning, forethought, ingenuity, a sacred animal

wildflower natural beauty; the short, perhaps unhappy, life • *see also* the names of specific flowers

will o' the wisp *see* **fox fire**

willow sadness; mourning; desperation; grief; abandonment; sterility; celibacy; forsaken love; eloquence; poetry; joy, but in later times, mourning; misery; quick growth; endurance; femininity; slenderness; associated with miraculous births, Pisces, the archangels Gabriel, Sandalphon, Asariel; emblem of the East, the rising sun • **willow branch** mercy • **willow switch** associated with whipping; punishment • **willow basket** protection • **willow wreath** bereavement; death; mourning • **male willow tree** purity • **Ainu** material of the first man • **Akkadian** the Cosmic Tree; sacred to Zeus • **Bud-**dhist meekness • **Celtic** imagination; intuition; vision; attribute of Esus; associated with the moon, moonstone, April/May • **Chinese** yin; the lunar; Spring; power over demons; purification; artistic ability; parting; femininity; grace; charm; emblem of meekness; attribute of Guanyin • **Christian** the Gospel; occasional substitute for a palm on Palm Sunday • **Far Eastern** immortality • **flower language** *weeping willow:* love forsaken, mourning; *French willow:* bravery and humanity; *water willow:* freedom • **Greco-Roman** emblem of Artemis/Diana; sacred to Europa; birthplace of Hera/Juno; attribute of Prometheus • **heraldic** pliancy; serenity; patience; friendship; perseverance • **Hindu** emblem of Avalokitesvara • **Japanese** perseverance; patience • **Jewish** mourning; associated with the Feast of the Tabernacles • **North American Indian** (prairie tribes) seasonal rebirth; *turtle dove with willow leaves in its beak:* messenger of the cycle of rebirth • **Russian** associated with death • **Sumero-Semitic** happiness; rejoicing; triumph; emblem of Tammuz; *willow branch:* emblem of Artemis, childbirth • **Taoist** strength in weakness • *see also* **osier**

willow-herb • **flower language** *spiked willow-herb* pretension

wimple • **white wimple and black robe** mourning • **German** attribute of married women

wind destruction; evil powers; air in its active and violent aspects; desire; regeneration; freedom; inconstancy; fickleness; instability; empty-headedness; transience; elusiveness; caprice; inducer of ecstasy, poetic inspiration; life force; vital breath of the universe; messenger of the gods; the spirit; time; nothingness; speed; madness; harbinger of change • **North wind** destruction; creativity; Winter; frost; cold; religious persecution • **South wind** heat; warmth; Summer • **East wind** morning; bringer of rain; wantonness; comforter; an ill omen • **West wind** mildness; gentleness; fertility; the Autumn; evening; death • **Christian** the Holy Spirit • **Islamic** messenger of God • **Jewish** God's breath; messenger of God • **Zoroastrian** world foundation; cosmic and moral balance keeper • *see also* **breeze; Khamsin; whirlwind**

wind chimes the ability to maintain harmony in emotional turbulence

winding sheet *see* **shroud**

windlass compulsion • *see also* **capstan**

windmill fertility; harvest; combines the symbolism of air or wind, and the wheel; emblem of the Netherlands • **children playing with toy windmills** allegory of Air • **windmill with a**

balance attribute of the personification of Temperance • **Christian** attribute of St. James the Less; *windmill with ship and fish:* attribute of St. Mary of Cleophas • **Spanish** *knight charging a windmill:* Don Quixote

window consciousness; possibility; communication; receptivity; penetration; the eyes; vigilance • **square window** terrestrial receptivity • **round window** spiritual receptivity • *see also* **rose window** • **red lattice window** an alehouse • **Masonic** *three windows:* South, East, and West

wine blood; sacrifice; youth and eternal life; the spiritual nature of love and wisdom; a spiritual drink; intoxication; inspiration; revelation; wisdom; resurrection; lust; truth; violence; putrefaction; gladness; rejoicing; revelry • **pouring wine on the ground** bloodletting in ritual sacrifice; offering to underworld gods; libation for the dead • **spilled wine** death omen • **mixed wine** euphemism for semen • **bread and wine** man and divinity respectively; the feminine and masculine respectively; androgyny; the visible manifestation of the spirit and divine ecstasy respectively; food of funerals • **wine and water** the solar and the lunar respectively; the blending of divine and human nature respectively • **wine and bread** the masculine and feminine respectively; the balanced product of agriculture • **alchemic** the process of Fermentation, the spiritualization of matter • **Christian** *water mixed with wine at the Eucharist:* Christ's humanity and divinity respectively, the spirit acting upon acting upon the earthly, the mingling of the divine and the human; *napkin and cruse of wine:* attribute of the Good Samaritan; *bread and wine:* the Eucharist, the two natures of Christ, the body and blood of Christ • **Greco-Roman** associated with Dionysus/Bacchus • **Islamic** the drink of the elect in Paradise • **Jewish** joy; *glass of wine set out on Seder nights:* gift for Elijah; *wine as intoxicant:* the blindness of those who lack faith; *ten drops of wine poured out on Passover:* the ten plagues visited upon Egypt

wine press the wrath of God; slaughter; destruction; thirst; Christ; patient or solitary labor or suffering • **Strength personified standing on a wine press** the conquest of the spirit over the heart

wineskin sin; evil-mindedness; heavy conscience; attribute of Silenus, satyrs

wings spirituality; spiritualization; imagination; thought; intelligence; justice; the possibility of spiritual evolution; divine mission; victory; healing; misfortune; chance; elevation; virtue; authority; power; glory; protection; time; speed; fancy; meditation; the soul; resurrection; divinity; personification of a fleeting occurrence; healing; attribute of angels, heavenly beings, Father Time, the personifications of Fame (usually with trumpet), History (usually with tablet), Peace (usually with doves), Fortune (usually with blindfold and globe), Opportunity, Fate, Night (usually with two infants), Melancholy (usually sitting) • **wings of skin** perversion of the higher qualities of wings; attribute of the devil, infernal creatures • **four wings** ubiquity • **angel with three pairs of wings** a seraph • **winged head** a cherub • **winged orb** spiritual elevation • **winged animals** the sublimation of that animal's specific positive virtues (for example, a winged bull may represent courage, nobility) • **spread wings** aspiration • **winged serpent** the union of spirit and matter • **winged hand** attribute of Poverty personified • **winged lion** androgyny; the union of two natures; emblem of Venice; attribute of Venice personified • **alchemic** volatility • **Assyrian** *eagle-headed god with wings and disk, or winged disk alone:* Ashur • **Buddhist** *two wings:* wisdom and method • **Chinese** *winged dragon:* celestial power, vital spirit; *blue man with wings, claws, drum, mallet and chisel:* Lei-kung; *two birds with a shared wing:* fidelity, lovers, indissoluble unity; *red and yellow bird with six feet and four wings:* chaos • **Christian** *winged head:* occasional early symbol of Christ; *winged man:* occasionally St. Matthew; occasional early Christian symbol of Christ; *winged deacon:* St. Josaphat; *bat wings:* attribute of the devil, demons • **Egyptian** occasional attribute of Neith; *winged ram with four heads:* the North wind, Qebui; *four-winged snake-headed man:* the East wind, Henkhisesui; *lion-headed man with four wings:* the South wind, Shehbui; *lion with four wings:* the South wind, Shehbui; *four-winged, ram-headed man:* the West wind, Hutchaiui • **Greco-Roman** attribute of Aphrodite/Venus, Artemis/Diana, Athena/Minerva, Eros/Cupid, Iris, Nemesis/Invidia, Eos/Aurora, Erinyes/Furies; Nike/Victoria; *four wings:* attribute of Chronos; *dark wings:* attribute of Hypnos/Somnus; *winged shoes and/or hat:* attribute of Hermes/Mercury, Perseus; *man making wings:* Dedalus; *man and youth flying with wings:* Dedalus and Icarus respectively; *wings of Icarus:* functional insufficiency; *butterfly wings:* attribute of the Horae, Zephyr; *purple wings:* attribute of Aquilo, Boreas • **heraldic** protection; swiftness; *wings on a shield:* the joy of flourishing prosperity • **Hindu** *winged white horse:* Devadatta, steed of Kalki • **Islamic** *green wings:* attribute of the archangel Gabriel • **Jewish** *winged man:* West; *wings of many colors:* attribute of the archangel Gabriel; *winged ox:* North • **Maori** strength; valor; *the Bird Man:* the divinity, the all-seeing, the all-wise • **Mithraic** *four wings:* the four winds, the four seasons • **Persian** *winged disk:* Ahura, Mazda, Ormuzd • **Slavic** *large winged dog:* Simargl • **Sumero-Semitic** *winged sun disk:* Shamash; *four wings:* the four winds, the four seasons, occasional attribute of El; *six wings:* occasional attribute of El • **Ural-Altaic** *winged horse:* guide to the underworld; *bird wings:* communication between this world and the spirit world • **Zoroastrian** *bearded man in a winged circle holding a ring:* Ahura Mazda

winnowing sublimation; selection; choice; separation of the good from the bad • **winnowing fan** associated with fertility rites • **Greco-Roman** attribute of Dionysus/Bacchus, occasionally Hermes/Mercury • **Hindu** *winnowing basket:* attribute of Dhumavat; *winnowing fan worn on the head:* attribute of Sitala

Winter old age; death; dormancy; hate; darkness; misery; coldness; involutive death with the promise of rebirth; associated with Capricorn, Aquarius, Pisces • **Greco-Roman** sacred to Hephaestus/Vulcan

Winter solstice gateway from which light emerges • **Chinese** corresponds to the abyss, the feet • **Hindu** inaugurates the Way of the Gods • **Pythagorean** gate of the gods

wintergreen calmness; refreshment • **folkloric** breaks hexes

wisteria welcome; the gentleness and devotion of womanhood • **heraldic** playfulness; spontaneity; welcome • **Japanese** happiness

witch the Terrible Mother; the evil demiurge; the dark unconscious of woman; bringer of an alternate level or reality; the fruit of repression; the primitive female aspect that survives in the male subconscious; *three witches:* associated with Macbeth • **Christian** priestess of devil worship • **Greek** Medea • **Lithuanian** Ragana • *see also* **sorcerer**

witch hazel protection against fairies, witches, evil spirits; used for divination • **flower language** a spell • *see also* **hazel**

wizard *see* **sorcerer**

Woden • **Anglo-Saxon** conductor of the dead; associated with Wednesday • *see also* **Odin**

wolf rapacity; rapine; hunger; hypocrisy; lust; cruelty; anger; aggression; fraud; deceit; the devil; war; warrior; cunning; ferocity; corruption; heresy; darkness; masher; a thief; untamed nature; inversion; murder; avarice; greed; false doctrine; a false prophet; the principle of evil; the lesser instincts taking control of more human instincts but with the possibility of improvement; untamed energies; swiftness; poverty; melancholy; night; light; the sun; Winter; protection; cowardice; valor; fertility; a man 50 to 60 years of age; attribute of gods of the dead, the personifications of Avarice, Gluttony; associated with Mars (planet), the archangels Michael, Samael • **wolf devouring children** fear of incest • **wolf with lamb** peace • **alchemic** antimony • **Algonquin** ruler of the kingdom of the dead • **Aztecan** *howling wolf:* the god of dance • **Celtic** devourer of the sun at night • **Chinese** greed; rapacity; *Celestial Blue Wolf:* dynastic founder • **Christian** evil; the devil; despoiler of the flock; cruelty; craftiness; obstinacy; heresy; attribute of St. Maurus; *tame wolf:* attribute of St. Francis of Assisi; *female wolf:* emblem of the papacy • **Egyptian** attribute of Khenti-Amentiu, Upuaut • **Greco-Roman** fierceness; valor; conductor of souls of the dead; sacred to Ares/Mars, Apollo, Silvanus; *female wolf:* attribute of Romulus and Remus, occasional form of Hecate; *man attacked by wolves, hands trapped in an oak tree trunk:* Milo of Croton • **heraldic** caution in attack; prudence; martial cunning; reward for perseverance in long sieges or works; the papacy • **Hindu** night • **Islamic** *hell wolf:* obstacle to pilgrims on the road to Mecca • **Jewish** bloodthirstiness; persecution; cruelty; attribute of the archangel Michael; *wolf with lion:* associated with the tribe of Benjamin • **Mongolian** *blue wolf:* Er Toshtuk • **Norse** bringer of victory; attribute of Belen; steed of Odin; *wolf with eagle:* emblem of the elect of Valhalla; *Fenrir the wolf:* bringer of evil; *twin wolves:* emblem of Freki and Geri; *wolf with human eyes:* a berserker • **Spanish** steed of warlocks • **Turkish** *Gray Wolf:* Mustafa Kemal • **witchcraft** form assumed by a werewolf; steed of warlocks, witches

wolfsbane deadliness; illicit love; remorse; vendetta; associated with Cancer • **flower language** misanthropy • **Greco-Roman** crime; poison words; coolness; witchcraft; associated with Cronus/Saturn, Cerberus

wolverine • **American** emblem of Michigan

woman the passive principle in nature; receptiveness; the changing and intuitive; the lunar; submissiveness; the mother; the unconscious; the involutive; associated with the left side; the anima; the Great Mother; the Great Goddess; often used as the personification of an idea or principle, such as Summer, Europe, Justice, etc.— they are differentiated by their attributes, such as sword, globe, serpent, etc. • **woman as captive** higher nature held latent by desires • **woman with two or three heads** Prudence personified • **man's head on a woman's body** solid and profound judgment • **seven women** the seven virtues (faith, hope, charity, temperance, prudence, fortitude, justice — these may be identified by their attributes— globe, serpent, scales, etc.) • **serpent coiled around a woman** the male-female relationship • **Christian** *child being suckled by a woman:* charity; *woman with veiled or blindfolded eyes:* the Synagogue personified • **Norse** *half-white/half-black goddess:* Hel • *see also* **hag; maiden; old woman; prostitute; Virgin; wild woman;** and specific women: **Eve; Helen; Virgin Mary,** etc.

womb beginning; morning; night; the tomb; protection from reality; the matrix; the Great Mother; the Earth Mother; the unmanifest; receptivity; spiritual regeneration; a mine; associated with Pisces, Cancer, Scorpio, Taurus, Virgo, Capricorn • **return to the womb** regression • **alchemic** a mine; the athanor • **Hindu** associated with the first chakra

wood primordial substance; wisdom; mother; life and death; celestial goodness in its lowest corporeal plane; associated with 5th wedding anniversaries • **touching or knocking on wood** a charm against evil • **burnt wood** wisdom; death • **touching wood** touching the Cosmic Tree, which was a place of sanctuary and protection • **Chinese** associated with blue, green; corresponds to East, Spring; *as an element:* associated with acid taste, learnedness, heat, wheat, sheep, the spleen, green, the bones, joy, -3- • **Christian** the Cross • **heraldic** love that does not injure that which it clings to • **Hindu** the primordial substance; Brahman • **Tibetan** the primordial substance • *see also* specific kinds of trees and their woods (**ebony; palm;** etc.)

wood pigeon *see* **pigeon**

wood sorrel • **flower language** joy; maternal tenderness; praise of God

woodbine *see* **honeysuckle**

woodcock goodwill; affection; fool; dupe; simpleton

woodpecker presage of a storm; perseverant action; fertility; lust; immortality; distinction; magic power; prophet; guardian of kings and trees; protection; security • **Christian** the devil; heresy; the repentant sinner petitioning God •

Greco-Roman Picus; lucky omen for hunters; sacred to Ares/Mars, Zeus/Jupiter, Silvanus, Tiora, Triptolemos; guardian of Romulus and Remus • **North American Indian** *prairie tribes:* could avert storms, lightning • **Pawnee** assurance of the continuity of life

woodruff • **flower language** modest worth

woods *see* **forest**

woof *see* **weaving**

wool a homely, simple life; noiselessness; vagueness; fertility; warmth; shroud; associated with 7th wedding anniversaries • **basket of wool** fertility; women's quarters; women's housework • *see also* **fleece; sheep**

woolsack • **British** wealth; emblem of the Lord Chancellor in Great Britain

word the first element in the process of manifestation; creative force; the savior; the manifestation of the individual • **Christian** Jesus Christ • **Greek** reason; the intellect; divine thought • **Jewish** that which by God made all things • **New Caledonian** the First Act • **South American Indian** life; immortality

work the endeavor of the soul to attain perfection; duty; obligation; drudgery

works • **days related to works** *Sunday:* light; *Monday:* divination; *Tuesday:* wrath; *Wednesday:* science; *Thursday:* politics, religion; *Friday:* love; *Saturday:* mourning • *see also* **Creation**

World (tarot) transitory life; the body; the senses; the manifest world as a reflection of creative activity; major fortune; the attainment of unveiled truth; the final blending of personal consciousness with universal completion; perfection as the end of creation out of Chaos; final crown of the initiate; truth and spiritual evolution attained on earth; cosmic consciousness; merging of the subconscious and super-conscious with the conscious; personal fulfillment; associated with the archangels Cassiel, Lumiel

worm death; dissolution; baseness; the devil; lowliness; contempt; weakness; cringing; insignificant man; death; the insidious destroyer; conscience; wiles; laziness; secrecy; sin; hell; a killing libidinal figure; life reborn from corruption and death; the destructive force of the libido • **Chinese** *silk worm:* emblem of industry

wormwood affection; purification; false judgment; punishment; bitter labor; intoxication; weaning; distress; torment; grief, especially that caused by absence; a perversion of the procreative drive • **wormwood and gall** bitterness • **Christian** the King of Babylon • **flower language** absence • **Greco-Roman** sacred to Ares/Mars

Wotan *see* **Woden; Odin**

wound punishment; the conscience; sacrifice to placate powerful forces; damage to the soul; martyrdom • **wound in the neck** poet's stigma • **Christian** *three wounds:* attribute of St. Cecilia; *five wounds:* the wounds of Christ in the Passion

woundwort associated with Venus (planet)

wreath eternity; celebration; mourning; victory; valor; resurrection; memory • **wreath on the head** honor • **bay wreath** death; mourning • **cypress wreath** mourning • **ivy wreath** conviviality • **bay laurel wreath** distinction in literature or music • **myrtle wreath** attribute of brides, initiates • **oak wreath** strength; hospitality; victory on the seas • **olive wreath** peace • **willow wreath** bereavement; death; mourning • **yew wreath** immortality • **Arabian** *orange blossom wreath:* fertility; attribute of brides • **Celtic** *serpent wreath:* fertility, charm against evil • **Chinese** *olive wreath:* literary merit • **Greco-Roman** *cypress wreath:* attribute of Hades/Pluto; *fennel wreath:* worn at rites of Sabazios; *flower wreath:* attribute of Flora; *grass wreath:* reward for Roman life savers, military heroes; *hawthorn wreath:* marriage; *bay laurel wreath:* victory at the Pythian games, attribute of Apollo, Clio; *oak wreath:* reward for saving a life, attribute of Zeus/Jupiter; *olive wreath:* victory at the Olympic games; *myrtle wreath:* attribute of brides; *parsley wreath:* victory at the Nemean games; *pine wreath:* victory at the Isthmian games, attribute of Pan/Faunus; *rose wreath:* attribute of Roman emperors; *verbena wreath:* marriage; *willow wreath:* attribute of Hera/Juno • **heraldic** *oak leaf and acorn wreath:* service saving a life or in homeland defense • **Phrygian** *fennel wreath:* worn at rites of Sabazios

wren modesty; maternity; heroism; lust; death; consolation; small size; insignificance; the Spirit; a witch • **Celtic** corresponds to the priestly caste; sacred to Taliesin • **English, French** killed at Christmas and buried in a church yard signaling the death of the old year • **Greek** sacred to Triptolemos • **heraldic** freedom • **North American Indian** greets the sun at dawn • **Scottish** killing a wren brought bad luck

wrestling stimulating fertility

writing table • **Christian** attribute of St. Ambrose

wryneck feminine lust

wyvern guardianship; Satan; war; pestilence • **heraldic** protection; valor • *see also* **lindworm**

X

X negation; inversion; perfection; completion; balance; elimination; a variable quantity; an unknown; illiteracy; spiritual love; signature; a kiss; associated with abnegation, responsibility, humaneness, -6- • **American** an inferior product; pornographic material; *XXX (19th century):* hard liquor; *XXX (20th century):* hardcore pornographic material • **Christian** St. Andrew's cross; the Cross of Christ; emblem of Christ • **Roman** boundary marker; barrier; the numeral for -10-

xanthium • **flower language** rudeness; pertinacity

xeranthemum • **flower language** cheerfulness under adversity

XP, X.P. (Chi Rho) usually shown with the staff of the P bisecting the X • **Chaldean** emblem of the sky god (circa 2500 BCE) • **Christian** said to have come to Constantine in a dream and first used as his personal emblem, later attributed to the first two letters for Christ in Greek • **Greek** abbreviation of "chreston," meaning a good thing, or a good omen, and used in a text to mark an important passage • **heraldic** Christianity; good omen

X-ray enhanced vision; perceptiveness; insight

Y

Y an unknown quantity; the figure of a man; associated with the search for the esoteric or the mystic, -7- • **alchemic** androgyny • **Christian** cross of the Thieves of Calvary; *on a chasuble:* the arms of Christ when hanging on the cross • **medieval** occasionally the Roman numeral for 150 • **Pythagorean** emblem of human life

yang *see* **yin and yang**

yantra • **Hindu** male and female divine energies; *predominately red:* emphasis of female energies; *predominately white:* emphasis of male energies; *circle:* water energy; *square:* earth energy; *triangle:* fire energy; *diagonal lines:* air energy; *horizontal lines:* water energy; *vertical lines:* fire energy; *point:* ether energy

yarmulke • **Jewish** submission to God

yarn • **heraldic** *fusil of yarn:* negotiation

yarrow *see* **achillea millefolium**

yeast fermentation; love; high spirits; agitation; promoter of increase; protection against plague • *see also* **leaven**

yellow associated with Gemini, Leo, Judaism, earth, the mind of man, intellect, intuition, marriage, deceit, bombast; journalistic sensationalism, sunlight, gold, the third heaven • **bright yellow** the sun; the solar; fruitfulness; beneficence; joy; faith; truth; kingship; intuition; magnanimity; fruitfulness; divine wisdom; goodness; glory; partakes of the symbolism of gold • **dark yellow** cowardice; inconstancy; adultery; treachery; betrayal; faithlessness; jealousy; death; avarice; ambition; melancholy; enmity; lowest rank; infernal light; degradation; treason; secrecy; deceit; unpleasantness; decay; heresy • **dull yellow** deceitfulness • **yellow cross** sign of the plague • **orange-yellow** divine wisdom or goodness; glory • **yellow-green** associated with Virgo • **yellow flag** disease; quarantine • **Amerindian** the setting sun; West • **Aztecan** *blue and yellow:* colors of Huitzilopochtli • **Buddhist** renunciation; desirelessness; humility; associated with South, charity; attribute of monastics, Ratnasambhava • **Chaldean** *golden yellow:* emblem of the sun; *pale yellow:* emblem of Venus (planet) • **Chinese** the national color; sacred to the emperor and his son; yin; associated with earth, South, the Center, metal, the lunar hare, the Ch'ing dynasty; *yellow clouds:* prosperity • **Christian** *bright yellow:* associated with divinity, revealed truth, the Robe of Glory, feasts of confessors, God the Son; *dark yellow:* associated with treachery, deceit, Jews, heretics, Judas Iscariot; *yellow shield:* attribute of Judas Iscariot; *bright yellow cloak:* attribute of SS Peter, Joseph • **Egyptian** associated with gold; *yellow skin:* attribute of the immortals • **German** *yellow star in Nazi Germany:* Jews were forced to wear a yellow Star of David • **Greco-Roman** *girls in yellow robes:* participants in rites of Artemis/Diana; *golden yellow:* attribute of Apollo • **Hindu** light; life; truth; immortality; West • **Islamic** has magical properties; associated with gold, the sun, the true believer; *yellow carpet:* rank, power, attribute of palaces and mosques • **Kabalistic** beauty; associated with the archangel Michael • **Kalmyk** North • **Mayan** associated with maize, fertile soil, South • **Mexican Indian** associated with the beginning of the rainy season • **Mithraic** *golden yellow:* attribute of Mithras • **North American Indian** *prairie tribes:* South • **Pueblo** North • **Spanish** attribute of the executioner in the Inquisition • **Tierra del Fuegan** associated with rocks, thunder, the dead, West

yew death; sadness; mourning; immortality; sorrow; constancy; faith; forgetfulness; sacred to Druids; associated with the archangel Cassiel • **yew wreath** immortality • **Celtic** illusion; immortality; transference; passage; a magic wood; wood of the White Wand • **Christian** immortality • **flower language** sadness; despair; sorrow • **heraldic** death; eternal life; resurrection; faith

Yggdrasil • **Norse** wisdom; the All Father; Tree of Life; fountain of life; eternal life; immortality; connection between the underworld, earth, and heaven; tree on which Odin sacrificed himself; meeting place of the gods • *see also* **ash tree**

yin and yang spirit and matter; perfect harmony and balance; mutual interdependence; Cosmic Egg; androgyny; two forces in tension but not in antagonism; life and form; good and evil; any pair of related opposites; the two opposing aspects of the Great Mother —creator/destroyer, birth/death, etc. • **yin** (the dark color) the material; the feminine; primordial darkness; primordial waters; the passive; intuition • **yang** (the light color) the spiritual; the masculine; the light of creation; the active; rationality;

yoga meditation; discipline; self-mastery; that which links various levels of reality

yogi one's higher self

yoke union; discipline; control; agriculture; balance; tyranny; slavery; toil; patience; sacrifice; burden bearing; the Law; patient service; trials; meekness; obedience; attribute of the personifications of Obedience, Patience, Toil • **Christian** Christ bearing the sins of the world; the law of Christ • **Jewish** attribute of Cain; *broken yoke:* associated with Nahum

yolk principal substance

youth *see* **man; boy**

Z

Z the thing that completes perfection; an unknown quantity; superfluity; associated with lightning, potential for good and/or evil, the stomach, -8- • **medieval** occasionally the Roman numeral for both -7- and -2000- • *see also* **zigzag**

Zachariah • **Christian** spiritual healing through faith and obedience

Zadkiel, Archangel associated with Jupiter (planet), violet (color), tin, brass, bronze, West, South, amethysts, lapis lazuli, sapphires, turquoise, -14-, -18-, the justice of God, freedom, benevolence, mercy, Sagittarius, Pisces, Thursday, the 6th heaven, elephants, whales, fish, eagles, chestnut trees, fig trees, junipers, Norway spruce, oaks, poplars • **Jewish** associated with staying the hand of Abraham when he was going to sacrifice Isaac • **Kabalistic** associated with -4-, blue • **tarot** associated with the Wheel of Fortune

zebra individuality

Zechariel, Archangel *see* **Zarachiel, Archangel**

zenith the point at which one passes out of time into timelessness; the midst of life

zephyr *see* **breeze; wind**

zephyr • **flower language** expectation

Zerachiel, Archangel supervises guardian angels; leads souls to judgment; associated with healing, the sun, children, the earth

zero *see* -0-

Zeus/Jupiter • **Greco-Roman** superconsciousness; the intuition of the supernatural; judgment; the will; the king; the universality of force; broad vision; the spirit and light of human intellect; intuitive thought; source of truth; associated with Thursday

ziggurat • **Babylonian** the cosmic mountain; the link between heaven and earth • see also **Babel, Tower of**

zigzag disquiet; confusion; the material world; lightning; thunderbolt; electricity; lightning; fecundity; waves of the sea; regeneration; spiritual purification and rebirth; emblem of storm gods; sudden change in thoughts, beliefs, ideas • **Babylonian** attribute of Adad • **Egyptian** water; the Nile • **Greco-Roman** emblem of Zeus/Jupiter • **Norman** the course of life • **zodiacal** *two zigzags:* emblem of Aquarius

zinnia • **flower language** thoughts of absent friends • **heraldic** lasting affection; constancy; remembrance; goodness

zircon wisdom; honor; riches; associated with Capricorn, Virgo, Aquarius; birthstone for December; charm for travelers and protection from plague, injuries, lightning, evil spirits • **blue zircon** stone for a 4th wedding anniversary • **yellow zircon** stone for an 11th wedding anniversary

zither the cosmos; the synthesis of heaven and earth; the strings correspond to the various levels of the universe • **Greco-Roman** attribute of Apollo, Terpsichore

Ziz • **Jewish** the power of air; food at the End Time; protector of all smaller birds

zodiac the year; the dignity of labor • **the first six signs** (Aries, Taurus, Gemini, Cancer, Leo, Virgo) relate to involution or matter • **the last six signs** (Libra, Scorpio, Sagittarius, Capricorn, Aquarius, Pisces) relate to evolution or materialization • **days related to the zodiac** *Sunday* the sun; *Monday* Cancer; *Tuesday* Scorpio; *Wednesday* Gemini; *Thursday* Sagittarius; *Friday* Taurus; *Saturday* Capricorn • *see also* separate zodiac signs such as **Aries; Taurus; Gemini**

zombie the resurfacing of ideas or beliefs thought dead

Zu • **Persian, Sumerian** servant and guardian of Enlil; divine storm bird; personification of the South Wind and Thunder Clouds; associated with cosmogony, the Tree of Life